Sheila Lukins All Around The World Cookbook

SHEILA LUKINS

ILLUSTRATIONS BY STEVEN GUARNACCIA

All Around The World Cookbook

WINE AND BEER ESSAYS BY BARBARA ENSRUD

WORKMAN PUBLISHING NEW YORK

*I dedicate my book to my most magical daughters,
Annabel and Molly, who have given me
their love, joy, and support
in ways none of us could have imagined.
And of course, to Richard, my dear husband
and extraordinary traveling companion, who so enthusiastically
planned many of the trips.*

Library of Congress Cataloging-in-Publication Data
Lukins, Sheila.
Sheila Lukins all around the world cookbook/by Sheila Lukins.
p. cm.
Includes index. ISBN 1-56305-636-4—ISBN 1-56305-237 (pbk.)
1. Cookery, International. I.Title II. Title: All around the world cookbook.
TX725.A1L814 1994
641.59—dc20 94-2421 CIP

Cover design: Paul Hanson
Cover food photographs: Walt Chrynwski
Book design: Lisa Hollander with Lori S. Malkin

Workman Publishing Company, Inc.
708 Broadway
New York, NY 10003

Manufactured in the United States of America
First printing April 1994
10 9 8 7 6 5 4 3 2

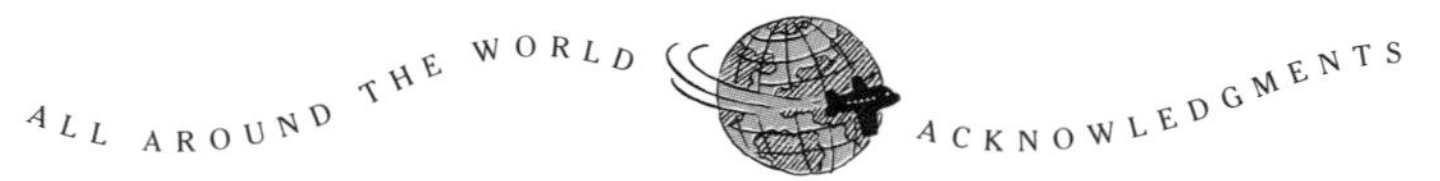

ALL AROUND THE WORLD

Acknowledgments

Usually a project of this magnitude is years in the dreaming stage. It happened quite differently for me. Peter Workman, my publisher, envisioned this journey over lunch on a rainy March day in 1991 at Chez Jacqueline in Greenwich Village. For his insight and trust I will always be grateful.

Without the love, support, devotion, and expertise from so many people, my book would never have been possible.

....

First and foremost, great thanks goes to Laurie Griffith, who appeared at my side one day from Paris via Kansas and became invaluable in the kitchen and throughout every other aspect of this endeavor. I will always treasure her talent, friendship, and total commitment.

....

Barbara Ensrud worked long and hard, eloquently contributing her vast knowledge of the wines and beers of the world, while Peggy Cullen shared her marvelous baking talent. A million thanks.

....

Arthur Klebanoff, my agent and very special friend, gave me his guidance, understanding, patience, and encouragement with an unfailing magical sense of humor. I will always love him.

....

Lula Mae Green never once failed to give me much needed help and care, and always with that beautiful smile on her face.

....

Walter Anderson, editor of Parade Magazine, has been a great inspiration for years and has shown tremendous faith and confidence in me through the good times and the difficult times. He is the best boss a girl could have. God bless Fran Carpentier, my Parade editor, a great person, a total joy to work with, and very funny too!

......

Love and thanks to my sweet sister, Elaine Yanell, and my beautiful mother, Berta Olderman. Peerless friends Anne Rosenzweig, Lily and Andy Freedman, and Suzy Davidson have so generously given of themselves, be it support, inspiration, or just a great night out whenever I needed it. Also, to Matt Franjola for bringing the words to the top.

....

This book never would have come to be without my extraordinary editor and friend, Suzanne Rafer, who gives new meaning to early morning phone calls, along with a brilliant sense of humor. I love her and don't want to have my coffee and toast without her.

....

A million thanks to art director, Paul Hanson, who not only named my book, but designed the best cover ever, and to Lisa Hollander, for a beautiful book design. Thanks, too, to Lori S. Malkin for helping bring that design to life.

....

Gratitude goes to Barbara Ottenhoff, Margery Tippie, and Jane Sigal for their editorial work on the book. And many thanks to the rest of my Workman family, including Andrea Glickson, David Schiller, Bert Snyder, Janet Harris, Sheilah Scully, Nancy Murray, Steve Pesola, Ruth Hochbaum (at BPE), Shannon Ryan, and Carolan Workman.

....

With great thanks and appreciation to the many people who helped lead the way to special restaurants, markets, and cooks all over the world. First and foremost to Priscilla Hawk, for the awe-inspiring task of arranging my safe passage all around the world. Also to Aglaia Kremezi, Karitas Mitrogogos, Chris Veneris, Stelios Boutaris, Hilde Xinotroulias, Joseph Petrocik, Marciel Presella, Camellia Panjabi, Singh Oberoi, Paddy Nichols, John and Sally McKenna, my friends at Nisho Iwai, Patricia Testa, Eduardo Galatzan, Jessica Harris, Wendy Posner, Mark Miller, John and Barbara Berkenfield, Dave Hoemann, Adrian and Nani Forastier, Gretel Goldsmith, Christine and Martin Leimdorfer, Jerilyn Brusseau, Svetlana Antonova, and Irina Yesimova.

....

Last, but not least, everlasting appreciation for the people who gave me the second half of my life: W. Jost Michelsen, Steve Price, Audrey Ehrmann, Jackie Ross, Gail Simon, John Schaefer, Diane Rudolph, Joanne Edelmann, and Teresa Iodice.

ALL AROUND THE WORLD

Contents

INTRODUCTION: AROUND THE WORLD IN 730 DAYS XI

Room Service
1

A PERFECT START 2

Sumptuous starts for special days include Jamaican Banana Brunch Soup, Nani's Tortilla de Patatas, and a flavorful Turkish Western Omelet.

BREAKFAST IN BED 18

When traveling, breakfast in a hotel dining room or in a great bed can be a real treat. Here's my diary of luxurious favorites.

Wish You Were Here
29

APERITIFS 30

Drinks that are elegant and soothing or fiery and lively. Enjoy a Rouge Tropical, a Margarita, a Rhumlet, or a Chilean White Peach Melba Sangria with friends, and celebrate the bewitching hour.

FIRST BITES & SMALL PLATES 42

Zakuski, meze, and tapas; slathers, empanadas, böreks, croquettes, and quesadillas; a selection of luscious palate-teasers to accompany a welcome glass of spirit.

SALADS 91

An Oriental Spinach Salad with Chinese Vinaigrette, a Samba Waldorf Salad, a Nordic Cobb, and a Chilean Avocado. Tossed and composed salad plates that belie any boundaries.

Great Melting Pot

125

SOUPS 126

An around-the-world collection of soups to invigorate and nourish—Indonesian Chicken Noodle Soup, Scandinavian Smoky Pea Soup, Gingered Crème de Crécy, Pappa al Pomodoro, and Cha-Cha Corn Gazpacho, to name just a few.

ALL AROUND THE WORLD MENUS 171

Serve friends and family a Highland Winter Luncheon, an Indonesian Rijsttafel, a Moroccan Couscous Dinner, or a Singapore Supper. Suggested menu ideas to help you plan extraordinary meals using the recipes in this book.

Marketplace

191

VEGETABLES 192

A wealth of vegetable dishes inspired by the world's glorious marketplaces. From Russia comes Beet Bread Pudding; from Marrakech, Sugar Mashed Carrots. Try the Sultan's Pillows, with their Turkish flavors, and a Coconut Ratatouille that fuses the best of Thailand and France.

TO MARKET, TO MARKET 226

A tour of some of the lushest marketplaces in the world; they are the inspiration for so many of the recipes in my book.

CONDIMENTS AND SPICES 235

Raitas and salsas; compotes and chutneys; spice mixes and hot sauces. A sizzling condiment repertoire to help enliven any entrée.

GRAINS AND BEANS 262

Dishes deserving of a place of honor on your table, including a lush fruit-studded pilaf, a creamy mushroom-topped polenta, spicy Frijoles Negros, and alluring Mexican Lentils with Pineapple and Bananas.

NOODLING AROUND.............. **288**

Not just pasta. Instead, a worldwide selection of comforting yet exciting noodle dishes. Fresh Crab Pad Thai, Malay Curried Noodles, Catalan Romesco "Sauce" Rotelli, Sesame Butterfly Noodles, and some updated favorites.

The Grand Tour

311

THE LAND........................... **312**

Jamaican Jerk Pork Ribs, Rio's Feijoada, Spiced Peloponnesian Lamb Shanks, Mexican Pot Roast, and Luscious Beef Hash—heavenly meat dishes make for hearty, satisfying entrées.

THE AIR.............................. **357**

Splendid poultry hailing from everywhere—Sweden to India—marinated, cooked, and sauced to perfection. Including Black Currant Duck Breasts, Honey and Ginger-Glazed Chicken, Chicken Rogan Josh, Chinese Squabs, and Roasted Pheasant with Prince Charles Sauce.

THE SEA.............................. **395**

A grand tour of the world's best fish and seafood. From Andalusia, an olive- and shrimp-rich Salad Parador; from Portugal, garlicky Steamed Clams Alentejo; from Istanbul, herb-scented Halibut Lemon Kebabs; from Thailand, Sweet and Sour Flounder. And oceans more.

Side Trips

431

HANDS ACROSS THE SEA............................ **432**

Sandwiches and other hands-on favorites, including a Thai Crab "Club," a Provençal Pan Bagna, a selection of smørrebørd ideas, a "Reuben" Pita, and Great Turkish Hamburgers.

WHISTLE STOPS: TIME FOR TEA..................... **452**

Delicate sandwiches, buttery scones, and sweet cakes to accompany a refreshing cup of tea. Plus "The Proper Way to Make Tea" and "Tea Sandwich Musts."

MY FAVORITE AFTERNOON TEAS 474

Tea at the Ritz in London, at the Caledonian in Edinburgh, on the beach in Rio, and at a friend's home in St. Petersburg. Memories of some favorite afternoon tea stops.

OVEN-FRESH BREAD 481

Enjoy warm thick slices of Irish Soda Bread or Portuguese Sweet Bread. Spread light, crisp Lavash with a favorite slather. Nibble on fragrant Rosemary-Olive Bread. Here is a selection of baked goods that are worth every minute of preparation time.

THE NEW CHEESE PLATE 494

Some favorite cheeses to enjoy from Spain, Portugal, Denmark, Sweden, Holland, and Greece.

The Light Fantastic

507

A WORLD OF DESSERTS 508

Cherry Compote, Quince Spoon Sweet, Turkish Fig Pastries, Scarlet Summer Pudding, Caribbean Coconut Tart, Banana Rum Ice Cream. Lush, intoxicating, gooey, and totally satisfying desserts.

CONVERSION TABLE 558

ALL AROUND THE WORLD COOKBOOK INDEX 559

ALL AROUND THE WORLD PHOTO CREDITS 590

INTRODUCTION

Around the World in 730 Days

Much of my childhood was spent in awe of the magical songs, stories, and mysteriously delicious foods that my grandparents brought with them when they emigrated to America from Russia. My grandmother would tell me wonderful tales about growing up in Kiev, as she nimbly made tiny meat pastries or crêpes to be filled with cherries or sweetened cheese mixtures. And my grandfather, dressed in a soft white shirt with a red embroidered collar, sang to me in a beautiful, haunting language that I longed to learn more about.

I can't remember which came first, my desire to visit their far away land, or my wish to cook like my grandmother. Throughout the years, these memories blended. When I think back on those times, I realize that was when this book was born.

My sense of adventure and longing to travel grew as I did. By the time I was in my late twenties, I was married, living in Paris, and fascinated by the extraordinary food markets there and all the pleasures of the table. Over the years this fascination drew me into a whole new world of food. I began my own catering business—The Other Woman Catering Company—and later went into partnership to open the Silver Palate specialty food shop. A line of packaged foods and three cookbooks followed. When the Silver Palate was eventually sold, and the last of the cookbooks—*The New Basics*—was completed, it was time for a journey of another kind.

First Stop, Moscow

One rainy March afternoon, just after returning from Spain, I was at lunch with my publisher and editor, waxing ecstatic about *tapas* bars, olives, and the new influence of Mediterranean cuisine that was taking America by storm. And this was only one of the many cuisines that was currently changing the ways we were eating. My publisher proposed to send me around the world to adopt, assimilate, adapt, and create for my next cookbook. I needed time to process this amazing suggestion. This was an opportunity not to be missed. Soon after, my journey to experience and discover began.

When I visited Bali, I went to see the breathtaking Legong Kraton perform outside an ancient temple in the town of Ubud.

From the outset I knew which cuisines were my favorites and which were influencing cooking in the United States. Those were the countries I targeted to visit. I remembered my grandparents and their food and I felt in my heart that my first trip would be to Russia. Since I had never seen Southeast Asia, that would have to follow. I loved Thai food, and I was longing to visit Bali and Singapore. The aromatic food of Morocco was so splendid, and how could I miss Tunisia? Memories of the marvelous foods of Japan were still very fresh in my mind. There, ancient cultures, customs, and rituals are brought to life in every meal. After a long formal *kaiseki*, Japan's majestic and delicate *dégustation*, I was ready to give up western food altogether. Yet time allows for a return to reality, and I did want to learn more about the great cuisines of India.

During the next two years, I visited 33 countries, immersing myself in the food of the world. Sometimes I encountered many political hot spots, including my first stop, Russia.

There were barricades around the White House when I visited Moscow. Yeltsin was on his way in and Gorbachev on his way out. Street signs were being changed from "Leningrad" back to "St. Petersburg" the day I arrived there. While most grocery stores were scantily stocked, I was amazed to see the huge central food markets brimming with everything from red bell peppers, berries, wild mushrooms, meat, and fish to the expected pickles and sauerkrauts. I learned later that these were controlled by the all-powerful Russian mafia. As I was on my way to Tblisi in Georgia to cook for a week in a private home, another revolution began and I missed my opportunity to learn more, first hand, about that wonderful cuisine. Russia, as expected, was beautiful yet cloaked in sadness and uncertainty. It was not the Russia of my fantasies.

Guess who joined me for dinner in Moscow... well, sort of.

Next on the agenda were Thailand and Indonesia, where the hot and spicy Malaysian cupboard blends with the best of Chinese offerings. The melding of both cuisines results in the most delicious dishes.

The scope of flavors influenced by Thai, Indian, and Indonesian ingredients—chili pastes, garlic, coconut, and cinnamon abound—was like nothing I had ever tasted, and was an intriguing introduction to Nonya and Baba cooking.

The bristling excitement of Bangkok, the old-world charm of Singapore, and the tranquil beauty of Bali, hardly prepared me for the impending chaos towards the end of the trip. After several stops in northern India, where I was dazzled by the foods, I was forced to leave Bombay in the middle of the night as a series of terrorist bombs disrupted the city. This abrupt change in plans caused me to miss visiting Goa in southern India and sampling the fiery vindaloos I was so looking forward to. But as happens, some good came out of the bad. My departure from India was on KLM and there was a stopover in Amsterdam. Not one to waste an opportunity, I managed to indulge in two spectacular *rijsttafels*, and a sunflower break at the magnificent Van Gogh Museum.

I yearned to see Cuba for the adventure it promised—and to sample the black beans, roasted pork, and renowned toasted sandwiches that I knew would be the best in the world. Restricted for travel to so many of us since the early 60s, the visit proved to be a challenge for my husband Richard, who was helping me plan some of my trips. It was only while visiting Jamaica, where I was in search of a great jerk sauce, that he managed to find a way to Havana. Flying in a pre-World War II prop plane was almost excitement enough, but lively, ever-hopeful Cuba did not disappoint. Great meals and a surprisingly lavish show at the Tropicana nightclub, left me hoping for the return of normalized relations between the U.S. and Cuba. During our stay, our guide proudly lead us to palm-ringed courtyards in old Havana for concerts, and then on to gracious lunches served against the gentle background sounds of guitars and maracas. Be it the old man rolling cigars or the waiter at a beloved ice cream parlor, the Cubans seemed to enjoy the opportunity to once again talk to an American family. This enthusiasm underpins an unfailing national optimism.

In Havana, the nightclub scene still includes some high-kicking show girls.

During all this travel, I tried very hard to keep my family life intact. Christmas was the ideal time for all of us to travel together. And so one year we set off for the Caribbean, focusing on Martinique and its great *colombo* curries and extraordinary Creole

Look what Santa left me at the Christmas fair in Mexico City.

At La Cinacina, a ranch in Argentina, where the gauchos are handsome and the barbecue is fantastic.

food. The following Christmas we spent in Mexico, mostly around Oaxaca, which during the holidays has some of the best festivals in the world. The extraordinary seven *moles* of the region can stand up to great food anywhere, and I probably ate as much there as I did in India—which set new records for my appetite.

When planning my trip to South America, I deliberatedly avoided Peru. The political turmoil there made travel too dangerous. I decided to save learning more about its many great potato dishes for another time. Instead I chose to search out great barbecue in Argentina. My destination was the gaucho town of San Antonia de Areco, where I found the perfect *estancia* (ranch) La Cinacina, which served a spectacular *asado*. Dashing gauchos barbecued the meats, in contrast to the elegant restaurants of Buenos Aires where I ate succulent beef in classic European style. Colorful Rio de Janiero was wild along the Copacabana and Ipanema beaches in preparation for *carnaval*. The festive food offerings added to the spectacle. Farther north, in Salvador, I found the mysterious Bahian food a fascinating blend of West African and Caribbean cuisines.

More trips followed but my final outing was to the British Isles. Miraculously, I found myself on a beautiful, sun-drenched farm in southern Ireland, followed by a visit to Scotland and England. A luxurious tea at Claridge's in London proved to be a perfect ending to an extraordinary two years.

A New Direction

Being given total freedom to explore cooking around the world has been a great privilege. Once home, I needed to approach this book with a fresh point of view and a well-thought-out game plan. I began to think of my kitchen as a blank canvas. After spending so much time visiting the most beautiful marketplaces in the world, I had to think of a way to capture the essence of my experiences.

When I returned from each trip, I developed palettes for the countries I had visited, based on the predominate aromas, colors, and tastes that make up the distinct flavors of their cuisines. These palettes ranged from hot to cool. When I visited the hotter cultures, the colors and intense flavors ignited. Blazing chilies and spices married in a blast of devilish dishes. The cultures in the colder climates

So fresh, so fragrant—a grand spice display in Tunisia.

displayed cooler colors and more reserved flavors. Interestingly, cilantro seemed to appear everywhere—Lisbon, Russia, Bangkok, Oaxaca, Bombay, and Marrakech—and soon became a tie that bound as I traveled.

I began my recipe development by reviewing the palettes. Some days I became the alchemist and others the artist. And I discovered that when the palettes fuse, magic happens. That is how I created the recipes for this book. For me, this has become the most exciting way to cook.

My book presents some of everything I learned after going all around the world. I brought home the customs, flavors, and essences of each cuisine and reinterpreted them in my kitchen. My recipes are not traditional, rather a blend of my views on the best the world has to offer. In visiting country after country, two basic premises of good cooking were costantly reinforced. First, using ingredients that are in season is paramount for the most electric flavors. Second, no good cook lets anything go to waste. Throughout the world the stems and often the roots of herbs are used to intensify sauces, broths, and stocks. As I cooked, I became fastidious about this.

Plenty of offerings at this market in Amsterdam, which I passed on my way to the Van Gogh Museum.

I've arranged the book somewhat traditionally, although I do begin with a collection of lovely breakfast ideas and take time out for tea (and an occasional side trip), since they became two meals I really learned to love. Chapters are peppered with essays by Barbara Ensrud on the wines and beers of the world, which have proliferated and gained importance over the last few years.

My hope is that the recipes, tales, cultural insights, and the food lore in this book will inspire you, as I was inspired by my grandparents years ago, to begin your own journey all around the world, at home in your kitchen.

Sheila Lukins

Sheila Lukins
New York City

ENGLISH MIXED GRILL · TURKISH WESTERN OMELET

MY FAVORITE RUSSIAN BREAKFAST · BALI SUNRISE BRUNCH

ON THE BEACH IN RIO · ODJA · JAMAICAN BLUE MOUNTAIN COFFEE · BUTTER RUM SAUCE

BANANA CINNAMON PANCAKES · BANANA BRUNCH SOUP

SCRAMBLED EGG AND SALT COD HASH · SAUSAGES

BREAKFAST IN GREECE · HONEY

MORNING MUESLI

CARIBE WESTERN OMELET · SPANISH HOT CHOCOLATE

SOFTLY SCRAMBLED EGGS WITH ASPARAGUS AND CURED HAM

Room Service

PROSCIUTTO DI PARMA · NANI'S TORTILLA DE PATATAS

THE PERFECTLY POACHED EGG

SWEDISH PANCAKES · SUNDAY MORNING IN CUBA

BRIOCHE IN JAPAN

MISS MAUD'S BREAKFAST BANANA BREAD

TORRIJAS · IRISH PORRIDGE

ROOM SERVICE

A Perfect Start

Whenever I check into a hotel room I begin an inexplicable ritual. Once settled, I leaf through the leather binders holding the guest services information until I find the room service menu. Gleefully anticipating what lies ahead, I always zero in on the breakfast menu. When I'm traveling, the early hours of the morning are my favorite time to get some work done and are thoroughly enhanced by the arrival of a beautiful breakfast served by handsome men, saying things like *Bonjour, Buon giorno, Buenos días, Eet smakeigk, Dobar tek,* and *Ohayo gozaimas*. What a treat! Rarely will someone look you in the eye and for me, at those hours, that's just fine.

This chapter includes some of my favorite breakfast memories. Some were enjoyed room service style, others in local restaurants and dining rooms. All make special starts for special days.

IRISH PORRIDGE

When I sat down to breakfast my first morning in Ireland, I was greeted by gorgeous breads, gooseberry preserves, and a steamy bowl of Irish oatmeal. Oatmeal is as essential to the Irish diet as is rice to Japan's and China's. There are many ways to make oatmeal, and the preferred consistency can range from thick to thin. This version is made from Ireland's finest oatmeal—the whole oats have a wonderful nutty flavor and their texture is similar to barley. These oats are the real McCoy and require 30 minutes of cooking time. Serve this porridge with a coarse-grain, dark brown sugar, a pitcher of cream (at least once—if you can stand it), plump raisins, honey, chopped walnuts, and ground allspice or cinnamon for sprinkling. If made ahead, the oatmeal can be reheated in the top of a double boiler over simmering water. If it seems to thicken a bit as it stands, add some milk to thin it to your desired consistency.

5 cups water
1 teaspoon salt
1 cup Irish oatmeal, such as McCann's
Dark brown sugar, for serving
Heavy (or whipping) cream or milk, for serving

Bring the water and salt to a rolling boil in a saucepan. Slowly add the oats while stirring constantly with a wooden spoon. When the oats begin to thicken (the water will be cloudy and feel somewhat thicker but the oats will still be granular), reduce the heat to a simmer. Cook uncovered 30 minutes, stirring often. Spoon into bowls and pass the brown sugar, cream, and any other additions that strike your fancy.

Serves 4

MORNING MUESLI

It was during the hippy 60s that Americans first became aware of muesli—the Swiss breakfast cereal for the health conscious. Although traditional muesli includes "raw" oats, toasting brings out their best flavor as well as the flavor of the coconut and almonds. Dried cherries and apricots add great taste and a nice chewy texture to the mix. For a breakfast cereal, serve with yogurt or milk. Muesli is lovely sprinkled over fresh fruit, ice cream, or frozen yogurt.

2 cups rolled oats
½ cup shredded coconut
½ cup sliced almonds
½ cup unprocessed coarse bran
½ cup dried cherries
¼ cup coarsely chopped dried apricots
¼ cup sunflower seeds
1 tablespoon (packed) light or dark brown sugar
⅛ teaspoon ground cinnamon

1. Preheat the oven to 350°F.

2. Spread the oats on a baking sheet and toast in the oven until lightly browned and fragrant, about 10 minutes, shaking the pan once during cooking. Transfer to a large bowl.

3. Place the coconut and almonds on the baking sheet and toast in the oven until lightly browned, 6 to 7 minutes, shaking the pan once or twice during cooking. Add to the oats along with all of the remaining ingredients. Toss well and cool. Muesli keeps for several weeks stored in an airtight container.

Makes 4 cups, enough for eight ½-cup servings

BANANA BRUNCH SOUP

The Jamaicans enjoy their abundant fruits in every conceivable way, and while there, I got the idea for this luscious soup. Although light, it is rich, so serve it in small portions in little cups or ramekins.

3 medium ripe bananas
4 tablespoons fresh lime juice
2 cups nonfat plain yogurt
¼ teaspoon ground cinnamon

1. Slice 2 of the bananas and toss with 3 tablespoons of the lime juice in a bowl. Add the yogurt and sprinkle with the cinnamon. Mix together, then process in a food processor or blender until nearly smooth with just a bit of texture remaining. Refrigerate covered for at least 1 hour.

2. To serve, divide the chilled soup between 4 ramekins. Thinly slice the third banana and toss it with the remaining tablespoon of lime juice. Lay the slices atop the soup for garnish. Serve chilled.

Serves 4

Wende,
Love the straw bags at the market in Montego Bay. Stalls overflow with habanero chilies, wild thyme and allspice—jerk sauce necessities.
Kisses,
Sheila

Jamaica
12 FEB
2-PM
1990

CHOCOLATE A LA TAZA
Hot Chocolate

The real thing in Spain is made with top-quality chocolate bars, and a bit of all-purpose flour is added to thicken the drink slightly. The absolutely authentic version is made with water, but I think the use of milk in this recipe adds just the right body and richness. Since good quality Spanish chocolate is not readily available in the U.S., this is an instance where authenticity must bow to practicality.

3 ounces bittersweet chocolate, such as Lindt Swiss bittersweet chocolate
2 cups milk
1 teaspoon all-purpose flour

1. Chop the chocolate very fine with a paring knife and place the pieces in a small saucepan with the milk. Place the pan over medium-high heat and stir constantly with a wooden spoon until the chocolate melts and the mixture comes to a boil. Remove from the heat.

2. Place the flour in a small bowl, whisk ½ cup of the hot chocolate into the flour in a slow stream, and continue to whisk until the mixture is completely smooth. Whisk this mixture back into the hot chocolate and bring to a boil again, whisking constantly.

3. Serve hot in pretty china cups.

Serves 2

SOUVENIR TO SAVOR

Spanish Hot Chocolate

Eating chocolate originated in Mexico with the Aztecs, who used crushed cocoa beans to concoct a hot drink. The chocolate drink that the Spanish conquistadors first tasted was very different from the hot chocolate we know today. Over the years it evolved from the bitter brew they first sampled into a sweet luxury.

An article in *Gourmetour* magazine, a Spanish trade journal, revealed great tales of how hot chocolate became so important to and beloved by the Spanish. "It is a traditional story in the northern Spanish region of Asturias that when Charles I visited Spain for the first time as its new monarch in 1517, he landed by mistake in the little Asturian village of Tazones, instead of the Basque coast. The locals, thrilled and awestruck to be the first to encounter the new king, served him the most luxurious refreshment they had: a cup of chocolate.

"Like so many legends, the story may be completely apocryphal. Even so, the lack of precise information about when cocoa and chocolate were introduced into Spain makes it possible that it might be true."

BALI SUNRISE BRUNCH

The colors of Bali are wildly intoxicating. The green of the rice paddies, the golden sunrises, the vivid reds and purples of the flowers dazzle the senses. While asparagus, red peppers, eggs, and shallots may not seem so exotic to us, the flavors and colors capture the beauty of a Balinese morning. This dish is perfect for brunch or luncheon, since the vegetables are easily prepared ahead. Just before serving, close your eyes and dream a bit.

12 ounces thin asparagus (you need 32 spears)
4 red bell peppers, halved lengthwise and roasted (page 202)
½ cup Apple Cider Vinaigrette (page 109)
4 large eggs
1 tablespoon white wine vinegar
4 teaspoons finely chopped shallots
Freshly ground black pepper, to taste
4 teaspoons chopped flat-leaf parsley

1. Snap the tough ends off the asparagus. Blanch the spears in boiling water until just crisp-tender, 1 to 2 minutes, depending on size. Drain, refresh under cold water, and pat dry. Set aside.

2. Place 2 roasted pepper halves in the center of each of 4 plates, then arrange 8 spears asparagus, 2 per side, in a log-cabin fashion to frame the peppers on each plate. Drizzle the vegetables evenly with the cider vinaigrette.

3. Poach the eggs in water mixed with the

The Perfectly Poached Egg

Bring 4 cups water and 1 tablespoon of white wine vinegar to a gentle simmer in a medium-size saucepan. Break an egg into a cup and then slip the egg into the simmering water. It is best to cook just one egg at a time as they tend to stick to each other, but if you must poach more than one, use a bigger pan and fill it with water. Cook for 3 to 4 minutes, depending on desired consistency. Remove the egg from the water with a slotted spoon and immediately dip it into a bowl of cold water to stop further cooking. To keep the egg from cooling off, gently slip it in a bowl of warm water until you are ready to serve. Before serving, drain the eggs on a paper towel and trim any ragged egg white.

Poached eggs are delicious atop a salad of frisée lettuce tossed with chunky sautéed bacon and a warm vinaigrette, on a bed of mashed potatoes sprinkled with sliced shallots and chopped tomatoes, and afloat in a cozy chicken noodle soup.

vinegar, following the instructions for poaching on page 6. Place the eggs atop the peppers in the center of the asparagus "frame."

4. Sprinkle with the chopped shallots, a grind of black pepper, and the chopped parsley. Serve immediately.

Serves 4

CARIBE WESTERN OMELET

Akee and salt cod is highly regarded as the national dish of Jamaica. I poked around some Jamaican restaurants in New York and tasted akee dishes, before I left on my trip to the island. But because it is unavailable fresh in the United States, canned akee was used. Mild tasting, this fruit resembles scrambled eggs in texture, taste, and appearance.

Miss Maud, a cook we met at our hotel in Jamaica, introduced me to the real thing. One morning I found her busily cleaning something very unusual in the kitchen. On the counter were large glossy black-purple seeds attached to fleshy yellow fruit resembling two lobes. She pointed to one of the trees outside on which hung opened red pods. "The akee tree," she said. "I'll make this dish for breakfast." She separated the flesh from the seeds and proceeded to sauté the fresh akee with cod, bacon, bell peppers, and scallions. I thought it the best "Western" omelet I'd ever tasted. Here is my version, taking poetic license. I've used fresh cooked cod, but smoked whitefish or salmon would be an acceptable substitute. Perfect for brunch with a hot cup of Jamaican Blue Mountain coffee.

6 slices bacon, cut crosswise into 1-inch pieces
1 green bell pepper, stemmed, seeded, and cut into ½-inch dice
4 scallions (3 inches green left on), sliced ¼ inch thick
3 ripe medium tomatoes, cored, seeded, and cut into ½-inch dice
1 tablespoon fresh thyme leaves
½ cup flaked cooked cod or smoked whitefish
6 large eggs
Dash of Tabasco or other hot sauce
Salt and freshly ground black pepper, to taste
2 ripe tomatoes, thinly sliced

1. Cook the bacon in a medium-size skillet over medium heat until the fat is rendered and the bacon is cooked but not completely crisp. Remove the bacon to a paper towel to drain.

2. Add the bell pepper and scallions to the rendered bacon fat and cook over medium heat to wilt the vegetables, 8 to 10 minutes. Add the diced tomatoes and reserved bacon to the vegetables. Season with the thyme and cook another 3 minutes. Gently fold in the flaked cod. Remove the skillet from the heat.

3. In a bowl, beat the eggs with the Tabasco, salt, and pepper. Return the skillet to medium heat. Pour the eggs over the vegetable mixture. Stir gently and constantly (but do not scramble) until the eggs are set, 4 to 5 minutes. To serve, arrange the tomato slices on serving plates and spoon the eggs atop. Serve immediately.

Serves 2 or 3

A TASTE OF THE WORLD

Spanish Palette

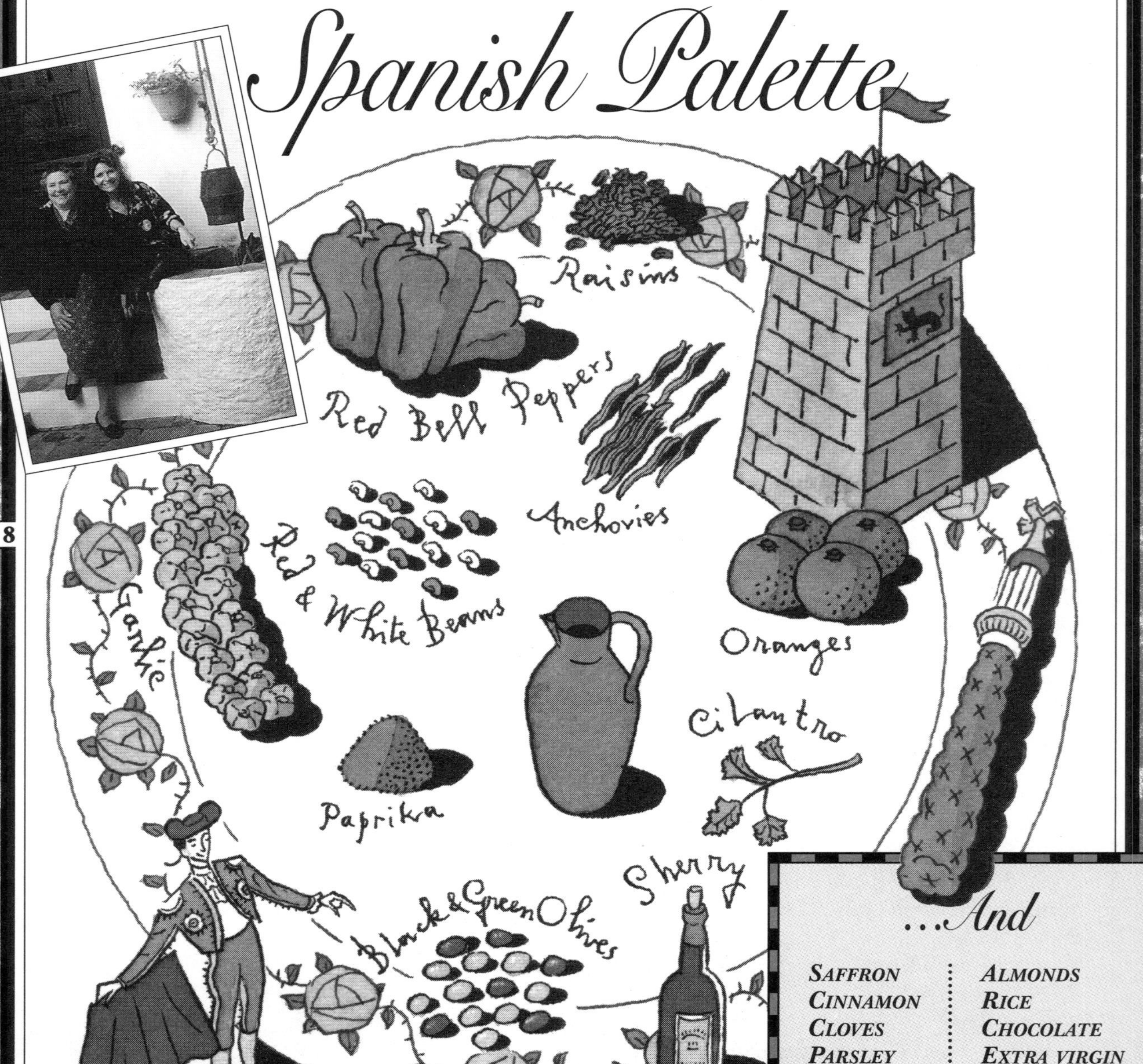

...And

SAFFRON
CINNAMON
CLOVES
PARSLEY
CAPERS
TOMATOES
ALMONDS
RICE
CHOCOLATE
EXTRA VIRGIN OLIVE OIL

Photo: With the Señora at the oldest house in Carmona, Spain.

NANI'S TORTILLA DE PATATAS

During a springtime visit to Spain, I first met Señor Adrian Forastier, who became a friend as well as a business associate. We spoke a lot about regional dishes. One in particular—*tortilla de patatas*—was something I told him I longed to taste. Each woman of the house has her own particular version of this delicious potato and onion "omelet," and it is as much a staple dish in Spain as scrambled eggs are in America. When he and his wife, Nani, came to New York from Barcelona, I invited them to my house for a lesson.

Nani explained to me that the dish is made from staple ingredients always present in a Spanish kitchen—lots of good Spanish olive oil, potatoes, onions, eggs, some coarse salt, and pepper. As we talked, she cooked and I wrote. There are actually no set rules for this recipe other than a long slow cooking of potatoes and onions in good-quality olive oil. (Don't let the quantity of oil in the recipe scare you, because most is drained off after the potatoes and onions are cooked.)

My rule would be: Do not overcook the eggs. I like my eggs set soft; 3 to 5 minutes is a good guide, but you must check carefully the first time you make the tortilla.

We gobbled this up immediately, piping hot, but it is also lovely served at room temperature or cold, cut into bite-size portions as a *tapas,* with a dab of mayonnaise.

4 large Idaho potatoes (about 2½ pounds), peeled
2 cups Spanish olive oil, for frying
1½ cups thinly sliced onions
6 large eggs
Salt and coarsely ground black pepper, to taste

1. Cut the potatoes into irregular ⅛-inch-thick slices, so that they take on a homey look.

2. Heat the oil in a 10½-inch nonstick skillet over medium heat until it just starts to shimmer in the pan. To test the heat of the oil, drop in a potato slice; if bubbles form around it, it's ready. It should not be hot enough to crisp the potatoes.

3. Stir in the potato slices, coating them well with the oil. Partially cover the skillet and cook for 5 minutes, stirring once and pressing down slightly on the potatoes with the back of a wooden spoon, so that the potatoes begin to color and soften slightly.

4. After 5 minutes, add the onions, stir well to combine with the potatoes, and continue to cook, partially covered, until the onions wilt, 15 minutes more. Stir every 5 minutes from underneath and press down on the mixture with the back of wooden spoon to break it up slightly.

5. Remove the cover and cook 15 minutes longer, stirring well. The potatoes and onions should be very soft and lightly golden but not crusty. During cooking, adjust the heat if necessary to keep it from cooking too fast.

6. Over a bowl, drain the vegetables in a coarse strainer, tapping the strainer a bit to remove as much oil as possible. Reserve the oil for frying other vegetables.

7. In a large bowl, lightly beat the eggs. Add the drained potatoes and onions. Season well with salt and pepper. Add about 1 teaspoon of the reserved oil to the skillet and heat over medium heat. Add the egg mixture, reduce the heat to medium-low, and if it begins to stick to the bottom of the pan, shake the pan slightly to move the mixture around or loosen it a bit with a spoon or spatula. Cook until the bottom is pale golden, 4 to 5 minutes, and invert it onto a flat plate.

8. Add another teaspoon of oil to the skillet if necessary and slip the omelet back in, uncooked side down. Cook until the eggs are cooked but still a bit soft on the inside, another 3 to 5 minutes, depending on desired consistency.

9. Invert the omelet onto a serving platter, and if you can bear it, let rest for 5 minutes before cutting into serving wedges and eating.

Serves 6

SOFTLY SCRAMBLED EGGS WITH ASPARAGUS AND CURED HAM

After hours of *tapas* and cocktails, dinnertime was upon us in Sevilla. At 11 P.M. we sat down to eat in the Alfonso XIII dining room, amidst the glorious Moorish architecture. The appetizer I chose—eggs and wild asparagus gently scrambled with Jabugo ham—was a marvel. The Jabugo, the lean, black-footed pig of Spain, forages mainly for nuts. There is a definite sweet, deep, rich flavor to the ham, and unlike prosciutto, it isn't very salty. Until it is made available in the United States, prosciutto will have to be substituted. At 11 A.M. this dish is ideal for brunch.

8 ounces very thin asparagus
2 ounces dried cured ham, such as prosciutto or serrano, thinly sliced
1 tablespoon extra virgin Spanish olive oil
4 large eggs
1 tablespoon sour cream
Salt and freshly ground black pepper, to taste
2 teaspoons unsalted butter
2 teaspoons snipped fresh chives, for garnish

1. Snap the woody ends off the asparagus and cut the spears into 1-inch lengths. Shred the sliced ham into 2 x ¼-inch pieces.

2. Heat the oil in a large nonstick skillet over medium heat. Add the asparagus and cook until bright green and just tender, about 2 minutes. Add the ham and cook another minute, shaking the skillet constantly. Remove the asparagus and ham and set aside. Clean the skillet.

3. Lightly beat the eggs, sour cream, salt, and pepper together, then stir in the asparagus and ham.

4. Melt the butter in the cleaned skillet over low heat. Add the egg mixture and cook, stirring constantly with a fork, until the eggs are set but still soft, 2½ to 3 minutes. Do not overcook. Serve immediately, garnished with the snipped chives.

Serves 4 as an appetizer, 2 as a brunch entrée

SCRAMBLED EGG AND SALT COD HASH

The ingredients most often used in other countries fuse beautifully with some of our best ideas. For instance, hash is one of America's favorite dishes. Instead of the traditional version with corned or roast beef, I cast my mind back to a great brunch I loved in Portugal and prepared some salt cod to get started.

Salt cod, onions, and potatoes have a great affinity for each other. For this hash, the cod is cooked gently with the onions, then the potatoes are sautéed to a golden brown. Everything is then folded together with softly scrambled eggs. Thick slices of toasted peasant bread and a cup of steamy hot chocolate is all that is necessary for a perfect Sunday morning brunch.

12 ounces salt cod, soaked overnight in water to cover
2 Idaho potatoes, peeled and cut into ¼-inch dice
4 tablespoons extra virgin olive oil
1 large onion, halved and slivered
Coarsely ground black pepper, to taste
8 large eggs
2 teaspoons chopped fresh cilantro, for garnish

1. Slice the cod about ¼ inch thick on the diagonal into large shreds. Set aside.

2. Cook the potatoes in boiling salted water to cover until just tender, about 5 minutes. Drain and set aside.

3. Heat 2 tablespoons of the oil in a large nonstick skillet. Add the onion and cook over medium heat to wilt, 10 to 12 minutes.

4. Add the shredded cod to the onions and fold together. Reduce the heat and cook, covered, until the fish is opaque and flakes when tested with a fork, about 15 minutes.

5. While the cod is cooking, heat the remaining 2 tablespoons oil in another large skillet and add the potatoes. Cook, shaking the skillet occasionally, over medium heat until the potatoes brown, about 10 minutes. Sprinkle with black pepper as they cook. With a spatula, carefully fold the potatoes into the onions and cod.

6. In a bowl, lightly beat the eggs.

7. Add the eggs to the potato mixture and cook over medium heat until the eggs are just set, about 5 minutes. Using a rubber spatula, occasionally fold the eggs from the bottom over the top. Sprinkle chopped cilantro over the top and serve immediately.

Serves 4

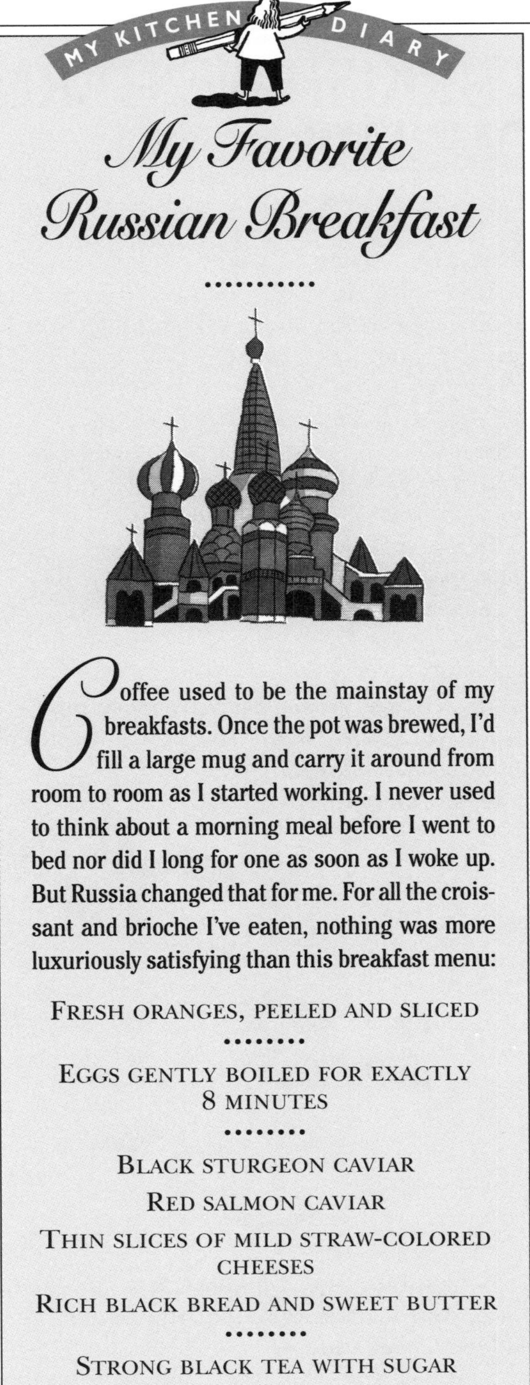

MY KITCHEN DIARY

My Favorite Russian Breakfast

Coffee used to be the mainstay of my breakfasts. Once the pot was brewed, I'd fill a large mug and carry it around from room to room as I started working. I never used to think about a morning meal before I went to bed nor did I long for one as soon as I woke up. But Russia changed that for me. For all the croissant and brioche I've eaten, nothing was more luxuriously satisfying than this breakfast menu:

FRESH ORANGES, PEELED AND SLICED

EGGS GENTLY BOILED FOR EXACTLY 8 MINUTES

BLACK STURGEON CAVIAR

RED SALMON CAVIAR

THIN SLICES OF MILD STRAW-COLORED CHEESES

RICH BLACK BREAD AND SWEET BUTTER

STRONG BLACK TEA WITH SUGAR

TURKISH WESTERN OMELET

This is my version of a Western omelet with a Turkish touch. It brings the lush flavors of the Mediterranean to your breakfast table. Top off with a cooling dollop of yogurt.

2 ripe plum tomatoes, seeded and coarsely chopped
¼ cup diced (¼ inch) feta cheese
1 ounce pastrami, cut into ¼-inch dice
2 tablespoons coarsely chopped red onion
2 tablespoons flat-leaf parsley, plus 2 teaspoons chopped, for garnish
6 large eggs
¼ cup milk
Salt and coarsely ground black pepper, to taste
4 teaspoons unsalted butter
2 tablespoons nonfat plain yogurt, for garnish

1. Combine the tomatoes, feta, pastrami, onion, and 2 tablespoons of the parsley in a small bowl. Set aside.

2. Whisk the eggs, milk, salt, and pepper together in a bowl.

3. Melt 2 teaspoons of the butter in a large nonstick skillet over medium-high heat until it foams. Pour in half of the egg mixture and stir the eggs gently until they begin to set. Stop stirring; run a spatula around the side of the skillet and shake the pan slightly to loosen the omelet from the bottom of the pan.

4. When the eggs are cooked to desired doneness (I prefer them slightly loose), spoon half of the filling onto the omelet and then roll it out onto a plate. Repeat the process to make a second omelet. Dollop each omelet with a tablespoon of yogurt and sprinkle with a teaspoon of chopped parsley.

Serves 2

ODJA

Tunisian Western Omelet

At Restaurant Bergere in Hammamet, halfway between Tunis and Sousse, I sat overlooking the turquoise Mediterranean and sandy beaches beyond the ancient medina, listening to the haunting sound of the muezzin call the faithful to prayer. I thought I was in heaven. In reality, I was at lunch—but what a heavenly lunch! Lightly scrambled eggs blended beautifully with chunky red and green peppers in a tomato sauce. The seasoning mixture of garlic and caraway along with a spoon of *harissa* (a piquant condiment made from dried chili peppers) was just delicious. For meat lovers, I suggest adding some small cubes of spicy chorizo along with the sautéed vegetables. Serve with warm pita bread and chilled crisp white wine.

4 cloves garlic, peeled
½ teaspoon caraway seeds
¼ teaspoon salt
3 tablespoons extra virgin olive oil
1 medium onion, peeled and cut into ½-inch dice
1 green bell pepper, stemmed, seeded, and cut into 1-inch dice
1 red bell pepper, stemmed, seeded, and cut into 1-inch dice
1 bay leaf
1½ cups prepared tomato sauce
1 ripe large tomato, cored, seeded, and cut into ½-inch dice
1 tablespoon Harissa (page 239)
4 large eggs, broken into a bowl
2 tablespoons coarsely chopped flat-leaf parsley, for garnish

1. Finely chop the garlic, caraway, and salt together. Set aside.

2. Heat the oil in a large nonstick skillet. Add the onion, bell peppers, and bay leaf. Cook, stirring, over medium-low heat for 5 minutes.

3. Add the tomato sauce, chopped tomato, and *harissa*; cook for 5 minutes longer to heat through.

4. Carefully slip in the eggs. With a wooden spoon, break the yolks and move the eggs around in the vegetable mixture until they set up and the whites look just slightly runny, about 2 minutes. Serve immediately, garnished with parsley.

Serves 4

ENGLISH MIXED GRILL

There are certain gastronomic moments in life that are truly unforgettable, and building upon them over the years has made my interest in food grow more and more. One such moment came in 1964, in England, when my husband Richard and I were invited to Royal Ascot, the glorious horse race which is held each year mid June. We were staying at Brown's Hotel and it was there that we had our first mixed grill breakfast. I was absolutely amazed to see a platter of grilled lamb chops, sausages, kidneys, and a rasher of bacon presented, accompanied by a grilled tomato and fried egg. To say I was watching my diet and passed on this would be a downright lie. In awe, we both gobbled down this incredible feast. It was delicious and fortifying. Every time I am back in London, I am tempted to indulge again but good sense and age tell me differently. Still a mixed grill is classic, and, if you have very low cholesterol, it is definitely a treat once in a while. (P. S. On my past visit to Britain I was once more seduced by the dish after a bowl of Irish porridge.)

1 thick white veal sausage (boudin blanc), about 4 ounces
2 small pork sausage links
2 small, thick loin lamb chops, well trimmed
2 thick slices slab bacon, rind discarded, or 2 pieces of Canadian bacon
1 ripe large tomato, halved crosswise
1 tablespoon unsalted butter
Salt and freshly ground black pepper, to taste
2 large eggs
1 teaspoon chopped flat-leaf parsley, for garnish

1. Preheat the broiler. Preheat the oven to 250°F if these units are separate.

2. Lightly score the white sausage 2 times on both sides.

3. Arrange the sausages, lamb chops, bacon, and tomato halves, cut sides up, on a heavy grilling or broiler pan. Broil 3 inches from the heat for 10 minutes, turning the sausages, chops, and bacon once after 5 minutes. Sprinkle with salt and pepper and let rest in the warm oven, or if not there, covered in a warm spot.

4. Melt the butter in a nonstick skillet over medium-low heat and fry the eggs for 2½ to 3 minutes or until desired doneness. Sprinkle with salt and pepper. Remove each egg to a large plate.

5. To serve, cut the veal sausage in half crosswise and divide the meat and tomatoes equally between the 2 plates. Sprinkle with the parsley and serve immediately.

Serves 2

SWEDISH PANCAKES

Splendid served for breakfasts or late-night suppers, these tissue-thin crêpes are delicious brushed with melted butter, folded into quarters, dusted with confectioners' sugar, and dolloped with Cherry Compote or other fresh sweetened berries. Experiment and serve them your favorite way. The crêpes can be made in advance, stacked, and wrapped well in plastic. They can be refrigerated for a few days or frozen and then wrapped in aluminum foil and warmed in a 350°F oven.

3 large eggs
2½ cups milk
1¼ cups all-purpose flour
1 tablespoon granulated sugar
½ teaspoon salt
2 tablespoons unsalted butter, melted
Approximately 1 teaspoon unsalted butter, for cooking the crêpes
2 to 4 tablespoons unsalted butter, melted for serving (optional)
¼ cup confectioners' sugar, for serving
1 cup Cherry Compote (page 510), for serving

1. Whisk together the eggs and 1 cup of the milk in a bowl.

2. Sift the dry ingredients together and then add to the egg mixture, whisking well.

3. Whisk in the remaining 1½ cups milk and the melted butter.

4. Melt ½ teaspoon butter in a 10-inch nonstick skillet over medium heat. Swirl the butter around in the pan to coat it as well as possible and heat until it's melted and very hot. Pour ¼ cup of the batter into the hot skillet and, working quickly, rotate the pan with a turn of the wrist so that the batter evenly coats the bottom of the pan. Cook the crêpe until golden brown on the bottom, or about 1½ minutes. Turn the crêpe over and cook it 1 minute longer. Remove to a plate. Continue with the remaining batter, adding a bit more butter to the pan if the crêpes begin to stick and stacking the crêpes as they are finished.

5. If serving the crêpes the same day, cover them with a kitchen towel until ready. For later use, wrap the crêpes well in plastic and refrigerate or freeze.

6. Just before serving, brush the crêpes lightly with the remaining melted butter, if desired, and dust with confectioners' sugar. Fold into quarters and place on dessert plates. Top with a spoonful of cherry compote or sweetened berries of your choice.

Makes 18 crêpes, enough for 6 servings

MY KITCHEN DIARY

Jamaican Blue Mountain Coffee

There is a Jamaican folk song that goes there is nothing like "a bowl of boiling coffee in the morning." Jamaican Blue Mountain beans are extremely aromatic with a sweet, gentle, mild flavor. They make coffee that is perfect for any occasion—and certainly worth singing about.

Jamaican Blue Mountain coffee is ranked the best in the world. It is the combination of topography, geology, and climate that results in a coffee with an almost perfect balance of aroma, body, acidity, and sweetness, creating a clean flavor and bouquet. Its scarcity and high demand make it the most expensive coffee in the world.

Coffee arrived in Jamaica in 1725 with Governor Sir Nicholas Lawes from Martinique. He planted seven Arabica seedlings on his estate in the foothills of the Blue Mountains at St. Andrew. Suitable conditions led the seedlings to flourish, and by the beginning of the 19th century, there were over 600 coffee plantations in Jamaica.

Soaring to 7,402 feet in the eastern part of the island, the Blue Mountains are the highest in Jamaica. The altitude and latitude of these mountains produce a climate that is always cool and misty yet never cold. Premium Blue Mountain coffee must grow above 5,000 feet and within a ten-mile radius of the Blue Mountain peak to claim its denomination as the world's richest tasting coffee.

BANANA CINNAMON PANCAKES

Do I ever owe a debt of gratitude to Miss Maud, a Jamaican cook, who made the most delicious banana pancakes for my family. Following is a version of her recipe which will certainly warm your heart on any cold winter morning. I've made a butter rum sauce to pour on top. These also would make a splendid dessert, stacked three high with hot butter rum sauce drizzled over them and a scoop of banana ice cream on top.

1 cup all-purpose flour
1¼ teaspoons baking powder
½ teaspoon ground cinnamon
Pinch of salt
1 cup milk
¼ cup (packed) light brown sugar
3 tablespoons corn oil
1 large egg
1 teaspoon pure vanilla extract
1 cup mashed ripe bananas (2 to 3 bananas)
1 tablespoon unsalted butter, melted
Butter Rum Sauce (recipe follows)

1. Combine the dry ingredients in a large bowl.

2. In a separate bowl mix together the milk, sugar, 2 tablespoons of the oil, the egg, and vanilla extract. Add to the dry ingredients and stir until the mixture is almost smooth. Fold the bananas into the batter. Let rest, loosely covered, for 20 minutes.

3. Combine the melted butter with the remaining tablespoon oil in a small ramekin for cooking the pancakes.

4. Place a nonstick skillet over medium heat. Pour a scant teaspoon of the butter and oil mixture in the skillet and heat. For each pancake, pour ¼ cup batter into the pan and cook until small bubbles form on the top, about 1 minute. Turn the pancake over and cook an additional 30 to 45 seconds. Proceed with the rest of the batter, adding more of the butter and oil mixture to the pan as necessary. Serve warm with the butter rum sauce.

Makes twelve 3-inch pancakes, enough to serve 4

BUTTER RUM SAUCE

When I was thinking of what to pour over banana pancakes, it seemed clear to me that maple syrup just wouldn't do. Easily prepared in the microwave, this sauce just hits the spot. The flavor of rum adds zest, while a pat of butter smooths the flavors together. It is also excellent at room temperature served over ice cream.

½ cup pure maple syrup
1 tablespoon unsalted butter
2 tablespoons dark Jamaican rum

1. Combine all the ingredients in a 4-cup microwave-safe measuring cup.

2. Cook on medium-high power for 2 minutes, until the butter is melted. Stir and serve hot.

Makes ⅔ cup

Note: This recipe was prepared in a 600- to 750-watt carousel microwave at medium-high power. If your microwave is less powerful, adjust the cooking time.

MISS MAUD'S BREAKFAST BANANA BREAD

During our stay in Jamaica, the smell of Miss Maud's fresh-baked banana bread would awaken us each morning. It's both moist and delicious and especially good sliced, toasted, and topped with guava jelly. Anyway you eat it, try it once out in the sun with some vintage Harry Belafonte calypso music on a hot summer day just to put yourself in the Caribbean mood.

1 cup (2 sticks) unsalted butter, at room temperature
1 cup (packed) light brown sugar
6 large eggs
2 cups all-purpose flour
2 teaspoons baking powder
¼ teaspoon ground nutmeg
Pinch of salt
3 ripe bananas, mashed
1 teaspoon pure vanilla extract

1. Preheat the oven to 350°F. Butter and lightly flour a 9 x 5-inch loaf pan.

2. Cream the butter and brown sugar in a large bowl with an electric mixer. Add the eggs one by one, beating well after each addition.

3. Combine the dry ingredients in a small bowl and add to the butter mixture, a little at a time, beating well after each addition.

4. Add the bananas and vanilla and mix to combine.

5. Pour the batter into the prepared pan. Bake until a skewer inserted in the center of the loaf comes out clean, about 1½ hours.

6. Cool the loaf in the pan for 10 minutes and then turn it out onto a rack to cool completely.

Makes 1 loaf

TORRIJAS

Spanish "French" Toast

There is nothing like breakfast in bed with cinnamon-dazzled Spanish French toast accompanied by Chocolate a la Taza, the great Spanish hot chocolate (see Index). Some ripe, long-stemmed strawberries alongside make for perfect nibbling and a perfect morning.

2 cups milk
2 large eggs
3 tablespoons granulated sugar
2 teaspoons ground cinnamon
2 tablespoons confectioners' sugar
4 thick slices (½ inch) crusty peasant bread, cut from a large round loaf, halved crosswise
2 tablespoons extra virgin Spanish olive oil

1. In a bowl large enough to soak the bread, whisk together the milk, eggs, granulated sugar, and 1 teaspoon of the cinnamon.

2. Combine the remaining teaspoon of cinnamon with the confectioners' sugar in a small bowl. Set aside.

3. Dip the bread in the batter to coat well.

4. Heat the oil in a nonstick skillet over medium-high heat. Lightly brown the bread in the oil, in batches if necessary (using more oil as needed), until nicely toasted, about 2½ minutes on each side.

5. Place 2 pieces of French toast on each plate and, using a strainer, sprinkle with the cinnamon sugar. Serve immediately.

Serves 4

ROOM SERVICE

Breakfast in Bed

There is probably no meal that I love more when I travel than a hotel breakfast, especially a room service breakfast. As a rule, it offers the little luxuries I never allow myself at home—endless pots of hot coffee or tea; great selections of fine jams and preserves; a vast array of warm muffins, sweet rolls, croissants, brioche, breads, and toast; local cheeses; fresh juices; and perfectly ripe fruit. And at home, would breakfast ever be served by a tuxedo-clad waiter sporting the morning paper and a pleasant attitude? Or would we bother to set a table beautifully with crisply laundered linens and a single perfect flower in a decorative yet elegant vase? Not likely. It's no wonder I love, and make the most of, away-from-home breakfasts.

Here then are some of my favorite morning meals.

Breakfast in Marrakech

Time:
about 8:30 A.M.

Place:
The Mamounia Hotel, Marrakech.

The order:
A Moroccan breakfast in my room.

The Moroccan breakfast turned out to be much too extensive to be served on a tray; therefore, a good-size table arrived and was placed on my terrace with a wonderful view of the hotel's palm gardens. The table was draped with delicate peach-colored linen, and a Lalique-style vase held full-blown, blood-red roses.

To begin, there were chilled fresh orange and grapefruit juices and a choice of yogurts. Baskets of muffins, croissants, and *pains au chocolat* rested near a small bowl of lush, deep purple grapes. Next came *harira,* the national soup of Morocco, made with lamb, lentils, chickpeas, and vegetables. This is traditionally served to break the fast during Ramadan and is always accompanied by some small sweet such as dried dates.

Following was the *beghir l'ghaif au miel et beurre*. These are thin honey-combed pancakes drizzled with fresh honey and melted butter. Immediately after arrived a rust-colored ceramic *tagine saloui,* a round, shallow dish with a conical lid. The dish inside was a bit more difficult for me to figure out. It was called *khlii aux oeufs*. When I looked under the lid, I saw lots of baked eggs surrounded by some form of cubed meat. A call to the chef revealed it to be sun-dried lamb cured with garlic, coriander, oil, and vinegar.

"The table was draped with delicate peach-colored linen, and a cut Lalique-style vase held full-blown, blood-red roses."

Scenes from the marvelous Mamounia in magical Marrakech, left to right: A rose on the breakfast table. The perfect bed for a morning meal, in a room with a garden view. A beautiful tagine keeps breakfast warm.

Quite a spread for 8:30 A.M. The feast was completed by a glass of perfumed *thé à la menthe*. The wonderful memories linger, but the next morning I ordered black coffee, toast, and some jam.

Room Service at the Hotel Gellert

For me, there is only one place to stay in Budapest—the Hotel Gellert, an Art Nouveau jewel built in 1918 at the foot of the Liberty Bridge on the Buda side of the Danube, in the shadow of Gellert Hill.

Upon entering the domed and pillared hall, it is clear why this hotel has been host to the grand and famous over the years. Recently restored, but not nearly to its once glorious self, one can still imagine what its finer days must have been like.

A stay at the hotel includes the use of its renowned spa. The Gellert's thermal baths are the most elegant in Budapest (Budapest sits atop a wealth of thermal springs), intricately tiled in different shades of green and blue interspersed with shiny gold. Between the men's and women's baths is a grand indoor swimming pool. My stay included luxurious mornings of steaming, soaking, and a good pummeling by the house masseuse, then breakfast in my room, which seemed to arrive as soon as I returned.

A tiny glass of fresh orange juice started the meal followed by copious amounts of steaming coffee. Two fried eggs perched on thinly sliced Hungarian smoked ham, accompanied by two gherkin pickles, lay waiting under a silver dome. A small basket held poppy seed-speckled rolls, whole-grain breads, and a delicious bun with broiled Parmesan cheese, all served with sweet butter, cream cheese, and a pot of cherry preserves. The grand finale was a golden, flaky pastry package filled with a luscious cheese mixture and dusted with confectioners' sugar. What splendor!

Sunday Morning in Cuba

After a glamorous night at the Tropicana night club in Havana, I couldn't wait to wake up and see what was for breakfast. (The Tropicana is about the only night club open in Cuba these days; although it is a little rough around the edges, I had a wonderful time.) In the morning, I took the elevator to the lobby which, I discovered, was overflowing with visiting South Americans and Europeans. I had been inquiring all over as to where the best Sunday brunch in Havana was served. All roads led to the few hotel dining rooms, and it made sense to go no further than the dining room of the Inglaterra, where I was staying. The walls of this lovely room were adorned with elaborate Spanish tiles in white, yellow, and blue patterns.

Top to bottom: The newest rose in old Havana. Scenes from the Tropicana '92 —it could have been Vegas!

The floor was all of marble, large pink and black squares, clean and polished. The elaborately carved white ceilings were decorated with gold paint. Heavy, dark, wooden Spanish tables were draped in crisp white linen and a generous buffet was set and waiting. Before approaching the food, coffee was definitely in order. Since the cups were tiny, I asked for two. The coffee was dark, strong, and heavily sweetened with a sugar syrup.

The first platter on the buffet table held toast, small twirled rolls, and crackers. Dishes of plum jam and orange marmalade were placed nearby. Then on to the parade of eggs. Eggs boiled for 5 minutes—or so said the accompanying card—nested in a large bowl of coarse salt to keep them warm. Next came a serving dish filled with hard-cooked eggs. Following, arranged in a chafing dish, were scrambled eggs garnished with strips of roasted pimiento and mortadella. There was a tray of black bread slices spread with something that closely resembled Spam or Pennsylvania Dutch scrapple. I passed on the sandwiches.

At the far end of the buffet table were urns filled with milk and a liquid yogurt drink. Another table opposite the eggs was set with platters of shredded cabbage and carrot salads. Large arrangements of cut fruits—pineapple, melons, oranges, and grapefruit—completed the display. Slices of orange bread, similar to a tea loaf, were offered.

For years there was a great Russian presence in Cuba. Although this is no longer the case, their breakfast influence still, obviously, exists. The brunch offerings, while not spectacular, were certainly good, and were made even better by my excitement about being in Cuba.

"The Tropicana is about the only night club open in Cuba these days; although it is a little rough around the edges, we had a wonderful time."

Breakfast at Café Tacuba

Café Tacuba is housed in a restored colonial convent in Mexico City's historic downtown district. My husband Richard, and my daughters, Annabel and Molly, and I were seated at a round table, surrounded by pristine white plastered walls decorated with blue and yellow Talvera tiles from Puebla, and elaborate wrought iron sconces. Since I wanted to taste everything on the menu, as usual, we ordered too much.

First came a large frothy pitcher of freshly made pineapple juice with about ten plastic straws placed inside. We all opted for glasses. Beautiful slices of pound cake topped with toasted almonds and lots of granulated sugar were served next. Then four large glasses of warm milk were set in the center of the table along with a small carafe of very strong coffee. The idea was to pour a bit of coffee into the milk for *café con leche*.

I could not resist ordering the *huevos rancheros*: two fried eggs perfectly cooked atop crisp tortillas drizzled with a hot chili-sparkled tomato sauce. Molly went for the hotcakes topped with butter and a type of maple syrup. Richard ordered a *tortilla española* (Spanish omelet), and Annabel chose *revueltos a la mexicana* (eggs scrambled with tomatoes, onions, green peppers, and red chilies served with refried red beans, *queso blanco*, and a dollop of *crema*—similar to sour cream—on top.) Served on beautifully decorated ceramic dishes, everything was delicious and festive. We all had big cups of Mexican hot chocolate with our splendid breakfasts.

On the Beach in Rio

Breakfast overlooking the Copacabana and Ipanema beaches in Rio was spectacular. In the seductive morning hours before the beaches swarm with some of the best bathing-suited bodies I've ever seen, the sand is vibrantly dotted with striped lounge chairs, umbrellas, and cabanas in brilliant shades of flamingo pink, dazzling turquoise, and blazing tangerine. The spectacular Sugarloaf Mountain looms in the background, highlighting Rio's distinctive natural beauty and setting the scene that has become famous around the world. Small stands draped and piled high with coconuts await the beginning of the business day when the throngs will line up to buy sweet coconut milk.

"In the seductive morning hours... the sand is vibrantly dotted with striped lounge chairs, umbrellas, and cabanas in brilliant shades of flamingo pink, dazzling turquoise, and blazing tangerine."

Breakfast began with freshly pressed apple juice followed by honeydew melon, sliced oranges, and ripe, red papayas. As expected, the coffee was luscious, thick and dark, and accompanied by foamy hot milk. Platters of thinly sliced ham and small wedges of local white cheese followed. Baskets of tiny brioche, croissants, melba toasts, and rolls were on the table, as were butter, honey, and a choice of lovely preserves. A small coconut flan was creamy and the perfect dessert touch to this simple, yet delicious, breakfast.

A Nordic Breakfast Buffet

A Nordic-style breakfast buffet is as incredible as it is unending. Table after table is laid out with appealing choices—the rest of life's decisions should only be so tough. My hotel in Helsinki, Finland, offered up one of the best of these buffets.

The first table held cut-glass pitchers of milk and different juices in a rainbow of colors, glass bowls filled with different blends of muesli, and an array of flavored and plain yogurts poking out of crushed ice. The next table was laden with luscious ripe fruit: sliced melons, berries of every variety, grapefruit halves, oranges, crispy red and green apples. Platters were spiraled with sliced tomatoes and cucumbers. Alongside, a table was arranged with trays of thinly sliced Swedish cheeses—Grevé, Hushållsost, Sveciaost, and Mesost—thinly sliced cured ham and smoked reindeer, a Finnish "must try." A rustic country basket covered with a quilted cozy kept boiled eggs snug and warm. The herring offerings were vast: smoked, pickled, with sour cream, home cured, marinated, and fried. Crocks were filled with rich cream cheese with chives, tarama, and unsalted butter. Strawberry and apricot preserves glistened alongside. An entire table was devoted to overflowing baskets of thickly sliced whole-grain breads, rolls, coffeecakes, and crisp flatbreads. Finally, steaming hot coffee and tea were served in big breakfast cups by the staff once you returned to a table with your embarrassingly ladened plateful.

"Table after table is laid out with appealing choices—the rest of life's decisions should only be so tough."

Left: Spectacular Guanabara Bay in Rio. Right: Ipanema at carnival time—the festive umbrellas are as impressive as the bathing suits.

On the Island of Crete

After learning of the extraordinary breakfast served at Hotel Doma in Chania, on the island of Crete, my husband Richard and I postponed our departure by a day so that we could enjoy an 11 A.M. feast on a Sunday morning. It didn't disappoint.

We were seated near a window framed by fuchsia

and bougainvillaea that overlooked the blue-green Aegean dappled with rugged sand-colored rocks. A brilliant

Left and right: The best breakfast in Crete is served at the Hotel Doma overlooking the Aegean.

blue sky capped the beauty of a moment that surely the Fauves would have envied.

A cut-glass compote dish offered blushing ripe peaches, apricots, and blood-red cherries. A single full-blown pink rose was placed next to the fruit. Small bowls were filled with mizithra (a mild feta cheese), salt-cured olives, and wild thyme honey. Pots of homemade orange marmalade and cherry preserves waited to be spread on sesame-covered, doughnut-shaped koulouria and rusks (hard barley toasts). The *pièce de résistance* was a bowl of rich, creamy yogurt spiced with cinnamon and ginger and topped with a sweetened plump black cherry sauce, sprinkled with pistachio nuts. Herbal teas completed the meal. Upon hearing that this is a typical field worker's breakfast, I could understand where all their energy comes from.

Early Morning in Istanbul

The gentle rap on the door of my room at the Istanbul Hilton at 7 A.M. announced a waiter carrying a tray laden with cheese, olives, sliced tomatoes, breads, wild thyme honey, preserves, and assorted breads. This was exactly what I was hungry for.

The cheese, beyaz penir, made from sheep's milk, resembles pot cheese and has a soft spreadable consistency similar to a young chèvre. *Siyah zeytia* are small, wrinkled, salt-cured, mild, black olives, with a sweet undertaste.

The best approach to this early gastronomic bliss, although a bit sticky, is to begin with a slice of crusty bread spread with cheese. Drizzle with honey and top with a slice or two of tomato. Nibble on olives as you go along, while sipping herbal tea. The only addition I would have made was a small dish of candied bitter orange peel—heaven!

SOUVENIR TO SAVOR

A Japanese Breakfast in Amsterdam

As I traveled around the world, I noticed more and more Japanese tourists everywhere I went. Several hotels worldwide are now accommodating these visitors by including their version of a typical Japanese breakfast on their menus. This is a simple but lovely version from Amsterdam. The gentler flavors of the miso soup and salmon are offset by the crunchy, sharp radishes and slightly bitter green plums. An interesting contrast to eggs and pancakes.

Miso Soup
Broiled Salmon
Boiled Rice
Roasted Seaweed
Pickled Radishes
Salted Green Plums
Green Tea

Brioche in Japan

In Tokyo, I had two totally different breakfast experiences. On my first visit, I was fortunate enough to stay at the Okura Hotel, a majestic structure that would have easily pleased Frank Lloyd Wright with its tasteful simplicity and grandeur. As expected, my breakfast at the hotel was equal in its tasteful simplicity. First, a ripe, juicy, bright green muskmelon turned out to be one of the most delicious pieces of fruit that I have ever tasted. Next, the famous Okura cinnamon toast was layered piece by piece in a stacked bamboo bento box. On the snowiest morning in New England, I have never had cinnamon toast to match this. Perhaps it was the thick, freshly baked brioche that made it so extraordinary. Perhaps it was the way the flavor was set off by a cup of steaming green tea. Perhaps it was the idea of this hardly traditional Japanese dish being offered at all. For me, it was a perfect way to start the day.

On the other hand, when I woke up at 3 A.M. for a predawn visit to Tsukiji, Tokyo's famed wholesale fish market, I was more than happy to huddle with a steamy hot bowl of noodle soup at a packed little sidewalk restaurant stand.

Frank Lloyd Wright might have felt right at home in Tokyo's sweeping Okura Hotel.

Continental Breakfast in Denmark

....

At the Hotel d'Angleterre in Denmark, continental breakfast takes on a whole new dimension. About 8 A.M. each day, a white linen-covered trolley adorned with a single white rose arrived in my room. A generous pot of coffee, tea, or hot chocolate stood beside a delicate basket filled with four different kinds of fresh bread, thickly sliced and generously embellished with the best grains. There was always one flaky Danish pastry, a different filling for each day of my stay! I understand why the Danes are famous for their delicate, not too sweet, buttery pastries. If coffee was not one's preference, fresh orange juice and a peach melba yogurt drink were served. There were also little jars of orange blossom honey and different jams, including black currant, my choice, along with a crock of sweet Danish butter. A pretty card with the daily weather forecast prepared me for another delightful day in Copenhagen.

Tulips and Gouda in Amsterdam

....

One of my favorite pleasures in Amsterdam was the Dutch breakfast. In my hotel dining room, which overlooked the canal below, I noticed, while sitting at a table covered with white linen and topped with a sumptuous bouquet of Dutch tulips, that the reflection of the oddly shaped facades of the brick houses across the way was disturbed only by the swimming ducks.

Breaking this reverie was breakfast: a large basket of white and whole-wheat breads and *ontbijtkoek,* or Dutch spice cake, a platter of thinly sliced Gouda cheese (naturally, this being Holland), ham, salami, tomatoes, and little pots of strawberry preserves and butter. Here were all the fixings for creating one's own open-faced sandwiches. A boiled egg and a huge pot of steaming tea began the day perfectly.

Breakfast at Ballymaloe

....

My first breakfast in Ireland was everything I had been waiting for from the moment I planned my trip. Ballymaloe is a marvelous grand country house owned by the Allen family in County Cork, where hospitality and food reign supreme. The accommodations are quartered within the main house and in a converted stable,

Above: The statue of Hans Christian Andersen's Little Mermaid rests in Copenhagen Harbor. Right and far right: At Ballymaloe, the morning tea arrives on a gingham-covered tray and is a welcome sight.

which was painted pale pink and covered in full blown lavender wisteria when I visited.

Great new friends, Sally and John McKenna, authors of *The Bridgestone Guides,* the best hotel and restaurant guides to Ireland, and food writers for *The Irish Times,* joined me and guided me through my morning meal while they planned the rest of my day.

Breakfast was served in one of the small dining rooms. Sun spilled onto the intimate round table covered in a blue and white gingham cloth. Bowls of gooseberry preserves and orange marmalade were laid next to irresistible baskets of coarse brown, just-baked Irish breads. Ballymaloe prides itself on serving only farm-churned sweet butter.

In awe, I sipped from a glass of fresh grapefruit juice, then dug in. Bowls of steamy hot oatmeal porridge sprinkled with coarse brown sugar and drizzled with cream arrived, followed by an amazing mixed grill. Each plate was arranged with a fried egg, grilled tomato, a rasher of bacon, one grilled pork sausage, grilled black pudding, and a sausage stuffed with pork and oats. A serving of mushrooms completed the dish. About this time a huge basket of hot scones was served; all was washed down with pots of tea and coffee.

Instead of the expected too-stuffed-to-move feeling, I was completely exhilarated by the magnificent Ballymaloe good morning.

"Bowls of gooseberry preserves and orange marmalade were laid next to irresistible baskets of coarse brown, just-baked Irish breads."

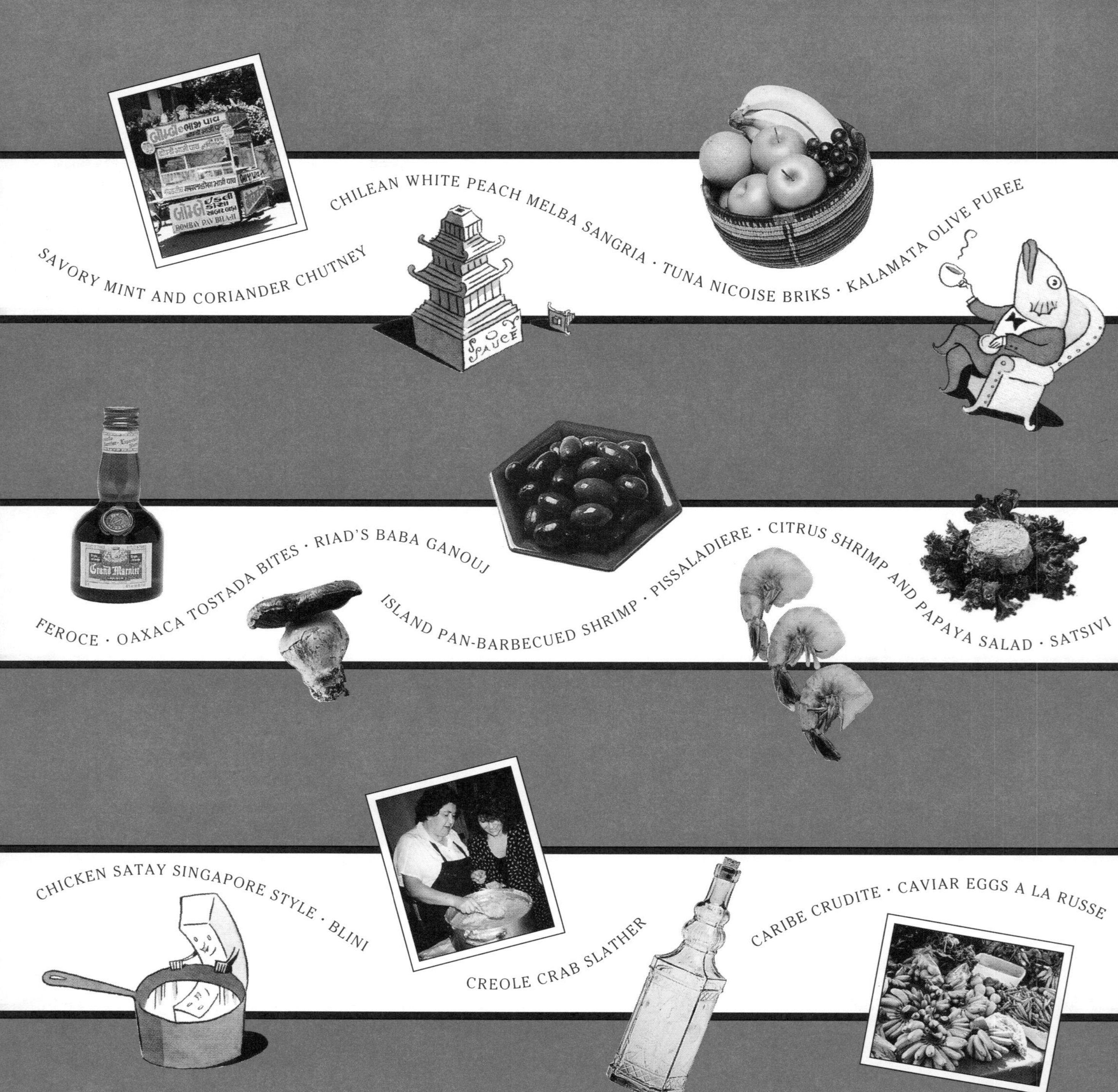
SAVORY MINT AND CORIANDER CHUTNEY
CHILEAN WHITE PEACH MELBA SANGRIA · TUNA NICOISE BRIKS · KALAMATA OLIVE PUREE
SAUCE
Grand Marnier
FEROCE · OAXACA TOSTADA BITES · RIAD'S BABA GANOUJ
ISLAND PAN-BARBECUED SHRIMP · PISSALADIERE · CITRUS SHRIMP AND PAPAYA SALAD · SATSIVI
CHICKEN SATAY SINGAPORE STYLE · BLINI
CREOLE CRAB SLATHER
CARIBE CRUDITE · CAVIAR EGGS A LA RUSSE

SPANAKOPITA · TURKISH EGGPLANT SALAD
BADAM SANDHEKO
THOSE TROPICAL SPLENDIFEROUS DRINKS
Wish You Were Here
PINA MARTINIQUE · THOD MUN PLA
CUBA LIBRE · TINY POTATO CROQUETTES · LAURIE'S BASIC GUACAMOLE
PLAKA TSATSIKI
THAI CRAB SPRING ROLLS · SASHA'S APPLE CRAB COCKTAIL · ZAKUSKI · SUNSHINE SALAD

Aperitifs

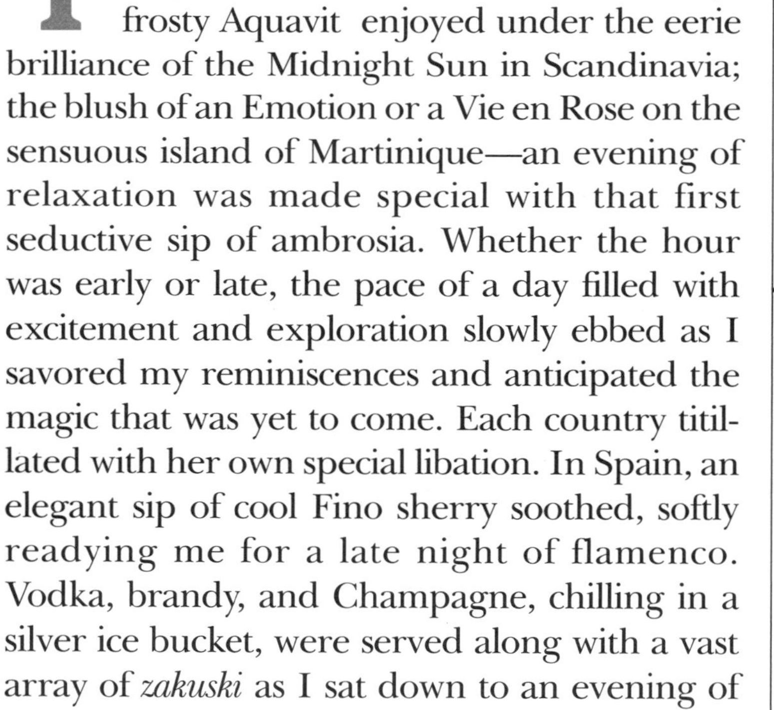

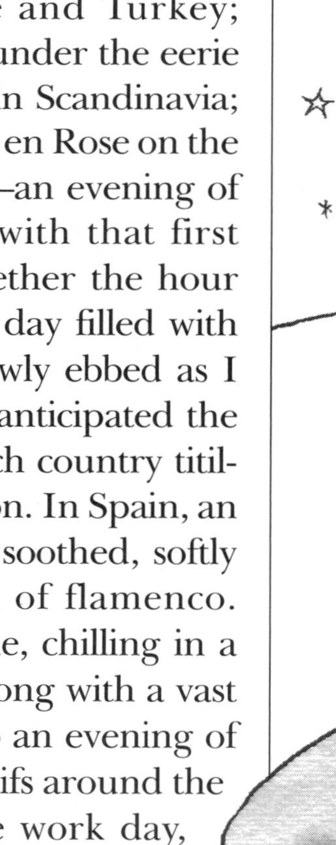

The cool clear fire of ouzo and raki judiciously sipped while overlooking the Aegean Sea in Greece and Turkey; frosty Aquavit enjoyed under the eerie brilliance of the Midnight Sun in Scandinavia; the blush of an Emotion or a Vie en Rose on the sensuous island of Martinique—an evening of relaxation was made special with that first seductive sip of ambrosia. Whether the hour was early or late, the pace of a day filled with excitement and exploration slowly ebbed as I savored my reminiscences and anticipated the magic that was yet to come. Each country titillated with her own special libation. In Spain, an elegant sip of cool Fino sherry soothed, softly readying me for a late night of flamenco. Vodka, brandy, and Champagne, chilling in a silver ice bucket, were served along with a vast array of *zakuski* as I sat down to an evening of feasting in St. Petersburg. Aperitifs around the world welcome the end of the work day, glasses brimming with conviviality and anticipation.

MARGARITAS

A Mexican favorite, margaritas are much beloved by so many of my friends, and every one of them has their own special secret to making this potent brew just right. The rim of the glass is either dipped in coarse salt or not, served over ice or straight up or frozen and slushy. Here is my friend Ellen White's version; it is sublime.

4 tablespoons coarse salt
2 lime wedges
4 ounces tequila (preferably Cuervo Gold)
1 ounce Grand Marnier or other orange liqueur
3 ounces fresh lime juice
Ice cubes or crushed ice
2 lime slices, for garnish

1. Sprinkle salt on a small plate.

2. Rub the rims of 2 cocktail glasses with the lime wedges and then dip them into the salt.

3. Pour the tequila, Grand Marnier, and lime juice into a cocktail shaker filled with ice cubes or crushed ice. Shake well and pour or strain half the mixture into each glass. Garnish each with a lime slice.

Makes 2 drinks

MY KITCHEN DIARY

Ouzo and Raki

Throughout the tavernas in Greece and Turkey, lazy days and spirited nights are celebrated with leisurely conversation and small glasses of an anisette-flavored aperitif—ouzo in Greece and fiery raki in Turkey. These potent spirits are distilled from wine grape residuals, and other fruits such as dates and figs. When mixed with water and ice, ouzo and raki turn a cloudy white, which the Turkish call "lion's milk," referring more to its strength than its appearance. Ouzo, milder only in comparison to raki, can be found spiced delicately with star anise, lime, and coriander. To keep your senses balanced, accompany these aperitifs with *meze* (see First Bites & Small Plates for a selection) or a simple bite of nuts or fresh fruit.

FRESH GRAPEFRUIT SPRITZ

Light, simple to prepare, and delicious, I enjoyed this refreshing drink in Jamaica. Wait until pink grapefruits are in season and squeeze up this naturally sweet drink. It's just right with hot and spicy food.

2 cups fresh grapefruit juice (2 pink grapefruits)
1 tablespoon sugar (optional)
Ice cubes
1 large bottle (23.5 ounces, 750 ml) sparkling water
4 fresh pineapple spears (each 3 inches long)
4 fresh mint sprigs

1. Pour ½ cup grapefruit juice in each of 4 glasses. Sweeten with a bit of sugar if desired. Add a few ice cubes and fill each glass with sparkling water.

2. Garnish each drink with a pineapple spear and a sprig of mint.

Makes 4 drinks

SOUVENIR TO SAVOR

The Rum of Martinique

Driving along the small and winding sun-drenched roads through the century-old sugar cane plantations in Martinique, we wove our way to Domaine Clement, one of the finest rum distilleries on the island. There we sampled the great plantation rums called rum *agricole,* many of which might easily compete with France's fine Armagnacs and Cognacs. These rums are not manufactured from residual sugar in a factory, but from cane juice pressed right there on the plantation.

Little has changed on the great plantations since the early 1600s when sugar cane and sun began working together to produce the pure white juice from which the finest rums are made. Sugar cane is still harvested by hand with a cutlass or machete, which ensures that it is cut at the bottom of the stalk, where it is richest in sugar. The top ends, which contain many impurities, are removed and most often used for molasses.

Once the juice is pressed from the cane, it is filtered, purified, concentrated, and distilled. White rum is aged in oak casks, and the longer it matures, the finer it will taste. Dark rums are aged for six to ten years in oak casks that have been burned inside with a torch. By some marvelous and mysterious alchemy, the rum acquires an incomparable finesse and a rich, deep amber color.

Both white and dark rums are the *raison d'être* for so many spectacular tropical drinks throughout the luscious sun-drenched Caribbean, but which to choose for each drink can sometimes be a puzzlement. I prefer to use white rum when mixing up light, fruity favorites such as daiquiris. An excellent aged dark rum can be enjoyed on its own, much as you would a fine Cognac. I also like a dark rum mixed into planter's punch. It tends to give the drink substantial body. And although white rum is usually poured for a Cuba Libre, when made with dark rum, it is quite delicious.

Santé! to the glorious tropical drinks that rum has inspired.

CARIBBEAN DAIQUIRIS

Daiquiris are elegant, smooth cocktails. They are delicious in their basic form and festive as sort of icy slushes with the addition of sweet, ripe fruits. The rule of thumb when making a basic daiquiri is to put it in a cocktail shaker, shake hard, and strain into a cocktail glass. When making a fruity variation, all ingredients get blended together and poured directly into a cocktail glass. Sip slowly. Cheers!

A BASIC DAIQUIRI

Crushed ice or ice cubes
1½ ounces white rum
Juice of 1 lime
1 tablespoon Simple Sugar Syrup (page 34)
Thin slice lime, for garnish

Half fill a cocktail shaker with the ice. Add the rum, lime juice, and syrup, and shake well. Strain into a cocktail glass. Garnish with a lime slice and enjoy.

Makes 1 drink

STRAWBERRY OR MANGO DAIQUIRI

Fresh fruit daiquiris, everything from strawberries to bananas, make the most delectable cocktails. Use smooth Caribbean white rum and fruit in perfect condition. Dig out the pink paper parasols and use them to garnish your drinks, along with a sprig of fresh mint or a small piece of fruit.

½ cup sliced ripe strawberries or chopped ripe mango
3 ounces white rum
Juice of 2 limes
1 ounce Simple Sugar Syrup (page 34)
1 cup crushed ice
2 whole strawberries or 2 fresh mint sprigs, for garnish

Combine all the ingredients except the garnish in a blender and process at high speed until mixed, 30 seconds. Pour into daiquiri glasses. Garnish each strawberry daiquiri with a fresh strawberry or each mango daiquiri with a mint sprig and serve.

Makes 2 drinks

BANANA DAIQUIRI

1 ripe banana, cut into large chunks
Juice of 2 limes
1 ounce Simple Sugar Syrup (recipe follows)
3 ounces white rum
1 cup crushed ice
2 fresh mint sprigs or pineapple spears

Combine all the ingredients except the garnish in a blender and process at high speed until mixed, 30 seconds. Pour into daiquiri glasses. Garnish each with a mint sprig or pineapple spear and serve.

Makes 2 drinks

SOUVENIR TO SAVOR

The Daiquiri

While sitting in the lobby of the Hotel Inglaterra in Havana, I read a little story about a Cuban barman by the name of Constante Ribalaiqua. Constante is credited with perfecting the daiquiri around the end of the 19th century at the glamorous Floridita Bar, which then bestowed on itself the distinction of being "the cradle of the daiquiri." The drink originated with the hardened warriors of the Liberation army. In order to combat against the weariness felt from years of struggling for independence from Spain, they tied to their saddles small bottles filled with a mixture of strong rum, honey, and lemon juice called *canchachara,* a vigorous stimulant for the long treks on horseback and exhausting battles. When U.S. troops arrived in Cuba in 1898, they added crushed ice to the *canchachara.* This first occurred near the shores of Daiquirí in the province of Orinte, and hence the new and lasting name.

SIMPLE SUGAR SYRUP

2 cups water
1 cup sugar

1. Combine the ingredients in a saucepan and simmer until the sugar is dissolved, stirring occasionally.

2. Cool to room temperature, pour into a glass jar, cover, and store in the refrigerator until ready for use.

Makes 2½ cups

MOJITO

Mojito . . . para empezar agrada, etona y alegra. Pon a trabajar el bar! "The *mojito* sparks your life and makes you happy. Let the bar work!" This is a famous Cuban version of the mint julep.

2 tablespoons very finely chopped fresh mint leaves
1 teaspoon sugar
1 tablespoon fresh lime juice
Crushed ice
2 ounces white rum
Club soda
2 fresh mint sprigs, for garnish

Mix the chopped mint leaves, sugar, and lime juice in a small pitcher. Fill 2 tall glasses with crushed ice. Pour the mint mixture over the ice, add rum to each glass, and top up with club soda. Garnish each glass with a mint sprig.

Makes 2 drinks

CUBA LIBRE

At the end of Batista's rule in Cuba, when Castro took control of the country, there was much celebrating to be done. The drink that welcomed Castro and celebrated "free Cuba" in the late fifties was the "Cuba Libre"—white or dark rum is the choice for this cola drink.

1 lime, halved
Ice cubes
3 ounces white rum
Cola
2 lime slices, for garnish

Squeeze the juice of half a lime into each of 2 tall glasses and drop in the lime halves. Fill the glasses with ice cubes, add the rum, and top with cola. Garnish each glass with a lime slice.

Makes 2 drinks

PUNCH MARTINIQUE

The rum of Martinique is extremely potent—up to 50 percent alcohol—so if that's where your rum is from serve the punch in small glasses. There is really no official recipe for this luscious drink as it is usually made to please the individual palate by adjusting the quantity of sugar syrup added. The only rule is to pour the sugar syrup into the glass first, followed by the rum and the lime juice. Stir the syrup before adding, or it will get too thick to mix well.

2 ounces Simple Sugar Syrup (facing page)
6 ounces white rum
Juice of 2 limes
Ice cubes
2 thin strips of lime zest, for garnish

Combine the syrup, rum, and lime juice in a shaker or small pitcher, stirring well, and pour over ice cubes in 2 tall glasses. Add a strip of lime zest to each glass.

Makes 2 drinks

PINA MARTINIQUE

This rosy-hued variation on the basic piña colada is enhanced by the subtle orange flavor of Cointreau and sweetness of crushed fresh strawberries. This version of the Caribbean classic is more sensuous than ever.

3 ounces white rum
1 ounce Cointreau
1½ ounces coconut cream, such as Coco Lopez
3 tablespoons crushed strawberries
3 tablespoons crushed pineapple
2 cups crushed ice
2 whole strawberries, for garnish

Combine all the ingredients except the garnish in a blender, and process at high speed until mixed, 1 minute. Pour into 2 tall glasses. Garnish with whole strawberries.

Makes 2 drinks

A TASTE OF THE WORLD

Caribbean Palette

Photo: Yes, we have plenty of bananas!

...And

Allspice
Thyme
Curry
Oregano
Pepper
Cilantro
Mint
Garlic
Scallions
Capers
Scotch bonnet chilies
Avocados
Tomatoes
Yams
Collard greens
Coconuts
Bananas
Limes
Raisins
Soy Sauce
Worcestershire sauce
Sugar
Rice
Beans
Dried peas
Dried salt cod

PLANTEUR

Martinique's planter's punch combines both white and dark rum with sweet-tart pineapple juice and citrusy orange juice. The garnishes of fresh pineapple, mint, and cherries are bright and festive, reflecting the colors of the gay Madras plaids worn on festival days by the women chefs of Martinique. If you can find them, add the finishing touches—a long turquoise straw and a bright pink parasol.

4 ounces fresh orange juice
4 ounces pineapple juice
2 ounces white rum
Dash of grenadine syrup
Dash of Angostura bitters
Ice cubes
1 ounce dark Jamaican rum
1 fresh pineapple spear, for garnish
1 fresh mint sprig, for garnish
1 maraschino cherry, for garnish

Combine the orange and pineapple juices with the white rum, grenadine, and bitters. Pour over ice cubes in a tall glass and drizzle the dark rum on top. Garnish with a pineapple spear, mint sprig, and cherry.

Makes 1 drink

Vermouth Cassis

Although black currants are not grown fresh in America, we can savor the taste of these juicy berries, native to France and northern Europe, through aromatic, velvety crème de cassis liqueur or black currant syrup. Black currant preserves make lovely fillings for miniature tarts or cookies but are not as widely available as other imported preserves may be. If you find a jar in a specialty food shop, it's worth the buy.

Considered the "most famous French long drink," vermouth cassis is a refreshing aperitif. My longtime friend Italian master chef Donaldo Soviero, makes the best I've ever tasted. For each drink, drop 2 ice cubes into a tall, thin highball glass, pour in 3 ounces chilled dry French vermouth, top with 3 ounces chilled sparkling water, and swizzle once. Slowly drizzle in 2 tablespoons crème de cassis, letting it gently float down into the glass. Do not stir! Garnish with a twist of lemon or orange zest. This makes 1 drink.

LA VIE EN ROSE

As I overlooked a deserted Caribbean beach while admiring a perfect island sunset and sipping *la vie en rose*, I could only imagine strains of Edith Piaf wafting softly by. At home, I put on my favorite Piaf album and serve up this rose-colored drink. Very romantic.

6 ounces pineapple juice
1 ounce raspberry liqueur
2 ounces white rum
Ice cubes
Fresh raspberries, for garnish

Combine all the ingredients except the ice cubes and garnish in a cocktail shaker. Shake well and pour over ice cubes in 2 tall glasses. Garnish with raspberries.

Makes 2 drinks

EMOTION

This restorative fruity island creation with the dramatic name tastes just right with a light addition of rum. Tonic adds the effervescence needed as you lazily gaze out at a waning summer sunset.

8 ounces fresh orange juice
½ ripe banana, cut into large chunks
2 tablespoons strawberry syrup
3 ounces white rum
Ice cubes
Tonic water

Combine all the ingredients except the ice cubes and tonic water in a blender and process at high speed until mixed, 1 minute. Pour over ice cubes in 2 tall glasses to the halfway point and top each glass with tonic water.

Makes 2 drinks

LE DAUPHIN

The names of the drinks served at the Bakoua Hotel in Martinique were almost as delicious and fascinating as the taste of the drinks them-

Those Tropical Splendiferous Drinks

How many times have you heard someone say while fantasizing about an upcoming Caribbean vacation, "I can't wait to lie on the beach and sip a planter's punch or a piña colada!"

Here they are. The best long cool drinks of Martinique. All fruity and frothy and waiting to be sipped. Delicious even without a nearby sea. Follow the basic recipes and feel free to adjust the ingredients to your taste. Have lots of pineapple spears, cherries, and other fruit on hand for garnishes. Tall, frosty glasses and long, pretty, colored straws are essential to the complete sybaritic sensation.

selves. *Le dauphin,* the name at one time given to the oldest son of the King of France, is a smooth, cool, coconut- and mint crème-de-menthe-imbued drink. Serve in wide Brandy Alexander glasses because this is a "cocktail" that only wants to be sipped. Royal, indeed.

3 ounces white rum
3 ounces white crème de menthe
3 ounces coconut cream, such as Coco Lopez
Ice cubes
Pineapple juice
2 fresh pineapple spears, for garnish
2 fresh mint sprigs, for garnish

Combine the rum, crème de menthe, and coconut cream in a cocktail shaker. Shake well. Add ice cubes, shake, and pour into glasses. Top each glass with pineapple juice. Garnish each with a pineapple spear and a sprig of mint.

Makes 2 drinks

ROUGE TROPICAL

Smooth pear nectar combined with luscious raspberry liqueur creates the perfect base for this rich yet cooling drink. The addition of tonic water brings this blushing fantasy to just the right consistency.

2 ounces pear nectar
1 tablespoon raspberry syrup or liqueur
4 ounces white rum
Ice cubes
Tonic water

Combine all the ingredients except the ice cubes and tonic water in a blender and process at high speed until mixed, 1 minute. Pour over ice cubes in 2 tall glasses to the halfway point and top each glass with tonic water.

Makes 2 drinks

RHUMLET

A grind of fresh nutmeg and a dash of spicy bitters enlivens this simple rum- and lime-based Caribbean drink. Decorative straws are a must for serving.

1 ounce Simple Sugar Syrup (page 34)
2 ounces white rum
1 ounce fresh lime juice
Pinch of ground nutmeg
Dash of Angostura bitters
Crushed ice
2 lime slices, for garnish

Combine all the ingredients through the bitters and stir well. Fill 2 tall glasses with crushed ice and pour in the mixture. Garnish each glass with a lime slice.

Makes 2 drinks

NAPOLEON BONAPARTE

In 1796 Napoleon married Josephine, a beautiful Creole who hailed from Martinique. It was in his honor that this stunning drink was named. As blue as the Caribbean sea, this drink bespeaks the best of a tropical paradise. Dazzling turquoise Curaçao blends well with the sweetness of Cointreau and the spark of fresh grapefruit juice. Well-chilled Champagne poured just before serving finishes each flute to perfection.

1 tablespoon Cointreau
1 teaspoon Curaçao blue
4 ounces fresh grapefruit juice, chilled
Ice cubes
Champagne, chilled

Combine the Cointreau, Curaçao, grapefruit juice, and ice cubes in a cocktail shaker. Shake well and strain into 4 champagne flutes. Top each glass with chilled Champagne.

Makes 4 drinks

CHILEAN WHITE PEACH MELBA SANGRIA

In Chile, February begins the long hot summer, the season for perfect sun-bathed white peaches. After hours of visiting every food market possible, I found nothing more deliciously refreshing at the end of the day than a cool white peach sangría. The secret, of course, is perfectly ripe peaches soaked for an hour or two in a semi-dry white wine, such as a Chenin Blanc, which gives the peaches the opportunity to release all their intoxicating juices. I've added fresh raspberries for color and just the right little tang of flavor. A splash of sparkling water and sprigs of fresh mint decorate beautifully.

6 ripe white or golden peaches
1 cup fresh raspberries
1 bottle (750 ml) Chenin Blanc or other semi-dry white wine
1 ounce Cointreau liqueur
2 cups sparkling water, chilled
Ice cubes
6 fresh mint sprigs, for garnish

1. Peel, pit, and finely dice the peaches. Place the peaches and raspberries in a large glass pitcher. Pour in the wine and Cointreau. Let stand at room temperature for 1 to 2 hours.

2. Before serving, add the sparkling water. Serve in wineglasses over ice and garnish with mint sprigs.

Serves 8 to 10 (1 glass each)

BARBARA ENSRUD'S RED WINE SANGRIA

This sparkling drink, originating in Spain, is most welcome and popular during the warm weather, especially with pungent and spicy foods like dishes from Mexico, Cuba, and Brazil. As is the case with most punches, the ingredients are variable and optional. The object is to include deliciously succulent fruit that will release its nectar into the punch. I personally love ripe red plums at their juiciest peak added to sangría. This sangría is also lovely made with white or rosé wine.

1 bottle (750 ml) Rioja red wine
1 ounce brandy or vodka, or to taste
Juice of ½ lemon
Juice of ½ orange
¼ cup superfine sugar, or more to taste
8 to 10 ounces sparkling water
Ice cubes
Thin lemon and orange slices, for garnish

Combine all the ingredients except the lemon and orange slices in a large pitcher. Stir thoroughly. Garnish with lemon and orange slices.

Makes about 1 quart

Elaine,

Pepe took me to see the oldest house in Carmona, about 1 hour from Sevilla. Wine, water jugs and ivy cover the beautiful walls.

Love,
Sheila

First Bites & Small Plates

No matter where I traveled—from Russia to Thailand—the twilight hour was a special time of day. The world seemed to stop, breathe a sigh, pull up a café chair, and order a little something tasty to accompany a glass of something refreshing.

The wonderful cocktail hour aperitifs I collected in the previous chapter were not meant to be sipped unaccompanied. They need a small tidbit to properly set them off. While these "first bites" change from country to country—robust *zakuski* in Russia, exotic spring rolls in Southeast Asia, garlicky *meze* in Greece and Turkey, stunning *tapas* in Spain—this worldwide ritual of relaxed predining dining often goes on for hours with everyone lingering over one more *blinchiki* or spicy sweet shrimp or empanada.

During the course of two years and 33 countries, I was lucky enough to indulge in an exquisite array of cocktail hour and first course food. To me, this tradition of sitting and savoring is splendid. They afforded me some of my most enjoyable moments. I hope they do the same for you.

BRAZILIAN ONION BITES

Along with a great seafood salad, spicy olives, and thinly sliced buffalo mozzarella, I was served little onion toasts sprinkled with Parmesan cheese as a prelude to a luscious dinner in Rio de Janeiro. I asked for the recipe because they were so light and delectable, and it turned out to be very easy to make those onion bites. Bake and serve as an hors d'oeuvre or at teatime, along with little cocktail napkins.

1 small onion, quartered lengthwise and thinly slivered crosswise
6 tablespoons mayonnaise
Salt and freshly ground black pepper, to taste
6 thin slices white bread, crusts removed
3 tablespoons freshly grated Parmesan cheese

1. Preheat the oven to 350°F.

2. Mix the onion with 5 tablespoons of the mayonnaise and salt and pepper to taste. Set aside.

3. Spread 3 slices of bread on one side with the remaining mayonnaise. Cut these into quarters.

4. Cut the remaining 3 slices of bread into quarters and spread each square evenly with the onion mixture. Top with the reserved bread squares, mayonnaise side up. Place these on a baking sheet and sprinkle the tops generously with Parmesan cheese.

5. Bake until lightly golden and slightly puffy, about 15 minutes. Serve immediately.

Makes 12 bites

OAXACA TOSTADA BITES

When it's cocktail hour in Mexico everyone longs for those foamy pitchers of margaritas to be poured. I've always found it necessary to have a nibble along with my drink or else! These cocktail nacho-type chips seem just right. Black beans, mashed with fresh tomatoes, lime juice, spices, and cocoa—reflecting the spectacular Oaxaca *moles*—cover the bottom of these crispy chips. Next comes smooth buttery avocado, then grated jalapeño Jack for extra bite. The ingredients all hold together well so that they're not difficult to eat out of hand. Serve at room temperature or heated.

1½ cups cooked black beans
1 large clove garlic, minced
2 ripe plum tomatoes, seeded and cut into ¼-inch dice
Finely grated zest of 1 lime
3 tablespoons fresh lime juice
3 tablespoons chopped fresh cilantro leaves
2 dashes Tabasco sauce
½ teaspoon unsweetened cocoa powder
½ teaspoon ground cumin
Pinch of ground cinnamon
Salt and coarsely ground black pepper, to taste
1 ripe avocado, preferably Haas, pitted and peeled
1 tablespoon sour cream
30 small round tortilla chips
¾ cup grated Monterey Jack cheese with jalapeños
3 pale romaine lettuce leaves, thinly shredded

1. Place the beans in a bowl and coarsely mash with the back of a wooden spoon. Add the garlic, tomatoes, lime zest, 2 tablespoons of the lime juice, 1 tablespoon of the cilantro, the Tabasco sauce, cocoa powder, cumin, cinnamon, salt, and pepper. Mix all the ingredients together well.

2. In another bowl, mash the avocado with the remaining 1 tablespoon lime juice, the sour cream, and salt to taste.

3. Spread 1 tablespoon of the bean mixture on each of the tortilla chips. If you are serving at room temperature, top each with ¼ teaspoon of the avocado mixture, then a sprinkling of grated cheese and the shredded lettuce. Sprinkle the remaining 2 tablespoons cilantro over all. If you would like to melt the cheese, top the beans with the cheese, place the chips on a baking sheet, and heat in a preheated 350°F oven for 3 to 5 minutes. Then top with the avocado, lettuce, and cilantro. To serve, arrange the chips on a festive platter.

Makes 30

SALMON RIBBON BITES

Whether it's teatime or the cocktail hour, these delicate sandwiches are perfect little bites served with chilled Champagne, icy vodka, or citrus-steeped black tea. You easily can substitute smoked sturgeon for the salmon or, for added interest, alternate layers of salmon and sturgeon. Fill a favorite small antique pitcher with some full-blown pink roses for a touch of romance and place it alongside the sandwich platter.

DILL CAPER BUTTER:
½ cup (1 stick) unsalted butter, at room temperature
2 tablespoons chopped fresh dill
1 tablespoon drained capers, minced

5 thin small slices pumpernickel bread (about 3 inches square and ⅛ inch thick)
4 ounces sliced smoked salmon
4 fresh dill sprigs

1. For the dill caper butter, combine the softened butter with the chopped dill and capers in a small bowl.

2. Spread one side of 4 slices of bread with the butter, reserving the last unbuttered slice for the top. Lay a piece of salmon atop each of the 4 buttered slices of bread, stack them one on top of the other, and finish with the last unbuttered slice.

3. Wrap the sandwich in plastic. Place the sandwich on a plate and weight it with another plate and a few small cans. Refrigerate for 1 hour.

4. To serve, cut the sandwich into 9 even wedges. Serve on a pretty little plate, garnished with dill sprigs.

Makes 9 bites

MEDITERRANEAN SPICED OLIVES

These olives are boldly spiced with the flavors of the Mediterranean but also sweetly mellowed by the addition of honey. They are marvelous alone or served with a selection of tangy chèvres, crusty grilled slices of peasant bread and ripe purple figs.

12 ounces Picholine or other imported green olives, rinsed with cold water and drained well
1 tablespoon finely grated orange zest
3 tablespoons extra virgin olive oil
1 teaspoon honey
2 cloves garlic, minced
½ teaspoon dried thyme
⅛ teaspoon ground allspice
¼ teaspoon coarse salt
¼ teaspoon coarsely ground black pepper
1 tablespoon chopped flat-leaf parsley

Place the olives, orange zest, oil, honey, and garlic in a bowl and mix well, using a rubber spatula. Add the thyme, allspice, salt, and pepper; fold to combine.

Fold in the parsley. Pack the olives into an airtight container and refrigerate, covered, at least 6 hours and up to 3 days for the flavors to meld.

Makes 12 ounces

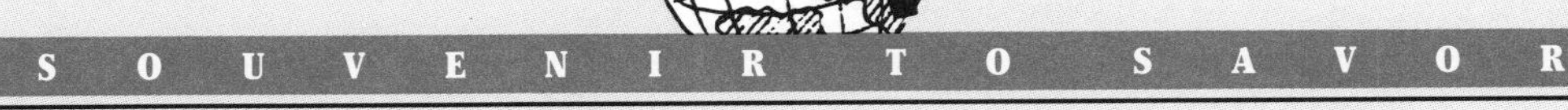

A Visit to Aegina

When the sun shines through in Athens, it beckons you to the closest island, if only for a short visit. My husband, Richard, and I boarded a hydrofoil bound for Aegina, one of the five Saronic islands and once the capitol of Greece, to visit Janette "Hilde" Xinotroulia, owner of the Ambrosia cooking school in Athens.

Upon approaching the bustling crescent-shaped harbor dappled with small pastel buildings, we longed to explore. After greeting Hilde, off we three went to an *ouzerie* for our first "snack" of the day. Seated on brightly painted blue chairs with rugged rush seats, we chose among an array of *meze* that were brought to the table for our consideration. We settled on giant white beans stewed with tomato sauce, tuna fish, golden browned zucchini slices drizzled with Kalamata olive oil and lemon juice, sliced tomatoes, cucumbers, and olives, and tender grilled octopus. A basket of bread completed the selection. I ordered Greek coffee, respectful of the 10 A.M. meal; Richard ordered ouzo!

As we ate we watched the floating morning market. Majestic boats backed into the harbor laden with wooden crates of tomatoes, peaches, lemons, zucchini (blossoms in profusion), and massive bunches of garlic. The scales hung from the masts waiting to serve the lines of shoppers.

After our mini feast we strolled to the end of the port to visit the local Friday morning market. Donkeys sporting large baskets filled with wild greens, zucchini blossoms, and garlic replaced modern shelving and refrigerators.

We continued on across the rugged terrain studded with pine trees to the island's featured attraction, the temple of Aphaia, one of the best preserved on the Greek islands. Along the way we passed masses of pistachio trees heavy with fruit.

After a late lunch at Hilde's house, we bought a bag of local pistachios and boarded the hydrofoil back to Athens, with splendid memories of our perfect day.

BADAM SANDHEKO
Spiced Roasted Peanuts

When my husband Richard was planning our trip to India, he couldn't resist a stop in Nepal. He said he'd meet me at the airport in New Delhi after he'd seen Katmandu. He arrived with thrilling tales and this delicious spiced nut recipe. While most visitors to Katmandu, along with many locals, frequent the popular Indian, Chinese, and Tibetan restaurants, he sought out the best Nepalese restaurant. It was housed in a three-story traditional building and featured several small dining rooms and a lovely top floor lounge. It was there that his amiable host offered him these zesty peanuts along with his drink. He brought a jar of them to India, and we nibbled them on our way to the Taj Mahal.

8 ounces roasted peanuts (not dry roasted)
2 tablespoons peanut oil
1 tablespoon minced peeled fresh ginger
1 tablespoon minced garlic
2 teaspoons chopped fresh cilantro leaves
¼ teaspoon chili powder

1. Mix all the ingredients together in a bowl.

2. Place the mixture in a medium-size nonstick skillet and cook over medium heat until the peanuts smell fragrantly toasty, 5 minutes, shaking the skillet often.

3. Cool the peanuts to room temperature and store in an airtight container.

Makes 1 cup

MY KITCHEN DIARY

An Opulent Fruit and Nut Display

The most opulent display of dried fruits and nuts is housed within the walls of the Egyptian spice market in Istanbul. To create your very own display, begin with a circular or rectangular brass or copper tray polished to sparkle. Gather very small brown bags from the grocery store and carefully fold them down about 1 inch from the top. Open the bags fully so that they stand on their own. Fill some of the bags to the brim with a variety of dried apricots, figs, dates, and cherries. Fill other bags with pistachios, almonds, walnuts, pecans, and roasted chickpeas. Stand all the filled bags upright on the tray and intersperse them with tiny white votive candles. Dapple any free space with bowls of pungent green and black olives and candied orange rind.

HIGHLAND PATE

Throughout Scotland, my assistant, Laurie, and I enjoyed smooth game liver pâtés slathered over Scottish Oatcakes with a dab of Cumberland Sauce. The pâté had a robust flavor and was creamy and delicate at the same time. I've combined equal amounts of pheasant, duck, and chicken livers with Scotland's renowned Drambuie and spiked them with green peppercorns for just the right balance of tastes. Once the pâté is puréed, pack it into a decorative serving pot before refrigerating. Remove from the refrigerator and let warm at room temperature for about 20 minutes before serving for all the flavors to come through.

8 ounces pheasant livers (see Note)
8 ounces duck livers
8 ounces chicken livers
6 tablespoons (¾ stick) unsalted butter
¾ cup chopped onion
1 tablespoon minced garlic
1½ teaspoons dried thyme
3 tablespoons Drambuie
¾ teaspoon ground allspice
¾ teaspoon salt
2 tablespoons green peppercorns packed in brine, drained and rinsed
⅓ cup heavy (or whipping) cream
Scottish Oatcakes (page 493)
Cumberland Sauce (page 345)

1. Wash and clean the livers well. Drain and pat dry.

2. Melt the butter in a large heavy skillet over low heat Add the onions and cook, stirring, until wilted, for about 10 minutes. Add the garlic and cook to soften, another 2 minutes. Transfer to a large bowl with a slotted spoon.

3. Add the livers to the skillet, sprinkle with the thyme, and cook over medium-high heat until well browned, about 10 minutes, shaking the pan, stirring, and turning the livers as they cook. Add the livers and cooking juices to the bowl with the onions.

4. Add the Drambuie, allspice, salt, and 1 tablespoon of the green peppercorns to the bowl and stir to mix. Place the liver mixture in a food processor and process until smooth.

5. With the machine running, add the cream through the feed tube and process until blended. Scrape the mixture into a bowl. Fold in the remaining tablespoon of green peppercorns and adjust the seasonings to taste. Cool to room temperature.

6. Scrape the pâté into a decorative crock or bowl and refrigerate covered for 4 to 6 hours. Serve with Scottish oatcakes or other biscuits and cumberland sauce.

Serves 12

Note: If you can't find pheasant livers, but still wish to make this pâté, just double the amount of chicken livers.

CHEVRES BATHED IN HERBS AND EXTRA VIRGIN OLIVE OIL

Summertime in Provence is bathed in the perfume of lavender, thyme, and rosemary. Ripe purple figs long to be plucked from their fruit-laden branches. Green fruity olive oils grace both delicate and pungent chèvres, and the Bandol wines abound. Use these flavors to create a colorful ceramic platter of chèvres marinated in herbs and oil. Halve ripe figs and surround the cheese. Garnish your platter with fresh herb sprigs and sprinkle liberally with coarse black pepper. Serve grilled thick slices of peasant bread in a rustic basket and keep the Bandol rosé chilled in a clay wine cooler. Soak up the sun and these extraordinary tastes.

12 large fresh thyme sprigs
12 large fresh rosemary sprigs
1 teaspoon crumbled dried lavender
1 soft mild chèvre log (about 11 ounces), without ash, cut crosswise into 8 rounds
1½ cups extra virgin Niçoise olive oil
Coarsely ground black pepper, to taste
16 fresh ripe figs, halved

Arrange half the thyme, rosemary, and lavender in the bottom of a shallow nonreactive dish just large enough to hold the chèvres in a single layer. Place the 8 chèvres on top and cover with the remaining herbs. Drizzle the oil over the cheese and herbs so it covers them completely. Sprinkle with pepper to taste. Cover with plastic wrap and let sit at room temperature for 24 hours. Serve, or store covered in the refrigerator and let warm to room temperature before serving. Before serving, arrange the figs decoratively around the cheese.

Serves 8

BHEL POORI

India's favorite snack! All over the country there are marvelous brightly decorated wooden vendor wagons that sell this wonderful nibble, which is made from a base of the best crispies and crunchies I've ever tasted, tossed with spices, chutneys, potatoes, garbanzos, onions, fresh mint, and cilantro, and topped with tomatoes and yogurt. The *bhel poori* mecca is Chowpatty Beach in Bombay where thousands throng for their evening sunset stroll.

Pao'Bhajee, my favorite vendor, laid out all his ingredients beautifully in decorative bowls and worked as fast as lightning to combine them. One had to eat nearly as fast so that the bowl and fork could be cleaned for the next anxious customer.

Stateside I first experimented with this recipe using puffed rice from the supermarket, which was good, but a visit to an Indian food shop in Manhattan produced the real McCoy—chickpea flour chips and crispy noodles. They are marvelous and well worth the effort to find them (see Note).

It's great fun and very easy to host a *bhel poori* party. Simply lay out all the ingredients in baskets and bowls on a counter or table, stack small bowls and piles of forks alongside, and let everyone make their own. This recipe includes instructions for premixing the *bhel poori.*

2 cups papdi gathiya (chickpea flour chips), slightly broken up (see Note)
1 cup puffed rice (available in supermarkets)
½ cup thin sev (thin, broken chickpea flour noodles; see Note)
1 teaspoon salt
¼ teaspoon freshly ground black pepper
½ teaspoon chili powder
Pinch of cayenne pepper
1 Idaho potato (8 ounces), cooked, peeled, and cut into ¼-inch dice
½ cup cooked chickpeas (garbanzo beans), drained and rinsed
¼ cup diced red onion
2 tablespoons chopped fresh cilantro leaves
Finely grated zest of 1 lemon
2 ripe plum tomatoes, seeded and cut into ¼-inch dice
1 teaspoon Savory Mint and Coriander Chutney (recipe follows)
1 tablespoon tamarind sauce (store bought or see recipe page 50 for a substitute)
1 cup nonfat plain yogurt, for garnish

1. In a bowl, combine the chickpea chips, puffed rice, noodles, salt, pepper, chili powder, and cayenne.

2. Add the potato, chickpeas, onion, cilantro, and lemon zest. Toss well.

3. Just before serving, add the tomatoes, chutney, and tamarind sauce; mix well to combine. Serve immediately, dolloped with yogurt.

Serves 6

Note: *Papdi gathiya* and *thin sev* are available from Indian markets. I bought mine at Little India, 128 East 28th Street, New York, NY 10016; (212) 683-1691. Little India will mail order.

SAVORY MINT AND CORIANDER CHUTNEY

Garden fresh, pungent, and a bit spicy, too, this classic, vibrant green condiment is used in India as often as an ingredient as it is served on its own. A spoonful or two mixed into a cup of plain yogurt makes for the most delicious *raita* to cool down the hottest curry. It also lends

great taste to Bhel Poori when mixed among the crispies. This is splendid fresh but will keep refrigerated for up to 3 days.

2 cups fresh mint leaves
2 cups (loosely packed) fresh cilantro leaves and tender stems
2 tablespoons minced peeled fresh ginger
1 tablespoon minced garlic
2 ripe plum tomatoes, seeded and chopped
½ green jalapeño chili, seeds and ribs removed, finely chopped (about 1 teaspoon)
3 tablespoons fresh lemon juice
1 teaspoon ground cumin
½ teaspoon ground ginger
¼ teaspoon salt
¼ teaspoon freshly ground black pepper
1 cup plain nonfat yogurt (optional)

Place all the ingredients except the yogurt in a food processor and process until the ingredients form a rough paste. Stop once or twice to scrape down the side of the bowl. Remove to a serving bowl or mix 2 tablespoons chutney into the yogurt and serve in a small serving bowl as a *raita*.

Makes 1¼ cups

NOT-REALLY-TAMARIND SAUCE

The tamarind tree, widely grown in India, produces long, flat pods that encase slightly sour pulp and seeds. The pods, green and hard when unripe, turn a deep brown color and soften slightly as they mature. Dried tamarind pulp is often found sold in small blocks. A chunk of dried tamarind can be rehydrated in warm water and then squeezed to extract the juice for use in recipes calling for tamarind. It is also possible to find a thick sauce made from concentrated tamarind juices sold in jars in Indian grocery stores. Available everywhere in India but difficult to find in America, this sweet-and-sour brown sauce is a key ingredient in many of the Indian dishes I tasted. Although not exactly the real thing, a close version is easy to duplicate. Some chefs I spoke to suggested I combine a little jaggery, a molasses-flavored type of brown sugar, with malt vinegar. I did, but remembered the tamarind sauce tasting more lemony. In order to create an adequate substitute, I bought a block of tamarind at an Indian grocery store. I broke off small bits and sucked on them as I was mixing this sauce. With fresh lemon juice instead of vinegar, the sauce turned out to be quite good. This will keep for weeks refrigerated, and it thickens up a bit. Use a spoonful or two as needed.

¼ cup (packed) dark brown sugar
3 tablespoons fresh lemon juice
½ teaspoon molasses

Combine all the ingredients in a very small saucepan over low heat, stirring until the sugar melts. Or, microwave it in a small microwave-safe container on full power for 30 seconds (see Note).

Makes ¼ cup

Note: This recipe was tested in a 600- to 750-watt carousel microwave at full power. If your microwave is less powerful, adjust the cooking time.

SALMON CAVIAR EGG SALAD

Since we are so conscious of eating healthily these days, I feel obliged to warn you that this dish is not for the meek of heart. This luxurious indulgence of chopped eggs slathered with crème fraîche and tossed with salmon caviar is splendid enough to be your cheat for the year. Just a sprinkle of fresh dill as a garnish adds the right contrast. Serve Swedish or Finnish whole-grain crisp breads alongside.

Interesting to me is that although I indulged in this luxurious salad while on a visit to Sweden, the eggs and caviar assembled in the same way would have made a splendid *zakuska* in St. Petersburg. In fact, the dish that follows is, more or less, the Russian version.

¼ cup mayonnaise
¼ cup crème fraîche
Salt and coarsely ground white pepper, to taste
12 hard-cooked eggs, peeled and coarsely chopped
3 tablespoons finely chopped red onion
4 ounces fresh salmon caviar, gently drained in a fine sieve to remove any excess liquid
1 tablespoon chopped fresh dill, for garnish

1. In a bowl, mix the mayonnaise, crème fraîche, salt, and pepper.

2. In a large bowl, combine the chopped eggs and onion.

3. Lightly toss the egg mixture with the mayonnaise mixture. Using a rubber spatula, gently fold in the caviar.

4. Chill in the refrigerator up to 1 hour. Serve small portions garnished with the chopped dill, on pretty little dishes as this is much too lavish to serve in a large bowl.

Serves 8 to 10

CAVIAR EGGS A LA RUSSE

Those childhood favorites, deviled eggs, have grown up in this recipe, with a topping of salmon caviar replacing that little sprinkle of paprika. In fact, all the traditional caviar garnishes are represented here, making for neater eating and delicious flavors. These little eggs are great for a cocktail party or as part of a Russian *zakuski* table (see pages 67 and 110).

6 hard-cooked eggs, peeled
3 tablespoons sour cream
1½ teaspoons finely grated onion
1 teaspoon finely chopped fresh dill
6 teaspoons fresh salmon caviar, gently drained in a fine sieve to remove any excess liquid
12 tiny fresh dill sprigs, for garnish

1. Cut the eggs lengthwise in half and remove the yolks to a bowl. Reserve the whites. Mash the yolks smooth with a fork.

2. Add the sour cream, onion, and chopped dill to the yolks and mix together until well blended. Mound the yolk mixture in the egg whites. Top each with ½ teaspoon caviar, covering the yolk completely. Garnish each with a sprig of dill. Serve on a delicate platter, lined with an attractive lacy paper doily.

Makes 12

Caviar

When you want luxury and indulgence, nothing satisfies more than caviar. While there are many pretenders to the throne, true caviar are the eggs from sturgeon, with the royal family being beluga, osetra, and sevruga from the Caspian Sea.

Sturgeon have been harvested for their precious roe on both the Russian and Iranian sides of the Caspian for generations. Due to the recent political climate and because the Iranians cure the roe with borax, illegal in the United States, Iranian caviar is unavailable in America, which leaves us in the hands of the Russian caviar masters.

The caviar master evaluates the roe of each fish for quality, ripeness, and freshness; then each batch is salted by hand. Top-grade fresh Russian caviar is marked "malossol" to indicate that it is lightly salted (less than 5 percent salt).

Each caviar has a distinctive taste and color. Beluga, the rarest, is the largest berry and mildest in flavor. The berries range in color from gray to black, all with a pearly luster. Osetra is a medium-size berry of greenish, golden, or grayish hue and is intensely flavorful with a nutty quality to it. Sevruga is the smallest and blackest of the caviars and favored by many to be the most delicious. Also available is pressed caviar made from broken eggs. It takes five pounds of eggs to make one pound of this intense jammy caviar and is best slathered atop blini.

When you have a great caviar, enjoy it simply with crisp toast points to let the full flavor of the beads burst in your mouth. Handle it gently so the berries do not break and avoid silver utensils because they react with the caviar and give it a metallic taste. So, as long as you're splurging, find a mother-of-pearl or bone spoon to serve the caviar.

Fresh toast points encircle a lavish amount of osetra caviar—now where's the Champagne?

BLINI

In St. Petersburg I was happily able to savor blini from sunrise to sunset. Basic blini were always waiting on the breakfast buffet—some with cheese worked into the batter and some with carrot purée. I preferred the pure version as they were lighter. Made from a leavened batter, these savory little pancakes are about ¼ inch thick. They are served either at room temperature or, if made ahead of time, wrapped in aluminum foil and placed in a preheated 350°F oven for 10 minutes until warmed through. They're delicious topped with sour cream or crème fraîche, drizzled with melted butter and honey, or spread lightly with sour cream and topped with black sturgeon caviar or fresh red salmon caviar. At about 9 A.M. I often could be found placing a large spoonful of black cherry preserves on mine.

1 teaspoon active dry yeast
2¾ cups all-purpose flour, sifted
2 cups milk
4 large eggs, separated
1¼ cups lukewarm milk
¼ teaspoon salt
3 teaspoons Clarified Butter (recipe follows)

1. Stir the yeast, ½ cup of the flour, and 2 cups milk together in a large bowl. Cover and let rest in a warm place, 30 minutes.

2. Add the remaining 2¼ cups flour, the egg yolks, warm milk, and salt to the yeast mixture and blend well.

3. Beat the egg whites until they hold stiff peaks and fold them gently into the batter with a rubber spatula. Let rest covered in a warm place until doubled in bulk, about 1 hour.

4. Heat ½ teaspoon clarified butter in a nonstick skillet over medium heat. Cook the blini 3 at a time if space permits. Spoon 1 tablespoon of batter per blini into the hot skillet and cook until light golden brown, 1 to 1½ minutes. Turn and cook the other side until golden, about 1 minute more. Remove to a plate and repeat with the rest of the batter. Add more butter to the skillet as necessary.

Makes approximately forty-five 3-inch blini

CLARIFIED BUTTER

Clarified butter is ideal for cooking pancakes, blini, and crêpes because it can be heated to high temperatures over a long period of time without burning. This recipe yields quite a bit, but it can easily be reduced by using 1 stick of butter.

1½ cups (3 sticks) unsalted butter

1. Place the butter in a small heavy saucepan and melt over low heat. Remove from the heat and let rest for 5 minutes.

2. With a spoon, carefully remove the foamy white butter fat that has risen to the top and discard. Spoon the next layer of clear golden liquid into a bowl. This is the clarified butter. Discard any remaining solids that remain in the saucepan.

3. Cool the clarified butter and place it in a

covered container. Refrigerate for up to 3 weeks or freeze it and use as needed.

Makes 1 cup

BUCKWHEAT BLINI

Traditional buckwheat blini and fresh caviar, preferably beluga, sevruga, or osetra, are a perfect marriage. Buckwheat flour is combined half and half with all-purpose wheat flour for these savory little pancakes. Serve warm with some crème fraîche alongside if you like to garnish your caviar with cool white dollops.

2 packages active dry yeast
1 cup lukewarm milk
1 cup buckwheat flour
1 cup all-purpose flour
½ teaspoon sugar
¼ teaspoon salt
3 large eggs, separated
½ cup warm water
4 tablespoons (½ stick) unsalted butter, melted
3 teaspoons Clarified Butter (page 53)

1. Place the yeast and milk in a small bowl and stir to combine.

2. Sift together the flours, sugar, and salt in a large bowl. Add the egg yolks and mix well. Add the yeast mixture, water, and melted butter. Mix to combine. Cover and let the batter rest in a warm place until doubled in bulk, about 1 hour.

3. Beat the egg whites until they hold stiff peaks and fold them gently into the batter with a rubber spatula. Let rest 1 hour.

4. Heat ½ teaspoon clarified butter in a nonstick skillet over medium heat. Cook the blini 3 at a time if space permits. Spoon 1 tablespoon of batter per blini into the hot skillet and cook until light golden brown, 1 to 1½ minutes. Turn and cook the other side until just golden brown, about 1 minute. Remove to a plate and repeat with the rest of the batter. Add more butter to the skillet as necessary.

Makes approximately twenty-eight 3-inch blini

A Well-Seasoned Pan

For perfect crêpes it is important to begin with a well-seasoned pan to prevent the crêpes from sticking. The best is a classic iron 7-inch crêpe pan which turns out a 6-inch crêpe, just right for main courses and dessert crêpes. The pan should be heavy enough to distribute heat evenly, yet light enough so that you can swirl the batter and "flip" the crêpes.

Before you use your crêpe pan for the first time, it should be scrubbed with steel wool to remove its protective coating and then washed with warm soapy water. Rub the inside well with a paper towel and vegetable oil and your pan is ready. Never wash your crêpe pan once it has been seasoned. After each use, simply wipe it out with a paper towel. If particles begin to stick to the bottom of the pan or if it has been washed, rub it with a paper towel and some coarse salt and then again with oil.

WILD MUSHROOM BLINCHIKI

At one of the meals I enjoyed during my stay in St. Petersburg, these delicious savory crêpes were served as a second course after an array of cold *zakuski* (pages 67 and 110). Chilled Champagne filled our glasses and chilled sour cream topped the hot *blinchiki*. Try to find fresh wild mushrooms for these or substitute cultivated white mushrooms—don't use dried. The herbs can be chosen to your taste.

1 cup all-purpose flour
1 tablespoon sugar
Pinch of salt
3 large eggs
1⅓ cups whole milk
⅔ cup buttermilk
8 ounces fresh wild mushrooms, such as cèpes, shiitake, or porcini
1 tablespoon unsalted butter
Salt and freshly ground black pepper, to taste
2 tablespoons chopped flat-leaf parsley or dill
2 tablespoons Clarified Butter (page 53)
2 tablespoons unsalted butter, melted
½ cup sour cream or crème fraîche, for garnish

1. Sift the flour, sugar, and salt into a mixing bowl. Make a well in the center of the dry ingredients. Break the eggs into the well and mix the eggs with a fork until well combined.

2. Add the milk and buttermilk in a steady stream, whisking constantly, while drawing in the flour. The batter should have the consistency of thin cream. Let the batter rest for 30 minutes.

3. Remove the tough stems from the mushrooms (reserve for another use) and wipe the caps clean with a damp paper towel. Cut the mushrooms into ⅛-inch-thick julienne strips.

4. Melt 1 tablespoon butter in a sauté pan. Add the mushrooms and cook over medium heat for 2 minutes, stirring constantly. Remove the pan from the heat and season the mushrooms with salt, pepper, and parsley. You should have about ½ cup. Add the seasoned mushrooms to the crêpe batter and stir well.

5. Heat a 7-inch nonstick skillet or crêpe pan over medium heat. Brush the pan lightly with a small amount of clarified butter to prevent the crêpes from sticking.

6. Ladle ⅓ cup batter into the pan and, working quickly, rotate the pan with a turn of your wrist so that the batter evenly coats the bottom. Cook the crêpe until it is set and golden, 45 to 60 seconds, then loosen it with a spatula and turn it over. Cook until just set, about 10 seconds longer. The underside should be paler than the top side. Repeat with the remaining batter. If the crêpes begin to stick, add a bit more butter to the pan.

7. Stack the finished crêpes on a plate and cover until ready to use. To keep warm, place the plate, loosely covered with aluminum foil, over a saucepan of boiling water.

8. To serve hot, fold the crêpes in half and arrange them, slightly overlapping, on an ovenproof platter. Drizzle with melted butter, cover with aluminum foil, and place in a preheated 350°F oven for 10 minutes. Dollop with sour cream and serve immediately.

Makes 8 to 10 six-inch blinchiki, serves 4 to 6

HERBED ORANGE CHEVRE SLATHER

Chèvre from France and giant green olives from Spain, brightened with orange zest and freshly snipped chives, blend together for a delicate, creamy slather that is splendid served with thin slices of pumpernickel raisin bread and a chilled glass of dry Spanish Fino sherry.

8 ounces soft mild chèvre without ash, such as Montrachet, at room temperature
¼ cup sour cream
Finely grated zest of 1 large orange
Freshly ground black pepper, to taste
⅓ cup chopped pimiento-stuffed Spanish olives
1 scallion (3 inches green left on), thinly sliced
2 teaspoons finely snipped fresh chives

1. Mash the chèvre with the sour cream in a medium-size bowl. Stir in the orange zest and pepper.

2. With a rubber spatula, gently fold in the olives, scallion, and 1 teaspoon of the chives. Spoon into a decorative bowl and garnish with the remaining chives. Refrigerate covered until ready to serve.

Makes about 1¼ cups

ZESTY YOGURT SLATHER

Most Greek and Turkish *meze* platters include a spiced yogurt dish. The yogurt served in those countries is thicker than American varieties, so I suggest extracting any excessive liq-

Slathers

When I began to refer to my spreads as "slathers," I saw them in a very luxurious light. Not for the meek or mild of palate, they are both bold in flavor and rich in texture, just perfect served as appetizers or included in a selection of *meze*. In the case of these recipes, a light schmear won't do. According to Webster's Dictionary, slather means to spread or pour lavishly. You'll want to be just a bit extravagant with your portion to get the true taste sensation.

A slather of herbed Greek white beans or delicate pink tarama is just as delicious on a thick slice of ripe tomato as it is on toasted coarse peasant bread. Discard your inhibitions and thoroughly enjoy the luscious global flavors of these exciting dishes.

uid by draining the yogurt in cheesecloth. Garlic adds spice and walnuts the depth in this spread. Orange zest and mint leaves lend freshness, and a bit of honey smooths all the flavors together. The consistency of the finished dish is very much like that of an herbed Boursin cheese. Just spread on toasted rustic bread and top with sliced tomatoes and cucumbers. Pungent Kalamata olives are the ideal accompaniment.

1 quart (32 ounces) nonfat plain yogurt
¼ cup finely chopped walnuts
½ small clove garlic, peeled and pressed through a garlic press
2 tablespoons coarsely chopped fresh mint leaves, plus 1 teaspoon, for garnish
2 teaspoons finely grated orange zest
1 teaspoon honey
Pinch of coarse salt
Pinch of coarsely ground black pepper

1. Line a strainer with 2 layers of cheesecloth and place it over a bowl. Add the yogurt and close the cheesecloth with a twistie. Let drain for 3 hours at room temperature.

2. Place the drained yogurt in a bowl and stir in the walnuts, garlic, 2 tablespoons of the mint, the orange zest, honey, salt, and pepper.

3. Transfer the mixture to a serving bowl and sprinkle with the remaining teaspoon of chopped mint. Refrigerate covered for up to 3 hours before serving. Twenty minutes before serving, remove the yogurt slather from the refrigerator.

Makes 1 cup

RIGANI WHITE BEAN AND GARLIC SLATHER

Greece inspires me to new heights with its heady bean dishes and spreads that are enlivened with garlic, *rigani* (oregano), and deep, fruity-tasting olive oils. There for the picking, pungent *rigani* blankets the mountain slopes of the Hellanas and aptly translates into "joy of the mountains."

The diverse flavors of this slather take on a delicate finesse with the addition of crème fraîche. To complement the plate, serve alongside bowls of deep purple Kalamata olives and green Picholines from France.

1 medium Idaho potato (8 ounces), peeled and cubed
Coarse salt, to taste
¼ cup extra virgin olive oil
2 cups chopped yellow onions
¼ cup chopped garlic
1 can (19 ounces) white kidney beans (cannellini), drained
2 tablespoons chopped fresh oregano leaves or 1 teaspoon dried
2 teaspoons shredded fresh thyme leaves, or ½ teaspoon dried
Coarsely ground black pepper, to taste
4 tablespoons crème fraîche
Toasted thickly sliced peasant bread or Pita Chips (page 66)

1. Cover the potato with water in a saucepan, add salt, and bring to a boil. Reduce the heat and cook until the potato is tender, about 10 minutes. Drain well.

2. Heat the oil in a large skillet over low

heat. Add the onions and garlic. Cook, stirring, until the onions are translucent and tender, about 15 minutes.

3. Add the potato, beans, oregano, thyme, and coarse salt and pepper to taste. Cook, stirring, over very low heat for 5 minutes. Let cool slightly.

4. Place half the bean mixture and 2 tablespoons crème fraîche in a food processor. Pulse 8 to 10 minutes until slightly smooth. Remove to a bowl and repeat with the remaining bean mixture and crème fraîche. Combine the batches and season generously with salt and pepper. Cool completely, then refrigerate covered until ready to use. Twenty minutes before serving, remove the slather from the refrigerator. Serve slathered on toasted peasant bread or with pita chips.

Makes 3½ cups

PROVENCAL CHICKPEA SLATHER

Nice is famous for the abundant use of chickpeas and chickpea flour in its cooking. To infuse the peas with a robust flavor before puréeing, I gently cook them with fennel, garlic, and anise-flavored Pernod. This also enhances the flavor of fennel. Serve a bowl of ripe purple figs or peaches alongside for a taste of sweet.

6 tablespoons extra virgin olive oil
1 cup finely chopped fennel bulb
1 cup finely chopped onion
4 cloves garlic, minced
1 teaspoon anise seeds
1 can (19 ounces) chickpeas, (garbanzo beans) drained
2 tablespoons dry white wine
1 tablespoon Pernod
Coarse salt and freshly ground black pepper, to taste
2 tablespoons coarsely chopped fennel ferns

1. Warm 4 tablespoons of the olive oil in a large nonstick skillet over medium-low heat. Add the fennel, onion, garlic, and anise seeds. Cook, stirring occasionally, until the vegetables are very tender, about 15 minutes.

2. Add the chickpeas, white wine, Pernod, salt, and pepper. Cook, stirring, over medium-low heat until most of the liquid is absorbed and the flavors blend together, 6 to 8 minutes. Stir in the fennel ferns.

3. Coarsely purée the mixture in batches in a food processor, adding up to 2 tablespoons more oil if desired. Adjust the seasonings and cool to room temperature.

Makes about 2 cups

CREOLE CRAB SLATHER

After enjoying endless traditional *crabes farcis* (stuffed crabs) in Martinique, I decided to transform all the ingredients into a spread for crostini. In the islands stuffed crabs seem overwhelmed with bread crumbs. This purer version eliminates the crumbs and unmasks the flavors, making for a fresh and lively tasting crab slather. Serve it atop toasted or grilled thin slices of French bread or on Belgian endive leaves.

2 tablespoons olive oil
2 tablespoons unsalted butter
3 large shallots, finely chopped (about ½ cup)
1 tablespoon minced garlic
½ teaspoon ground allspice
¼ teaspoon ground cardamom
Pinch of cayenne pepper
8 ounces fresh lump crabmeat, picked over for shell and cartilage
1 tablespoon chopped fresh thyme leaves
1 tablespoon chopped flat-leaf parsley
½ cup dry white wine
Salt, to taste

1. Heat the oil and butter in a large nonstick skillet over low heat. Add the shallots and garlic and cook, stirring, until wilted, 5 to 7 minutes. Stir in the allspice, cardamom, and cayenne pepper.

2. Add the crabmeat, thyme, and parsley and stir together well, breaking up the crab a bit. Add the wine and cook, stirring, over medium-low heat until the liquid is reduced, about 8 minutes. Remove to a bowl and let cool to room temperature. Season with salt, cover, and chill until ready to use.

Makes 1½ cups or 10 to 12 servings

TARAMA SLATHER

Indulging a love for tarama, a creamy smooth fish spread, definitely requires perseverance, for the necessary Greek-style carp or cod roe can be difficult to come by. The roe is distributed in America by Krinos, a food company specializing in Greek products. It is often available in specialty food shops and some upscale supermarkets. Found in most *meze* selections, tarama can be either strong or mild. I prefer the salty flavor of the roe tamed with fresh lemon juice and lush crème fraîche. Spoon it into a small crock or serve it *meze* style: Spread the tarama in the center of a small oval dish, garnish it with cracked green olives, and place a basket of toasted sliced peasant bread and thickly sliced tomatoes alongside.

3 slices white bread, crusts removed, torn into small pieces
2 tablespoons grated onion
½ teaspoon minced garlic
⅓ cup carp roe or smoked cod roe (tarama)
2 tablespoons fresh lemon juice
2 tablespoons olive oil
½ cup crème fraîche
Coarsely ground black pepper, to taste

1. Place the bread, onion, and garlic in a food processor and pulse on and off about 5 times. Add the fish roe and process just until smooth.

2. With the machine running, drizzle in the lemon juice through the feed tube. Drop by drop, drizzle in the olive oil and process until it is completely incorporated. Remove the mixture to a bowl.

3. Gently fold in the crème fraîche and season with pepper. Refrigerate covered for 1 hour before serving.

Makes 1 cup

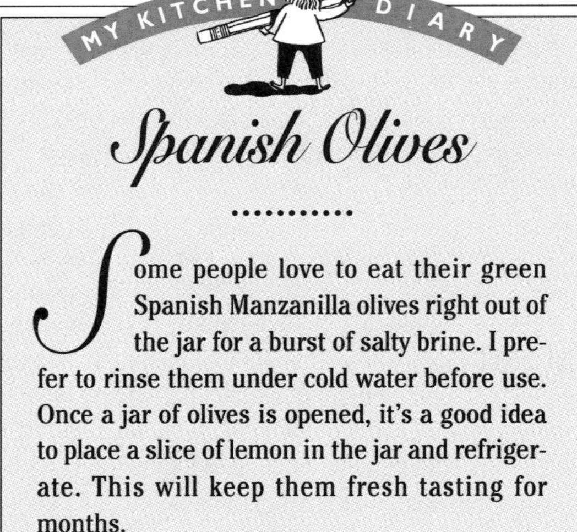

Spanish Olives

Some people love to eat their green Spanish Manzanilla olives right out of the jar for a burst of salty brine. I prefer to rinse them under cold water before use. Once a jar of olives is opened, it's a good idea to place a slice of lemon in the jar and refrigerate. This will keep them fresh tasting for months.

SPANISH OLIVE TAPENADE

The French love their olive spread made from lusty black Niçoise olives. The Italians choose rich Gaeta olives for theirs. I, on the other hand, have come to love a fruitier-tasting version made from Spanish Manzanilla olives—the small, slightly sweeter green olives available on most supermarket shelves. Blended with extra virgin Spanish olive oil, which has a smooth, sweet flavor reminiscent of fruit and almonds, the bite of the *tapenade* is mellowed and then brightened with the addition of lemon juice and cilantro. Spread on large croutons, brushed with oil and toasted, and serve with a Fino sherry for a perfect hors d'oeuvre. Have small bowls of almonds and dried cherries alongside to sweeten the palate.

1½ cups pitted Spanish Manzanilla olives
1 clove garlic, finely chopped
1 teaspoon capers, drained
¼ cup extra virgin Spanish olive oil
1 teaspoon lemon juice
2 tablespoons chopped fresh cilantro leaves
Freshly ground black pepper, to taste

1. In a food processor, combine the olives, garlic, and capers. Process until just smooth, scraping down the sides of the bowl if necessary. With the machine running, slowly drizzle in the oil and lemon juice through the feed tube and process until well combined.

2. Transfer the mixture to a bowl and fold in the cilantro and pepper. Let rest at room temperature for 1 hour for the flavors to come out.

Makes about 1 cup

KALAMATA OLIVE PUREE

Kalamata olives, from the town of Kalamata, have always been an essential feature in the Greek diet. These glossy, black purplish olives exude a pungent flavor and their firm meaty texture and almond shape distinguish them from other black olives. I enjoy using Kalamatas in Greek salads or puréed into a lusty *tapenade* to spread on *crostini* and pita chips.

½ cup pitted Kalamata olives
2 small cloves garlic, peeled
1 tablespoon extra virgin olive oil
1 tablespoon fresh lemon juice
1 tablespoon fresh oregano leaves, or 1 teaspoon dried oregano mixed with tablespoon chopped flat-leaf parsley

Combine all the ingredients in the bowl of a food processor and process until just puréed. It should retain a bit of texture. If necessary, stop and scrape down the sides of the bowl with a spatula. Transfer to a small decorative bowl and serve at room temperature. This purée will keep covered in the refrigerator for up to 1 week.

Makes ½ cup

LAURIE'S BASIC GUACAMOLE

Smooth, creamy, deep green avocados proliferate in Mexico and show up puréed in a velvety sauce, sliced into salads, or coarsely mashed as a sandwich spread. But the avocado dish that has leaped the borders with the greatest success is guacamole. Literally translated as "avocado mixture," guacamole is traditionally made by pounding the avocado with a pestle in a stone mortar, called a *molcajete,* and mixing it up with cilantro, tomato, onion, and hot chilies. This delicious dish is typically served with tortilla chips. After four years in the Southwest, my assistant Laurie became an expert at making guacamole. Playing around with other flavorings, she added lime for a sweet-tartness, sour cream for smoothness and then dolloped it on scrambled eggs. Served with a great salsa, it was the best meal of the day. When serving guacamole on its own, find your most festive small bowl to pack it up in.

3 ripe avocados, preferably Haas, pitted and peeled
2 tablespoons fresh lime juice
¼ cup sour cream
¼ teaspoon ground cumin
3 dashes Tabasco sauce
Salt and coarsely ground black pepper, to taste
3 ripe plum tomatoes, seeded and cut into ¼-inch dice
¼ cup diced (¼ inch) red onion
¼ cup chopped fresh cilantro leaves or flat-leaf parsley

1. Place the avocado in a bowl, toss well with the lime juice, and mash coarsely with a fork.

2. Fold in the sour cream and season with the cumin, Tabasco, and salt and pepper to taste.

3. Stir in the tomatoes, red onion, and cilantro. Transfer to a festive bowl and serve.

Makes 3 cups

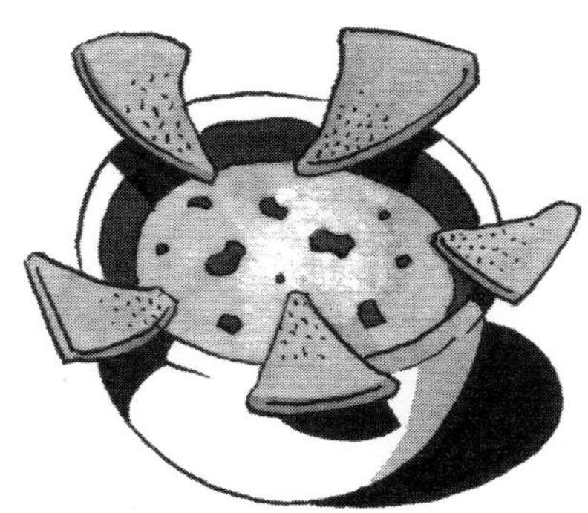

FEROCE

I first ate this rich avocado dish as an appetizer in Martinique. The authentic version brought to mind a kind of cross between a Mexican guacamole and a French brandade. Traditionally it is made with dried salt cod that has been soaked in water overnight, then cooked and mixed with plenty of Scotch bonnet chilies and hot, hot pepper sauce—therefore the name *feroce,* or ferocious. Instead of salt cod I've used cooked fresh cod, but smoked salmon or smoked flaked whitefish can be substituted as well. When folding the ingredients together, proceed gently and do not overmix. The flavor and consistency should personify freshness. Serve *feroce* with grilled baguette slices or delicate croutons for slathering.

1 cup water
½ cup dry white wine
2 bay leaves
4 black peppercorns
2 branches fresh thyme
8 ounces fresh cod fillets or steaks
1 ripe avocado, preferably Haas
2 tablespoons fresh lime juice
1 tablespoon extra virgin olive oil
1 teaspoon minced garlic
Dash of Tabasco or other hot sauce, or more to taste
Salt and freshly ground black pepper, to taste
6 fresh basil leaves, finely slivered

1. In a skillet bring the water, wine, bay leaves, peppercorns, and thyme to a boil. Reduce the heat and add the cod. Simmer covered until the fish flakes easily when tested with a fork, 12 to 15 minutes. Remove the fish from the liquid and let stand until cool enough to handle, flake the cod off the bone, and measure ½ cup cooked fish.

2. Peel the avocado and remove the pit. In a bowl, coarsely mash the avocado with the lime juice and olive oil. Fold in the garlic and flaked fish, then season with the Tabasco, salt, and pepper. Gently fold in the fresh basil. Transfer to an attractive bowl for serving.

Makes 1 cup or 8 appetizer servings

BRANDADE

The farther I traveled, the greater my list of favorites became. While brandade, a heady blend of salt cod, olive oil, and garlic has its roots in Provence, the Italians, Portuguese, and Cubans each make their own distinctive versions. I love those that are puréed with mashed potatoes, milk, and garlic, but it seems that each addition moves another inch away from the classic.

In this recipe, poetic license runs free. The cod is soaked overnight and cooked in a free-wheeling court bouillon. Onions that have been wilted in a generous amount of green, fruity extra virgin olive oil are added along with crème fraîche. This is folded all together with riced Yukon Gold potatoes, the great creamy potatoes. Finally it's seasoned with lots of fresh thyme and generous pinches of coarse black pepper. Adjust the olive oil, crème fraîche, and other seasonings to your taste. Serve at room temperature with thick toast slices and slightly chilled Bandol rosé.

1 cup dry white wine
1 cup water
6 black peppercorns
1 bay leaf
1 pound salt cod, soaked overnight (see box)
1 pound Yukon Gold or other waxy potatoes, peeled and halved
½ cup extra virgin olive oil
½ cup minced onion
1 tablespoon coarsely chopped garlic
1 cup crème fraîche
1 tablespoon fresh thyme leaves
Coarsely ground black pepper, to taste

1. Place the wine, water, peppercorns, and bay leaf in a large saucepan. Bring to a boil, then reduce to a simmer. Add the salt cod and simmer until the fish is cooked through, about 10 minutes. Remove the fish from the cooking liquid, cool to room temperature, and remove any bones. Flake the fish into medium-size pieces and set aside.

2. Place the potatoes in a medium-size saucepan, and add cold water to cover. Bring to a boil and boil uncovered until tender, about 20 minutes. Drain. While the potatoes are still warm, press them through a ricer or mash them.

3. Heat the oil in a large nonstick skillet over medium heat. Add the onion and cook to soften, 10 minutes. Remove from the heat and add the garlic, crème fraîche, thyme, and pepper. Fold the mixture into the mashed potatoes. They should be moist and fluffy.

4. Stir in the flaked fish. Adjust the seasonings. Serve immediately with a green salad and crusty bread.

Serves 6

Salt Cod

Around the world, particularly in those countries that border the Mediterranean, salt cod—cod that has been preserved and dried in salt—turns up in many guises and is widely enjoyed as a staple food. In the south of France, it is puréed with potatoes, onion, lots of garlic, and the best green extra virgin olive oil for a smooth and velvety *brandade de morue. Bacalà* in Italy usually appears in a less smooth state; the potatoes are thinly sliced, as are the onions. *Bacalhau* in Portugal most often appears flaked with eggs, onions, and potatoes.

For all these dishes, it is essential to soak and prepare the salt cod before using it. When you first see a piece of salt cod, don't be surprised. Cut from the side of the fish, it is long, rather stiff, and weighs about 1½ pounds. It can have quite a pungent aroma, so store it well wrapped until use. Preferably you'll have bought one without bones. If not, carefully remove them before soaking.

To prepare the salt cod, cut it into large pieces and place in a large bowl. Cover with cold water and soak overnight, changing the water 2 or 3 times. The next day, drain the fish, rinse it under cold water, and drain again.

Salt cod usually can be found in ethnic markets or ordered through your local fish shop.

A TASTE OF THE WORLD

Greek Palette

Photo: The Parthenon with those splendid Doric columns.

...And

Cinnamon	Bell peppers
Coriander	Zucchini
Oregano	White beans
Vanilla	Figs
Mint	Lemons
Thyme	Raisins
Rosemary	Currants
Dill	Hazelnuts
Marjoram	Pistachios
Garlic	Almonds
Cucumbers	Olive Oil
Red onions	Yogurt
Spinach	Lamb

SKORDALIA SAUCE

There is a thick, creamy garlic and almond sauce served all over Greece that I fell in love with. I enjoy eating it on its own with some pita bread, but for a *meze* course it's lovely served with Tarama Slather, Riad's Baba Ghanouj (see Index), and freshly roasted vegetables or grilled small fish. Of all the renditions I tasted, there was none as delicious as that served at Periyali, the great three-star Greek restaurant in New York City. This is their recipe, which also appears in *The Periyali Cookbook* by Holly Garrison with Nicola Kotsoni and Steve Tzolis.

1 small (4 ounces) Yukon Gold or other waxy potato
5 slices stale white bread, such as Pepperidge Farm, crusts removed
3 tablespoons fresh lemon juice
3 tablespoons white wine vinegar
3 tablespoons extra virgin olive oil
¾ teaspoon salt, plus more to taste
½ teaspoon sugar
½ cup blanched almonds, coarsely chopped
2 cloves garlic, peeled and pressed through a garlic press
Coarsely ground black pepper, to taste
Pita Chips (page 66)

1. Place the potato in a small pan, cover with water, and boil until tender, 12 to 15 minutes. Cool to room temperature and peel. Set aside.

2. Fill a bowl with water. Drop the bread, one slice at a time, into the water. Remove it from the water, and squeeze it out very slightly. Place the bread in a bowl and set aside.

3. Mix the lemon juice, vinegar, oil, ¾ teaspoon salt, and sugar together in a measuring cup. Set aside.

4. Place the almonds, garlic, and reserved potato in a food processor. Pulse the machine on and off until just smooth. Do not overprocess.

5. With the machine running, add the reserved bread along with any water in the bowl that might have accumulated alternately with the lemon juice mixture. Stop occasionally to scrape down the sides of the bowl.

6. Remove the mixture to a bowl and season with salt and pepper. Refrigerate covered for several hours. Serve at room temperature with the pita chips.

Makes 1½ to 2 cups

PLAKA TSATSIKI

Cucumber and Yogurt Dip

In 1965 Richard and I got married and went to Greece on our honeymoon for three glorious weeks. He coyly mentioned to me that his college roommate Dick Johnson lived in Greece, and we really should invite him to join us on our travels. My mother said, "Who takes someone with them on their honeymoon?" But after a night of drinking ouzo in Piraeus and dancing until dawn, I not only invited Dick Johnson, but also his two friends visiting him, Lois and Manoles, to come along on a sail through the Cyclades islands. Before we embarked, Dick invited us for drinks at his apartment. Richard and I wandered through the Plaka, the Greenwich Village of Athens, weaving our way through vendors selling beautifully patinaed antique brass and copper and richly colored and patterned rugs. When we arrived at Dick's apartment, he brought out ouzo and *plaka tsatsiki,* and we gazed in awe at the Acropolis against a brilliant blue sky.

1 quart (32 ounces) nonfat plain yogurt
1 hothouse (seedless) cucumber
4 cloves garlic, coarsely chopped
½ cup walnut pieces
½ cup extra virgin olive oil
1 scallion (white only), thinly sliced on the diagonal
¼ cup fresh dill, chopped
¼ teaspoon coarse salt
¼ teaspoon coarsely ground black pepper
Pita Chips (recipe follows), for serving

1. Line a strainer with 2 layers of cheesecloth and place it over a bowl. Add the yogurt and gather and close the top of the cheesecloth with a twistie. Let drain for 3 hours at room temperature.

2. Peel and cut the cucumber lengthwise in half. Coarsely chop one of the halves and cut the other into ¼-inch dice.

3. Place the coarsely chopped cucumber, the garlic, walnuts, and drained yogurt in a food processor. Pulse on and off until combined but still a bit chunky. Remove the mixture to a bowl. Fold in the olive oil, scallion, dill, salt, and pepper, then stir in the diced cucumber.

4. Chill covered in the refrigerator for 1 hour before serving. Serve in a pretty bowl with pita chips to scoop.

Makes 2½ cups

PITA CHIPS

These plump toasted pita wedges are even better than tortilla chips for dipping. To store, keep the wedges in a plastic bag and reheat in the oven, spread out on a baking sheet, to crisp them up a bit.

4 pita breads (7-inch diameter), cut into 8 wedges each

1. Preheat the oven to 350°F.

2. Arrange the pita wedges on 2 baking sheets and bake until just crisp, about 5 minutes. Cook up to 5 minutes longer for crispier wedges.

Makes 32 chips

RIAD'S BABA GHANOUJ

Adam Reiss, the owner of Doc's Restaurant in New Preston, Connecticut, told me that his chef manager, Riad Aamar, made the best "baba" he'd ever tasted. Of course I ordered it and had to agree—it's awfully good. Riad learned this recipe from his mother in Jerusalem and happily shared the family secret. It's important once the eggplants are baked to remove and discard the bitter seeds. Tahini sauce smooths out the sharp flavors of garlic and lemon and fresh mint finishes the dish. Serve with warmed pita bread or crispy Lavash flatbread (see Index).

2 eggplants (about 1½ pounds each)
1 tablespoon tahini sauce
Juice of 1 lemon
2 cloves garlic, minced
3 teaspoons chopped flat-leaf parsley
2 teaspoons chopped fresh mint leaves
Salt and coarsely ground black pepper, to taste
1 tablespoon extra virgin olive oil

1. Preheat the oven to 425°F.

2. Pierce the eggplants in several places with the tines of a fork. Wrap them separately in aluminum foil and place on a baking sheet. Bake until soft, about 45 minutes.

3. Unwrap the eggplants and let stand until cool enough to handle. Halve the eggplants lengthwise and carefully remove all of the flesh, discarding the seeds and the skin.

4. Coarsely chop the eggplant flesh and place it in a bowl. Add the tahini, lemon juice, garlic, 2 teaspoons of the parsley, the mint, and salt and pepper. Mix well.

5. Place the eggplant mixture in a small serving bowl, drizzle the olive oil over the top, and sprinkle with the remaining teaspoon of parsley. Serve at room temperature.

Makes 2½ cups

SOUVENIR TO SAVOR

Meze, Tapas, and Zakuski

Throughout Turkey, Greece, Spain, and Russia, vibrantly flavored small plates are always at the ready. Accompanied by a favorite drink, they take the edge off an appetite, and say "welcome." Called *meze* in Greece and Turkey, *tapas* in Spain, and *zakuski* in Russia, some dishes are elaborate preparations, while others might be as simple as a slice of cheese or a small bowl of nuts. In feeling, they are not too unlike those old favorites—the antipasti of Italy.

The balance of textures and flavors served is of utmost importance. In Turkey and Greece, dishes such as marinated olives and Turkish-style leeks begin the feast and are followed by calamari or other fried seafood with a pungent garlic sauce. In Spain, a basket of substantial crispy fresh potato chips are never far from reach. In Russia, sliced smoked fish begin a *zakuski* presentation, accompanied by a plate of fresh herbs, tomato wedges, and cucumbers. All countries have their "slathers," or luscious purées—tarama in Greece and Turkey (and one not too dissimilar in Russia), *tapenade* in France—meant to be scooped up on crunchy bread toasts.

These delicious small plates are, from my point of view, the best way to eat. With the generous selections offered, I rarely make it to the main course, which often seems a bit boring following such a spread. In Spanish, Greek, and Turkish restaurants, *meze* and *tapas* usually arrive on oversized trays, dishes carefully balanced one with the other. *Zakuski,* on the other hand, are already set out to look at and admire. Most often these dishes can be prepared ahead of time and have good staying power, which makes them ideal for large dinners or cocktail parties. Plates can be arranged in small stacks for your guests to serve themselves. Cocktail napkins, either cloth or paper, are appropriate to have nearby.

What to drink? In Spain, they usually serve a chilled dry Fino sherry. In Russia, a small bottle of vodka rests in a bucket filled with ice or a bottle of brandy is placed on the table. In Turkey and Greece, glasses of raki or ouzo are served.

A gracious sense of hospitality permeates the atmosphere as soon as one's guests feast their eyes upon these welcoming tables.

ISLAND PAN-BARBECUED SHRIMP

Caribbean islanders love their food nice and spicy. This dish combines the celebrated herbs of Provence—rosemary and thyme—with island-hot cayenne, black pepper, and garlic. Quickly cooked in a hot skillet atop the stove, these shrimp make a great appetizer. Serve with a splash of fresh lime juice to cool things down a bit. Jumbo shrimp are very delicious and dramatic but feed fewer and require a longer cooking time than large shrimp. When cleaning the shrimp, remove the vein along the back side, and the shrimp will fan out nicely when they cook.

1 pound large or jumbo shrimp, peeled and deveined, tails left on
2 tablespoons olive oil
1 tablespoon minced garlic
1 tablespoon chopped fresh rosemary leaves
1 tablespoon chopped fresh thyme leaves
½ teaspoon freshly ground black pepper
¼ teaspoon cayenne pepper, or to taste
¼ teaspoon salt
2 limes, halved

1. Combine the shrimp with the oil, garlic, rosemary, thyme, both peppers, and the salt. Let marinate at room temperature for 1 hour.

2. Heat a dry nonstick skillet over medium-high heat until hot. Lay the shrimp in the pan and cook, turning once, for 4 to 8 minutes depending on the size of the shrimp. They should be just cooked through. Brush the shrimp with the remaining marinade before turning. Serve with lime halves alongside.

Serves 4 as an appetizer

GOONG WAAN
Spicy Sweetened Shrimp

Cooking class at the Oriental Hotel in Bangkok was exciting, informative, and lots of fun. A full program consisted of three-hour classes, five mornings a week, with lunch served at the conclusion of each session. Most of the participants were American or British, longing to take a permanent taste of Southeast Asia back home. While certain ingredients are available in areas of the United States (fish sauce is essential), others can be substituted with more easily available products. For this shrimp recipe, palm sugar was needed. I substituted light brown sugar and the result was equally delicious. The slightly sweet flavor of the fish sauce and sugar balance beautifully with spicy garlic and crushed peppercorns. Serve with icy Thai or Chinese beer.

1 pound large shrimp in their shells
½ cup water
¼ cup (packed) light brown sugar
3 tablespoons Thai Fish Sauce (page 254; see Note)
2 cloves garlic, minced
2 tablespoons minced fresh cilantro roots and stems, strings removed
1 teaspoon white peppercorns, lightly crushed
4 whole cilantro sprigs, for garnish

1. Rinse the shrimp under cold water. Drain and set aside.

2. Mix the water, brown sugar, and fish sauce together in an 8- to 10-inch-wide saucepan. Cook, stirring, over low heat until the sugar dissolves, about 2 minutes.

3. Add the garlic, minced cilantro, and pepper. Bring the mixture to a boil over medium heat and continue to boil until the sauce reduces and thickens slightly, 6 to 7 minutes.

4. Add the shrimp and cook, stirring constantly and coating the shrimp with sauce, over medium heat, until opaque and just cooked through, 1½ to 2 minutes. Remove to a bowl and let cool to room temperature.

5. Chill the shrimp in the refrigerator up to 1 hour, tossing the shrimp twice in the sauce. With a slotted spoon, remove the shrimp to a bowl and garnish decoratively with cilantro sprigs. Have small bowls or plates alongside to serve the shrimp and to hold the shells.

Serves 10 to 12 as an hors d'oeuvre, 4 as an appetizer

Note: If you'd rather buy fish sauce, it is available in Asian grocery stores or Asian sections of supermarkets.

A TASTE OF THE WORLD

Southeast Asian Palette

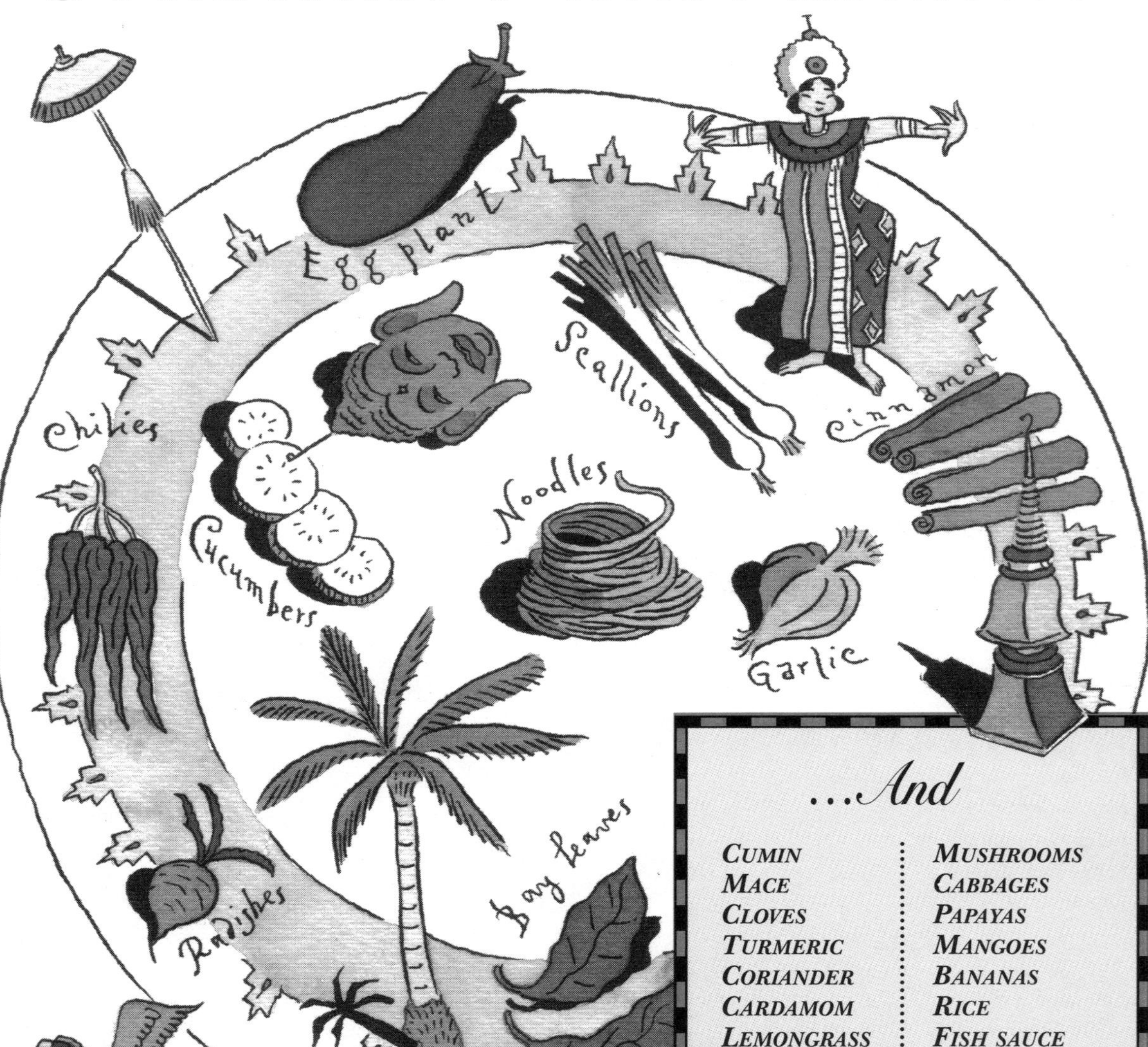

...And

CUMIN	MUSHROOMS
MACE	CABBAGES
CLOVES	PAPAYAS
TURMERIC	MANGOES
CORIANDER	BANANAS
CARDAMOM	RICE
LEMONGRASS	FISH SAUCE
CILANTRO	SOY SAUCE
MINT	CHILI PASTE
BASIL	SHRIMP PASTE
GINGER	COCONUT MILK
MUNG BEAN SPROUTS	BROWN SUGAR
	SHRIMP

CHICKEN SATAY SINGAPORE STYLE

Singapore today is a modern metropolis—even the legendary Raffles Hotel has been gorgeously refurbished with its overhead fans gently whirring and its potted palms all in a row. But it was on the sprawling veranda of a private home that I dined on the most delicious, aromatic satay I have ever eaten. It was prepared by the family cook, whose hand with spices worked magic. For this satay, the chicken must be fresh and tender, but the real secret lies in the two sauces. One is the marinade and the other the peanut sauce used for dipping. Both are triumphs in texture, flavor, and consistency.

MARINADE:
3 tablespoons peanut oil
1 tablespoon soy sauce
1 teaspoon honey
3 cloves garlic, minced
1 tablespoon minced peeled fresh ginger
1 tablespoon curry powder
1 teaspoon ground coriander
1 teaspoon ground turmeric
1 teaspoon ground cumin
1 very small dried chili, finely crumbled
Salt and freshly ground black pepper, to taste

2 pounds boneless, skinless chicken breasts
Saus Kacang (recipe follows)

1. Soak at least 24 bamboo skewers (12 inches long) in water overnight.

2. Mix all the marinade ingredients together in a large bowl.

3. Cut the chicken along the grain into strips about 3 inches long and ½ inch wide. Mix well with the marinade and let rest covered at room temperature for 2 hours.

4. Just before serving, preheat the oven to 450°F.

5. Thread the chicken pieces lengthwise on the bamboo skewers and place them on baking sheets. Bake until just cooked through, about 5 minutes. Do not overcook.

6. Serve at room temperature with *saus kacang*.

Makes 24 skewers

SAUS KACANG
Indonesian Peanut Sauce

Perhaps one of the most familiar flavors of the Indonesian palate is Saus Kacang or, as we know it, peanut sauce. You will always find this dipping sauce alongside grilled meat satays in a *rijsttafel* or accompanying *gado gado*, the Indonesian equivalent of *salade niçoise*. The consistency of this sauce should be rich and creamy. If you prefer your sauce a bit thicker or thinner, experiment with the quantities of peanut butter and coconut milk.

¼ cup peanut oil
1 small onion, finely chopped
2 cloves garlic, finely chopped
2 teaspoons curry powder
1 teaspoon chili paste (available in specialty food shops) or ½ teaspoon crushed red pepper flakes
¼ cup coconut milk (page 252 or available in specialty food shops)
¼ cup water
¼ cup creamy peanut butter
3 tablespoons fresh lemon juice
2 teaspoons white wine vinegar
3 tablespoons (packed) light brown sugar
1 cinnamon stick (3 inches long)
1 bay leaf
2 tablespoons finely chopped peanuts (optional)
¼ cup boiling water
2 teaspoons chopped fresh basil leaves

1. Heat the oil in a large nonstick skillet over low heat. Add the onion and garlic and cook, stirring, until wilted, about 5 minutes.

2. Add the curry powder and chili paste; cook 2 to 3 minutes to mellow the flavors. Stir in the coconut milk and water, then stir in the peanut butter, lemon juice, vinegar, brown sugar, cinnamon stick, and bay leaf. Mix together well.

3. Bring the mixture to a boil and immediately reduce the heat to low. Simmer gently, stirring, until the sauce thickens, about 5 minutes. Stir in the chopped peanuts if using.

4. Remove the cinnamon stick and bay leaf. Place the mixture in a food processor and process until smooth, adding the boiling water through the feed tube to bind the sauce.

5. Scrape the sauce into a serving bowl and cool to room temperature. Store covered in the refrigerator. Let warm to room temperature 15 to 20 minutes before serving. If the peanut sauce separates a bit before serving, whisk in a few drops, up to 1 teaspoon, of boiling water, and the sauce will come together. Garnish with a sprinkling of chopped basil.

Makes about 1½ cups

SATSIVI

Chicken Bathed in Walnut Sauce

Soviet Georgian food absolutely fascinates me. Its flavors are extremely complex, the result of lavish ingredients. With my first taste of *satsivi* in a Georgian restaurant in St. Petersburg, I began making notes for a recipe. There, a rather mild walnut sauce was spooned over cut-up pieces of boiled chicken as part of a *zakuski,* accompanied by pickled beets and cabbage and a bowl of sliced cucumbers and tomatoes covered with fresh parsley sprigs. The second time I tasted this dish was in a Georgian restaurant in Moscow. The chicken was shredded from the bones and the walnut sauce coated the meat. The flavor was intense and I loved it.

A rich chicken broth, tenderly simmered chicken, walnuts, garlic, and bright, fresh herbs are the components of this dish. The velvety consistency comes from a liaison of egg yolks and sauce. This is a perfect dish for the *zakuski* table, as it can be prepared ahead and served at room temperature. In fact, *satsivi* means "eaten cold." Have plenty of Lavash-style bread—light crisp flat bread with a rich delicate flavor (see Index)—in a basket as well as coarse black bread for dipping in the sauce.

BROTH:
1 chicken (3 to 3½ pounds), cut into 8 pieces
1 large onion, halved, peel left on
2 ribs celery with leaves on
2 carrots, quartered
2 parsnips, quartered
2 cloves garlic, peeled and lightly bruised (page 153)
1 ripe large tomato, cored, seeded, and coarsely chopped
4 fresh parsley sprigs
4 fresh dill sprigs
4 cups defatted Chicken Broth (page 127)
3 cups water
Salt and freshly ground pepper, to taste

WALNUT SAUCE:
2 cups walnut pieces
6 large cloves garlic, coarsely chopped
¾ cup coarsely chopped fresh cilantro leaves and stems
¼ cup chopped fresh dill leaves and stems
1 tablespoon grated lemon zest
1 teaspoon coarse salt, or more to taste
2 tablespoons unsalted butter
2 cups diced (¼ inch) onions
1 tablespoon all-purpose flour
3½ cups defatted broth (see above)
2 large egg yolks
¼ teaspoon ground cinnamon
Pinch of cayenne pepper, or more to taste
3 tablespoons fresh lemon juice

GARNISH:
2 tablespoons coarsely chopped fresh cilantro leaves, plus 8 whole sprigs
1 tablespoon chopped fresh dill

1. For the broth, place the dark meat of the chicken, the onion, celery, carrots, parsnips, garlic, tomato, parsley, dill, chicken broth, and water in a large stockpot. Bring slowly to a boil, then reduce the heat and simmer uncovered for 15 minutes.

2. Add the white chicken meat (breasts and wings) and simmer another 30 minutes over medium-low heat. The chicken should be cooked through. Season with salt and pepper.

3. Remove the chicken from the broth and let cool. Increase the heat under the broth to medium and cook an additional 15 minutes. Taste and adjust the seasonings. Strain the broth and let cool. Remove any fat that rises to the surface or pour through a gravy separator to defat it. Measure 3½ cups broth and save the rest for another use.

4. Remove the skin from the chicken and shred the meat from the bones in large pieces. Place the meat in a bowl and set aside. Discard the skin and bones.

5. For the sauce, combine the walnuts, garlic, cilantro, dill, lemon zest, and coarse salt in a food processor. Pulse on and off until the mixture resembles coarse meal. Remove and set aside.

6. Melt the butter in a medium-size heavy saucepan over medium-low heat. Add the onions and cook, stirring, until wilted, about 10 minutes. Sprinkle with the flour and cook, stirring, 1 minute.

7. Add the 3½ cups broth and cook, stirring, over low heat for 5 minutes to thicken slightly. Stir in the walnut mixture and cook, stirring, another 2 minutes. Do not boil.

8. Place the egg yolks in a small bowl, whisk slightly, and then very gradually whisk in 2 cups of the hot walnut broth to temper the yolks. Gradually whisk the egg mixture back into the pot of walnut broth. Add the cinnamon, cayenne, and salt to taste. Cook, whisking constantly, over very low heat another 3 minutes. Do not boil. The sauce will be slightly thickened.

9. Remove the sauce from the heat and stir in the lemon juice and reserved chicken. Cool to room temperature, then cover and refrigerate overnight.

10. Before serving, let the dish warm to room temperature. Fold in the chopped cilantro and dill and transfer to a decorative bowl. Garnish with cilantro sprigs and serve.

Serves 8 to 10 as an appetizer

YAKITORI

The name of this Japanese dish is familiar, but the meaning may not be. Yet it does get right to the point: *yaki* means broiled or baked and *tori*, chicken. These tender little bites of boneless chicken breast are marinated in a sweetened soy mixture that is enlivened with garlic and fresh ginger. Therefore, they need no dipping sauce. A quick grill or broil delivers a delicate, satisfying hors d'oeuvre. When using small bamboo skewers, it is necessary to either soak them in water overnight or wrap the ends in foil so that they won't burn.

3 whole skinless, boneless chicken breasts
2 tablespoons soy sauce
2 tablespoons dry sherry
1½ tablespoons sugar
1 tablespoon finely chopped garlic
1 tablespoon finely chopped peeled fresh ginger

1. Soak 24 bamboo skewers (12 inches long) in water overnight.

2. Cut the chicken breasts into 1½-inch cubes and place them in a bowl.

3. In a separate bowl, mix together the remaining ingredients. Pour the marinade over the chicken and toss well., Let marinate covered for 1 to 2 hours at room temperature.

4. Prepare hot coals for grilling or preheat the broiler.

5. Thread 2 pieces of chicken onto each skewer and reserve the marinade. Wrap the remaining exposed skewer with a small piece of aluminum foil so that it doesn't burn while grilling.

6. Grill or broil the skewers 3 to 4 inches from the heat until the chicken is just cooked through, about 2 minutes per side, brushing occasionally with the remaining marinade. Serve hot or at room temperature.

Makes 24 skewers

THOD MUN PLA

Tiny Thai Croquettes

One of the best dishes I brought back with me from the cooking classes I attended in Bangkok was piquant fish croquettes. These crispy savory bites are an exciting surprise—I find them irresistible. I've made several ingredient substitutions so that they could be made right in our own kitchens. The original recipe called for freshwater fish and I've chosen catfish for its texture and sweet flavor. Kaffir lime leaf shreds became grated lime zest and winged beans became green beans. Two Thai ingredients that proved essential are fish sauce and red curry paste, which can be found in Asian grocery stores. These croquettes are great in miniature for hors d'oeuvres, or if made slightly larger, as an appetizer. Serve hot with Thai Sweet and Sour Sauce for a perfect flavor burst!

12 ounces catfish fillets
12 ounces green beans, trimmed and cut into ⅛-inch rounds
1 cup fresh basil leaves, coarsely chopped
3 tablespoons Thai Fish Sauce (page 254; see Note)
1 tablespoon red curry paste
1 tablespoon finely grated fresh lime zest (2 limes)
1 teaspoon (packed) dark brown sugar
¼ teaspoon freshly ground black pepper
1 large egg, lightly beaten
2 tablespoons vegetable oil, plus more if needed
Thai Sweet and Sour Sauce (recipe follows)

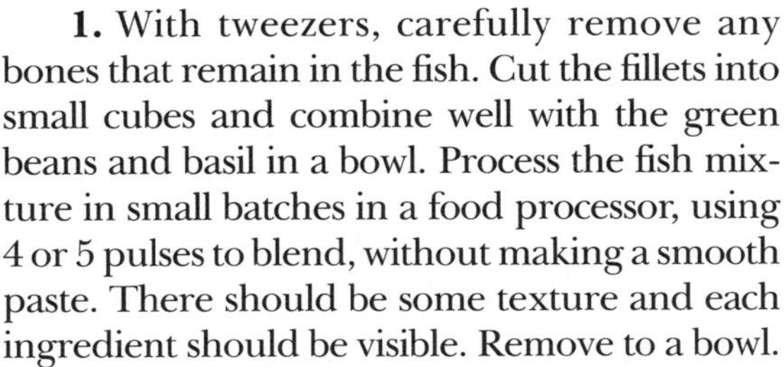

1. With tweezers, carefully remove any bones that remain in the fish. Cut the fillets into small cubes and combine well with the green beans and basil in a bowl. Process the fish mixture in small batches in a food processor, using 4 or 5 pulses to blend, without making a smooth paste. There should be some texture and each ingredient should be visible. Remove to a bowl.

2. To the fish mixture, add the fish sauce, curry paste, lime zest, sugar, and black pepper and mix well with a fork. Fold in the egg to bind the mixture. Form into 16 roundish croquettes, 2 inches across, or 32 croquettes, 1 inch across.

3. Heat the oil in a nonstick skillet over medium heat. Add the croquettes in small batches and sauté on both sides until golden, about 2 minutes per side for the larger and 1 minute per side for the smaller. Add more oil to the skillet, if necessary. Serve hot with the sweet and sour sauce.

Serves 16 as an hors d'oeuvre, 8 as an appetizer

Note: If you'd rather buy fish sauce, it is available in Asian grocery stores or Asian sections of supermarkets.

THAI SWEET AND SOUR SAUCE

Thai sauces have a perfect harmony of flavors and textures. Sweet and sour tastes are achieved by blending vinegars, sugars, chilies, and garlic. Cucumbers infuse their flavor and add a delicate crunch. If you are making the 2-inch croquettes, leave the cucumbers in slices; for the smaller croquettes, dice the cucumbers. This sauce also goes well with other fried fish and satay dishes.

1 cup rice wine vinegar
½ cup water
½ cup granulated sugar
¼ cup (packed) light brown sugar
1 to 2 tablespoons finely chopped fresh red chilies (seeds and ribs removed)
1 teaspoon salt
1 teaspoon minced garlic
1 teaspoon finely chopped fresh cilantro stems and roots, strings removed
1 cup halved, seeded, and thinly sliced cucumbers
8 cilantro leaves, for garnish

1. Combine the vinegar, ½ cup water, both sugars, the chilies, salt, garlic, and chopped cilantro in a saucepan. Cook over low heat for 2 minutes, stirring to dissolve the sugars. Remove to a bowl and let cool to room temperature.

2. Stir in the cucumber slices, garnish with the cilantro leaves, and serve immediately.

Makes 2 cups

TINY POTATO CROQUETTES

Richard and I arrived in St. Tropez on a hot sun-drenched August day. We quickly unpacked and, of course, headed right to a restaurant. We sat outdoors under a creamy canvas umbrella, and feeling wonderfully celebratory, ordered Champagne. Just after the cork was popped, we were treated to tiny potato croquettes—Provence infused with lots of freshly chopped garlic and rosemary. Dollops of Orange-Rosemary Mayonnaise atop are an added kiss of sunshine.

2 large Idaho potatoes (about 1½ pounds), peeled
3 large eggs, lightly beaten
2 tablespoons all-purpose flour
Finely grated zest of 1 orange
⅓ cup minced garlic
2 tablespoons chopped flat-leaf parsley
1 tablespoon finely chopped fresh rosemary or 1 teaspoon crumbled dried
2 teaspoons coarse salt
1 teaspoon freshly ground black pepper
⅓ cup olive oil
⅓ cup vegetable oil
Orange-Rosemary Mayonnaise (recipe follows)

1. Bring a medium-size pot of water to a boil. While waiting for the water to come to a boil, coarsely grate the potatoes into a bowl of cold water. Drain and cook them in the boiling water for 2 minutes. Drain the cooked potatoes well and pat dry with a paper towel.

2. Place the potatoes in a bowl. Add the eggs, flour, orange zest, garlic, herbs, salt, and pepper. Combine well.

3. To form the croquettes, roll 1 tablespoon of the potato mixture in the palms of your hands to form a ball, then flatten it slightly, so that it is about 1½ inches across and ½ inch thick.

4. Heat the oils in a large nonstick skillet over medium heat. Cook the croquettes in batches of 6 to 8 for 2½ to 3 minutes on each side until light golden brown. Drain on paper towels. Serve warm with the orange mayonnaise. To reheat the croquettes, spread them out in a single layer on a baking sheet and heat for 5 minutes in a preheated 375°F oven.

Makes 30 croquettes

ORANGE-ROSEMARY MAYONNAISE

In this easily made mayonnaise, the thick orange syrup imparts a beautiful flavor and fresh rosemary infuses its aromatic scent. Let rest refrigerated at least 1 hour before serving for the flavors to come out.

1 cup fresh orange juice
¼ cup mayonnaise
¼ cup sour cream
¾ teaspoon finely chopped fresh rosemary or ¼ teaspoon crumbled dried
Salt, to taste

1. Place the orange juice in a small saucepan over medium heat. Cook, swirling the pan, until the juice is reduced to a thick syrup, 10 to 12 minutes. You should have about 1½ tablespoons.

2. Combine the mayonnaise and sour cream in a small bowl. Add the orange syrup, rosemary, and salt and stir well. Cover and refrigerate for 1 hour before serving.

Makes about ½ cup

THAI CRAB SPRING ROLLS

These beautiful, crispy little spring rolls are both delicate and wonderfully flavored. For truly superb eating, just wrap one up in a tender lettuce leaf, with mint and cilantro leaves tucked in for freshness. Or if you're serving these for a special occasion, create a Thai centerpiece (page 396) for a greater variety of garden vegetables. Dip it all into Sweet Garlic Sauce or Indonesian Soy Sauce.

3 tablespoons plus ½ cup peanut oil, or more if needed
1 cup finely shredded green cabbage
1 cup finely slivered snow peas
½ cup slivered leeks or scallions
½ cup mung bean sprouts
2 tablespoons chopped fresh cilantro leaves
2 tablespoons minced garlic
1 tablespoon minced peeled fresh ginger
8 ounces fresh lump crabmeat picked over for shell and cartilage
1 teaspoon Thai Fish Sauce (page 254; see Note)
1 teaspoon soy sauce
Dash of chili oil
1 tablespoon cornstarch
1 tablespoon water
5 spring roll wrappers, 8 inches square (available in Asian markets)
2 heads Boston lettuce, leaves separated, rinsed, and patted dry
2 cups fresh mint leaves, plus a few mint sprigs, for garnish
½ cup fresh cilantro leaves, plus a few cilantro sprigs, for garnish
¾ cup Sweet Garlic Sauce and/or Indonesian Soy Sauce (recipes follow)

1. Heat 1 tablespoon of the peanut oil in a large nonstick skillet over medium heat. Add the cabbage and sauté for 3 minutes, tossing constantly. Remove the cabbage to a bowl. Add ½ tablespoon oil to the skillet, add the snow peas, and sauté for 3 minutes. Add the snow peas to the cabbage. The vegetables should be softened but still retain some crunch. Add another 1½ tablespoons oil to the skillet, add the leeks, bean sprouts, cilantro, garlic, and ginger, and sauté for 2 minutes. Stir in the crabmeat, fish sauce, soy sauce, and chili oil. Add to the cabbage and snow peas and toss all the ingredients together well. Set aside.

2. In a bowl, mix the cornstarch and water.

3. Cut the spring roll wrappers diagonally in half from point to point and then in half again so that there are 4 triangles from each wrapper.

4. Place a triangle in front of you on a clean work surface with the long side facing you. Place 1 tablespoon of the crab mixture in the center of the long side about ½ inch from the edge. Fold the ends of the long side in towards the center over the filling. Brush the opposite tip of the wrapper with the cornstarch mixture, then roll the spring roll towards the tip and press lightly to seal. Repeat the process until all the filling has been used.

5. Heat the remaining ½ cup peanut oil in a nonstick skillet over medium heat until hot. Fry the spring rolls in small batches about 2 minutes per side until golden. Add more oil to the skillet if necessary. Drain on paper towels.

6. To serve, decorately arrange the lettuce leaves on one side of a large serving plate and the hot spring rolls on the other. Pile the mint and cilantro leaves in the center. Garnish with a few sprigs of mint and cilantro. Place the dipping sauces in bowls and serve alongside.

Makes 20 spring rolls

Note: If you'd rather buy fish sauce, it is available in Asian grocery stores or Asian sections of supermarkets.

SOUVENIR TO SAVOR

The Mystery Fruit

On a very steamy Sunday in April, 1991, I was on a bus traveling from Bangkok to Ayuthaya. Halfway through the three-hour trip, the guide handed out as refreshment a somewhat dry, bright yellow oval-shaped fruit that was unfamiliar to me. The texture was both spongy and velvety. The aroma was quite strong, somewhat reminiscent of a papaya, but not nearly as pleasant. This was jackfruit and it definitely called for further investigation.

The jackfruit is an unusual large tropical fruit with Indian origins that is available year round in southeast Asia. Grown on evergreens, the fruit can become as long as 3 feet, as wide as 20 inches, and can weigh as much as 90 pounds. (The smaller fruits are saved for exporting!) Jackfruit has a thick green, knobbly and scaled rind covering pale cream, yellow, or pink flesh. It is much like a papaya or pineapple, a bit less juicy, but sweet and fragrant. The underripe fruit is often used in curries, salads, and vegetable dishes. As it ripens it becomes strongly perfumed and is most often used in fruit salads. The seeds can be roasted and eaten as a snack or used in curries.

Stateside, jackfruit is rarely available fresh, but canned jackfruit sometimes is found in Asian grocery stores. Jackfruit is most certain to become more familiar in American markets in the years to come. On a recent wander through Chinatown in New York, I was amazed to see very large jackfruits hanging proudly from the awnings in fruit and vegetable shops. They were all tied up and decorated with blue ribbons as if they'd won first prize at the local fair!

SWEET GARLIC SAUCE

In this Indonesian dipping sauce, a rich, deep, sweet flavor is achieved by long and slow simmering. Serve with lightly fried prawn rolls, chicken and meat satays, and grilled vegetables.

½ cup rice wine vinegar
1 cup water
½ cup (packed) dark brown sugar
3 tablespoons finely chopped garlic
2 teaspoons chili paste (available in specialty food shops)
½ teaspoon salt

Place all the ingredients in a small heavy saucepan. Simmer uncovered over medium-low heat until the sauce has reduced and thickened to a creamy consistency, 30 to 35 minutes. Cool to room temperature before serving. The sauce can be stored tightly covered in the refrigerator up to 2 weeks.

Makes ¾ cup

INDONESIAN SOY SAUCE

Soy sauce is frequently called for as an ingredient or condiment in Indonesian cooking, but Japanese or Chinese soy sauce may be a bit too salty to harmonize with the more complex Indonesian flavors. I've made a smoother, more mellow version based on the traditional Indonesian *kecap manis.*

⅓ cup (packed) dark brown sugar
⅓ cup water
⅓ cup soy sauce
2 tablespoons light molasses
1 teaspoon minced peeled fresh ginger
¼ teaspoon ground coriander
⅛ teaspoon freshly ground white pepper

1. Place the brown sugar and water in a small heavy saucepan and cook, stirring, over low heat for 1 minute to dissolve the sugar. Increase the heat to medium and cook at a very slow boil until the mixture thickens slightly, about 2 minutes.

2. Reduce the heat to low and stir in the soy sauce, molasses, ginger, coriander, and pepper. Simmer another 2 minutes, stirring frequently. The sauce may be stored tightly covered in the refrigerator up to 2 months.

Makes ¾ cup

PRATHAAD LOM

Prawn Rolls

Simple to prepare and delicious tasting, these prawns (shrimp) are marinated for just 15 minutes in an aromatic blend of garlic, cilantro roots, white pepper, and fish sauce. I've wrapped just the middle of the prawns in wonton skins and let the tails show through decoratively. Serve hot and crisp as an hors d'oeuvre with small bowls of Sweet Garlic Sauce and

Indonesian Soy Sauce alongside for dipping. Have a tiny plate at hand for the tails.

2 cloves garlic, minced
6 white peppercorns, crushed
1 teaspoon finely chopped fresh cilantro roots, small strings discarded
1 tablespoon Thai Fish Sauce (page 254; see Note)
24 large shrimp, partially peeled (tails left on) and deveined
12 wonton skins (3½ inches square), cut in half crosswise
½ cup peanut oil
¾ cup Sweet Garlic Sauce and/or Indonesian Soy Sauce (page 79)

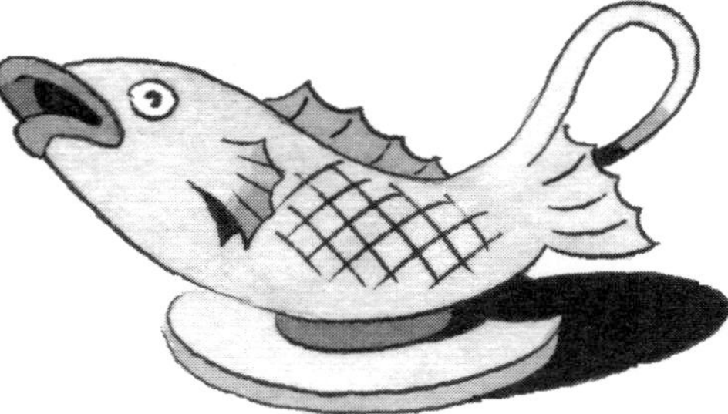

1. Combine the garlic, peppercorns, cilantro, and fish sauce in a bowl. Add the shrimp, toss well, and set aside to marinate for 15 minutes. Drain the shrimp.

2. Wrap a wonton skin around the center of each, so that the tip and the tail are exposed. Dip your finger in a little water and dampen the open edge slightly to seal.

3. Heat the peanut oil in a large skillet over medium heat. Add the prawn rolls, 6 at a time, and fry 1 minute on each side, until nicely golden. Drain on a paper towel and repeat with the remaining prawn rolls. Serve immediately with one or both of the sauces for dipping.

Makes 24 prawn rolls

Note: If you'd rather buy fish sauce, it is available in Asian grocery stores or Asian sections of supermarkets.

PISSALADIERE

In this delicate version of the classic Niçoise onion tart, I've used puff pastry instead of the traditional heavier bread dough for ease and lightness of texture. The natural sweetness of the onions comes out as they slowly cook in a fruity extra virgin olive oil, making a perfect flavor foil for the pungent anchovies and briny olives that decorate the top of the tart. The tart is lovely served as an appetizer or an hors d'oeuvre.

¼ cup extra virgin olive oil
5 medium onions, peeled, halved, and thinly slivered
1 teaspoon dried thyme
Salt and freshly ground black pepper, to taste
1 sheet prepared puff pastry (about 8½ ounces), thawed according to package directions, and then kept chilled
2 cans (about 2 ounces each) anchovy fillets (30 in all), drained
10 imported black olives, pitted and halved
1 tablespoon coarsely chopped flat-leaf parsley

1. Heat the oil in a large heavy pot over low heat. Add the onions and cook, stirring occasionally, until the onions are very soft, about 20 minutes. Season with the thyme, salt, and pepper. Set aside.

2. Preheat the oven to 350°F.

3. Sprinkle a clean work surface and a rolling pin with flour. Roll the sheet of puff pastry to a 14 x 11-inch rectangle. Place the pastry on a baking sheet (with no sides). Prick the pastry all over with a fork.

4. Spread the onion mixture over the dough, leaving a 1-inch border around the sides. Make a lattice pattern over the onions with the anchovies. Arrange the olive halves in the spaces of the lattice pattern.

5. Place the tart on the lowest rack of the oven and bake until golden brown, 20 to 25 minutes. Remove from the oven and sprinkle with the chopped parsley. Cut into 12 pieces and serve hot.

Makes 12 squares, serves 6 as an appetizer

TUNA NICOISE BRIKS

When I began working on this book, one reason I wanted to go to Tunisia was to taste and learn to make *briks*—tissue-thin pastry envelopes with local fillings and always a perfectly cooked egg. Authentically *briks* are made from a delicate, thin pastry called *warka*. Since *warka* is not available in America, I tried working with both phyllo dough and spring roll wrappers and found spring roll wrappers were best. Making *briks* takes practice and patience because you must break an egg into the center of the wrapper over the filling. Kiss one or two good-bye and then you'll be an expert.

Once assembled and shaped into a triangular package, the *brik* is cooked in hot oil. The egg must be done to the perfect consistency, runny but not raw. Besides learning how to make a *brik,* you must learn how to eat it. Pick the cooked *brik* up, by two diagonally opposite corners, holding one corner high. Bite off the lower bottom corner and slowly suck the cooked egg out. It must not get on your face or your plate. Once again, this is worth the effort because they're just delicious.

1 can (6⅛ ounces) tuna, drained and flaked
¼ cup chopped flat-leaf parsley
2 tablespoons chopped sun-dried tomatoes packed in oil
1 tablespoon drained tiny capers
1 tablespoon finely chopped shallots
1 teaspoon fresh lemon juice
Coarsely ground black pepper, to taste
4 spring roll wrappers (8 inches square; available in Asian markets and some supermarkets)
4 small super-fresh eggs
1 egg white
Vegetable oil, for frying
Lemon wedges, for garnish

1. Combine the tuna, parsley, sun-dried tomatoes, capers, shallots, lemon juice, and pepper in a bowl. Set aside.

2. Place a spring roll wrapper in front of you on a clean work surface with the point of the square facing you like a diamond. In the center of the lower half of the diamond, place 2 tablespoons of the tuna mixture. Use the back of the spoon to make an indentation big enough to break an egg into.

3. Gently break an egg into the center of the tuna mixture. Using a pastry brush, brush the edges of the spring roll wrapper with egg white. Fold the top half of the diamond over the egg and filling and press the edges together. Brush the edges again with egg white, fold the edge over ½ inch, as if you were preparing a papillote, and press gently to seal. Form 3 more packets.

4. Heat about ¼ inch vegetable oil in a medium-size skillet over medium heat until a small piece of bread sizzles when it is added.

5. Using a large spatula (or two if necessary), carefully lift the *brik* and place it in the hot oil. Fry the brik for 2 minutes on the first side, then gently turn it over with a spatula and fry about 2 minutes longer on the other side, until it is golden brown. Remove to a paper towel and repeat with the remaining *briks*. Serve immediately with lemon wedges.

Serves 4

Note: This recipe uses lightly cooked eggs. To avoid any illness problems that can sometimes be caused by eggs that are not fully cooked, use only eggs you know to be farm fresh and kept refrigerated.

Working with Phyllo

Thin, flaky phyllo makes the most wonderful pastry for wrapping both savory and sweet fillings, from cocktail bites to desserts. Although difficult to find fresh, phyllo pastry is available in the freezer section of most supermarkets across America in 1-pound boxes containing approximately 24 to 30 sheets. Phyllo is easy to work with, although it can take some trial and error to get started. Defrost the unopened package in the refrigerator or at room temperature. Phyllo can dry out and become brittle very quickly so lay the sheets on a kitchen towel and cover them with a sheet of waxed paper followed by a dampened kitchen towel. Only remove sheets when you are ready to use them. Always work on a flat, clean surface. When brushing the sheets with butter, use a very light hand. A little goes a long way. Most recipes in this book call for between 8 ounces and 1 pound of phyllo. The remainder should be well wrapped in plastic and stored in the refrigerator. It will keep for up to a week.

CHILEAN EMPANADAS

Chilean cooks produce delicious, savory empanadas that are second to none. During my stay in Chile, I managed to enjoy them more often than I would have imagined possible. For my adaptation of this South American specialty, I've shredded cooked corned beef instead of the traditional boiled beef because I love its moist pungent flavor. Raisins, black olives, chopped hard-cooked egg, and parsley add their own special tastes and textural contrasts. Dark rum and sweet cinnamon fuse all the flavors together. The Chileans typically wrap empanadas in a substantial pastry made with lard instead of butter. I prefer phyllo dough for a lighter, flakier pastry. These are delicious served as a party hors d'oeuvre with icy Margaritas (see Index) or a chilled Latin American beer.

½ cup golden raisins
2 tablespoons dark rum
3 tablespoons olive oil
1 small onion, chopped
¼ teaspoon ground cinnamon
Pinch of crushed red pepper flakes
12 ounces cooked corned beef, shredded
½ cup chopped pitted black olives
4 hard-cooked eggs, peeled and coarsely chopped
¼ cup chopped flat-leaf parsley
Salt, to taste
1 pound phyllo dough (see Note)
1 cup Clarified Butter (page 53)

1. Toss the raisins with the rum in a small bowl and let plump for 30 minutes.

2. Heat the oil in a heavy casserole over low heat. Add the onion and cook, stirring, until wilted, about 10 minutes. Stir in the cinnamon and pepper flakes, then add the corned beef and stir to combine. Add the raisins and rum along with the olives. Stir well and transfer the mixture to a large bowl.

3. Fold in the eggs and parsley. Add salt and adjust the seasonings to taste. Cool to room temperature. Refrigerate, covered, or freeze until ready to use.

4. Preheat oven to 350°F.

5. Lay the phyllo pastry sheets on a clean dry dish towel. Keep covered with a piece of waxed paper and a slightly dampened dish towel so that the phyllo does not dry out.

6. Place 1 sheet of phyllo lengthwise in front of you on a clean work surface. Using a pastry brush, lightly cover the surface with clarifed butter. Cover with a second sheet of phyllo and brush again with butter. Cut the phyllo into six 3-inch-wide strips (the short way). Place 1 teaspoon of the filling 1 inch from the bottom in the center of each strip. Fold a corner across the filling, then continue to fold the triangle, as if folding a flag, to the end of the strip.Tuck the end under. Place the triangles as you finish them on a baking sheet and brush with butter. Bake each filled sheet until golden brown, about 15 minutes. Serve hot.

Makes 60 empanadas

Note: Phyllo dough is readily available frozen in 1-pound boxes. Follow the package directions for thawing the dough.

THE BEERS OF

Latin America

When south-of-the-border spices set up a mouth-tingling clamor for something soothing, a cool beer is sometimes the best solution. All of the Latin American countries produce beer, sizable quantities in some cases. Few are exported to the U.S., however, except for several from Mexico and Brazil. Argentina and Chile are better known for wine than for beer. But Mexican beers have always been popular in this country, particularly in California, Texas, and the Southwest, where the Mexican culinary influence is strongest.

Curiously, Corona, the Mexican beer that developed a cult following in the eighties, is perhaps the least typical of Latin American beers. Corona is a light, bland, sweetish brew, bottled in clear glass. Far more interesting in terms of character are amber beers—Dos Equis, Carta Blanca Dark, and Indio Oscura among them—full-bodied and malty, excellent with spicy Latin meat dishes, rich sauces like *mole,* and Caribbean specialties, like Jamaican Jerk Chicken or Porc Colombo. Brazil's lively Xingu, occasionally found in the U.S., is another good example of this style.

Latin America's traditional lagers, paler in color, crisper, and somewhat drier, usually have a stronger accent of hops along the lines of a Pilsener. Again, what we see here is mostly from Mexico, like the bracing Dos Equis Lager Especial, and others, such as Carta Blanca, Bohemia, and Tecate.

Incidentally, when in Mexico, be on the lookout for

one of the country's most distinctive brews, Negra Modelo from the Yucatán, a rich, creamy, reddish-brown beer with a hint of chocolate in its malty flavor. It is now available in some parts of the U.S. Most Mexican beer companies also make Christmas beers, like the dark, malty Noche Buena and Commemorativa, but they are rarely exported.

"Amber beers—full-bodied and malty, excellent with Latin meat dishes, rich sauces like mole, and Carribean specialties, like Jamaican Jerk Chicken or Porc Colombo."

Left: The glorious beaches of Ixtapa in festive Mexico. Top to bottom: A display of spices on the streets of Rio de Janeiro. Enjoy Brazil's solid Xingu and malty Negra Modelo with spicy foods. Argentinian wall art—as electric as its beers and red wine—and we haven't even talked tango!

GORDON'S QUESADILLAS

When I visited Mexico, one of my goals was to find the ultimate quesadillas, a dish I learned to love at Gordon's, Bruce Paltrow's and Gordon Naccarato's former restaurant in Aspen, Colorado. I was surprised when not one in Mexico compared. Gordon is now chef at The Monkey Bar in Los Angeles. Happily I found him and convinced him to share his splendid recipe. I've added shredded duck to the original and it's great. Gordon served his quesadillas with chipotle salsa and a light Mexican cream. I've whipped up a delicate Avocado Cream to dollop on top. Serve with Fiesta Corn Salsa or Thai Fruit Salsa. Olé!

8 large flour tortillas (7½-inch diameter)
4 ounces Monterey Jack cheese with jalapeños, grated
4 ounces Montrachet or other soft goat cheese, crumbled
1 cup shredded cooked duck or dark meat chicken
4 large white mushrooms, stems trimmed and thinly sliced
2 scallions (2 inches green left on), very thinly sliced crosswise
1 tablespoon finely chopped fresh cilantro leaves or flat-leaf parsley
2 limes, quartered, for serving
Fresh cilantro sprigs, for garnish
½ cup Avocado Cream (recipe follows), for serving
Fiesta Corn Salsa or Thai Fruit Salsa (page 246)

1. Place 4 tortillas on a work surface and sprinkle each with 1 tablespoon Monterey Jack and ½ ounce Montrachet, making sure the cheeses are evenly distributed over the surface.

2. Scatter ¼ cup shredded duck over each, then sprinkle evenly with the sliced mushrooms, scallions, and chopped cilantro. Cover with the remaining cheeses. Place a second tortilla over each, creating a sandwich, and press down on the ingredients with the palm of your hand.

3. Heat a dry nonstick large skillet over medium heat until very hot. Using a large spatula, place a quesadilla in the skillet and cook, pressing down with the spatula, and turning once, until the cheese melts and the tortillas brown slightly, 3 to 4 minutes per side. Remove to a low oven (250°F) to keep warm. Repeat with the remaining quesadillas.

4. To serve, cut each quesadilla into quarters and serve hot, garnished with quartered limes, cilantro sprigs, and a dollop of avocado cream. Serve with a bowl of salsa alongside.

Makes 4

AVOCADO CREAM

Rich, velvety texture with a delicate under flavor, this cream is pefect dolloped atop quesadillas or into a steamy bowl of soup. Think of it as the new Mexican sour cream.

1 ripe avocado, preferably Haas, pitted, peeled, and cut into large pieces
Juice of 1 lime
½ cup sour cream
Salt, to taste

Place all the ingredients except the salt in a food processor and process until completely smooth. Scrape into a bowl and season to taste with salt. Serve immediately.

Makes 1 cup

PASTRAMI BOREKS

I was running everyone ragged in Istanbul looking for a meat *börek,* a small phyllo pie. Although cheese *böreks* were plentiful, meat-filled ones were scarce. But finally, eureka! There they were in the window of a pastry shop in the village of Sariyer, about a half hour outside of Istanbul along the Bosporus. These *böreks* were so delicious, and filled not with boiled beef or lamb, as I had thought, but rather cured beef—pastrami—all sautéed up with peppers, tomatoes, and parsley. Rolled up in phyllo into little triangular pillows, these are elegant served as an hors d'oeuvre, hot out of the oven. Have small, pretty cocktail napkins at hand.

2 tablespoons olive oil
4 Italian frying peppers, stemmed, seeded, and cut into ¼-inch dice
8 ounces pastrami, excess fat removed, cut into ¼-inch dice
¼ cup shallots, coarsely chopped
4 plum tomatoes, cored, seeded, and cut into ¼-inch dice
2 teaspoons dried oregano
Salt and coarsely ground black pepper, to taste
¼ cup chopped flat-leaf parsley
1 pound phyllo dough (see Note)
1 cup Clarified Butter (page 53)

1. Heat the oil in a nonstick skillet over low heat. Add the peppers and cook, stirring, until softened, 8 to 10 minutes. Add the pastrami and shallots and cook 5 minutes. Stir in the tomatoes and oregano, then season with salt and pepper. Cook 5 minutes longer over low heat, stirring occasionally. Stir in the parsley and cool to room temperature.

2. Preheat the oven to 350°F.

3. Lay the phyllo pastry sheets on a clean dish towel. Keep covered with a piece of waxed paper and a slightly dampened dish towel so that the phyllo does not dry out.

4. Place 1 sheet of phyllo lengthwise in front of you on a clean work surface. Using a pastry brush, lightly cover the surface with clarified butter. Cover with a second sheet of phyllo and brush again with butter. Cut the phyllo into six 3-inch-wide strips (the short way). Place 1 teaspoon of the filling 1 inch from the bottom in the center of each strip. Fold a corner across the filling, then continue to fold the triangle, as if you were folding a flag, to the end of the strip. Tuck the ends under. Place the triangles as you finish them on a baking sheet and brush with butter. Bake until golden brown, about 15 minutes. Serve hot.

Makes 48 triangles

Note: Phyllo pastry is readily available frozen in 1-pound boxes. Follow the package directions for thawing the dough.

COCKTAIL COULIBIAC

When I visited Russia, I was dying to have a classic *coulibiac* because the whole notion was so romantically Tolstoyesque. Unfortunately there was nothing so dramatic to be had, but I did get to eat some of its components in individual dishes. A traditional *coulibiac* has layers of fresh salmon, rice, mushrooms, hard-cooked egg, and fresh dill mounded between 2 layers of brioche pastry, which is formed into the shape of a whole decorated fish. As this preparation is rather cumbersome for today's cuisine, it has more or less gone the way of beef Wellington. I've recreated it using a lighter touch and folded the filling between layers of flaky phyllo. These little triangles are both delicate and light—perfect to serve at cocktail hour with chilled sparkling Champagne.

2 cups water
1 cup dry white wine
2 fresh dill sprigs
6 black peppercorns
1 bay leaf
2 salmon steaks (12 ounces each and 1½ inches thick)
½ cup cooked barley or white rice
⅓ cup chopped fresh dill
8 ounces crimini or shiitake mushrooms
2 tablespoons unsalted butter
¾ cup finely chopped onion
2 hard-cooked eggs, coarsely chopped
Salt and coarsely ground black pepper, to taste
1 cup crème fraîche or sour cream
1 pound phyllo dough (see Note)
1 cup (2 sticks) Clarified Butter (page 53), melted

1. Place 2 cups water, the wine, dill sprigs, peppercorns, and bay leaf in a shallow pan large enough to hold the salmon in a single layer. Bring to a boil, then reduce the heat and add the salmon and more boiling water if necessary to completely cover the fish. Simmer until the fish is just cooked through, about 15 minutes; it should flake easily when tested with a fork. Remove to a plate with a slotted spatula. Cool to room temperature.

2. When the salmon is cool enough to handle, remove and discard any bones, skin, and fat. Carefully flake apart the flesh and set aside.

3. Place the cooked barley in a large bowl. With a fork, mix in the dill.

4. Clean the mushrooms well with a damp towel, trim the stems, and coarsely chop the caps.

5. Melt the 2 tablespoons butter in a large nonstick skillet over medium-low heat. Add the onion and cook until wilted and translucent, about 8 minutes. Add the mushrooms and increase the heat to medium. Cook, stirring, for 5 minutes. Add the mushrooms to the cooked barley and toss to combine.

6. Add the flaked salmon and chopped eggs and combine with a fork, working from underneath, and being careful not to break up the salmon too much. Season with salt and pepper. Gently fold in the crème fraîche with a rubber spatula, working from the bottom of the bowl to blend the ingredients.

7. Preheat the oven to 350°F.

8. Remove the phyllo pastry from the box and lay the sheets on a clean dish cloth. Cover the pastry with a sheet of waxed paper and then a slightly dampened dish cloth.

9. Place one sheet of phyllo pastry on a work surface with one long side in front of you. Brush the pastry sparingly all over with melted butter. Cover with a second sheet of phyllo and brush it with butter. Cut the phyllo into six 3-inch-wide strips the short way. Place 1 teaspoon of the salmon filling in the center of each strip 1 inch from the bottom. Fold a corner across the filling and then continue to fold as if you were folding a flag until the strip is all folded. Tuck under the edges. Place the triangles on a baking sheet and brush with butter. Repeat with the remaining phyllo and filling.

10. Bake until golden brown, about 15 minutes. Serve immediately.

Makes about 80 triangles

Note: Phyllo dough is readily available frozen in 1-pound boxes. Follow the package directions for thawing the dough.

SOUVENIR TO SAVOR

Aquavit

Aquavit is a thrilling Scandinavian potato-based spirit infused with aromatic seeds and spices—most often caraway, anise, fennel, or bitter orange. A contraction of the Latin *aqua vita*—"water of life"—Aquavit has been made for over 500 years and had its beginnings when "Northerners" learned the techniques of distillation. What began as a medicine rapidly gained popularity as a beverage. The idea of flavoring Aquavit came from the belief that these flavorings had therapeutic benefits in addition to disguising the slightly unpleasant flavor of the alcohol.

Not only does Aquavit complement the many different elements of Scandinavian cuisine—smoky soups and stews, salt-cured salmon, creamy salads, and rich shellfish—it is also said to aid in the digestion of these delicacies.

At home, Aquavit is best when stored in the freezer and served icy, in tiny stemmed glasses. A lovely serving idea is to place the Aquavit bottle in a clean, empty, half-gallon milk carton that is roughly the same height and slightly wider than the bottle. Fill the container with water, add rose petals, delicate evergreens, or dill flowers, and freeze. Just before serving time, tear the milk carton away from the ice-molded bottle. Tie a pretty linen napkin around the base and underside of the mold and serve in a silver ice bucket.

Aquavit is the beverage of preference, accompanied by a beer chaser, to sip with *smörgåsbord.* It is also perfect as an accompaniment to gravlax drizzled with a dilled mustard sauce and thick slices of black bread.

Some of the perfume-infused Aquavits available in America are:

SKÅNE (Swedish): Spiced with caraway, anise, and fennel with a mild caraway flavor.

BLACK CURRANT (Swedish): Flavored with black currants.

O. P. ANDERSON (Swedish): Spiced with caraway seeds and anise, has a full caraway flavor.

HERRGÅRDS (Swedish): Spiced with caraway seeds and whiskey, this aquavit is slightly sweet and draws its flavor from storage in old sherry barrels.

AALBORG (Danish): Spiced with caraway seeds.

AALBORG JUBILAEUMS (Danish): Spiced with dill seeds and coriander.

LØITEN LINIE (Norwegian): Mild caraway flavor. Stored in sherry barrels.

ARSTA (Swedish): Spiced with bitter orange.

SKÅL!

Next time you serve smoked salmon or gravlax, accompany it with a caraway-spiced Aquavit.

SPANAKOPITA

We are accustomed to enjoying spinach, mixed with cheese and eggs, in these flaky phyllo triangles, but in Greece each cook performs his or her special alchemy with *horta,* the wild greens reminiscent of dandelion greens, which appear in abundance in every little marketplace throughout Greece. Use this recipe as an opportunity to be as creative as you'd like. Instead of spinach, I've cooked up fennel, dandelion greens, and Swiss chard to make my filling for this flavorful pie. To avoid a soggy crust, it is essential to squeeze out as much moisture as is possible from the cooked greens. Another trick is to sprinkle the bottom layers of phyllo with Parmesan cheese before adding the greens to absorb any extra liquid. Brush each sheet of phyllo generously with butter while layering.

12 ounces dandelion greens, rinsed, tough stems removed
12 ounces Swiss chard, rinsed, tough stems removed
2 tablespoons olive oil
2 fennel bulbs (about 1½ pounds total), cut into ¼-inch dice
1 medium onion, cut into ¼-inch dice
2 tablespoons chopped shallots
4 ounces feta cheese, crumbled
½ cup low-fat cottage cheese, drained
2 tablespoons chopped fresh dill
¼ teaspoon ground nutmeg
Salt and coarsely ground black pepper, to taste
½ cup Clarified Butter (page 53)
4 tablespoons freshly grated Parmesan cheese
12 sheets phyllo dough, cut into 9-inch squares, (keep phyllo covered with waxed paper and a damp kitchen towel; see Note)

1. Place the dandelion greens, still slightly damp from rinsing, in a large heavy pot. Cover and steam over medium-high heat until just wilted, 1 to 2 minutes, tossing the greens once or twice for even cooking. Drain well, then place the greens in a dish towel and squeeze out any remaining moisture. Repeat the process with the Swiss chard. Coarsely chop the greens and place in a large bowl.

2. Heat the oil in a large nonstick skillet over medium-low heat. Add the fennel and onion and cook, stirring occasionally, until wilted, 10 to 12 minutes.

3. Add the fennel and onion to the greens. Add the shallots, feta, cottage cheese, dill, nutmeg, and salt and pepper to taste; stir well. Place the mixture in a sieve and, using the back of a spoon, press out any remaining liquid in the mixture.

4. Preheat the oven to 350°F.

5. Lightly brush a 9-inch square baking pan with clarified butter. Sprinkle the bottom of the pan with 2 tablespoons Parmesan cheese. Fit 1 phyllo square in the bottom of the pan and brush it all over with clarified butter. Repeat this step 5 times for 6 layers of phyllo. Sprinkle evenly with the remaining 2 tablespoons Parmesan cheese.

6. Spoon the vegetable mixture into the pan and spread it evenly over the pastry. Top with 6 phyllo squares, brushing each one with clarified butter. Neatly cut the unbaked pie into 16 even squares.

7. Bake until the phyllo is deep golden in color, about 40 minutes. Cool slightly and serve. (The first square may be slightly difficult to remove from the pan neatly.)

Makes 16 small squares

Note: Phyllo pastry is readily available frozen in 1-pound boxes. Follow the package directions for thawing the dough.

Salads

Roasted red bell peppers nestle against pale green cucumbers, deep purple Kalamata olives, and pristine white feta cheese in an updated Greek Salad. Bananas, apples, and pineapples blend lusciously in a Chilean-inspired version of a classic Waldorf. For me, salads can be the most creative outlets in a culinary repertoire. And when I think that not so long ago salad primarily meant a wedge of iceberg lettuce, I'm delighted to be leaving those years behind. Yesterday's obligatory afterthoughts have been transformed into beautiful works of art; from country to country, the discoveries I made are glorious.

The abundance of greens readily available these days has had a significant hand in changing the dull plates of iceberg into plates of splendor. Endive and *mâche* are simply dressed in a vinaigrette and tossed with vegetables, nuts, and Roquefort cheese. And when you take fresh crab meat, place it atop dressed arugula, and surround it with sliced bananas and stuffed eggs sprinkled with chives, you're talking colors that rival the Fauve palette. Tossed or composed, there are simply no limits when it comes to salads.

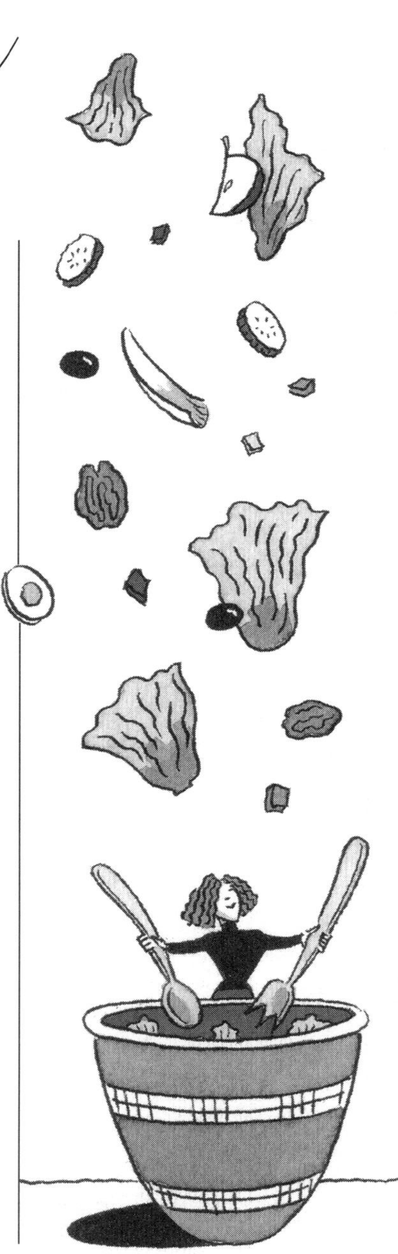

CARIBE CRUDITES

In both France and the Caribbean, crudités connote lots of thinly slivered vegetables arranged beautifully on large plates. They make a lovely appetizer or salad course served with simple fish or meat dishes. To dress up the vegetables, I've spooned a pungent roasted pepper vinaigrette over the top.

4 cups very finely slivered red cabbage
2 Belgian endives, rinsed and very thinly sliced crosswise
2 ripe large tomatoes, thinly sliced
½ hothouse (seedless) cucumber, peeled and thinly sliced
¼ cup Roasted Red Pepper Vinaigrette (recipe follows)
1 cup diced (¼ inch) ripe cantaloupe
¼ cup chopped fresh mint leaves, plus 6 small sprigs, for garnish

1. Cover the bottoms of 6 dinner plates with the red cabbage. Sprinkle the endive over the cabbage and arrange the tomato and cucumber slices decoratively on top.

2. Just before serving, drizzle each portion evenly with vinaigrette. Sprinkle the cantaloupe and chopped mint on top of the salads and garnish with the small mint sprigs.

Serves 6

ROASTED RED PEPPER VINAIGRETTE

½ red bell pepper, roasted (page 202)
2 tablespoons red wine vinegar
½ teaspoon sugar
⅛ teaspoon salt
Pinch of freshly ground black pepper
¼ cup olive oil

1. Combine the roasted red pepper, vinegar, sugar, salt, and pepper in a food processor; pulse on and off until the pepper is smoothly puréed.

2. With the machine running, slowly drizzle in the oil through the feed tube and process until the oil is incorporated and the vinaigrette is slightly thickened. Store covered in the refrigerator for up to 2 days. Bring to room temperature before using.

Makes ½ cup

INSALATA D'ESTATE

This beautiful summer salad is resplendent with flavors and colors of the Italian Riviera: arugula, oranges, tomatoes, a splash of fruity extra virgin olive oil, and balsamic vinegar. It can be transformed easily into a light entrée by attractively arranging thinly sliced prosciutto di Parma atop all.

3 large tomatoes (about 8 ounces each), peeled
3 large navel oranges, peeled
2 bunches arugula, rinsed well and patted dry
1 tablespoon plus 2 teaspoons extra virgin olive oil, or to taste
1 tablespoon plus 2 teaspoons balsamic vinegar, or to taste
Coarse salt and coarsely ground black pepper, to taste
3 tablespoons thinly slivered fresh basil leaves

1. Remove the tomato cores. Cut each tomato lengthwise in half and then into thin wedges. Set aside in a shallow bowl.

2. Thinly slice the oranges crosswise and set aside in a shallow bowl.

3. Remove and discard any tough stems from the arugula and place the leaves in a bowl. Just before serving, toss with 1 tablespoon each of the oil and vinegar and sprinkle with salt and pepper.

4. Drizzle the tomatoes and oranges each with 1 teaspoon oil and 1 teaspoon vinegar. Sprinkle with salt and pepper.

5. Divide the arugula among 6 salad plates. Arrange the orange slices in the center of each salad. Surround with the tomato wedges and sprinkle each salad with basil.

Serves 6

ORIENTAL SPINACH SALAD

The light and crisp taste of the Orient comes through in a classic American favorite. Fresh bean sprouts lend a welcome bite to spinach and mushrooms, and a garnish of hard-cooked eggs and scallions adds a freshness. Serve alongside Hong Kong Pork Chops and Sesame Butterfly Pasta (see Index) accompanied by an icy cold Chinese beer.

2 bunches spinach (about 8 ounces each), tough stems removed
8 ounces white mushrooms, stems trimmed
¾ cup mung bean sprouts, rinsed and drained
2 hard-cooked eggs
3 scallions (3 inches green left on), trimmed
Coarse salt and coarsely ground black pepper, to taste
¼ cup Chinese Vinaigrette (recipe follows), or to taste

1. Rinse the spinach well in at least 2 changes of water. Shake dry and let drain completely. Coarsely tear the leaves and place in a large bowl.

2. Wipe the mushrooms with a damp paper towel and thinly slice. Add to the spinach along with the sprouts and toss lightly.

3. Coarsely chop the eggs and set aside. Thinly slice the scallions on the diagonal and set aside.

4. Just before serving, sprinkle the spinach salad well with salt and pepper. Dress with the vinaigrette and remove to a large serving bowl. Sprinkle the top with the chopped eggs and sliced scallions. Serve immediately.

Serves 6 to 8

A TASTE OF THE WORLD

French Palette

...And

BAY LEAVES	*FRESH BEANS*
CHERVIL	*LEEKS*
MINT	*GRAPES*
TARRAGON	*HAZELNUTS*
THYME	*WALNUTS*
BOUQUET GARNI	*CHESTNUTS*
NUTMEG	*DRIED BEANS*
GARLIC	*CHEVRE*
SHALLOTS	*HEAVY CREAM*
ONIONS	*DIJON MUSTARD*
TOMATOES	*OLIVE OIL*
WILD MUSHROOMS	*WALNUT OIL*
PEAS	*WINE VINEGAR*
ARTICHOKES	

CHINESE VINAIGRETTE

This lightly pungent vinaigrette with the flavors of the Orient is delightful tossed over dark greens such as fresh spinach. It is not necessary to add salt because of the soy sauce. A generous grind of black pepper is always a welcome addition.

1 teaspoon grated orange zest
2 tablespoons fresh orange juice
1 tablespoon rice wine vinegar
1 tablespoon white wine vinegar
2 teaspoons soy sauce
½ teaspoon Dijon mustard
¼ cup peanut oil
1 tablespoon dark sesame oil

Whisk the orange zest and juice, both vinegars, the soy sauce, and mustard together in a small bowl. While whisking constantly, slowly drizzle in both oils and continue whisking until emulsified. Store covered in the refrigerator for up to 2 days. Bring to room temperature before using.

Makes ½ cup

LA COUPOLE SALAD

When I visited Paris in the 70s, I raced over to La Coupole on the Boulevard Montparnasse to eat roast chicken and the best *frites* ever. I began my meal with this great salad, classically made of beets, endive, and *mâche*. I've done my best to recreate it, adding a few extras such as walnuts and a crumble of Roquefort cheese. I've tossed it all up with a walnut oil vinaigrette, dressing the beets separately so that they don't bleed onto the greens. To this day I can't think of a better way to serve the salad than with roast chicken.

1 large head Belgian endive
6 small bunches mâche or other tender, sweet greens, roots removed (about 4 cups leaves)
½ cup walnut halves, slightly broken
1 cup cubed Roasted Beets (page 194; about 4 small)
¼ cup Walnut Oil Vinaigrette (recipe follows)
Coarse salt and coarsely ground black pepper, to taste
2 ounces Roquefort cheese, crumbled

1. Trim the root end of the endive. Separate the leaves, rinse well, and pat dry. Stack the leaves in small batches and cut lengthwise into thin slivers. Place in a large bowl.

2. Rinse the *mâche* and shake dry. Add to the endive with the walnuts and toss well.

3. Place the beets in a small bowl and toss with 2 tablespoons of the walnut oil vinaigrette. Set aside.

4. Just before serving, sprinkle the greens with salt and pepper and toss with the remaining 2 tablespoons vinaigrette. Divide the salad among 6 small salad plates. Sprinkle evenly with the beets and Roquefort cheese. Serve immediately.

Serves 6

WALNUT OIL VINAIGRETTE

When a salad calls for a great nutty flavor, this vinaigrette is both a subtle and harmonious addition to sweet as well as bitter greens. Because walnut oil is quite expensive and spoils quickly, I find it best to buy it in small quantities.

¼ cup red wine vinegar
1 teaspoon Dijon mustard
1 teaspoon sugar
Salt and freshly ground black pepper, to taste
6 tablespoons walnut oil

Combine the vinegar, mustard, sugar, salt, and pepper in a small bowl. While whisking contantly, slowly drizzle in the oil and continue whisking until emulsified. Use immediately.

Makes about ½ cup

CAESAR SALAD

Thought to originate in Tijuana, Mexico, this favored salad is nevertheless redolent with Italy's great flavors (not surprising since the creator is believed to have been an Italian immigrant). In the classic recipe, the salad bowl is rubbed with garlic and an egg is cooked in boiling water for just a minute and tossed over the greens, but I have chopped hard-cooked eggs and combined them with garlic, anchovies, and Parmesan cheese in the dressing. This method is easier and it results in a dressing that coats the greens beautifully, while eliminating worries about possible salmonella in a barely cooked egg.

3 tablespoons white wine vinegar
1 teaspoon finely grated lemon zest
2 tablespoons fresh lemon juice
1 clove garlic, peeled and pressed through a garlic press
1 teaspoon Dijon mustard
1 small can (2 ounces) anchovy fillets, finely chopped
2 hard-cooked eggs, finely chopped
2 tablespoons freshly grated Parmesan cheese
Coarsely ground black pepper, to taste
½ cup olive oil
1 head romaine lettuce, tough outer leaves removed, rinsed well, and patted dry
2 cups Garlic Croutons (recipe follows)

1. Place the vinegar, lemon zest and juice, garlic, mustard, anchovies, eggs, cheese, and pepper in a bowl and mix together well. While whisking constantly, slowly drizzle in the olive oil and continue whisking until the mixture is emulsified.

2. Gently tear the lettuce into small pieces and place in a serving bowl with the croutons. Toss well with the dressing and serve immediately.

Serves 6 to 8

GARLIC CROUTONS

This is a very simple method of preparing croutons; no messy sautéing! Accustomed to seeing these crisp bites in a Caesar salad, I was quite taken when I found them atop my hot Russian borscht. There are so many uses for them. For a different flavor, substitute thyme, tarragon, or oregano for the garlic, and they're perfect as a base for your favorite stuffing.

2 cups cubed (1 inch) good-quality French bread
1½ teaspoons minced garlic
Salt and freshly ground black pepper, to taste
2 tablespoons olive oil

1. Preheat the oven to 350°F.

2. Place the bread in a bowl. Mix the garlic, salt, and pepper with the olive oil. Drizzle this mixture over the bread cubes and toss well to combine.

3. Spread out the bread cubes on a baking sheet. Bake, tossing once, until golden brown, 15 to 20 minutes. Watch the croutons carefully after 15 minutes to avoid burning.

Makes about 2 cups

MY KITCHEN DIARY

Pomelos

Pomelos are the largest fruit in the citrus family. Generally, they are yellow, round to pear shaped, with the fruit buried under a thick layer of peel and pith. The flesh ranges in color from lemon yellow to deep red. Originating in Asia, pummelos have long been savored as an ingredient in Thai dishes. A combination of firm grapefruit segments and fresh bean sprouts can be substituted in recipes calling for the fruit. Bean sprouts sound unusual, but they simulate the citrus fibers of the pomelo. Besides being a refreshing addition to composed salads or fish and poultry dishes, these wonderful bites of sunshine are lovely for a special breakfast or an exotic snack.

MAMBO FRUIT SALAD

When it's hot and steamy outside, cool fruits atop zesty dressed salad greens make for lovely summer dining. Caribbean-inspired, this is an excellent appetizer salad when chicken or fish is on the grill.

1 ripe large tomato, cut into ¼-inch dice
1 ripe avocado, preferably Haas, pitted, peeled, and cut into ¼-inch dice
¼ cup fresh lime juice
1 cup diced (¼ inch) ripe cantaloupe
1 cup diced (¼ inch) ripe pineapple
¼ cup fresh orange juice
4 to 6 cups mixed salad greens, rinsed well and patted dry
¼ cup Lime-Garlic Vinaigrette (recipe follows)
¼ cup chopped fresh mint leaves, plus 4 small mint sprigs, for garnish
½ cup crème fraîche
1 tablespoon finely grated orange zest

1. Toss the tomato and avocado with the lime juice in a bowl. Add the cantaloupe, pineapple, and orange juice and toss again.

2. Just before serving, toss the salad greens with the vinaigrette. Toss the fruit mixture with the chopped mint. Mix the crème fraîche and orange zest.

3. To serve, divide the salad greens between 4 large plates and spoon the fruit salad over the center. Top each salad with a dollop (about 1 tablespoon) of crème fraîche and garnish with a fresh mint sprig.

Serves 4

LIME-GARLIC VINAIGRETTE

A refreshing vinaigrette for delicate seafood, vegetable, and fruit salads.

2 tablespoons red wine vinegar
2 tablespoons fresh lime juice
1 clove garlic, minced
¼ teaspoon salt
3 tablespoons olive oil
1 tablespoon finely chopped fresh basil leaves

Whisk the vinegar, lime juice, garlic, and salt together in a small bowl. Slowly drizzle in the oil, whisking constantly, until thickened. Stir in the basil just before using.

Makes about ½ cup

SUNSHINE SALAD

Sweet and savory flavors make this Caribbean-hued salad perfect to lead off a meal featuring Chicken Picadillo Enchiladas and Sunny Sweet Potato Salad (see Index). Velvety avocado, crisp, sharp greens, and red onion are all favorites. Sweet oranges stand out as the unusual ingredient here, but coupled with tomatoes, they mellow the briny olives.

2 bunches arugula or watercress
3 navel oranges
1 ripe avocado, preferably Haas
1 small red onion
½ cup Spanish Manzanilla olives
3 ripe plum tomatoes
3 to 4 tablespoons extra virgin Spanish olive oil
2 to 3 tablespoons sherry vinegar
Coarse salt and coarsely ground black pepper, to taste
1 tablespoon finely snipped fresh chives, for garnish
1 tablespoon coarsely chopped flat-leaf parsley, for garnish

1. Rinse the arugula or watercress well, remove any tough stems, and pat dry.

2. With a sharp knife, cut the rind from the oranges, being sure to remove any bitter white pith. Cut the oranges into ¼-inch-thick slices

3. Halve, pit, and peel the avocado, then cut into ¼-inch dice. (If preparing the avocado in advance, toss it with 1 tablespoon lemon juice to prevent discoloration.)

4. Peel, halve, and thinly sliver the onion. Rinse the olives under cold water. Drain and pat dry. Seed the tomatoes and cut into ¼-inch dice.

5. To assemble the salad, arrange the arugula on a serving platter. Place orange slices decoratively on top. Sprinkle the avocado over the oranges. Add the onion and olives decoratively, then top with the tomatoes.

6. Lightly drizzle the olive oil and vinegar over the salad and sprinkle with salt and pepper. Garnish with the chives and parsley and serve.

Serves 6

A TASTE OF THE WORLD

Caribbean Fruit Basket

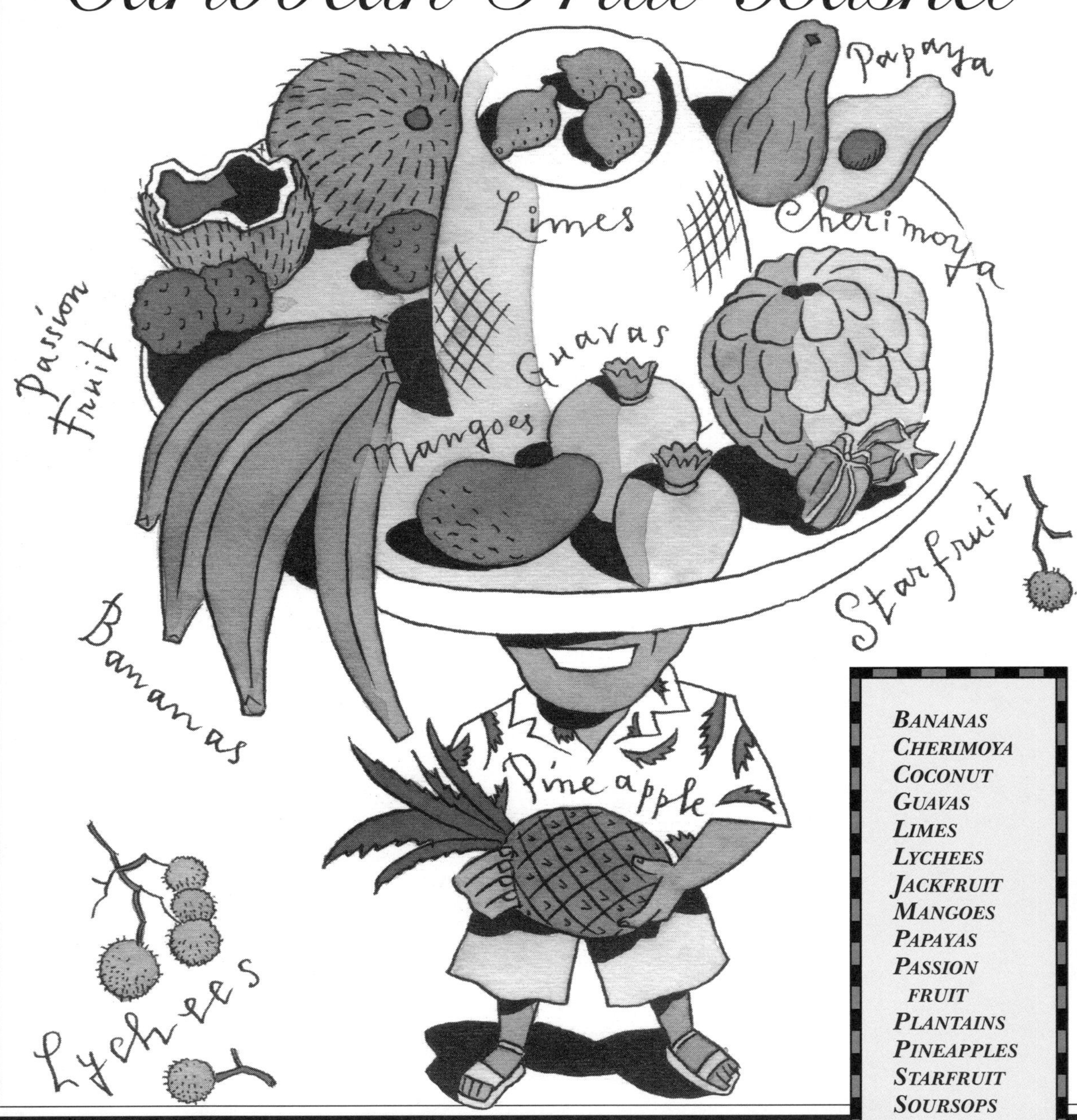

BANANAS
CHERIMOYA
COCONUT
GUAVAS
LIMES
LYCHEES
JACKFRUIT
MANGOES
PAPAYAS
PASSION FRUIT
PLANTAINS
PINEAPPLES
STARFRUIT
SOURSOPS

SAMBA WALDORF SALAD

Waldorf salad is a great American favorite, but I was fresh back from Chile when I made this version. My choice of fruits tells it all: Pineapple adds sweet lightness, and bananas provide a velvety foil when combined with the bright bites of red grapes, celery, crisp tart apples, and almonds. All tossed together with orange mayonnaise, this Waldorf salad is a burst of South American flavor.

2 bananas, peeled, halved lengthwise, and cut into ½-inch slices
1 Granny Smith apple, cored and cut into ½-inch pieces
Juice of 1 lime
2 cups diced (½ inch) pineapple
2 ribs celery, cut into ¼-inch dice
1 cup seedless red grapes, halved
½ cup coarsely chopped almonds
Salt and freshly ground black pepper, to taste
1 cup Sunrise Orange Mayonnaise (recipe follows)

1. Toss the bananas and apple with the lime juice in a large bowl. Add the pineapple, celery, grapes, and almonds and toss well to combine. Season with salt and pepper.

2. Gently fold in the mayonnaise, combining thoroughly. Serve at once.

Serves 8

SUNRISE ORANGE MAYONNAISE

A simple creamy mayonnaise is elevated to new heights by blending in a thick fresh orange syrup and finely grated zest. This is excellent tossed over delicate fruit and seafood salads.

2 cups fresh orange juice
½ cup mayonnaise
½ cup sour cream
Finely grated zest of 1 orange

1. Place the orange juice in a small pan, bring to a boil, reduce the heat slightly, and cook, swirling the pan occasionally, until reduced to 3 to 4 tablespoons very thick syrup, 25 to 30 minutes.

2. Mix the mayonnaise and sour cream together in a bowl. Stir in 2 tablespoons of the orange syrup and the orange zest. Store covered in the refrigerator for up to 4 hours.

Makes 1 cup

ROASTED PEPPERS AND HARICOTS VERTS

Chez Henri, a favorite bistro in Paris, serves up this wonderfully satisfying, yet light first course. The crimson red color and velvety texture of the peppers provides a lovely contrast to the green, crisp haricots verts (slim green beans). Reminiscent of the south of France, this dish adds a pleasant freshness to any meal, or if you love it as much as I do, it is a meal in iself! Soak up the extra garlicky vinaigrette with crusty peasant bread!

8 ounces haricots verts
Salt
4 red bell peppers, halved lengthwise and roasted (page 202)
½ cup Lemon-Garlic Vinaigrette (recipe follows)
4 teaspoons snipped fresh chives, for garnish
8 whole chives, for garnish

1. Snap just the stem ends off the haricots verts. Blanch the beans in boiling salted water to cover until just crisp-tender, about 2 minutes. Drain the beans, refresh with cold water, and set aside.

2. Cut each roasted pepper half lengthwise in half so that you have 16 pieces.

3. To arrange the salad, toss the beans with ¼ cup of the vinaigrette and place them lengthwise in the center of each of 4 salad plates.

4. Arrange 2 pepper pieces on each side of the beans, rounded ends facing out, so that the assemblage resembles a butterfly. Drizzle the remaining vinaigrette over the peppers. Sprinkle each portion with 1 teaspoon chives, then place 2 whole chives pointing out where the peppers join the beans to resemble antennae. Serve immediately.

Serves 4

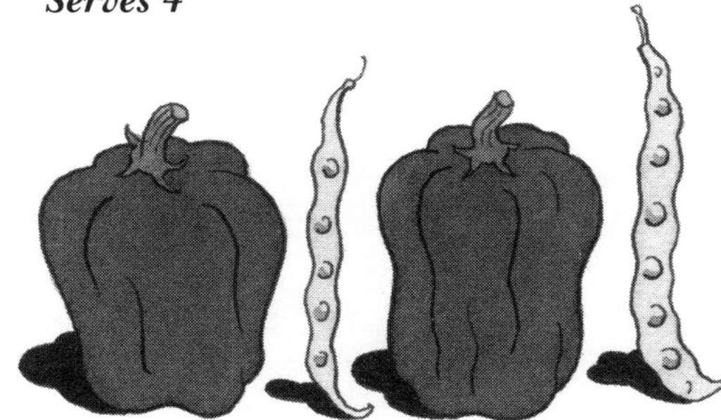

LEMON-GARLIC VINAIGRETTE

Mincing the garlic clove with salt greatly heightens the garlic's flavor, and the lemon juice adds a lovely fresh taste. This vinaigrette is excellent with robust vegetable salads.

1 small clove garlic
¼ teaspoon coarse salt
1½ teaspoons Dijon mustard
2 tablespoons fresh lemon juice
¼ cup extra virgin olive oil
¼ cup pure olive oil
Small pinch of sugar
Salt and freshly ground black pepper, to taste

1. Finely mince the garlic with the coarse salt. Place in a bowl with the mustard and lemon juice. Whisk together.

2. Slowly drizzle in both olive oils, whisking constantly, until thickened. Season with the sugar, salt, and pepper. Store covered in the refrigerator up to 2 days. Bring to room temperature before using.

Makes a generous ½ cup

SEVILLA TAPAS SALAD

While soaking up the sun at a small café on a beautiful Spanish afternoon, I was served two delicious *tapas*. One, fresh white anchovies drizzled with extra virgin olive oil and sprinkled with parsley, was delectable, with a head of roasted garlic, placed alongside, to spread on some rustic Spanish bread. This salad was also served, and set off the fish perfectly. It would also be ideal as topping for a *bruschetta* appetizer.

1 pound ripe plum tomatoes, cored, seeded, and cut into small dice
½ red onion, finely diced (about ½ cup)
¼ cup drained tiny capers
2 tablespoons extra virgin olive oil
¼ teaspoon coarsely ground black pepper
Salt, to taste
2 tablespoons chopped flat-leaf parsley

In a bowl combine the tomatoes, onion, capers, oil, and pepper. Season with salt and add parsley. Toss gently with a fork. Serve within 1 hour for the freshest taste.

Serves 6

CHILEAN AVOCADO SALAD

I had a gorgeous entrée salad for lunch in Santiago, Chile. The avocado was not shyly presented but rather regaled the plate, along with ripe tomatoes, cantaloupe, and roasted red pepper—all topped with a lemon-mint yogurt dressing. If preparing your ingredients ahead of time, rub the avocados with fresh lime juice to prevent discoloration. For this recipe, you could substitute chives or cilantro for the mint in the dressing.

8 ripe small plum tomatoes, quartered
2 cups diced (¼ inch) ripe cantaloupe
4 ripe avocados, preferably Haas, halved, pitted, and peeled
2 red bell peppers, halved lengthwise and roasted (page 202)
1 cup Lemon-Mint Yogurt Dressing (recipe follows)
2 tablespoons chopped fresh chives or cilantro leaves, for garnish

1. Cut each tomato quarter lengthwise into 3 thin wedges.

2. To assemble the salad, evenly divide the tomatoes among 4 plates. Sprinkle each plate with ½ cup cantaloupe.

3. Arrange 2 avocado halves, flat side down, in the center of each plate. Drape a roasted red pepper half over the avocado halves. Drizzle each plate with ¼ cup of the dressing. Sprinkle evenly with chopped chives or cilantro. Serve immediately.

Serves 4

LEMON-MINT YOGURT DRESSING

This light and creamy dressing is unusual but very well suited to drizzle over the Chilean Avocado Salad as well as toss with dark peppery greens such as watercress, arugula, and purslane.

1 cup (8 ounces) nonfat plain yogurt
1 tablespoon fresh lemon juice
1 teaspoon finely grated lemon zest
¼ cup extra virgin olive oil
¼ teaspoon coarsely ground black pepper
2 tablespoons chopped fresh mint leaves

Whisk the yogurt and lemon juice and zest together in a small bowl. While whisking constantly, slowly drizzle in the olive oil and continue to whisk until smooth and slightly thick. Fold in the pepper and mint just before serving.

Makes 1¼ cups

DILLED CUCUMBER SALAD

This light, refreshing Scandinavian salad is a welcome contrast to most of the creamy sauced salads that appear on a typical smorgasbord table. If you use hothouse cucumbers with very few seeds, it is unnecessary to seed the cucumbers. I prefer not to salt the cucumbers to remove excess liquid because they will not be crisp when served, and to keep them crisp toss the salad just before serving. Sweet apple cider vinegar adds the right amount of tang without a sharp bite. This is lovely with shrimp, beet, and egg salads.

2 chilled hothouse (seedless) cucumbers, peeled and thinly sliced on the diagonal (if you use regular cucumbers, halve lengthwise, seed, and slice on the diagonal)
2 tablespoons sugar
Salt, to taste
¼ cup apple cider vinegar
Coarsely ground black pepper, to taste
2 tablespoons chopped fresh dill

1. Place the cucumbers in a bowl.

2. In a small bowl, stir the sugar and salt in the vinegar to dissolve. Toss the dressing with the cucumbers. Add a generous grinding of pepper and adjust the salt to taste. Add the dill and toss gently with the cucumbers. Serve immediately, if possible. If not, store covered in the refrigerator for up to 4 hours.

Serves 8

FLAGEOLET SALAD

Although I'm used to eating these small, pale green beans warm, nestled next to pink slices of roasted leg of lamb, they make a delightful salad as well. This delicate bean from Brittany and central France is harvested in August and September before it has matured. While seldom sold fresh, they usually can be found canned or dried. Although they are not readily available on your supermarket shelf, they can be found in specialty food shops. These French beans lend themselves beautifully to the flavors of Tuscany: sage, celery, Parmesan, and prosciutto di Parma. A strong, fruity olive oil ties the flavors together.

12 ounces (1½ cups) dried flageolets, or 2 cans (16 ounces each), rinsed and drained
2 cups defatted Chicken Broth (page 127)
½ cup diced (¼ inch) carrots
1½ cups thinly and diagonally sliced celery (4 ribs)
4 ripe plum tomatoes, seeded and cut into ¼-inch dice
¼ cup extra virgin olive oil
1 clove garlic, minced
2 tablespoons chopped fresh sage leaves
1 teaspoon coarse salt
¼ teaspoon coarsely ground black pepper
16 thin slices prosciutto di Parma
Thinly shaved Parmesan-Reggiano cheese, for garnish

1. Rinse the dried beans and soak overnight in 6 cups of water. Discard any beans that float to the top.

2. Drain the beans, rinse well, and place them in a large heavy pan. Cover with 8 cups fresh water and the chicken broth. Bring to a boil, then reduce the heat and simmer partially covered until tender but not mushy, about 1½ hours. (If you are using canned beans, simmer in the broth for 15 minutes.)

3. While the beans are cooking, cook the carrots in boiling water for 4 to 5 minutes. Drain and set aside.

4. Drain the cooked beans and place them in a bowl with the carrots, celery, and tomatoes. Add the olive oil, garlic, sage, salt, and pepper and toss to combine.

5. To serve, lay 2 slices of prosciutto on each of 8 plates. Top with the bean salad and garnish with shavings of Parmesan cheese.

Serves 8

THE WINES OF

Greece

The West's wine heritage owes everything to Greece, a country that has been producing wines continuously since antiquity from the world's most ancient vineyards. The word *symposium* originally meant "gathering to drink wine," but for Socrates and friends it was primarily an occasion to exchange views on hot topics of the day—like love and politics.

Most of us think first of Retsina when we think of Greek wine. Understandably, perhaps, since it is not only the most widely exported Greek wine but makes up 35 percent of production in Greece. In a sense Retsina, with its minerally character and resinated flavors, is the quintessential Mediterranean wine, offering a brisk counterpoint to cuisines heavily based on olive oil. It is a great favorite with seafood in its home country, as well as with the native olive that grows so prolifically throughout

"In Greece, as in other Mediterranean countries, wine is food—meals are simply not complete without it."

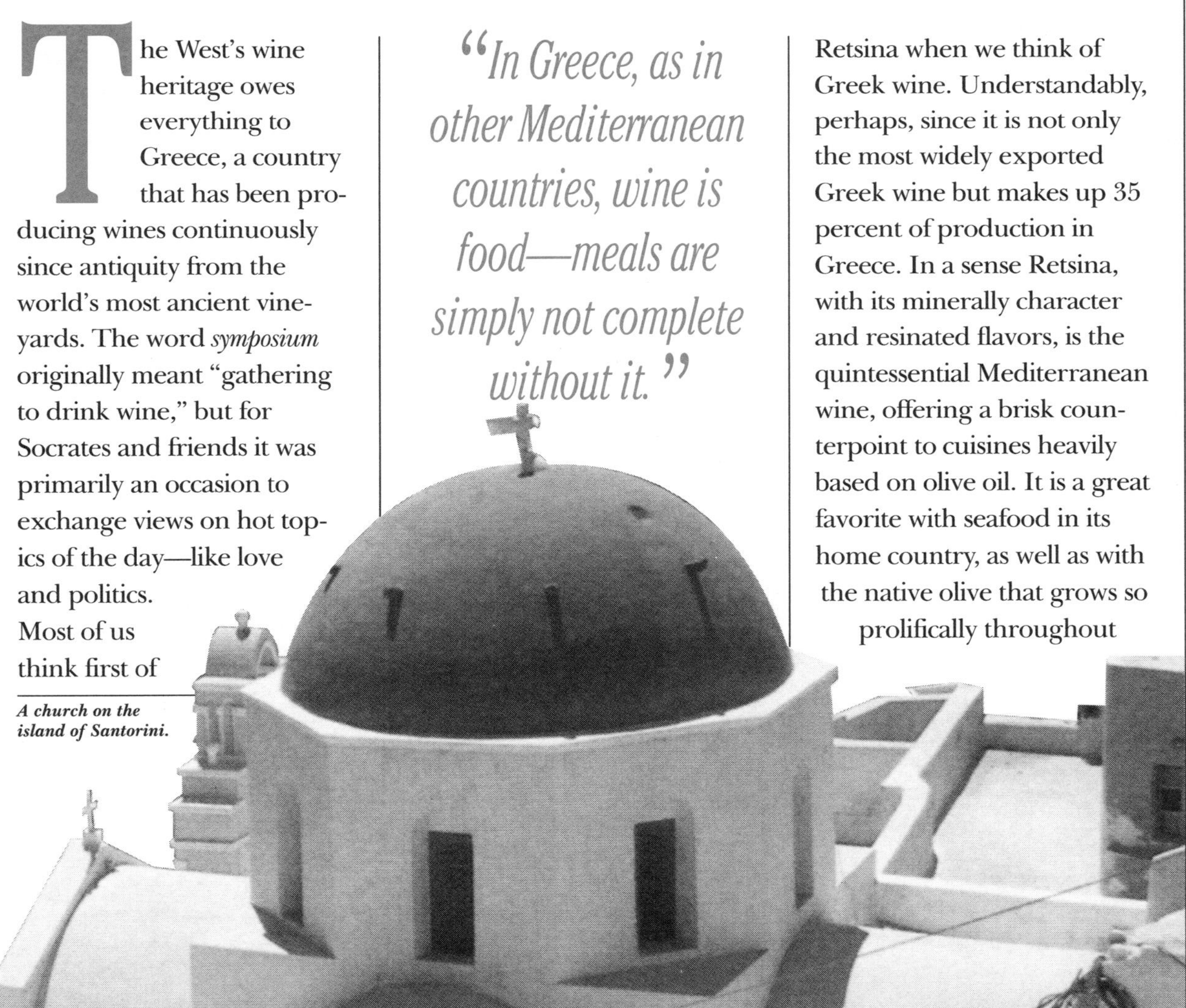

A church on the island of Santorini.

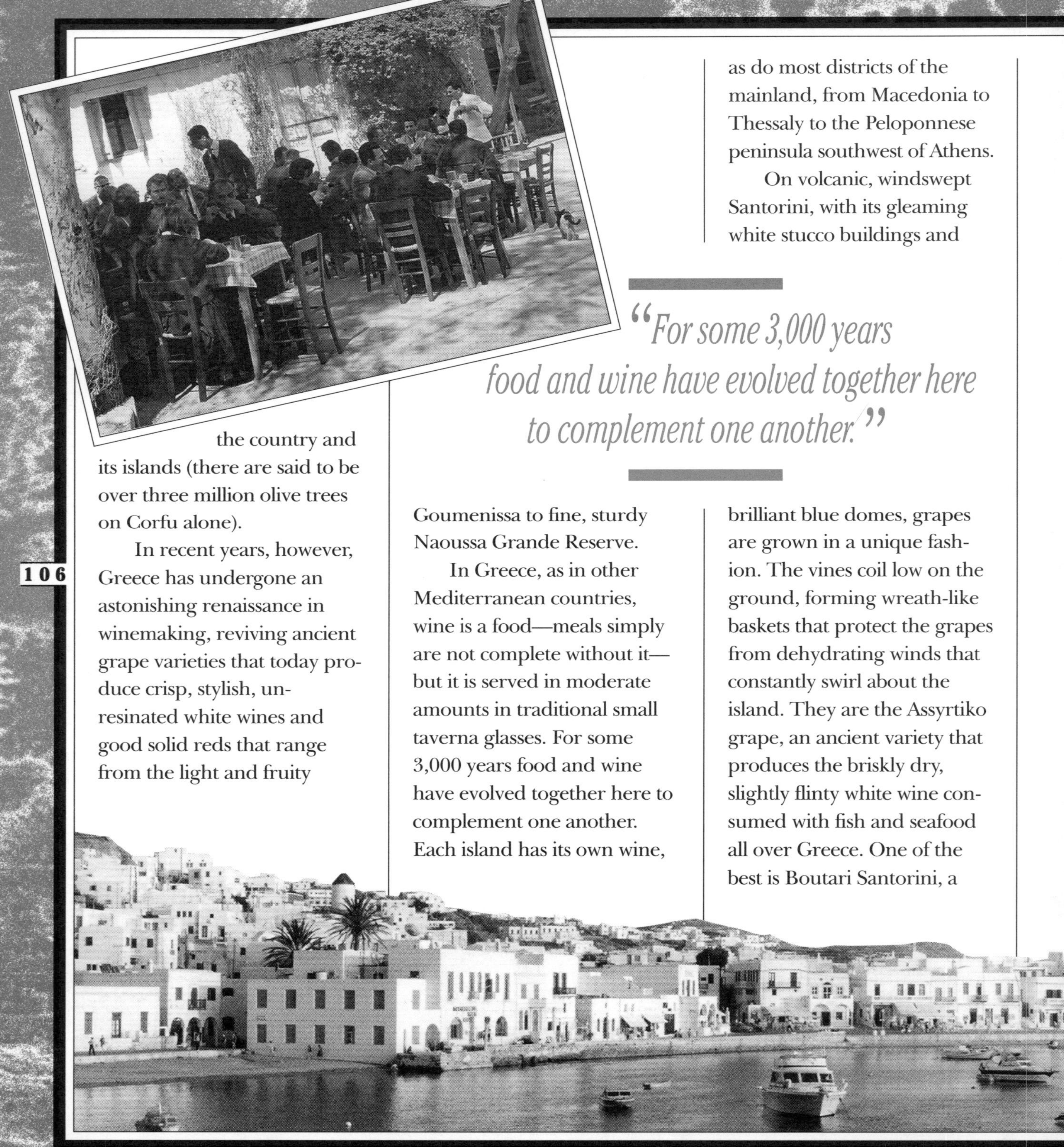

the country and its islands (there are said to be over three million olive trees on Corfu alone).

In recent years, however, Greece has undergone an astonishing renaissance in winemaking, reviving ancient grape varieties that today produce crisp, stylish, unresinated white wines and good solid reds that range from the light and fruity Goumenissa to fine, sturdy Naoussa Grande Reserve.

In Greece, as in other Mediterranean countries, wine is a food—meals simply are not complete without it—but it is served in moderate amounts in traditional small taverna glasses. For some 3,000 years food and wine have evolved together here to complement one another. Each island has its own wine, as do most districts of the mainland, from Macedonia to Thessaly to the Peloponnese peninsula southwest of Athens.

"For some 3,000 years food and wine have evolved together here to complement one another."

On volcanic, windswept Santorini, with its gleaming white stucco buildings and brilliant blue domes, grapes are grown in a unique fashion. The vines coil low on the ground, forming wreath-like baskets that protect the grapes from dehydrating winds that constantly swirl about the island. They are the Assyrtiko grape, an ancient variety that produces the briskly dry, slightly flinty white wine consumed with fish and seafood all over Greece. One of the best is Boutari Santorini, a zingy, dry white now widely available in the U.S. Here, it would be just the sort of wine to drink with citrus-flavored fish kebabs, but also with slices of feta and Kalamata olives.

Other white wines worth looking for are Kourtakis Kritikos from Crete, Boutari's Lac des Roches, Côtes de Meliton from Thessaly, and the fragrant Robola of Cephalonia. Greece's zesty, dry rosé, Roditys, can be just right with *meze* or the Russian *zakuski,* the savory appetizers so popular in Eastern Europe and the Middle East.

Greece also has made great strides with red wine. There is the sturdy Nemea, often with a lion on the label (a reference to Hercules' struggle with the lion of Nemea); its dry warmth is excellent with moussaka or the spicy veal stew known as *stifado.* The Peloponnese also produces the fruity Patras made from the St. George grape. Perhaps the best reds come from Macedonia in northern Greece—where the ancient grape, Xinomavro, is used to produce Naoussa (Boutari's very good Grande Reserve)—and also from Thessaly, where European varieties, such as Cabernet and Merlot, are grown and blended into the likes of Château Carras. Any of these wines would suit some of the lamb dishes included in this cookbook, as well as Pastitsio, and Mediterranean Roast Chicken, with its flavors of garlic and rosemary (see the Index for these).

The perfect finale to a Greek meal is a glass of dessert wine, and two date to Homeric times, perhaps to the Olympian gods themselves. Samos, a sweet (but not cloyingly sweet) golden Muscat from the Aegean island of Samos is best when lightly chilled. Mavrodaphne is red, dark, sweet, and somewhat stronger, probably the wine Homer had in mind when he spoke of the "wine-dark sea."

Top left: Ouzo at a sunny taverna in Athens. Bottom: Mykonos, from the Aegean. Above: You need a good burro or good sneakers to get a view of Santorini from this high up.

RUSSIAN SALAD

When I think of vegetables à la russe, I think of mayonnaise-bound cubes of potatoes, peas, and carrots. I've tried to lighten the salad a bit by tossing the vegetables individually with a sweet, delicate apple cider vinaigrette. This separation also prevents the beets from turning everything else a deep magenta color. The individual tastes and colors make a much more dazzling presentation when arranged separately. Serve this salad as part of a *zakuski* table or with a platter of smoked fish, accompanied by good Russian black bread.

2½ pounds Idaho potatoes (about 5), peeled and cut into ¼-inch dice
2 large carrots, peeled and cut into ¼-inch dice
3 medium Roasted Beets (page 194), peeled and cut into ¼-inch dice
1 hothouse (seedless) cucumber, peeled and cut into ¼-inch dice
½ cup Apple Cider Vinaigrette (recipe follows), plus more for serving
5 tablespoons chopped fresh dill
3 scallions (3 inches green left on), thinly sliced
1 hard-cooked egg, coarsely chopped, for garnish
6 small fresh dill sprigs, for garnish

1. Boil the potatoes in water to cover in a medium-size saucepan until tender, about 10 minutes. Drain and set aside.

2. Boil the carrots in water to cover

Mommy,
How do you like my matrushka? I lined up all 15 in my room in St. P. to keep me company. Now on to Moscow.

Love,
Sheila

in a small saucepan until tender, about 10 minutes. Drain and set aside.

3. Toss the potatoes, carrots, beets, and cucumber each separately in a small bowl with 2 tablespoons apple cider vinaigrette and 1 tablespoon chopped dill.

4. Arrange the vegetables on a large plate (about 14 inches in diameter) in a decorative fashion, placing the beets in the center and alternating the potatoes, carrots, and cucumber twice around the edge. Sprinkle the scallions and remaining 1 tablespoon dill atop the vegetables. Sprinkle the chopped egg over all and garnish with the dill sprigs.

5. Toss the salad at the table or serve it as is. Pass the additional vinaigrette.

Serves 8 to 10

APPLE CIDER VINAIGRETTE

When a sweeter and milder vinaigrette is in order, apple cider vinegar is an ideal choice. Purists would stay away from the added sugar, but I've never minded bending the rules a bit. Choose this vinaigrette for vegetable and egg dishes and more delicately flavored greens.

1 1/2 teaspoons Dijon mustard
1 1/2 teaspoons sugar
1/4 teaspoon salt
1/4 teaspoon freshly ground black pepper
1/3 cup apple cider vinegar
1 tablespoon chopped flat-leaf parsley
2/3 cup vegetable oil

Whisk the mustard, sugar, salt, pepper, vinegar, and chopped parsley together in a bowl. Slowly drizzle in the oil, whisking constantly, until thickened. Adjust the seasonings to taste. Store covered in the refrigerator for up to 2 days. Bring to room temperature before using.

Makes 1 cup

RUSSIAN GARDEN SALAD

We all enjoy summer vegetables, but Russians truly savor their cucumbers, radishes, scallions, and fresh herbs. Light yogurt and fresh dill bring the crispness together in this simply prepared salad. Remember to toss the dressing with the vegetables just before serving. This salad is a wonderful accompaniment to Baltic Sturgeon Salad in this chapter.

10 to 12 firm red radishes (about 8 ounces), cleaned and trimmed
1 hothouse (seedless) cucumber, peeled
6 scallions (3 inches green left on), trimmed
2 tablespoons chopped fresh dill
Freshly ground black pepper, to taste
1 cup nonfat plain yogurt
1/4 cup sour cream
Salt, to taste
8 fresh dill sprigs, for garnish

1. Cut the radishes and cucumber into 1/4-inch dice (about 2 cups each). Combine them in a large bowl.

2. Thinly slice the scallions on the diagonal and add them to the vegetables along with the chopped dill and pepper. Toss to combine. Refrigerate, covered, no longer than 2 hours before serving.

3. In a separate bowl, mix the yogurt and sour cream together. Just before serving, toss the yogurt mixture with the vegetables and season with salt. Garnish with dill sprigs.

Serves 8

SOUVENIR TO SAVOR

Zakuski

Chicken, well-dressed and garnished, makes a beautiful zakuski presentation.

Before I left for Russia, I was asked by my hosts what I was most interested in learning about during my visit. Perhaps because I loved the name or the idea, I answered "traditional *zakuski*." *Zakuski* are a delightful assortment of small hot and cold appetizers which are eaten before a meal or main course. In years past, the amount and type of *zakuski* served reflected the prosperity and stature of the host's family.

Akin to Turkish *meze* and Spanish *tapas, zakuski* possibilities are vast: everything from delicious Georgian *satsivi* (delicate pieces of chicken bathed in a walnut sauce) to thin *blinchiki,* laden with wild mushrooms; caviar-slathered hard-cooked eggs (see the Index for recipes); smoked meats and sausages; rich black breads; pickled beets, cabbages, and cucumbers; and cold fish and vegetable salads all join the party. Once everyone is seated, there begins a nonstop array of food and drink to indulge the largest appetites. Don't even think of other ways to start your next fete. This is informal dining at its very best.

The welcoming colors and ambiance of Russian *zakuski* tables somehow evoke an old-fashioned Victorian Christmas for me. The tables are laid with crisp white cloths, which are often embroidered or decorated with a bit of green trim. The wooden dishes are lacquered bright red, trimmed with bands of gold and black, and embellished with golden leaves and flowers all outlined in black. A silver ice bucket is filled to chill the vodka and Champagne. The green stemmed glassware is lined up at the ready. Dishes are laden with snowy white sturgeon and jet black, pearly caviar; bright red peppers and tomatoes and crispy cucumbers nestled in their dark green skins come alive under blankets of fresh flat-leaf parsley, feathery dill, and delicate cilantro; snow white salads are bound with fresh mayonnaise—all echo the colors of the setting. What pleasure and gaiety. What a warm, inviting, totally civilized way to begin any evening meal or festive luncheon.

A TASTE OF THE WORLD

Russian Palette

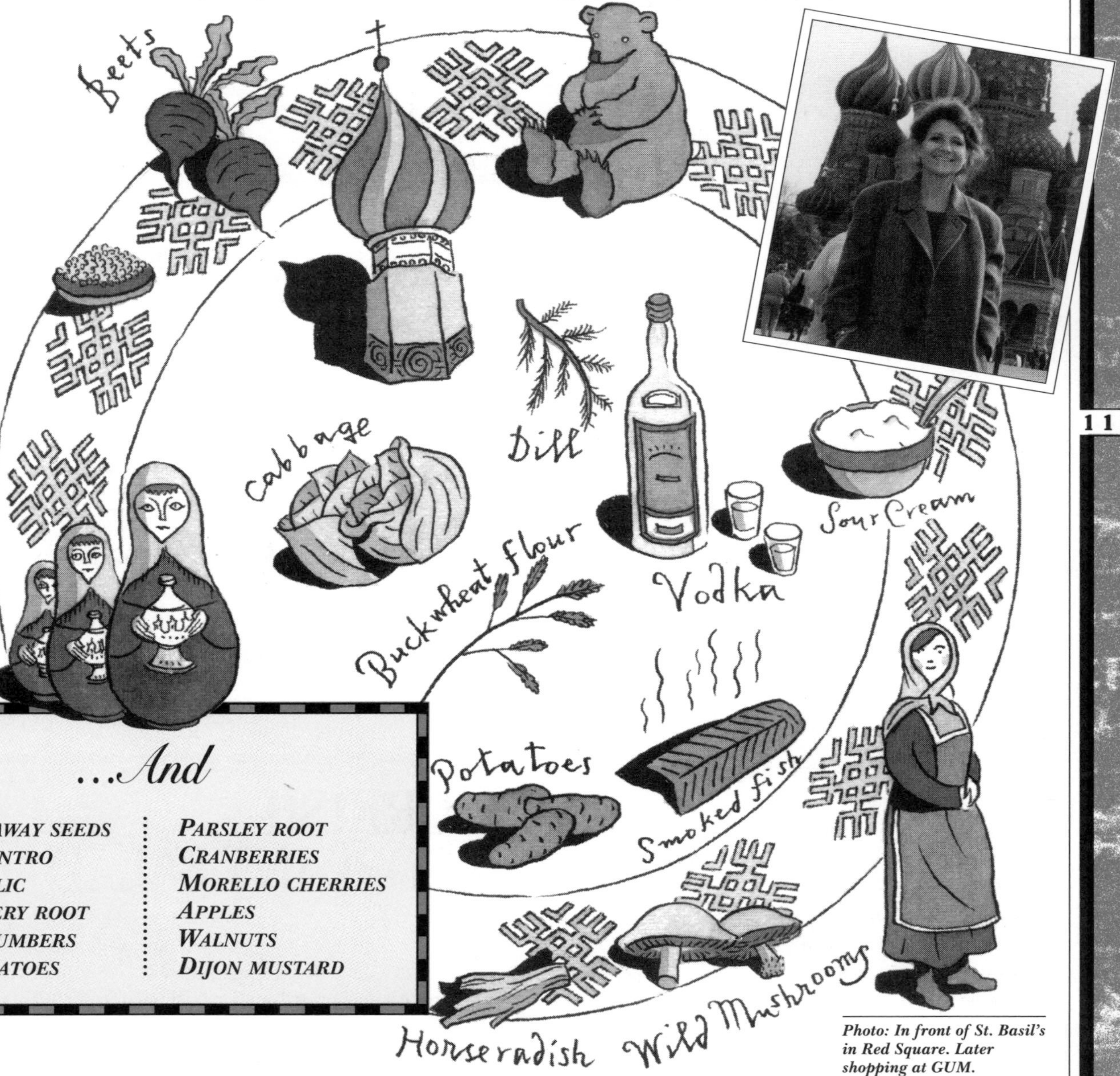

...And

Caraway seeds	*Parsley root*
Cilantro	*Cranberries*
Garlic	*Morello cherries*
Celery root	*Apples*
Cucumbers	*Walnuts*
Tomatoes	*Dijon mustard*

Photo: In front of St. Basil's in Red Square. Later shopping at GUM.

GREEK SALAD

Too often when ordering a Greek salad, I've been served a plate of thick green pepper rings, thin white onion rings, feta cheese chunks, underripe tomato wedges, and a few olives. A wonderful trip to Greece helped me to rethink that static combination. I've eliminated the pepper rings in favor of roasted red peppers and transformed the pungent Kalamata olives into a succulent purée for slathering on toasted peasant bread. The flavors are brightened by a lemon vinaigrette and a garnish of fresh mint leaves. Seek out a fresh feta cheese if possible to make the salad extra special.

This salad stands on its own as an entrée but is an excellent accompaniment to roast lamb or grilled seafood as well. Be sure to prepare the olive purée, peppers, and vinaigrette ahead of time so that the salad can be easily assembled just before serving.

8 romaine lettuce leaves (preferably the pale green inner leaves), torn into 1-inch pieces
½ hothouse (seedless) cucumber, peeled, quartered lengthwise, and cut into ½-inch cubes
4 tablespoons Lemon-Garlic Vinaigrette (page 102)
4 ripe plum tomatoes, cut into 8 wedges each
2 scallions (3 inches of green left on), thinly sliced on the diagonal
¼ cup chopped flat-leaf parsley
4 slices (½ inch thick) round peasant bread, lightly toasted
4 tablespoons Kalamata Olive Purée (page 60)
8 ounces feta cheese, coarsely crumbled
½ cup Kalamata olives
2 red bell peppers, halved lengthwise and roasted (page 202)
2 tablespoons chopped fresh mint leaves, for garnish

1. In a bowl, toss together the lettuce leaves, cucumber, and 2 tablespoons of the vinaigrette and set aside.

2. In another bowl, toss the tomatoes, scallions, and parsley with the remaining 2 tablespoons vinaigrette and set aside.

3. Spread each slice of toast with 1 tablespoon of the olive purée and place on the side of each of 4 large plates.

4. Divide and arrange the greens on the plates. Spoon the tomato mixture on top of the greens. Top with the feta cheese and garnish with a few olives. Cut each pepper half in half. Lay 2 pieces of roasted red pepper decoratively on each salad. Garnish with chopped fresh mint leaves.

Serves 4

TURKISH EGGPLANT SALAD

Yogurt adds a subtle tang and creamy texture to this puréed eggplant spread, which is further brightened with lemon, dill, and sweet tomatoes. Serve with slices of grilled or toasted peasant bread.

2 large eggplants (about 1 pound each)
1 tablespoon extra virgin olive oil
1 teaspoon fresh lemon juice
Salt and coarsely ground black pepper, to taste
½ cup nonfat plain yogurt
2 tablespoons chopped fresh dill
½ teaspoon finely grated lemon zest
¼ cup seeded and diced (¼ inch) plum tomato, for garnish

1. Preheat the oven to 350°F.

2. Pierce each eggplant a few times with the tip of a small paring knife, then wrap each one in aluminum foil. Bake on a baking sheet until tender, about 1 hour.

3. Let the eggplants stand until cool enough to handle, then unwrap them. Halve each one lengthwise and scoop the softened pulp into a food processor, discarding most of the seeds.

4. Add the oil, lemon juice, salt, and pepper to the eggplant and pulse on and off about 6 times. The ingredients should be combined but the texture should still be coarse. Remove the mixture to a bowl and gently fold in the yogurt, dill, and lemon zest. To serve, spoon the purée into a decorative bowl or spread it in a small oval dish. Garnish the top with the diced tomato.

Makes 1½ cups

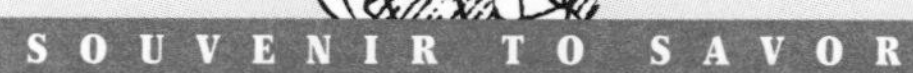

SOUVENIR TO SAVOR

Salad Splendor

To wax ecstatic about the salads served in Turkey may seem, at face value, inappropriate, but I assure you that these bursts of freshness are glorious. Usually served along with the *meze* to begin a meal, they are left on the table throughout. Platters are heaped with large, dark green, peppery arugula leaves, tasting like the first harvest of spring. Pale green, crisp wedges of iceberg lettuce (yes, you read me right) are arranged on the arugula, and next to them, peeled juicy slices of sun-ripened tomatoes abound alongside crisp wedges of cucumber. No fancy dressing weighs down these salads; they are sprinkled instead with a perfect balance of lemon juice and extra virgin olive oil. I hope our palates haven't become too jaded to enjoy these simple pleasures.

POTATO PRIMAVERA SALAD

When I'm writing a cookbook, there tend to be extra ingredients around my kitchen at all times. One day I happened to have a beautiful salmon fillet in my refrigerator and, since I'm always well stocked on potatoes, I put together a light and delicate salmon-potato salad with all the freshness of springtime. Employing both the Balinese and Scandinavian palettes, I tossed it all together with an orange-sweetened mayonnaise and brightened it with cucumbers, tomatoes, and crisp chives. A small dollop of fresh salmon caviar atop each portion would make for a very elegant first course.

4 cups water
4 flat-leaf parsley sprigs
1 bay leaf
4 black peppercorns
8 ounces salmon fillet
2 Idaho potatoes, peeled and cut into ¼-inch dice
3 plum tomatoes, seeded and cut into ¼-inch dice
1 cup peeled, seeded, and diced (¼ inch) cucumber
3 hard-cooked eggs, coarsely chopped
2 teaspoons drained tiny capers
1½ tablespoons snipped fresh chives
Salt and coarsely ground black pepper, to taste
¾ cup Orange-Rosemary Mayonnaise (page 76)
6 teaspoons fresh salmon caviar (optional)

1. Place the water, parsley, bay leaf, and peppercorns in a large wide pot and bring to a boil. Reduce the heat and simmer for 10 minutes. Add the salmon fillet and cook, partially covered, until the salmon flakes easily with a fork, about 5 minutes. Remove from the cooking liquid and set aside.

2. Place the potatoes in a pot with salted water to cover. Bring to a boil, reduce the heat to medium, and cook until just tender, 5 to 8 minutes. Drain, remove to a large bowl, and cool to room temperature.

3. Add the tomatoes, cucumber, hard-cooked eggs, capers, and chives to the potatoes. Pat the salmon dry and carefully break the salmon into large flakes, discarding any skin and bones, and add it to the salad. Season with salt and pepper.

4. Add the orange-rosemary mayonnaise and gently fold all the ingredients together with a large rubber spatula.

5. Divide the salad among 6 salad plates and dollop each portion with 1 teaspoon salmon caviar.

Serves 6

NORDIC COBB SALAD

Cobb salad, an American favorite, is vividly enhanced by the Danish food palette. Shrimp, beets, chopped eggs, and pickles are combined and brought together with a tangy Danish blue cheese dressing. This is a moment to employ your creativity and artistic sensibilities by arranging the ingredients in a stunning pattern. Typically the ingredients are arranged in stripes, but you can choose whatever design pleases you.

DRESSING:
¼ cup apple cider vinegar
1 teaspoon Dijon mustard
1 tablespoon sugar
Salt, to taste
¼ cup vegetable oil
4 ounces Danish blue cheese, crumbled
Coarsely ground black pepper, to taste

SALAD:
1 pound large shrimp, peeled and deveined
2 Idaho potatoes, peeled and cut into ¼-inch dice
1 cup peeled and diced (¼ inch) carrots
2 medium Roasted Beets (page 194), peeled
2 ripe avocados, preferably Haas, pitted, peeled, and cut into ¼-inch dice
1 tablespoon fresh lemon juice
1 head romaine lettuce, rinsed, dried, and torn into small pieces
1 large head Bibb lettuce, rinsed, dried, leaves left whole
4 hard-cooked eggs, peeled and coarsely chopped
1 large dill pickle, cut into ¼-inch dice
Salt and coarsely ground black pepper, to taste
2 tablespoons chopped flat-leaf parsley

1. For the dressing, combine the vinegar, mustard, sugar, and salt in a food processor. With the machine running, slowly drizzle in the oil through the feed tube and continue to process until the mixture is slightly thick. Add the blue cheese and process just to combine the cheese slightly. Some texture should remain. Transfer to a bowl, add pepper, cover, and set aside.

2. For the salad, cook the shrimp in boiling water for 1 minute. Drain, rinse under cold water, and pat dry. Cut crosswise into small pieces.

3. Cook the potatoes in boiling water to cover until tender, 5 to 7 minutes. Drain and set aside.

4. Cook the carrots in boiling water to cover until just tender, about 2 minutes. Drain and set aside.

5. Cut the roasted beets into ¼-inch dice. Set aside.

6. Toss the avocados with the lemon juice to prevent discoloration. Set aside.

7. To arrange the salad, place the romaine lettuce in the bottom of a large salad bowl. Arrange the Bibb lettuce leaves decoratively around the rim of the bowl.

8. Place the shrimp on top of the greens in the center of the bowl. Arrange the potatoes, carrots, beets, avocados, eggs, and dill pickle decoratively around the shrimp.

9. Sprinkle the salad with salt and pepper to taste and the parsley.

10. To serve, present the arranged salad bowl (you deserve some applause for your efforts). Then spoon the dressing over the top and toss gently to coat the ingredients. Serve immediately.

Serves 8

SASHA'S APPLE CRAB COCKTAIL

One evening in St. Petersburg I was feted by a group of Soviet Georgians in a lovely restaurant that is only open for private functions. From the minute I arrived, Georgian Cognac flowed and toasts proliferated. The table was laid with a colorful cold *zakuski*—bowls of tomatoes, cucumbers, and red peppers garnished with parsley, slices of roast chicken stuffed with dried apricots, small perfect tomatoes filled with mayonnaise-tossed grated cheese and garnished with lots of scallion greens, and large wineglasses filled with crabmeat and tart apple cocktail. The rims of the glasses had been rubbed in sugar syrup and dipped in chopped fresh dill. There was a dollop of pink sauce atop the crab. When I asked Chef Sasha what it was, he replied, "Russian dressing." For my version I've created a tomato-chive garnish.

SALAD:
2 Granny Smith apples, cored and cut into ¼-inch dice
Juice of 2 lemons
1 pound jumbo lump crabmeat, picked over for shell and cartilage
¼ cup chopped fresh dill
2 tablespoons snipped fresh chives
Salt and freshly ground black pepper, to taste

DRESSING:
½ cup mayonnaise
Finely grated zest of 1 lemon
1 tablespoon fresh lemon juice
1 tablespoon Dijon mustard

GARNISH:
2 ripe plum tomatoes, cored, seeded, and cut into ⅛-inch dice
2 teaspoons snipped fresh chives
8 fresh dill sprigs

1. For the salad, toss the diced apples with the lemon juice in a bowl to prevent discoloration.

2. Place the crabmeat in another bowl. Drain the apples, pat them dry, and add to the crabmeat along with the dill, chives, salt, and pepper. Toss gently to combine.

3. For the dressing, whisk the mayonnaise, lemon zest, lemon juice, and mustard together. Gently fold the dressing into the salad with a rubber spatula, being careful not to break up the crab too much. Refrigerate covered for about 1 hour to allow the flavors to develop.

4. For the garnish, toss together the tomatoes and chives.

5. Divide the salad among 8 large wineglasses. Sprinkle the tops with the tomato garnish and place a sprig of dill atop each portion.

Serves 8

SOUVENIR TO SAVOR

A Most Splendid "Entrée"

On most menus abroad, the word "entrée" presents appetizers or first courses, instead of the main course as it does in America. I tasted one of my favorites, both for its simplicity and its flavor, in a lovely restaurant in Seville. A large plate was generously laden with slices of perfectly ripe tomatoes. The tomatoes were blanketed with thin slices of Jabugo ham, a lean, cured prosciutto-style ham, which was lightly drizzled with an intense extra virgin olive oil and then splashed with sherry vinegar. A generous coarse grinding of fresh black pepper completed the dish. Simply delicious!

THE WINES OF

Russia

A decade ago the U.S.S.R. ranked sixth in world wine production. A considerable amount of that output came from Soviet bloc countries that are now independent republics, such as Romania, Bulgaria, Hungary, and Moldova. Georgia, too, is rich in history and wine lore. Although the region remains a principal area for wine grape growing, the heavy, sweet table wines produced by its wineries are losing favor.

Currently Ukraine is the source of Russia's best table wines and its largest producer of sparkling wines. Most are on the sweetish side, though there is certainly the potential for drier wines and better quality. The most widely planted grape varieties are Saperavi for red wines and Rkatsiteli for whites. There are also vineyards planted with such European varieties as Cabernet Sauvignon, Riesling, Chardonnay, Merlot, and Pinot Noir; these will undoubtedly be expanded in the future.

A splendid Georgian white with a gorgeous label.

The Crimea is noted for very fine dessert wines. The esteemed Massandra winery boasts cellars that still hold vintages of its Sauternes-like sweet wines dating to the 1770s. Uzbekistan, Azerbaijan, and other areas in Central Asia produce primarily fortified dessert wines, including the very good port-like red Uzbekistan, made from Saperavi grapes and known for its healing qualities.

Wines from the disbanded Soviet Union may eventually make their way to these shores but probably not before considerable upgrading of quality and the adoption of modern techniques takes place. This will take time, but the potential is enormous.

PALTEROVICH CREAMY APPLE HERRING

My friend Bruce Paltrow makes the most marvelous pickled herring in cream salad, which somehow missed the deadline for *The New Basics Cookbook*. I wasn't taking any chances this time and called him for the recipe as soon as I got back from Russia. His family, originally named Palterovich, came from the Polish Russian region of Minsk. We can thank them for bringing this recipe to America. It makes a lovely addition to a *zakuski* table or a great starter for Sunday brunch.

2 jars (12 ounces each) sliced herring packed in vinegar and spices
2 tablespoons fresh lemon juice
1 Granny Smith apple, cored
1 large sweet onion (preferably red Maui or Vidalia), thinly sliced
1½ cups sour cream or crème fraîche
¼ cup drained prepared white horseradish
¼ cup finely chopped fresh dill
Freshly ground black pepper, to taste
Fresh dill sprigs, for garnish

1. Drain the herring well, and if the slices are very large, cut them into smaller pieces. Discard any of the pickling spices that may cling to the herring.

2. Pour the lemon juice into a large bowl. Cut the apple into irregular 1-inch pieces about ¼ inch thick. Add to the lemon juice and toss to prevent discoloration. Add the herring and onion and combine gently.

3. In a separate bowl, mix the sour cream, horseradish, and chopped dill together. Fold into the herring mixture. Season with pepper and combine well. Refrigerate covered at least 4 hours before serving. Serve in a pretty cut-glass bowl, garnished with dill sprigs.

Serves 12

TARAMA SALMON BLUSH

I never much liked *vitello tonnato* (cold veal with tuna sauce), but this dish offers a variation on the theme that I find appealing for a sophisticated luncheon. The briny, pungent flavor of tarama becomes refined when slathered on sweet, ripe slices of tomato. When shopping for smoked salmon, avoid lox or other heavily salted varieties. Irish or Canadian Gaspé smoked salmon is lovely in this delightful salad. Studded with fresh salmon caviar and capers, the presentation is dazzling.

2 ripe large beefsteak tomatoes, sliced crosswise about ½ inch thick (4 slices in all)
4 tablespoons Tarama Slather (page 59)
1 tablespoon drained capers
1 tablespoon fresh salmon caviar,
8 ounces thinly sliced smoked salmon
4 fresh mint sprigs, for garnish

Arrange a tomato slice in the center of each of 4 small salad plates. Lightly spread 1 tablespoon of the tarama slather over each tomato slice. Spoon the capers and caviar decoratively atop the tarama for a polka dot effect. Arrange the salmon slices decoratively around the tomatoes. Garnish each plate with a mint sprig.

Serves 4

KHALED KOUHEN'S SALAD MICHWIYA

Grilled Vegetable Salad

I love listening to my assistant Laurie Griffith's Tunisian tales. Laurie vividly recounts summers spent in Tunis as a guest of her friend Khaled Kouhen. Khaled's mother is a marvelous home cook with a wide repertoire, but this typical staple salad always enthralled. Simple yet time consuming, it is definitely worth the effort.

Madame Kouhen also uses this salad as a basis for a terrific Tunisian sandwich. She slices the top off of a sandwich-size piece of baguette and hollows out some of the inside. She then fills it with salad *michwiya* and lays chunks of tuna, hard-cooked egg slices, capers, and pitted olives atop. Accompanied by wedges of ripe watermelon, this is a most luscious summer lunch. I've included the eggs and tuna in this recipe, but the salad is delicious on its own.

1 medium onion, peeled and halved
2 red bell peppers, stemmed, seeded, and halved
2 green bell peppers, stemmed, seeded, and halved
1½ pounds ripe plum tomatoes, halved lengthwise and seeded
2 large cloves garlic, peeled
1 teaspoon caraway seeds
½ teaspoon coarse salt
2 tablespoons olive oil
2 tablespoons fresh lemon juice
2 hard-cooked eggs, peeled and quartered lengthwise (optional)
8 imported black olives, or more to taste
¾ cup canned solid white albacore tuna, drained (optional)
2 tablespoons drained capers, for garnish

1. Preheat the broiler. Line a baking sheet with aluminum foil.

2. Place the onion and bell pepper halves cut side down on a baking sheet. Broil 3 inches from the heat until the skins are blackened. Remove the peppers to a plastic bag, tie it shut, and set aside. Remove the onion to a plate and set aside.

3. Place the tomato halves cut side down on the same baking sheet. Broil 3 inches from the heat until the skins blacken slightly, about 5 minutes. Slip off the skins and discard.

4. Chop the garlic, caraway seeds, and coarse salt together. Set aside.

5. Remove and discard the charred skins from the bell peppers and the outer layer of the onion when they are cool enough to handle. Coarsely chop and place in a large bowl.

6. Coarsely chop the tomatoes and drain in a strainer to remove any excess liquid. Add to the peppers and onion.

7. Add the garlic mixture, oil, and lemon juice and stir well. To serve, spread the mixture over the surface of a large plate or individual small plates. Place the egg quarters, if using, and olives decoratively around the outside of the plate. Sprinkle flakes of tuna, if using, atop the salad and top with capers.

Makes 3 cups, serves 6 as a salad

Tunisian Palette

...And

Bay leaves	*Turnips*
Cloves	*Pumpkins*
Basil	*Oranges*
Garlic	*Raisins*
Capers	*Dates*
Olives	*Almonds*
Okra	*Pine nuts*
Tomatoes	*Chickpeas*
Bell peppers	*Anchovies*
Yams	*Tuna*
Chilies	*Olive oil*
Red onions	*Harissa*

TURKISH MUSSEL SALAD

One of the lighter *meze* I tasted in Istanbul was an excellent mussel salad, tossed with finely diced sweet green peppers, tomatoes, shallots, and cornichons. Back home, I recreated the salad and enjoy serving it with Rigani White Bean and Garlic Slather (see Index), sliced tomatoes, cucumbers, and peppery greens, and plenty of crusty bread.

6 dozen small mussels
1 cup water
4 ripe plum tomatoes, seeded and cut into ¼-inch dice
1 Italian frying pepper, stemmed, seeded, and cut into ¼-inch dice
16 cornichons, cut into ¼-inch slices
4 teaspoons finely chopped shallots
¼ cup olive oil
2 tablespoons fresh lemon juice
¼ cup chopped flat-leaf parsley
Salt and coarsely ground black pepper, to taste

1. Scrub the mussels thoroughly under cold running water to remove any sand, then snip off the beards. Place the mussels in a large heavy pot and add the water. Bring to a boil, cover the pot, and steam, shaking the pan once or twice, until the mussels open, 6 to 8 minutes. Discard any mussels that do not open and drain.

2. Let the mussels stand until cool enough to handle, then remove them from their shells and place them in a large bowl.

3. Add the tomatoes, pepper, cornichons, shallots, oil, lemon juice, parsley, salt, and pepper to the mussels and toss together gently. Serve at room temperature or chill covered in the refrigerator for up to 30 minutes before serving.

Serves 6 as an appetizer

JAMAICAN CRAB SALAD COMPOSEE

What I enjoyed about the salads that I had in the Caribbean was that they appeared so fresh and always seemed to be made of flourishing local ingredients. Bananas, crab, lime, and pineapple proliferated, and curry powders and mango chutneys appeared when least expected, fusing all the various cultural influences. This lovely summer entrée salad combines the best of the Caribbean.

½ cup nonfat plain yogurt
½ teaspoon minced garlic
1½ teaspoons finely grated lime zest
2 tablespoons fresh lime juice
⅛ teaspoon paprika
6 hard-cooked eggs
⅓ cup mayonnaise
1 tablespoon best-quality curry powder
1 tablespoon finely chopped mango chutney
8 ounces jumbo lump crabmeat, picked over for shell and cartilage
2 cups mixed salad greens, preferably mesclun (baby lettuces), rinsed and dried
2 tablespoons Lime-Garlic Vinaigrette (page 98)
1 banana, thinly sliced on the diagonal
2 tablespoons finely snipped fresh chives, for garnish

1. To make the yogurt dressing for the crab, process the yogurt, garlic, lime zest, 1 tablespoon of the lime juice, and the paprika in a food processor until smooth. Remove to a bowl until ready to use. (Makes about ½ cup.)

2. Peel and halve the hard-cooked eggs lengthwise. Remove the yolks, finely chop them, and set aside the whites.

3. In a bowl, mix together the egg yolks, mayonnaise, curry powder, and chutney. Spoon the mixture into the egg white halves and set aside, loosely covered.

4. Toss the crabmeat with ¼ cup of the yogurt dressing in a bowl. Reserve the rest of the dressing for another use, such as atop grilled chicken or vegetables.

5. To assemble the salad, toss the salad greens with the vinaigrette and place it in the center of 4 dinner plates. Spoon the dressed crab evenly atop the greens.

6. Toss the banana slices with the remaining tablespoon of lime juice. Alternate the stuffed eggs (3 halves per person) and banana slices around the greens and crab. Sprinkle the salads with the snipped chives.

Serves 4

CITRUS CREAM SHRIMP AND PAPAYA SALAD

The extraordinary pink and golden papayas of Bali and the Caribbean inspired this delicate summer salad. It's creamy yet light and the cucumber's crunch adds just the right texture.

4 cups water
1 pound medium shrimp, peeled and deveined
2 tablespoons white wine vinegar
2 tablespoons fresh orange juice
1 tablespoon light honey
2 teaspoons Dijon mustard
Salt and freshly ground black pepper, to taste
½ cup olive oil
¼ cup heavy (or whipping) cream
1 tablespoon finely grated orange zest
1 teaspoon chopped fresh tarragon leaves or 1 teaspoon dried
1 ripe papaya (about 1 pound), peeled, seeded, and cut into ½-inch dice
1 hothouse (seedless) cucumber, peeled and cut into ½-inch dice
1 head red radicchio, leaves separated, rinsed, and patted dry
1 tablespoon snipped fresh chives, for garnish

1. Bring the water to a boil in a medium-size saucepan, add the shrimp, and cook for 1 minute. Drain and let the shrimp cool.

2. To make the dressing, combine the vinegar, orange juice, honey, mustard, salt, and pepper in a small bowl. Whisking constantly, slowly drizzle in the oil and continue to whisk until the dressing thickens. Gradually whisk in the cream. Fold in the orange zest and tarragon. (Makes 1 cup.)

3. Combine the shrimp, papaya, and cucumber in a bowl. Toss with ¼ cup of the creamy dressing, reserving the remainder for another use. To serve, arrange the radicchio leaves on a platter, spoon the salad over the center, and sprinkle with the chives.

Serves 6

BALTIC STURGEON SALAD

A simple potato salad is easily transformed into a succulent appetizer, brunch dish, or cold *zakuska* with the addition of smoked sturgeon and a garnish of salmon caviar. I love this dish served with Russian Garden Salad (page 109) with its burst of crispy freshness. Serve Russian black bread alongside.

1½ pounds Idaho potatoes (2 to 3)
1 pound thinly sliced smoked sturgeon
1 cup peeled, seeded, and diced (¼ inch) cucumber
3 tablespoons finely snipped fresh chives
Finely grated zest of 1 large lemon
½ cup nonfat plain yogurt
¼ cup sour cream
Salt and freshly ground black pepper, to taste
2 ounces fresh salmon caviar (optional)
8 whole chives, for garnish

1. Peel the potatoes and cut into ¼-inch dice (about 3 cups). Boil in water to cover in a medium-size saucepan until tender, 4 to 5 minutes. Drain, cool, and place in a large bowl.

2. Set aside 8 of the best slices of sturgeon. Shred the remaining sturgeon into the potatoes. Add the cucumber, chives, and lemon zest and gently toss to combine.

3. In a separate bowl, mix the yogurt and sour cream together, then fold it into the potato mixture. Season with salt and pepper. The salad can be refrigerated up to 4 hours before serving.

4. To serve, place a slice of sturgeon on each of 8 plates, then spoon about ½ cup salad on each serving of sturgeon. Divide the caviar equally in small dollops atop the salad and garnish with the whole chives.

Serves 8

ITEK TIM
MINESTRONE
MULLIGATAWNY SOUP · CHILEAN PISTOU WITH CILANTRO PESTO
FEZ-STYLE TOMATO SOUP · WORLD-CLASS CHICKEN SOUP
RICH BEEF BROTH
SPICED PRAWN AND PINEAPPLE SOUP · PAPPA AL POMODORO
MEDITERRANEAN WHITE BEAN SOUP · CHA-CHA CORN GAZPACHO · SOTO BANJAR
CHRISTMAS RED PEPPER SOUP · BOTVINYA

GINGERED CREME DE CRECY · MALAY OXTAIL SOUP

CREAMY WILD MUSHROOM SOUP

HARIRA SOUP

Great Melting Pot

CARLOS' BLACK BEAN SOUP · HOT RUSSIAN BORSCHT

CURRIED GOLDEN SQUASH SOUP · SOPA ALENTEJANA

HUNGARIAN BLACK CHERRY SOUP

SCANDINAVIAN SMOKY PEA SOUP · CASBAH CARROT SOUP

WENDE'S AVGOLEMONO SOUP

Soups

America, more than any other country, opened its doors at the turn of the 19th century, to welcome an extraordinary wealth of cultures. This diverse collection of people brought with them—among so many wonderful treasures—recipes for some of the world's best soups. On some level, they are what we all were served at home to comfort and soothe during our childhood. Seeking out the sources became a fierce challenge, but the results are extremely gratifying. For I also discovered "new melting pots" that are just emerging as we approach another century turn.

From teeming North African medinas in the soft light of dawn to spirited fiestas on summer evenings in Ixtapa, soup nourishes the body as well as invigorates the soul. A bowl of warm spiced Moroccan Harira, a cool vibrant Mexican Gazpacho, steaming Hot Russian Borscht, lusty Italian Minestrone, spicy Caribbean red bean soup—there are so many exceptional choices.

CHICKEN BROTH

Throughout this book, chicken broth is called for since it is essential to many soups and stews and provides the base for flavorful sauces. Some recipes call for a large amount of broth and others only a cup or two. As most of us are not in the restaurant business, it is not possible to have a stockpot simmering away on the back burner at all times. Therefore, it is well worth the effort to make a large batch of broth every once in a while. Once strained and defatted, it can be frozen in plastic containers or ice cube trays. This way you can vary the portion sizes and choose what you need for different recipes.

When I'm preparing vegetables for a broth that is going to be strained, I rinse them off but do not peel them. The skins are full of important nutrients and give the broth a deep, rich color. I always like to add parsnips, tomatoes, and a few whole cloves for their naturally sweet flavor. Parsley is a must, and if you like the flavor, a few sprigs of fresh dill add a lovely taste.

Every cook has certain rules for making broth, but one that is fairly universal is to not stir it once it begins to simmer. Stirring may cause the broth to become cloudy. Once the broth has finished cooking, let it rest at room temperature to cool before straining and defatting.

6 pounds chicken backs and wings
4 ribs celery with leaves
4 carrots, peels left on and halved
2 medium onions, skins left on and halved
2 parsnips, peels left on and halved
1 large ripe tomato or 3 plum tomatoes, halved
4 cloves garlic, lightly bruised (page 153)
8 sprigs flat-leaf parsley
4 sprigs fresh dill (optional)
2 large branches fresh thyme
6 black peppercorns
4 whole cloves
1 bay leaf
1 tablespoon coarse salt, or to taste
4 quarts water

1. Rinse the chicken pieces well, removing any excess fat. Place the chicken in a large soup pot and add all the remaining ingredients.

2. Bring to a boil over medium-high heat. Reduce the heat to medium and simmer gently, partially covered, for 1½ hours, carefully skimming any foam that rises to the surface. Adjust the seasonings and cook 30 minutes longer. Remove the pot from the heat.

3. Strain the broth, then pour it through a fine sieve once more to clear it. Let cool to room temperature.

4. If the broth is to be used immediately, set it aside for 15 minutes to allow the fat to rise to the surface. Then, degrease the broth completely (see How to Defat Chicken Broth, page 128). If the broth is not for immediate use, transfer the cooled broth to a storage container and refrigerate covered. Remove the hardened layer of fat from the top before using. Use the broth within 3 to 4 days or freeze for up to 3 months.

Makes about 4 quarts

MY KITCHEN DIARY

How to Defat Chicken Broth

When a recipe calls for chicken broth, it should always be defatted. This is especially important for cold dishes, where any fat will congeal. Defatting a broth is a very simple process that requires only a little planning.

If you need to use a hot homemade broth immediately, remove the solids with a slotted spoon and pour the hot liquid through a fine strainer to clear it. Set the clear liquid aside for 15 minutes to allow the fat to rise to the surface. Carefully remove the top layer of fat with a shallow metal spoon. If you need a small amount of broth, pour the quantity required for your recipe through a gravy separator, discarding any fat that remains.

The foolproof way to defat is to strain the finished broth and let it cool to room temperature. Ladle the broth into containers and let cool completely. Refrigerate covered overnight so that the fat solidifies on the top. Before use, remove the hardened fat and discard it. Your broth is now defatted and ready for use.

RICH BEEF BROTH

A long-simmered rich beef broth is a great luxury to have on hand in the refrigerator or freezer for both soups and sauces. It's quite easy to make your own and all you really need is a few hours at home one afternoon to tend the simmering pot. To begin you want good beef bones and a nice piece of soup meat to give the broth added flavor and richness. I chop up vegetables, always adding some tomatoes for sweetness, and spread them in the bottom of a roasting pan. Next I lay the bones and meat over the vegetables and bake them together in a hot oven. Once they've cooked for an hour or so, I put everything in a large soup pot, add water, and simmer it slowly for about 3 hours. Be sure not to add salt at the beginning because as the broth cooks it reduces and the flavors become more concentrated. I add mine halfway through the cooking time. Once the broth is strained, cooled, and defatted, you're in business.

4 medium onions, peels left on
4 ribs celery with leaves
4 medium carrots, peels left on
4 tomatoes
3 parsnips, peels left on
3 leeks, trimmed
4 cloves garlic, peels left on
3 pounds flanken or other soup beef with bones
3 pounds beef bones
4 quarts water
8 black peppercorns
6 whole cloves
4 large fresh thyme sprigs
1 bay leaf
Coarse salt to taste

1. Preheat the oven to 450°F.

2. Rinse and coarsely chop the onions, celery, carrots, tomatoes, parsnips, and leeks. Place them in the bottom of a roasting pan, add the garlic, and arrange the meat and bones over the top. Bake uncovered for 1 hour.

3. Remove the meat, bones, and vegetables to a very large soup pot.

4. Pour 1 quart of the water into the roasting pan and bring to a hard boil over high heat, scraping up any browned bits on the bottom of the pan. Pour it into the soup pot and add the remaining 3 quarts of water as well.

5. Add the peppercorns, cloves, thyme, and bay leaf. Bring to a boil, skimming off any foam that rises to the surface. Reduce the heat to medium-low and simmer, partially covered, for 2 hours. Uncover and simmer 1 hour more. Halfway through the cooking time, add salt to taste.

6. Remove the meat and bones, then strain the broth and let cool to room temperature. (The vegetables will have given much of their flavor to the broth, but can be enjoyed as a purée or used puréed to thicken soups and stew sauces. The meat, too, is good with freshly steamed potatoes and carrots, and a pungent horseradish sauce.)

7. Transfer the broth to a storage container and refrigerate covered. Remove and discard the hardened layer of fat from the top before using. Use the broth within 3 to 4 days or freeze in 8-ounce containers for up to 3 months.

Makes 5 cups

FRESH VEGETABLE BROTH

When a vegetable soup or stew calls for vegetable broth, it should be an intensely flavored alternative to chicken and beef broth. For nutritional value, flavor, and color, I've added all the vegetables unpeeled to the pot and slowly simmered the broth, uncovered, over low heat. Parsnips, tomatoes, and carrots add a rich sweetness. Once the broth is strained and cooled, it freezes beautifully for up to 3 months.

1 medium onion, peels left on, studded with 4 whole cloves
2 cloves garlic, peels left on and lightly bruised (page 153)
2 ribs celery with leaves, cut into large chunks
2 carrots, peels left on and cut into large chunks
2 leeks, trimmed and cut into large chunks
8 white mushrooms, halved
2 medium tomatoes, quartered
4 medium new red potatoes, halved
8 parsley sprigs
2 fresh dill sprigs
1 bay leaf
8 black peppercorns
1 teaspoon coarse salt
10 cups water

1. Rinse all the vegetables well. Place all the broth ingredients in a large heavy pot. Bring to a boil, reduce the heat, and simmer uncovered for 1 hour. Adjust the seasonings to taste and simmer for 30 minutes longer.

2. Strain the broth, reserving the vegetables for a purée to eat as is or to thicken soups and stew sauces. Let the broth cool to room temperature, then refrigerate covered in a storage container or freeze. Refrigerated it will keep about 4 days. This recipe may be doubled.

Makes 4 cups

FISH STOCK

Fish stock is easy to make and I recommend cooking up a flavorful batch and keeping it on hand in the freezer. I find that 8-ounce plastic containers are the most convenient size for use in most recipes.

2 to 2½ pounds fish trimmings (heads, tails, and bones)
2 medium onions, quartered
2 medium carrots, coarsely chopped
2 ribs celery with leaves, coarsely chopped
4 white mushrooms, wiped, cleaned and quartered
6 flat-leaf parsley sprigs
2 fresh thyme sprigs
6 black peppercorns
6 cups water
2 cups dry white wine

1. Rinse the fish trimmings well in several changes of water until the water runs clear. Place them and all the remaining ingredients in a large heavy pot. Bring to a boil, reduce the heat, and simmer uncovered for 25 minutes.

2. Remove the fish trimmings and flavoring vegetables with a slotted spoon and discard. Cool the stock slightly and strain through a double thickness of cheesecloth.

3. Cool the broth to room temperature. Refrigerate covered for up to 2 days or freeze in 8-ounce containers for up to 3 months.

Makes 6 cups

LAMB STOCK

Ever wonder what to do with the bone from a leg of lamb? When I was in Russia, I tasted a deep amber broth dappled with tomatoes, beets, herbs, and millet. The base of the soup was a rich lamb stock, completely defatted and quite delicious. To begin, I roasted the bone from a 6- to 7-pound leg of lamb atop a bed of vegetables, discarded the fat, combined the ingredients in a soup pot, and proceeded. This flavorful stock is a lovely base for soups and stews and freezes well.

4 ribs celery with leaves, halved
2 carrots, peels left on and halved
2 parsnips, peels left on and halved
2 large onions, cut into 8 pieces each, peel left on
4 cloves garlic, peel left on and halved
1 bone from a roasted 6- to 7-pound leg of lamb, or about 2½ pounds of other roasted lamb bones
10 cups water
8 fresh thyme sprigs
4 parsley sprigs
8 black peppercorns
4 whole cloves
Salt, to taste

1. Preheat the oven to 400°F.

2. Rinse the celery, carrots, and parsnips well, then spread them along with the onions and garlic in the bottom of a shallow roasting pan large enough to hold the lamb bone. Place the bone atop the vegetables and bake uncovered for 1 hour.

3. Remove the bone and vegetables to a large soup pot. Pour off any fat in the roasting pan and add 4 cups of the water. Place the pan over high heat and bring to a boil, scraping up any brown bits in the bottom of the pan. Add this liquid to the soup pot.

4. Add the remaining 6 cups water to the soup pot along with the thyme, parsley, peppercorns, and cloves. Slowly bring to a boil, skimming off any foam that rises to the surface. Reduce the heat to low and simmer partially covered for 1½ hours. Season with salt.

5. Strain the stock and discard the solids. Let cool to room temperature, then refrigerate overnight in a covered container. Remove the hardened layer of fat that has formed on the top and discard it before you use the stock or before you freeze it. Refrigerated it will keep for 3 to 4 days; frozen up to 3 months.

Makes 4 cups

HEARTY IRISH BEEF SOUP

Beef marrow bones encased in tender meat lend their pungent flavor to this soup. Once the meat has been cooked and shredded back into the soup, it becomes more of a stew, perfect for serving on cold winter nights. After shredding the meat from the bones, scoop the marrow out onto a slice of toasted peasant bread—this is the cook's treat. For the soup, bake up a loaf of Irish Soda Bread (see Index) and serve it along with a large wedge of tangy Cheddar cheese for a memorable feast.

8 ounces dried baby lima beans
3 pounds beef marrow bones with meat, cut 1 inch thick
5 quarts water
1 teaspoon coarse salt
½ teaspoon coarsely ground black pepper
2 cups coarsely chopped onions
5 cloves garlic, thinly slivered
2 leeks, trimmed, rinsed well, and coarsely chopped
2 cups coarsely chopped celery
2 small parsnips, peeled and coarsely chopped
2 cups coarsely chopped carrots
1 can (28 ounces) plum tomatoes
8 fresh thyme sprigs
1 bay leaf
4 cups cabbage cut into 1-inch pieces
8 ounces green beans, cut into ½-inch pieces
½ cup coarsely chopped flat-leaf parsley

1. Place the lima beans in a bowl, cover with water, and soak overnight.

2. Rinse the beef bones under cold water. Place them in a large soup pot and add the water. Bring to a boil, skimming off any foam that rises to the top. Add the salt and pepper. Reduce the heat and simmer, partially covered, for 1 hour.

3. Drain the lima beans and add them to the pot along with the onions, garlic, leeks, celery, parsnips, carrots, tomatoes, thyme, and bay leaf. Simmer partially covered for 2 hours.

4. Add the cabbage and green beans. Simmer uncovered for another 45 minutes.

5. Remove the meat bones from the pot. Shred the meat from the bones. Discard the bones and return the meat to the pot. Stir in the parsley and simmer uncovered an additional 5 minutes. Adjust the seasonings and serve hot.

Serves 8 to 10

MALAY OXTAIL SOUP

Aziza Ali created one of Singapore's first Malay restaurants, Aziza's, and it was with great pride that she regaled us with fascinating stories about her native cuisine.

Her rich oxtail soup was one of my favorite dishes, although if it is not your favorite meat, short ribs may be substituted. The clear beef broth is infused twice in this preparation. The first infusion is with cinnamon, cilantro, cumin, chilies, and other perfumed spices. The broth is then strained and cooked again with freshly slivered ginger, garlic, and fresh cilantro leaves. I love this soup served over very thin noodles.

1 oxtail (2 to 2½ pounds), cut into 2-inch pieces
1 medium onion, halved, peel left on
4 cloves garlic, lightly bruised (page 153) and peeled
3 fresh cilantro sprigs, roots and stems lightly crushed
1 cinnamon stick (3 inches long)
1 teaspoon ground cumin
½ teaspoon whole coriander seeds
1 dried red chili
4 cups defatted Rich Beef Broth (page 128)
Salt and freshly ground black pepper, to taste
3 tablespoons finely slivered peeled fresh ginger, cut into 1-inch lengths
1 tablespoon finely slivered garlic
½ cup coarsely chopped fresh cilantro leaves
2 cups cooked angel hair pasta or pearl barley (optional)

1. Place the oxtail, onion, garlic, cilantro sprigs, cinnamon stick, cumin, coriander, and chili in a heavy soup pot. Add the broth and water to cover the ingredients by 1½ inches.

2. Bring just to a boil, reduce the heat, and simmer covered for 1¼ hours, skimming any foam that rises to the surface. Season with salt and pepper and cook uncovered for another 15 minutes. The oxtail should be very tender. (If you substitute short ribs of beef, the cooking time will be about 30 minutes longer.) Remove from the heat. Remove the oxtail and shred the meat from the bones, discarding the bones and any fat. Cover the meat and set aside.

3. Strain the broth twice through a very fine strainer. Cool for at least 1 hour so that the fat rises to the top. Skim off all the fat and discard. (The recipe can be made up to this point 1 day ahead. Refrigerate the broth overnight and skim the fat from the surface before proceeding with the recipe. Refrigerate the meat as well.)

4. Return the broth to the soup pot. Add the ginger and slivered garlic. Bring to a boil, reduce the heat, and simmer for 10 minutes. Return the shredded meat to the broth and cook another 5 minutes. Stir in the cilantro and cook 1 minute longer.

5. Divide the pasta or barley between 8 soup bowls and ladle the hot soup atop. Serve immediately.

Serves 8

Note: Because the flavor is very rich, I recommend small servings.

HOT RUSSIAN BORSCHT

In Russia, there are endless borscht variations depending on available ingredients, regional preferences, and personal taste. Some are made from just beet broth and finely chopped herbs, some with lots of lard, and others with cooked white beans—just to name a few. Succulent short ribs of beef, a rich broth, and roasted beets are the basis for my luscious hearty take on this soup. I find experimenting with the contrast of sweet and savory tastes to be the challenge and the fun. Tomatoes and parsnips sweeten the broth while it simmers. Sweet potatoes add their unique and delicate flavor. Lemon juice, to your taste, creates the contrast and balance. Fresh herbs and garlic added just before serving brighten the flavors, and a dollop of cold sour cream is an ideal garnish. Russians like garlic, and they will often serve pungent garlic croutons alongside hot borscht. For a complete meal, have a bowl of kasha for each person and plenty of black bread and sweet butter on the table.

2¼ to 2½ pounds beef short ribs
1 onion, peel left on and halved
2 ribs celery with leaves, halved
1 carrot, quartered
1 parsnip, quartered
4 fresh dill sprigs
4 cups defatted Rich Beef Broth (page 128)
4 cups water
1¼ pounds raw beets with stems
2 sweet potatoes (about 1 pound), peeled and cut into ½-inch cubes
4 cups thinly slivered green cabbage
4 to 6 tablespoons fresh lemon juice
½ teaspoon caraway seeds
Salt and freshly ground black pepper, to taste
¼ cup chopped fresh dill leaves and stems
¼ cup chopped flat-leaf parsley
1 teaspoon minced garlic
1 cup sour cream, for garnish

1. Preheat the oven to 350°F.

2. Place the beef, onion, celery, carrot, parsnip, and dill sprigs in a large soup pot. Add the broth and water. Bring slowly to a boil, reduce the heat, and simmer covered until the beef is very tender, about 1½ hours, skimming off any foam that rises to the top. Remove the short ribs and set aside to cool.

3. While the broth is cooking, rinse the beets well and trim the stems to 1 inch. Wrap individually in aluminum foil and bake until tender, 1 to 1½ hours, depending on size. Wearing thin rubber gloves if you don't want to dye your hands, slip the skins off the beets and coarsely grate. Set aside.

4. Strain the broth, cool slightly, and skim off any fat that rises to the top. Return the defatted broth to a clean soup pot. Shred the meat from the bones, discarding the bones and any fat; set aside.

5. Add the sweet potatoes to the broth. Partially cover the pot and bring to a boil over medium heat. Add the cabbage and cook, partially covered, 5 minutes. Reduce the heat to a simmer and add the meat, beets, lemon juice to taste, caraway seeds, salt, and pepper. Simmer another 5 minutes.

6. Just before serving, stir in the dill, parsley, and garlic and simmer for 1 minute. Serve piping hot, garnished with a dollop of sour cream.

Serves 8

THE BEERS OF

China and Japan

Brewing dates to the mid-1800s in China and Japan, and the arrival of the German Navy to the Chinese port of Tsingtao and Commodore Perry's American Navy to Japan in 1853.

Pilsener and German-style lagers, well-flavored with imported hops, are most prevalent in both countries. Americans are most familiar with Tsingtao (pronounced Ching-dow), an excellent Pilsener made in the port town of the same name on the Shantung peninsula, a beer now widely available in the United States.

Most cities of any size in China today have a brewery, but the Chinese thirst for beer has increased tremendously in recent decades. In fact, several Western countries, such as Great Britain and Germany, have teamed with local companies to produce dark and light beers.

Kirin, an American favorite, but seek out the new greats from Asia.

Kirin, Japan's first brew, was produced by American brewers but eventually passed into Japanese control and became an international favorite. The kirin is a mythical beast, half horse and half dragon, that supposedly sired the great Chinese sage Confucius. Kirin is Japan's largest brewer, with several breweries situated around the islands. Though best known for its hoppy Pilsener-style lager, Kirin also produces a strong, dark lager known as Black Beer, and a hearty stout.

Sapporo, Asahi, and Suntory also have large breweries, producing somewhat milder, less hoppy lagers. Asahi, however, is responsible for launching a new beer style in the 80s, the brisk light Super Dry, that has since prompted a global wave of crisp "dry" beers noted for little or no aftertaste.

Japanese beers are the

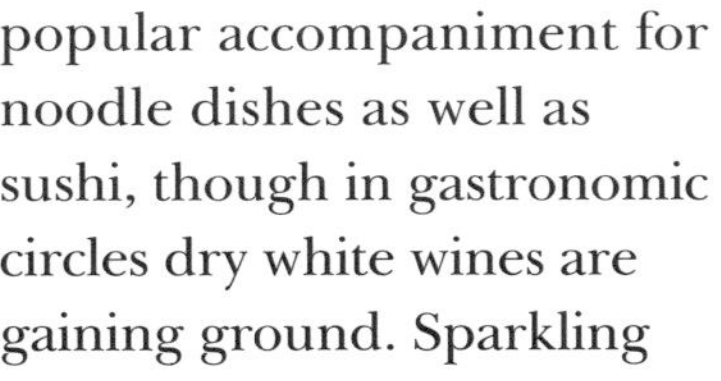

popular accompaniment for noodle dishes as well as sushi, though in gastronomic circles dry white wines are gaining ground. Sparkling wines in particular are considered good partners for sushi because they are better able than still wine to handle the formidable green horseradish known as wasabi that accompanies it.

> *"Japanese beers are the popular accompaniment for noodle dishes as well as sushi, though in gastronomic circles dry white wines are gaining ground."*

The notion that beer is the best (or only) accompaniment to Chinese food is an insult to the intricacies of this ancient and complex cuisine. There are numerous wines better suited to certain dishes than beer, even the best beer. Dry Riesling is superb with many fish specialties, even those flavored with ginger, and excellent, too, with deep-fried fish or chicken (though not sweet and sour versions, where beer is indeed a better choice). Pinot Gris (and Italian Pinot Grigio) are also versatile with a variety of fish, chicken, and vegetarian dishes. Pinot Noir, Merlot, and Syrah (or Australian Shiraz) make excellent companions for Chinese roast duck or squab.

Even the Chinese seem to recognize that wine can bring out the best in food and have begun to grow and produce wine on a limited basis. Recent plantings of wine grapes near Beijing and in western regions show some promise, and others are being explored. Japan also produces wine, but so far it is uneven in quality and style.

The tops of the hops!

ELLEN'S HOT AND SOUR SOUP

My great friend Ellen White, long past chef of The Silver Palate kitchens, always made a great hot and sour soup. This popular Szechuan recipe, brimming with vegetables, is both light and satisfying. The soup is seasoned with hot chili oil to suit my palate, but more may be gingerly added if you prefer the soup more fiery. Rice wine vinegar adds a mellow bite to the soup, but white wine vinegar will add a bit more punch. Enoki mushrooms add a crisp texture and delicate flavor to the soup. If you cannot find them, thinly slivered fresh white mushrooms are an acceptable substitute.

8 cups defatted Chicken Broth (page 127)
1 ounce dried shiitake mushrooms, rinsed well
½ cup rice wine vinegar
⅓ cup soy sauce
3 scallions (3 inches green left on), finely julienned
1 small carrot, peeled and finely julienned
2 ounces snow peas, finely julienned
¼ cup bamboo shoots, finely julienned
4 cloves garlic, minced
1 tablespoon minced peeled fresh ginger
4 ounces shrimp, peeled, deveined, and coarsely chopped
8 ounces pork tenderloin or boned pork chops, coarsely chopped
½ teaspoon hot chili oil, or more to taste
¼ cup cornstarch
1 ounce enoki mushrooms, stems trimmed, or 4 ounces white mushrooms, cleaned, stems trimmed, and thinly slivered
8 ounces fresh bean curd, cut into ¼-inch cubes
½ cup cooked peas
Salt to taste
Crispy fried noodles, for garnish

1. Bring 2 cups of the chicken broth to a boil in a small saucepan. Add the shiitake mushrooms and remove from the heat. Let stand for 1 hour.

2. Drain the shiitake mushrooms, straining the liquid through a fine mesh sieve lined with cheesecloth and set aside. Remove and discard the tough stems and thinly slice the mushroom caps. Refrigerate the reserved liquid until slightly chilled.

3. In a soup pot, combine the remaining 6 cups chicken broth, the vinegar, and soy sauce and bring to a boil. Add the shiitake mushrooms, scallions, carrot, snow peas, bamboo shoots, garlic, ginger, shrimp, and pork. Return the soup to a boil, then reduce the heat and simmer gently for 8 minutes.

4. Combine the chilled liquid from the shiitake mushrooms with the chili oil and cornstarch. Slowly add it to the soup, while stirring gently.

5. Add the enoki mushrooms, bean curd, and peas. Simmer, stirring constantly, until the soup thickens slightly, about 2 minutes. Season with salt to taste. Serve garnished with crispy fried noodles.

Makes 12 cups, enough to serve 8

HARIRA SOUP

My version of *harira,* while still robust, is a bit more delicate than the authentic Moroccan mutton-flavored soup. Accompanied by a thick slice of peasant bread topped with roasted tomatoes, the soup will provide a most satisfying meal.

SOUVENIR TO SAVOR

A Step Back in Time

Walking through Djemaa el Fna, the intoxicating open square bordering the old walled city of Marrakech, is either like touring Cecil B. DeMille's movie set for *The Ten Commandments* or stepping into another world, a few centuries back in time. The square is medieval in feeling, vibrating with the traditional sights, smells, and sounds of Morocco. Snake charmers vie for attention alongside acrobats, musicians, and vendors selling everything from *djellabas* (caftans) and baskets to richly patterned rugs. Here's where some of the best street foods I've ever tasted anywhere is sold.

To make the scene even more magical, smoke is ever present, rising above grills charring spicy sausages, fish, and chicken alongside perfumed tagines. Tables are laid with olives in every hue from purple to red brown to green, all lavishly coated in peppers and spices.

Brilliant red chilies with a few green leaves still on the stems rest abundantly on a patterned turquoise cloth. Alongside, a pot of boiling potatoes wait to be chopped and scooped into round Arabic breads along with hard-cooked eggs and a drizzle of hot oil. Long tables covered in paper offer up glazed ceramic bowls of *harira,* a chicken, lamb, vegetable, and legume soup. Beside each bowl rests a small square of paper with about 6 plump dried dates to eat along with the soup. Sometimes I wonder if the Moroccan sense of color wouldn't give Matisse a run for his money.

1 chicken (3½ to 4 pounds) with giblets (not the liver), cut into 10 serving pieces (not counting wing tips and back; reserve for another use), rinsed and patted dry
1¾ pounds lamb shoulder on the bone, cut into 3-inch pieces
2 tablespoons olive oil
2 medium onions, coarsely chopped
4 ribs celery with leaves, cut into ½-inch dice
2 cloves garlic, minced
½ teaspoon ground ginger
½ teaspoon salt
¼ teaspoon freshly ground black pepper
¼ teaspoon crushed saffron threads
1 cinnamon stick (3 inches long)
8 cups defatted Chicken Broth (page 127)
1 can (28 ounces) plum tomatoes, drained and crushed
8 flat-leaf parsley sprigs, stems lightly crushed
½ cup (4 ounces) dried red lentils, rinsed
1 can (15½ ounces) chickpeas (garbanzo beans), drained and rinsed
½ cup small macaroni, such as ditalini
3 tablespoons fresh lemon juice
½ cup chopped flat-leaf parsley

1. Preheat the oven to 400°F.

2. Place the chicken, giblets, and lamb in a small, shallow roasting pan. Bake for 15 minutes just to sear the meat. Let cool slightly, then discard any fat in the pan.

3. Heat the olive oil in a large heavy pot over medium heat. Add the onions and celery and cook, stirring, until the onions are slightly wilted, 5 minutes. Add the garlic, and cook until lightly golden, 5 minutes longer. Add the ginger, salt, pepper, saffron and cinnamon stick; toss to coat the vegetables. Cook, stirring, for 1 minute.

4. Add the seared meat, the chicken broth, tomatoes, parsley sprigs, and lentils. Bring to a boil, reduce the heat to medium-low, and cook covered for 30 minutes. Add the chickpeas and cook uncovered over medium-low heat for 20 minutes. Increase the heat to medium and add the macaroni; cook for 10 minutes. The lentils and macaroni should be soft.

5. Remove the chicken, chicken giblets, and lamb and cool slightly. Remove and discard the parsley sprigs and cinnamon stick.

6. When the meat is cool enough to handle, shred the chicken from the bones, discarding the skin. Chop the giblets. Shred the lamb from the bones. Return the shredded chicken and lamb to the soup.

7. Before serving, heat the soup through and adjust the seasonings. Stir in the lemon juice and parsley and serve immediately.

Serves 8 to 10

COCK-A-LEEKIE SOUP

Scottish Chicken, Leek, and Barley Soup

This is one of Scotland's most comforting soups and is rich enough to be a one-dish meal if served with coarse brown bread and a sharp Cheddar cheese. One of the original versions was cooked with prunes and served as a stew. If you'd like to add prunes, which will thicken the broth and sweeten it a bit, add ½ cup coarsely chopped pitted prunes after 45 minutes of cooking. If the soup seems too thick, it may be necessary to add more liquid as it cooks. I would suggest a bit of chicken broth.

8 large leeks (about 3 pounds), 3 inches green left on
2 tablespoons vinegar
1 chicken (about 3½ pounds), quartered
6 medium carrots, cut on the diagonal into 1-inch pieces
¾ cup pearl barley
6 black peppercorns
4 whole cloves
3 quarts water
Salt and coarsely ground black pepper, to taste
5 tablespoons chopped flat-leaf parsley

1. Trim the roots from the leeks and cut a 2-inch-deep X in the white end. Cut an X in each green end to just above the white bulb. Place in a large bowl with the vinegar and cover with cold water. Let soak for 30 to 40 minutes. Rinse well under cold running water. Cut on the diagonal into 1-inch pieces.

2. Rinse the chicken well and remove any

excess fat. Place the chicken in a large soup pot and add the leeks, carrots, barley, peppercorns, and cloves. Cover with the 3 quarts water and season with salt and pepper.

3. Bring to a boil, skimming off any foam that rises to the top. Reduce the heat to medium and simmer, partially covered, until the chicken is cooked through, about 1 hour. Stir occasionally and add more water or chicken broth if necessary.

4. Remove the chicken to a plate and let stand until cool enough to handle. Remove the skin and bones, shred the meat, and return the meat to the pot along with 4 tablespoons of the parsley. Adjust the seasonings.

5. Serve in large ceramic soup bowls. Sprinkle with the remaining tablespoon of chopped parsley.

Serves 8

MULLIGATAWNY SOUP

This famous Indian soup was originally developed by cooks who served in English homes during the period of India's colonization in the 18th century. Originally mulligatawny was made with peppers, hence its name, derived from the word *mullaga*—pepper. The soup was adjusted and modified to suit Western tastes so that over the years it changed greatly from chef to chef. In the latter half of this century, its mild curry flavor has made it delicate and pleasing enough to have won it accolades at many ladies' luncheons across America.

I have made my version with fresh chicken for a rich broth and infused it with celery, carrots, onions, ginger, and garlic. Apples and tomato add a sweet depth of flavor. While a good-quality curry powder is acceptable for this soup, I've combined a mixture of cloves, coriander, turmeric, and cayenne. The addition of coconut milk towards the end of cooking gives the soup its luscious velvety consistency. A dollop of cool yogurt and a sprinkle of tomatoes and parsley just before serving adds a fresh brightness.

1 chicken (2½ to 3 pounds), cut into 8 pieces
1 large onion, peeled
8 whole cloves
3 ribs celery with leaves, halved
2 carrots, peeled and halved
2 ripe plum tomatoes, halved
1 Granny Smith apple, quartered and cored
6 cloves garlic, peeled
1 piece (2 inches) fresh ginger, peeled
4 flat-leaf parsley sprigs
1 bay leaf
½ teaspoon salt
6 black peppercorns
10 cups water
½ cup yellow split peas
1 tablespoon unsalted butter
1 teaspoon ground coriander
½ teaspoon ground turmeric
¼ teaspoon ground cloves
Pinch of cayenne pepper
½ cup coconut milk (page 252 or available in specialty food stores)
½ cup nonfat plain yogurt, for garnish
3 ripe plum tomatoes, seeded and cut into ¼-inch dice, for garnish
2 tablespoons chopped flat-leaf parsley, for garnish

1. Rinse the chicken pieces well and place them in a large heavy pot.

2. Stud the onion with the cloves and add it to the chicken along with the celery, carrots, tomatoes, apple, garlic, ginger, parsley, bay leaf, salt, and peppercorns.

3. Cover with the water and bring to a boil over medium-high heat, skimming the foam as it rises to the top. Reduce the heat to medium and simmer until the chicken is cooked through, about 45 minutes. Remove the chicken pieces from the broth and let stand until cool enough to handle. Remove the skin and shred the chicken meat from the bones. Place the chicken in a bowl, cover, and refrigerate until ready to use.

4. Remove and discard the cloves from the onion; discard the bay leaf. Return the onion to the soup. Add the split peas to the soup and cook, partially covered, over medium heat until the peas have blended into the soup, about 1½ hours.

5. While the soup is cooking, melt the butter in a small skillet over low heat. Add the coriander, turmeric, cloves, and cayenne. Cook, stirring constantly, for 1 minute to mellow the spices and bring out the flavors. Add to the soup and cook to integrate the flavors, 5 minutes more.

6. Remove the soup from the heat and purée it in a food processor or blender in small batches until smooth. Return it to the pot.

7. Whisk in the coconut milk, stir in the chicken, and adjust the seasonings to taste.

8. To serve, heat the soup through over low heat. Serve in shallow soup bowls, garnished with a dollop of yogurt and sprinkled with the chopped tomatoes and parsley.

Serves 6

WORLD–CLASS

Chicken Soup

Have you ever looked at a steaming pot of homemade chicken soup and thought it could be even better? Actually it's very easy to transform Mom's treasured soup recipe into a Mexican fiesta, a Turkish thrill, or a Singapore sensation. First decide what you're in the mood for, then choose the flavoring palette from your desired country and begin with your basic recipe. The following chart shows what ingredients can be added, and when, to your simmering broth to give it a new national identity.

Starters give the initial flavor to a great pot of chicken soup and remain essentially the same throughout the world. On the other hand, the vegetables you add will vary greatly according to cultural preference. In Russia, you would rarely come upon a pot of any soup without some cabbage, potatoes, or beets, while in Mexico or Chile, corn and tomatoes are essential. Spices should be added early—before the liquid—in order to mellow their flavors. As you can imagine, these too vary from country to country. Chilies are found in soups from Southeast Asia to India, while a cinnamon stick would never be left out of North Africa's finest pots. When it comes to thickeners, noodles, rice, and beans show up in endless variety and are used worldwide to add lushness and body to a broth. Fresh herbs are a must in chicken broth, and depending on the amounts used, will add a delicate essence or a powerful punch. For instance, dill used in a Turkish soup will take on a totally different character than dill used more frugally in Russian kitchens.

For a final touch as a soup finishes cooking, you can do as the Chinese do and sprinkle in a little chili oil or as the Spanish do and drizzle in a little dry sherry. Then garnish with a flourish and you've got a world-class chicken soup.

	STARTERS & ✿ VEGETABLES	SPICES	THICKENERS	HERBS	SPARKLERS	GARNISHES
JAPANESE	garlic, ginger ✿ shiitake mushrooms		rice, noodles	chives	rice vinegar, soy sauce	scallions, tofu, chives, cress
CHINESE	garlic, ginger ✿ shiitake mushrooms, snow peas, bok choy, mung bean sprouts	chilies	bean curd, noodles	cilantro	chili oil, sesame oil, soy sauce, scallions	scallions, chives, crispy noodles
INDONESIAN	garlic, ginger ✿ tomatoes	chilies	thin noodles	lemongrass, basil, mint	lime juice	hard-cooked eggs, toasted coconut, cilantro, mung bean sprouts, fried shallots
SOUTHEAST ASIAN	garlic, ginger, onions ✿ mung bean sprouts, scallions, mushrooms	chilies	noodles	coriander, mint	fish sauce, coconut milk, lime juice	coconut milk, hard-cooked eggs, cilantro fried shallots
RUSSIAN	onions, garlic ✿ wild mushrooms, beets, cabbage, celery root	caraway seeds, dill seeds	potatoes, apples, barley	dill, parsley	lemon juice	hard-cooked eggs, garlic croutons, sour cream
HUNGARIAN	onions, garlic, bacon ✿ parsnips, mushrooms, green bell peppers, cabbage	paprika	spaetzle, noodles, dumplings	dill, marjoram, parsley		sour cream
SCANDINAVIAN	✿ red cabbage, mushrooms, beets		potatoes	tarragon, dill, chives		
INDIAN	onions, garlic, ginger ✿ tomatoes, spinach, apples, cauliflower	chilies, curry powder, turmeric, cinnamon sticks, cloves	lentils	mint, cilantro	lime juice	yogurt, coconut milk, toasted coconut
MEXICAN	onions, garlic ✿ corn, tomatoes, red bell peppers	cinnamon, cumin, red chilies	beans, rice	cilantro, thyme, oregano	lime juice slivered corn tortillas	avocado, scallions,
CHILEAN	onions, garlic ✿ corn, fava beans, tomatoes		rice	basil, cilantro	orange juice	avocado
BRAZILIAN	garlic, scallions ✿ butternut squash, collard greens		rice, black beans	cilantro	lime juice	pineapple

	STARTERS & ✿ VEGETABLES	SPICES	THICKENERS	HERBS	SPARKLERS	GARNISHES
ARGENTINEAN	onions, garlic ✿ carrots, tomatoes, butternut squash, escarole	chilies, cumin	rice, chickpeas			chorizo, almonds, olive oil
CARIBBEAN	garlic, ginger ✿ okra, collard greens, tomatoes	chilies, allspice, curry powder	sweet potatoes, red beans	mint, cilantro	lime juice, pineapple	bananas, toasted coconut, avocado
PORTUGUESE	onions, garlic, cured ham ✿ potatoes	chilies		cilantro		extra virgin olive oil, cilantro, hard-cooked eggs, orange zest
SPANISH	onions, garlic ✿ bell peppers	saffron, paprika, cinnamon	rice, beans	parsley	sherry, orange juice	orange zest
FRENCH	onions, garlic ✿ carrots, Swiss chard, peas, green beans		potatoes, dried beans	chervil, basil, tarragon, chives, flat-leaf parsley		pistou (pesto), crème fraîche, croutons, Gruyère cheese
ITALIAN	onions, garlic, pancetta ✿ Swiss chard, tomatoes	dried oregano, dried red chilies	pasta, cannellini beans	basil, flat-leaf parsley		Parmesan cheese, extra virgin olive oil
BRITISH	onions ✿ leeks, mushrooms, parsnips, Brussels sprouts		barley	dill	sherry	cress
TURKISH	onions, garlic ✿ tomatoes, green beans	dried oregano, dried thyme	white beans, rice	dill	lemon juice	yogurt
GREEK	onions, garlic ✿ tomatoes, spinach, zucchini	dried thyme	rice, beans, lentils	mint, flat-leaf parsley	lemon juice, honey	extra virgin olive oil, yogurt, Kasseri cheese
TUNISIAN	onions, garlic ✿ okra, bell peppers, tomatoes, turnips, leeks	cumin	chickpeas, potatoes	mint	lemon juice	hard-cooked eggs
MOROCCAN	onions, garlic ✿ yams, tomatoes, carrots, turnips, zucchini	cinnamon sticks, cloves, cumin	chickpeas, prunes, dates	mint, cilantro	*harissa*, lemon juice	hard-cooked eggs

CHILEAN CORN AND CHICKEN CHOWDER

I was visiting Chile in February, which was during their summer, and the sweet white corn was in season. They don't serve corn on the cob but instead use it in favorite dishes, such as the specialty, *pastel de choclo*. Here the corn is cooked and stirred for hours with an abundance of sugar to make the "crust" layers that rest over an empanada-like filling.

For those of us not quite ready to spend hours at the stove in the summer, I've made a light summer chowder from the basic *pastel* ingredients. Start with a chowder of chicken, corn, and potatoes. Fresh tomatoes, velvety avocado, lime juice, and parsley stirred in just before serving add a fresh garden smoothness any time of year.

BROTH:

1 small chicken (about 2¼ pounds), cut into 8 pieces, rinsed well
1 onion, peel left on and halved
1 rib celery with leaves
1 carrot, halved
2 cloves garlic
8 flat-leaf parsley sprigs
6 black peppercorns
1 bay leaf
1 large fresh thyme sprig
Salt, to taste

CHOWDER:

4 ounces slab bacon, rind removed, cut into ¼-inch dice
1 medium onion, peeled and cut into ¼-inch dice
3 tablespoons all-purpose flour
1 pound Idaho potatoes, peeled and cut into ¼-inch dice
2 tablespoons chopped fresh thyme leaves or 1 teaspoon dried
1 cup half-and-half
3 cups corn kernels, preferably fresh (about 3 ears)
Salt and coarsely ground black pepper, to taste
4 ripe plum tomatoes, peeled, seeded, and cut into very small dice
1 avocado, preferably Haas, pitted, peeled, and cut into small dice
1 teaspoon fresh lime juice, or more to taste
¼ cup coarsely chopped flat-leaf parsley

1. For the broth, place the chicken pieces and remaining broth ingredients except the salt in a large heavy pot. Add just enough water to cover (about 2 quarts). Bring to a low boil, reduce the heat to medium-low, and simmer, partially covered, skimming any foam, for 30 minutes. Salt the broth to taste and continue to cook uncovered until the chicken is cooked through, 20 minutes longer.

2. Remove the chicken from the broth and let stand until cool enough to handle. Discard the skin and shred the meat from the bones. Place the chicken in a bowl, cover, and refrigerate until ready to use. Strain the broth and measure 6 cups for the chowder. Refrigerate or freeze the remaining broth for another use.

3. For the chowder, wilt the bacon in a large heavy pot over low heat until it gives off its fat, about 5 minutes. Add the onion and cook, stirring, until wilted, another 10 minutes. Do not brown.

4. Sprinkle in the flour and cook, stirring constantly, another 5 minutes.

5. Add the reserved broth and stir until blended with the flour. Add the potatoes and thyme. Cook, stirring occasionally, over medium-low heat until the potatoes are just tender, about 10 minutes.

6. Off the heat, stir in the half-and-half, corn, and shredded chicken. Cook, stirring, over low heat for 5 minutes. Season generously with salt and pepper.

7. Before serving, reheat the soup over low heat. Stir in the tomatoes, avocado, lime juice, and parsley and serve immediately.

Serves 8

SOUVENIR TO SAVOR

Nonya and Baba

Close to 200 years ago, men seeking fortune and adventure set sail off the coast of southern China en route to Malaysia. Happy with what was found, these Chinese men married Malaysian women and became integrated in a unique society. Today the mingling of these two worlds is known as the Peranakan culture. The women are the Nonya and the men, the Baba. The basis of their cuisine is Chinese, yet the Nonya influence predominates. The Malaysian women added their rich collections of spices, herbs, and roots—the mainstays of the Nonya kitchen—where chili pastes and garlic abound. The scope of flavor was further influenced by Thai, Indian, and Indonesian ingredients. The hot and spicy Nonya kitchen results in a most intriguing cuisine.

SOTO BANJAR

Indonesian Chicken Noodle Soup

If I had just one word with which to describe Indonesian soups, I think "perfumed" would be my choice. Although each region of Indonesia has its specialties, I came across one in particular that I love, *soto banjar,* from the capital of South Kalimantan, Banjarmasin, in southern Borneo. Both cinnamon and cardamom are essential ingredients to this regional style of cooking. In addition to the wonderful flavors, the arrangement of the prepared ingredients—chicken, potatoes, thin noodles, and hard-cooked eggs—garnished with crispy shallots and garlic, celery leaves and a slice of lime, is decorative and perfectly suited for either a very special first course or a cozy family dinner. Since the whole meal is presented in one large shallow bowl, this dish would be lovely to eat gathered around a blazing fire.

4 cups defatted Chicken Broth (page 127)
3 cups water
4 large flat-leaf parsley sprigs
2 fresh cilantro sprigs, roots and stems slightly crushed
1 whole chicken breast (1 to 1¼ pounds), rinsed well
3 medium boiling potatoes (about 12 ounces), peeled and cut into ½-inch cubes
4 ounces shallots, peeled
4 large cloves garlic, peeled
3 tablespoons olive oil
1 tablespoon minced peeled fresh ginger
1 teaspoon ground cardamom
1 cinnamon stick (3 inches long)
Coarse salt and freshly ground black pepper, to taste
2 cups cooked angel hair pasta
3 hard-cooked eggs, peeled and quartered
¼ cup chopped green celery leaves or fresh cilantro leaves
1 lime, thinly sliced

1. Combine the chicken broth, water, and parsley and cilantro sprigs in a medium-size soup pot. Bring to a boil and add the chicken breast. Reduce the heat and simmer, partially covered, until the chicken is just cooked through, about 30 minutes. Remove the chicken and let cool slightly. Shred the meat from the bones in 1½ x ½-inch pieces, discarding the skin and bones. Set aside covered.

2. Strain the broth and return it to the pot. Add the potatoes to the broth.

3. Cut half the shallots and half the garlic lengthwise into very thin slices. Heat the oil in a medium-size nonstick skillet over low heat. Add the sliced shallots and garlic and cook, stirring, until lightly golden and crisp, about 10 minutes. Remove with a slotted spoon to a paper towel to drain. Reserve for garnish.

4. Finely mince the remaining shallots and garlic and the ginger together with the cardamom. Add to the skillet and cook uncovered, stirring, over low heat until aromatic, 3 to 4 minutes. Add this mixture to the broth along with the cinnamon stick, salt, and pepper. Cook covered over medium heat until the potatoes are tender, 12 to 15 minutes. Remove the potatoes from the broth with a slotted spoon.

5. To assemble, lay out 4 to 6 shallow soup or pasta bowls. Arrange the chicken, pasta, eggs, and potatoes in sections in each bowl, so that it resembles 4 wedges.

6. Heat the broth until piping hot and adjust the seasonings. Discard the cinnamon stick. Ladle the broth into the bowls and sprinkle with the reserved shallots and garlic. Sprinkle the celery leaves or cilantro atop and float a lime slice in the center of each bowl.

Serves 6 as a first course, 4 as an entrée

ITEK TIM

Peranakan Duck, Tomato, and Pineapple Soup

Welcome to the world of Nonya cooking—real Indonesian mommy food! I first learned of this unique Peranakan style of cooking from my travel companion and husband, Richard, who had read up on it in a guide to Singapore that we picked up. He described a cuisine that meshed the best of Chinese and Malay ingredients and traditions. So, shortly after landing in Singapore, we raced to Nonya and Baba Restaurant on River Valley Road for lunch. A feast it was! Dolly Yeo, chief cook and part owner, prepared the most exotic-sounding dishes; yet they seemed to us simple, fresh, and delicious. I never was able to obtain a written recipe for the *itek tim* that we ate, but when I got home I created one from the menu description: "A classical Peranakan Soup, the way grandma used to cook. Choice pieces of duck cooked with fresh tomatoes, salted vegetables, and sour plum cooked over a slow fire until the duck meat is tender. To add extra bite, green chilies are added to the soup before serving."

Believe me, the effort of making the duck broth is well worth it. The rich flavor it imparts "makes" this soup. The broth and pickled cabbage can be done ahead of time. The soup is then quickly prepared and definitely a standout. Each individual flavor is necessary for this taste sensation.

BROTH:
1 duck (about 5 pounds), cut into 8 pieces
1 large onion, peel left on and quartered
4 cloves garlic, peel left on and lightly bruised (page 153)
1 piece (1 inch) fresh ginger, peeled
6 fresh cilantro stems with roots, lightly crushed
10 white peppercorns
6 whole cloves
4 cups defatted Chicken Broth (page 127)
6 cups water
Salt, to taste

SOUP:
2 tablespoons thinly sliced fresh lemongrass
2 tablespoons minced peeled fresh ginger
2 cups Sweet Pickled Cabbage (page 237)
8 ripe plum tomatoes, seeded and cut into ½-inch dice (about 2 cups)
2 cups diced (½ inch) fresh ripe pineapple
½ cup coarsely chopped shallots
1 tablespoon minced fresh green chili
½ cup coarsely chopped fresh cilantro leaves

1. For the broth, rinse the duck well and trim off any lumps of excess fat. Place the duck in a large soup pot along with the onion, garlic, ginger, cilantro, peppercorns, cloves, chicken broth, and water. Bring to a boil over medium heat. Reduce the heat to medium-low and simmer uncovered for 40 minutes, skimming any foam that rises to the surface. Remove the duck breasts and set aside. Season the broth with salt and simmer until the legs and thighs are cooked through, about 15 minutes longer.

2. Remove the remaining pieces of duck and let cool to room temperature. Remove all the fat and shred all the meat from the bones in pieces about 2½ x ½ inch. Cover the meat and set aside. (If working 1 day ahead, refrigerate it overnight.)

3. Strain the broth, discarding the solids, then strain again through a double layer of cheesecloth. To defat the broth quickly, pour it through a gravy separator and discard the fat. You should have about 9 cups broth. (If working ahead, cool the broth to room temperature and refrigerate it overnight. Before proceeding, remove and discard all the fat that has risen to the top.)

4. For the soup, pour the defatted broth into a clean soup pot. Add the lemongrass and minced ginger. Simmer over medium heat for 10 minutes. Divide the pickled cabbage evenly between 8 shallow soup bowls.

5. Add the tomatoes, pineapple, shallots, and duck to the broth; simmer 2 minutes longer. Stir in the green chili and cook another 30 seconds. Stir in the cilantro. Ladle the hot soup over the pickled cabbage in the bowls. Serve immediately.

Serves 8

A TASTE OF THE WORLD

Indonesian Palette

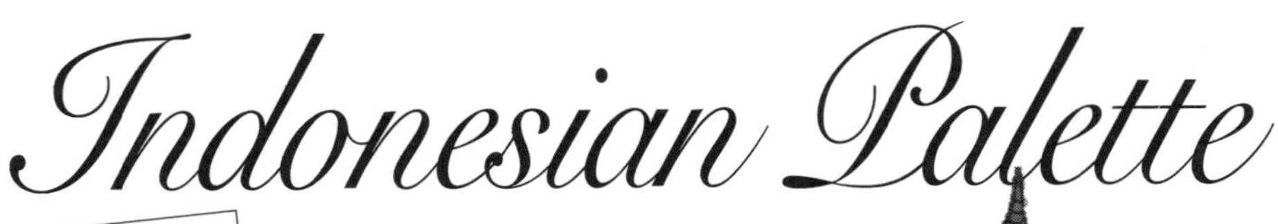

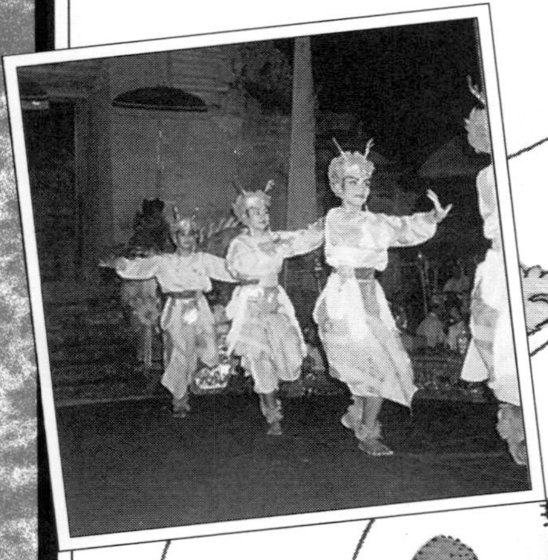

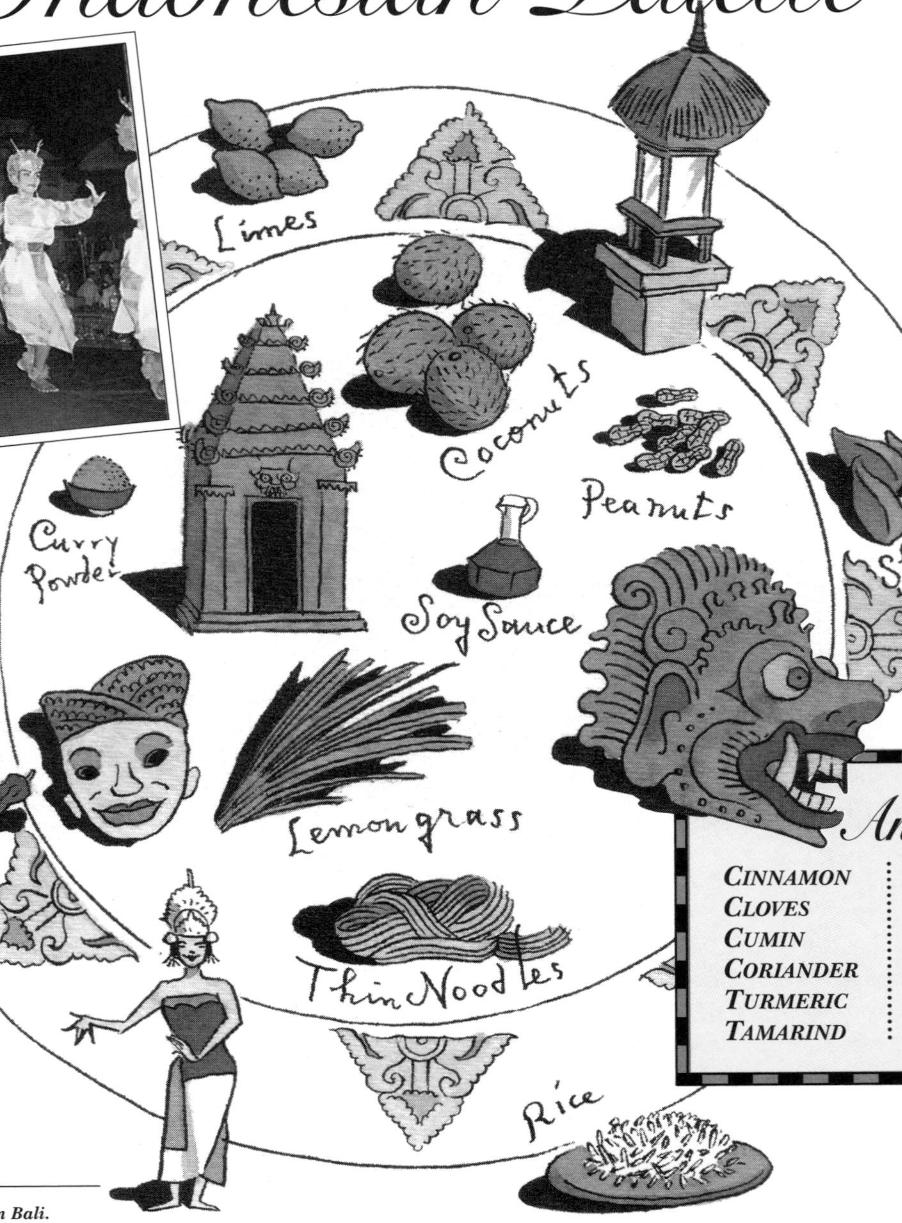
Limes
Coconuts
Peanuts
Shallots
Curry Powder
Soy Sauce
Lemongrass
Chilies
Thin Noodles
Rice

And

CINNAMON	NUTMEG
CLOVES	GARLIC
CUMIN	GINGER
CORIANDER	CILANTRO
TURMERIC	PEANUT OIL
TAMARIND	SUGAR

Photo: The Legong in Bali.

SPICED PRAWN AND PINEAPPLE SOUP

The cultures of Indonesia and Thailand interweave into beautifully flavored dishes. Lemongrass, ginger, cilantro, and peppermint perfume the palate. In this dish I've combined the Peranakan soup, *wang kuah nanas,* which blends Malaysian and Chinese cuisines with a spiced prawn soup, *tom yaam goong,* from Thailand. I've substituted fresh green chilies for the dried hot, red Thai chilies and added fresh pineapple for a touch of Peranakan intoxication. The prawns are stirred in at the last minute, and the freshest of herbs just before serving. Because this soup cooks rather quickly, be sure to have all your ingredients prepared before you begin.

5 cups Fish Stock (page 130)
8 white peppercorns, crushed
1 tablespoon finely minced fresh cilantro root, tiny strings removed
3 stalks fresh lemongrass, very thinly sliced
2 tablespoons finely julienned peeled fresh ginger
¼ cup fresh lime juice
3 tablespoons Thai Fish Sauce (page 254; see Note)
1 tablespoon finely minced fresh green chili (seeds and ribs removed), or more to taste
2 cups diced (½ inch) fresh ripe pineapple
1 pound large shrimp, peeled and deveined
1 tablespoon finely grated lime zest
2 tablespoons coarsely chopped fresh peppermint leaves
2 tablespoons coarsely chopped fresh cilantro leaves

1. Bring the fish stock to a boil in a large saucepan. Add the peppercorns and cilantro root and simmer uncovered for 2 minutes to flavor the broth.

2. Add the lemongrass and ginger and simmer another 2 minutes.

3. Add the lime juice, fish sauce, and green chili; slowly bring to a boil. Add the pineapple, reduce the heat, and simmer 1 minute longer.

4. Add the shrimp and lime zest and simmer until the shrimp are just cooked through, 1½ to 2 minutes. Stir in the peppermint and cilantro and serve immediately in large shallow soup bowls.

Serves 6

Note: If you'd rather buy fish sauce, it is available in Asian markets or Asian sections of supermarkets.

MINESTRONE

Luscious, thick, fresh vegetable soups the world over reflect the best seasonal produce and culinary preferences of each country, and more specifically, highlight the pride of regionality. In Italy, one is likely to feast upon a pale minestrone, thick with white beans or rice, throughout the north. Heading south, one meets up with the heady flavors of minestrone perfumed with tomatoes, basil, and garlic.

In contrast to the anemic vegetable soup that we are often served in America, the vegetable soups of Italy are made voluptuous with the addition of fresh pumpkin, dried beans, and pastas. I add split peas to my minestrone, a tip I picked up from the old Bleecker Luncheonette, at one time a hangout in New York City. I believe their addition of split green peas thickens the soup to perfection. I also add diced ripe tomatoes and coarsely chopped basil just before serving for a burst of freshness.

2 tablespoons extra virgin olive oil
8 ounces pancetta, or other unsmoked bacon, cut into ½-inch cubes
6 medium carrots, peeled, halved lengthwise, and sliced ½ inch thick
3 medium onions, cut into ¼-inch dice
4 cloves garlic, minced
2 leeks (3 inches green left on), rinsed well and cut into ¼-inch dice
1 small head green cabbage (1½ pounds), cored and cut into 1-inch pieces
1 Idaho potato, peeled and cut into ¼-inch dice
½ cup green split peas
8 cups defatted Chicken Broth (page 127)
½ cup chopped flat-leaf parsley
2 teaspoons dried thyme
1 teaspoon dried tarragon
Salt and coarsely ground black pepper, to taste
4 medium zucchini (1¼ pounds), cut into ½-inch cubes
12 ounces Swiss chard, leaves and stems rinsed and cut crosswise into 1-inch-thick slices
6 ripe plum tomatoes, seeded and cut into ½-inch pieces
½ cup coarsely chopped fresh basil leaves

1. Heat the olive oil in a large, heavy soup pot over medium-low heat. Add the pancetta and cook until some of the fat is rendered, 10 to 12 minutes.

2. Add the carrots, onions, garlic, and leeks. Cook, stirring occasionally, over low heat until the onions are wilted, about 15 minutes.

3. Fold the cabbage, potato, and split peas into the vegetables and continue to cook for 10 minutes.

4. Add the chicken broth, parsley, thyme, tarragon, salt, and pepper. Bring to a boil, reduce the heat, and simmer uncovered for 30 minutes.

5. Add the zucchini and simmer 15 minutes longer, stirring occasionally from the bottom.

6. Add the Swiss chard and simmer 8 to 10 minutes. Stir in the tomatoes and basil and simmer 5 minutes longer. The split peas should be cooked through and the vegetables soft but not mushy. Serve piping hot.

Serves 8 to 10

MEDITERRANEAN LENTIL VEGETABLE SOUP

Favorite flavors of the Middle East and North Africa come together in this satisfying vegetable soup. Truly a meal in itself, this rich soup on a cold autumn night is perfect served along with Boiled Potatoes and Sliced Tomatoes (see Index), a bowl of oil-cured black olives, and warm bread.

2 tablespoons olive oil
6 carrots, peeled and sliced ¼ inch thick
4 ribs celery with leaves, cut into ¼-inch dice
2 medium onions, cut into ½-inch dice
4 cloves garlic, coarsely chopped
8 cups defatted Chicken Broth (page 127)
1 can (35 ounces) plum tomatoes, crushed with their juices
1 cup dry red wine
¾ cup lentils
½ teaspoon ground cumin
¼ teaspoon ground allspice
2 cinnamon sticks (each 3 inches long)
Salt and coarsely ground black pepper, to taste
½ cup pitted prunes, quartered
½ cup chopped flat-leaf parsley
¼ cup chopped fresh mint leaves

1. Heat the oil in a heavy soup pot over low heat. Add the carrots, celery, and onions and cook, stirring, until the onions are wilted, about 10 minutes. Add the garlic and cook 1 minute longer.

2. Add the broth, tomatoes, wine, lentils, cumin, allspice, cinnamon sticks, salt, and pepper. Bring to a boil, reduce the heat to medium-low, and simmer uncovered, stirring occasionally, until the lentils are just tender, about 30 minutes.

3. Add the prunes and parsley and continue to simmer another 15 minutes. Before serving, remove the cinnamon sticks, adjust the seasonings, and stir in the mint.

Serves 8

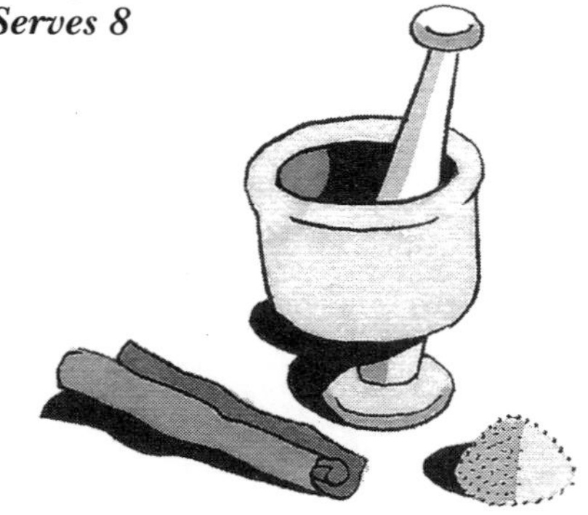

MY KITCHEN DIARY

To Skin Fresh Fava Beans

When the favas first come into season in the spring, they are most often small and tender. Later on in the season the beans are slightly larger and can have a heavy outer skin on them which is tough when cooked. I prefer to remove the skin before adding the beans to recipes. Fortunately, this is a very simple process: Bring a small pot of water to a boil. Drop in the fava beans and cook for 30 seconds until the skins just turn white. Drain and cool under cold running water. Carefully slip the beans out of their skins and proceed with the recipe.

CHILEAN PISTOU WITH CILANTRO PESTO

Every summer in Santiago, Chile, great cooks await the harvesting of the famous *porotos granados,* fresh white and green haricots, to add to their lush garden vegetable soups. Being there at just the right time, I was fortunate enough to enjoy not only the beans but all the fresh corn as well. Reminded of great Provençal *pistous,* I made a pesto of fresh cilantro to dollop onto this soup just before serving. Because I couldn't wait until summertime to make this recipe, I used the first springtime fava beans which came to the market. As the summer goes on, other fresh beans that become available can be used instead of the favas.

CILANTRO PESTO:
2 cups fresh cilantro leaves
2 small cloves garlic, coarsely chopped
¼ cup freshly grated Parmesan cheese
½ cup extra virgin olive oil

SOUP:
2 tablespoons vinegar
3 medium leeks (about 1½ pounds), roots trimmed, 3 inches green left on
4 medium carrots, peeled and cut into ½-inch pieces
1 pound Idaho potatoes, peeled and cut into ½-inch pieces
8 ripe plum tomatoes, peeled, seeded, and cut into ½-inch dice
3 large fresh thyme sprigs
4 cloves garlic, lightly bruised (see To Bruise Garlic, facing page) and peeled
12 cups Fresh Vegetable Broth (page 129)
4 ounces uncooked penne pasta
3 zucchini (about 8 ounces), cut into ½-inch pieces
4 ounces haricots verts (thin green beans), stem ends trimmed, halved crosswise
1 cup fresh basil leaves
2 cups corn kernels, preferably fresh (about 2 ears)
3 pounds fresh fava beans, or other fresh seasonal beans, shelled (about 1 pound) and outer skins removed (page 151)
Freshly grated Parmesan cheese, for garnish

1. For the pesto, place the cilantro, garlic, and Parmesan cheese in a food processor. Pulse the machine on and off until the mixture is well chopped but not puréed. Then, with the machine running, slowly drizzle the olive oil through the feed tube and process until the mixture is well combined and smooth.

2. For the soup, fill a large bowl with water and add the vinegar. Cut a 2-inch-deep X in the leeks at the white end and a 3-inch-deep X at the green end. Place the leeks in the vinegar water and soak for 30 minutes. Rinse well under cold running water. Cut the leeks lengthwise in half, then slice crosswise ½ inch thick.

3. Place the leeks, carrots, potatoes, tomatoes, thyme, and garlic in a large soup pot. Cover with the vegetable broth. Bring to a boil, reduce the heat to medium low, and simmer uncovered for 30 minutes.

4. Increase the heat to medium-high and add the pasta, zucchini, haricots verts, and basil. When the soup starts to boil, adjust the heat and simmer gently until the pasta is just tender, about 15 minutes.

5. Add the corn and fava beans and cook until both are tender, 2 to 3 minutes.

6. Serve the soup in shallow bowls. Top each serving with a generous dollop of the cilantro pesto and grated Parmesan.

Serves 8

SOPA ALENTEJANA

Garlic and Cilantro Bread Soup

When I visited Portugal while researching this book, my first meal in Lisbon was lunch at Restaurant Tagide, overlooking the Tagus River and the Alfama, the old Moorish quarter. It had been years since I had visited Portugal and all I could remember eating was lots of grilled sardines. Happily times have changed. A

cuisine resplendent with fresh cilantro, garlic, and rich fruity olive oil never disappoints. My first taste at lunch was this extraordinary soup, a luxuriant broth adorned with a perfect poached egg. When I tried to get the recipe from the maitre d', he told me that the chef crushed garlic and cilantro in the bottom of the bowl, added corn bread, and covered it with boiling water. Not much help at all! Figuring out the recipe has been quite a challenge. I began by rejecting the notion of using just boiling water and instead substituted defatted chicken broth infused with garlic and cilantro. I think all the effort in this seemingly simple soup is well worthwhile. It gives a 90s meaning to the 80s concept of "flavor bursts."

ENRICHED BROTH:
12 cups defatted Chicken Broth (page 127)
10 cloves garlic, lightly bruised and peeled (see box, below)
10 fresh cilantro sprigs with stems and roots, roots lightly crushed
3 tablespoons extra virgin olive oil
4 black peppercorns

SOPA:
6 cloves garlic, coarsely chopped
1 tablespoon coarse salt
Finely grated zest of 1 lemon
1 cup coarsely chopped fresh cilantro leaves and stems
3 tablespoons extra virgin olive oil, plus ¼ cup for garnish
6 large eggs, at room temperature
6 thin slices corn bread, lightly toasted (use other peasant bread if necessary)
3 tablespoons coarsely chopped cilantro leaves, for garnish

1. For the enriched broth, place the broth, garlic, cilantro, olive oil, and peppercorns in a large heavy pot. Bring to a boil, reduce the heat to medium-low, and simmer uncovered for 20 minutes. Strain the broth and return it to the pot. Keep warm.

2. For the *sopa,* place the chopped garlic, salt, and lemon zest in a food processor and pulse on and off until finely chopped. Add the cilantro and process until just smooth. With the machine running, drizzle in 3 tablespoons oil through the feed tube and process until just smooth. Scrape the purée into a bowl and set aside.

3. Bring the strained broth to a simmer and poach the eggs in the broth for 2 minutes (see page 6 for preparing perfect eggs). Remove with a slotted spoon and set aside.

4. Re-strain the broth if desired and simmer until heated through.

5. To serve, place 2 teaspoons of the cilantro purée in the bottom of each of 6 shallow soup bowls. (Pasta bowls may be used.) Lay a slice of toasted corn bread on top of the purée. Top the bread with a poached egg and ladle the hot broth over the eggs. Garnish with the 3 tablespoons chopped cilantro and drizzle each serving with a bit more olive oil. Serve immediately.

Serves 6

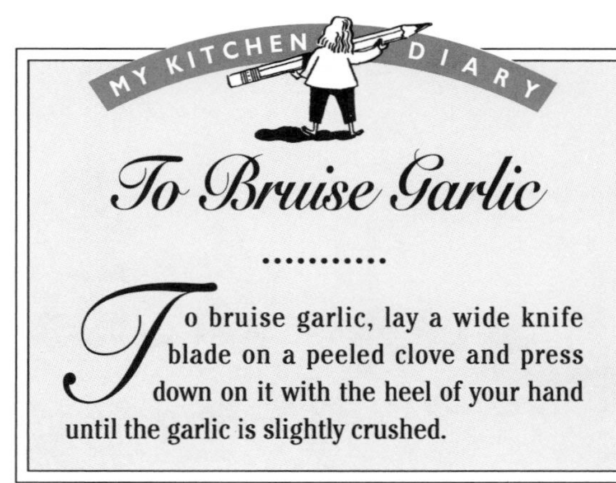

To Bruise Garlic

To bruise garlic, lay a wide knife blade on a peeled clove and press down on it with the heel of your hand until the garlic is slightly crushed.

THE WINES OF

Portugal

Portugal is best known for port, the potent fortified red wine that is a pet of connoisseurs. Legions of wine drinkers, however, may be more familiar with fruity Portuguese rosés, particularly the mildly sparkling versions from Mateus and Lancer's. For export, these wines are often sweetened a bit. However, in Portugal drier wines are preferred, and some of the best everyday wines are produced there.

In the north, for instance, the charming, super-dry white of the Minho region is known as *vinho verde* ("green wine"). The name refers not to the color—which is pale as straw for the white wines and cherry garnet for the reds—but to the youthful vibrancy of these wines. Only the white is export-ed; the astringent bite of the red is something of an acquired taste. Being young, *vinho verde* contains a high degree of malic acid and even the white is too acidic for some.

In the last decade, Portugal has undergone a transformation of sorts. The old-style, rather oxidized whites have now given way to livelier, fresher wines—both red and white. Producers such as João Pires, Herdade de Esporão, Fernandes, J. M. da Fonseca, Reguengos de Monsarraz (a cooperative in Alentejo), and Quinta de Bacalhõa are making excellent wines.

Fans of rich, sturdy red wines can certainly still find them among Portugal's well-aged, traditional reds—especially those labeled Garrafeira or Reserve Particular from regions like Bairrada, the Dão, and the Douro. Quality producers include Ferreira (Barca Velha is tops), Borges & Irmão, Carvalho, Ribeiro & Ferreira, Quinta do Cotto, and Cavas São João.

Old Lisbon—the best place for "fado," the haunting songs of sailors.

RESTO DES AMIS' FRENCH ONION SOUP GRATINEE

The French really know how to cook for those cold winter nights *en famille*. Their luscious onion soup gratinée has just the right country feeling when it comes bubbling hot out of the oven with melted, nutty-tasting Gruyère cheese blanketing the top. The best onion soup gratinée I've ever tasted was not in France but at Resto des Amis in Atlanta, Georgia. Little wonder, as the restaurant is co-owned by chefs Guenter Seeger of The Dining Room at the Ritz Carlton in Atlanta and Jean-Louis Palladin of Jean-Louis in the Watergate Hotel in Washington, D.C. *Merci bien! C'est délicieux.*

2 cups cubed (¾ inch) sourdough bread
¼ cup olive oil
5 tablespoons chopped fresh thyme
3 tablespoons chopped fresh rosemary
Salt and freshly ground black pepper, to taste
3 large Vidalia onions or other sweet onions, sliced in thin rings
4 cloves garlic, thinly slivered
⅔ cup dry sherry
2 cups defatted Chicken Broth (page 127)
2 cups defatted Rich Beef Broth (page 128) or veal stock
1½ cups grated Gruyère cheese

1. Preheat the oven to 350°F.

2. Place the cubed bread on a baking sheet. Drizzle with 2 tablespoons of olive oil, then sprinkle with 1 tablespoon each of thyme and rosemary, and season with salt and pepper. Bake until crisp, about 15 minutes, shaking the pan occasionally. Set aside.

3. Heat the remaining 2 tablespoons olive oil in a large heavy pot over medium-low heat. Add the onions and cook until lightly browned and caramelized, about 45 minutes, stirring occasionally. Add the garlic and cook for 1 minute more.

4. Raise the heat and add the sherry to the onions and garlic; bring to a rapid boil. Add the broths, bring to a boil, reduce the heat, and simmer gently, covered, for 20 minutes.

5. Add the remaining thyme and rosemary and additional salt and pepper, if desired. (At this stage the soup may be cooled and refrigerated covered for later use, although the fragrance of the fresh herbs will soften.)

6. To serve, preheat the broiler.

7. Place 4 ovenproof crocks on a baking sheet and ladle in the soup to ½ inch from the rim. Make sure each serving gets plenty of onions. Float a handful of croutons on the top of each bowl and cover well with grated cheese. Place the crocks under the broiler, about 3 inches from the heat source, and broil until bubbly and golden brown. Serve immediately.

Serves 4

PAPPA AL POMODORO

Italian Tomato Bread Soup

I count Italy's great tomato bread soup as one of my favorites. There are two yearly events which occur simultaneously for me and which always result in my first batch of this soup on Memorial Day weekend. At my farm in Connecticut, the herb garden starts to flourish with chives, tarragon, and masses of marjoram, and tomatoes in the markets seem to be making their metamorphosis from winter's pale, mealy variety into the lush, red, juicy orbs that herald summer.

A generous splash of fruity extra virgin olive oil starts the soup. Next come softly wilted onions and garlic. Peeled, seeded tomatoes with all their sweet juice make the base of the soup.

SOUVENIR TO SAVOR

The World's Best "Bred" Soups

From my point of view, the bread soups of Italy and France shine brilliantly with color and flavor. In fact, on a hot sunny day in mid-August when ripe tomatoes are bursting on the vine, there seems nothing more delicious or satisfying to eat than *pappa al pomodoro,* the great bread soup from southern Italy. A simmering pot brimming with tomatoes, onions, garlic, and fruity extra virgin olive oil is prepared to receive day-old Italian or sourdough bread, transforming the soup into a robust "stew."

According to *Larousse Gastronomique, soupe* originally meant the bread on which was ladled the *potage,* or the contents of the cooking pot.

When properly made, Tuscany's *ribollita* (reboiled) vegetable soup sends minestrone scurrying down the ladder to second place. Thin slices of toasted Italian peasant bread laden with garlic are layered between wilted garden vegetables and baked with chicken broth and fresh Parmesan cheese until bubbling hot, ready to warm the soul in the cold of winter. The bread adds substance and depth to this "soup stew."

The French follow along the way with their lusty *garbure,* dazzled traditionally with a confit of preserved goose. Best suited for winter, the soup mingles thinly slivered cabbage with sliced potatoes, green beans, peas, and dried haricots. Fresh thyme perfumes these vegetables cooked in a rich vegetable broth. Towards the end of cooking, whole-grain or whole-wheat bread is added, lending a thick lushness to this peasant preparation.

And where would steamy onion soup gratinée be without slices of toasty day-old baguette bathed in a melted Gruyère. Or where would the smoky split pea soup *potage Saint-Germain* be without its crisp-toasted herb croutons floating atop.

The Russians and especially Ukrainians wouldn't think of serving a steaming pot of borscht without floating garlic-scented croutons as a garnish. Portugal's gift to the world is its heady *sopa alentejana,* brimming with corn bread, garlic, and cilantro and topped off with a poached egg.

Rich, satisfying bread soups—they are certainly a very practical and delicious use of a day-old loaf.

Chicken or vegetable broth should be rich and full flavored. I add marjoram from my garden to the soup, but fresh basil is a perfectly acceptable substitute. Once the soup is lightly simmered, day-old bread is torn in pieces and allowed to rest in the soup for one hour. The soup is best served at room temperature with some freshly grated Parmesan stirred in just before serving. This is a splendid way to begin a lusty meal of grilled butterflied leg of lamb, ratatouille, and herb-spiked roasted potatoes.

⅓ cup fruity extra virgin olive oil
1 cup diced (¼ inch) onion
4 cloves garlic, finely chopped
6 pounds ripe tomatoes, peeled, seeded, and chopped, juices reserved (see How to Peel Tomatoes, page 242)
½ cup fresh marjoram or basil leaves, coarsely chopped
4 cups defatted Chicken Broth or Fresh Vegetable Broth (page 127 or 129)
Salt and freshly ground black pepper, to taste
1 long sourdough baguette, cut into 10 to 12 ½-inch-thick slices
2 tablespoons freshly grated Parmesan cheese, plus more for passing at the table

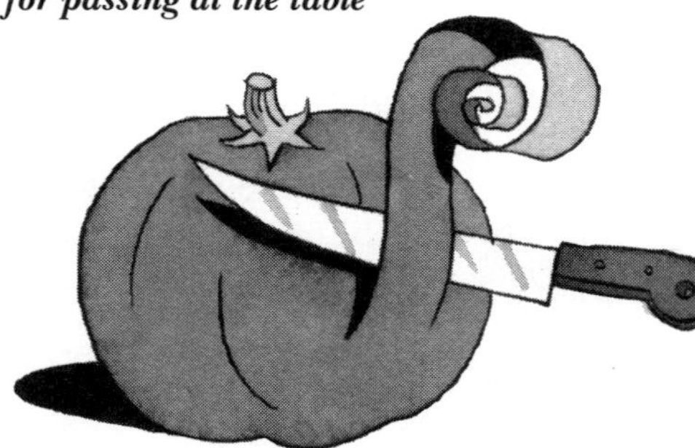

1. Heat the oil in a large heavy soup pot over low heat. Add the onion and cook, stirring, until wilted, about 10 minutes. Stir in the garlic and cook for another 3 minutes.

2. Add the tomatoes with all their juices. Stir in the marjoram and broth, then season with salt and pepper. Simmer, partially covered, over medium-low heat for about 10 minutes to blend the flavors.

3. Break up the bread and stir it into the soup. Remove from the heat and let rest covered for 1 hour. Adjust the seasonings to taste.

4. Before serving, stir in the 2 tablespoons Parmesan. Serve at room temperature in large shallow soup bowls and pass additional Parmesan to sprinkle atop.

Serves 8

WENDE'S AVGOLEMONO SOUP

Wende, famous for her Bloody Mary in *The Silver Palate Good Times Cookbook,* has become a connoisseur of Greek cooking since her marriage to Aristedes Kambanis. This version of a classic Greek recipe has been in her husband's family for quite a while. The use of escarole pays homage to the great love of Italian food we all share. Fresh dill contributes its sweet delicacy as the final addition.

3 tablespoons olive oil
2 medium onions, coarsely chopped
2 heads escarole, rinsed well, trimmed, and cut into 1-inch pieces
8 cups defatted Chicken Broth (page 127)
2 large eggs, lightly beaten
Juice of 2 lemons
Salt and coarsely ground black pepper, to taste
2 tablespoons chopped fresh dill, plus small dill sprigs for garnish

1. Heat the olive oil in a large heavy pot over low heat. Add the onions and cook, stirring occasionally, until softened, about 10 minutes. Add the escarole, increase the heat to medium, and cook, stirring, for 1 minute.

2. Add the chicken broth and simmer the soup until the escarole is tender, about 20 minutes. Cool the soup slightly.

3. Beat the eggs and lemon juice together in a small bowl. Whisking constantly, slowly pour 1 cup of the warm soup broth into the egg mixture to temper it. Whisk this mixture gradually back into the soup. Season with salt and pepper and stir in the chopped dill. Reheat the soup very gently over low heat. (Do not boil or the eggs will curdle.) Garnish each bowl with a dill sprig.

Serves 6 to 8

CURRIED GOLDEN SQUASH SOUP

There's a gentle warmth and sweetness to summer's sunniest squash. Cooked along with mellow curry powder and smooth tangy yogurt, it becomes a delightful choice for lazy Indian summer evenings. The ripest tomatoes and freshest parsley bring the bright flavors of the garden to your prettiest table.

3 tablespoons unsalted butter
2 medium onions, chopped
2 tablespoons best-quality curry powder
6 cups Fresh Vegetable Broth or defatted Chicken Broth (page 129 or 127)
2 medium Idaho potatoes (about 1 pound), peeled and cut into ¼-inch dice
1 teaspoon salt
6 yellow summer squash (about 2 pounds), trimmed and sliced
2 cups nonfat plain yogurt
1 small green zucchini, trimmed and cut into ¼-inch dice
3 ripe plum tomatoes, seeded and cut into ¼-inch dice, for garnish
2 tablespoons chopped flat-leaf parsley, for garnish

1. Melt the butter over low heat in a large heavy pot. Add the onions and cook, stirring, until the onions are wilted, about 10 minutes.

2. Add the curry powder and cook, to smooth out the flavor, another 2 minutes, stirring continuously.

3. Add the broth and potatoes and simmer uncovered over medium heat for 15 minutes. Season with the salt.

4. Add the yellow squash and simmer another 10 minutes.

5. Remove 1 cup of the broth from the soup. Place 1 cup of the yogurt in a bowl and slowly whisk in the warm broth to temper the yogurt. Slowly stir this mixture back into the soup.

6. Purée the soup until smooth in a food processor or blender in small batches. Return the soup to the pot. Adjust the seasonings to taste.

7. Before serving, stir in the zucchini and heat the soup (do not boil) through over low heat. Garnish each serving with a dollop of the remaining yogurt and a sprinkle of chopped tomato and parsley.

Serves 8

CHRISTMAS RED PEPPER SOUP

During the Christmas season, Mexico has to be one of the most festive places on earth! The sights, sounds, and colors are thoroughly enticing—as is this cinnamon-spiked, richly roasted red pepper soup. The flavor is both sweet and savory; orange juice added towards the end of cooking adds a sweet tang. A dollop of cool, vibrant green avocado cream atop this soup gives it a richness, and crisp tortilla strips scattered over all add a festive crunch to the texture.

6 large red bell peppers, 3 halved lengthwise and roasted (page 202), the remainder stemmed, seeded, and diced
3 tablespoons extra virgin olive oil
2 medium onions, halved lengthwise and cut into ¼-inch slivers
½ teaspoon ground cinnamon
Pinch of cayenne pepper
6 cups Fresh Vegetable Broth or defatted Chicken Broth (page 129 or 127)
½ cup fresh orange juice
¼ cup vegetable oil
4 corn tortillas (6- to 7-inch diameter), cut into 2 x ½-inch strips
¾ to 1 cup Avocado Cream (page 86)
¼ cup coarsely chopped flat-leaf parsley

1. Cut the roasted bell peppers into 1-inch dice and set aside.

2. Heat the olive oil in a heavy soup pot over low heat. Add the onions and raw red pepper dice; cook, stirring, until the onions are wilted, about 15 minutes.

3. Add the diced roasted peppers, cinnamon, and cayenne and stir well. Add the broth and bring to a boil. Reduce the heat to medium-low and simmer for 25 minutes, stirring occasionally.

4. Stir in the orange juice and simmer 5 minutes longer.

5. Cool the soup to room temperature. Purée until smooth in a food processor or blender in batches. Return the soup to the pot.

6. Heat the vegetable oil in a large nonstick skillet over medium-high heat. Add a quarter of the tortilla strips and fry for 1 minute, shaking the pan for even cooking. Remove the strips to paper towels to drain. Repeat with the remaining tortilla strips, cooking them in 3 batches.

7. Just before serving, gently heat the soup through. Ladle into bowls and dollop each serving with 1 to 2 tablespoons of the avocado cream. Scatter a few tortilla strips over the soup and sprinkle with the chopped parsley.

Serves 6 to 8

FEZ-STYLE TOMATO SOUP

The food of Fez is considered the very best to be had in Morocco. Precious spices, lavishly used, add the most extraordinary flavors to just about any dish. Cinnamon is the prize. When combined with velvety honey, a simple tomato soup absorbs all the richness of flavor one could possibly want. A sprinkling of fresh mint makes a nice ending touch.

2 tablespoons vegetable oil
2 cups coarsely chopped onions
1 tablespoon minced garlic
2 cans (28 ounces each) plum tomatoes
2 cups defatted Chicken Broth (page 127)
Juice and finely grated zest of 2 oranges
2 tablespoons honey
2 cinnamon sticks (each 3 inches long)
1 teaspoon ground allspice
¼ teaspoon ground nutmeg
2 Idaho potatoes, peeled and sliced ¼ inch thick (32 slices)
Salt and coarsely ground black pepper, to taste
2 tablespoons chopped fresh mint leaves, for garnish

1. Heat the oil in a large heavy pot over medium-low heat. Add the onions and cook until just softened, 5 minutes, stirring occasionally. Add the garlic and cook to soften, 5 minutes more.

2. Crush the tomatoes and add them with their juices. Add the broth, orange juice and zest, honey, cinnamon sticks, allspice, and nutmeg. Bring the soup to a boil, reduce the heat, and simmer uncovered to blend the flavors, 30 minutes.

3. While the soup is simmering, place the potatoes in a large saucepan and cover with water. Bring to a boil, reduce the heat, and simmer uncovered until just tender, about 8 minutes. Drain and set aside.

4. Remove the cinnamon sticks. Purée the soup until very smooth in a food processor or blender in batches. Return the purée to the pot and season to taste with salt and pepper.

5. Before serving, warm the soup gently. To serve, place 4 potato slices in the bottom of each soup bowl, ladle the hot soup atop, and sprinkle with the chopped mint.

Serves 8

CASBAH CARROT SOUP

The carrots in Morocco are of indescribable sweetness. They are served most often as small salads, either mashed or cut into chunks, but always bathed in sugar and lavished with fresh mint. While prowling through the intoxicating spice displays in the souks (marketplaces), I was amazed to see Moroccan curry powder, paler and a bit less pungent than the Indian varieties. I've combined curry and ginger to enrich this carrot soup and sparkled it with fresh mint just before serving.

2 tablespoons olive oil
1 cup coarsely chopped onion
1 tablespoon minced peeled fresh ginger
¼ cup raw long-grain rice
1 teaspoon best-quality curry powder
2 pounds carrots, peeled and sliced ¼ inch thick
10 cups defatted Chicken Broth (page 127)
Salt and coarsely ground black pepper, to taste
2 tablespoons coarsely chopped fresh mint leaves, for garnish

1. Heat the oil in a large heavy pot over medium-low heat. Add the onion and ginger and cook until the onion is wilted, 10 minutes, stirring occasionally. Add the rice and curry powder and cook for 1 minute, stirring well.

2. Add the carrots and broth. Increase the heat and bring the broth to a boil. Reduce the

heat and simmer uncovered until the carrots and rice are tender, about 30 minutes.

3. Let the soup cool slightly, then purée it in a food processor or blender in small batches. Return the soup to the pot. Season to taste with salt and pepper and heat through. Garnish with the fresh mint just before serving.

Serves 8

GINGERED CREME DE CRECY

A soft, velvety carrot soup with the gentle sparkle of crystallized ginger gets a final touch of cream added just at the end. This soup is lovely to begin a meal of robust Coq au Vin (see Index). As it is rich, small portions are all that is necessary. When reheating the soup, be sure not to boil it. A light grating of nutmeg on top is a lovely addition.

6 medium carrots (about ¾ pound), peeled
2 ribs celery with leaves
1 cup thinly sliced onion
¼ cup chopped crystallized ginger
7 cups defatted Chicken Broth (page 127)
½ cup cooked white rice
Salt, to taste
½ cup heavy (or whipping) cream
6 to 8 watercress sprigs, for garnish

1. Slice the carrots and celery crosswise.

2. Place the carrots, celery, onion, and ginger in a large heavy pot and add the broth.

3. Bring the broth to a boil over high heat. Reduce the heat to medium and simmer covered until the vegetables are very tender, about 20 minutes. Remove from the heat and add the rice. Season with salt and let rest, partially covered, for 15 minutes to cool slightly.

4. Purée the soup in small batches in a blender until smooth. Return to the pot and stir in the cream. Adjust the seasoning.

5. Pinch the top 2 inches off the watercress sprigs.

6. To serve, heat the soup through but do not boil. Ladle into small cups or bowls and garnish each portion with a sprig of watercress.

Serves 6 to 8

JADE SOUP

One look at the ingredients and you'll quickly understand where the name of this lovely soup comes from. Vibrant green mint mingles with peas and fresh chives to make this superb soup. Served either hot or cold, it is both light and delicate. Once the soup is strained, which is essential for removing the pea skins, it becomes quite thin and just the right consistency to begin a Japanese or Chinese meal.

2 bunches scallions (about 8) trimmed, 3 inches green left on
1 medium onion, thinly sliced
2 packages (10 ounces each) frozen green peas, thawed
6 cups defatted Chicken Broth (page 127)
Salt and freshly ground black pepper to taste
⅓ cup fresh mint leaves
1 tablespoon snipped fresh chives, for garnish

1. Coarsely slice the scallions and combine them with the onion, peas, and chicken broth in a heavy pot. Bring to a boil, reduce the heat, and simmer, partially covered, until the vegetables are soft, about 20 minutes. Remove from the heat. Season with salt and pepper and cool to room temperature.

2. Purée the pea mixture in small batches in a blender until smooth, adding the mint leaves to the last batch. Pass the soup through a strainer to remove the pea skins.

3. To serve the soup cold, chill it in the refrigerator for up to 4 hours. To serve it hot, gently heat it through just before serving.

4. Ladle the soup into small bowls or cups and sprinkle with chives.

Serves 4 to 6

SCANDINAVIAN SMOKY PEA SOUP

Fresh ginger, the secret ingredient, distinguishes Scandinavia's dried pea soup from others, such as *potage Saint-Germain*. I've resisted adding anything other than the basic ingredients—a smoky ham hock, onions, garlic, and carrots—to present this soothing winter soup in its purest state. To prevent the soup from tasting too salty, I've boiled the ham hock first to remove some of the salt. Serve this soup hot with buttered black pumpernickel topped with a thin slice of roast beef for a perfect winter Sunday supper.

1 meaty smoked ham hock (about 12 ounces)
2 tablespoons olive oil
2 cups chopped onions
3 small carrots, peeled and finely chopped
2 tablespoons minced garlic
1 pound yellow split peas, picked over and rinsed
12 cups defatted Chicken Broth (page 127)
1 piece (1 inch) fresh ginger, peeled and lightly crushed
4 fresh dill sprigs
2 flat-leaf parsley sprigs
1 teaspoon ground allspice
⅛ teaspoon coarsely ground black pepper
Coarse salt, to taste
2 tablespoons chopped fresh dill, for garnish

1. Place the ham hock in a medium-size saucepan and cover with cold water. Bring to a boil and continue to gently boil for 15 minutes. Drain and rinse under cold water. Pat dry.

2. Heat the oil in a heavy soup pot over low heat. Add the onions and carrots and cook, stirring, until the onions are wilted, about 10 minutes. Add the garlic and cook 1 minute longer.

3. Add the ham hock, peas, chicken broth, ginger, dill and parsley sprigs, allspice, and pepper. Bring to a boil, reduce the heat to low, and simmer, partially covered, for 1¼ hours, stirring constantly.

4. Remove the ham hock and cool slightly. Shred the meat from the bone and return it to the soup. Remove the ginger and dill and parsley sprigs and discard. Adjust the seasonings, adding salt if needed, and serve piping hot, garnished with the chopped dill.

Serves 6

CREAMY WILD MUSHROOM SOUP

Walking through the Scandinavian markets at summer's end, one is bound to come upon a plethora of wild mushrooms just harvested from the magnificent outlying woods. So it's no wonder that it was in Denmark that I enjoyed a lush mushroom soup. Fresh morels floated atop this cream-enriched soup, seasoned with just the right amount of allspice. I don't completely purée the soup, but instead leave a bit of texture which gives body to this homage to autumn.

1 ounce dried wild mushrooms, such as morels, cèpes, or shiitakes
7 cups defatted Chicken Broth (page 127)
¼ cup tawny port
2 tablespoons unsalted butter
1 cup coarsely chopped onions
1½ pounds fresh white mushrooms, wiped clean, stems trimmed, and coarsely chopped; reserve 8 whole mushroom caps for garnish
1 teaspoon ground allspice
Salt and coarsely ground black pepper, to taste
1 cup heavy (or whipping) cream
3 tablespoons snipped fresh chives

1. Rinse the wild mushrooms well in a strainer under cold water to remove any dirt. Place the mushrooms in a bowl. Bring 1 cup of the chicken broth and the port to a boil and pour over the mushrooms. Let the mushrooms soak for at least 1 hour. Drain the mushrooms, reserving the liquid, and set aside. Strain the liquid through a double layer of cheesecloth.

2. Melt the butter in a heavy soup pot over low heat. Add the onions and cook until wilted, stirring occasionally, for 10 minutes. Add the fresh mushrooms, increase the heat to medium-low, and cook to bring out their flavor, stirring occasionally, for 15 minutes.

3. Add the remaining 6 cups chicken broth, the allspice, salt, and pepper. Bring to a boil, reduce the heat, and simmer, partially covered, for 15 minutes. Add half the reserved wild mushrooms with all the soaking liquid. Cook, partially covered, 15 minutes longer.

4. Purée half of the soup in a food processor or blender and return it to the pot. Add the remaining wild mushrooms along with the cream. Heat another 10 minutes to warm the soup through.

5. Julienne the reserved mushroom caps and garnish each serving with the julienned mushrooms and snipped chives.

Serves 8

BOTVINYA

Sorrel Potato Soup

It's amazing to see how many transformations the potato goes through in Russian cooking and how the same accents such as egg and cucumber are used in new and surprising ways over and over again. Fresh seasonal produce, such as lemony sorrel, excites the imagination and the palate for this springtime soup. Garnishes of yogurt, cucumber, eggs, and dill dazzle.

2 bunches sorrel or spinach (about 12 ounces)
1 tablespoon olive oil
1 tablespoon unsalted butter
1 large onion, diced
6 scallions (3 inches green left on), thinly sliced
1 cup coarsely chopped flat-leaf parsley
6 cups defatted Chicken Broth (page 127)
2 Idaho potatoes (8 ounces each), peeled and cut into ¼-inch dice
1 bay leaf
Salt and freshly ground black pepper, to taste
½ cup nonfat plain yogurt or sour cream, for garnish
2 hard-cooked eggs, peeled and coarsely chopped, for garnish
1½ cups peeled and julienned hothouse (seedless) cucumbers, for garnish
2 tablespoons chopped fresh dill, for garnish

1. Rinse the sorrel well. Remove and discard the tough stems. Coarsely chop the leaves and set aside.

2. Heat the oil and butter in a heavy soup pot over low heat. Add the onion, scallions, and ½ cup of the parsley and cook, stirring occasionally, until wilted, about 10 minutes.

3. Add the broth, potatoes, and bay leaf; cook over medium heat until the potatoes are just tender, about 10 minutes. Season with salt and pepper.

4. Remove the bay leaf and add the sorrel. Cook for 3 minutes to wilt the sorrel. Adjust the seasonings, stir in the remaining ½ cup parsley, and cook 30 seconds longer.

5. Ladle the hot soup into shallow soup bowls and top with a dollop of yogurt, chopped egg, julienned cucumbers, and chopped dill.

Serves 6 to 8

MEDITERRANEAN WHITE BEAN SOUP

It seems that every country throughout the Mediterranean has an affinity for bean soups, and each region enhances its own with favorite local flavorings. Fresh fennel, both the bulb and the feathery ferns, perfume this soup. A smoky ham hock, bay leaves, and allspice impart depth and flavor. A confetti of carrots and tomato add a cheerful flourish along with a dollop of cool crème fraîche.

1 pound dried large white beans, such as cannellini or Great Northern
8 cups cold water
2 fennel bulbs (1¾ pounds each), rinsed
2 tablespoons olive oil
4 medium onions, cut into ½-inch dice
4 large cloves garlic, coarsely chopped
1 smoked ham hock (about 8 ounces)
10 cups defatted Chicken Broth (page 127)
1 teaspoon dried thyme
4 allspice berries
2 bay leaves
2 carrots, peeled and cut into ¼-inch dice
3 ripe plum tomatoes, seeded and cut into ¼-inch dice, for garnish.
½ cup crème fraîche, for garnish

1. Rinse the beans and soak overnight in the cold water. Drain, rinse, and set aside.

2. Remove the ferns from the fennel bulbs. Coarsely chop them and set aside. Trim the bulbs and cut into ½-inch cubes.

3. Place the oil in a heavy soup pot. Add the fennel bulbs, onions, and garlic; wilt the vegetables over low heat, stirring occasionally, for 15 minutes.

4. Add the beans, ham hock, broth, thyme, allspice, and bay leaves. Bring the soup to a boil, reduce the heat, and simmer, partially covered, until the beans are tender, about 1½ hours. Remove the ham hock, allspice, and bay leaves. Let the ham hock stand until cool enough to handle, then shred the meat from the bone.

5. Purée 2 cups of the soup in a food processor or blender until smooth. Stir the purée back into the soup along with the fennel ferns and meat from the ham hock. Reheat over low heat.

6. Meanwhile, cook the diced carrots in boiling water to cover until just tender, 3 to 5 minutes. Drain and stir into the soup.

7. Serve the soup in large shallow bowls, garnished with diced tomatoes and a dollop of crème fraîche.

Serves 8

MONTEGO RED PEA SOUP

The cooks of Montego Bay, Jamaica, love their red peas (or red beans as we know them). One of the island's staple foods, they're mixed with rice, served over rice, served on their own—thick and creamy—or used for robust soups. Instead of a heavy preparation, I prefer "red peas" as the base in this lighter vegetable soup. After wilting onions and carrots, I caramelize them with a bit of brown sugar to give the soup a base for a sweet and sour taste and then add Jamaican allspice for richness. The sweetness plays nicely off the smoky flavor of the ham hock. The fresh lime juice added just before the soup is ready completes the sweet and sour effect. Velvety, ripe avocado, as a garnish, provides a perfect contrast to this soup, rich in island ingredients.

8 ounces dried red kidney beans
2 tablespoons unsalted butter
2 tablespoons olive oil
2 medium onions, cut into ½-inch dice
6 cloves garlic, minced
4 carrots, halved lengthwise, then cut crosswise into 1-inch pieces
2 tablespoons light brown sugar
2 cans (28 ounces each) plum tomatoes, crushed, with their juices
6 cups defatted Chicken Broth (page 127)
1 smoked ham hock (about 12 ounces)
¾ cup dry red wine
1 teaspoon ground allspice
¼ teaspoon freshly ground black pepper
Salt, to taste
3 tablespoons fresh lime juice
½ ripe avocado, preferably Haas, pitted, peeled, and cut into ¼-inch dice, for garnish

1. Rinse the beans well and place them in a large bowl. Cover with cold water and let soak overnight. The next day drain, rinse the beans, and set aside.

2. Heat the butter and olive oil in a medium-size soup pot over low heat. Add the onions, garlic, and carrots; cook, stirring, until the onions are wilted, about 10 minutes. Sprinkle with the brown sugar and continue to cook another 15 minutes to caramelize the vegetables.

3. Add the beans, tomatoes, chicken broth, and ham hock. Bring to a boil, reduce the heat to medium-low, and simmer uncovered, stirring occasionally, until the beans are just tender, about 1 hour. Add the wine, allspice, and pepper. Simmer uncovered over low heat another 25 minutes. Add the salt and 2 tablespoons of the lime juice.

4. Remove the ham hock, let cool, and shred the meat from the bone. Return the meat to the soup.

5. Toss the diced avocado with the remaining tablespoon of lime juice.

6. Reheat the soup before serving. Divide it between 6 bowls and garnish each serving with diced avocado. Serve immediately.

Serves 6

CARLOS' BLACK BEAN SOUP

So many dishes that I prepare these days and enjoy in my travels remind me of my wonderful friend and onetime cook, Carlos Carresquera, from Venezuela. He taught me his native cuisine and demonstrated a great inventive flair for coming up with perfectly balanced sweet and sour tastes. Brown sugar, red bell peppers, lots of capers, pickling brines, vinegar, and citrus juices were his "secret ingredients."

In all my travels I have not tasted better black beans or black bean soup than those Carlos made. When he first prepared this soup for me, cilantro wasn't as fashionable as it later became in the late 80s with the flourishing of Southwestern and Pacific Rim cuisines. Now that it is so widely available, a cilantro garnish is as easy as it is lovely. Carlos' black bean soup first appeared in *The Silver Palate Cookbook* but without the fanfare it deserved. The time is right now to prepare this excellent soup. For an exquisite soup and sandwich combination, serve the soup with roasted tomato and red bell pepper *bruschetta.*

2 pounds black beans
¼ cup olive oil
3 cups diced onions
8 cloves garlic, lightly bruised (page 153) and peeled
1 meaty ham bone or smoked ham hock
6 quarts water
2 tablespoons plus 1 teaspoon ground cumin
1 tablespoon dried oregano
3 bay leaves
2 teaspoons freshly ground black pepper
Pinch of cayenne
6 tablespoons chopped flat-leaf parsley
6 tablespoons chopped fresh cilantro leaves
1 teaspoon salt
2 medium red bell peppers, stemmed, seeded, and cut into ¼-inch dice; reserve ¼ cup for garnish
¼ cup dry sherry
1 tablespoon (packed) brown sugar
1 tablespoon fresh lime juice
1 cup crème fraîche or sour cream

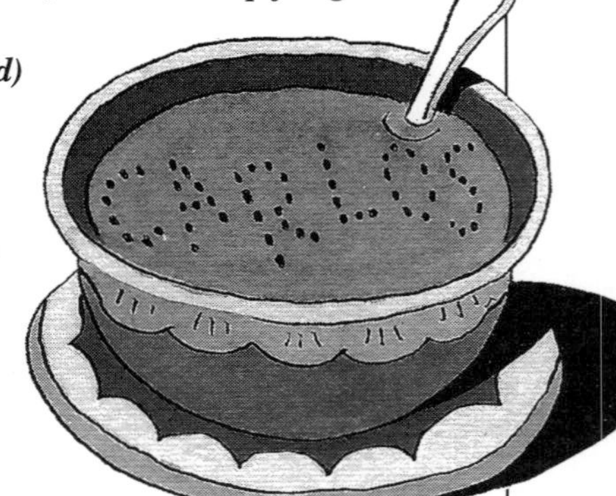

1. Rinse the beans well and place them in a large bowl. Cover with cold water and let soak overnight. The next day, drain, rinse, and set aside.

2. Heat the oil in a large soup pot over low heat. Add the onions and garlic and cook over low heat until the onions are wilted, about 10 minutes.

3. Add the beans with the ham bone and the water to the pot. Stir in 2 tablespoons of the cumin, the oregano, bay leaves, black pepper, cayenne, and 2 tablespoons each of the parsley and cilantro. Bring to a boil, reduce the heat, and simmer uncovered until the beans are very tender and the liquid is reduced by about three-quarters. This will take 1½ to 2 hours.

4. Transfer the ham bone to a plate and let cool slightly. Finely shred any meat on the bone and return it to the pot.

5. Stir in the remaining 4 tablespoons parsley, 2 more tablespoons of the cilantro, the salt, all but ¼ cup of the bell pepper, the remaining 1 teaspoon cumin, the sherry, brown sugar, and lime juice. Simmer another 30 minutes, stirring frequently. Adjust the seasonings and serve very hot. Garnish each serving with a dollop of crème fraîche and a sprinkling of the remaining diced red pepper and chopped cilantro.

Makes 10 to 12 small portions

MEXICAN GAZPACHO

Although I did not eat gazpacho when I visited Mexico, I came home inspired by their markets full of colorful ingredients. Here, I begin my soup with roasted peppers to add a subtle smoky flavor and substance to the tomato base. Fresh cucumbers and ripe tomatoes add the tastes of a summer garden, and an avocado and hard-cooked egg garnish adds the perfect final touch. Serve chilled in chunky mugs or bright bowls.

2 red bell peppers, halved lengthwise and roasted (page 202)
2 cups canned tomato juice
½ cup red wine vinegar
⅓ cup extra virgin olive oil
⅓ cup coarsely chopped red onion
1 hothouse (seedless) cucumber, peeled and coarsely chopped
1 large red bell pepper, stemmed, seeded, and coarsely chopped
4 ripe plum tomatoes, cored and coarsely chopped
Salt and coarsely ground black pepper, to taste
2 dashes Tabasco sauce
1½ tablespoons chopped flat-leaf parsley
1 ripe avocado, preferably Haas, pitted, peeled, and finely diced, for garnish
2 hard-cooked eggs, coarsely chopped, for garnish

1. In a blender, purée the roasted peppers with 1 cup of the tomato juice and pour it into a large bowl. Whisk in the vinegar, olive oil, and remaining 1 cup tomato juice.

2. Add all the fresh vegetables through the tomatoes to the tomato juice mixture. Working in small batches, place the mixture in the food processor and pulse on and off 6 to 8 times until blended but still chunky. Remove to a second large bowl.

3. Season with salt, pepper, and the Tabasco sauce. Stir in the parsley. Refrigerate at least 6 hours before serving. Serve chilled, garnished with the avocado and hard-cooked egg.

Serves 6

SOUVENIR TO SAVOR

La Noche de los Rábanos

When Richard and I planned our Christmas trip to Mexico, he made sure that we would be in the city of Oaxaca by the evening of December 23 to celebrate "The Night of the Radishes." This festival, held every year, is the first of many special events of the long, elaborate Christmas celebration. The edges of the Zócola, Oaxaca's magnificent central square, are made magical with dioramas composed of dried corn husks, dried flowers, and, last but not least, carved hybrid red radishes. Depicting everything from nativity scenes to folkloric dances, each outlying community group strives to outdo the other with their remarkable displays. Thousands of people move around the Zócola in orderly serpentine lines to view this amazing show.

The first scenes are artfully crafted from dried corn husks. Following the corn husks are ornate displays crafted from tiny dried flowers, called *flores immortales,* portraying traditional nativity scenes. At last you come to the radishes, and the expressions of delight become increasingly contagious.

Many radish figurines are as tall as 12 inches. The long red, hybrid radishes are carved into castles with every brick and stone defined to create authentic scenes and tell a story. Carvings of folk dancers and musicians in elaborate costumes with every intricate pattern and detail in place come alive. I was particularly awed by eight women dancers wearing long full skirts with billowing sleeved blouses, all carved to look like lace. Not a detail was missing. If rickrack was supposed to line the hem of a skirt, it was there. Not a gem was absent from a wise man's coat in a nativity scene.

The pride and skill that goes into these perfect works of art is unlike anything I have ever seen. Simple passion meets pure talent when, once a year, these artisans imbue the humble radish with new meaning.

These intricately carved Oaxacan radishes steal the show at Christmastime.

CHA-CHA CORN GAZPACHO

Light, cool, and crisp, this vibrant summer soup revels in the colors and flavors of a Mexican fiesta. Fresh corn and red bell peppers contrast well with cool cucumbers and dill. After stripping the kernels, I've simmered the cobs in chicken broth to infuse it with a rich sweetness. Serve chilled in brightly colored mugs along with your favorite fajitas or quesadillas for light summer dining.

4 cups defatted Chicken Broth (page 127)
2 ears corn, kernels removed (about 2 cups), cobs reserved and halved crosswise
4 fresh dill sprigs with stems
4 new red potatoes, scrubbed and cut into ¼-inch dice (about 2 cups)
3 medium cucumbers
2 cups nonfat plain yogurt
1 small red bell pepper, stemmed, seeded, and cut into ¼-inch dice
Coarsely ground black pepper, to taste
2 tablespoons chopped fresh dill

1. Place the chicken broth, corn cobs, and dill sprigs in a medium-size heavy pot. Bring to a boil, reduce the heat, and simmer uncovered for 10 minutes. Remove and discard the cobs and dill sprigs.

2. Add the potatoes to the broth and cook until tender, about 8 minutes. Add the corn kernels and cook for 1 minute longer. Remove from the heat and pour the soup through a strainer, reserving the vegetables and broth separately.

3. Peel, halve, and seed the cucumbers. Coarsely chop 2 of the cucumbers and cut the last cucumber into ¼-inch dice.

4. Place the yogurt and coarsely chopped cucumbers in a food processor and pulse the machine on and off just to combine but not purée. With the machine running, pour in 1 cup of the reserved chicken broth through the feed tube and pulse the machine just to combine the ingredients. Remove the mixture to a bowl.

5. Stir in the reserved potatoes and corn, the diced cucumber, red pepper, and chopped dill. Season with pepper. Refrigerate for up to 4 hours. Serve chilled.

Makes 6 cups or 6 servings

HUNGARIAN BLACK CHERRY SOUP

Cherries herald the awakening of summer, the most luxurious season of all. In Turkey as well as throughout Hungary, they blanket the markets and fruit carts after a long gray winter. It was, in fact, the Turks who introduced the cherry to Hungary in the 16th century. Cherries have always been a favorite fruit of mine, and when they're in season, I pile them in bowls on the kitchen table so that we can nibble on them every time we pass. I know that they're just right when some blood red juice wiggles down my chin.

Cherry soup is time consuming to prepare, but it's one of those spectacular dishes that is well worth the effort. For this soup, cook the cherries along with a sweet Tokay, one of Hungary's greatest wines, made from the nectar of overripe grapes. Today, Tokay is still considered the only great wine made east of the Rhine. Cherry soup makes a lovely cool beginning to the many fiery Hungarian *paprikás* dishes. It is also a perfect start for an elegant meal of Rack of Lamb with Tarragon Herb Rub (see Index).

3 pounds fresh Bing cherries, rinsed
¼ cup sugar
1 tablespoon finely grated orange zest
2 teaspoons finely grated lemon zest
½ cup fresh orange juice
¼ cup fresh lemon juice
4 cups water
1 cup sweet Tokay or Riesling wine
Salt, to taste
6 tablespoons crème fraîche or sour cream, for garnish
6 fresh mint sprigs, for garnish

1. Set aside 18 cherries. Remove the stems of the remaining cherries, and pit them with a cherry pitter.

2. Place the prepared cherries in a nonreactive soup pot. Toss with the sugar and orange and lemon zests and juices. Add the water.

3. Bring the soup to a boil. Add the wine, reduce the heat to medium-low, and simmer uncovered until the cherries are soft, about 15 minutes. Skim any foam that rises to the surface and stir occasionally as it cooks. Season the soup with salt. Remove from the heat and let cool to room temperature.

4. Remove the cherries with a slotted spoon to a food processor or blender and process until smooth, adding a bit of liquid if necessary. Return the cherry purée to the soup liquid. Refrigerate 4 to 5 hours to chill the soup completely.

5. To serve, ladle the soup into 6 shallow bowls. Garnish each with a tablespoon of crème fraîche, 3 reserved cherries, and a sprig of mint.

Serves 6

Menus

It was not until I got married that I taught myself to cook and entertain. I read cookbooks of every variety and when I began to put together my first few dinner parties, I always found it helpful to have a list of menus to refer to. I enjoyed learning which dishes worked best together. After following menus for years, I became adept at creating my own. The selections I've chosen for this chapter were developed keeping several important things in mind: taste, texture, color, and compatability. Within each menu, the dishes are organized in a logical serving sequence, with the exception of banquet fare, which you should feel free to lay out all at once in a dramatic and gorgeous display. I've also suggested some exciting national menus, taking poetic license, which I hope will lead you on new and adventurous gastronomic journeys. Barbara Ensrud, a wine and beer authority, has made appropriate suggestions for each menu.

As you study the recipes menus, you will find that there are some variations in serving amounts, but in general most of the menus will serve 6 to 8. It may be necessary to adjust some recipes accordingly, but in most cases, the dish is easily increased. Before you go shopping, be sure to adjust your quantities to suit the amount of people you'll be feeding.

BREAKFASTS AND BRUNCHES

Caribe Breakfast on the Balcony

FRESH GRAPEFRUIT SPRITZ

BANANA CINNAMON PANCAKES
WITH
BUTTER RUM SAUCE

SOFTLY SCRAMBLED EGGS WITH
ASPARAGUS AND CURED HAM

SALADE TROPICALE
DE FRUITS

COFFEE

Irish Country Breakfast

FRESH FRUIT JUICES

IRISH PORRIDGE WITH
CREAM, BROWN SUGAR, AND HONEY

ENGLISH MIXED GRILL

DORSET SCONES AND IRISH SODA BREAD
WITH
PRESERVES AND SWEET BUTTER

IRISH BREAKFAST TEA

COFFEE WITH HOT MILK

A Café Tacuba Breakfast

FROTHY FRESH PINEAPPLE JUICE

BANANA BRUNCH SOUP

SCRAMBLED EGGS

HOT CORN TORTILLAS

SAUN'S FRESH SALSA VERDE AND
CRÈME FRAÎCHE

MISS MAUD'S
BREAKFAST BANANA BREAD

CAFÉ CON LECHE

CHOCOLATE A LA TAZA

A Summer Mediterranean Brunch

FRESH BLOOD ORANGE JUICE AND
WATERMELON JUICE

CURED BLACK OLIVES

FRESH MANOURI CHEESE WITH
WILD THYME HONEY

SOFT-BOILED EGGS

CREAMY YOGURT TOPPED WITH
CHERRY COMPOTE AND
PISTACHIO NUTS

BASKET OF BREADS AND RUSKS
WITH
ASSORTED PRESERVES AND SWEET BUTTER

COFFEE AND TEA WITH WARM MILK

RIPE PEACHES, NECTARINES,
AND CHERRIES

A Tunisian Brunch

Tuna Niçoise Briks

Odja
(Tunisian Western Omelet)

Roasted Peppers and Haricots Verts

Cumin Curry Rolls

Vin Gris de Mourvèdre
or
Grenache Rosé

Turkish Fig Pastries

Ripe peaches

LUNCHES

Lunch From A Swedish Market

Salmon Caviar Egg Salad

Lisa's Rosy Shrimp Salad

Swedish Crayfish

Scandinavian cheeses

Limpa Bread

Wheat Berry Bread

Oregon Pinot Gris, Australian Sémillon, or
Carlsberg Elephant beer

Boston lettuce salad with
Apple Cider Vinaigrette

Spice Cake with Coffee Frosting

Fresh raspberries

Highland Winter Luncheon

Highland Pâté

Scottish Oatcakes

Wheat Berry Bread

Sparkling Saumur (Bouvet-Saphir Brut)

Cock-a-Leekie Soup

Roasted Pheasant with
Prince Charles Sauce

Garlic Mashed Potatoes
with Arugula

Red Burgundy
(Beaune 1er Cru)

Watercress and arugula salad
with Apple Cider Vinaigrette

Cranachan

Scottish Shortbread

Scottish Coffee

Framboise

Indian Summer, Mid Day

Casbah Carrot Soup

Yummy Grilled Cheese Sandwiches

Fiesta Corn Salsa

Chilled Beaujolais-Villages or *Fleurie*

Radicchio, endive, and bibb lettuce salad
with Lily Lime Vinaigrette

Moroccan Pumpkin Tea Loaf with
sweetened whipped cream

Ripe plums

Vineyard Luncheon

Minestrone

Focaccia

Vernaccia di San Gimignano

Roasted Red Peppers

Spinach Catalan

Thinly sliced Prosciutto di Parma

Parmigiano-Reggiano cheese

Red and green grapes

Chianti Classico

Summer Plum Tart

Sweet Malvasia

Soup and Sandwich Cuban Style

Carlos' Black Bean Soup

Cuban Sandwich

Salsa Carnaval

Dos Equis beer or *Rioja Dry Rosé*

Tia Maria Ice Cream

Gingersnaps

Lunch on the Lanai

Plaka Tsatsiki with Pita Chips

Jamaican Crab Salad Composée

Jamaican Jerk Ribs and Chicken

Sunny Sweet Potato Salad

Cool Down Salsa

Kiwi Salsa

Salsa Carnaval

Mosel Riesling or *Amber beer*

Pineapple Upside-Down Cake

Vanilla Bean Ice Cream

Lunch at the Beach

Khaled Kouhen's Salad Michwiya on crusty baguettes garnished with chunks of tuna, hard-cooked egg slices, and olives

Chilean Quinoa Tabouleh

Riad's Baba Ghanouj

Lavash

Chilean Sauvignon Blanc

Jamaican Gingerbread

Watermelon wedges

Déjeuner sur l'Herbe

Provençal Chickpea Slather

Chèvres
Bathed in Herbs and
Extra Virgin Olive Oil

Niçoise olives

Crusty bread

Bandol Rosé
or
Rosé de Syrah

Pissaladière

Ratatouille

Provençal Pan Bagna

Côtes-du-Rhône Villages

Orange Pound Cake

Steffi Berne's Chocolate Skinnies

Ripe peaches
and
cherries

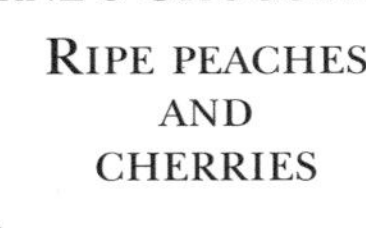

Summer Sunday Luncheon

Chilean White Peach Sangria

Mambo Mango Pork

Sunny Sweet Potato Salad

Roasted Peppers and Haricots Verts

Fumé Blanc

Gingersnaps

Iced Coffee
with
scoops of
Tia Maria
Ice Cream

Riviera Luncheon

Chèvres Bathed in Herbs and
Extra Virgin Olive Oil

Rosemary-Olive Bread

Penne Pasta Salad Niçoise

Sancerre

Velvety Tarte au Citron

Raspberry Ruby Sorbet

TEAS

Russian Samovar Tea

Galina's Berry Tea or Orange
Spiced Tea

Caviar Eggs à la Russe

Salmon Ribbon Bites

Blini with Red Salmon Caviar

Sweet Blinchiki with sweet butter,
honey, and Cherry Compote

Irish Lace Tea

Variety of teas with lemon slices and milk

Ritzy Egg Salad Tea Sandwiches

Gaspé Smoked Salmon Tea Sandwiches

Cucumber and Tiny Sprout Tea Sandwiches

Herbed Cherry Chicken Salad Tea Sandwiches

Dorset Scones with clotted cream and strawberry jam

Linzer Tart

Velvety Tarte au Citron

Spice Cake with Coffee Frosting

Scottish Shortbread

Tea and Sympathy

Variety of teas with lemon slices and milk

Anne's Ham and Cheese Salad Tea Sandwiches

Cucumber and Tiny Sprout Tea Sandwiches

Herbed Cherry Chicken Salad Tea Sandwiches

Caviar Eggs à la Russe

Hungarian Cherry Tea Cake

Moroccan Pumpkin Tea Loaf

Little Swedish Lingonberry Tea Cake

Finnish Cardamom Tea Loaf

João Pires Muscat, Bual Madeira, or *Chilled Tawny Port*

French Goûter d'Hiver

Kugelhopf with preserves and sweet butter

Linzer Tart with sweetened whipped cream

Chocolate a la Taza

Armagnac

CELEBRATIONS

Italian Antipasto Festival

Sparkling Venegazzú Prosecco

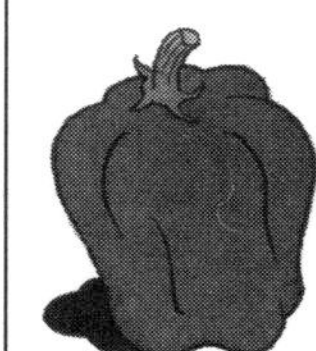

Proscuitto di Parma

Roasted Tomatoes

Roasted Bell Peppers

Flageolet Salad

Lentils

Gaeta olives

Fresh ricotta cheese

Focaccia

Arugula and radicchio salad with Lemon-Garlic Vinaigrette

Sweet Gorgonzola and Parmigiano-Reggiano cheeses

Ruffino Libaio, Rosso di Montalcino, and *Vino Nobeli*

Ripe figs and peaches

Hazelnut-Almond Biscotti

Rijsttafel

Shrimp crackers

Thai Crab Spring Rolls
with
Sweet Garlic Sauce,
Indonesian Soy Sauce,
and Thai Fish Sauce

Goong Waan
(Spicy Sweetened Shrimp)

· · · · · · · · · · ·

Soto Banjar
(Indonesian Chicken
Noodle Soup)

· · · · · · · · · · ·

A-Jaad (Thai Cucumber Cool Down)

Sweet Pickled Cabbage

Thai Pickled Carrots

Thai Pickled Cucumbers

Thai Coconut "Ratatouille"

Cool Down Salsa

Sambal
(chili paste)

Serunding

White rice

Thai Fried Rice and Egg

Lamb Satay

Chicken Satay Singapore Style
with
Saus Kacang

Honey and Ginger-Glazed Chicken

Gaeng Kua Goong
(Curried Pineapple and Prawns)

Pla Preeo Wan
(Sweet and Sour Flounder)

Banana Leaf Curry

*Singha lager, Alsace Riesling,
or
Tocai del Friuli*

· · · · · · · · · · ·

Indonesian Ribbon Cake

Russian Zakuski Party

Beluga or Osetra caviar

Blini and Buckwheat Blini

Caviar Eggs à la Russe

Baltic Sturgeon Salad

Salmon Ribbon Bites

Cocktail Coulibiac

Sasha's Apple Crab Cocktail

Palterovitch Creamy Apple
Herring

Satsivi

Griottes

Assorted black breads

Iced Russian Vodka

· · · · · · · · · · ·

Sunday Farmhouse Roast Pork
with
Savory Plum Conserve

Russian Salad
with
Apple Cider Vinaigrette

Sugared Mashed Carrots

Dilled Cucumber Salad

Rigani White Bean and
Garlic Slather

Provençal Chickpea
Slather

Lalli's Turkish Pilaf
Tomatoes

*Bulgarian Merlot
or
Cabernet Sauvignon*

Meze Celebration

Mediterranean Spiced Olives
Berra's Turkish Leeks
Mussel Salad
Skordalia Sauce
Plaka Tsatsiki
Tarama Slather
Rigani White Bean and Garlic Slather
Riad's Baba Ghanouj
Fresh feta cheese
Lavash, Pita Chips, and crusty bread
Raki and *Ouzo*

Hot Shrimp in a Pot
Pastrami Böreks
Sultan's Pillows
Savory Salmon Croquettes
Pinot Bianco or *Soave Classico*

Quince Spoon Sweet
Banana Bliss

Ice Cream Dream Party for the Kids

La Heladeria Coppelia Sundae
Havana Jelly-Roll Cake
Steffi Berne's Chocolate Skinnies
Salade Tropicale de Fruits
Chocolate Sauce

All Around the World Cocktails

Prathaad Lom with Sweet Garlic Sauce
Gordon's Quesadillas with Avocado Cream
Salmon Ribbon Bites
Chicken Satay Singapore Style with Saus Kacang
Velvety Curried Shrimp
White rice
Delicate Herbed Potato Pancakes with Orange-Rosemary Mayonnaise
Tarama Salmon Blush
Pastrami Böreks
Rigani White Bean and Garlic Slather
Feroce

Champagne

DINNERS

Mediterranean Tastes

Pappa al Pomodoro

Spinach Risotto
Halibut Lemon Kebabs
Lagrein Rosato

Insalata d'Estate

Profiteroles

Santa Lucia Dinner

MINESTRONE

ORVIETO SECCO (CAMPOGRANDE)

OSSO BUCCO WITH BABY ARTICHOKES AND MINT GREMOLATA

LEMON ORZO

GATTINARA OR *BARBARESCO*

ARUGULA SALAD WITH LEMON-GARLIC VINAIGRETTE

RIPE PEACHES AND FIGS

HAZELNUT-ALMOND BISCOTTI

GRAPPA

Mediterranean Pasta Dinner

MEDITERRANEAN SPICED OLIVES

CHÈVRES BATHED IN HERBS AND EXTRA VIRGIN OLIVE OIL
WITH
CRUSTY HERBED BREAD

ROSÉ DE SYRAH

INSALATA D'ESTATE

PASTA ARRABIATA

CÔTES-DU-RHÔNE-VILLAGES

PÊCHES AU BANDOL

HAZELNUT-ALMOND BISCOTTI

A Homey Mediterranean Dinner

BRAISED GLOBE ARTICHOKES

SAUVIGNON DE TOURAINE

POULET CHASSEUR

CLASSIC POLENTA

DILLED CARROTS

CHINON

TENDER ROMAINE AND ENDIVE SALAD
WITH
LEMON-GARLIC VINAIGRETTE

ASIAGO CHEESE

BOSC PEARS

WARM BAGUETTE

CHÂTEAUNEUF-DU-PAPE

SUMMER PLUM TART

VANILLA BEAN ICE CREAM

Provençal Supper

HERBED ORANGE CHÈVRE SLATHER
WITH
LARGE GARLIC CROUTONS

BRAISED GLOBE ARTICHOKES

BRANDADE

CÔTES-DU-RHÔNE BLANC
(GUIGAL, GOUBERT, OR *LA VIEILLE FERME)*
OR *SAUVIGNON BLANC*

LA COUPOLE SALAD

TARTE TATIN

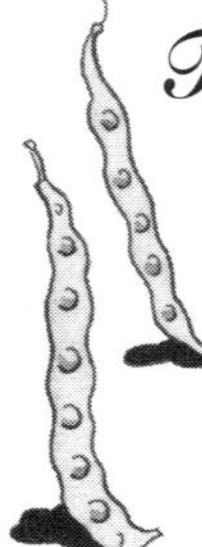

The Flavors of Summer

Mediterranean Spiced Olives

Jumbo Shrimp Ragout

Summer Tomato Risotto

Gavi

Roasted Peppers and Haricots Verts

Sweet Gorgonzola cheese with Rosemary-Olive Bread

Recioto Amarone della Valpolicella

Ripe melon

Après Ski

Highland Pâté with a warm baguette

Griottes, cornichons, and pickled onions

Vouvray

Resto des Amis' French Onion Soup Gratinée

Sunday Farmhouse Roast Pork

Garlic Mashed Potatoes with Arugula

Dilled Carrots

Savory Plum Conserve

Bourgogne Rouge

or

Australian Shiraz-Cabernet

Boston lettuce salad with Walnut Oil Vinaigrette

Linzer Tart

Scottish Coffee

Un Dîner en Ville

La Coupole Salad

Provençal Rabbit in Tawny Port

Herbed Wild Mushrooms

Garlic Mashed Potatoes with Arugula

Domaine Tempier Rouge

Selection of French cheeses

Châteuneuf-du-Pai

Velvety Tarte au Citron

Muscat Beaumes-de-Venise

Heavenly Harvest Dinner

Gingered Crème de Crécy

St. Veran

Coq au Vin

Buttered wide noodles

Bandol

Sunshine Salad

Tarte Tatin

Calvados

Moroccan Couscous Dinner

Khaled Kouhen's Salad Michwiya
Black olives
Crusty bread

Seven Vegetable Couscous
Yacout Tomato Marmalade
Harissa
Dry white Bordeaux (Entre-Deux-Mers or Château Bouvet)

Oriental Oranges
Watermelon wedges
Mandarin Liqueur

1,001 Nights

Minted Sweet Carrot Salad
Sweetened Emerald Zucchini
Yacout Tomato Marmalade
Lavash
Baby Bisteeyas

Lamb and Prune Tagine
Dry Greek Rosé Roditys, Rosé of Cabernet Franc, or Zinfandel Rosé

Oriental Oranges

The Andalusian

Spanish Olive Tapenade
Rosemary-Olive Bread
Verdujo de Rueda

Mediterranean Lentil Vegetable Soup

Andalusian Steak Rollos
Roasted Peppers and Haricots Verts
Rioja Gran Riserva (Marqués de Riscal)

Orange Flan

La Costa del Sol

Herbed Orange Chèvre Slather
Spanish Olive Tapenade
Peasant bread

Caesar Salad with Garlic Croutons

Zarzuela
Lemon Orzo
Albariño or Rueda

Pavlova

Portuguese Tango Dinner

Sopa Alentejana

João Pires Dry Muscat

Mediterranean Roasted Chicken

Tomatoes Provençale

Portuguese Cabernet (Quinta do Bacalhõa)

Serra and Serpa cheeses

Pão-Doce (Portuguese Sweet Bread)

Late-bottled vintage Port

Ripe figs and oranges

A Dinner for the Gods

Wende's Avgolemono Soup

Rigani White Bean and Garlic Slather with Pita Chips

Greek Salad

Spiced Peloponnesian Lamb Shanks

Dill-flecked white rice

Greek Naoussa or Merlot

Galatoboureko

A Plaka Supper

Kalamata Olive Purée

Tarama Salmon Blush

Pita Chips

Santorini

Spanakopita

Individual Moussakas

Goumenissa

Tender romaine leaves with Lemon-Garlic Vinaigrette

Galatoboureko

Quince Spoon Sweet

Santorini Splendor

Tarama Salmon Blush

Greek Salad

Pastitsio

Boutari's Grand Réserve

Creamy Yogurt topped with Quince Spoon Sweet

Turkish Delight

Pastrami Böreks
Berra's Turkish Leeks
Hot Shrimp in a Pot
Halibut Lemon Kebabs
Fumé Blanc

Iceburg lettuce, arugula, and watercress Salad with Lemon-Garlic Vinaigrette

Cherry Compote
Confetti Lemon Sorbet
Watermelon slices

A Sultan's Feast

Turkish Eggplant Salad
Mediterranean Spiced Olives
Lavash

Yogurt Kebabs
Robola de Cephalonia or *Pinot Blanc*

Tender romaine, arugula, and purslane salad with Lemon-Garlic Vinaigrette

Oriental Oranges
Turkish Fig Pastries

The Dubliner

Irish smoked salmon with buttered black bread
Harp lager

Dublin Corned Beef and Cabbage with Orange Horseradish Cream and Cumberland Sauce
Guinness stout or *Black & Tan (half stout/half ale)*

Irish Oatmeal Cookies
Irish coffee

Midnight Sun Celebration

Aquavit
Gravlax with Sweet Dilled Mustard Sauce
Seared Gravlax
Swedish Crayfish
Dilled Cucumber Salad
Ida's Beet Salad
Limpa Bread
Wheat Berry Bread
Tokay d'Alsace (Pinot Gris)

Pavlova

Nordic Nosh

Gravlax with
Sweet Dilled Mustard Sauce

Champagne Brut Rosé

Black Currant Duck Breasts

Dilled Carrots

Delicate Herbed Potato Pancakes

Red Burgundy (Chambolle-Musigny)
or
Australian Shiraz

Summer
Plum Tart

St. Martin's Day Feast

Gravlax with
Sweet Dilled Mustard Sauce

Dilled Cucumber Salad

Iced Polish Vodka
or
Champagne Brut Rosé

St. Martin's Day Roasted Goose

Braised Red Cabbage

Delicate Herbed Potato Pancakes
with
Swedish lingonberries

Red Burgundy
(Echézeaux)

Sachertorte

Black Muscat
(Quady Elysium)

Bites Before the Bolshoi

Buckwheat Blini with Caviar

Hot Russian Borscht

Granny's Mushroom Kasha

Champagne

Miniature Pavlovas

Russian Nights

Botvinya (Sorrel Potato Soup)

Wild Mushroom Blinchiki with
sour cream

Russian Cod Ragout

Marsanne

Vanilla Bean Ice Cream

Cherry Compote

A Blushing Beet Bash

Hot Russian Borscht

Meat Loaf à la Lindstrom

Garlic Mashed Potatoes with Arugula

Rhubarb-Beet Compote

Hungarian Merlot

Oakleaf lettuce salad with Apple Cider Vinaigrette

Sachertorte with sweetened whipped cream

Apricot Liqueur

Magyar Magic

Salmon Ribbon Bites

Pinot Gris

Hungarian Black Cherry Soup

Russian Garden Salad

Magyar Goulash

Creamy Paprika Potatoes

Egri Bikaver or *Merlot*

Linzer Tart with sweetened whipped cream

A Dinner with Japanese Influences

Thai Pickled Carrots

Maguro sushi (finest quality red meat tuna)

Blanc de Noir Brut

Stir-Fried Scallops and Asparagus

Yakitori

Soy sauce

Kirin beer

Confetti Lemon Sorbet

Gingersnaps

Tokyo Tailgate

Cold Sake

A-Jaad (Thai Cucumber Cool Down)

Oriental Spinach Salad with Chinese Vinaigrette

Tokyo Fried Chicken with Basil Teriyaki Sauce

Sesame Butterfly Noodles

Sapporo beer

Melon Coupe Sasha

Gingersnaps

Singapore Supper

Prathaad Lom (Prawn Rolls)
with Sweet Garlic Sauce
and Indonesian Soy Sauce

Chilled Dolcetto d'Alba, Cabernet Franc,
or *Singha beer*

Roast Duck, Melon, and
Mango Salad

Oriental Oranges

Confetti Lemon Sorbet

Malay Festival Nights

Lamb Satay

Chicken Satay Singapore Style
with Saus Kacang

Sparkling Brut Rosé
or
sparkling Vouvray

Spiced Prawn and Pineapple Soup

Golden Chicken Curry

Malay Curried Noodles

Cool Down Salsa

Raita Cool Down

Asian beer

Confetti Lemon Sorbet

Ripe Papaya and watermelon

A Thai Table

Thod Mun Pla
(Tiny Thai Croquettes)
with Thai
Sweet and Sour Sauce

Thai Crab
Spring Rolls
with Sweet Garlic Sauce

Gaeng Kua Goong
(Curried Pineapple
and Prawns)

Thai Fried Rice and Egg

Thai Fruit Salsa

Singha lager

Watermelon wedges

Chinese Cook-in Dinner

Ellen's Hot and Sour Soup

Hong Kong Pork Chops

Sesame Butterfly Noodles

Lightly chilled Brouilly

Oriental Spinach Salad

Ripe muskmelon

A Taj Table

Bhel Poori
with
Savory Mint and Coriander Chutney

Curried Golden Squash Soup

Exotic Lamb Curry

Spiced Vegetable Dal

Indian Creamed Spinach

Spicy Marigold Rice

Tomato-Apricot Chutney

Minted Banana Raita

Dry Riesling
or
Pilsen-style lager beer

Condiments with Coffee

Cozy Fireside Supper

Gordon's Quesadillas
with
Avocado Cream

Blazing Squash Chili with
white rice or barley

Insalata d'Estate

Christmas ale or *Bock beer*

Orange Flan

Casual Mexican Summer Supper

Barbara Ensrud's Red Sangria

Laurie's Basic Guacamole

Ranchero Salsa Rosa

Tortilla chips

Oaxaca Tostada Bites

Cha-Cha Corn Gazpacho

Pepitos (Mexican Steak Sandwiches)

Dos Equis

Orange Pound Cake

Coconut Cream Ice Cream

Mexican Fiesta

Christmas Red Pepper Soup

Gordon's Quesadillas with
Avocado Cream

Spanish Cava Brut

Mexican Pot Roast

Mexican Lentils with
Pineapple and Bananas

Fiesta Corn Salsa

Spanish Pesquera

Sunshine Salad

Mexican Christmas Bread
Pudding

*Ruby Port (Sandeman
Founder's Reserve)*

Rio Revelry

Rio's Feijoada

Bahia Butternut Mash

Copacabana Collards

La Bamba Rice

Argentine Cabernet or *Malbec*

Caribbean Coconut Tart

Coconut Cream Ice Cream

Amaretto

Chilean Tastings

Chilean White Peach Sangria

Chilean Empanadas

Chilean Avocado Salad with Lemon-Mint Yogurt Dressing

Chilean Pistou with Cilantro Pesto

Chilean Quinoa Tabouleh

Chilean Merlot

Lime Baked Bananas

Mardi Gras Magic

Sunshine Salad

Island Grilled Red Snapper with Sauce Chien

Mexican Lentils with Pineapple and Bananas

Sauvignon Blanc or *Tecate beer*

Orange Pound Cake

Coconut Cream Ice Cream

Paradise Island Dinner

Caribe Crudités

Banana Daiquiri

Minty Avocado Shrimp Salad with Lily Lime Vinaigrette

Honey and Ginger-Glazed Chicken

Thai Fried Rice and Egg

Jamaican Gingerbread

Riesling

Confetti Lemon Sorbet

Fresh raspberries

Passion Fruit Liqueur

Caribbean Carnaval

Feroce

Island Pan-Barbecued Shrimp

Jamaican Jerk Chicken

Fiesta Corn Salsa

Martinique Green Beans

White Zinfandel
or
crisp lager
(Red Stripe)

Banana Rum Ice Cream

Lime Baked Bananas

Reggae Evening

Montego Red Pea Soup

Home-Style Jamaican Chicken

La Bamba Rice

Pinot Noir, Zinfandel,
or
Red Stripe beer

Rum Raisin Ice Cream

Gingersnaps

Viva Havana

Señorita Shrimp Boats

Cuba Libre

Mambo Mango Pork

Moros y Cristianos

Chilean Caliterra

Sunshine Salad

Havana Jelly-Roll Cake

Coconut Cream Ice Cream

Salade Tropicale de Fruits

Tropicana al Fresco

Samba Waldorf Salad

Home-Style Jamaican Chicken

Mexican Lentils with Pineapple and Bananas

Copacabana Collards

Jamaican dark beer or *Dragon stout*

Havana Jelly-Roll Cake

Raspberry Ruby Sorbet

SWEET GARAM MASALA
SULTAN'S PILLOWS · THAI COCONUT RATATOUILLE · BEET BREAD PUDDING · BLAZING SQUASH CHILI
MALAY CURRIED NOODLES · FRESH CRAB PAD THAI · SALSA CARNAVAL
BERRA'S TURKISH LEEKS · COPACABANA COLLARDS
PAN CON TOMATE · TOMATO APRICOT CHUTNEY · LEMON ORZO
Hungarian Sweet
PAPRIKA
59¢ Per oz
SPICY MARIGOLD RICE · POLENTA WITH CRIMINI MUSHROOM SAUCE

GARLIC MASHED POTATOES WITH ARUGULA
SAVORY PLUM CONSERVE · GRIOTTES
APPLE-PINEAPPLE RAITA
Sharwood's
INDIA
CURRY POWDER
HOT MADRAS
Market-place
INDIAN CREAMED SPINACH · BYZANTINE PILAF
GREY POUPON
DIJON MUSTARD
AVOCADO BUTTER · SWEETENED EMERALD ZUCCHINI
TARTE PROVENCALE · PENNE PASTA SALADE NICOISE · SUGAR MASHED CARROTS
MEDITERRANEAN DUCK AND TWO-BEAN PASTA

Vegetables

My passion for beautifully arranged vegetables and fruits—all scarlet, golden, purple, and green—grew even greater as my journey brought me from the open markets of Spain to Bangkok to St. Petersburg to Cuba. The riot of colors, shapes, and scents became more intoxicating the farther I went. Vendors in Turkey and Greece could only be challenging the palettes of Gauguin and Matisse when they arranged mounds of blood red-cherries alongside the ripest scarlet tomatoes, and the pinkest of peaches. When arranging a still life, was there ever an artist clever enough to string rows of bananas and corn together, the pale yellow intensified by long bunches of dark red chilies?

The markets of the world are the places where each country's unique palette is splendidly displayed. I will never forget the excitement I felt upon first visiting a Provençal market and selecting just the right purple eggplant, red pepper, bright green zucchini, and violet-hued garlic to go into a ratatouille. Markets have given me my greatest source of recipe inspiration.

BRAISED GLOBE ARTICHOKES

Every once in a while there comes along a perfect vegetable preparation that can serve as an appetizer, salad, or a light entrée. Here's a prime example. These artichokes are particularly lovely because all the fuss is done before cooking. White wine, vegetables, and garlic infuse the cooking liquid and enhance the delicate taste of the artichokes. Then, all you need to do is prepare a red wine vinaigrette or a creamy sauce for dipping the leaves. If you would prefer to serve this as an entrée, accompany it with Boiled Potatoes and Sliced Tomatoes (see Index). To make more, divide the artichokes and other ingredients between two pots and proceed with the recipe. Sprinkle with fresh parsley before serving.

Juice of 1 lemon
6 medium artichokes
2 large onions, finely chopped
4 carrots, peeled and finely diced
4 cloves garlic, finely chopped
2 teaspoons dried thyme
Salt and freshly ground black pepper, to taste
¼ cup extra virgin olive oil
⅔ cup dry white wine
2 cups water
¼ cup coarsely chopped flat-leaf parsley

1. Place the lemon juice in a large bowl and fill three-quarters full with cold water.

2. Cut the stems off the artichokes and remove the tough bottom leaves. Cut about 1½ inches off the tops. With scissors, trim the tops of the remaining leaves. Place the artichokes in the acidulated water to prevent discoloration.

3. When ready to cook them, drain the artichokes and place them with all the remaining ingredients except the parsley in a large pot.

4. Partially cover the pot and cook over medium-low heat until the artichokes are tender, about 1 hour, shaking the pot occasionally. If necessary, add a bit more water.

5. When the artichokes are tender (a leaf will detach easily), remove them from the liquid with tongs and place them upside down on paper towels to drain.

6. To serve, place the artichokes in a large shallow bowl or on a deep platter. Spoon the vegetables and some cooking liquid over the artichokes. Sprinkle with the parsley and serve at room temperature.

Serves 6

ASPARAGUS SAUTE

When asparagus are first in season, prepare them the Spanish way—quickly sautéed in a fruity olive oil—for intense flavor.

About 12 ounces medium asparagus
1 tablespoon extra virgin Spanish olive oil
Coarse salt, to taste

1. Snap off the woody ends of the asparagus spears. Peel the outer layer from the bottom half of each spear.

2. Heat the oil in a large cast-iron skillet over medium-high heat. Add the asparagus and sauté until the asparagus is bright green and with just a tad of brown, about 2 minutes. Sprinkle with salt and serve immediately.

Serves 4

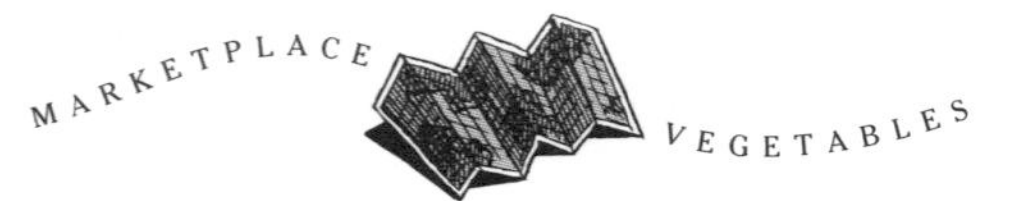

IDA'S BEET SALAD

At Ida Davidsen's Restaurant in Copenhagen, I enjoyed a wonderful, thinly sliced smoked duck breast served with perfectly boiled yellow potatoes that had been sautéed in the duck's fat. The *pièce de résistance* was a creamy beet salad enlivened with tiny slivers of red cabbage, minced red onions, and sweet pickles. The vegetables were bathed in a crème fraîche horseradish sauce. I've tossed my beets, cabbage, and onions with salt, pepper, and cider vinegar before adding the sauce and let them rest for 10 minutes so that the cabbage and onion can wilt slightly. This salad is quite rich, so only small portions are necessary.

6 medium Roasted Beets (recipe follows), peeled
1 small red cabbage (about 1 pound), cored and tough outer leaves removed
¼ cup minced red onion
3 tablespoons minced sweet gherkin pickles
½ teaspoon coarse salt
⅛ teaspoon finely ground white pepper
1 tablespoon apple cider vinegar
1½ cups crème fraîche
½ cup sour cream
3 tablespoons drained prepared white horseradish

1. Cut the beets into ¼-inch dice and place in a large nonreactive bowl.

2. Slice a quarter of the cabbage leaves into fine slivers, discarding any tough white sections. Chop the slivers into small pieces; there should be about 1 cup. Reserve the remaining cabbage for another use.

3. Add the cabbage, onion, and gherkins to the beets. Sprinkle with salt, pepper, and vinegar. Fold together well and let rest for 10 minutes.

4. In another bowl, combine the crème fraîche, sour cream, and horseradish. No more than 1 hour before serving, gently fold the dressing into the vegetables. Adjust the seasonings and serve at room temperature.

Serves 8

ROASTED BEETS

Roasting dramatically intensifies the flavor, texture, and color of many vegetables. Being a beet lover, I have experimented with many methods of preparation and have found that a roasted beet is a delicious beet. It's important to remember not to pierce or cut into the beet before cooking, so leave at least an inch of stem and root on the beet when you trim them. Otherwise they will bleed away their color, flavor, and vitamins. Once cooked and peeled, the beets are ready for use in any recipe.

8 raw medium beets (about 2 pounds)

1. Preheat the oven to 350°F.

2. Rinse the beets well and trim the stems and roots, leaving 1 inch of each on the beets.

3. Wrap the beets individually in aluminum foil, place them on a baking sheet, and bake until tender, about 1½ hours. Remove from the oven and let stand until cool enough to handle. Wearing rubber gloves if you don't want to dye your fingers, unwrap the beets and slip the skins off. Cover and store in the refrigerator until ready to use.

Serves 4 to 6 in desired recipes

BEET BREAD PUDDING

I found a packet of recipe cards in Russia in which a beet bread pudding particularly struck my interest. I had someone translate the Cyrillic writing for me, and I came home with a side dish recipe that was quite intriguing, but I knew there were changes to be made. I've used chicken broth instead of water to soak the bread and added golden raisins for sweetness, which plays off the savory flavor of rye bread. Roasting the beets gives extra richness to this sweet and savory pudding.

1 small loaf rye bread with seeds (about 14 ounces), cut into ¼-inch-thick slices
12 ounces Roasted Beets, (facing page), peeled
4 cups defatted Chicken Broth (page 127)
1 cup golden raisins
2 teaspoons unsalted butter, for the pan
4 large eggs
½ cup sugar
2 tablespoons chopped fresh dill
Finely grated zest of 1 orange
Salt and freshly ground black pepper, to taste
¾ cup sour cream (optional)

1. Let the rye bread slices dry uncovered overnight or lightly toast them and let dry at room temperature for 30 minutes.

2. Coarsely grate the roasted beets. Set aside.

3. Tear the bread into large pieces, place in a bowl with the chicken broth and raisins, and mix well. Let rest for 1 hour.

4. Preheat the oven to 325°F. Generously butter a 13 x 9-inch baking dish.

5. In a separate bowl, whisk the eggs, sugar, dill, orange zest, salt, and pepper together. Gently fold most of the egg mixture into the soaked bread mixture.

6. Spread half the bread mixture evenly in the prepared baking dish. Cover evenly with the grated beets, then spread the remaining bread mixture over the beets. Pour the remaining egg mixture evenly over all.

7. Bake in the center of the oven until lightly golden and set, about 40 minutes. Let rest for 10 minutes before cutting into 12 squares. Serve warm or at room temperature with dollops of sour cream.

Serves 12

BRAISED RED CABBAGE

I always thought that good bacon was necessary to make a flavorful red cabbage dish until I discovered this delicate Swedish version, which I find more to my liking. By combining red wine vinegar, red currant jelly, and dried cherries, the balance of sweet and sour is just right. Once all the ingredients are tossed together, the pot is covered and braised for 1 hour, making the preparation rather effortless and the result superb. An essential served with any roasted goose feast, this vegetable also goes beautifully with duck and roasted pork dishes.

1 large red cabbage (about 2½ pounds), cored, halved, and tough outer leaves discarded
2 tablespoons unsalted butter
1 cup dried cherries
¼ cup red wine vinegar
¼ cup apple juice
¼ cup red currant jelly
1 tablespoon sugar
Salt and coarsely ground black pepper, to taste

1. Preheat the oven to 325°F.

2. Cut the red cabbage into thin slices and set aside.

3. Melt the butter in a large, heavy, oven-proof pot over medium heat. Add the cherries and cook until they begin to soften, 2 minutes, stirring.

4. Add the cabbage, vinegar, apple juice, red currant jelly, sugar, salt, and pepper. Cook over low heat until the cabbage begins to wilt, 5 minutes, stirring occasionally. Cover and braise in the oven for 1 hour. The cabbage will be tender and the liquid slightly thickened. Serve hot. This dish may be stored covered in the refrigerator for up to 3 days.

Serves 6 to 8

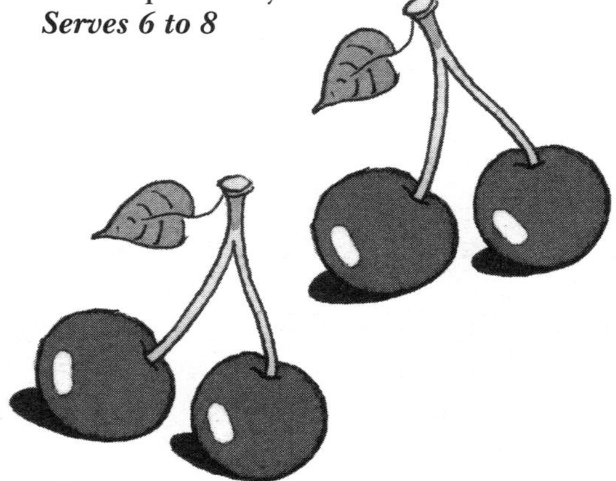

Beer of the Czech Republic

One of the most original and universally appreciated styles of beer evolved around the town of Pilsen in the Czech Republic, the famed Bohemia of old. Pils, or Pilsener, is the most widely produced style of beer made today—a clear golden lager, brisk and dry, with pronounced flavor of hops. The original Pilsener, Pilsener Urquell, remains one of the world's top premium beers, zesty with hops, and is still the prototype for this style.

The Czech Republic has one of the oldest and strongest brewing industries in Europe. The original Budweiser was made there, in the city of Ceské Budějovice in the south near the border of Austria. Today, the local beer is known as Budvar (shortened to "Bud") since Anheuser-Busch beat them to the punch in trademarking the Budweiser name in 1875.

DILLED CARROTS

Simple sweet carrots, prepared the Danish way with garlic and fresh dill, transcend the mundane to become an exciting vegetable served with simple roast meats, game birds, and poultry ragouts. The garlic adds extraordinary flavor which I am partial to, but if you prefer a bit less, adjust the amount to your taste.

6 medium carrots (about 1 pound), peeled and sliced on the diagonal ⅛ inch thick
2 tablespoons olive oil
2 teaspoons minced garlic
Salt and coarsely ground black pepper, to taste
3 tablespoons chopped fresh dill

1. Bring a medium-size pot of salted water to a boil. Add the carrots and boil until just tender, about 5 minutes. Do not overcook. Drain and set aside.

2. Heat the oil in a large nonstick skillet over low heat. Add the garlic and cook, stirring occasionally, until lightly golden, 5 to 6 minutes.

3. Add the carrots and combine well. Season with salt and pepper. Cook 1 to 2 minutes just to heat through. Stir in the dill. Serve immediately.

Serves 4 to 6

SUGARED MASHED CARROTS

These coarsely mashed carrots were served as part of a grand salad display at the Yacout, a restaurant in Marrakech. If there was a jewel to use to describe the intensity of color of this small dish, I would love to find it. The taste is also spectacular, and the rough texture is important because it provides additional interest to the dish. Adjust the sugar syrup as you see fit. Serve at room temperature.

6 to 8 medium carrots, peeled and cut into 1-inch lengths
4 cups water
¼ cup sugar
3 to 4 tablespoons Simple Sugar Syrup (page 34)
2 fresh mint sprigs, for garnish

1. Combine the carrots, water, and sugar in a medium-size saucepan. Bring to a boil, reduce the heat to medium, and simmer until tender, about 30 minutes. Drain and remove to a bowl.

2. Add the sugar syrup and coarsely mash the carrots with a fork. Cool to room temperature.

3. To serve, spread the mashed carrots on a small round or oval plate, flattening them slightly with the back of a fork. Garnish with the mint sprigs.

Serves 8

COPENHAGEN CARROTS

Light and refreshingly spiked with ginger, these shredded carrots are the perfect accompaniment, along with Creamy Potato Salad, to Copenhagen Cod Cakes (see Index).

2 tablespoons apple cider vinegar
½ teaspoon Dijon mustard
½ teaspoon sugar
Salt and coarsely ground black pepper, to taste
¼ cup vegetable oil
2 tablespoons chopped flat-leaf parsley
1 tablespoon minced peeled fresh ginger
4 cups coarsely grated carrots

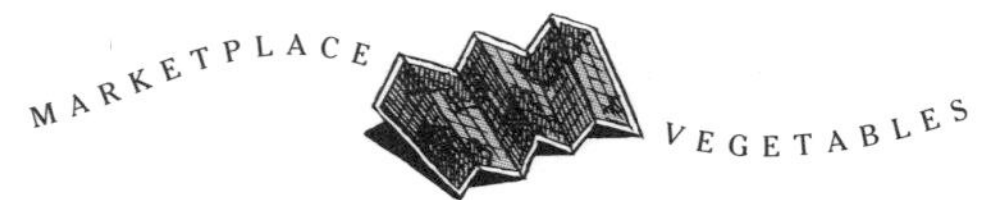

1. Combine the vinegar, mustard, sugar, salt, and pepper in a medium-size bowl. While whisking constantly, slowly drizzle in the oil and continue to whisk until the mixture is slightly thick. Stir in the parsley and ginger.

2. Add the grated carrots to the bowl and toss with the dressing. Cover and refrigerate until ready to serve.

Serves 6 to 8

MINTED SWEET CARROTS

Here's a delicious way to enjoy the natural sweetness of carrots. Enhanced with a bit of sugar syrup, in the Moroccan style, the fresh bite of mint makes this vegetable dish delectable.

8 medium carrots, peeled, halved lengthwise, and cut into 1-inch lengths
3 tablespoons Simple Sugar Syrup (page 34)
2 tablespoons chopped fresh mint leaves

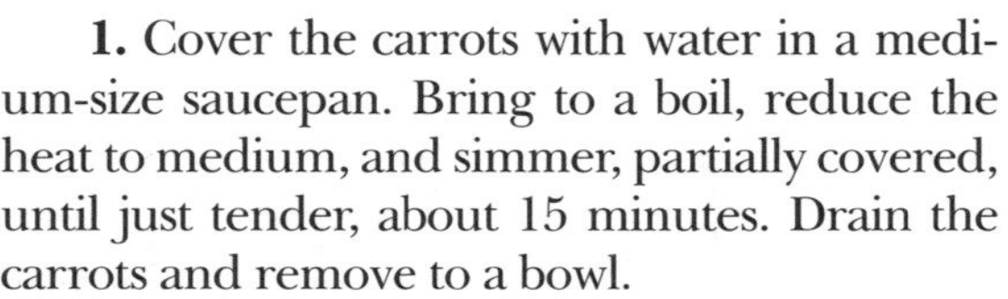

1. Cover the carrots with water in a medium-size saucepan. Bring to a boil, reduce the heat to medium, and simmer, partially covered, until just tender, about 15 minutes. Drain the carrots and remove to a bowl.

2. Toss the carrots with the sugar syrup, then lightly toss with the mint leaves. Serve at room temperature on a small round or oval plate.

Serves 8

COPACABANA COLLARDS

While in Brazil, I had a version of collard greens that I thought was terrific. Finely diced slab bacon, garlic, coarse salt, and freshly ground black pepper impart all the flavor they need. Because the greens shouldn't be too soft, I've cooked them for just 10 minutes, in a small amount of chicken broth. The dish is easily prepared—most of the work is in slivering the dark green leaves—and the payoff is worth it. These are great served with corned beef and pork dishes.

2 pounds collard greens, tough stems removed and leaves rinsed well
4 ounces slab bacon, rind discarded, cut into ¼-inch cubes
1 tablespoon minced garlic
Salt and coarsely ground black pepper, to taste
¼ cup defatted Chicken Broth (page 127)

1. Stack 4 to 6 collard leaves at a time one on top of the other and roll them up on the diagonal. Thinly slice on the diagonal. Set aside.

2. Place the bacon in a large heavy pot and cook, stirring, over low heat to render the fat, about 5 minutes. Add the garlic to the bacon and cook, stirring, for 2 minutes.

3. Add the collard greens, in batches if necessary, until they all fit. Combine well and season with salt and pepper.

4. Drizzle the greens with the chicken broth. Cover the pot and cook, stirring occasionally, over medium-low heat until just tender but still slightly crunchy, 10 to 12 minutes. Serve immediately.

Serves 6

A TASTE OF THE WORLD

South American Palette
Argentina, Brazil, and Chile

...And

- Chilies
- Basil
- Cilantro
- Garlic
- Scallions
- Calabaza
- Collard greens
- Hearts of palm
- Onions
- Tomatoes
- Bananas
- Coconuts
- Grapefruits
- Limes
- Oranges
- Papayas
- Peaches
- Raisins
- Black beans
- Chickpeas
- Black olives
- Rice
- Coconut milk
- Beef
- Dried salt cod
- Suckling pig

MARTINIQUE GREEN BEANS

It seems to me that no matter what country I visit there is always some version of green beans prepared in a rustic style. In Martinique I ate green beans sautéed with wild country onions and lots of wild thyme. In order to recreate the flavor of those onions, I've substituted shallots and garlic. These beans are delicious served with Caribbean Chicken and Le Colibri Porc Colombo (see Index). A generous squeeze of fresh lime juice brightens all the flavors.

1 pound tender green beans, stem ends trimmed
2 tablespoons extra virgin olive oil
1 cup coarsely slivered shallots
6 cloves garlic, slivered
¾ cup defatted Chicken Broth (page 127)
6 ripe plum tomatoes, seeded and cut into ¼-inch dice
2 tablespoons fresh thyme leaves
Salt and coarsely ground black pepper, to taste
3 fresh limes, halved, for serving

1. Bring a large pan of water to a boil. Add the beans and cook until just crisp-tender, 3 to 5 minutes. Drain, rinse under cold water, and drain again. Set aside.

2. Heat the oil in a large skillet over medium heat. Add the shallots and garlic. Cook, stirring, to wilt the vegetables, 5 minutes. Add the broth and cook until the shallots are soft, about 7 minutes. Add the tomatoes, thyme, salt, and pepper and cook an additional 3 minutes.

3. Toss in the cooked green beans and fold together well. Cook an additional 2 minutes. Adjust the seasonings and serve hot, topped with the fresh lime halves for squeezing over the beans.

Serves 6

BERRA'S TURKISH LEEKS

Berra Koc, Russian born but raised in Ankara, the capital of Turkey, brought her beautiful recipes with her when she moved to America. Traditionally cold olive oil dishes begin the renowned turkish *meze*, and this dish is a perfect example of the rich silky result. Berra says it's essential to serve it with plenty of lemon wedges.

1 tablespoon vinegar
2 pounds leeks
3 medium carrots, peeled
½ cup olive oil
½ cup water
1 teaspoon sugar
1 teaspoon salt
Juice of 1 small lemon
2 tablespoons raw long-grain rice
6 generous lemon wedges, for serving

1. Place the vinegar in a large bowl and fill it with cold water.

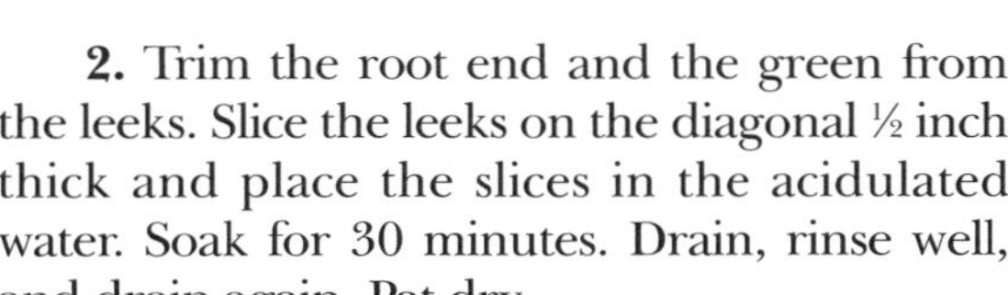

2. Trim the root end and the green from the leeks. Slice the leeks on the diagonal ½ inch thick and place the slices in the acidulated water. Soak for 30 minutes. Drain, rinse well, and drain again. Pat dry.

3. Slice the carrots on the diagonal ¼ inch thick.

4. Heat the olive oil in a large heavy pot over medium heat until hot. Add the leeks and carrots; cover and cook, shaking the pan often, until the vegetables begin to absorb the oil, about 15 minutes.

5. Add the water, sugar, salt, and lemon juice to the pot. Add the rice and stir very gently just to combine. Cover and simmer until the rice is tender and the water has been absorbed, about 20 minutes. Serve at room temperature with the lemon wedges.

Serves 6

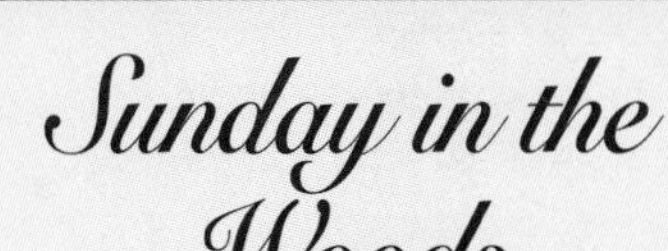

SOUVENIR TO SAVOR

Sunday in the Woods

Indian summer in St. Petersburg is the season for hunting wild mushrooms. It is one of the most cherished forms of relaxation, and each family has their favorite place in the woods to seek out the luscious harvest. There are no mushrooms cultivated to sell in Russia, yet there are many dishes prepared with mushroom sauces. When overflowing baskets are brought back to family kitchens, some mushrooms will be eaten fresh, but the majority will be carefully sliced, dried, and stored for use all year round. The pungent flavors are very similar to dried porcini and cèpes. Some bring their harvest overflow to the large city markets, so that others who were not able to gather their own have an opportunity to store up for the winter.

HERBED WILD MUSHROOMS

There are few countries around the world—from Russia to Denmark and on to France—that aren't obsessed with their wild mushrooms, especially in the prime gathering seasons of fall and spring. Sundays are reserved for the hunt, when everyone takes to the woods with their baskets ready to hold the precious harvest. The earthy flavors of the mushrooms in simple preparations make a wonderful accompaniment to game birds as well as simple roast chicken. Because the mushrooms are wild, they tend to be quite dirty, but resist any temptation to run them under cold water for they'll be ruined. Instead, clean them with a soft mushroom brush or use a damp kitchen towel or paper towels to wipe them off. To enhance their flavor in this recipe, I've added dried thyme, lots of parsley, and some lemon zest. These tastes complement rather than overwhelm.

2 pounds fresh wild mushrooms, such as shiitakes and chanterelles, stems removed
2 tablespoons extra virgin olive oil
4 large shallots, coarsely chopped
2 large cloves garlic, coarsely chopped
1¼ teaspoons dried thyme
⅓ cup chopped flat-leaf parsley
2 tablespoons unsalted butter
1½ teaspoons freshly ground black pepper
1 to 1½ tablespoons finely grated lemon zest
Salt, to taste

1. Wipe the mushroom caps with a damp paper towel, then cut into ½-inch pieces. Set aside.

2. Heat the olive oil in a large nonstick skillet over medium-low heat. Add the shallots, garlic, and thyme; cook, stirring, until the shallots soften slightly, about 3 minutes. Increase the heat to medium-high and stir in the mushrooms. Cover and cook until the mushrooms soften, 5 to 6 minutes.

3. Add the parsley, butter, pepper, and lemon zest. Cook, stirring, until the mushrooms give off some of their liquid, 4 to 5 minutes. Season with salt and additional pepper to taste.

Serves 6

ROASTED BELL PEPPERS

I think I may roast peppers more often than I boil water. They're wonderful in recipes and great to have on hand in the refrigerator. They'll keep for five days if they are drizzled with a little olive oil and lemon juice. In the winter, adapt your BLTs to BLPs when tomatoes are not quite up to par.

4 large bell peppers, red, green, yellow, or orange, stemmed, halved lengthwise, and seeded
2 tablespoons extra virgin olive oil
2 teaspoons fresh lemon juice

1. Preheat the broiler. Line a baking sheet with aluminum foil.

2. Flatten each pepper half slightly with the palm of your hand. Lay the peppers, skin side up, in a single layer on the prepared baking sheet. Place under the broiler about 3 inches from the heat source and broil until the skins are charred black, 12 to 15 minutes. Remove the peppers to a paper or plastic bag, close tightly, and let the peppers steam for about 15 minutes. Slip off the charred skins.

3. Place the peppers in a flat plastic container and drizzle with the oil and lemon juice. Stir to coat the peppers. Cover and refrigerate until ready to use. Serve at room temperature.

Serves 4

DELICATE HERBED POTATO PANCAKES

Most potato pancakes are sturdy little disks, bound together with eggs and flour, but not these. This delicate Swedish version looks more like a lace doily than anything else and is bursting with the flavors of fresh garden herbs and pungent black pepper. They're lovely served with Black Currant Duck Breasts, St. Martin's Roasted Goose (see Index), or on their own with Swedish lingonberries.

2 medium Idaho potatoes, peeled
2 tablespoons snipped fresh chives
2 tablespoons chopped fresh tarragon leaves
Coarse salt and coarsely ground black pepper, to taste
2 tablespoons unsalted butter
2 tablespoons vegetable oil

1. Coarsely grate the potatoes into a bowl. Work quickly to prevent the potatoes from discoloring too much. The potatoes will give off a starchy liquid but don't drain them. Add the chives, tarragon, salt, and pepper and mix well.

2. Heat 1 tablespoon each of the butter and oil in a large nonstick skillet over medium-high heat until quite hot and slightly foamy. Add 2 tablespoons of the potato mixture per pancake to the skillet, flattening the pancakes with the back of a spatula. Cook until the pancakes are golden brown, 2 to 3 minutes per side. Add the remaining butter and oil to the pan as necessary, and fry the remaining pancakes. Serve immediately or cover with aluminum foil and keep warm in a low (250°F) oven.

Makes 10 pancakes, serves 4 to 5

GERMAN POTATO SALAD

This is not an authentic German potato salad but more a Franco-German combination since I've added bacon and onion, which are often found in French-style salads. The creamy dressing is enlivened with mustard and cider vinegar and adds character to the potatoes. It is lovely served alongside grilled sausages, especially Polish kielbasa, or with other roasted meats, accompanied by a light cucumber salad.

4 large Idaho potatoes (about 2 pounds)
Salt, to taste
8 ounces slab bacon, rind discarded, cut into ¼-inch cubes
1 medium onion, chopped
2 tablespoons apple cider vinegar
1 teaspoon Dijon mustard
1 teaspoon sugar
Freshly ground black pepper, to taste
1 cup sour cream
1½ tablespoons chopped flat-leaf parsley, for garnish

1. Peel the potatoes and cut crosswise into ¼-inch-thick slices. Place in a pot and cover with salted water. Bring to a boil, reduce the heat, and simmer uncovered until tender but not mushy, about 8 minutes. Drain well and place in a large bowl.

2. Place the bacon in a nonstick skillet and cook over low heat until the fat is rendered, about 10 minutes. Add the onion and cook until wilted, about 10 minutes. Drain and discard the fat from the bacon and onion and add them to the potatoes. Fold together with a rubber spatula.

3. For the dressing, combine the vinegar, mustard, sugar, and salt and pepper, to taste. Whisk together well, then fold in the sour cream. Toss the salad with the dressing while the potatoes are still warm. Adjust the seasonings. Serve warm or at room temperature, sprinkled with the parsley.

Serves 8

THE BEERS OF

Germany

Germany is the world's largest producer—and consumer—of beer. There are some 1,400 breweries in the country as a whole (now including what formerly was East Germany, which had 200). Germans drink nearly 150 liters per capita annually. They produce not only the most beer, they make it in more different styles than any other country. Various regions and even towns have their specialties.

German beers range from the light, effervescent, almost wine-like Berliner Weisse, the famous wheat beer of Berlin, to the dark, richly malted bock beers of Bavaria. There are the copper-hued Altbiers of Düsseldorf, the golden ales (Kölsch) of Cologne, the smoky Rauchbiers of Bamberg, the brisk, dry Pilsen-style lagers from Bremen and Hamburg (such as Beck's and St. Pauli Girl). There are 800 breweries in Bavaria alone. The city with the most breweries, however, is not Munich but Cologne, where there are twelve within the city limits.

The brewing industry of Germany is exceedingly old, documented to the Middle Ages, and probably much older than that. The Pure Beer Law of 1516 (*Reinheitsgebot*),

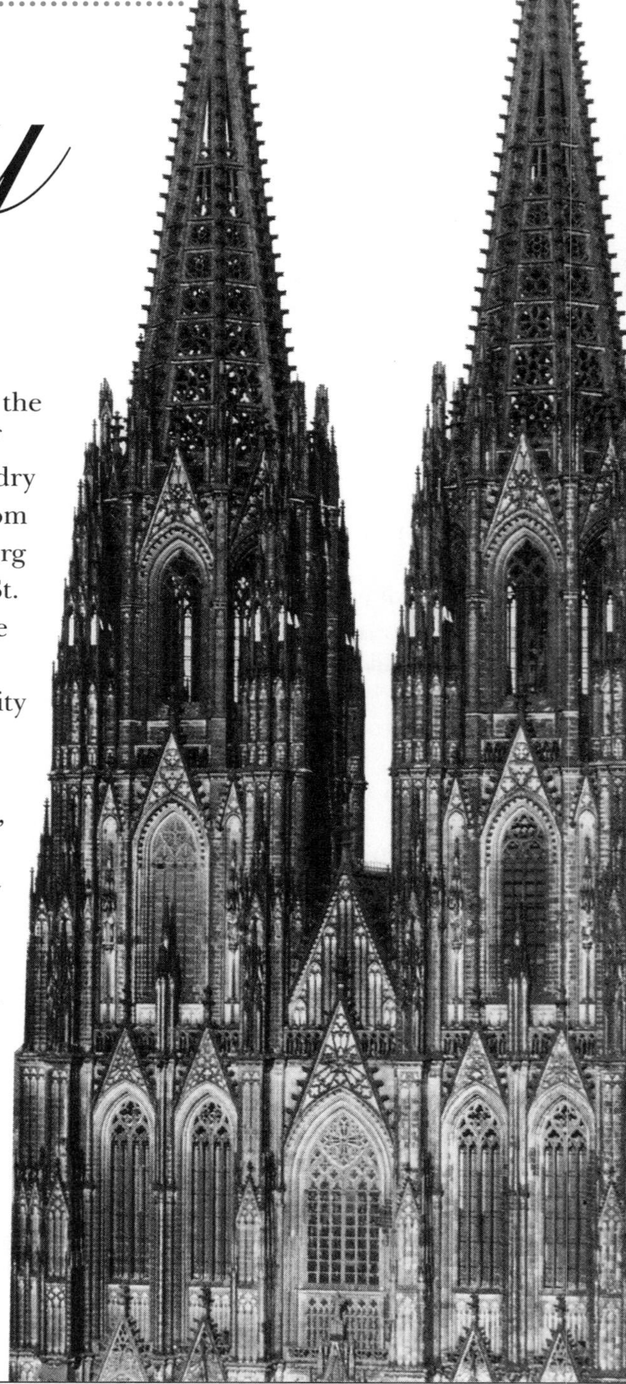

The gothic spires of the Cologne Cathedral.

> "There are some 1,400 breweries in the country as a whole. They not only make the most beer, they make it in more different styles than any other country."

4.2 percent in lager, whether dark or light. Though bock is made in various places, the original bock developed in Einbeck and was popularized in Munich. It is usually dark in color but pale versions also exist.

still followed today by quality brewers, decreed that beer could be made only from malt (malted barley), hops, yeast, and water. No additives whatsoever were permitted. Just as legitimate, however, are the lighter styles of such specialties as Weizenbier, or wheat beers, which Munich claims to have originated sometime around a thousand years ago in a local monastery.

German traditions greatly influenced the brewing industry worldwide, largely determining the styles of beer available everywhere. Lager, for example, denoting a pale or clear golden beer, comes from the German term meaning "to store" or "cellar," during which time the beer aged, mellowed, and clarified. Bockbier, said to have been a favorite of Martin Luther, is darker and stronger than lager, somewhat higher in alcohol, usually between 5 and 6 percent over the more usual 3.2 to

Above and right: Scenes from the festive Oktoberfest in Munich—pass the stein!

GRATIN DAUPHINOIS

This rustic potato dish, a staple in most French households, is classically made from three basic ingredients: potatoes, garlic, and cream. Most cooks have their favorite recipe, adding a bit of this or that as preferred. Grated Gruyère cheese is sometimes scattered between the layers and atop the gratin. I like mine simple, creamy, and completely comforting. I prefer using crème fraîche rather than heavy cream because it adds a mild tangy flavor and a luscious consistency. I also use lots of coarsely ground black pepper for zest. Any way you make it, you'll have great potatoes to serve along with roasted poultry and other meats.

1 clove garlic, peeled and halved
1 teaspoon unsalted butter, for the dish
4 Idaho potatoes (about 2 pounds), peeled and thinly sliced
Salt and coarsely ground black pepper, to taste
2 cups crème fraîche
½ cup milk

1. Preheat the oven to 350°F. Rub a 13 x 9 x 2-inch baking dish all over with the cut side of the garlic, then butter the dish.

2. Place the sliced potatoes in a large saucepan and cover with salted cold water. Bring to a boil and boil for 1 minute. Drain and pat dry. Place the potatoes in a bowl and season generously with salt and pepper.

3. Mix the crème fraîche and milk together in a small bowl.

4. Layer half the potatoes in the baking dish, then cover with half the crème fraîche mixture. Repeat with the remaining potatoes and crème fraîche.

5. Bake until the potatoes are tender and bubbly and golden on top, 50 to 60 minutes.

Serves 8

CREAMY PAPRIKA POTATOES

Known in Hungary as "poor man's goulash," these potatoes, flavored with sweet paprika and enriched with sour cream, would be delicious served with Hungarian sausages and a green salad. They're not bad with Magyar Goulash (see Index) either.

2 tablespoons olive oil
1 large onion, coarsely chopped
1 tablespoon sweet paprika
4 large Idaho potatoes (about 2 pounds), peeled and cut into ½-inch dice
2 cups defatted Chicken Broth (page 127)
½ cup sour cream
Salt, to taste
⅓ cup chopped flat-leaf parsley or fresh dill

1. Place the oil in a medium-size heavy pot over medium-low heat. Add the onion and cook, stirring, until wilted, about 10 minutes.

2. Remove the pot from the heat and stir in the paprika. Add the potatoes and broth. Bring to a boil, reduce the heat to medium, and simmer uncovered until the potatoes are tender, about 15 minutes.

3. Stir in the sour cream and gently simmer 2 to 3 minutes to allow the flavors to blend. Season with salt and stir in the parsley. Serve immediately.

Serves 4

Paprika

The king of Hungarian cuisine is, without doubt, the vivid red spice called paprika. Introduced by the Turks during their 16th-century occupation of Hungary, the world's finest paprika is produced here. Varying in strength and color from mild and sweet to hot and pungent and from bright red to slightly brown, it is a tremendously versatile spice. Paprika is the finely ground powder obtained from dried peppers known as *Capsicum annum.* These aren't the bell peppers that we are accustomed to but rather a conical, horn-shaped pepper that grows about 4 to 6 inches long and 1 to 2 inches in diameter. Fields of these colorful peppers stretch across southern Hungary near Szeged, the paprika capital. The peppers are harvested in late summer, dried, and then ground into different strength paprikas depending on the ratio of flesh, seeds, and ribs used. There are six varieties of paprika:

KÜLÖNLEGES: Delicate with a bright red color. Hardly spicy at all and by far the most beautifully hued.

CSMEGES: Mild mannered with just a touch of heat.

EDES NEMES: Known as "noble sweet" in spice circles. It is by far the most popular of paprikas, and since it is only slightly hot, it is the most versatile. It is the one you are probably most familiar with.

Félédes: A semisweet powder just a little hotter than *Edes nemes.* You don't need much to add a bit of fire to dishes.

RÓZSA: Rose colored, this variety is paler, spicier, and more perfumed than the others. Used in spicy dishes.

ERÖS: Hot and very spicy. The color varies from slightly yellow to brown.

Your choice of paprika depends on your taste, but generally the milder ones are used in cooking, while the hotter versions appear tabletop for the personal addition of fire to dishes.

Amazingly versatile, paprika isn't like most other spices that are doled out in pinches and tiny spoonfuls. It is boldly scooped and measured into many soups, stews, and sauces. Paprika is best known for its presence in Hungary's national dish—goulash. Paprika also adds lovely color to recipes and varying amounts of fire depending upon your choice of strength.

When cooking with paprika, the best flavor is obtained by sprinkling the paprika over onions that have been gently cooked in bacon or lard. Be sure that the temperature isn't too hot, since this can ruin the flavor and the color of the paprika. Most important, as with all spices, is to buy paprika in small, manageable quantities so that it is always fresh and packed with flavor. It also freezes very well, so that it can be used bit by bit when called for.

More kinds of paprika than you thought existed exist.

A TASTE OF THE WORLD

Hungarian Palette

...*And*

Poppy seeds	*Parsnips*
Cinnamon	*Red and green bell peppers*
Parsley	*Plums*
Tarragon	*Apricots*
Marjoram	*Cottage cheese*
Garlic	*Lard*
Onions	*Wide noodles*
Cucumbers	*Dumplings*
Potatoes	

GARLIC MASHED POTATOES WITH ARUGULA

There is nothing more comforting in the world than a warm bowl of mashed potatoes. I remember those of my childhood with deep affection—they were buttery, a bit lumpy, and a perfect part of our 6 o'clock family dinners. Today mashed potatoes have been elevated to haute cuisine—the lumps are gone, and roasted garlic and other additions grace them with new honor. In this recipe, garlic and olive oil, as well as the arugula that is woven in towards the end, enhance the flavor. Feel free to adjust the amounts of milk and oil to your preference. Some of us like our mashed potatoes very creamy, others fluffy, and some a bit drier. I still don't think any of us appreciate lumps. They're great served with all roasted meats and poultry.

3 large cloves garlic, unpeeled
¼ cup plus 1 teaspoon extra virgin olive oil
Salt and freshly ground black pepper, to taste
3 pounds Idaho potatoes, peeled
Defatted Chicken Broth (page 127) or 1 chicken bouillon cube plus cold water, for cooking the potatoes
2 bunches arugula, rinsed well, tough stems removed
2 tablespoons unsalted butter
1¾ cups hot milk, or more if needed

1. Preheat the oven to 350°F.

2. Place the garlic cloves on a small piece of aluminum foil. Drizzle with 1 teaspoon oil and sprinkle with salt and pepper. Close the foil loosely and bake in a small baking pan until the garlic is soft, about 40 minutes. Remove and set aside.

3. Cut the potatoes into large chunks and place them in a pot. Cover with the broth or cold water to which you've added the bouillon cube. Bring to a boil, reduce the heat slightly, and gently boil uncovered until the potatoes are very tender, 20 to 25 minutes.

4. While the potatoes are cooking, bring a small pot of water to a boil. Dip the arugula in quickly to blanch it and squeeze it dry in paper towels. Pull the leaves apart and reserve.

5. Drain the cooked potatoes and return them to the pot. Shake the pot over low heat for 15 seconds to remove excess moisture.

6. Press the potatoes through a ricer into a large bowl or mash them with the back of a large fork. Squeeze the roasted garlic out of the skins into the potatoes and add the butter and hot milk little by little, continuing to mash until smooth. Drizzle in ¼ cup olive oil and season generously with salt and pepper. Stir in the arugula. Serve immediately. (This recipe may be halved for 4 portions.)

Serves 6 to 8

STOCKHOLM STREET POTATOES

On a rainy, gray August afternoon in Stockholm, I visited the Wasa Museum. There, bathed in a ghostly light, is the royal flagship (the Wasa) which sank on its maiden voyage in the early 17th century and was brought to the surface in 1961. It was a breathtaking experience. I left the museum around 4 P.M., entranced and hungry, and on that dank day, nothing seemed more appealing than the hot baked potatoes mounded with dreamy, dill-flecked shrimp salad offered by a street vendor. Another topping he offered was thick yogurt mixed with red salmon caviar.

On its own, the shrimp salad is a lovely light luncheon salad, but when combined with warm potato pulp, the dish is bold enough to satisfy a hearty appetite. If you prefer to serve the shrimp as a salad, omit the baked potatoes in the recipe.

8 ounces shrimp, shelled, deveined, and cooked
3 hard-cooked eggs, peeled
2 tablespoons finely diced red onion
1 tablespoon drained tiny capers
2 tablespoons finely chopped fresh dill
4 baked potatoes, halved lengthwise
Salt and freshly ground white pepper, to taste
¼ cup mayonnaise
¼ cup crème fraîche
1 teaspoon honey mustard

1. Cut each shrimp crosswise into 4 small pieces and place in a bowl.

2. Separate the cooked egg whites from the yolks, cut the whites into small pieces, and add them to the shrimp. Reserve the yolks for another use.

3. Add the onion, capers, and dill to the shrimp.

4. With a small melon baller, scoop out 4 balls from each potato half, leaving a generous amount of potato inside the skins. Add the potato balls to the shrimp, gently combine, and season with salt and pepper.

5. To make the dressing, mix the mayonnaise, crème fraîche, and mustard together. With a rubber spatula, gently fold it into the salad.

6. Before serving, warm the potato shells on a baking sheet in a preheated 350°F oven for 10 to 12 minutes. Mound the shrimp salad equally into the 8 potato halves. Serve while the potatoes are still warm.

Serves 8

BOILED POTATOES AND SLICED TOMATOES

My favorite travel discoveries are the many dishes created from seasonal produce abundant in the marketplace. They are usually easy to prepare and show off native ingredients to great advantage. I'm a big fan of potatoes and was particularly taken by this dish served on Martinique. Sliced potatoes, lightly coated with a good olive oil and a grind of black pepper, are layered on top of ripe juicy tomato slices and served with diced avocado and lime wedges for a burst of freshness. Wow! Perfect with grilled fish and the best sandwiches.

3 large Idaho potatoes (about 1½ to 2 pounds)
4 ripe large tomatoes, cored and sliced ¼ inch thick
3 tablespoons extra virgin olive oil
Freshly ground black pepper, to taste
Coarse salt, to taste
1 ripe avocado, preferably Haas, pitted, peeled, and cut into ¼-inch dice
1 tablespoon fresh lime juice
2 teaspoons fresh thyme leaves
3 limes, quartered, for garnish

1. Place the potatoes in a large saucepan and cover with water. Bring to a boil, reduce the heat, and simmer uncovered until tender, 15 to 20 minutes. Drain. When the potatoes are cool enough to handle, peel them and slice crosswise ¼ inch thick.

2. Arrange the tomato slices in a single layer over the bottom of a serving platter. Drizzle with 1 tablespoon of the olive oil and a coarse grind of black pepper.

3. Place the potato slices in a bowl and gently toss with the remaining 2 tablespoons olive oil and salt and pepper to taste. Arrange the potatoes on top of the tomatoes, overlapping the slices a bit.

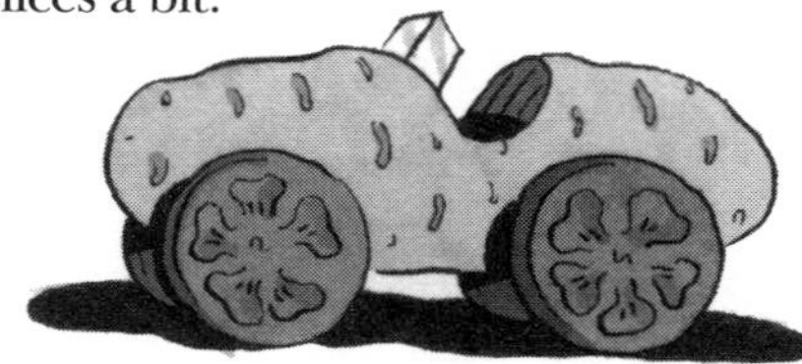

4. Toss the avocado with the lime juice and sprinkle atop the potatoes along with the fresh thyme leaves. Arrange the lime wedges on the side of the platter.

Serves 6

SOUVENIR TO SAVOR

Hot Potato Party

Strange but true: It was while reveling in the great street food of Turkey that I had a vision of a Super Bowl party. The inspiration was a shiny black cart painted with hot pink letters announcing FIRINDA PATATES (baked potatoes). An array of garnishes sat ready to embellish the potatoes. The fresh garnishes included bowls of chopped, seeded ripe tomatoes; finely diced red bell peppers; sliced raw mushrooms tossed in olive oil and lemon juice with a healthy grinding of black pepper; chopped flat-leaf parsley; and a finely diced potato and green pea salad all dressed up with mayonnaise and dill. The only false note was a plastic bottle of ketchup standing alongside these otherwise fresh offerings.

First the hot potatoes were cut in half lengthwise, then the insides were mashed with a liberal pat of butter (you can eliminate this). Once mashed, the two potato halves were fitted into a plastic dish. Each half was then topped with as many of the garnishes as possible and then came the inevitable ketchup squirt—if desired.

A baked potato buffet really is perfect on Super Bowl Sunday. Bake up a bunch and set out the toppings. Let everyone help themselves—and enjoy the game!

SUNNY SWEET POTATO SALAD

A luscious curried mayonnaise sweetened a bit with mango chutney coats sweet and baking potatoes. It is critical not to overcook the sweet potatoes; so follow the timing and test them with the sharp tip of a paring knife. Bright and crisp scallions add the right flavor and texture. This golden potato salad is a must with Jerk Chicken and Jerk Pork Ribs (see Index) for perfect Caribbean taste sensations.

Coarse salt, to taste
2 sweet potatoes (about 1 pound), peeled and cut into ½-inch cubes
2 Idaho potatoes (about 1 pound), peeled and cut into ½-inch cubes
Freshly ground black pepper, to taste
1 cup mayonnaise
3 tablespoons mango chutney, finely chopped
2 to 3 tablespoons best-quality curry powder
4 scallions (3 inches green left on), thinly sliced on the diagonal
1 tablespoon chopped flat-leaf parsley

1. Bring 2 medium-size pots of salted water to a boil. Cook the sweet potatoes in one pot until just tender, 5 to 6 minutes. Do not overcook. Cook the Idaho potatoes in the other pot until tender, 8 to 10 minutes. When the potatoes are finished cooking, drain them and combine in a bowl with salt and pepper to taste.

2. For the dressing, mix together the mayonnaise, chutney, and curry powder; gently fold it into the potatoes with a rubber spatula. Fold in the scallions and parsley. Serve at room temperature. This potato salad keeps covered in the refrigerator for up to 2 days.

Serves 8

MY KITCHEN DIARY

Eggplants

Along the Mediterranean, eggplant is often referred to as the staff of life. Certainly in Greece and Turkey, it is nearly ubiquitous—sautéed, baked, boiled, or puréed or transformed in slathers, salads, and stews. Each country contributes its flavored herbs, spices, and oils to this subtle-tasting vegetable. India gives us dazzling curries, the Middle East adds tahini (sesame paste), to create *baba ghanouj*, the South of France contributes spreads redolent with garlic, thyme, and parsley. Dill, yogurt, garlic, and lemon juice predominate in Turkey, while tomatoes sweeten and add dimension throughout Greece. Each distinctive preparation can be eaten with bread or served on its own as a salad or appetizer. After baking eggplants to soften the pulp, be sure to discard the seeds and any liquid that escapes because they tend to impart a bitter taste.

THAI COCONUT RATATOUILLE

This light and unusual blend of vegetables is a bit reminiscent of the ratatouille of Provence in that tomatoes, eggplant, and garlic are gently stewed together, but that is where the similarities end. Once the banana, ginger, lemongrass, and cilantro are added, this Thai "ratatouille" takes on its own national character. The vegetables and fruits are bound together in a creamy coconut milk sauce, and the result is delicate and delicious. A sprinkling of spiced toasted coconut (*serunding*) adds a welcome contrast. Serve coconut ratatouille as part of a *rijsttafel,* as a side dish with a favorite curry, or as a light entrée, as presented here.

12 ounces small Japanese or Italian eggplants, unpeeled, cut into ½-inch dice
2 teaspoons coarse salt
1½ cups defatted Chicken Broth (page 127)
4 ounces green beans, sliced French style on the diagonal
8 ounces green cabbage, shredded ½ inch wide
1 medium onion, coarsely chopped
2 tablespoons minced peeled fresh ginger
2 tablespoons minced garlic
1 tablespoon thinly sliced fresh lemongrass
1 tablespoon minced fresh cilantro stems
2 cups diced (¼ inch) banana
1 cup coarsely chopped seeded plum tomatoes
1 cup coconut milk (page 252 or available in specialty food stores)
¼ cup chopped fresh cilantro leaves
6 cups hot cooked rice (1½ cups, raw)
1½ cups Serunding (spiced toasted coconut; page 257)

1. Sprinkle the eggplants with 1 teaspoon of the salt and let stand for 15 minutes. Rinse and pat dry.

2. Heat the chicken broth in a large pot over medium heat. Add the eggplants and cook for 5 minutes. Add the green beans, cabbage, onion, ginger, garlic, lemongrass, cilantro stems, and remaining 1 teaspoon salt. Cook covered over medium heat for 10 minutes.

3. Stir in the banana, tomatoes, and coconut milk; simmer uncovered 10 minutes longer. Remove from the heat and stir in the cilantro leaves.

4. Divide the rice between 8 shallow soup bowls. Ladle the vegetables atop the rice and sprinkle each bowl evenly with *serunding*. Serve immediately.

Serves 8

RATATOUILLE

In the summer of 1990, I was fortunate enough to be able to spend some time in a rented house in St. Tropez. Those were dreamlike days. Typically I would head to the market at about 7 A.M. avoiding the wild traffic crunch, scoop up the brilliant purple eggplants, red peppers, verdant zucchini, and perfectly ripe summer tomatoes necessary for this classic Provençal dish. I had masses of thyme in my garden and hedges of rosemary. The garlic was crisp and fresh and the extra virgin olive oil from Nice was as green as the zucchini. What an intense ratatouille it made.

This dish lasts for a few days in the refrigerator, so make plenty. It's perfect served hot or at room temperature for lazy summer entertaining. Be sure to get the best-quality olive oil possible. When shopping for eggplants, try to select the ones with flat, rounded bottoms (opposite the stem end). These are the males. They have very few seeds and are less likely to have a bitter flavor. The females have a small indentation on the bottom and have many more seeds inside.

2 medium eggplants (about 2½ pounds), unpeeled, cut into 1-inch cubes
1 tablespoon coarse salt
6 tablespoons extra virgin olive oil
2 medium onions, coarsely chopped
2 tablespoons minced garlic
2 large red bell peppers, stemmed, seeded, and cut into 1-inch pieces
4 medium zucchini, quartered lengthwise and cut into 1-inch chunks
2 teaspoons herbes de Provence (French dried herb blend)
Salt and coarsely ground black pepper, to taste
2 cans (28 ounces each) plum tomatoes, drained (juices reserved) and coarsely chopped
2 tablespoons tomato paste
½ cup chopped flat-leaf parsley
1 tablespoon chopped fresh thyme leaves

1. Sprinkle the eggplant with the coarse salt. Let drain in a colander for 30 minutes, then pat dry.

2. Preheat the oven to 350°F. Line a baking sheet with aluminum foil.

3. Spread the eggplant on the prepared baking sheet and toss with 2 tablespoons of the olive oil. Cover well with another sheet of foil. Bake until soft, about 45 minutes, tossing once or twice. Set aside.

4. Heat 2 tablespoons of the remaining olive oil in a large heavy pot over medium-low heat. Add the onions, garlic, and peppers and cook uncovered, stirring occasionally, until wilted, 10 to 12 minutes.

5. Add the zucchini, baked eggplant, and herbes de Provence; cook uncovered, stirring, to soften the zucchini and blend the flavors, 10 minutes. Season generously with salt and pepper.

6. Add the tomatoes, 1 cup of the reserved juices, and the tomato paste. Simmer uncovered 30 minutes, stirring occasionally. Add the remaining 2 tablespoons olive oil and cook for 5 minutes longer.

7. Stir in the parsley and thyme. Adjust the seasonings. Serve hot, cold, or at room temperature.

Serves 12

GLAZED ROASTED SHALLOTS AND GARLIC

Shallots and garlic lose their biting flavor when baked and caramelized in a skillet with butter and sugar. Wonderfully sweet and tender, they're almost like candy as far as I'm concerned, and are beautiful served as a vegetable along with roast pork, game birds, and lamb.

2 pounds large shallots, peeled
1 head garlic (about 16 cloves), separated into cloves and peeled
½ cup defatted Chicken Broth (page 127)
1 tablespoon fresh lemon juice
1 tablespoon sugar
½ teaspoon salt
¼ teaspoon freshly ground black pepper
1½ tablespoons unsalted butter

1. Preheat the oven to 375°F.

2. Place the shallots and garlic in a single layer in a shallow baking pan. In a small nonreactive saucepan, combine the broth and lemon juice; bring to a boil over high heat. Pour the hot broth over the shallots and garlic and sprinkle with the sugar, salt, and pepper. Cover with aluminum foil and bake for 45 minutes.

3. Remove the foil, stir gently, and bake uncovered until the shallots and garlic are very tender, 20 to 30 minutes.

4. Melt the butter over medium heat in a large nonstick skillet. Add the shallots and garlic with their cooking liquid. Increase the heat to medium-high and cook, shaking the pan frequently, until the shallots and garlic are golden brown and caramelized all over, 5 to 7 minutes. Transfer to a serving dish and serve hot.

Serves 6

Purslane

Purslane, an unusual green, finds itself on salad plates all over Turkey and Greece but is rarely found in our markets. Even when it is available, we tend to overlook it, as we do many other somewhat obscure greens. Purslane has a tingly peppery taste that adds a refreshing bite to any salad of greens. Its fleshy leaves are succulent with a nice crunch. If purslane is unavailable in your area, arugula or watercress are good substitutes. Purslane is delicious on its own or tossed with Lemon-Mint Yogurt Dressing (see Index).

INDIAN CREAMED SPINACH

American creamed spinach recipes call for a heavy thickened white sauce, but Indian cooks seem to be masters, producing a smooth, creamy dish without the use of flour. I abandoned American principles and added Indian flavors—cumin, turmeric, coriander, fresh ginger, and tomatoes—for great flavor and substance. For a smooth consistency I've thinned the cooked spinach with a rich broth and added less cream than traditionally called for. This spinach side dish is excellent served with curries, *dal, raita,* and rice when you prepare your own Indian feast. If preparing this dish ahead, reheat it in a double boiler over slowly boiling water or covered in a microwave oven.

2 pounds fresh spinach
4 tablespoons (½ stick) unsalted butter
1 teaspoon cumin seeds
½ teaspoon ground coriander
¼ teaspoon ground turmeric
1 medium onion, finely chopped
3 cloves garlic, finely chopped
1 tablespoon finely chopped peeled fresh ginger
1 teaspoon finely chopped mild green chili (seeds and ribs removed)
2 ripe plum tomatoes, cut into ¼-inch dice
½ teaspoon finely chopped red chili (seeds and ribs removed)
⅓ cup defatted Chicken Broth or Fresh Vegetable Broth (page 127 or 129)
¼ cup heavy (or whipping) cream
Salt, to taste

1. Remove the tough stems from the spinach (reserve for another use—see the following recipe). Rinse the leaves well, shaking off some of the water. Put the wet spinach into a large heavy pot. Cook covered over medium-high heat until completely wilted, 3 to 4 minutes, stirring well once or twice to cook evenly. Drain well, coarsely chop, and set aside.

2. Melt the butter in a heavy saucepan over low heat. Add the cumin seeds, coriander, turmeric, and cook, stirring, for 2 minutes. Add the onion and garlic and cook, stirring, until wilted and lightly golden, 5 to 8 minutes.

3. Stir in the ginger and green chili; cook for 1 minute. Add the tomatoes and red chili, increase the heat to medium, and cook, stirring, for 8 minutes.

4. Add the chopped spinach and cook, stirring, over medium-high heat for 5 minutes. Stir in the broth and cream and season with salt. Cook to heat through, 1 minute more. Serve immediately.

Serves 4

WHAT TO DO WITH THOSE STEMS

When preparing tender spinach leaves, it seems a shame to discard the stems. This Sephardic preparation makes great use of them and, of course, you can more than double the recipe. For an appetizer, poach an egg and serve on top.

Stems from 1 bunch fresh spinach, trimmed
1 tablespoon extra virgin Spanish olive oil
1 teaspoon minced garlic
⅛ teaspoon sweet paprika
Coarse salt, to taste

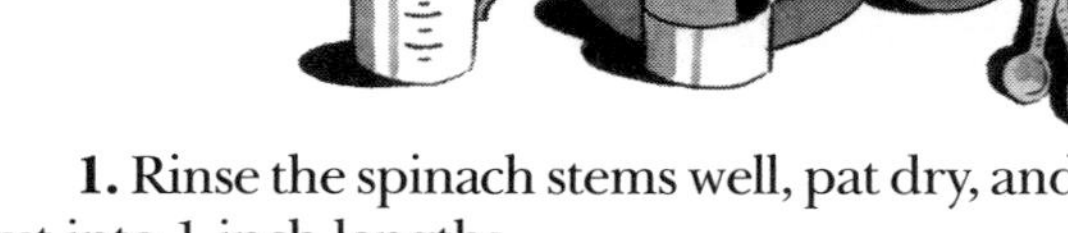

1. Rinse the spinach stems well, pat dry, and cut into 1-inch lengths.

2. Heat the oil in a medium-size cast-iron skillet over medium-high heat. Add the spinach stems, garlic, and paprika and sauté until just tender, 1 to 1½ minutes. Season with salt and serve immediately.

Serves 2 as a small side dish

SPINACH CATALAN

Sweet and savory flavors predominate in many Catalan dishes. In this dish either spinach or Swiss chard marries well with golden raisins, toasted pine nuts, and fruity olive oil. A heavy cast-iron skillet and high heat cook the greens quickly, before they have a chance to release their liquid.

About 8 ounces tender fresh spinach
1 tablespoon extra virgin Spanish olive oil
¼ cup pine nuts
½ cup golden raisins
Finely grated zest of 1 orange
Coarse salt and freshly ground black pepper, to taste

1. Remove the stems from the spinach leaves (reserve for another use—see this page). Rinse the leaves well and pat dry with paper towels.

2. Heat the oil in a large cast-iron skillet over low heat. Add the pine nuts and cook, shaking the skillet and stirring the nuts, until golden, about 3 minutes.

3. Add the spinach leaves, raisins, and orange zest to the nuts. Increase the heat to medium-high and cook stirring constantly, until the spinach wilts, 1 to 2 minutes. Season with salt and pepper and serve immediately.

Serves 2

BAHIA BUTTERNUT MASH

The most amazing tastes come out of Brazil, where the marketplace is alive with splendid produce. When I visited, I was surprised to find the great orange calabaza pumpkin displayed throughout the markets. Although I had first seen it all over the Caribbean and next in Barcelona, it was in Brazil that I got the inspiration for this dish. Occasionally calabazas can be found in Latin American markets throughout the U.S., but because the supply is uncertain, I've substituted butternut squash and combined it with carrots for a most luscious vegetable dish. Instead of puréeing it, I've coarsely mashed the squash and carrots with a small amount of butter, ginger, salt, and pepper. The flavor is both pungent and delicious.

1 butternut squash (2 pounds), seeded, peeled, and cut into 1-inch chunks (see Note)
6 medium carrots, peeled and cut into 1-inch chunks
Salt, to taste
1 tablespoon unsalted butter
⅛ teaspoon ground ginger
Freshly ground black pepper, to taste

1. Place the squash and carrots in a large heavy pot and cover with salted water. Bring to a boil, reduce the heat, and simmer uncovered until tender, 15 to 20 minutes. Drain well and remove to a bowl.

2. Add the butter and ginger and coarsely mash the vegetables with a fork. Season generously with salt and pepper and serve piping hot.

Serves 8

Note: Butternut squash can be difficult to cut because the pulp is very firm and the outer skin is slightly tough, so work carefully. Cut the squash in half crosswise at the base of the large neck, then carefully cut each piece in half lengthwise. Scoop out any seeds in the cavity and slice the halves into 1-inch lengths crosswise. Peel the skin from each piece and continue with the recipe.

BLAZING SQUASH CHILI

The bright golden colors of the Indian flavor palette fuse with the red-hot excitement of Mexico in this lush, pungent vegetarian chili. Butternut squash, red peppers, beans, cumin, chili powder, oregano, and cilantro pay homage to the American Southwest. Thinly sliced scallions add their cool crispness atop the chili served over brown rice or barley.

2 tablespoons olive oil
2 medium onions, cut into ¼-inch dice
2 tablespoons finely chopped garlic
2 medium red bell peppers, stemmed, seeded, and cut into ½-inch dice
3 tablespoons chili powder
2 tablespoons ground cumin
1½ tablespoons dried oregano
¼ teaspoon ground allspice
Pinch of crushed red pepper flakes
2 cans (28 ounces each) plum tomatoes, chopped with their juices
½ cup dry red wine
2 butternut squash, seeded, peeled, and cut into ½-inch dice (see Note)
Finely grated zest of 1 orange
Salt and coarsely ground black pepper, to taste
2 cans (15¼ ounces each) dark red kidney beans, drained
2 tablespoons chopped fresh cilantro leaves
2 tablespoons chopped flat-leaf parsley
3 scallions (3 inches green left on), thinly sliced on the diagonal, for garnish

1. Heat the oil in a large heavy pot over medium-low heat. Add the onions, garlic, and peppers. Cook, stirring occasionally, until the vegetables have wilted, about 10 minutes. Add the chili powder, cumin, oregano, allspice, and red pepper flakes and cook for 1 minute longer, stirring to coat the vegetables well with the spices.

2. Stir in the tomatoes with their juices, the red wine, butternut squash, orange zest, salt, and pepper. Bring to a boil, reduce the heat to medium-low, and simmer uncovered until the squash is tender, about 20 minutes. Adjust the seasonings to taste.

3. Fold in the kidney beans and simmer 10 minutes longer. Just before serving, stir in the cilantro and parsley. Serve garnished with the scallions.

Serves 8

YACOUT TOMATO MARMALADE

This little Moroccan dish, inspired by one I had at the restaurant Yacout, gives new meaning to the word marmalade. Slow, long cooking slightly caramelizes the tomatoes into a sweet, lush consistency. When served alongside Sugared Mashed Carrots and Sweetened Emerald Zucchini (see Index), you have a veggie feast fit for a pasha. Bread is not a necessity because ideally these dishes should be eaten off the tip of a fork so that their intense flavors are thoroughly appreciated. Savory Lentil Salad (see Index) provides an interesting complement to the trio.

3 pounds ripe plum tomatoes, seeded and coarsely chopped
¼ cup sugar

1. Place the tomatoes and sugar in a large heavy pot and cook uncovered over low heat for 1¼ to 1¾ hours, depending on how watery the tomatoes are. You can raise the heat towards the end of the cooking time to speed up the process. Stir often as the tomatoes cook. Cool to room temperature.

2. To serve, spread the tomatoes on a small round plate, flattening them slightly with the back of a fork. Serve at room temperature.

Serves 8

PAN CON TOMATE

In the late 80s, as the wildly explosive food decade began to ebb, Italian *bruschetta* was so popular that the term became almost generic. It spoke of toasted or grilled bread slices overflowing with herbed and oiled ripe tomato salad. Putting trendy aside for the moment, the Spanish have long savored their own version of this dish. The key to *pan con tomate* is large, perfectly ripe summer tomatoes, which are rubbed over toasted bread so that the juice and pulp are absorbed. This simply prepared dish should be arranged on a large flat basket, garnished with pungent herbs, such as basil, rosemary, and cilantro.

4 thick slices (1 inch) peasant bread, grilled or toasted
4 teaspoons extra virgin olive oil
2 large cloves garlic, peeled and cut lengthwise in half
2 ripe large beefsteak tomatoes, cut crosswise in half
Coarse salt, to taste

Drizzle each slice of bread with 1 teaspoon olive oil. Rub each slice with the cut side of a garlic clove half, then rub with the cut side of a tomato half, squeezing the juices and pulp over the surface. Sprinkle with coarse salt and serve immediately.

Serves 4

Bruschetta the Greek Way

The Greeks have a delectable version of *bruschetta.* It's a bit different yet the star is still the tomato. They begin with large, hard barley rusks brushed with olive oil and rubbed with garlic. They then grate tomatoes over the large holes of a hand-held grater to capture the pulp and loosen the skin atop. For a more elaborate presentation, dapple with Kalamata Olive Slather (see Index) and sprinkle with chopped fresh oregano.

ROASTED TOMATOES

When sun-dried tomatoes appeared on the scene in the 80s, I think we were all dazzled by their sensational taste. I remember them being slightly smoky, dried yet still plump, and certainly succulent. As the supply grew and they began turning up in almost every conceivable dish, the quality diminished. They became tough, chewy, and rather dark brown. I hope that roasted tomatoes will take over in the 90s. Their sweetly caramelized flavor is glorious on grilled bread, simple roasted fish, or as a filling for a tomato tart. Drizzled with a little oil and sprinkled with fresh herbs, they are perfect as a simple vegetable dish or as a component of a salad.

6 ripe large tomatoes

1. Preheat the oven to 250°F. Line a baking sheet with aluminum foil.

2. Cut each tomato crosswise into 3 thick slices. They should be at least ¾ inch thick.

3. Arrange the slices in a single layer on the prepared baking sheet and slowly roast until most of the liquid has caramelized, 1¾ to 2 hours. Remove from the baking sheet with a metal spatula and use as desired. These will keep covered in the refrigerator for 2 to 3 days.

Serves 6, allow 1 tomato per serving

TOMATOES PROVENCALE

Although I have never been served these tomatoes in France, the flavor of the crumbs, redolent with garlic, thyme, and parsley, remind me of the best tastes of Provence. The secret is the fresh bread crumbs, a hint of thyme, and fresh flat-leaf parsley. Baked for a short while, the tomatoes become luxuriously soft and sweet. Finished under the broiler, the tops will be perfectly toasty.

1 large slice coarse bread (¾ inch thick)
1 medium clove garlic, coarsely chopped
3 tablespoons chopped flat-leaf parsley
¼ teaspoon dried thyme
Salt and coarsely ground black pepper, to taste
6 ripe medium tomatoes (about 6 ounces each)
4 tablespoons extra virgin olive oil

1. Lightly toast the bread, then tear it into large pieces.

2. Place the toasted bread in a food processor with the garlic and parsley. Pulse the machine on and off for about 15 seconds. The bread should be in medium-size crumbs. Remove the mixture to a bowl and season with the thyme and generously with salt and pepper.

3. Preheat the oven to 350° F.

4. Halve the tomatoes crosswise. Using a small melon baller, scoop out some of the center pulp. Discard the seeds, finely chop the pulp, and add it to the crumbs. Add 2 tablespoons of the olive oil and mix well.

5. Divide the crumb mixture evenly among the tomato halves. Place on a baking sheet and drizzle the tops evenly with the remaining 2 tablespoons olive oil.

6. Bake until bubbly, 20 minutes; remove from the oven.

7. Before serving, preheat the broiler.

8. Broil the tomatoes 4 to 5 inches from the heat until the tops are golden, about 30 seconds. Serve immediately.

Serves 8

TARTE PROVENCALE

A magnificent vine-ripened tomato tart pays homage to the South of France. The tomatoes are luxuriously baked in a rustic pie crust filled with Comté cheese and perfumed with herbes de Provence, awakening memories of a summer afternoon in Nice.

TART CRUST:
¾ cup all-purpose flour
¾ cup whole-wheat flour
1 tablespoon herbes de Provence (French dried herb blend)
½ teaspoon coarsely ground black pepper
4½ tablespoons unsalted butter, chilled
¼ cup solid vegetable shortening, chilled
¼ cup ice water

FILLING:
6 ripe plum tomatoes, cut into ¼-inch-thick rounds
Coarse salt, to taste
2 cups grated Comté or Emmenthal cheese
½ teaspoon grated nutmeg
¼ teaspoon coarsely ground black pepper
2 tablespoons chopped fresh opal basil leaves
1 tablespoon slivered opal basil leaves
1 tablespoon extra virgin olive oil
8 pitted Niçoise olives

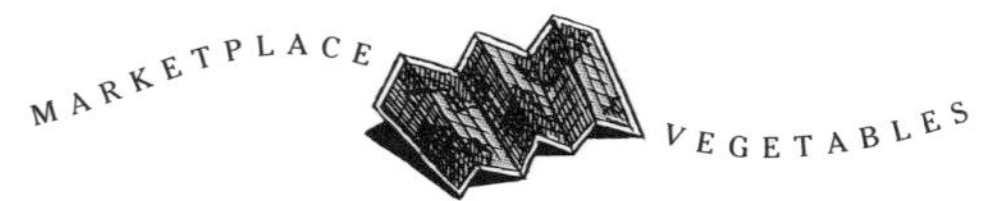

1. Three hours ahead of time, prepare the tart crust: Combine the flours in a medium-size mixing bowl, then stir in the herbes de Provence and the pepper. Cut the butter and the shortening into small pieces, then cut them into the flour with two knives or a pastry blender until the mixture resembles coarse meal.

2. Add the ice water, a tablespoon at a time, mixing it in with a fork until the mixture forms a ball (you may need a bit more water). Flatten the dough into a disk and cover it with plastic wrap. Refrigerate for 3 hours.

3. For the filling, sprinkle the sliced tomatoes with coarse salt and let drain on paper towels for about 30 minutes. Pat dry.

4. Preheat the oven to 375°F.

5. Roll out the chilled dough on a lightly floured surface to form a round about ⅛ inch thick. Carefully lay the dough over the bottom of a 9-inch tart pan with removable bottom and pat it in place, leaving the sides slightly thicker. Trim off the excess.

6. Prick the bottom of the crust with a fork and line it with aluminum foil. Fill with pie weights or dried beans.

7. Bake the crust for 10 minutes. Carefully remove the weights and foil and bake 12 minutes longer. Allow the crust to cool slightly. Leave the oven on.

8. Spread the cheese over the bottom of the tart shell. Arrange the tomatoes on top of the cheese in an overlapping circular pattern, covering the surface. Sprinkle with the nutmeg, pepper, chopped basil, and slivered basil. Drizzle the top with the olive oil and dot with olives.

9. Bake the tart for 40 minutes. Let it rest for 10 minutes. To serve, carefully remove the side of the tart pan and run a thin spatula under the crust to loosen it from the bottom. Place the tart on a platter and serve hot or at room temperature.

Serves 6

SULTAN'S PILLOWS

Light as pillows, these sweet and savory little phyllo triangles are worthy of a sultan's table. Filled with plump prunes, sweet red peppers, tomatoes, fresh rosemary, and cinnamon, they capture the culinary spirit of the Ottoman Empire. Served hot and flaky, they are a perfect accompaniment to a succulent roasted leg of lamb.

2 tablespoons olive oil
¼ cup chopped shallots
1 red bell pepper, stemmed, seeded, and cut into ¼-inch dice
1 ripe beefsteak tomato, seeded and coarsely chopped
1 cup pitted prunes, quartered
1 tablespoon honey
2 tablespoons chopped fresh rosemary leaves
¼ teaspoon ground cinnamon
Salt and coarsely ground black pepper, to taste
12 sheets phyllo dough (see Note)
1 cup (2 sticks) Clarified Butter (page 53), melted

1. Heat the oil in a medium-size nonstick skillet over low heat. Add the shallots and pepper and cook for 15 minutes, stirring frequently.

2. Stir in the tomato, prunes, honey, rosemary, cinnamon, salt, and pepper. Increase the heat to medium, and cook, stirring occasionally, until all the liquid has been absorbed, about 10 minutes.

3. Preheat the oven to 350°F.

4. Remove the phyllo pastry from the box and lay the sheets on a dish towel. Cover the pastry with a sheet of waxed paper and then a slightly dampened dish towel.

5. Place 1 sheet of phyllo lengthwise in front of you on a clean work surface. Brush it all over with butter. Cover with a second sheet of phyllo and brush it with butter. Cut the phyllo the short way into six 3-inch-wide strips. Place 1 teaspoon of the filling 1 inch from the bottom in the center of each strip. Fold a corner across the filling and then continue to fold to the end as if you were folding a flag. Tuck under the edges. Place the triangles, as completed, on a baking sheet and brush with butter. Repeat five more times for 36 triangles in all. Bake until golden brown, about 15 minutes. Serve immediately.

Makes 36 triangles

Note: Phyllo dough is readily available frozen in 1-pound boxes. Follow the package directions for thawing the dough.

SWEETENED EMERALD ZUCCHINI

Here zucchini is tenderly simmered in sweetened water, which removes that slight bitterness that it sometimes has. I had this dish as part of a Moroccan salad selection and found it just delicious in its simplicity. I don't really encourage these Moroccan salads being served in large portions because they are so delicate and special on their own. They deserve the limelight. This is best served at room temperature.

¼ cup sugar
2 tablespoons water
1 pound zucchini, ends trimmed, quartered lengthwise, and cut into 1-inch lengths
¼ cup chopped fresh mint leaves

1. Place the sugar and 2 tablespoons water in a medium-size saucepan. Bring to a boil and cook until the sugar is completely dissolved.

2. Reduce the heat to low, add the zucchini, and stir well to coat with the syrup. Cover and cook, stirring once or twice, until the zucchini is tender but not mushy, about 8 minutes.

3. Drain the zucchini in a strainer, reserving the juices.

4. Toss the zucchini gently with the mint and ¼ cup of the reserved juices. Serve at room temperature on a small oval or round plate as an appetizer salad.

Serves 6 to 8

BANANA LEAF VEGETABLE CURRY

My rendition of vegetable curry was inspired by a visit to Banana Leaf Apolo in Singapore (see the box on the facing page). Gentle flavors and colors are the base for this curry. Carrots, potatoes, and cauliflower are enriched by the addition of honey, cinnamon, garbanzo beans, and golden raisins. A garnish of toasted coconut sets it all off with a nice crunch. Serve this atop a bed of snowy rice on a banana leaf (or in a shallow bowl) with Golden Chicken Curry (see Index) alongside.

2 tablespoons olive oil
1 cup coarsely chopped yellow onion
2 tablespoons minced garlic
1½ tablespoons best-quality curry powder
6 medium carrots, peeled, halved lengthwise, and cut into 1-inch lengths
3 Idaho potatoes, peeled and cut into ½-inch dice
1 medium cauliflower, trimmed and cut into small florets
4 cups Fresh Vegetable Broth (page 129)
2 tablespoons honey
1 cinnamon stick (3 inches long)
1 can (19 ounces) chickpeas (garbanzo beans), drained
½ cup golden raisins
2 cups seeded, diced plum tomatoes
½ cup coarsely chopped flat-leaf parsley or fresh cilantro leaves
4 cups cooked long-grain white rice (about 1¼ cups dry)
1 cup toasted coconut (page 514), for garnish

1. Heat the oil in a large heavy pot over medium heat. Add the onion and cook until wilted, 8 to 10 minutes, stirring occasionally. Add the garlic and cook, stirring, 2 to 3 minutes more. Sprinkle the curry powder into the pot and cook over medium heat, stirring constantly to mellow the flavors, 1 to 2 minutes.

2. Add the carrots, potatoes, cauliflower, broth, honey, and cinnamon stick. Bring to a

boil, reduce the heat to a simmer, and cook uncovered until the vegetables are tender, about 20 minutes. Add the chickpeas and raisins, and simmer another 15 minutes, stirring occasionally. The raisins should be plumped.

3. Just before serving, stir in the tomatoes and parsley and cook to heat through, 1 to 2 minutes. Serve atop rice and garnish with toasted coconut.

Serves 8

SOUVENIR TO SAVOR

Little India, Singapore

To wander the streets of Little India in Singapore is to weave through a pastel maze of beautiful small and ancient buildings. With all your senses feasting on the intoxicating aroma of fresh jasmine that pervades the air, you may come across the famous Banana Leaf Apolo, tucked away between rows of Indian restaurants on Race Course Road. It is *the* place to enjoy a great banana leaf curry.

The Banana Leaf Apolo is one of several southern Indian-style banana leaf restaurants where superb curries are served. It is not a fancy place. Rather, it is arranged like a cafeteria with long tables in the center of the room and smaller tables along the side. Richard and I walked in and went right to the counter, where the ready-cooked curries were kept hot in steam trays. I chose a spicy vegetable curry, he chose a chicken curry, and we ordered a fish head curry to share. Considered to be Singapore's national dish, a whole fish head is actually cooked until tender in a hot gravy laden with fresh okra and eggplant, spices and chilies. It is hotter than hot, but a real flavor experience as well as a visual experience—as that fish head just gazes up at you. Cool beers, fresh lime juice served over lots of ice, and chilled yogurt or *raita* help temper the fire.

On the way to the table, we passed blue plastic drums filled with golden rice studded with vegetables, which we chose over the plain white rice. As soon as we sat down, a banana leaf the size of a placemat was set in front of each of us. First, our rice of choice was spooned into the center of our leaves. The vegetable and chicken curries were ladeled on top of the rice. The fish head curry was presented in a bowl alongside, as were some stewed vegetables. We were also served pappadum, wafer-thin, deep-fried lentil crackers.

We knew these curries were to be eaten with our hands (the right one)—which actually requires a certain amount of skill and finesse. The locals of course are whizzes at this. It was a major test of hand-eye coordination for us, and when I asked the server for napkins, he pointed to an open bathroom across the room with rows of sinks . . . I loved it! The meal, redolent with spices and sauces was as delicious and exotic as it was fun. I kept thinking what a great idea for picnics—get lots of banana leaves to use instead of dishes and bring lots of damp towels for cleaning up.

To Market, To Market

Visiting the markets of a country is, to me, as important as visiting its greatest museums, its most renown historical sites. A good market is the heart and soul of a place, and has been the source of great inspiration. There is nothing more spectacular than the freshest produce artfully arranged. It is an invitation—a challenge—to create something worthy of such natural beauty.

I enjoy visiting a marketplace at the height of activity, when it vibrates with people: Merchants calling out to attract customers; shoppers poking, sniffing, arguing, buying; others just wandering. Here are souvenirs of some of the favorite markets I visited on my travels for this book.

To Market in Mexico

Oaxaca city, the capital of the state of Oaxaca in southern Mexico, is a magical place to visit. A showcase of Mexico's 16th-

> "It's best to arrive at about 8 A.M. to get the lay of the land before the throngs descend on the grand riot of fruit, vegetables, meat, fish."

century art and architecture, it also features the nearly mystical Zapotec and Mixtec ruins of Mitla and Monte Albán.

Should you visit this glorious city, be sure that your stay includes a Saturday and allow plenty of time for a visit to Mercado Central de Abastos, one of the world's greatest markets. The name literally means "to supply," and that it does! It's best to arrive at about 8 A.M. to get the lay of the land before the throngs descend on the grand riot of fruit, vegetables, meat, fish, and all the other wonderful ingredients, such as large brown blocks of vanilla and chocolate, that make up one of the world's most festive cuisines. As you continue along, walk through the aisles of chilies, cinnamon, and other spices that are destined to culminate in Oaxaca's renowned *mole negro*. My journey through some very exotic-looking sausage stalls came to a halt in front of a perfectly cleaned pig's head with a dark green jalapeño chili sticking out of its mouth to look like a tongue,

At the Mercado Central de Abastos, Oaxaca, left to right: Baskets of chilies of every description. Each grower tends an array of beautiful produce. A marketplace sign. She's simply marketing, but I'd wear that dress out to dinner!

S O U V E N I R T O S A V O R

An Indian Market

Although most visitors come to Agra to see the exquisite 17th-century Taj Mahal, the minute I arrived at the vegetable market in the rural section of the city, I knew what I had come to India for. It began when a gentle man gave me a mass of perfumed dark red roses from his burlap sack. I felt I might be in heaven as I buried my face in their heady perfume. As I lifted my face from the roses with some reluctance, I noticed the sea of brilliant orange marigolds around me. With each step the colors seemed to become more thrilling. The women were beautifully wrapped in saris of pinks, reds, oranges, yellows, and turquoises with occasional gold patterns that sparkled under the sun.

Calming down a bit, I was able to wander deeper into the market, being careful not to get in the way of the rather large, fuzzy, dark gray pig walking about everywhere looking for something to eat. I was even more careful to avoid the muzzled fawn-colored camels bending down to pick up bunches of herbs. In their own way they are as gentle as the beautiful white cows that wander freely. Sweet brown and white goats accompanied me throughout the market as I continued on. Because animals are sacred in India and live with the people, they are calm and unthreatening and very pleasant to have around. But since this wasn't a trip to study animal husbandry, I sought out the vegetables.

Working within their own aesthetic of market artistry, Indians arrange their wares in like colors, which only heightens their drama. Tomatoes are packed by like size in gorgeous large baskets. Cauliflowers with small compact white heads are dazzling nestled in their dark green leaves. Red onions are laid out in masses on burlap cloths. The small heads of garlic are separated from large heads of garlic. Various brown potatoes are piled next to mounds of fresh ginger. There are peas galore and the cilantro never stops. The vegetables are lovingly attended to by the vendors who are proud to show off the bounty they've brought to sell. It's easy to see the inspiration for the magnificent vegetable dishes for which India is so well known.

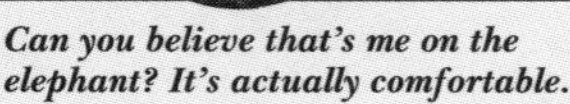

Can you believe that's me on the elephant? It's actually comfortable.

making for one of those great photo opportunities I'm always on the lookout for. Along the way, I was tempted by cooked peeled yams sold with small plastic bags filled with honey to drizzle atop.

Either before you begin your market adventure or as a small break halfway through, have a rich, foamy hot chocolate served out of a rustic glazed ceramic bowl at one of the great breakfast counters located strategically around the market. Accompany it with a small *pan de yerma,* a luscious, eggy, sweet, and soft breakfast bread. The more adventurous might prefer a small crisp tortilla drizzled with puréed black beans and *salsa verde*, and topped off with the best *queso blanco* (a mild white cheese). Happy and fortified, you'll be ready to wander through the beautiful displays of jade green pottery, woven baskets, and brightly patterned cloths and linens. My most useful purchase was an orange plaid shopping bag to carry my treasures safely home.

Great hedge cutting in King Edward VII Park in Lisbon. That's one bit of gardening I'm glad not to do.

"The heady perfume of fresh cilantro fell over me like a veil of hand-tatted Portuguese lace."

Shopping in Lisbon

Walking through the stately doors of Lisbon's Mercado da Riberia, the majestic central food market, just after 10 on a Saturday morning was just a bit overwhelming. The heady perfume of fresh cilantro fell over me like a veil of hand-tatted Portuguese lace. The singular perfume was disturbed only occasionally by a hint of burning incense. The two-story building with its leaded glass ceiling seemed reminiscent of the train stations in 1930s thriller spy movies. Instead of porters and suitcases, however, the market was filled with wooden and brightly colored plastic crates holding more and more cilantro, cabbages, onions, ropes of garlic, tomatoes, leeks, and more cilantro.

Radishes, beets, and huge squashes lay on top of wooden crates on the first floor. The second-story balcony was home to small stalls selling hanging ropes of red-brown *chourico*, a paprika-infused sausage similar to Spanish chorizo. The color was further boosted by lavish ropes of white, pink, and purple-hued garlic. There always seemed to be something spectacular in each market stall. Just around the corner from the sausages hung masses of dried red chilies in huge bunches interspersed with dried yellow corn and ropes of onions. The next stall held garlands of deep green bay leaves on their stems alongside more garlic, onions, and chilies. Butternut squash broke up the brilliant red and yellow every once in a while. A stall nearby had—surprisingly—ripe pineapples suspended from stainless-steel hooks and ropes. Every once in a while bags of oranges and tomatoes appeared alongside huge dark green melons. Nearby were stalls of fresh- and salt-water fish. The artistry and apparent pride in both ingredients and display was spectacular.

Carolyn—

When its watermelon-time in Turkey - each display is decorated with red flowers or a tomato - to show just how ripe and perfect the crop is.

Off to Greece—
Sheila

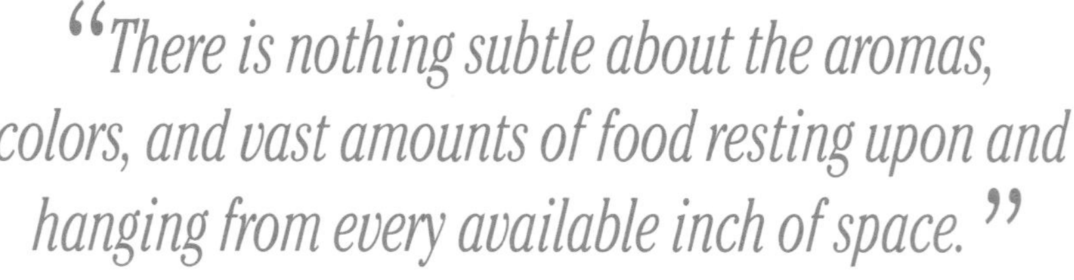

"There is nothing subtle about the aromas, colors, and vast amounts of food resting upon and hanging from every available inch of space."

At Lisbon's majestic Mercado da Riberia, the fish are fresh caught and displayed with pride.

What I loved most was how each vendor, especially the women, set up shop and personalized their spaces. Homey plants in colored ceramic pots rested on boxes or cabinets under the skylighted ceiling. Occasionally on a ledge rested a cozy Thermos, filled I imagine, with hot soup or coffee. The atmosphere was so caring, I kept thinking, why aren't there more markets like this in America?

The Spices of Turkey

Planning my trip to Istanbul conjured up memories of my honeymoon twenty-seven years before, and I knew I had to pay a return visit to the Misir Carsisi, Istanbul's intoxicating spice bazaar.

The small, low-roofed, rectangular building, with its unadorned exterior, is surrounded by exotic views of mosques, their majestic minarets ascending into the blue-gray Turkish sky. The faint high-pitched trilling as the muezzin calls the faithful to prayer mingles with the harsh noises of modern Istanbul traffic.

Before delving into the fray, I stopped for lunch at Pandeli, a not-to-be-missed restaurant above the bazaar. I was immediately struck by the intensity of the turquoise tiles that covered the walls. Diamond-shaped royal blue tiles and tiny squares of white added to the brilliant effect. Richly patterned kilim rugs covered the cushions of the banquettes that encircled the main dining room. Dark wooden tables draped with crisp white linens set the turquoise afire.

Lunch was simple and began with a delicate assortment of *meze*, consisting of shrimp, tarama, stuffed vine leaves, smoked salmon, and ripe tomato slices. My entrée of sea bass en papillote was enchanting. The parchment was folded origami-style into a Turkish hat. The fish rested in a light lemon butter sauce and was topped by a single slice of tomato. Under other circumstances, I would have lingered over a tiny cup of rich Turkish coffee but the bazaar awaited.

Upon entering the market, one is immediately and magnificently overwhelmed. There is nothing subtle about the aromas, colors, and vast amounts of food resting upon and hanging from every available inch of space. Reminiscent of the souks of Arabia,

Cicek Pasaji

A favorite spot in Istanbul is the Flower Passage—Cicek Pasaji—a lovely old arcade filled with tavernas that exude the sort of mysterious atmosphere I adore. Locals and tourists alike linger for hours, chatting animatedly over small plates of *meze* and glasses of milky white raki. Smoke mingles with rays of sunlight that pass through the skylights. It is not unusual to hear a plate, or two, crash to the ground. Just outside is the Balikcilar Carsisi, the fish market, with the most dazzling collages of the day's fresh catch. These silvery creatures of the sea reflect the strings of tiny lights laced around the tented alleyways. There are flower stalls, spice shops, and kitchen utensils everywhere. The pyramids of fruits and vegetables are beautiful in their simplicity. Apricots and cherries—at a peak of perfection rarely seen in our markets—glow with the dew of ripeness.

Outside the Flower Passage in Istanbul.

each vendor has a small crowded space to display his wares. Huge white burlap sacks overflowing with plump dried apricots sit next to sacks bursting with golden sultanas, pistachios, peanuts, walnuts, and roasted chickpeas. Deep red, black, golden, and blue striped cloths are wrapped around the sacks to hold them in place. They are lined up front to back as deeply as possible in each space. Snowy sugar-coated *lokum* (or Turkish delight, a chewy confection that is popular in the Middle East) are stacked in bins and on shelves behind the fruit and nuts. Alongside, glass and tin display cabinets are filled with stacks of luxurious honeycomb. Liquid honey is spooned from deep trays. Beyond the honey stall, a bright red meat slicer thinly cuts pastrami, a favorite Turkish cured meat. Next, the flaxen-hued cheeses roughly cut into large chunks wait to be sold.

As I continued to meander through the aisles, I came upon huge sacks filled with chartreuse- and peppermint green-colored raw henna, sculpted into pyramid shapes rising one foot above the sacks. Then came pyramids of russet, deep brown, and black peppers offset by golden saffron. Clear cellophane bags of

S O U V E N I R T O S A V O R

Marketing in Budapest

Budapest's grand Central Market, to my great disappointment, was closed during my visit. This grand iron and red brick structure built in 1895 at the foot of the Liberty Bridge will be closed for major restoration for several years. But I did find a small cozy makeshift market in some old warehouses where a handful of the vendors had set up shop. I knew I was in the right place when I saw all the dried peppers strung outside the entryway. The beautiful red peppers against the brick walls created a stunning play of colors and warmed me immediately. Upon entering, I found myself in a long narrow hallway filled with meat, poultry, fruit, and vegetable stalls interspersed with a few pickle shops. The main attraction in most of these pickle shops was a huge wooden vat filled with sauerkraut. Hungarians prefer sauerkraut to fresh cabbage in most dishes, so I was not overly surprised by the amounts of sauerkraut I saw being sold. But the pickle shops also sold a dazzling variety of pickled vegetables and peppers. Boughs of dried red peppers, garlic, and long Hungarian salamis decorated every available space. Tiny cellophane bags of paprika, in several different strengths, were also in good supply. The winter's bounty of oranges made the whole place festive and warm. So, sad as I was that the Central Market was closed, I felt I had discovered a lovely surprise that few other visitors would get to see.

spices hung from the ceiling like an earthen-hued rainbow. Sacks of celadon green sage rested beside bright green basil, oregano, and mint. This amazing sensory world seemed to extend forever tended by affable, proud merchants who respectfully displayed the elements for great Turkish cuisine.

> "A woman balancing a bamboo pole across her shoulders carted buckets of squid to a waiting stall keeper."

The Chinese not only make an art of slicing and dicing, they prepare their vegetables beautifully for market.

The Chinese Way to Shop

The Chinese shop every day. Originally this was due to lack of refrigeration and adequate storage room, but today more than anything they want all their ingredients to be fresh. Fish, for example, is not considered really fresh unless it's swimming. While most Westerners in Hong Kong rely on supermarkets for their food, on my trips, I enjoyed wandering through the open-air produce markets that dot the island. Not knowing Cantonese did not curtail my shopping. Pointing did the trick with the friendly hawkers who weigh everything on their age-old scales. Fruit, vegetables, and seafood are sold by the catty, which is roughly $1\frac{1}{3}$ pounds. The smells, sounds, and buzzing atmosphere made every trip an experience to be savored.

A man toting two large woven wicker baskets full of live chickens brushed by. Splashing carp and garoupa sprinkled me with fresh water. A woman balancing a bamboo pole across her shoulders carted buckets of squid to a waiting stall keeper. Mounds of winter melon, bunches of Chinese parsley (cilantro), scallions, and choy sum (sort of a cross between spinach and collard greens), huge locally grown carrots, and fat onions rubbed shoulders with hairy rambutan, bok choy, mangoes, two-foot-long string beans, and ripe tomatoes.

I couldn't resist a side of roasted pork and stopped to buy a catty, which was swiftly and smoothly hacked off by the butcher. Never having acquired a taste for the mud-caked delicacies, I passed up the thousand-year-old eggs, opting instead for a fist of knobby ginger and some garlic, which were placed in paper-thin pink plastic bags and tied with a sprig of chive. Adding to the exotic smells and sights, salted fish with iridescent scales dangled above displays of dried scallops and miniscule shrimp. I thought about what to buy and picked out some glistening purple eggplants, a few bright red "killer" chilies, and a large yellow capsicum. Then, I headed for the hotel.

"... I passed up the thousand-year-old eggs, opting instead for a fist of knobby ginger... which was placed in pink bags and tied with a sprig of chive."

This scallion seller in Hong Kong also deals in fiery chilies.

MARKETPLACE

Condiments and Spices

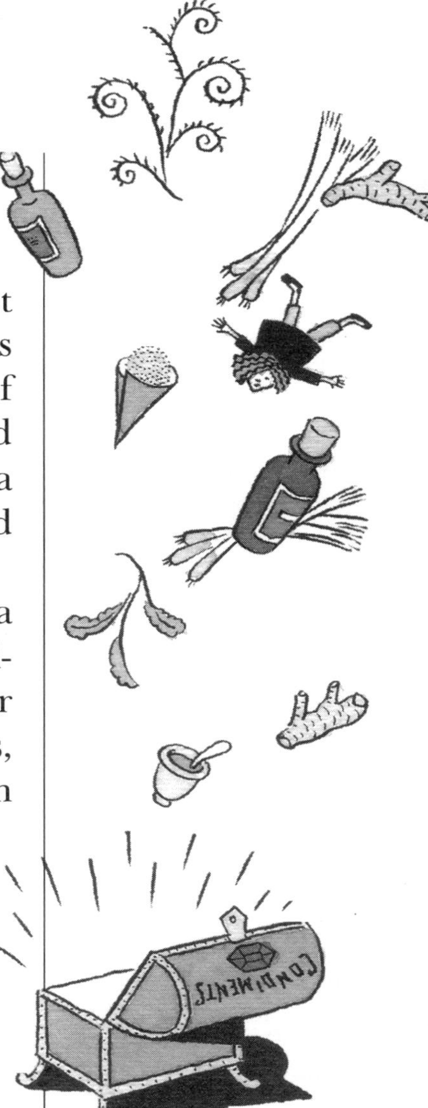

Having a great condiment repertoire is like having a well-stocked jewelry box. They add a burst of flavor, texture, and excitement to dishes from the simplest grilled fish to the most exotic curry. Condiments should surprise the palate with their balance of sweet and sour, smooth and chunky, or hot and cool. The good news is that many cuisines offer a terrific range of condiments so that no dish need ever go to the table underdressed.

As they are relatively easy to prepare, creating a spectacular condiment just requires a vivid imagination. I used my travels to spur my own, and offer up sour cherries pickled with cinnamon, cloves, and fresh tarragon that will spark anything from boiled potatoes to roasted meats; fiery Harissa to serve with subtle vegetable dishes; lush Rhubarb-Beet Compote to pair with game birds; and a zesty mango salsa, perfect for grilled fish, plus many more—of course.

And also included here are a few of my favorite homemade spice blends.

PRESERVED LEMONS

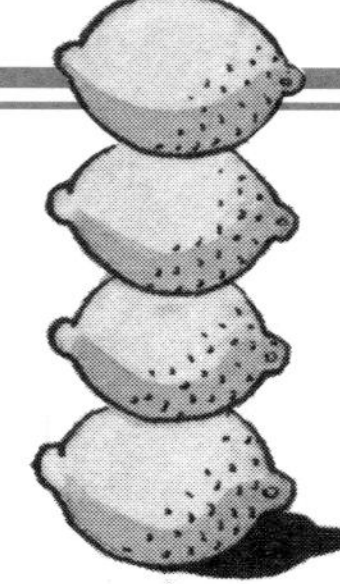

Preserved lemons are an essential ingredient in Moroccan cooking. As they rest in their juices, the lemons will tenderize and plump over time. For most recipes, the pulp is discarded and only the succulent, tangy, tender rinds are used. You want a pure lemon flavor so don't be tempted to add any spices. As lemons are often treated with disinfectants, it is necessary to scrub them well before using. These lemons will keep for months, refrigerated, and are well worth the time it takes to prepare them.

2 tablespoons plus 8 teaspoons coarse salt
8 medium thin-skinned lemons, scrubbed well
2 cups fresh lemon juice
Olive oil or water

1. Place 1 tablespoon of coarse salt in the bottom of each of 2 sterilized quart-size canning jars.

2. Using the palms of your hands, roll the lemons back and forth on a work surface to soften them slightly and release the juices.

3. Starting ½ inch down from the top of the lemon, cut all the way through and down to within ½ inch of the bottom end. Make a quarter turn and repeat the cutting so that there are 4 quarters joined at both ends. Squeeze the lemons over a bowl to remove as much juice as possible. Sprinkle the inside of each lemon with 1 teaspoon coarse salt.

4. Place 4 lemons in each jar. You may have to work them in, pushing down gently so that 4 fit snuggly. They will probably be pressed out of shape. If it is too difficult to get the whole lemons into the jars, they can be cut into quarters lengthwise.

5. Divide the juices collected from the lemons between the 2 jars. Add an additional 1 cup lemon juice to each and top up with olive oil or water to cover the lemons if necessary. Fill to within ½ to 1 inch of the top of the jar. Screw on the tops and let the jars stand in a warm place for 3 weeks. Turn the jars over once or twice during that time (let rest on their lids, then back on their bottoms). After 3 weeks, the rinds should be soft. Store in the refrigerator. Scrape out and discard the pulp before using. Rinse the rind under running water to remove any white film that has formed (don't worry, it's harmless). Preserved lemons keep for months in the refrigerator.

Makes 2 quarts

THAI PICKLED CARROTS

A colorful and delicately pickled condiment, these carrots have just the right bite in texture and flavor. When you make the Banana Leaf Curry (see Index), be sure to serve them alongside.

4 medium carrots (about 8 ounces), peeled and cut into 2½-inch-long matchsticks
1 tablespoon coarse salt
1 cup rice wine vinegar
2 tablespoons (packed) light brown sugar
2 to 3 tiny dried red chilies, such as Bird Eye Chinese, or other small red chilies

1. Place the carrots in a bowl and toss with the salt. Let sit for 1 hour, tossing once or twice. Drain well and return to the bowl.

2. Meanwhile combine the vinegar and sugar in a small saucepan. Lightly crush the chilies and discard the seeds, according to taste. (The heat is in the seeds.) Add the chilies to the saucepan. Cook over low heat until the sugar dissolves, 1½ to 2 minutes. Cool to room temperature.

3. Add the vinegar mixture to the carrots, toss to combine, and let rest for 1 hour more. Drain and serve, or store covered in the refrigerator, up to 2 weeks.

Makes about 1½ cups

THAI PICKLED CUCUMBERS

Unlike regular pickles, these thinly sliced cucumbers are salted first before they are infused with a piquant rice wine vinegar brine. There's a slight crispness to the texture, and they're always welcome as a condiment on the Thai table to enjoy atop rice, noodles, or just on their own. Try to find the long seedless cucumbers as they'll make the best pickles, but if these are unavailable, cut regular cucumbers lengthwise in half and remove the seeds before slicing.

1 hothouse (seedless) cucumber, unpeeled
1 tablespoon coarse salt
1 cup rice wine vinegar
2 tablespoons light brown sugar
2 to 3 tiny dried red chilies, such as Bird Eye Chinese, or other small red chilies

1. Halve the cucumber lengthwise, then cut crosswise into ⅛-inch-thick slices. Place the cucumber in a bowl and toss with salt. Let sit for 1 hour, tossing once or twice. Drain well and return to the bowl.

2. Meanwhile combine the vinegar and sugar in a small saucepan. Lightly crush the chilies and discard the seeds, according to taste. (The heat is in the seeds.) Add the chilies to the saucepan. Cook over low heat until the sugar dissolves, 1½ to 2 minutes. Cool to room temperature.

3. Add the vinegar mixture to the cucumbers, toss to combine, and let rest for 1 hour more. Drain and serve, or store covered in the refrigerator. These are best served within 8 hours.

Makes about 2 cups

SWEET PICKLED CABBAGE

Salted pickled cabbage is served as a condiment as well as used as an ingredient in Asian cooking. While some recipes require days of salting and soaking, this method is rather quick and the results produce a cabbage that is soft yet still maintains a nice crunch to it. The brown sugar in the brine smooths out the salty flavor.

If you like your pickles "hot," add more dried chilies and leave the seeds in the brine. Try this with Hot Russian Borscht (see Index).

8 cups finely shredded green cabbage (about 1 large head cabbage)
2 tablespoons coarse salt
1 cup rice wine vinegar
3 tablespoons (packed) light brown sugar
2 to 3 tiny dried red chilies, such as Bird Eye Chinese, or other small red chilies

1. Place the cabbage in a large bowl and toss with the salt. Let sit for 1 hour, tossing twice. After 1 hour, place the cabbage in a colander, rinse with cold water, and drain well. Return to the bowl.

2. Meanwhile combine the vinegar and sugar in a small saucepan. Lightly crush the chilies and discard the seeds, according to taste. (The heat is in the seeds.) Add the chilies to the saucepan. Cook over low heat until the sugar is dissolved, 1½ to 2 minutes. Cool to room temperature.

3. Add the vinegar mixture to the cabbage, toss to combine, and let rest for 1 hour more. Drain and serve, or store covered in the refrigerator up to 3 to 4 days.

Makes 3 cups

GRIOTTES
Pickled Sour Cherries

In America we bake sour cherries into the very best pies, but the French pickle them in the style of cornichons to accompany pâtés and cold meats. The Morello cherry season is extremely short but the effort of pickling them is well worth it as they'll last throughout the year. Late June or the first few weeks in July produce just enough cherries to make it essential to seize the moment.

Pickling these sour cherries is really a rather simple process. To begin, it is necessary to prick the cherries with a sterilized needle so that they will absorb the brine. Apple cider vinegar has a lovely sweetness, and I prefer it for my pickling brines. Brown sugar, cloves, cinnamon sticks, and fresh tarragon infuse the cherries with their delicate perfume. My favorite way to serve the cherries is with boiled new potatoes, runny raclette cheese softened by a fire fueled with pine cones, and thinly sliced cold roasted pork.

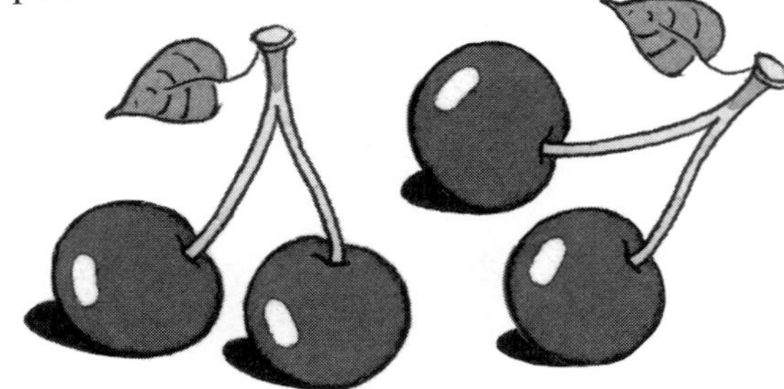

2 pounds fresh sour cherries with stems, leaves, and pits
12 fresh tarragon sprigs
6 cinnamon sticks (each 3 inches long)
36 whole cloves
2 cups apple cider vinegar
1 cup (packed) light brown sugar

1. Have ready 6 sterilized pint-size canning jars and lids and several sterilized needles.

2. Rinse the cherries and drain well. Prick each cherry 2 or 3 times with a sterile needle so they absorb the brine.

3. Place 2 sprigs of tarragon, a cinnamon stick, and 6 cloves in each jar. Divide the cherries among the jars.

4. Bring the vinegar to a boil in a noncor-

rosive saucepan. Add the brown sugar and stir until dissolved. Pour the hot liquid into the jars, making sure the cherries are completely covered but do not fill the jars past ½ inch from the rim. Cool and then cap the jars following the manufacturer's directions. Let the jars stand for 15 days before serving the cherries. Store in a cool, dark place.

Makes 6 pints

HARISSA

This fiery red paste is beloved as a condiment all over North Africa. It's often placed on the table along with bread, butter, and olives before a meal begins. It is also used in cooking to flavor broths for couscous and stews.

With an eye toward the American palate, I've tamed my *harissa* by combining roasted red bell peppers with dried hot red chilies. In North Africa, it is made solely with the chilies. You can adjust the heat by adding more. *Harissa* is sold in tubes at specialty food stores, although it will never be as fresh and delicious as your own. It lasts for weeks when stored refrigerated in a clean glass jar.

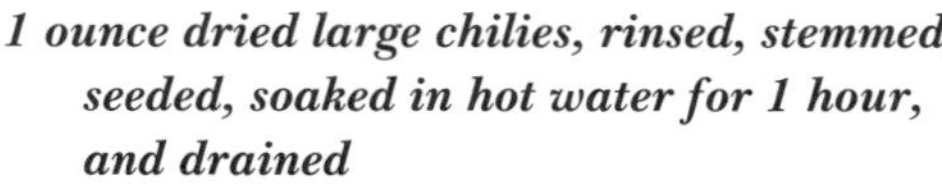

1 ounce dried large chilies, rinsed, stemmed, seeded, soaked in hot water for 1 hour, and drained
3 red bell peppers, halved lengthwise and roasted (page 202)
4 cloves garlic, halved and peeled
1 teaspoon coarse salt
1 teaspoon caraway seeds
1 teaspoon coriander seeds
1 teaspoon ground cumin
¼ cup olive oil

1. Place the rehydrated chilies, roasted red bell peppers, garlic, salt, caraway, coriander, and cumin in a food processor. Pulse on and off until well combined but not completely smooth.

2. With the machine running, drizzle the olive oil through the feed tube and continue processing until the oil is combined and the mixture is just smooth, about the consistency of mayonnaise.

3. Remove to a glass jar and keep refrigerated until use.

Makes 1¼ cup

SAVORY PLUM CONSERVE

For this rich condiment, Italian purple plums —available from August through the end of October—are combined with curry powder from India and cumin from North Africa. The result is this unusually lush conserve. Serve it alongside your favorite curries, game, roast pork, cheeses, and omelets.

4 pounds small Italian plums, halved and pitted
1 medium onion, halved and slivered
1 cup (packed) light brown sugar
¾ cup water
½ cup dry red wine
Juice of 1 orange
2 cinnamon sticks (each 3 inches long)
1 teaspoon best-quality curry powder
1 teaspoon ground cumin
1 teaspoon ground allspice
¼ teaspoon ground cloves

1. Place all the ingredients in a large heavy pot. Bring to a boil, reduce the heat, and simmer uncovered for 1 hour, breaking up the plums slightly with the back of a spoon and stirring occasionally.

2. Cool to room temperature, then cover and refrigerate up to 2 months.

Makes 6 cups

RHUBARB-BEET COMPOTE

One of the most unusual and delectable condiments I tasted on my journey through Scandinavia was a rhubarb-beet compote. It seemed well worth recreating. The natural sugar in the tender beets lessens the need for too much additional sugar, and fresh orange juice adds to the complexity as the compote simmers. I first enjoyed the compote alongside rare roasted leg of lamb in a tarragon cream sauce, but this fruit condiment would go beautifully with roasted pheasant, duck, or goose.

12 ounces Roasted Beets (page 194), peeled and cut into ¼-inch dice
1½ pounds rhubarb, leaves removed, rinsed, and cut into ½-inch pieces
¾ cup sugar
½ cup fresh orange juice
Finely grated zest of 1 orange

1. Place the beets, rhubarb, sugar, and orange juice in a large heavy pot. Bring to a boil and cook over medium-high heat, occasionally skimming off any foam that rises to the top, until slightly thickened, 10 to 12 minutes. Do not overcook.

2. Stir in the orange zest and cool. Serve at room temperature or refrigerate covered for up to 3 days.

Serves 12

CHEF BAYO'S TANZANIAN GREEN TOMATO CHUTNEY

My sister-in-law, Priscilla Hawk, has a love of world travel. One of her many trips took her to Tanzania's Gibbs Farm. Nestled high in the hills, between Ngorogoro Crater, a natural amphitheater, and Lake Manyara, where breathtaking birds mingle with herds of animals, this inn is an oasis of lush greenery, a sharp contrast to the dusty roads and vast plains below. Lush gardens, coffee plantations, a lily pond, and cozy cottages surround the inn. Priscilla says that as she sat in the well-shaded rustic chairs that were scattered along garden paths, she felt that she had been transported to the French countryside.

The dining room in the main house has paintings and crafts by local artisans displayed alongside low wooden tables set with colorful flowers and linens. It is the perfect setting for Chef Bayo's superb luncheon buffet. Among the selections was this outstanding chutney. Chef Bayo graciously filled a jar for Priscilla to bring back to me, so that I could try my hand at his green tomato chutney.

12 ounces green tomatoes or tomatillos, cored and cut into ½- inch dice
2 large yellow onions, cut into ½-inch dice (about 2 cups)
2 large green (underripe) papayas (about 12 ounces each), peeled, seeded, and cut into ½-inch dice
3 cups sugar
2 cups apple cider vinegar
1 teaspoon coarse salt
½ teaspoon ground nutmeg
½ teaspoon ground cinnamon
¼ teaspoon ground cloves

1. Place the green tomatoes, onions, and papayas in a large heavy pot. Add the sugar, vinegar, salt, and spices. Stir well.

2. Bring the mixture to a boil, reduce the heat slightly, and simmer uncovered until the mixture is thick, about 1 hour.

3. Cool to room temperature, then refrigerate covered until ready to use. The chutney will thicken slightly as it chills. If you prefer a less liquidy chutney, drain a bit off.

Makes 4 cups

Chutney

"The Indian woman's love for the sour, the piquant, and spicy is responsible for an appetite-building assortment of fresh chutneys without which no Indian meal—breakfast, brunch, lunch, tea, cocktail, and dinner—is complete," says Arvind Saraswat, Executive Chef of India's Taj Hotel chain. Major Grey's sweet mango variety has certainly not cornered the market on chutney as it is known in India. There, chutney takes on a whole different meaning than it does in America. The range of possibilities is vast, from sweet and fruity preserve-like chutneys to extraordinarily sour mouth-puckering varieties.

In India, there was always a balanced range of chutneys on the table. Any combination of fruits is perfectly acceptable. The chutneys I sampled and enjoyed included one made from chopped fresh mint, coriander, and tomatoes. I also had a sweet and sour tamarind chutney served alongside a sweet thick tomato and mango chutney. There were also raw chutneys such as finely chopped onions coated in hot chili spices. With so many wonderful chutneys to choose from, it was often tempting to simply "hold the entrée."

TOMATO APRICOT CHUTNEY

Ripe tomatoes combined with plump dried apricots make a luscious chutney. Ginger adds a piquant touch, and golden raisins, cinnamon, and allspice round out the flavors. Basically this condiment is cooked in one step and is quite easy to prepare. Don't limit this chutney to Indian specialties, for it is also lovely served with roast lamb, pork, or poultry.

4 pounds tomatoes, peeled and coarsely chopped
1 large onion, halved and thinly slivered
1 cup (packed) dark brown sugar
½ cup apple cider vinegar
½ cup dried apricots, coarsely chopped
½ cup golden raisins
¼ cup minced peeled fresh ginger
1 cinnamon stick (3 inches long)
1 teaspoon ground allspice
1 teaspoon salt

1. Place all the ingredients in a large heavy pot over medium-low heat and simmer gently uncovered for 1¼ hours, stirring often. Reduce the heat when the mixture starts to boil.

2. Remove the cinnamon stick and let the chutney cool to room temperature. Store in covered containers in the refrigerator until ready to serve. It will keep up to 4 weeks.

Makes 6 cups

MY KITCHEN DIARY

How to Peel Tomatoes

During my travels, I noticed that most tomatoes served in salads or as decorative garnishes were peeled. They always looked beautiful and tasted great. Since peeling them is easy enough, you might want to consider doing it more often than for the occasional soup. Here's how:

Bring a large pot of water to a boil. With a sharp paring knife, cut an X just through the skin on the bottom of each tomato. Drop the tomatoes, a few at a time, into the water for 30 seconds. Remove the tomatoes with a slotted spoon to a bowl filled with ice water to cool them down. The skin will easily slip off each tomato. If the tomatoes are to be cooked further, the ice water bath is unnecessary.

RANCHERO SALSA ROSA

When serving eggs in Mexico, it's customary to have a tomato sauce that is at once piquant, lightly cooked, and still fresh in flavor and appearance. This not-too-fiery sauce fits the criteria. If you prefer your sauce a bit hotter, add more jalapeños. I like to start my morning gently. Fresh cilantro may be substituted for the parsley.

6 ripe plum tomatoes (about 1½ pounds)
2 jalapeño chilies, halved lengthwise, seeds removed, and minced
1 tablespoon vegetable oil
1 small onion, finely diced
1 clove garlic, minced
Salt, to taste
1 tablespoon coarsely chopped flat-leaf parsley

1. Cut a small X in the bottom of each tomato. Drop into a pot of boiling water for 30 seconds. Remove to a bowl of ice water and slip off the skins. Halve the peeled tomatoes lengthwise, remove the seeds, and cut into small cubes. Place in a bowl and fold in the jalapeños.

2. Heat the oil in a small saucepan over low heat. Add the onion and cook until soft and translucent, about 10 minutes, stirring constantly. Stir in the garlic and cook 1 minute longer. Add to the tomatoes.

3. Coarsely purée one-third of the tomato mixture in a food processor or blender. Remove to a saucepan along with the remaining tomato mixture. Cook, stirring, over low heat for 10 minutes. Season with salt, stir in the parsley, and cool to room temperature. Use immediately or refrigerate covered up to 3 days. Serve at room temperature.

Makes 1½ cups

A TASTE OF THE WORLD

Mexican Palette

...And

Oregano	***Tomatoes***
Thyme	***Chayotes***
Cinnamon	***Red onions***
Cumin	***Lemons***
Cloves	***Oranges***
Vanilla	***Raisins***
Cilantro	***Rice***
Onions	***Dried beans***
Garlic	***Almonds***
Olives	

***Photo:** There's nothing like the Mercado Central de Abastos in Oaxaca on a Saturday.*

SALSA CARNAVAL

Sitting under a thatched umbrella on the beach at Ixtapa on the west coast of Mexico, I tasted a version of this refreshing salsa served atop perfectly grilled red snapper. The sweet fruits are beautifully enlivened by fresh lime juice, and the jalapeño and onion lend just the right bite. *Salsa carnaval* also makes a surprisingly good condiment for Jerk Chicken (see Index).

1 cup diced (¼ inch) ripe cantaloupe
1 cup diced (¼ inch) seeded ripe watermelon
1 cup diced (¼ inch) peeled hothouse (seedless) cucumber
4 ripe plum tomatoes, seeded and cut into ¼-inch dice
⅓ cup finely chopped red onion
1 teaspoon minced seeded jalapeño pepper
2 tablespoons fresh lime juice
2 tablespoons coarsely chopped flat-leaf parsley

Mix all the ingredients together in a bowl and let rest for at least 1 hour before serving.

Makes 4 cups

KIWI SALSA

Before preparing a fruit salsa, consider not only the flavor but also the texture and color of the fruits you're including. Kiwi along with its seeds adds nice crunchy texture. This salsa also works well with half an avocado substituted for half of the papaya. This is a zesty and refreshing sauce for grilled fish or poultry.

1 ripe papaya (about 1¼ pounds), peeled, seeded, and cut into ¼-inch dice
4 ripe kiwis, peeled and cut into ¼-inch dice
½ cup cored, seeded, and diced (¼ inch) ripe tomato
1 large shallot, minced
2 teaspoons finely grated lime zest
2 tablespoons fresh lime juice
¼ teaspoon minced jalapeño chili
Salt, to taste
2 tablespoons chopped fresh cilantro leaves

Place the papaya, kiwis, tomato, and shallot in a bowl. Add the lime zest, lime juice, and jalapeño and toss gently. Season to taste with salt and stir in the cilantro. Refrigerate up to 1 hour before serving.

Makes 3 cups

THAI FRUIT SALSA

Top off grilled salmon, swordfish, or tuna with this velvety, fresh salsa. Green chilies add a welcome bite. Stir in the chopped basil just before serving.

1 ripe mango, peeled, pitted, and cut into ¼-inch dice
1 ripe avocado, preferably Haas, pitted, peeled, and cut into ¼-inch dice
3 ripe plum tomatoes, seeded and finely diced
¼ cup finely diced red onion
2 teaspoons minced garlic
1 to 2 teaspoons minced jalapeño chili
5 tablespoons fresh lime juice
1 tablespoon finely grated lime zest
¼ cup chopped fresh basil leaves

In a large bowl combine all the ingredients except the basil. Refrigerate covered up to 2 hours. Just before serving, toss in the basil.

Makes about 4 cups

FIESTA CORN SALSA

This salsa captures the essence of summer in both flavor and texture. The sweetness of just-picked corn and ripe tomatoes is enhanced by velvety papaya and zesty fresh lime. Take care not to overcook the corn. Its crunch, along with the red onion, exudes freshness. Try it with Gordon's Quesadillas or Mambo Mango Pork (see Index).

1 cup fresh corn (2 ears), lightly cooked
1 ripe papaya, peeled, seeded, and cut into ¼-inch dice
⅓ cup finely diced red onion
2 ripe plum tomatoes, seeded and finely diced
1½ teaspoons minced garlic
1 tablespoon finely grated lime zest
¼ cup fresh lime juice
⅓ cup chopped fresh cilantro leaves

In a large bowl gently combine all the ingredients except the cilantro. Cover and refrigerate up to 2 hours. Just before serving, toss in the cilantro. Serve chilled.

Makes about 4 cups

SAUN'S FRESH SALSA VERDE

At Saun and Pancho Drohojowski's beautiful *casa* in Cuernavaca, I had the most marvelous

fresh *salsa verde* spooned over my *huevos rancheros* for breakfast on New Year's Day. Saun gave me her recipe, and here it is. You can increase the heat by adding more jalapeño.

8 ounces fresh tomatillos
2 scallions (3 inches green left on), sliced
1 teaspoon minced seeded jalapeño chili
½ teaspoon minced garlic
2 tablespoons fresh lime juice
½ cup coarsely chopped fresh cilantro leaves
Salt, to taste

1. Remove the papery outer skin and stems from the tomatillos. Cut into quarters and place in a saucepan. Cover the tomatillos with water and bring to a boil. Continue cooking until the tomatillos are just soft, 2 to 3 minutes. Drain, rinse under cold water, and drain thoroughly. Cool to room temperature.

2. Place the cooked tomatillos, the scallions, jalapeños, garlic, and lime juice in a food processor or blender. Pulse on and off about 10 times until well combined. Add the cilantro and pulse another 10 times.

3. Remove the salsa to a bowl and season with salt to taste. Serve at room temperature or refrigerate covered up to 3 days.

Makes 1 cup

COOL DOWN SALSA

The spices of Indonesia are intense and often quite hot. Chilies proliferate in soups, seafood, and curries. Cool downs offer up a good balance to the heat and help to increase the pleasures of the palate. For instance, in Ubud, Bali, I nibbled on a platter of sliced bananas and crisp cucumbers along with a very spicy duck curry. The salsa combines the cool tastes of cucumber, lime, and cilantro along with pineapple—which when sweet and ripe are perfect antidotes to an overheated palate. Of course, I couldn't resist the spark of a bit of garlic, red onion, and chili as well. Adjust the seasoning to your own taste and serve chilled.

2 cups diced (¼ inch) fresh ripe pineapple
2 cups diced (¼ inch) peeled hothouse (seedless) cucumber
½ cup diced (⅛ inch) red onion
1 fresh red chili
1 teaspoon minced garlic
2 teaspoons finely grated lime zest
½ cup fresh lime juice
2 tablespoons finely slivered fresh basil leaves
2 tablespoons coarsely chopped fresh cilantro leaves

1. Gently combine the pineapple, cucumber, and onion in a bowl.

2. Cut the chili in half and carefully remove and discard the seeds and ribs. Mince the chili and add 1 to 2 teaspoons, depending on taste, to the pineapple mixture. Toss in the garlic, lime zest, and lime juice. Cover and refrigerate up to 2 hours before use.

3. Toss in basil and cilantro just before serving so that the citrus juice doesn't discolor it. Serve chilled.

Makes 4 cups

A-JAAD
Thai Cucumber Cool Down

Thai dishes are most often hot, spicy, and sweet. Chilled crisp "cool downs" are the perfect condiments or salads to enjoy alongside to freshen the palate. Although the salads often have chilies in them, you can adjust the amount to suit your taste without altering the flavors. Be sure to choose firm, fresh cucumbers and shallots for this dish.

½ cup rice wine vinegar
2 tablespoons sugar
1 teaspoon salt
1 to 2 tablespoons minced fresh red chili (seeds and ribs removed)
1 cup halved and thinly sliced hothouse (seedless) cucumber
½ cup thinly sliced shallots (about 2 ounces)
1½ tablespoons chopped fresh cilantro leaves
8 small fresh cilantro leaves, for garnish

1. Combine the vinegar, sugar, and salt in a small saucepan. Cook, swirling the pan, over low heat until the sugar dissolves, about 2 minutes. Add the chili and let cool.

2. Place the cucumber and shallots in a bowl, pour the vinegar mixture over the top, and stir to combine.

3. Just before serving, toss in the chopped cilantro. Transfer to an attractive bowl and garnish with whole cilantro leaves.

Serves 4

CREAMY YOGURT

When drained, yogurt has a thick creamy consistency. It is lovely sweetened with a spoonful of honey, served atop a Cherry Compote (see Index), or used to dollop a hot, bubbly moussaka.

4 cups (32 ounces) nonfat plain yogurt

Place a strainer lined with a double layer of cheesecloth over a large bowl. There should be plenty of room between the bottom of the strainer and the bottom of the bowl. Pour the yogurt into the strainer and let drain at room temperature for about 2½ hours. Remove to a clean bowl. Chill and serve.

Makes 1 cup

RAITA COOL DOWN

Raita, a smooth Indian yogurt condiment, is the perfect "cool down" to accompany a pungent curry. Lightly sautéed ginger and cumin add depth of flavor. Sweet plum tomatoes, cucumbers, and scallions add just the right crunch, and fresh cilantro adds a cleanness. Make 2 to 3 hours before serving and refrigerate until serving.

2 teaspoons vegetable oil
1½ teaspoons minced peeled fresh ginger
½ teaspoon ground cumin
2 ripe plum tomatoes, seeded and cut into ¼-inch dice
1 cup diced (¼ inch) peeled hothouse (seedless) cucumber
4 scallions (3 inches green left on), thinly sliced on the diagonal
1 small clove garlic, minced
1½ cups nonfat plain yogurt
Dash of Tabasco sauce
Salt, to taste
¼ cup coarsely chopped fresh cilantro leaves

Place the oil, ginger, and cumin in a small skillet. Cook over low heat for 1 minute, stirring constantly. Scrape into a mixing bowl with a rubber spatula. Add the tomatoes, cucumber, scallions, and garlic. Stir well to combine. Add the remaining ingredients and fold gently to combine. Adjust the seasonings. Cover and refrigerate for at least 1 hour but no longer than 3. Stir well before serving.

Makes 2 cups

MINTED BANANA-COCONUT RAITA

I find satiny smooth *raitas* the most luxurious accompaniment to *dal* dishes (lentils which become smooth after a long cooking), curries, and many other spicy meat and poultry recipes. With plain nonfat yogurt so readily available and so receptive a base for fruits, chutneys, and crispy vegetables, *raitas* become the ultimate "cool down."

For this delicious and unusual *raita,* I've toasted sweetened coconut and mixed it with ripe bananas, lime juice, and pungent black mustard seeds. But use your imagination and experiment with different combinations for spectacular results. This simple condiment takes on new interest when you vary the fruits and herbs. Refrigerate *raitas* for 1 to 2 hours before serving so that they aren't too runny.

½ cup grated coconut
2 tablespoons unsalted butter
1 teaspoon black mustard seeds
2 ripe medium bananas, cut into ¼-inch dice
2 tablespoons fresh lime juice
1½ cups nonfat plain yogurt
2 tablespoons plus 1 teaspoon chopped fresh mint leaves
Pinch of salt

1. Preheat the oven to 350°F.

2. Spread the coconut in a small baking pan and bake, shaking the pan once or twice so that it doesn't burn, until just golden brown, 2 to 3 minutes. Set aside.

3. Melt the butter in a small nonstick skillet over medium-low heat. Add the mustard seeds, cover, and cook, shaking the pan, until they pop open, about 2 minutes. Add the coconut and mix well. Remove from the heat.

4. Place the bananas in a medium-size bowl and toss with the lime juice. Fold in the yogurt, 2 tablespoons of the mint, and the salt with a rubber spatula. Fold in the coconut mixture and remove to a serving bowl. Sprinkle the top with the remaining teaspoon of mint. Cover and refrigerate at least 1 hour but no longer than 2. Stir well before serving.

Makes 2¼ cups

APPLE-PINEAPPLE RAITA

Fresh ginger, apple, and sweet crushed pineapple combine to make this a most delicious *raita*. A healthy amount of fresh basil adds an intense licorice taste, and the grated apple adds great body. In this instance, canned crushed pineapple adds just the right texture. It is delicious served with fruited rice and lentil dishes.

1 tablespoon fresh lime juice
1 Granny Smith apple, cored
1 teaspoon minced garlic
1 piece (1 inch) fresh ginger, peeled and grated
1 cup crushed pineapple, drained
1½ cups nonfat plain yogurt
½ teaspoon salt
¼ cup chopped fresh basil leaves

1. Place the lime juice in a mixing bowl, coarsely grate the apple into the bowl, and toss with the lime juice.

2. Add the garlic, ginger, and pineapple and toss to combine. Transfer the mixture to a fine strainer, drain off the excess liquid, and return the fruit to the bowl.

3. Add the yogurt and salt and mix together, then fold in the basil. Cover and refrigerate at least 1 hour but no longer than 2. Stir well before serving.

Makes 2 cups

MANGO-TOMATO RAITA

Both sweet and savory flavors come together in this unexpected *raita*. The ripe mangoes and tomatoes blend into tangy yogurt mixed with a heady *garam masala* made from cinnamon, cardamom, cloves, and mace. The onion, jalapeño, and fresh cilantro add both crunch and complex character to the mixture. As the *raita* rests, all the flavors brighten. Serve it with Exotic Lamb Curry and Le Colibri Porc Colombo (see Index).

2 ripe mangoes (about 12 ounces each)
3 ripe plum tomatoes, seeded and cut into ¼-inch dice
¼ cup finely chopped red onion
1 teaspoon finely chopped jalapeño chili (seeds and ribs removed)
2 cups nonfat plain yogurt
½ teaspoon Sweet Garam Masala (page 259)
Salt, to taste
2 tablespoons chopped fresh cilantro leaves

1. Remove the skin and pits from the mangoes and cut the flesh into ¼-inch dice. Place in a bowl with the tomatoes, onion, and jalapeño and gently fold together.

2. In a separate bowl, mix the yogurt and *garam masala*. Fold the yogurt into the fruit, season with the salt, and gently fold in the cilantro. Cover and refrigerate at least 1 hour but no longer than 2. Stir well before serving.

Makes 3 cups

A TASTE OF THE WORLD

Indian Palette

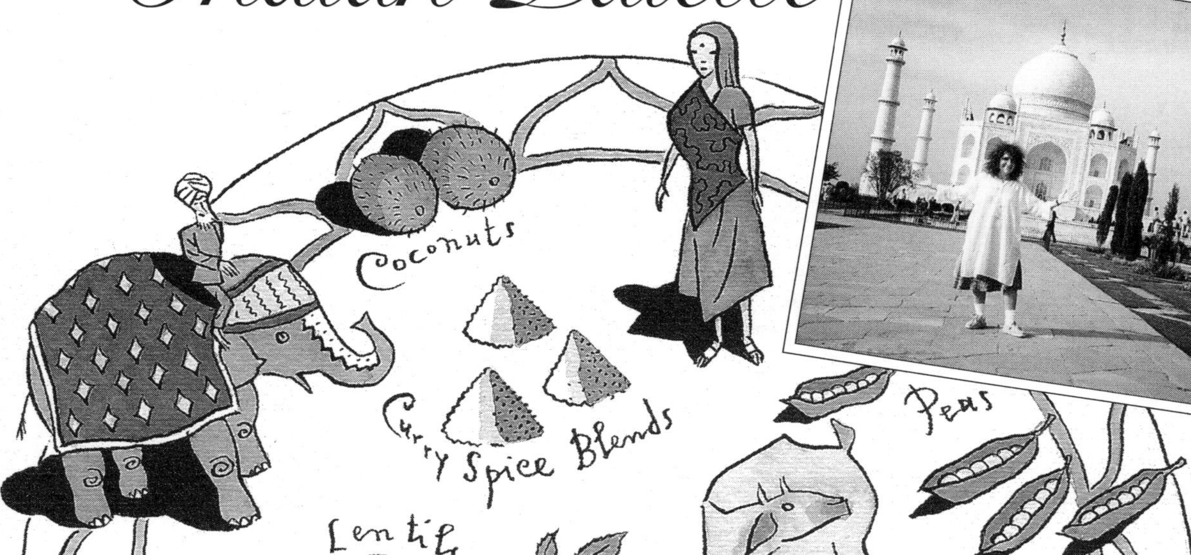

Photo: At the Taj—I hope they have a beauty parlor in there!

...And

CINNAMON	*POTATOES*
CARDAMOM	*SPINACH*
CUMIN	*EGGPLANTS*
CLOVES	*ONIONS*
MACE	*MANGOES*
MUSTARD SEEDS	*RAISINS*
ANISE	*APPLES*
TURMERIC	*LIMES*
PEPPERS	*CASHEWS*
CHILIES	*ALMONDS*
CILANTRO	*BASMATI RICE*
GARLIC	*YOGURT*
GINGER	*JAGGERY*
TOMATOES	*TAMARIND*

RICH COCONUT MILK

Coconut milk is an essential ingredient in both Thai and Indonesian dishes, and as these foods become more popular in America, coconut milk will become more widely available. Currently it can be found canned in many Asian markets or specialty food stores, but it's also quite simple to prepare at home. It will keep nicely in the refrigerator for a week.

2 cups milk
1 cup unsweetened dried coconut

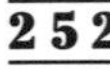

1. Bring the milk to a boil in a small heavy saucepan. Remove from the heat, add the coconut, and stir well to combine. Cover and set aside for 2 hours to steep.

2. Place the milk and coconut mixture in a food processor and process for 2 minutes.

3. Strain the mixture through a double layer of cheesecloth into a bowl and squeeze the coconut well to extract all moisture. Reserve the strained liquid and discard the coconut. Use at once or refrigerate covered for up to 3 days.

Makes about 2 cups

Dear Andy,
Bused it to the ancient city of Ayutthaya in the AM and returned by boat serving luncheon along the Chao Phya into Bangkok.
Love,
Sheila

MY KITCHEN DIARY

Scotch Bonnet Chilies

These little fiery red, orange, yellow, and green lantern-shaped chilies are in great abundance throughout the colorful Caribbean markets and add fire to many Jamaican dishes, including their famous jerk marinades. They are better known in the United States as habaneros, and throughout the Southwest are considered the king of chilies. It is said that this chili derives its name from Havana, where they may have originated.

A word of warning: One must proceed with caution when working with Scotch bonnets. The heat primarily comes from the seeds and the ribs. Add the chili to dishes judiciously, allowing the dish to cook a while before tasting it to determine whether it needs more. And be sure to wash your hands well with warm soapy water after preparing the chilies.

Handle with care—these are very hot Scotch bonnets.

JAMAICAN PEPPER SAUCE

Hot pepper sauces proliferate throughout the Caribbean. Some are tamed by the addition of sweet fruits—ripe mangoes and golden raisins mellow the Scotch bonnet chilies and island spices used in this chunky sauce. Slowly cooked to a rich thickness, Jamaican Pepper Sauce can be served with fish, meat, and poultry or spooned into a savory stew to enrich a sauce.

1 ripe mango, peeled, pitted, and diced
2 ripe large tomatoes, seeded and diced
1 Scotch bonnet or habanero chili, seeds and ribs removed and minced, or more to taste
½ cup golden raisins
4 shallots, finely chopped
1 tablespoon minced peeled fresh ginger
2 teaspoons ground allspice
½ teaspoon salt
½ teaspoon ground cinnamon
¼ teaspoon ground cloves
½ cup (packed) dark brown sugar
½ cup granulated sugar
½ cup red wine vinegar

Combine all the ingredients in a heavy saucepan. Cook, stirring occasionally, over low heat, until the sauce is thick and rich, about 1 hour. Cover and refrigerate for up to 2 weeks.

Makes 2 cups

SAUCE CHIEN

Sauce chien was only a rather odd-sounding name to me before I tasted it atop grilled red snapper in Martinique. What I was surprised to discover was how much it reminded me of the light Thai dipping sauces I had tasted in Bangkok. But laden with fire-power—provided by super hot Scotch bonnet chilies—this sauce is not as sweet as those from Thailand. It is more like an exotic vinaigrette. Creole cooks use their wild country onions in this sauce, but I've substituted fresh shallots for the indigenous ingredient. Try *sauce chien* as a salsa with grilled fish or poultry.

¼ cup finely diced shallots
1 ripe plum tomato, seeded and cut into ⅛-inch dice
1 to 2 teaspoons minced fresh red chili, preferably Scotch bonnet (habanero) chili, seeds removed, depending on desired hotness
½ cup fresh lime juice
¼ cup rice vinegar
Salt and freshly ground black pepper, to taste
2 tablespoons chopped fresh cilantro leaves
1 teaspoon finely snipped fresh chives

Mix all the ingredients together in a small bowl and serve within 2 to 3 hours. For a fresher taste, serve within 1 hour.

Makes 1 cup

THAI FISH SAUCE

Pungent, slightly salty, and sweet, fish sauce is an essential ingredient in Thai and other Southeast Asian cuisines. It is often available in Asian markets and specialty food stores. If you can't find it, here is an acceptable substitute.

1 can (2 ounces) anchovies, drained
2 cloves garlic, lightly bruised and peeled (page 153)
½ teaspoon (packed) dark or light brown sugar
¼ teaspoon salt
1¼ cups water

1. Place all the ingredients in a small heavy saucepan. Simmer over medium-low heat for 10 minutes without stirring.

2. Remove from the heat, cool slightly, then strain through a double layer of cheesecloth. Store covered in the refrigerator up to 2 weeks.

Makes about ¾ cup

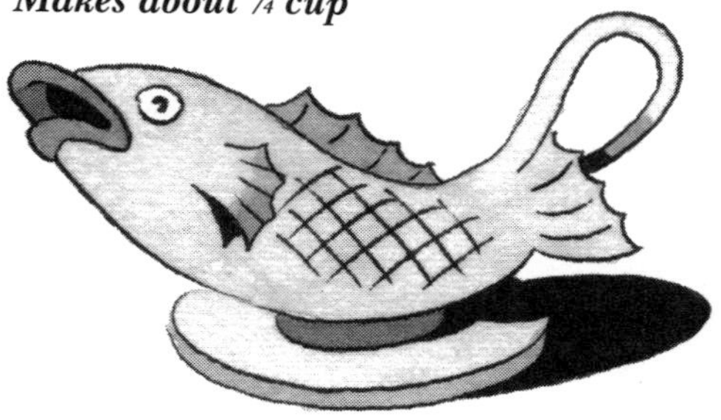

AVOCADO BUTTER

Creamy ripe avocados, fresh lime juice, and a dash of hot sauce make this a most luxurious butter. A slice melting over grilled chicken, steak, or red snapper is heavenly.

8 tablespoons (1 stick) unsalted butter, at room temperature
½ ripe avocado, preferably Haas, pitted, peeled, and cut into small chunks
1 tablespoon fresh lime juice
1 tablespoon chopped flat-leaf parsley
1 teaspoon Worcestershire sauce
½ teaspoon minced garlic
Dash of Tabasco or other hot sauce

1. Blend all the ingredients together in a small bowl.

2. Transfer the mixture to a piece of plastic wrap. Use the wrap to help form the butter into a log shape. Roll up in the wrap and twist the ends shut, creating a compact, evenly formed cylinder. Refrigerate until firm, at least 2 hours, or freeze up to 3 weeks.

Makes ¾ cup

The Wines of Mexico

Mexico produces huge quanties of wine, but 90 percent of it is made from lesser grapes and distilled into brandy. During the 70s and 80s, winegrowers in Baja and the central highland regions, such as Querétaro and Aguascalientes, began planting better varieties for table wine, including Cabernet Sauvignon, Merlot, Chardonnay, and Sauvignon Blanc, in order to combat high tariffs on imported wines. Since then, however, with the tariffs lowered or removed, imports from Europe and California have regained the market. A few producers persist, striving for quality in their better wines and achieving it more frequently than in the past. The top firms include Bodegas de Santo Tomás, Domecq, Luis Cetto, and Cavas de San Juan.

Mulegé, by the Golfo de California coast in Baja, California, is lush with beautiful date palm trees.

WINES AND BEERS OF

India and Pakistan

India's religious traditions, both Hindu and Muslim, did not encourage the development of alcoholic drinks. The coming of the British Raj, however, spawned a brewing industry that continues to thrive today in parts of India and Pakistan. The British favored lagers in the warm, subtropical climate, particularly in the Pilsener style (strongly flavored with hops), but they also prized bitter stout. The Mohan Meakin brewery in northern India continues to produce several lagers under labels such as Lion, Gymkhana, and Golden Eagle. Southern India, notably Hyderabad and Bangalore, produces crisp lager beers, such as Jubilee, Flying Horse, and Kingfisher, and also good bitter stout, again Kingfisher as well as Pelican and London.

If beer is not your choice for an Indian feast, this wine is a good alternative.

The Murree Brewery is Pakistan's leading brewer, and neighboring Rajasthan in India's Punjab region is known for its dry, well-hopped Black Label lager.

India is perhaps the world's youngest winegrower, with vineyards southeast of Bombay recently planted to Chardonnay and Cabernet Sauvignon. Launched in the mid-80s by a French-Indian company, Indage India Ltd. of Narayangoan, production includes red and white table wines under the Riviera label and highly regarded efforts with a sparkling wine known as Omar Khayyám.

Though we tend to drink imported beers from the Orient with spicy Indian food, we are beginning to discover how well certain wines go with many dishes. Milder meat curries and biryanis are complemented by Merlot, lighter Cabernet Sauvignon, or blends thereof. Sauvignon Blanc is an excellent choice with all but the hottest shrimp curries. Dry Rieslings from Alsace or the U.S. Northwest work very nicely with milder spicy chicken and fish dishes, as well as gentler vegetarian specialties. Other dry white wines to try include Pinot Blanc, Pinot Gris, and Sémillon.

CURRY BUTTER

A blend of Indian ingredients make for a delicious butter to slice over grilled fish, meat, or poultry. Rolled into a little log and frozen, ready for use at any time, these dressed-up pats enhance the simplest dish.

8 tablespoons (1 stick) unsalted butter, at room temperature
1½ teaspoons best-quality curry powder
1 tablespoon fresh lime or lemon juice
½ teaspoon ground ginger

1. Blend the ingredients together in a small bowl.

2. Transfer the mixture to a piece of plastic wrap. Use the wrap to help form the butter into a log shape. Roll up in the wrap and twist the ends shut, creating a compact, evenly formed cylinder. Refrigerate until firm, at least 2 hours, or freeze up to 3 weeks.

Makes ½ cup

SERUNDING

Malaysian restaurateur Aziza Ali lives in Singapore, where she owns the finest restaurant—Aziza's. Her spice combinations, especially this coconut condiment, fascinated me. In her *serunding* mixture, Aziza combines the coconut with sweet and savory spices. Delicate toasting brings out all the flavors. Serve it sprinkled over Malay Oxtail Soup, Thai Coconut Ratatouille, or Exotic Lamb Curry (see Index). I also like to serve this as a garnish for curries.

1 cup finely grated coconut, slightly moist
1 tablespoon minced garlic (about 2 large cloves)
1 teaspoon ground cinnamon
1 teaspoon ground cumin
1 teaspoon ground coriander
½ teaspoon crushed red pepper flakes, or to taste

1. Preheat the oven to 350°F.

2. In a large bowl lightly toss all the ingredients together with your hands, making sure that the garlic and spices are well distributed.

3. Spread the coconut mixture on a baking sheet and toast on the center rack of the oven, until pale golden, 5 to 7 minutes, shaking the pan twice. Check after 5 minutes to be sure the coconut doesn't burn. Remove to let cool and dry out slightly. Store in an airtight jar until use. This will keep 3 to 4 weeks.

Makes 1 cup

MASALA FOR MILDLY SPICED SAUCES

This *masala* is beautifully suited to vegetable and fish dishes. And, it also works well stirred into yogurt along with fruit for a cooling *raita*—try it in the Apple-Pineapple Raita or the Savory

MY KITCHEN DIARY

Masalas

The complex flavors of Indian cuisine are enhanced by an extraordinary array of carefully blended aromatic spice mixtures known as *masalas.* Each blend, with its own distinct characteristics, is suitable for a particular dish. The aromatic mixtures may contain cardamom, mace, nutmeg, cumin, and coriander, while the hotter ones are laced with chilies, pepper, and cloves.

What we in America think of as curry powder is just one type of the *masala.* Although there are many excellent blends available, you would rarely find an Indian cook using a commercial mix. To use just one curry powder would mean that all dishes would taste alike, and the fabulous subtleties in a true Indian meal would be lost.

To make a *masala,* ideally you would begin by dry roasting whole spices in a heavy skillet over medium heat for about 2 minutes, shaking the pan constantly. The heat draws out the natural oils, thereby enhancing and mellowing the flavor. Then you would grind the spices in a well-cleaned coffee mill or pepper grinder. They'll last about 4 months when stored in an airtight container in a cool place.

In the recipes for spice mixtures in this book, I've used combinations of ground spices since it's the most convenient method for American kitchens. Occasionally I've included a seed or two, such as fenugreek or fennel, but these easily can be ground before adding them to the mixture. If you prefer using whole spices, your flavors will be that much more intense.

Chilies for masala with heat.

Mint and Coriander Chutney (see Index). This recipe can be easily doubled or tripled.

2 tablespoons ground cardamom
2 teaspoons ground cumin
1 teaspoon ground cinnamon
½ teaspoon freshly ground black pepper

Combine all the ingredients in a bowl. Transfer to an airtight jar and store in a cool dry place.

Makes about 3 tablespoons

SAVORY MASALA FOR MEAT

Because the sweet and savory play of ingredients is so prevalent in both Indian and North African cooking, this *masala* is ideally suited to those luscious, pungent lamb preparations these cuisines are so well known for. Liberal amounts of ginger and black pepper introduce the right amount of heat.

2 tablespoons ground cumin
1½ tablespoons ground coriander
1½ tablespoons ground cardamom
½ teaspoon ground ginger
½ teaspoon ground cinnamon
¼ teaspoon freshly ground black pepper
¼ teaspoon ground cloves
¼ teaspoon ground mace
¼ teaspoon ground nutmeg

Combine all the ingredients in a small bowl. Transfer to an airtight jar and store in a cool dry place.

Makes ¼ cup

SWEET GARAM MASALA

This mixture uses the warm aromatic spices so prevalent in both India and North Africa. Stirred into the Mango-Tomato Raita (see Index)—it exudes a magical flavor. This recipe can easily be doubled or tripled.

1 tablespoon ground cardamom
1 teaspoon ground cinnamon
1 teaspoon ground coriander
½ teaspoon ground cloves
¼ teaspoon ground mace

Combine all the ingredients in a small bowl. Transfer to an airtight jar and store in a cool dry place.

Makes 2 tablespoons

COLOMBO CURRY POWDER

Caribbean curry powder is pungent and aromatic. The beauty of mixing your own is being able to adjust the spice amounts to your taste. Buy the freshest ground spices available and keep them at their peak by storing them in a cool dry place or freeze in plastic bags until ready to use. You can easily double or triple this recipe.

1 tablespoon ground coriander
1 teaspoon ground fenugreek
½ teaspoon ground cinnamon
½ teaspoon ground cumin
½ teaspoon ground black pepper
¼ teaspoon ground allspice
¼ teaspoon ground ginger
¼ teaspoon ground turmeric
¼ teaspoon ground cardamom
¼ teaspoon dry mustard
⅛ teaspoon ground mace
Pinch of cayenne pepper

Mix all the ingredients together in a small bowl. Transfer to an airtight jar and store in a cool dry place.

Makes just over 2 tablespoons

The large public spice market in Martinique is both heady in aroma and visually dazzling. Various sized and shaped bottles of vibrant red hot sauces are lined up together with clear golden honeys and rich dark brown spice sauces. Neat vertical piles of bagged spices create a pink-, peach-, and red-hued rainbow. Within these clear bags rest cinnamon, cloves, colombo (the curry powder of the island), saffron, ginger, and black and white peppers. Fawn-hued tamarind pods are laid out to dry next to baskets of smoky green bay leaves. Twiggy sarsaparilla branches and brownish purple nutmegs rest among the bottles and bags just waiting to be grated. Large jars of vanilla beans stand among enormous pieces of cinnamon bark and braids of garlic. Burlap sacks overflow with fresh mountain thyme. Where was my kitchen when I needed it—the desire to cook up something wonderful was overwhelming.

MY OWN CURRY POWDER

Before visiting India, I always found it perfectly adequate to use prepared curry powder for all my Indian cooking. There are certainly some perfectly acceptable commercial brands available. But after wandering through the wildly aromatic spice markets in Bombay, Agra, and Jaipur, I decided that I must try mixing my own. Feeling like a mad chemist, I worked up a blend that turned out to be quite delicious. Of course, just tasting the mixture on the tip of a spoon did not necessarily convince me that I had come up with a winner. I mellowed the flavors first by cooking them for a while in oil. It was then that I could appreciate the complex blending of all the spices.

For this mixture, it is necessary to grind the fenugreek seeds in a heavy spice mill, pepper grinder, or small well-cleaned coffee grinder. The flavor was a big surprise to me at first; instead of being very strong, the scent was mildly reminiscent of dried corn. My only disappointment was that my mixture was not bright golden in color, but once my sauce began cooking, the turmeric released its warm, magnificent color.

Once you get a feel for mixing your own blends, it's easy enough to change the proportions to suit your taste. For instance, if you prefer a hotter mixture, try increasing the amount of ginger and cayenne pepper, working in very small amounts as you make the adjustments. As I've mentioned before, these *masalas* are best after cooking has mellowed them a bit. Try this in Curried Squash Soup, Casbah Carrot Soup,

Banana Leaf Vegetable Curry, or Exotic Lamb Curry (see Index).

2 tablespoons ground cumin
1 teaspoon crushed or ground fenugreek seeds
1 teaspoon ground ginger
¼ teaspoon crushed dried dill
¼ teaspoon ground mace
¼ teaspoon ground cardamom
¼ teaspoon dry mustard
⅛ teaspoon ground turmeric
¼ teaspoon freshly ground black pepper
Pinch of cayenne pepper

Combine all the ingredients in a small bowl. Transfer to an airtight jar and store in a cool dry place.

Makes about ¼ cup

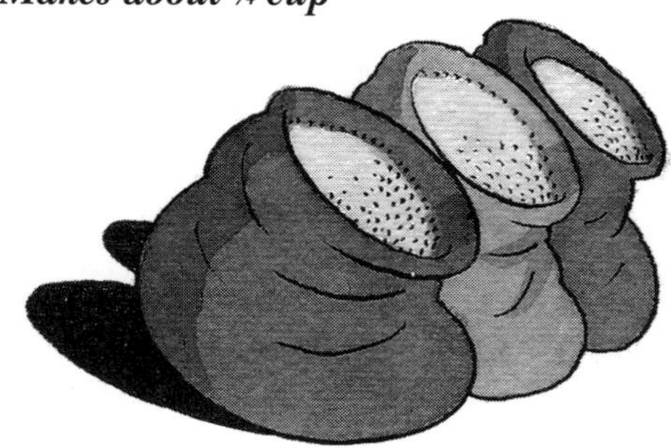

MARKETPLACE

Grains and Beans

Grains are integral to the cuisines of so many of the countries I visited. Asian countries go without saying, but in Spain, paella made with saffron-infused rice, is practically the national dish; in the Middle East, gorgeous fruit-studded pilafs shine; in North Africa, couscous is the *raison d'être* for many luscious poultry, lamb, and vegetable tagines; and in Russia, kasha—plain or mixed with wild mushrooms, herbs, and spices—is standard fare.

Grains and beans are partners in such a wonderful variety of hearty, healthful dishes, that the more I traveled, the more inspired I became by what I ate. I've combined black-eyed peas with barley for an unexpected, fresh approach to Island cuisine. And using typical Mediterranean and Caribbean ingredients, I've come up with a knock-out version of rice and beans.

If they aren't there already, I hope my recipes help convince you to move grains and beans to the place of honor on your table.

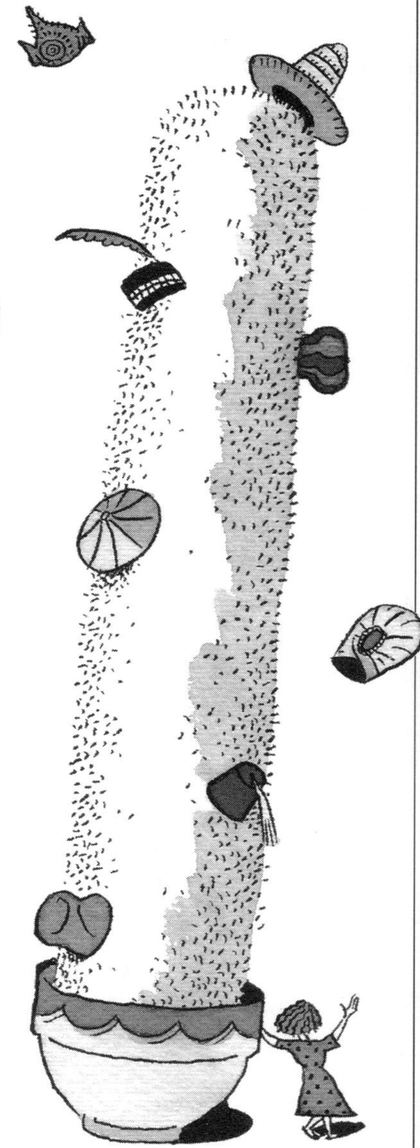

SPICY MARIGOLD RICE

Wonderful Sri Lankan friends Sassi and Nama, who moved from Jaffa to Paris several years ago, haven't deprived themselves of the delights of their native cuisine. Luckily for me, they generously share their hospitality—and recipes—with friends! Here is a special marigold-colored rice that will bring Jaffa to your table. The beautiful color of the rice is offset by tiny cubes of carrot, and the flavor is brightened with chopped cilantro. A touch of sweetness is added with golden raisins and toasted coconut.

1 cinnamon stick (3 inches long), lightly crushed
5 whole cloves
3 cardamom pods, lightly crushed
8 cups defatted Chicken Broth (page 127)
1 tablespoon ground turmeric
3 cups long-grain rice
1 cup diced (¼ inch) carrots
1 cup golden raisins
½ cup chopped fresh cilantro leaves
½ cup grated coconut, lightly toasted (page 514), for garnish

1. Place the cinnamon stick, cloves, and cardamom pods in a small skillet. Heat them for 2 minutes over medium-high heat, shaking the pan occasionally, to release the flavors. Remove from the heat and place the spices in a 5-inch square of cheesecloth; tie it securely with a piece of string.

2. Bring the chicken broth to a boil in a large heavy pot along with the spice bag and turmeric. When the broth is boiling, add the rice, stir it well, reduce the heat, and simmer covered until tender, 15 to 20 minutes. In the last 5 minutes of cooking, stir in the carrots and raisins to cook with the rice. When the rice is done, drain it, reserving ½ cup of the cooking liquid. Remove the spice bag.

3. Place the rice in a bowl and stir in the reserved cooking liquid. Add the chopped cilantro and combine. Sprinkle with the toasted coconut. Serve hot.

Serves 10 to 12

SOUVENIR TO SAVOR

Paradise Found

The closest I've ever come to Shangri-la was a stay at the Amandari Hotel, nestled among terraced emerald rice fields in southern Bali. The surrounding village of Ubud is truly paradise. Richard and I hired Amir, a fabulous guide, to lead us through the mystical world of gamelan music, *bayrong* dance, and the lacy shadow puppets of *wayang kulit.* Throughout our stay, as Amir took us from place to place, I plied him with questions—discreetly, I hope—about what he typically ate for breakfast, lunch, dinner, and late night snacks. His answers were pretty straightforward—a bowl of rice with a little green vegetable on top or a bowl of rice with a little fish on top. No frills—just basic, good, healthy eating.

LA BAMBA RICE

When I was looking around Mexico for great home-cooked dishes, I found that tomato-rice was so popular, it was served for breakfast, lunch, and dinner. Everybody seemed to have a favorite version. I created mine using plenty of tomatoes, chorizos, and green peas. For supper or brunch, just add a couple of fried eggs or serve with a big bowl of black beans alongside. It would also be excellent served with chicken.

3 tablespoons olive oil
1 medium onion, cut into ¼-inch dice
1 tablespoon finely chopped garlic
3 chorizo sausages (about 5 ounces), cut into ¼-inch cubes
2 cups long-grain rice
1 can (28 ounces) plum tomatoes, drained and crushed
4 cups defatted Chicken Broth (page 127)
Salt and freshly ground black pepper, to taste
10 ounces frozen green peas, thawed
½ cup coarsely chopped flat-leaf parsley

1. Heat the oil in a large heavy pot over low heat. Add the onion and cook, stirring, until wilted, about 10 minutes. Add the garlic and cook, stirring, for 2 minutes. Then add the chorizos and cook for another 10 minutes.

2. Add the rice and stir to coat and combine; cook for 3 minutes, stirring constantly.

3. Stir in the tomatoes and add the chicken broth. Season with salt and pepper. Bring to a boil, stir, and reduce the heat to medium low. Simmer covered until most of the liquid is absorbed, about 20 minutes.

4. When the rice is cooked, stir in the peas and parsley. Let sit 5 to 6 minutes to heat the peas, then serve hot.

Serves 8 to 10

VEGETABLE SPARKLED RICE

This delicately perfumed, vegetable-dappled rice is simple yet versatile enough to receive any topping of seafood or poultry. Tiny flecks of carrot, fresh ginger, cloves, and a hint of cinnamon infuse basmati, the long-grain Indian rice grown in the lower Himalayas. The taste is enriched by slow cooking in a flavorful vegetable broth.

1½ cups basmati rice
2 tablespoons unsalted butter
2 tablespoons vegetable oil
2 medium onions, cut into ¼-inch dice
2 tablespoons minced garlic
2 tablespoons minced peeled fresh ginger
2 medium carrots, peeled and cut into ¼-inch dice
1 cinnamon stick (1 inch long)
3 whole cloves
4 cups Fresh Vegetable Broth (page 129)
½ cup golden raisins

1. Rinse the rice in a strainer under cold water.

2. Heat the butter and oil in a large heavy pot over low heat. Add the onions, garlic, ginger, carrots, cinnamon stick, and cloves. Cook, stirring, over medium-low heat until the vegetables are slightly softened, 10 to 12 minutes.

3. Add the rice and cook, stirring, for about 2 minutes.

4. Add the broth and bring to a boil. Reduce the heat to medium and simmer covered until the rice is cooked and the liquid has been absorbed, about 20 minutes. Stir in the raisins, cover, and let stand off the heat for 5 minutes. Fluff the rice with a fork and serve hot.

Serves 6 to 8

SPINACH RISOTTO

Northern Italy is responsible for giving us this wonderful method of preparing rice. As risotto became the rage in the 80s, we all tried more and more inventive combinations, but I always return to the rather simple, classic preparations such as this dish. I prefer my risotto creamy and moist, so I only cook it briefly after the last addition of broth.

½ cup diced (¼ inch) pancetta
4 tablespoons olive oil
8 ounces fresh crimini, shiitake, or white mushrooms, stems trimmed, caps wiped clean with a damp paper towel, sliced
½ cup minced onion
5 cups defatted Chicken Broth (page 127)
1½ cups Arborio rice
½ cup dry white wine
1 bunch tender young spinach (about 8 ounces), tough stems removed, leaves rinsed and chopped (about 2 cups)
1 tablespoon unsalted butter
1 tablespoon freshly grated Parmesan cheese, plus more for serving
Salt and freshly ground black pepper, to taste

1. Cook the pancetta in a large nonstick skillet over medium-low heat until it is lightly browned and the fat is rendered, about 10 minutes. Remove the pancetta to a bowl with a slotted spoon and set aside.

2. Add 2 tablespoons olive oil to the fat in the skillet. Increase the heat to medium-high, add the mushrooms, and sauté until softened, 4 to 5 minutes. Add the mushrooms to the pancetta. Set aside.

3. Heat the remaining 2 tablespoons olive oil in a large heavy pot over medium-low heat. Add the onion and cook, stirring occasionally, until wilted, about 10 minutes.

4. While the onion is cooking, bring the chicken broth to a boil in a medium-size pan. Reduce the heat to a gentle simmer.

5. Add the rice to the onion and stir well with a wooden spoon for 1 minute so that all the grains are evenly coated with oil. Add the wine and cook, stirring, until it has been absorbed by the rice, 3 to 4 minutes. Add the chopped spinach and stir well.

6. Add the hot broth to the rice mixture, 1 ladle at a time (about ½ cup), and cook, stirring frequently, over medium heat until each addition of broth is absorbed into the rice before adding the next.

7. When the rice is tender and nearly all the broth has been absorbed, stir in the reserved pancetta and mushrooms.

8. When all the broth has been absorbed, add the butter and cheese and mix well. Season with salt and pepper. Serve immediately, passing a bowl of freshly grated Parmesan to sprinkle over the top.

Serves 4 to 6

SUMMER TOMATO RISOTTO

It is the amazing sweetness of summer's tomatoes at their peak that imbue this risotto with incredible taste, so I make sure to prepare it as often as possible in July and August. As the rice finishes cooking, add chopped fresh mint leaves for a surprising finish.

2 tablespoons olive oil
1 cup coarsely chopped onion
2 tablespoons minced garlic
4 large beefsteak tomatoes (about 2 pounds), peeled and coarsely chopped
1 tablespoon honey
1¼ cups Arborio rice
6 cups defatted Chicken Broth (page 127)
Salt and coarsely ground black pepper, to taste
¼ cup chopped fresh mint leaves

1. Heat the oil in a heavy pot over low heat. Add the onion and cook to wilt slightly, 5 minutes, stirring occasionally. Add the garlic and cook 4 minutes longer.

2. Add the tomatoes and honey, increase the heat to medium, and cook, stirring occasionally, until most of the liquid has evaporated and the mixture has thickened, 20 minutes.

3. When the tomatoes are nearly done cooking, bring the chicken broth to a boil in a medium-size pan. Reduce the heat to a gentle simmer.

4. Add the rice and stir well, making sure that all the grains are evenly coated with the tomato mixture.

5. Add ½ cup of the hot broth and cook, stirring frequently, until it has been absorbed into the rice, 3 to 4 minutes. Continue to cook, stir, and add broth ½ cup at a time until all has been absorbed.

6. Remove the risotto from the heat and add salt and pepper to taste. Stir in the mint and serve.

Serves 4

Barbara,

How can I ever go back to NY when I can buy tomatoes and peaches like these in the morning market in Lerici?

Ciao!
Sheila

LALLI'S TURKISH PILAF TOMATOES

A recent visit to Turkey and a sampling of the pilafs prepared there, gave me a far greater appreciation for these complex grain dishes. For my pilaf tomatoes, I've taken "cook's" license, incorporating what I learned into a recipe left for me years ago by a Turkish friend. A fragrant mixture of rice, dried cherries, and apricots makes a splendid filling for large tomatoes. These are delicious on their own or served with roast leg of lamb or grilled fish kebabs. I hope they do Lalli proud.

6 ripe large tomatoes (about 12 ounces each)
Coarse salt, to taste
⅓ cup dried cherries
⅓ cup golden raisins
⅓ cup dried apricots, cut into ¼-inch dice
1 cup boiling water
2 tablespoons olive oil
1 small onion, cut into ¼-inch dice
½ cup chopped walnuts
½ cup chopped blanched almonds
3 cups cooked brown or white rice (about ¾ cup raw)
2 tablespoons apricot preserves
2 tablespoons fresh orange juice
2 tablespoons honey
½ teaspoon ground cinnamon, plus more for sprinkling
½ teaspoon ground allspice
½ cup chopped fresh mint leaves
6 fresh mint sprigs, for garnish

1. Cut the tops off the tomatoes, and using a teaspoon, scoop out the pulp, leaving a ½-inch-thick wall. Core the pulp and discard as many seeds as possible. Coarsely chop enough pulp to measure ½ cup. Set aside.

2. Sprinkle the tomato cavities lightly with coarse salt and place cut side down on paper towels to drain for 30 minutes.

3. Place the dried fruits in a bowl, cover with the boiling water, and let soak for 30 minutes. Drain well.

4. Preheat the oven to 350°F.

5. Heat the oil in a large heavy saucepan over medium-low heat. Add the onion and cook, stirring, until wilted, 5 to 7 minutes. Add the nuts and cook, stirring, another 5 minutes. Remove from the heat.

6. Add the ½ cup tomato pulp, drained fruit, cooked rice, preserves, orange juice, honey, spices, chopped mint, and coarse salt to taste to the nut mixture and stir well with a fork.

7. Lightly oil the bottom of a shallow baking dish large enough to hold the tomatoes.

8. Spoon a generous ½ cup of the rice mixture into each tomato shell. Place in the prepared baking dish. Sprinkle the tops lightly with cinnamon. Bake until the tomatoes are just tender and heated through, about 20 minutes. Serve hot or at room temperature, garnished with mint sprigs.

Serves 6

A TASTE OF THE WORLD

Turkish Palette

Photo: Inspiration for a Pastrami Reuben.

...And

CINNAMON	CAPERS
CLOVES	OLIVES
NUTMEG	BELL PEPPERS
SAFFRON	EGGPLANTS
TURMERIC	WHITE BEANS
CUMIN	CUCUMBERS
ANISE	QUINCES
CAYENNE PEPPER	PUMPKINS
	POMEGRANATES
DILL	ALMONDS
BASIL	PISTACHIOS
MINT	WALNUTS
ROSEMARY	HONEY
THYME	PHYLLO PASTRY
SAGE	PASTRAMI
GARLIC	FETA CHEESE
SHALLOTS	YOGURT

ORIENTAL PILAF

I always like to cook rice or other grains in chicken or vegetable broth for added flavor. In this Middle Eastern-inspired pilaf, I've added chicken wings to the broth to enrich the dish even further. Before adding liquid, it's best to cook the rice for a minute or two in oil or butter to keep the grains from sticking together. Oriental pilaf is an ideal accompaniment to any simple roast poultry, lamb, or pork dish.

3 cups defatted Chicken Broth (page 127)
6 chicken wings, rinsed
1 tablespoon olive oil
1 tablespoon unsalted butter
½ cup diced (¼ inch) onion
⅓ cup pine nuts
¼ teaspoon crumbled saffron threads
1 cup long-grain rice
⅓ cup currants
1 cinnamon stick (3 inches long)
Salt, to taste

1. Place the chicken broth in a pan and bring to a boil. Add the chicken wings, reduce the heat, and simmer uncovered 15 minutes. Strain the broth and reserve the wings for another use (or remove the skin and nibble on them as you finish the pilaf).

2. In a large heavy pot, heat the oil and butter over low heat. Add the onion, pine nuts, and saffron. Cook, stirring constantly, until the nuts begin to brown, 6 to 8 minutes.

3. Add the rice and stir well to coat the grains with oil. Cook 1 minute, stirring constantly. Add the chicken broth, currants, and cinnamon stick. Bring to a boil, then reduce the heat and cover the pot. Simmer until the rice is tender, about 20 minutes. Remove the cinnamon stick, season with salt, and serve hot.

Serves 6

BYZANTINE PILAF

Replete with the precious spices of the Orient (saffron, allspice, cardamom, and cumin) and studded with ruby dried cherries and bright orange diced carrots, this fragrant rice brings to the present the feeling of ancient luxury. Bring it to the table steaming hot to accompany Lamb and Prune Tagine, Honey and Ginger-Glazed Chicken, or Chinese Squabs (see Index).

¾ teaspoon ground allspice
½ teaspoon ground cumin
½ teaspoon ground cardamom
¼ teaspoon crumbled saffron threads
¼ teaspoon salt
1 tablespoon unsalted butter
1 tablespoon olive oil
1 cup coarsely chopped onion
2 tablespoons minced garlic
4 medium carrots, peeled and cut into ¼-inch dice
1½ cups long-grain rice
3½ cups defatted Chicken Broth (page 127)
¾ cup dried cherries

1. Mix the allspice, cumin, cardamom, saffron, and salt together in a small bowl. Set aside.

2. Heat the butter and oil in a large heavy pot over low heat. Add the onion and cook, stirring occasionally, until slightly wilted, about 5 minutes. Add the garlic and carrots and cook for 5 minutes longer.

3. Add the spice mixture and cook for 1 minute, stirring constantly, to mellow the flavors.

4. Add the rice and cook for 1 minute, stirring constantly, to combine all ingredients well. Stir in the chicken broth and cherries. Increase the heat to medium-high and bring the rice to a boil. Reduce the heat, cover the pot, and cook until the liquid is absorbed and the rice is tender, about 15 minutes. Serve hot.

Serves 6

SOUVENIR TO SAVOR

Rijsttafel—A Gift From the Spice Islands

Indonesia, once known as the Dutch East Indies, is made up of thousands of tropical islands strung out between Asia and Australia. Although they boast of the famed *rijsttafel,* rice table, as their "national" meal, ironically the name is Dutch. Sometime during the 17th century, when the wealthy Dutch merchants first began occupying Indonesia and controlling the sea trade between the islands and Holland, they adopted the Indonesian concept of serving rice surrounded by a variety of small dishes. Holland is still considered by many, myself included, the best place to enjoy an Indonesian *rijsttafel.*

A cold beer heralds the feast and remains the beverage of choice throughout the meal. Bowls of *krupuk,* pastel-colored fish chips, are always on the table. Next, an appetizer of *pangsit goreng,* or fried wontons filled with a mixture of chicken, leeks, and garlic appears, accompanied by three dipping sauces: a sweet tomato sauce, a chili sauce, and a clear ginger sauce.

Then the banquet begins in earnest—a big deep bowl of white rice is brought to the table and surrounded by many smaller dishes of satays, meats, chicken, fish, eggs, vegetables, and pickles and chilies. Variety is important—a combination and balance of textures (crunchy, crispy, creamy, chewy), colors (black, red, gold, green), flavors (pungent, aromatic, sweet, sour, piquant), temperatures (hot, warm, room temperature) and spices (hot, bitter, sweet) are all essential. Each person is given a shallow soup bowl flanked only by a large soup spoon and a fork. Knives are rarely used.

Each diner places a generous serving of rice in the center of his or her plate and spoons the smaller dishes around the rice. One eats a bit of rice with every bite as it is meant to help temper the spicier dishes. Mixing dishes, however, is not considered good *rijsttafel* etiquette as this spoils the subtle tastes and perfect balance.

THAI FRIED RICE AND EGG

The fried rices of Thailand do not seem as oily as those from our favorite Chinese restaurants. Instead they are a bit smokier and more dense in flavor. I've used brown rice and a smoky bacon to create this effect. The rice is spiced with ginger and garlic and refreshed with cucumbers and crispy bean sprouts. Serve in large shallow bowls with a fried egg atop for a rich and satisfying luncheon or supper dish.

2¾ cups defatted Chicken Broth (page 127)
4 cloves garlic, lightly bruised (page 153) and peeled
1 cup long-grain brown rice
4 ounces thinly sliced bacon, coarsely shredded
1 pound large shrimp, peeled, deveined, and halved crosswise
2 tablespoons vegetable oil
⅔ cup coarsely chopped shallots (about 3 large)
2 tablespoons minced peeled fresh ginger
2 tablespoons minced garlic
1 cup peeled, seeded, and diced (¼ inch) cucumber
8 ounces fresh bean sprouts
4 tablespoons snipped fresh chives
4 tablespoons (½ stick) unsalted butter
6 large eggs
6 whole chives, for garnish

1. Place 2½ cups of the chicken broth in a medium-size saucepan. Add the garlic cloves and bring to a boil. Stir in the rice, reduce the heat, and simmer, tightly covered, until all the liquid is absorbed, about 50 minutes. Remove the garlic and discard. Place the rice in a bowl and fluff it with a fork.

2. Cook the bacon in a large nonstick skillet until just crispy, 5 to 7 minutes. Remove to a paper towel to drain and set aside.

3. Add the shrimp to the fat in the skillet and cook over medium-high heat until just cooked through, 1½ to 2 minutes. Remove with a slotted spoon and set aside.

4. Heat the oil in a large heavy saucepan over medium-low heat. Add the shallots, ginger, and minced garlic; cook, to wilt slightly, 2 minutes, stirring constantly. Add the reserved rice, remaining ¼ cup broth, the bacon, and cucumber. Cook, stirring to combine, 1 minute longer.

5. Stir in the shrimp, bean sprouts, and 3 tablespoons of the chives. Cook 30 seconds longer. Divide the rice evenly between 6 shallow soup or pasta bowls. Cover with aluminum foil to keep warm.

6. Melt 2 tablespoons butter in each of 2 large skillets. Fry 3 eggs in each skillet (sunny side up). Place 1 fried egg atop each bowl of rice. Sprinkle with the remaining tablespoon snipped chives and lay a whole chive across each. Serve immediately.

Serves 6

SCOTTISH FRIED RICE

The great Scottish rice and smoked haddock dish known as kedgeree is given a delicious traditional Chinese fried rice twist here. I have taken liberties with this Scottish tradition and scrambled the eggs rather than using chopped hard-cooked eggs. Piquant curry powder and a pinch of cayenne are mellowed by brief cooking before being tossed with the rice. I've used flaky moist, smoked whitefish or chub, which is readily available and a Sunday morning favorite around my house. A sprinkling of fresh chives livens all the flavors, making this a perfect brunch or late supper dish.

8 ounces smoked whitefish or chub
1 tablespoon unsalted butter
1 tablespoon vegetable oil
1 medium onion, cut into ¼-inch dice
4 cloves garlic, minced
1 tablespoon best-quality curry powder
Pinch of cayenne pepper
3 cups cooked rice
2 tablespoons chopped flat-leaf parsley
3 large eggs, lightly beaten
1½ tablespoons snipped fresh chives, for garnish

1. Remove the head, skin, and bones from the fish. Flake the flesh into large pieces and set aside.

2. Heat the butter and oil in a large nonstick skillet over medium-low heat. Add the onion and garlic and cook to wilt, 8 to 10 minutes, stirring occasionally. Add the curry and cayenne and cook, stirring to mellow the flavors, 1 minute longer.

3. Add the rice and parsley and combine well with a fork, fluffing the rice.

4. Make a well in the center of the rice, pushing it towards the sides of the skillet, and pour in the eggs. Cook the eggs for 1 to 2 minutes, stirring them with a fork until they scramble. Once they are scrambled, gently fold the eggs into the rice.

5. Remove the rice from the heat and gently fold in the flaked fish. Serve immediately, garnished with the chives.

Serves 6

POLENTA WITH CRIMINI MUSHROOM SAUCE

Whenever I head up to my house in Connecticut, I try to get to Doc's Restaurant in New Preston where I feast on Chef Riad's great polenta and mushrooms, the inspiration for this dish. I've molded the polenta in small ramekins and cut the rounds horizontally in half before frying, for a most attractive presentation. The hot crimini mushrooms in a rich sauce, spooned atop the polenta, make a beautiful starter.

Classic or Quick Polenta (recipes follow)
¼ cup plus 3 tablespoons olive oil, or more if needed
2 tablespoons unsalted butter
2 pounds crimini or other wild mushrooms, stems trimmed, caps wiped clean with a damp paper towel, sliced
¼ cup thinly sliced shallots
4 fresh thyme sprigs
1 cup dry white wine
1 cup defatted Chicken Broth or Fresh Vegetable Broth (page 127 or 129)
Salt and coarsely ground black pepper, to taste
2 tablespoons chopped flat-leaf parsley

1. Fill eight 4-ounce ramekins with the polenta while it is hot. Smooth the tops. Let rest at room temperature until set, about 1 hour, or refrigerate covered with plastic wrap until ready to use.

2. Meanwhile heat ¼ cup olive oil and 1 tablespoon of the butter in a large heavy pot over medium-high heat. Add the mushrooms and sauté, stirring and shaking the pan, until cooked through, about 5 minutes. Add the shallots and thyme and cook, stirring, for 2 minutes longer. Add the wine and the broth. Simmer uncovered over medium-high heat until the liquid is reduced by about half, 18 to 20 minutes. Add the remaining 1 tablespoon butter and simmer 2 minutes longer, shaking the pot and stirring. Remove the thyme sprigs and discard. Season with salt and pepper. Set aside.

3. Carefully unmold the polentas. Cut each one horizontally in half.

4. Heat the remaining 3 tablespoons olive oil in a nonstick skillet over medium-high heat. Fry the polenta rounds in batches until golden and crisp, 8 to 10 minutes per side, adding more oil if necessary.

5. Arrange 2 rounds of polenta on the center of each of 8 small plates.

6. Heat the mushroom sauce through and spoon equally over the polenta. Garnish with the parsley and serve immediately.

Serves 8

CLASSIC POLENTA

Italians give polenta the same nostalgia status that Americans reserve for mashed potatoes. We think of our mothers and grandmothers tending these cozy, comfortable dishes that warmed our spirits and keep us fondly remembering "the old days" long into our adulthood. Classic polenta requires 30 to 40 minutes of constant stirring, but sadly we don't always have this much time or energy. If you do and are a purist, here is the traditional way to make polenta. There are perfectly acceptable quick-cooking polentas widely available today, and I often use them for many of my recipes.

6½ cups water
2 teaspoons salt
1½ cups imported polenta or coarse yellow cornmeal
2 tablespoons unsalted butter

Bring the water to a boil in a large heavy pot and add the salt. With the water boiling rapidly, add the polenta in a slow, steady stream while stirring constantly. Reduce the heat to medium and cook, stirring constantly, until the polenta is thick and soft, 30 to 40 minutes. Stir in the butter. Serve immediately or let it set in a mold or molds for later use.

Serves 6 to 8

QUICK-COOKING POLENTA

There are still plenty of cooks who would never consider using anything but classic polenta. But for many of us, spending 30 minutes preparing the real thing is impossible. Now there are boxes of quick-cooking polenta widely available in most grocery stores. Although I'm not sure if this version is sold in stores throughout Italy, I find it an acceptable alternative for many recipes, especially when it is cooled, fried, and covered with a luscious sauce. The brand I

MY KITCHEN DIARY

Square Cut or Pear-Shaped—A Real Gem

Polenta—the classic cornmeal dish of northern Italy—is wonderful eaten soft and warm right out of the pot with a pat of added butter and a sprinkling of cheese, or cooled, cut into shapes, and fried until golden. More and more in the U.S., this fried version is showing up in restaurants, replacing small squares of toast as a perch for vegetables and small game birds.

Once the polenta is cooked, it is transferred to a baking dish or other mold. The top is smoothed off and the polenta is allowed to set. Then it is cut into shapes appropriate to the dish being served. Circles are both decorative and effective for appetizer portions, while small fried squares are lovely for a hot first course with, for instance, a duxelles of freshly sautéed wild mushrooms delicately spooned into the center. Two triangles, cut diagonally from a larger square of polenta, look perfect angled together in the center of a dinner plate to hold small game birds. And, there are those of us who always make sure there's enough leftover polenta to fry up in big squares in the morning. Blanketed in Vermont maple syrup, it makes the perfect breakfast.

have found in most supermarkets is Fattorie & Pandea Instant Polenta. The box describes it as pre-cooked maize meal.

6 cups water
2 teaspoons salt
1 package (13 ounces) imported quick-cooking polenta
2 tablespoons unsalted butter

Bring the water to a rapid boil in a large heavy pot. Add the salt and then the polenta in a slow, steady stream, stirring constantly. Cook, stirring with a wooden spoon, over medium heat until the polenta is thick and cleans the side of the pan, about 5 minutes. Vigorously stir in the butter. Serve immediately or let it set in a mold or molds for later use.

Serves 8

A TASTE OF THE WORLD

Moroccan Palette

...*And*

CINNAMON	*ONIONS*
CUMIN	*DATES*
CLOVES	*RAISINS*
TURMERIC	*PRUNES*
CORIANDER	*LEMONS*
MINT	*ORANGES*
PARSLEY	*PINE NUTS*
GARLIC	*OLIVE OIL*
CAPERS	*HONEY*
SQUASHES	*CHICKPEAS*
YAMS	*HARD-COOKED EGGS*
TURNIPS	*PHYLLO PASTRY*
TOMATOES	
CARROTS	

Photo: Charming your way into the Medina in Marrakech.

SOUVENIR TO SAVOR

Ras el Hanout

Before I left for Marrakech, I telephoned Paula Wolfert, the most knowledgeable person I knew on the subject, for information on where to go and what to see and eat. She suggested that I head directly for the spice market, and she was absolutely right. However, this turned out to be a bit of a trip. With a guide—a must in this maze-like souk (market)—Richard and I entered the medina and began weaving our way, passing through the wool-dying area, the leather-tanning area, and all manner of stalls selling copper, brass, antiques, and gold. Our senses began to tingle as we neared the pungent spices. It's hard to believe that in America we buy these riches sealed up in little glass jars. Our guide introduced us to a friend of his who presented me with various spices in brass measuring cups as I sat on a leather hassock in the middle of his spice shop. I was ready to smell, listen, and buy. I bought a bag of dried pink and purple roses, bags of saffron threads, and bags of glorious mixtures that he had prepared. First, there was a four-spice mixture that he told me to use when cooking fish. It was made up of ground nutmeg, ginger, coriander, and cardamom. It smelled sweet yet a bit savory.

But the best was still to come. The spice merchant began to tell me about the very "famous" Moroccan thirty-five-spice mixture, *ras el hanout* or "the house blend," mixed to the taste of the shopkeeper. It is traditionally used in cooking tagines primarily made of lamb, poultry, and game. He recited the spices, and I sat on my hassock and took copious notes. His *ras el hanout* contained paprika, chilies, ginger, coriander, cumin, nutmeg, and juniper, but I'm sure he held back on the "real" secret ingredients. I bought a large plastic bag full. Looking around some more, I saw that there were marvelous straw baskets filled with lavender, *harissa,* rosemary, and thyme, which made me think of herbes de Provence. I was a bit sad to leave the "spice school," but knew there was a marvelous lunch awaiting within the next hour, so I gathered up my plastic bags filled with riches and continued on my way.

SEVEN VEGETABLE COUSCOUS

This vegetable combination is one of my favorites to serve over delicate couscous. I've come across similar recipes in many books, and although the seven vegetables vary somewhat, traditionally they include pumpkin. When I was developing my version, pumpkins were nowhere to be found—so, no pumpkin shows up here. For my seven vegetables I gathered leeks, onions, carrots, zucchini, tomatoes, potatoes, and turnips. But as important as the vegetables is a great flavored broth to cook them in.

Defatted chicken broth or vegetable broth are ideal. The vegetables are cooked until tender but not overdone. When serving, a ladle or two of broth moistens the vegetables and grains beautifully. Prunes and golden raisins add a lushness to this dish and chickpeas introduce an interesting texture.

6 medium leeks (4 inches green left on)
1 tablespoon white vinegar
3 quarts defatted Chicken Broth or Fresh Vegetable Broth (page 127 or 129)
4 tablespoons olive oil
6 large fresh cilantro sprigs, rinsed, roots and stems crushed
8 cloves garlic, lightly bruised (page 153) and peeled
3 cinnamon sticks (each 3 inches long)
2 teaspoons ground cumin
2 teaspoons best-quality curry powder
¼ teaspoon crumbled saffron threads
1 teaspoon coarse salt
2 medium zucchini, ends trimmed
6 medium carrots, peeled, halved lengthwise, and cut into 2-inch lengths
3 Idaho potatoes, peeled and cut into quarters
8 ounces small white turnips, peeled and quartered
3 small yellow onions, peeled and halved
3 ripe large tomatoes, cored and quartered
1 can (16 ounces) chickpeas, drained and rinsed
1 cup pitted prunes, halved
½ cup golden raisins
4 tablespoons chopped cilantro leaves
8 cups cooked couscous (2⅔ cups dried), hot

1. Trim the roots from the leeks. Cut a 3-inch deep X through the white bulb and into the green of each leek. Place the leeks in a bowl and cover with water. Add the vinegar and let soak for 30 minutes to remove any sand. Drain and rinse under cold running water. Set aside.

2. While the leeks are soaking, prepare the seasoned broth: Combine the broth, oil, cilantro sprigs, garlic, cinnamon sticks, cumin, curry powder, saffron, and salt in a very large heavy pot. Bring to a boil, reduce the heat, and simmer uncovered for 30 minutes.

3. Using a potato peeler, peel the zucchini lengthwise at intervals to make 3 or 4 stripes in the skin. Cut the zucchini into 1½-inch lengths. Set aside.

4. Place the leeks, carrots, potatoes, turnips, and onions in the broth. Bring to a boil, reduce the heat, and simmer uncovered for 30 minutes.

5. Add the zucchini, tomatoes, chickpeas, prunes, and raisins. Stir gently so that the vegetables don't break up. Simmer 30 minutes longer.

6. Just before serving, gently heat the vegetables and broth through. Stir in 3 tablespoons of the cilantro.

7. Spoon the couscous into shallow bowls and top with the vegetables and broth. Garnish with the remaining tablespoon of cilantro. Serve hot. You'll love it.

Serves 6 to 8

THE WINES OF

Chile

Chile occupies a unique position in the Latin American wine industry—it is the only Latin country so far whose wines have gained serious international recognition, in the United States as well as Europe. Chile's Cabernet Sauvignons, Sauvignon Blancs, and, more recently, Merlots have gone head to head against some of Europe's best wines and held their own, even coming away with medals.

The potential for quality wine in Chile was recognized in the mid-18th century, but the first vines were planted much earlier. The grape arrived with the early Spanish padres who set up missions in the mid-16th century. They planted the same variety that came to be known as the Mission grape in California. Chile got its first significant boost toward quality in 1851, when several growers and winemakers introduced Bordeaux techniques in the vineyard and cellar and Bordeaux grape varieties—Cabernet Sauvignon, Merlot, Sauvignon Blanc, and others—to the inland winegrowing valleys. Fortunately, they arrived prior to

Left to right: Thousands of bottles of wine ready for drinking–you choose. The Osorno volcano rises high above Lake Llanquihue. Concha y Toro and Santa Rita are two of Chile's top producers.

Europe's tragic bout with *Phylloxera,* the root-eating bug that destroyed virtually all European vineyards later in the century. The little bug never made it across the Andes.

The next major impact on quality emerged in the 1980s, when the political climate that had long held Chile aloof from the rest of the world finally relaxed. Chilean wines were soon being discovered by the world's wine community, now considerably larger and more global in scope than ever before. As Chile's economy improved, well-established producers began exporting more of their wines. New investors from France, Spain, and the U.S. provided capital to upgrade technology.

The Bordeaux influence has continued and ripened. Chile produces excellent Cabernet, firm in its structure and flavor without being overly tannic or hard, drinkable sooner than many other Cabernets. The better producers now select their best lots for bottling as Reserves. Chile's Reserve Cabernets, more concentrated in fruit, represent some of the best values on the market, many ranging in price from $9 to $12 a bottle. They are excellent with lamb or beef, as are the somewhat lighter, elegant Merlots that are increasingly made and in greater demand by wine consumers.

Chile's white wines are very food-friendly, dry, and medium-bodied, lighter than their California counterparts, and less oaky. Sauvignon Blanc, for instance, is stylish and very dry, and had rather herbaceous flavors until recently. The latest styles of

"Chile produces excellent Cabernet, firm in its structure and flavor without being overly tannic or hard."

Top to bottom: Los Vascos represents Chile's new winemakers while Cousino Macul has distinguished itself for a long time. When bottling, attention is given to every detail.

Sauvignon have softened, though they are still crisp and slightly austere. Riesling has long been produced in Chile, and while traditionally it is dry, occasionally it is a little sweet for the American market.

> "Chile's Cabernet Sauvignons, Sauvignon Blancs, and Merlots have gone head to head against some of Europe's best wines."

Chardonnay is a relatively recent direction for Chilean winegrowers, but some of the wines are very attractive, with bright fruit flavors and little or no oak emphasis. A few Reserve Chardonnays are barrel-fermented and aged briefly in new oak, giving them a spicy vanilla accent. These wines will show more finesse in time; at the moment Sauvignon Blancs are the better value. Some Sémillon is grown as well, occasionally blended with Sauvignon Blanc.

Taking a cue from California, more producers are blending the Bordeaux red varieties to produce some very interesting, distinctively flavorful reds. Among the top producers are older firms like Cousino Macul, Concha y Toro, Undurraga, Santa Carolina, and Santa Rita. Among new firms that have achieved recognition for quality are Errazuriz, Los Vascos, Miguel Torres, Sergio Traverso, Caliterra, and Canepa.

CHILEAN QUINOA TABOULEH

Quinoa (KEEN-wah) is a delicate pearly grain that is delicious served either hot or cold in salads. Originating high in the Andes of South America, quinoa was an important part of the Incan diet. Readily available in supermarkets today, it makes a perfect base for a Chilean-inspired classic Middle Eastern dish. Avocados combine with tomatoes, corn, cucumbers, and fresh cilantro in this tabouleh. When you're working with quinoa, don't mix it vigorously; instead fold all the ingredients gently together with a rubber spatula or a fork so that it stays fluffy.

2 cups quinoa
4 cups water
¼ teaspoon salt
¼ teaspoon freshly ground black pepper
5 tablespoons fresh lemon juice
⅓ cup extra virgin olive oil
½ cup coarsely chopped fresh cilantro leaves
2 teaspoons minced garlic
1 ripe avocado, preferably Haas, pitted, peeled, and cut into ½-inch dice
1 cup fresh corn kernels, cooked
⅓ cup finely chopped red onion
4 plum tomatoes, cut into ½-inch dice
1 cup diced (½ inch) cucumbers

1. Rinse the quinoa well in a strainer under cold running water. Place the quinoa in a medium-size pan, add the water, and bring to a boil. Reduce the heat to medium-low and simmer covered until the liquid is absorbed, 10 to 12 minutes. The quinoa should be translucent. Remove from the heat and fluff it with a fork. Transfer the quinoa to a large bowl and cool to room temperature.

2. Sprinkle the grains with the salt and pepper and stir, folding from underneath the grains. Fold in 4 tablespoons of the lemon juice and the oil. Gently fold in the cilantro and garlic.

3. Toss the avocado with the remaining tablespoon of lemon juice to prevent discoloration.

4. Fold the corn, onion, tomatoes, cucumbers, and avocado into the quinoa. Adjust the seasonings to taste. Serve at room temperature within 2 hours of preparation.

Serves 8 to 10

GRANNY'S MUSHROOM KASHA

It took a bowl of kasha in Russia to awaken my childhood memories of Granny Reesman cooking pots of it when I was a child. Born in Ukraine, she grew up in Kiev, and when she moved to America, all her wonderful dishes came with her.

Admittedly, kasha can be an acquired taste. On my trip, I visited the town of Novgorod and had lunch at an historical restaurant, which still prepares all their dishes in the classic manner. After we enjoyed a few pieces of thinly sliced sturgeon with black bread, out came a steaming ceramic pot of borscht from a wood-burning oven and a bowl of kasha alongside. Although kasha can be quite simple fare, I've added sautéed mushrooms and onions with a bit of garlic and olive oil to give the buckwheat a "bite." It goes well with the Russian Cod Ragout (see Index).

8 ounces white mushrooms
2 tablespoons unsalted butter
2 tablespoons olive oil
1 large onion, cut into ¼-inch dice
1 teaspoon chopped garlic
1 cup kasha (roasted buckwheat groats)
½ teaspoon coarse salt
¼ teaspoon coarsely ground black pepper
2 cups defatted Chicken Broth (page 127), boiling

1. Trim the stems of the mushrooms and wipe the caps with a damp paper towel. Cut into quarters.

2. Melt the butter in a large nonstick skillet over medium-high heat. Add the mushrooms, and sauté until slightly browned, 5 minutes, shaking the pan constantly. Set aside.

3. Heat the oil in a large heavy saucepan. Add the onion and cook over medium-low heat until slightly wilted, about 5 minutes. Add the garlic and cook until the onion just begins to brown, about 5 minutes longer.

4. Stir the kasha into the onion mixture and cook, stirring constantly, over very low heat for 2 minutes. Add the mushrooms, salt, pepper, and boiling broth. Stir, cover, and cook over very low heat until all the liquid is absorbed, 12 to 15 minutes.

5. Remove the kasha from the heat and fluff it with a fork. Adjust the seasonings and let rest, partially covered, for about 10 minutes. Fluff with the fork again to separate the grains. Serve immediately.

Serves 6

MOROS Y CRISTIANOS

Black Beans and Rice

My first meal in Cuba was a great lunch at La Bodeguita del Medio in old Havana. One of my favorite dishes was *moros y cristianos, mano a mano*—Moors and Christians, hand to hand. The name of this classic Cuban recipe of black beans and white rice refers to the invasion of Spain by Moors in the 8th century. The Spanish were ultimately victorious. I have adapted the Cuban version adding only a little rice when the cooking is completed instead of using half beans and rice. I think it is better this way. Chorizos, a ham hock, and ripe tomatoes infuse the beans with their distinctive flavors.

1 pound dried black beans
8 cups water
2 tablespoons olive oil
8 ounces slab bacon, rind discarded, cut into ¼-inch cubes
1 large onion, chopped
1 tablespoon minced garlic
1 ripe large tomato, coarsely chopped
1 teaspoon ground cumin
Pinch of cayenne pepper
2 bay leaves
8 cups defatted Chicken Broth (page 127)
4 ounces chorizo sausages, cut into ½-inch slices
1 smoked ham hock (about 12 ounces)
1 tablespoon (packed) dark brown sugar
2 cups cooked white rice (about ½ cup raw)
1 tablespoon fresh lime juice

1. Pick through the beans, discarding any stones and rinse. Place the beans in a bowl, cover with the water, and soak overnight. Drain and rinse the beans.

2. Heat the oil in a large heavy pot over medium-low heat. Add the bacon and cook until the fat is rendered, 3 to 4 minutes. Add the onion, garlic, and tomato. Cook another 10 minutes to wilt the vegetables. Add the cumin, cayenne, and bay leaves; stir to combine.

3. Add the beans, broth, chorizos, ham hock, and brown sugar. Bring to a boil, reduce the heat, and simmer, partially covered, for 2 hours, stirring occasionally.

4. Remove the ham hock and let stand until cool enough to handle. Shred any meat from the bone and return the meat to the beans.

5. Before serving, heat the beans through and stir in the cooked rice and lime juice. Serve in shallow bowls. As this dish sets, it tends to thicken so that you may have to add a bit more chicken broth before serving. Store covered in the refrigerator for up to 2 days.

Serves 8

CALYPSO BEANS AND RICE

Flavors essential to Caribbean dishes, such as allspice and hot sauce, and to Mediterranean dishes, such as olives, capers, peppers, and cilantro, come together in these party beans and rice. With grains having become major factors in our diets, it's fun to experiment with the varieties available. Pearl barley makes a wonderful substitute for rice in this preparation. This makes a great companion to Sunshine Salad (see Index) and cold beer.

8 ounces slab bacon, rind discarded, cut into ¼-inch cubes
2 yellow bell peppers, stemmed, seeded, and cut into ½-inch pieces
1 medium onion, cut into ¼-inch pieces
8 cloves garlic, finely chopped
1 cup long-grain rice
4 cups cooked dark red kidney beans
2 cups Rich Beef Broth (page 128)
1½ cups pimiento-stuffed Spanish Manzanilla olives
3 ripe medium tomatoes, seeded and cut into ½-inch pieces
¼ cup drained capers
1 tablespoon dried basil
1 tablespoon dried oregano
1½ teaspoons ground allspice
¼ teaspoon hot sauce, such as Tabasco
Salt and freshly ground black pepper, to taste
½ cup thinly sliced scallions
¼ cup chopped fresh cilantro leaves

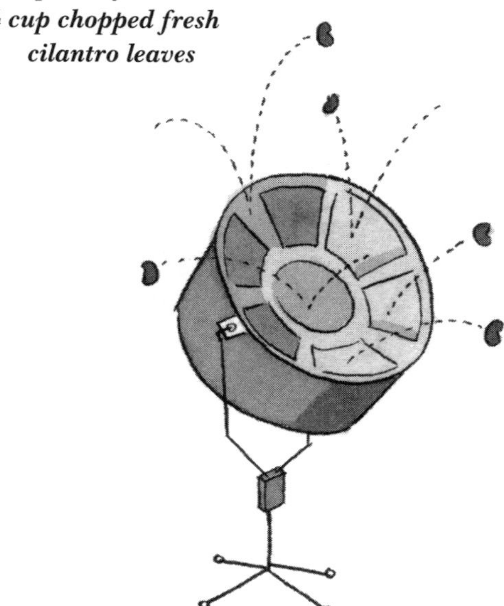

1. Sauté the bacon in a large heavy pot over low heat until the fat is rendered, about 8 minutes.

2. Add the bell peppers, onion, and garlic. Cook over low heat for 5 minutes to wilt the vegetables. Add the rice and cook, stirring, for 2 minutes.

3. Add the remaining ingredients except the scallions and cilantro. Stir, cover, and cook over medium-low heat until the liquid is absorbed and the rice is tender, about 20 minutes. Add the scallions and cilantro and gently combine. Serve hot. Store covered in the refrigerator for up to 2 days.

Serves 8

FRIJOLES NEGROS

I love black beans spooned over fried eggs on crispy tortillas, or on their own dolloped with sour cream, Avocado Cream (see Index), or sprinkled with a soft white cheese. I've made the flavor of these beans more complex with the addition of cocoa powder and a drizzle of olive oil. The cocoa cuts the rough edge of the chili powder and mellows it slightly. The beans make a great soup or a flavorful dish served over rice. An essential for Mexican cooking, these black beans are great to have on hand as an ingredient for fajitas, nachos, or just served on their own with grilled spicy sausages.

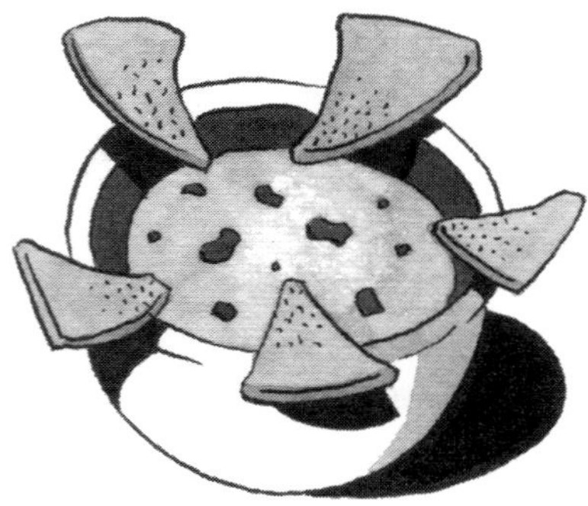

1 pound dried black beans
1 medium onion, peeled
4 whole cloves
8 cups water
8 ounces chorizo sausages
4 large fresh cilantro sprigs, stems crushed
1 large carrot, trimmed and halved
1 rib celery with leaves, halved
2 tablespoons olive oil
2 tablespoons unsweetened cocoa powder
1 tablespoon ground cumin
1 tablespoon chili powder
¼ teaspoon crushed red pepper flakes

1. Pick through the beans, discarding any stones, and rinse. Place the beans in a bowl, cover with the water, and soak overnight. Drain and rinse the beans.

2. Stud the onion with the cloves.

3. Place all the ingredients in a large heavy pot and bring to a boil. Reduce the heat to a simmer and cook uncovered until the beans are tender but not mushy, about 1½ hours.

4. Remove the flavoring vegetables and cilantro and discard. Slice the chorizos if desired and stir them back into the beans. Serve hot. Store covered in the refrigerator for up to 3 days.

Serves 8

BLACK-EYED PEAS AND BARLEY

Rice with beans is a wonderful meal all by itself, but for variety, I've used barley, one of my favorite grains, to make a new island dish.

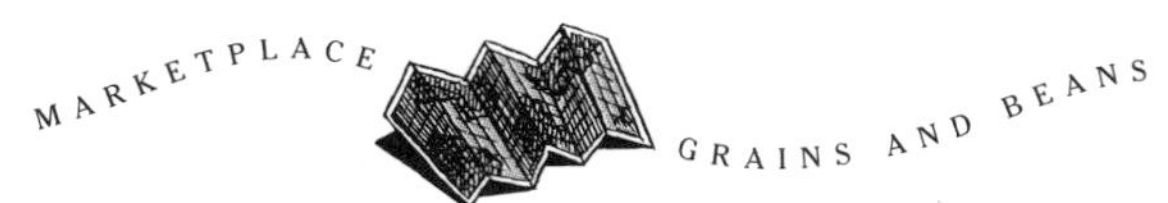

Jamaican allspice and shredded coconut add some sweetness to the smoky flavor released by the ham hock. Fresh lime juice added as the beans finish cooking and a chopped plum tomato garnish contribute an unexpected freshness to the dish. When preparing the barley, be sure not to overcook it. Leave it a bit firm and rinse it in a strainer with cold water to remove the excess starch before combining it with the cooked black-eyed peas. Serve hot in small bowls with chicken or pork barbecue.

8 ounces dried black-eyed peas
6 cups of water
¾ cup pearl barley
4 cups water
2 tablespoons olive oil
2 medium onions, chopped
1 smoked ham hock (about 12 ounces)
1 tablespoon chopped garlic
2 bay leaves
1½ teaspoons ground allspice
8 cups defatted Chicken Broth (page 127), or more if needed
¼ cup shredded coconut
Salt and freshly ground black pepper, to taste
¼ cup fresh lime juice
¼ cup chopped flat-leaf parsley
4 ripe plum tomatoes, seeded and cut into ¼-inch dice, for garnish

1. Pick through the peas, discarding any stones, and rinse. Place the peas in a bowl, cover with the water, and soak overnight. Drain and rinse the peas.

2. Place the barley in a medium-size saucepan and cover with the water. Bring to a boil over high heat, reduce the heat to medium, and simmer uncovered until tender but not mushy, 45 minutes. Drain the barley if necessary and set aside.

3. Heat the oil in a large heavy pot over low heat. Add the onions and cook until wilted, 5 to 7 minutes. Add the peas, ham hock, garlic, bay leaves, allspice, and chicken broth. Bring to a boil, reduce the heat to medium, and simmer uncovered until the peas are tender, 40 to 45 minutes, occasionally skimming off the foam that rises to the surface. Add a bit more broth if the peas seem dry.

4. Remove the ham hock and let stand until cool enough to handle. Shred any meat from the bones and return it to the peas.

5. Add the barley and coconut, season with salt and pepper, and stir gently to combine.

6. Before serving, heat through and fold in the lime juice and parsley. Serve in bowls and garnish with the diced tomatoes. Store covered in the refrigerator for up to 2 days.

Serves 8

MEXICAN LENTILS WITH PINEAPPLE AND BANANAS

These lentils, inspired by the Mexican notion of combining fruit with dried beans, is hearty yet totally refreshing as the pineapple chunks brighten every bite. Bananas and a tomato sauce enriched with raisins add an extra dimension. A squeeze of fresh lime juice over the lentils finishes the dish with a nice tingle. A perfect accompaniment to Mambo Mango Pork (see Index) or other savory meat dishes.

8 ounces lentils
6 cups Fresh Vegetable Broth or defatted Chicken Broth (page 129 or 127)
2 ribs celery with leaves, halved
1 medium carrot, trimmed and halved
8 flat-leaf parsley sprigs
2 tablespoons olive oil
½ cup diced (¼ inch) onion
2 cloves garlic, minced
1 can (28 ounces) plum tomatoes, drained, ¾ cup juice reserved, and crushed
½ cup golden raisins
Salt and coarsely ground black pepper, to taste
1 can (20 ounces) pineapple chunks, drained
2 slightly underripe bananas, peeled and cut into ¼-inch cubes

1. Pick through the lentils, discarding any stones, and rinse well in a strainer. Place in a large heavy pot along with the broth, celery, carrot, and parsley sprigs. Bring to a boil, reduce the heat to medium-low, and simmer uncovered until the lentils are tender but not mushy, 20 minutes. Some liquid will remain in the pot.

2. While the lentils are cooking, heat the oil in a large heavy saucepan over low heat. Add the onion and garlic and cook, stirring constantly, until the onion is wilted, about 10 minutes.

3. Add the tomatoes with the reserved juice and the raisins to the onion. Simmer uncovered, stirring occasionally, over medium heat for 10 minutes. Season with salt and pepper.

4. Stir in the pineapple and cook 5 minutes. Stir in the bananas and cook 2 minutes longer.

5. When the lentils are cooked, remove the celery, carrot, and parsley sprigs and drain. Return the lentils to the pot.

6. Add the tomato mixture and gently fold the ingredients together. Serve hot.

Serves 6 to 8

SPICED VEGETABLE DAL

In India's vegetarian households, *dal* (lentils) and vegetables often stand in for meat. They are high in protein and very delicious and satisfying when prepared in richly seasoned broths enhanced with aromatic spices such as cumin and cloves. Lots of fresh parsley and ripe tomatoes add their wonderful flavor to this spiced *dal* as they finish cooking. If you prefer your *dal* soupier, add more broth during the last 15 minutes of cooking. Serve *dal* as a side dish with a chicken or meat curry or with rice, a vegetable, or a vegetable *raita*.

1 cup red lentils
2 tablespoons unsalted butter
1 tablespoon vegetable oil
2 tablespoons minced peeled fresh ginger
1 tablespoon minced garlic
1 large onion, halved and slivered
2 teaspoons ground cumin
⅛ teaspoon ground cloves
Pinch of ground tumeric
4 cups Fresh Vegetable Broth (page 129)
4 ripe plum tomatoes, seeded and cut into ¼-inch dice
½ cup coarsely chopped flat-leaf parsley
Salt and freshly ground black pepper, to taste

1. Pick through the lentils, discarding any stones, and rinse well in a strainer.

2. Heat the butter and oil in a large heavy pot over medium-low heat. Add the ginger, garlic, and onion and cook, stirring, until wilted, about 10 minutes. Sprinkle in the cumin, cloves, and turmeric. Cook, stirring well, about another 2 minutes.

3. Stir in the lentils, add the broth, and bring to a boil over high heat. Reduce the heat to medium and simmer uncovered until soft but not mushy, 20 minutes, skimming off the foam as it rises to the top and stirring occasionally.

4. Stir in the tomatoes and the parsley. Continue to cook, stirring, another 15 minutes. The flavors should be well-blended and the lentils very soft. Season with salt and pepper, and serve hot or at room temperature. Store covered in the refrigerator for up to 3 days.

Serves 6 to 8

SAVORY LENTIL SALAD

Throughout North Africa and the Middle East, grains and legumes are prepared in the most delicious ways and are often accorded the place of honor in a meal. Great flavor is achieved by cooking legumes and grains in well-seasoned broths. Most dried beans must be soaked overnight and then cooked the following day, but lentils and split peas are tiny and a relatively short cooking period is all that is needed. What you want is a legume that is cooked until just tender but not mushy. Most package directions call for a too long cooking time; so before you think they're ready, begin testing—either tasting the beans or pressing them between your fingers—to be sure you catch them before they're mushy. This salad is lovely refreshed with a dollop of Lemon-Mint Yogurt Dressing.

2 cups dried brown or green lentils (16 ounces)
1 small onion, peeled
4 whole cloves
2 ribs celery with leaves, halved
2 cloves garlic, lightly bruised (page 153) and peeled
4 flat-leaf parsley sprigs
6 cups Fresh Vegetable Broth or defatted Chicken Broth (page 129 or 127)
2 tablespoons fresh lemon juice
1 tablespoon fruity extra virgin olive oil
Coarsely ground black pepper, to taste
¼ cup chopped fresh mint leaves or flat-leaf parsley
½ cup Lemon-Mint Yogurt Dressing (page 103)
6 to 8 fresh mint sprigs, for garnish

1. Pick over the lentils, discarding any stones, and rinse well in a strainer. Place in a heavy pot.

2. Stud the onion with the cloves and add it to the lentils along with the celery, garlic, parsley, and broth. Bring to a boil, reduce the heat to medium, and simmer uncovered until the lentils are just tender, about 20 minutes, skimming off the foam that rises to the surface. Do not overcook or the lentils will be mushy. Drain the lentils and discard the flavoring vegetables.

3. Gently toss the warm lentils with the lemon juice and olive oil. Season to taste with pepper, then toss in the mint. Serve each portion dolloped with a tablespoon of the yogurt dressing and garnished with a fresh mint sprig. Serve warm or at room temperature. Store covered in the refrigerator for up to 3 days.

Serves 6 to 8

Noodling Around

Pasta, sauced in all its Mediterranean glory, held court on our tables for an entire decade. But pasta has had to step aside of late with the growing popularity of noodle dishes from Singapore, Thailand, India, China, and Japan. The time of the noodle is now, and in this chapter there are curried noodles, *pad Thai*, farfalle dressed with a spicy peanut sauce. But because from time to time I find myself longing for an old favorite—a classic marinara with the deep taste of garlic and fruity olive oil—I made it my business to perfect one that really sings of Italy. It's here, too.

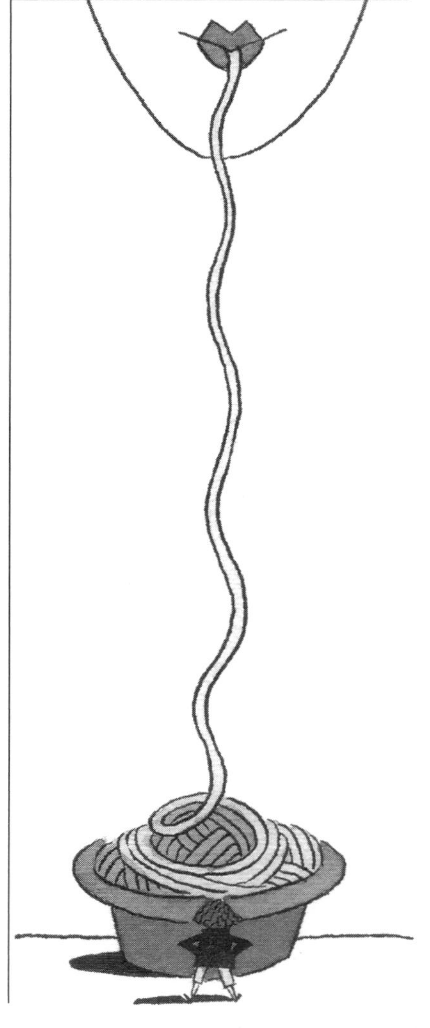

As I traveled, it seemed that one noodle dish tasted better than the next. My first impression of Tsukiji, the enormous Japanese fish market, was of workers huddled around tiny tables in open street-side restaurants, slurping up steaming hot bowls of noodles with a pair of chopsticks to get warm, stay warm, and be comforted. That's what noodles do. And for that reason, they are beloved everywhere.

AMANDARI SMOKED SALMON ANGEL PASTA

I first tasted this pasta while overlooking rice paddies at the beautiful Amandari hotel in Ubud, Bali. It seemed to me an unusual combination of ingredients for Indonesia but perfectly suited to the sensual surroundings. This is a lovely pasta dish to prepare for summer dining, for it's both fresh tasting and light. The recipe easily can be doubled for entertaining.

8 ripe plum tomatoes, cut into 8 pieces each
2 shallots, finely chopped
2 tablespoons drained tiny capers
2 tablespoons finely chopped fresh tarragon leaves or other fresh herb such as basil or dill
Finely grated zest of 1 orange
4 ounces thinly sliced smoked salmon, coarsely shredded or torn into small pieces
¼ cup plus 1 tablespoon extra virgin olive oil
⅛ teaspoon freshly ground black pepper
8 ounces dried angel hair (very thin) pasta
2 hard-cooked eggs, coarsely chopped, for garnish

1. In a bowl, combine the tomatoes, shallots, and capers. Add the tarragon, orange zest, and salmon, then the ¼ cup olive oil. Gently fold the ingredients together. Season with the pepper. Cover and let rest at room temperature for about 1 hour.

2. Shortly before serving, bring a large pot of water to a boil. Add the remaining tablespoon of oil and the pasta and cook until just tender. Drain the pasta and divide among 4 shallow pasta bowls. Top each portion evenly with the tomato and salmon mixture. Sprinkle each portion with chopped egg and serve immediately.

Serves 4

PENNE PASTA SALADE NICOISE

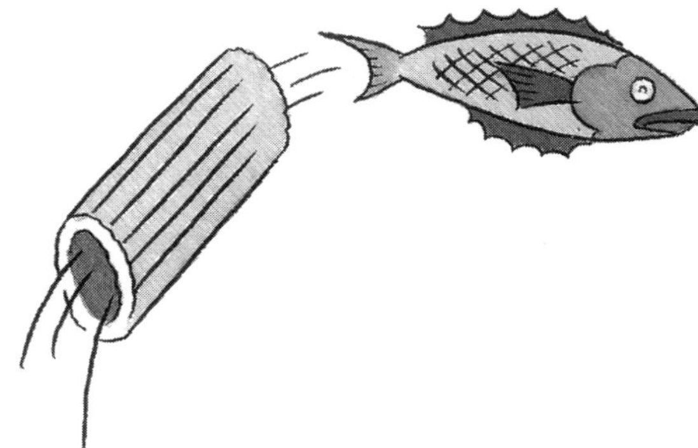

If traveling along the coast of France in the summer, it's almost a crime not to stop for lunch at an outdoor café in Nice. From your sunny post, settle in to watch the action, sip a lightly chilled Bandol rosé, and eat *salade niçoise* along with chèvres marinated in a great fruity olive oil and the freshest herbes de Provence. I love the *niçoise* flavors of tuna, potatoes, olives, capers, and anchovies, all tossed up with haricots verts (tiny green beans), fresh off the vine. To these ingredients I've added penne to make a rustic pasta salad, large enough to serve a luncheon crowd. Garnish the top with chopped eggs and lots of flat-leaf parsley.

¾ cup plus 1 tablespoon extra virgin olive oil
1 pound ribbed penne pasta
½ teaspoon minced garlic
⅓ cup halved and finely slivered red onion
½ cup pitted imported black olives, halved if very large
3 tablespoons drained capers
8 anchovy fillets, halved crosswise, or more to taste
½ cup plus 2 tablespoons coarsely chopped flat-leaf parsley
Coarsely ground black pepper, to taste
8 ounces haricots verts, stem ends trimmed, halved crosswise
2 Idaho potatoes, peeled and cut into ¼-inch cubes
2 cans (6½ ounces each) white meat tuna, drained and flaked into large pieces
3 ripe large tomatoes, cut into ½-inch cubes
3 hard-cooked eggs, peeled and coarsely chopped, for garnish

1. Bring a large pot of salted water to a boil. Add 1 tablespoon olive oil and the penne and cook until just tender. Drain, rinse under cold water, and drain well. Place the pasta in a large bowl.

2. Toss the pasta with the remaining ¾ cup olive oil. Fold in the garlic, onion, olives, capers, anchovies, ½ cup parsley, and a generous amount of pepper.

3. Bring a small pot of water to a boil and cook the haricots verts until just tender, about 3 minutes. Drain, cool under cold water, drain again, and pat dry. Add to the pasta.

4. Place the potatoes in a small pot with cold water to cover and bring to a boil. Cook until just tender, 7 to 8 minutes. Drain and add to the pasta.

5. Add the tuna and tomatoes. Using a large rubber spatula and working from underneath, fold all the ingredients together. Adjust the seasonings.

6. Transfer the salad to a large attractive serving bowl. Sprinkle the top with the chopped eggs and remaining 2 tablespoons parsley.

Serves 12

An Anchovy Tip: Store your anchovy tins in the refrigerator or a cool, dark place. Once they get warm, the anchovies become mushy and are difficult to work with.

MALAY CURRIED NOODLES

The flavors of Singapore come to life in these noodles, which are brimming with red peppers, shrimp, bean sprouts, and scallions, and spiced with Indian curry powder. Served at room temperature, they are excellent as a luncheon dish or included in a buffet. For this recipe (as for other wok recipes), all the ingredients should be prepared before you start cooking.

4 ounces dried angel hair (very thin) pasta
4 tablespoons plus 1 teaspoon corn oil
1 large egg, lightly beaten
1 medium onion, halved and cut into thin slivers
1 tablespoon best-quality curry powder
1 red bell pepper, stemmed, halved lengthwise, seeded, each half sliced crosswise into ¼-inch strips
1 pound medium shrimp, peeled and deveined
2 cups fresh mung bean sprouts
2 scallions (3 inches green left on), thinly sliced on the diagonal
¼ cup finely slivered fresh basil leaves, for garnish

1. Bring a large pot of water to a boil. Add 1 tablespoon corn oil and the pasta and cook until just tender. Drain, rinse with cold water, and drain again. Remove to a bowl and set aside.

2. To make the omelet, heat 1 teaspoon oil in a 10-inch nonstick skillet over medium-high heat. Swirl the oil in the pan so that it coats the entire bottom. When the oil sizzles slightly, pour the beaten egg into the center of the skillet and swirl the pan so that the egg covers the bottom. Cook 1 minute, then loosen the omelet from the sides of the pan with a spatula and gently turn it over. Cook 30 seconds longer. Remove to a plate, cut into ½-inch-wide strips, cover, and set aside.

3. Heat the remaining 3 tablespoons oil in a wok over medium-high heat. When the oil sizzles slightly, add the onion and sauté until just wilted, about 3 minutes. Sprinkle the curry powder over the onion and cook, stirring, 1 minute. Add the red pepper strips and sauté until slightly softened and the curry coats the vegetables well, about 2 minutes.

4. Add the shrimp and mix with the vegetables. Sauté until the shrimp are just cooked through, about 3 minutes.

5. Add 1 cup of the bean sprouts, the scallions, and cooked pasta. Reduce the heat to medium and gently lift the pasta from the bottom to combine it well with the other ingredients.

6. Divide the noodles between 6 to 8 shallow pasta bowls. Garnish with the omelet strips, remaining 1 cup bean sprouts, and the slivered basil leaves. Serve warm or at room temperature.

Serves 6 to 8

SOUVENIR TO SAVOR

Noodles at Narita

Listen—just in case you find yourself in Tokyo's Narita Airport with time on your hands and hunger pains in your stomach—as I did on my way to Hong Kong—here's a good tip.

From experience, I know that no connecting flight is ever ready when you are, so I wasn't surprised to be wandering around the airport with an unscheduled three-hour layover. That gave me plenty of time to explore, and I discovered a small cafeteria on the second floor of Narita's transit area, just above United Airline's arrivals and departures. This was truly the most atypical airport food because it was delicious. I wasn't up for a large meal at this point, but a snack seemed a soothing way to pass the time. Within minutes, I was served a bowlful of Japanese noodles shimmering in a delicious broth that was enhanced by some greens and one delicate slice of pork floating on top. Fresh scallions were sprinkled over all. Soon I was slurping along with the best of them. These noodles seemed more comforting at that moment than even my mother's delicious, rich noodle pudding!

I have since been to Narita on other trips and now you can bet I leave time for repeated airport noodling!

SOUVENIR TO SAVOR

Saucy Thai Tales

A typical Thai dinner is more of a mini-feast than a regular evening meal as we know it. Almost more important than the beautifully arranged main dishes are an array of sauces and dips served in small bowls woven among the entrées. They appear in myriad textures and colors. Some are thick and earthen hued. Others are broth-clear with vibrant ingredients floating about. These sauces and dips are essential to the Thai dining experience and complement the pungent and spicy flavors of the cuisine. They also satisfy the individual tastes of each diner, for while the cook prepares the main dishes to his or her liking, each person adds these seasonings to taste.

Everyone begins with a bowl of rice or noodles. Sauces are spooned over to begin the flavoring process, then selections from the entrées are added.

Thai food is often thought of as too hot and spicy for American palates, but this is a misconception. The harmony of the four primary tastes is what Thai seasoning is all about. Visiting a Thai noodle restaurant, you will find a ring of four condiments in small bowls on each table. They contain fish sauce, sugar, vinegar, and powdered chilies. These four tastes are reflected in Thai sauces and dips. The salty flavors come from fish sauce or the more familiar soy sauce. Sweet flavor comes from palm sugar, similar in taste to brown sugar, or regular granulated sugar. Sour tastes come from vinegar or lime juice, although rice vinegar has a mellow quality to it. The spice comes most often from Thailand's hot little chilies, but also from fresh ginger and garlic, which is how I like to get my kicks!

Rock,
This was the King of Siam's summer palace just outside of Bangkok—Shall we dance?
Love,
Sheila

FRESH CRAB PAD THAI

In Bangkok, you can hardly turn a corner without finding someone munching on the *pad Thai* they've bought from a nearby street vendor. Authentic *pad Thai* is a simple noodle dish made from rice noodles tossed with fish sauce, sugar, vinegar, chilies, shrimp, and egg. I've changed the recipe slightly, but there are certain essentials that must remain. Do try to find rice noodles or rice sticks in an Asian grocery store or the specialty food section of a supermarket. If you can't, the thinnest spaghetti will do. Instead of tossing the noodles with sugar and vinegar as is traditionally done, I find it much more inviting to serve the *pad Thai* with small bowls of Thai Sweet and Sour Sauce for sprinkling on during the meal. As the noodles are subtle in flavor, the sauce is necessary to give the dish a spark.

8 ounces dried thin rice noodles (rice sticks) or spaghetti
¼ cup peanut oil
1 tablespoon coarsely chopped garlic
6 tablespoons fresh lemon juice
2 tablespoons Thai Fish Sauce (page 254; see Note)
8 ounces fresh lump crabmeat, picked over for shell and cartilage
8 ounces fresh mung bean sprouts, rinsed and drained
4 scallions (3 inches green left on), thinly sliced crosswise
2 hard-cooked eggs, coarsely chopped, for garnish
⅓ cup peanuts, coarsely chopped, for garnish
⅓ cup coarsely chopped fresh cilantro leaves, for garnish
1 cup Thai Sweet and Sour Sauce (page 75), for serving

1. Bring a large pot of water to a boil. Remove it from the heat and add the rice noodles (sticks) and soak, uncovered, for 5 minutes. (If you are using spaghetti, prepare it following package directions.) Drain.

2. Heat the oil in a wok or a very large skillet over medium heat. Add the garlic and cook, stirring, until just golden, 2 minutes.

3. Add the noodles to the wok and toss with the oil and garlic. Add the lemon juice and fish sauce and toss well.

4. Add the crabmeat, sprouts, and scallions and toss gently to heat through, 2 minutes. Remove to a large shallow serving bowl. Sprinkle the eggs, peanuts, and cilantro over the noodles. Serve immediately with small bowls of Thai sweet and sour sauce to sprinkle on top.

Serves 4

Note: If you'd rather buy fish sauce, it is available in Asian grocery stores or Asian sections of supermarkets.

SESAME BUTTERFLY NOODLES

When spring comes, those long hours of stew simmering are definitely over. It's time for bright yet full-flavored meals that don't take hours to prepare. For this dish, butterfly noodles are slathered in a spicy peanut sauce subtly flavored with fresh ginger and garlic. The noodles are sprinkled with toasted sesame seeds and dazzled with a julienne of crisp, fresh snow peas.

2 tablespoons sesame seeds
4 ounces snow peas, strings and stem ends removed
Salt, to taste
1 tablespoon peanut oil
12 ounces dried butterfly noodles (farfalle)
1¼ cups Spicy Peanut Sauce (recipe follows)
Coarsely ground black pepper, to taste

1. Place the sesame seeds in a small, dry skillet over medium heat and toast, shaking the pan constantly, until golden brown, 3 to 4 minutes. Set aside.

2. Cut the snow peas into julienne strips. Blanch in boiling water for 30 seconds. Refresh immediately under cold running water and drain well.

3. Bring a large pot of salted water to a boil. Add the peanut oil and the noodles and cook until just tender. Drain and cool under cold running water. Drain well.

4. Place the noodles in a bowl and toss with the peanut sauce. Season with salt and pepper.

5. Transfer the noodles to a serving bowl. Scatter the julienned snow peas over the top and sprinkle with the toasted sesame seeds.

Serves 6

SPICY PEANUT SAUCE

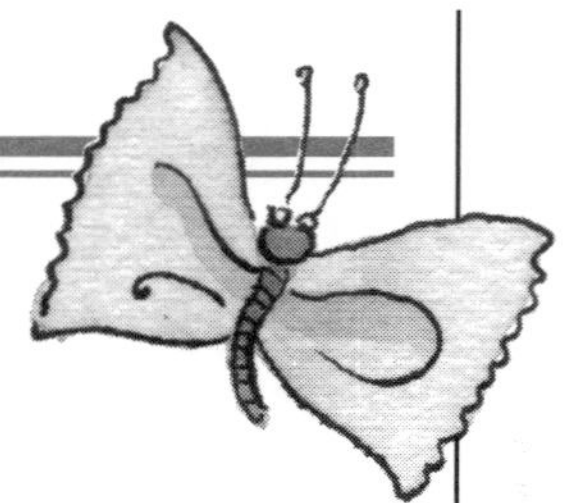

There are thick peanut sauces served in Indonesia for dipping satay, and there are others which grace noodles in Chinese restaurants across America. This sauce is not too thick; the texture resembles most a velvety mayonnaise. It is ideal for tossing with pasta for a cool summer feast and just the right consistency for combining with tender shredded chicken breasts. If you prefer yours a bit hotter, add a little more chili oil.

¼ cup soy sauce
¼ cup rice wine vinegar
6 tablespoons cold water
1 tablespoon sugar
½ teaspoon salt
2 teaspoons minced peeled fresh ginger
1 teaspoon minced garlic
6 tablespoons smooth peanut butter, at room temperature
3 tablespoons peanut oil
3 tablespoons Asian sesame oil
½ teaspoon chili oil

1. Place the soy sauce, vinegar, water, sugar, salt, ginger, and garlic in a blender. Process on high speed until the ginger and garlic are smoothed into the liquid, about 1 minute. Add the peanut butter and process for 1 minute longer.

2. Combine the oils and drizzle into the sauce with the blender running on low speed. Store covered in the refrigerator for up to 2 days. Bring to room temperature before serving.

Makes 1¼ cups

A TASTE OF THE WORLD

Chinese Palette

Photo: Chives, scallions, and cilantro at a Hong Kong market.

...And

- RED CHILIES
- CILANTRO
- SHALLOTS
- BEAN SPROUTS
- ONIONS
- BOK CHOY
- CABBAGES
- WONTON OR SPRING ROLL WRAPPERS
- RICE NOODLES
- SESAME SEEDS
- SESAME OIL
- PEANUT OIL
- CHILI OIL
- CHILI PASTE
- PLUM SAUCE
- HOISIN SAUCE
- RICE WINE VINEGAR
- PORK

THE WINES OF

Italy

Wine is such an integral part of *la tavola italiana* (the Italian table) that it is considered, defined as, a food. Just as Italian cooking has exploded across America, so have Italian wines, in all their delightful variety. And just as each of Italy's fascinating regions has evolved its own foods and flavors, each has developed wines that best complement the local cuisine. Among white wines, for instance, Gavi's racy fruit and faintly flinty character do wonders for seafood fished out of the Ligurian Sea—just as they do for our own sea bass, red snapper, Dungeness crab, and various seafood pastas.

> *"Just as each of Italy's fascinating regions has evolved its own food and flavors, each has developed wines that best complement the local cuisine."*

Pinot Grigio and Verdicchio go well with Adriatic-fished scampi or razor clam dishes. On our shores they prove a sound match for fresh cherrystones, steamed mussels, or our own versions of grilled shrimp.

Though enormous quantities of Italian whites are made from the widely planted (and blandly flavored) Trebbiano grape—Frascati, Orvieto, Toscano Bianco, and dozens of others—more flavorful varieties are gaining rapidly. They include the fragrant Pinot Bianco, for instance, as well as Malvasia, Sauvignon Blanc, and the ever popular Chardonnay, which is producing more complex, oak-aged whites from leading producers, such as Antinori, Ruffino, Gaja, Fontodi, Frescobaldi, Maculan, and Ca' del Bosco. Chardonnays from Trentino and Alto Adige, simpler perhaps but still dry and fruity, also offer excellent value, particularly those from such producers as Zenato, Zeni, Lageder, Brigl, Tiefenbrunner, Santa Margherita, and San Michaele.

Italy, however, thinks of itself as red wine country, and so does the world. Red wine production far outstrips white wine. The most illustrious and distinctive Italian wines are red, with names that are superbly operatic—

Left: Grapes for nibbling or pressing.
Right: In Verona we stopped for a Sambuco on our way to "Aida." Those elephants I didn't get to ride.

Barolo, Barbaresco, Brunello, Tignanello, Flaccianello, Gattinara, Taurasi, Amarone, to name but a few. They stand shoulder to shoulder with the other world greats—Bordeaux, Hermitage, Chambertin—and they are just as pricey in many cases. Happily, however, Italy's love of red wine

Left: From these vineyards will come the best Barbarescos and Barolos. Right: We may have come a long way with Chianti's like Ruffino's top Riserva Ducale, but empty straw-wrapped bottles did make great candle holders and lamps.

> *"Italian wine has undergone a massive revolution in the last two decades, as traditional styles have given way to newer, more vibrant ones."*

streaks across the price spectrum. There are plenty of moderate-priced reds that are tremendously versatile with many of the foods we like to eat today, especially grilled meats and vegetables, roast chicken and game birds, savory pizzas, and hearty pastas.

Italian wine has undergone a massive revolution in the last two decades, as traditional styles have given way to newer, more vibrant ones. It is perhaps most noticeable with Chianti, the Italian wine Americans knew first. Italy used to send us enormous shipments of jug-style Chianti, which was mostly fruity, sometimes a little *frizzante* but also a little sharp and acidic. Today's Chianti is much more flavorful and better balanced, with less bite and more charm. For best values in Italian reds, look for these names: Dolcetto d'Alba, Barbera, Rosso di Montalcino, Campo Fiorin, Montepulciano d'Abruzzo, Barco Reale, Rubesco, Salice Salentino, Monte Antico.

Finally, there are Italian rosés, the best of which are dry, fruity, and extremely agreeable to drink on their own or with food. Costadolio from Maculan near Vincenza is the very model of fresh appeal, and others worth seeking out are Lagrein Rosato, Lacryma Rosa, Taurino Rosato, and Rosato dei Masi.

MEDITERRANEAN DUCK AND TWO-BEAN PASTA

When I think back to the times we rented a vacation house in Italy years ago, I remember how much I enjoyed creating lunches from ingredients that were so fresh and perfect that very little effort on my part was needed. I had a favorite salad that I made from shredded roasted chicken, the thinnest green beans, a sprinkling of capers, lemon zest, and green, fruity extra virgin olive oil. A grind of pepper finished it off. Thinking about that time and salad led me to create this pasta dish with duck, cannellini beans, and delicate haricots verts. Lemon zest and juice add the spark to the rich tasting sauce, which is easily prepared ahead of time. Add the lemon juice just before serving so that the haricots don't lose their bright color. Toss the sauce with curly fusilli pasta.

2 to 2½ cups coarsely shredded cooked duck or dark meat chicken
Salt, to taste
6 ounces haricots verts, stem ends trimmed, halved crosswise
1 cup drained and rinsed cooked white cannellini beans
2 tablespoons drained tiny capers, rinsed
2 tablespoons finely grated lemon zest
6 ripe plum tomatoes, seeded and cut into ½-inch dice
8 tablespoons chopped flat-leaf parsley
Freshly ground black pepper, to taste
½ cup plus 1 tablespoon extra virgin olive oil
12 ounces dried fusilli pasta
2 tablespoons fresh lemon juice

1. Place the duck in a large bowl.

2. Bring a pot of salted water to a boil and cook the haricots verts until just tender, about 3 minutes. Drain under cold water and pat dry. Add to the duck along with the cannellini beans. Carefully fold together with a rubber sptaula so that the white beans don't break up.

3. Add the capers, lemon zest, tomatoes and 2 tablespoons of the parsley, a sprinkle of salt, a generous grind of pepper, and the ½ cup olive oil. Fold together well.

4. Bring a large pot of salted water to a boil. Add the remaining tablespoon of oil and the pasta and cook until just tender. Drain, rinse under hot water to remove starch, and drain again. Toss the hot pasta with the duck, vegetables, lemon juice, and remaining parsley. Serve immediately.

Serves 6

RUSTIC TOMATO-PANCETTA PASTA

Rustic, fresh, and creamy ricotta is subtly enriched by pancetta, shallots, and earthy-flavored sun-dried tomatoes. Coarsely chopped flat-leaf parsley and ripe plum tomatoes brighten the flavors of this easy sauce for a delicate yet exciting Italian pasta dish. Fresh arugula, lightly dressed with extra virgin olive oil and a splash of balsamic vinegar, will complete a beautiful meal.

3 cups ricotta cheese
3 tablespoons extra virgin olive oil
8 ounces pancetta or other unsmoked slab bacon, rind discarded, cut into ½-inch cubes
1 cup coarsely chopped shallots
1 cup coarsely chopped flat-leaf parsley
¼ cup finely chopped sun-dried tomatoes
4 ripe plum tomatoes, seeded and cut into ½-inch pieces
¼ teaspoon salt
¼ teaspoon black pepper
12 ounces large dried tubular pasta, such as rigatoni

1. Place the ricotta in a large bowl.

2. Heat 2 tablespoons oil in a large nonstick skillet over medium heat. Add the pancetta and cook, stirring, occasionally, until the fat is rendered, about 10 minutes. Transfer with a slotted spoon to the bowl with the ricotta.

3. Add the shallots to the rendered fat and oil, reduce the heat to medium-low, and cook, stirring, until wilted, about 10 minutes. Transfer to the ricotta with a slotted spoon.

4. Add all but 1 tablespoon of the parsley, the sun-dried tomatoes, plum tomatoes, salt and pepper to the ricotta; fold all together.

5. Shortly before serving, bring a large pot of salted water to a boil. Add the remaining tablespoon of oil and the pasta and cook until just tender. Remove ½ cup of the cooking liquid and reserve. Drain the pasta and toss it well with the ricotta mixture, adding about 2 tablespoons of the reserved cooking liquid, or more according to taste, to give a creamy texture to the sauce. Adjust the seasonings and serve immediately garnished with the remaining tablespoon of parsley.

Serves 6

PASTA ARRABIATA

I've called for penne in this recipe, as the bolder the sauce, the bolder the pasta should be. Rigatoni would also be just fine.

1 pound hot Italian sausages, cut into ½-inch pieces
3 tablespoons olive oil
1 fennel bulb, trimmed, cored, and cut into ½-inch-wide julienne strips
5 cups Marinara Sauce (recipe follows)
½ teaspoon coarsely ground black pepper
1 teaspoon crushed red pepper flakes, or to taste
Salt, to taste
1 pound dried penne pasta
1 cup pitted Kalamata olives, coarsely chopped
1 cup fresh basil leaves, slivered
Freshly grated Parmesan cheese, for serving

1. Place the sausage pieces in a large nonstick skillet over medium heat. Cook until browned and cooked through, 30 minutes, stirring occasionally. Remove with a slotted spoon and drain on paper towels. Discard the fat and wipe the skillet clean.

2. Heat 2 tablespoons oil in the skillet over medium heat. Add the fennel and cook, stirring, for 15 minutes. Return the sausage to the pan.

3. Add the marinara sauce, black pepper, and red pepper flakes and simmer uncovered for 10 minutes.

4. Bring a large pot of salted water to a boil. Add the remaining tablespoon of oil and the penne and cook until just tender. Drain the pasta and return it to the pot.

5. Add the olives and basil to the sauce, heat through, and add to the pasta. Toss and serve immediately with the Parmesan.

Serves 8

A TASTE OF THE WORLD

...And

Oregano	*Polenta*
Basil	*Arborio rice*
Rosemary	*Cannellini beans*
Sage	*Anchovies*
Flat-leaf parsley	*Salamis*
Dried red chilies	*Prosciutto di Parma*
Capers	*Sausages*
Wild mushrooms	*Parmigiano-Reggiano cheese*
Arugula	*Ricotta cheese*
Fennel	*Extra virgin olive oil*
Pears	
Hazelnuts	
Almonds	

***Photo:** The Colosseum in Rome needs little explanation—but what happened to all the traffic?*

MARINARA SAUCE

For a long time, I was disappointed in my tomato sauce. I wanted it to taste really Italian but it never quite did. Now I think I have discovered the secret. I begin with a great-quality extra virgin olive oil and use more than I normally would. Instead of mincing the garlic cloves, I crush them slightly and cook them whole until just lightly colored. Once all the ingredients are added, a slow 30-minute simmer finishes the trick. This marinara is perfect as is over a bowl of steaming pasta or in other recipes, such as the Pasta Arrabiata.

¼ cup extra virgin olive oil
4 large cloves garlic, lightly bruised (page 153)
4 cans (28 ounces each), plum tomatoes, drained and coarsely chopped
½ cup dry red wine
½ cup coarsely chopped flat-leaf parsley
½ cup fresh basil leaves, torn in half
2 teaspoons dried oregano
Salt and freshly ground black pepper, to taste
Pinch of sugar

1. Heat the oil in a large heavy pot over medium-low heat. Add the garlic and cook until it colors slightly but does not burn, 3 to 4 minutes. Remove from the heat and carefully stir in the tomatoes and the wine.

2. Return the pot to medium heat. Stir in the parsley, basil, oregano, salt, pepper, and sugar. Simmer uncovered, stirring occasionally, for 30 minutes. Serve immediately, or cool and store covered in the refrigerator for up to 2 days.

Makes 7 cups

PER VIA AEREA
PAR AVION

Burt –

never forget our
4:00 Campari and
soda as we sailed
into Portofino!

Ciao
Sheila

CATALAN ROMESCO "SAUCE" ROTELLI

Romesco sauce, cherished by the Catalonians, is considered essential to their cuisine. When summer sizzles and the local ingredients are bountiful, the sauce proliferates. The best red bell peppers, tomatoes, onion, garlic, and almonds are the components of this "dish." Classically the ingredients are finely ground to the consistency of a pesto and served along with grilled or fried fish. I decided not to purée them and to take a bit of license with seasonings. Chunky romesco makes a perfect pasta sauce tossed with rotelli or fusilli. Large tubes should not be used since you need a shape that will catch the sauce. You can also spoon the sauce over grilled poultry or mix it with garbanzo beans (chickpeas).

7 tablespoons extra virgin Spanish olive oil
8 large cloves garlic, thinly sliced
1 cup coarsely chopped blanched almonds
4 red bell peppers, stemmed, seeded, and cut into ¼-inch dice (about 4 cups)
2 medium onions, halved and thinly slivered
4 cups diced ripe plum tomatoes (about 2 pounds)
Juice and finely grated zest of 1 orange
Salt and freshly ground black pepper, to taste
⅓ cup coarsely chopped fresh cilantro leaves or flat-leaf parsley
1 pound dried rotelli or fusilli pasta
Freshly grated Manchego or Parmesan cheese, for serving

1. Heat 4 tablespoons of the oil in a large heavy saucepan over low heat. Add the garlic and cook until pale golden, about 5 minutes. Remove the garlic with a slotted spoon and set aside.

2. Add the almonds to the oil, increase the heat slightly, and cook, stirring, until the almonds are golden, about 3 minutes. Remove the almonds with a slotted spoon and add them to the garlic.

3. Add 2 tablespoons oil to the saucepan and heat over medium-low heat. Add the peppers and onions and cook, stirring occasionally, for 15 minutes to soften the vegetables. Add the tomatoes and orange juice and zest. Season with salt and pepper. Continue to cook for 5 minutes to blend the flavors.

4. Add the reserved garlic and almonds and cook to warm through, 2 minutes more. Adjust the seasonings and stir in the cilantro.

5. Bring a large pot of salted water to a boil. Add the remaining tablespoon of oil and the pasta and cook until just tender. Drain and toss with the sauce. Serve immediately. Pass grated Manchego or Parmesan cheese to sprinkle over the top.

Serves 8, sauce makes 6 cups

LESLIE RUSSO'S SUMMER PUTTANESCA

From that wonderful woman who brought you Leslie Russo's Negronis in *The Silver Palate Good Times Cookbook* comes a terrific Italian-inspired summer pasta. Fresh garden arugula marries with roasted red peppers, garlic, olives, and anchovies in an easily put together cold sauce. All you need to do is cook up some wide noodles and toss them with the vegetables before serving.

2 red bell peppers, halved lengthwise and roasted (page 202)
6 cups arugula, rinsed, tough stems removed
1 large clove garlic, minced
Coarsely ground black pepper, to taste
1 cup pitted imported black and green olives, coarsely chopped
1 can (2 ounces) anchovies, drained
⅓ cup plus 1 tablespoon extra virgin olive oil
8 ounces dried pappardelle or other wide noodles
Coarsely grated Parmesan cheese, for serving

1. Cut the peppers lengthwise into ¼-inch strips. Place the arugula in a large bowl. Sprinkle with the garlic and generously with black pepper. Add the pepper strips and chopped olives. Toss lightly.

2. Cut the anchovies crosswise in half and add them to the arugula mixture. Toss together with the ⅓ cup olive oil.

3. Bring a large pot of water to a boil. Add the remaining tablespoon of oil and the noodles and cook until just tender. Drain the noodles and rinse under warm water to remove excess starch. Toss immediately with the arugula mixture. Sprinkle with coarsely grated Parmesan cheese and serve at once.

Serves 6

LINGUINE WITH GARLIC AND OIL LIGURIA

Donaldo Soviero, brilliant Italian chef and author of *La Vera Cucina Italiana,* makes the most unusual and delicious version of an oil and garlic pasta I have ever tasted. He enhances it with pine nuts, golden and dark raisins, and toasted croutons, so that all it needs is a gentle toss with linguine—and a great bottle of Chianti alongside.

2 cups cubed (½ inch) day-old peasant bread
1 cup plus 1 tablespoon extra virgin olive oil
4 large cloves garlic, peeled, plus 2 cloves minced
Salt, to taste
12 ounces dried linguine pasta
½ cup golden raisins
½ cup dark raisins
½ cup pine nuts
¼ teaspoon crushed red pepper flakes
⅓ cup chopped flat-leaf parsley
Freshly ground pepper, to taste
Freshly grated Parmesan cheese, for serving

1. Preheat the oven to 350°F.

2. Place the bread on a baking sheet and toast, shaking the pan once or twice during cooking, until golden, 10 minutes. Set aside.

3. Heat the cup of oil in a large heavy pot over low heat. Add the whole garlic cloves and cook until they begin to color, about 10 minutes. Remove from the heat and discard the garlic cloves. Set the pot with oil aside.

4. Just before serving, bring a large pot of salted water to a boil. Add the remaining tablespoon of oil and the pasta and cook until just tender. Rinse under hot water, drain well, and place in a large serving bowl.

5. While the pasta is cooking, add the minced garlic, raisins, pine nuts, and red pepper flakes to the reserved oil and place the pot over low heat. Cook until the garlic just begins to brown, 8 to 10 minutes. Do not let it burn.

6. Add the oil mixture to the hot pasta along with the croutons and parsley. Toss well with a large spoon and fork. Season well with salt and pepper. Serve immediately with a bowl of freshly grated Parmesan.

Serves 6

S O U V E N I R   T O   S A V O R

Remembrances of Pastas Past

For two summers during the early 70s, Richard and I rented a house for the month of August in the small fishing village of Lerici, perched above the Golfo di Poeti and near the glamorous Italian Riviera towns of Portofino and Rapallo. Each day we planned different activities, but our favorite was walking from the house into town in the morning for coffee and again for a Campari and soda in the late afternoon. As we lingered at the café, we watched small, brightly painted fishing boats coming into port with the day's catch. The town, with its own aura of romance, had been home to Shelley, and the favorite haunt of Byron and Keats. Every day, as the sun waned, a small excursion boat shuttled across the gulf for a short ride to the tiny island of Portovenere, distinguished by a magnificent citadel and many excellent outdoor restaurants framing the water's edge. It was at one of these delightful places that I had my first taste of a marvelous curried seafood linguine. Silky golden ribbons studded with baby calamari and shrimp was our special favorite.

Oh those summers in Italy—they were poetic!

Until that time, I had rarely eaten pasta that wasn't tossed with a tomato-based sauce. Even pesto, today almost a cliché, was *avant garde* at the time. These curried noodles were sublime, accompanied by a perfectly chilled dry white wine. We ended our meals with fresh peaches beautifully presented in a bowl of cold water, just waiting to be peeled.

Before heading back to Lerici, we'd stroll along the quay, taking in the beauty of the softly lit citadel against a clear, starry sky. About midnight the boat slowly drifted across the Golfo di Poeti back to Lerici. We'd talk with the other passengers about Shelley, Keats, and Byron, the curried pasta, and about the beautiful place we were all lucky enough to be spending the summer. Over the past years, the curried seafood linguine lingers in my memory, but the name of the restaurant is long forgotten. If you make it to the Portovenere, I think it was the second from the last restaurant to the far right, looking toward the island from the water. If you get there, you know what to order.

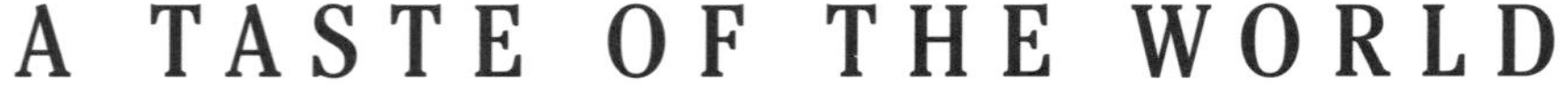

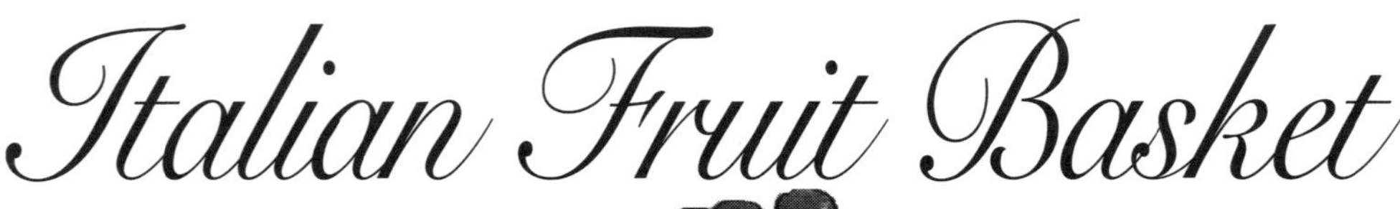

A TASTE OF THE WORLD

Italian Fruit Basket

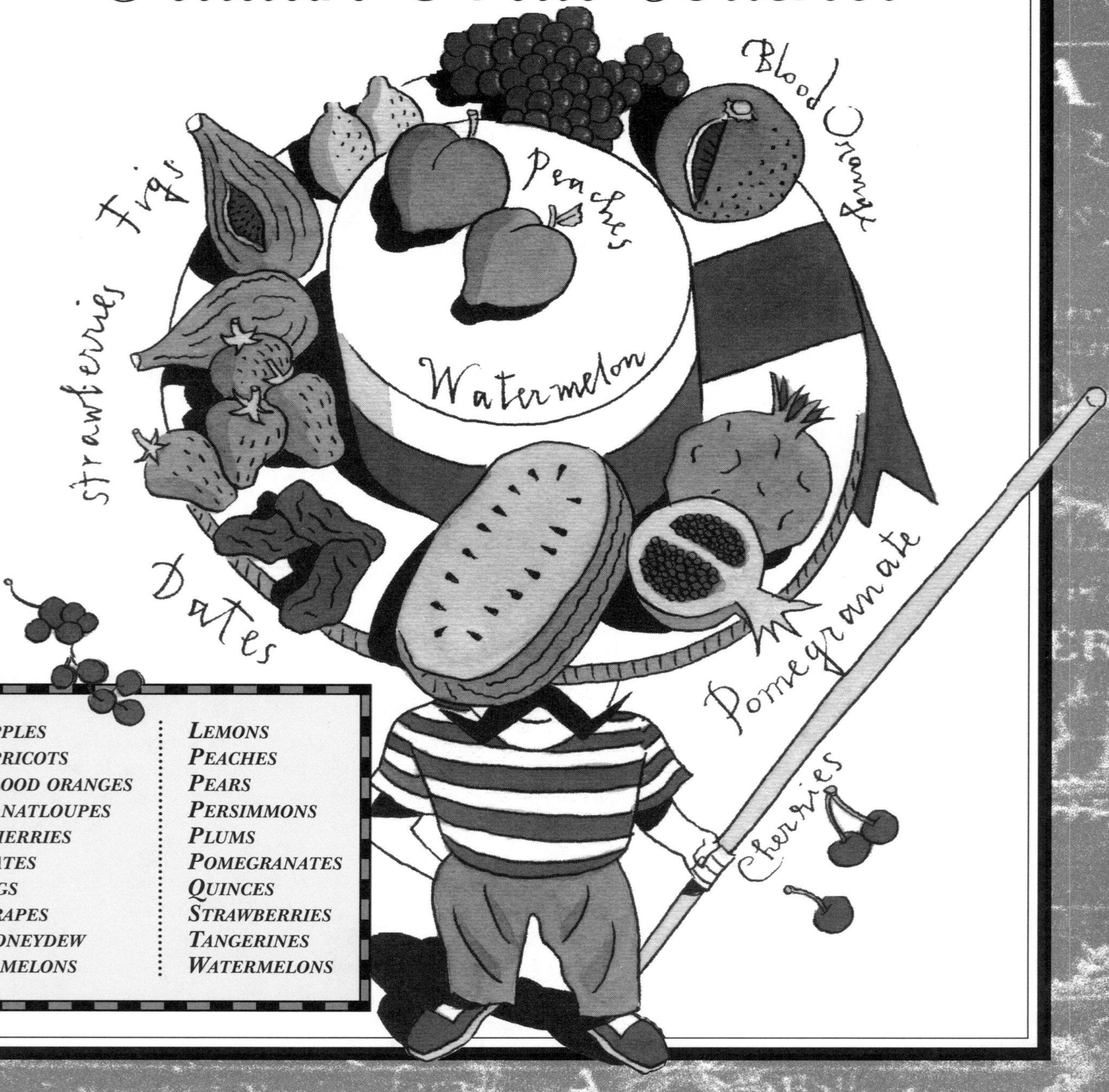

Apples	*Lemons*
Apricots	*Peaches*
Blood oranges	*Pears*
Canatloupes	*Persimmons*
Cherries	*Plums*
Dates	*Pomegranates*
Figs	*Quinces*
Grapes	*Strawberries*
Honeydew melons	*Tangerines*
	Watermelons

BERTA'S REALLY RICH NOODLE PUDDING

Once a year my mother, Berta, makes this yummy pudding for a special holiday gathering. I'm not sure where the recipe came from, but my Russian grandmothers made it before my mother took over the mantle. This version is quite caloric and perhaps not perfectly tailored to the 90s, but I wouldn't dare tamper. I don't cook it quite so long as Berta does, which I feel gives the pudding a lighter texture. If you choose, most of the ingredients can be substituted with reduced-calorie, no-cholesterol products. Enjoy it—once a year!

Salt, to taste
8 ounces medium dried egg noodles
½ cup milk
3 large eggs
1 cup creamy cottage cheese
1 cup sour cream
4 ounces cream cheese, at room temperature
4 tablespoons (½ stick) unsalted butter, melted
1 cup golden raisins
Pinch of ground cinnamon

1. Preheat the oven to 350°F.

2. Bring a large pot of salted water to a boil. Add the noodles and cook until just tender. Drain and reserve.

3. In a large bowl beat the milk and eggs together. Whisk in the cottage cheese, sour cream, cream cheese, and 2 tablespoons of the melted butter. Toss in the noodles, raisins, cinnamon, and salt to taste. Mix well.

4. With the remaining butter, grease a 13 x 9 x 2-inch shallow baking dish. Add the noodle mixture and spread it evenly in the pan. Bake on the center rack of the oven until the pudding is set and slightly browned on top, about 45 minutes. Let rest 10 minutes before cutting.

Serves 12

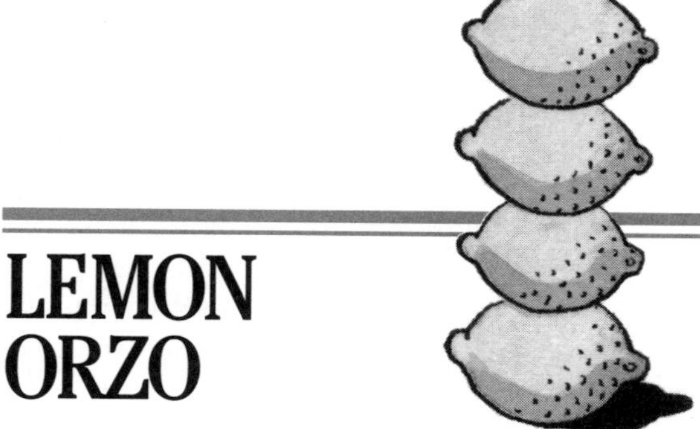

LEMON ORZO

Orzo is a small, delicate Italian pasta shaped like rice and it works perfectly served with both Chinese and Japanese dishes in place of rice. Fresh lemon juice and zest and spring green chives add the most delectable flavor to this "sweet" and versatile pasta. A little bit of peanut oil added once the pasta has been cooked smooths the textures and flavors together.

5 cups defatted Chicken Broth (page 127)
2 cups dried orzo pasta
¼ cup snipped fresh chives
2 teaspoons finely grated lemon zest
2 teaspoons peanut oil
2 teaspoons fresh lemon juice

1. Bring the broth to a boil in a medium-size saucepan. Add the orzo, reduce the heat, and simmer uncovered until just tender. Drain and return the pasta to the pan.

2. Add the remaining ingredients and toss well to combine. Serve hot.

Serves 4 to 6

SPANISH BELL PEPPER, TOMATO, AND OLIVE PASTA

The best ingredients of the Spanish palette define this sweet and robust tomato sauce. Green olives, anchovies, and capers add pungency, while golden sultanas mellow the flavors. To do it justice, a full-bodied sauce needs a wide or large noodle to cling to; therefore, choose pappardelle if you prefer ribbons or rigatoni if you favor tubes. This sauce is also delicious spooned over roasted fish and poultry.

5 tablespoons extra virgin Spanish olive oil
1½ cups thinly slivered onions
2 red bell peppers, stemmed, seeded, and cut into ¼-inch-wide strips
2 tablespoons coarsely chopped garlic
2 cans (28 ounces each) plum tomatoes
2 tablespoons tomato paste
1 can (2 ounces) anchovies packed in oil
1 cup pitted Spanish Manzanilla olives, halved
½ cup golden raisins
¼ cup drained capers
2 teaspoons dried oregano
½ teaspoon crushed red pepper flakes, or more to taste
Salt and coarsely ground black pepper, to taste
¼ cup plus 2 tablespoons chopped fresh cilantro leaves or flat-leaf parsley
1 pound dried pappardelle or rigatoni pasta

1. Heat 4 tablespoons of the olive oil in a large heavy pot over low heat. Add the onions and cook, stirring once or twice, until wilted, about 10 minutes.

2. Add the bell peppers and garlic; cook, stirring, over low heat another 10 minutes.

3. Coarsely chop the plum tomatoes, reserving their juices, and add both to the vegetables along with the tomato paste. Cook, stirring once, until the sauce just begins to thicken, 5 minutes.

4. Coarsely mash the anchovies and add them with their oil to the pot. Stir in the olives, raisins, capers, oregano, pepper flakes, salt, and pepper. Increase the heat to medium-low and simmer uncovered, stirring occasionally, until blended through, about 30 minutes. Stir in ¼ cup cilantro and cook for 1 minute longer.

6. While the sauce is simmering, bring a large pot of salted water to a boil. Add the remaining tablespoon of oil and the pasta and cook until just tender. Drain the pasta and divide among 6 to 8 pasta bowls. Top with sauce and sprinkle with the remaining 2 tablespoons of cilantro. Serve immediately.

Serves 6 to 8

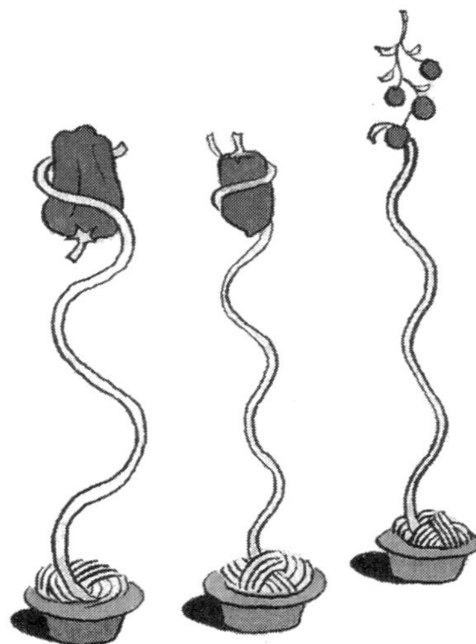

GRECIAN TOMATO SAUCE

There must have been a few gods missing from Mount Olympus the day someone stirred up this tomato sauce. Given my passion for tomatoes and my love for sweet and sour, I can't really say that I've ever tasted a better sauce. As might be expected, the tomatoes begin cooking with onions, garlic, and olive oil, but that's where the predictable ends. For magic comes from adding cinnamon sticks, honey, and wine, which impart an indescribable flavor. Just as the sauce finishes simmering, I brighten it with fresh mint leaves. Excellent served over pasta or as the cooking sauce for slowly braised meats, such as veal or lamb shanks.

¼ cup extra virgin olive oil
1 medium onion, cut into ¼-inch dice (about 1 cup)
3 cans (two 28 ounces each, one 14 ounces) plum tomatoes, drained but 1 cup juice reserved, tomatoes lightly crushed
1 tablespoon tomato paste
¼ cup honey
¼ cup dry red wine
2 large cloves garlic, lightly bruised (page 153)
2 cinnamon sticks (each 3 inches long)
¼ cup coarsely chopped fresh mint leaves

1. Heat the oil over low heat in a large heavy pot. Add the onion and cook to wilt, 10 minutes, stirring often.

2. Add the crushed tomatoes, with the reserved juice, the tomato paste, honey, red wine, garlic, and cinnamon sticks to the onion. Simmer uncovered, stirring occasionally, for 1 hour.

3. Remove the garlic and cinnamon sticks from the sauce and stir in the chopped mint. Serve immediately or cool slightly, transfer to a covered container, and refrigerate up to 3 days.

Makes 5 cups

RIO'S FEIJOADA · GAENG KUA GOONG · JERK CHICKEN

INDONESIAN PORK SATAY

STEAMED CLAMS ALENTEJO

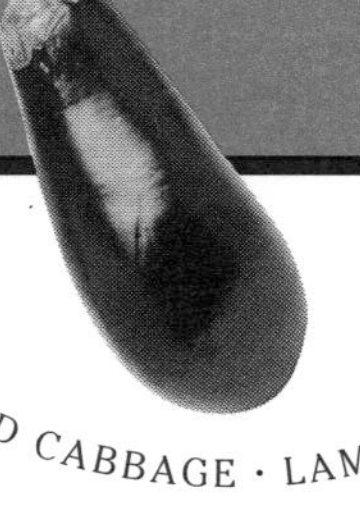

ANDALUSIAN STEAK ROLLOS · CHAKHOKBILI · DUBLIN CORNED BEEF AND CABBAGE · LAMB AND PRUNE TAGINE

PASTITSIO

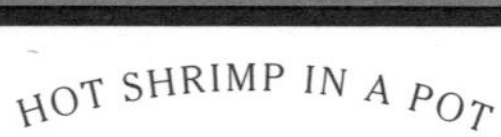

HOT SHRIMP IN A POT · THAI SEAFOOD SALAD · MEE SOTO · DANISH BEEF HASH

MU SHU CHICKEN BURRITO · POULET CHASSEUR

HALIBUT LEMON KEBABS · BLACK CURRANT DUCK BREASTS
RUSSIAN COD RAGOUT · MAMBO MANGO PORK
The Grand Tour
MADRAS CHICKEN SALAD
SPICED PELOPONNESIAN LAMB SHANKS
SRI LANKAN DEVILED BEEF RIBS
BLACK SEA BASS BAKED IN A SALT CRUST
ZARZUELA · SEARED GRAVLAX · ST. MARTIN'S DAY ROAST GOOSE

The Land

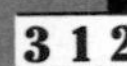

After not having eaten much meat in recent years, I had forgotten just how wonderful it could taste. It took a trip to Argentina to awaken my palate. I had gone there specifically to taste the beef and I was not disappointed. The highlight was the day I spent at an *asado,* a genuine barbecue, complete with handsome gauchos (Argentinian cowboys). Now, we're talking *real* beef (to say nothing of beefcake). Although there were no recipes to speak of, the quality of the meat was superb. Suddenly, meat preparations once more seemed innovative and exciting.

That Argentine visit led me to Brazil where I was inspired to create a Carnaval Corned Beef and a spectacular Feijoada. Around the world I continued, bringing back ideas for fiery Sri Lankan Deviled Beef Ribs, Japanese teriyaki dishes, the hottest of hot, spicy Jamaican Jerk Pork Ribs.

Once I started, the sky was the limit.

Although today we are unlikely to serve a meat dish to our guests, perhaps the times are changing again. Let's welcome meat back to the table.

SUNDAY FARMHOUSE ROAST PORK

There is nothing more delicious or pleasant than a simple French farmhouse lunch on a Sunday afternoon. Somehow a roast loin of pork served right from the oven or at room temperature, thinly sliced, perfectly complements a salad of buttery, green leaf lettuce dressed lightly with a delicate vinaigrette. A crusty baguette and a small selection of cheeses complete the meal. For the menu I'd choose simple cheeses, such as a ripe, creamy Camembert from Normandy and a regal sheep's milk Roquefort from southwest France. A crock of sweet creamy butter served with the cheeses enhances their flavors further. Small wooden bowls of large shelled walnuts and large, soft raisins and plump dried Turkish apricots are lovely accompaniments to the cheeses.

1 boneless pork loin (4 to 4½ pounds)
3 large cloves garlic, slivered
4 tablespoons (½ stick) unsalted butter, at room temperature
2 tablespoons Dijon mustard
1 tablespoon chopped fresh thyme leaves or 1 teaspoon dried
½ teaspoon coarsely ground black pepper
1 cup defatted Chicken Broth (page 127)
¾ cup dry white wine
1 tablespoon apricot jam or preserves

1. Preheat the oven to 350°F.

2. Cut deep slits in the pork loin with the tip of a small sharp knife and insert the garlic slivers. Place the pork in a shallow roasting pan. Set aside.

3. In a small bowl, mix together the butter, mustard, thyme, and pepper. Spread this evenly over the pork.

4. Heat the chicken broth, wine, and jam together in a small pan until the jelly dissolves and pour this over the pork.

5. Roast the pork on the center rack of the oven until cooked through (150° to 160°F on a meat thermometer), about 1½ hours or 20 minutes per pound; baste frequently, adding a bit more wine if necessary. Let the pork rest for 15 minutes before slicing.

Serves 8

HABANA LIBRA PORK ROAST

When we had our all too short visit to Havana, Cuba, we had lunch at La Bodeguita del Medio, Hemingway's favorite restaurant. Tucked away in a beautiful, old section of town, the buildings there still retain their gentle pastel colors. Soft guitars and red maracas carried through the palm-tree-lined courtyard. One memorable dish of our lunch was slices of roast pork smothered in soft onions. I've recreated it here, combining the spiciness and the sweetness that pervade so many Caribbean dishes. To enhance the flavors and aromas, I've studded the roast not only with garlic but also with slivered fresh ginger. Dark Jamaican rum, delicate cider vinegar, and a bit of broth make for a pungent basting liquid and succulent roast.

2 tablespoons olive oil
2 tablespoons unsalted butter
2 large onions, halved crosswise and slivered
1 boneless pork loin (about 3½ pounds)
3 cloves garlic, slivered
1 piece (1 inch) fresh ginger, peeled and slivered
½ teaspoon ground cloves
½ teaspoon ground cinnamon
½ teaspoon freshly ground black pepper
¼ cup honey
¼ cup plus 1 tablespoon (lightly packed) dark brown sugar
1 cup defatted Chicken Broth (page 127)
¼ cup apple cider vinegar
¼ cup dark Jamaican rum

1. Preheat the oven to 350°F.

2. Heat the oil and butter in a large skillet over medium heat. Add the onions and cook, stirring, until wilted, about 15 minutes. Place the onions in the bottom of a shallow roasting pan.

3. Cut deep slits in the pork loin with the tip of a small sharp knife and insert the garlic and ginger slivers. Mix the cloves, cinnamon, and pepper together and rub it all over the pork.

4. Place the pork loin on top of the onions. Drizzle the top of the pork with the honey, then sprinkle with the brown sugar. Combine the chicken broth, vinegar, and rum and pour this over the onions in the bottom of the pan.

5. Roast the pork until cooked through (150° to 160°F on a meat thermometer), about 1½ hours or 20 minutes per pound, basting frequently and moving the onions around in the liquid.

6. Remove the pork to a carving board, cover loosely with aluminum foil, and let rest for 15 minutes.

7. While the pork is resting, strain the sauce. Place the onions in a saucepan and pour the sauce through a gravy separator to remove any excess fat. Add the degreased sauce to the onions and heat over low heat.

8. To serve, thinly slice the pork and arrange on a platter. Top with the onion sauce.

Serves 8 to 10

SOUVENIR TO SAVOR

La Bodeguita del Medio

Considering it was Ernest Hemingway's favorite restaurant in Havana, it seems only appropriate that the place mats of La Bodeguita del Medio lean toward the literary. A marvelous poem, dedicated to the founder, is printed on the left side of the menu, and whimsical quips about the daily dishes are available on the right side.

Dedicated to The Little Grocery Store in the Center of Town and its founder, Angel Martinez.

The little grocery store is now a large grocery store,
In victory the banner waves in the air,
Whether it is a large grocery store or a small grocery store,
Our Cuba blossoms with good reason.

Whomever has money, cash, bread, green or dough,
will eat well there.
But if you don't have a dime and are very hungry,
There's always someone there who will care for you.

The cups are held high while the town sings its song.
While Martinez pours an abundance of vintage wine,
somewhere else.

I will be making a toast so that this story will repeat itself,
And so that the new large grocery store will
Never cease or forget to be the small, little grocery store.

—Nicolas Guillen

THE WINES OF

Spain

Spain was long a sort of sleeping giant in Europe, but becoming a full-fledged member of the European Economic Community (EEC) during the 80s brought dramatic changes. A surge of new energy swept through the country and its economy and enlivened the gastronomic scene along with everything else. Americans, who have recently discovered Spanish food, especially the delightful small plates called *tapas*, can now find some terrific wines to go with them—altogether new ones as well as traditional ones, like the inimitable sherry or Rioja, which have upgraded quality and become more stylish.

In Spain, the drink that accompanies *tapas* is dry sherry, typically Fino or Manzanilla, sometimes the darker dry Oloroso. Though imitations of sherry are made around the world, none has the warm, nutty, distinctive character of real Spanish sherry. Dry sherries, including the richer Amontillado, are best chilled. In addition to familiar brands—La Ina, Tio Pepe, Dry Sack, and La Gitana, one must add the

Top: A wine-cellar in Rueda—how do you get in? Bottom: A beautiful tile sign featuring a dry sherry from Sanlúcar de Barrameda, the center of the Manzanilla district. Right: The sign above the entrance to the Tinto Pesquera winery.

superb Lustau Fino and dark Almacenista Oloroso.

Spanish white wines have livened up significantly. Brightest among them is Albariño from Galicia in northern Spain, with its fresh, crisp, pear-like flavor, excellent with seafood dishes. The region of Rueda is also producing brisk, dry, appealing whites from the Verdejo grape under such labels as Martin Sancho, Marqués de Griñon, and Marqués de Riscal, excellent with shellfish and paella. Catalonia also has worthy white wines, including Torres Gran Vina Sol and Milmanda (both Cardonnay based) and Raimat Chardonnay.

Spain is better known for sturdy red wines. Rioja, especially Rioja Reserva and Gran Reserva (both of which are aged longer and more concentrated in flavor), has improved dramatically over the last decade, and is admirably suited to roast lamb or roast fowl and other meats. Those ranked among the top producers of Rioja include: Conde de Valdemar, Bilbainas, Cune, Loriñon, Bodegas Palacio Glorioso, Marqués de Arienzo, Marqués de Murrieta—most of whom also produce good dry white wines and dry, fresh *rosados* (rosés).

Red wines from other regions, however, are creating much of the excitement over Spanish wines. Among these are the dark, richly concentrated Pesquera from Bodegas Fernandez in Ribera del Duero, Lar de Barros from Extremadura, Gran Fuedo, Señorio de Sarria, and Toro Gran Colegiata, robust reds from Navarra, and the new, vigorously stylish versions of Cabernet and Merlot from Torres, Marqués de Grinon, Viña Magaña, and Raimat. These are reds that complement heartier meat dishes, game, and some of Spain's flavorful cheeses, like aged Manchego.

"Though imitations of sherry are made around the world, none has the warm, nutty, distinctive character of Spanish sherry."

MAMBO MANGO PORK

Inspired by the many delicious moist pork dishes and the cornucopia of luscious tropical fruit available throughout the Caribbean, I've married ripe, juicy pineapple and pungent mango chutney into a succulent basting sauce. Serve the pork thinly sliced with the sauce atop.

1 boneless pork loin (about 3½ pounds)
3 cloves garlic, thinly slivered
4 tablespoons (½ stick) unsalted butter
1 tablespoon Colombo Curry Powder (page 259) or best-quality curry powder
4 cups diced (½ inch) fresh pineapple
1½ cups pineapple juice
1½ cups defatted Chicken Broth (page 127)
½ cup mango chutney

1. Preheat the oven to 350°F.

2. Cut deep slits in the pork loin with the tip of a small sharp knife and insert the garlic slivers. Place the pork in a shallow roasting pan. Set aside.

3. Melt the butter in a large deep skillet over medium-low heat. Add the curry powder and cook, stirring, for 3 minutes to mellow the flavor. Add the pineapple and cook, stirring, over medium heat, for 5 minutes. The pineapple should be well coated with the curry butter. Stir in the juice and broth. Bring to a boil and continue to boil uncovered for 10 minutes. Remove the pineapple from the sauce with a slotted spoon and place it on and around the pork loin. Pour ½ cup of the sauce over the pork; reserve the rest for basting.

4. Roast the pork uncovered for 1 hour, basting occasionally. Spread the chutney over the top of the pork. Baste and roast until cooked through (150° to 160°F on a meat thermometer), about 30 minutes more; add more liquid to the pan if necessary for basting. Let rest for 10 to 15 minutes before slicing.

5. To serve, thinly slice the roast, transfer to a serving platter, and spoon the pineapple sauce atop.

Serves 8 to 10

HONG KONG PORK CHOPS

This recipe started out in my kitchen as a version of *char shu* pork (Chinese-style roast pork), but it finished up as pork chops marinated in Hong Kong flavors. The savory dipping sauce is essential to the chops and is quite charming served in small decorative bowls alongside each dish. As you cut the chops, you dip a bite. Remember that with the leaner pork these days, no more than 20 minutes cooking time is necessary or they will dry out.

DIPPING SAUCE:
6 tablespoons soy sauce
6 tablespoons hoisin sauce
4 teaspoons honey
2 teaspoons Chinese chili sauce (available in Asian markets)
2 teaspoons minced garlic

SOUVENIR TO SAVOR

Shopping in Hong Kong

Hong Kong's vast markets offer something for everyone. They also take into account certain sensibilities. The open-air meat markets here, for instance, thoughtfully have distinctive rows of red-shaded overhead lights so that vegetarians are forewarned of their presence. Every part of the butchered cow is proudly displayed on large metal hooks, forming garish curtains of slaughtered flesh in front of wall-less shops. A carnivore's delight. Nearby, huge pig carcasses, roasted or barbecued to a crusty brownish gold, are sold off by the catty—about 1½ pounds. The pork seller expertly hacked off a sizable chunk and wrapped it for me in brown paper.

I moved on. Past the snake shop with its curative wares of snake blood and snake meat. Past the stalls with their vats of pickled vegetables. Past the dried fish and barrels of shrimp, carefully segregated according to size. Past the three-foot-high mound of washed bean sprouts.

The streets are kept amazingly clean thanks to frequent hosing by the stall keepers. So there is constantly a thin sheet of water underfoot. Shoppers walk gingerly, avoiding puddles and the spray of the hose.

When I visited, durian was in season. You catch the unmistakable sewer-like aroma fifty feet away. Still, durian devotees are drawn to this bizarre, prehistoric-looking fruit like bees to honey. Huge and heavy as watermelons, the fruit has a thick and frighteningly prickly armor that encases the velvety smooth flesh. I wonder how long it took for someone to realize that there was anything worth eating inside. It is an acquired taste that I haven't yet acquired. The mangoes, on the other hand, smell marvelous, are readily available most of the year, and can be carted home without the aid of a pickup truck. I'll stick with them.

MARINADE:
3 tablespoons soy sauce
3 tablespoons Oriental sesame oil
3 tablespoons hoisin sauce
3 tablespoons dry sherry
1 tablespoon minced garlic
1 tablespoon minced peeled fresh ginger
1 shallot, finely chopped
½ teaspoon salt

6 thick (1½ inches) center-cut loin pork chops (about 4½ pounds)
2 tablespoons honey
2 tablespoons Oriental sesame oil

1. Prepare the dipping sauce by combining all the ingredients in a medium bowl; divide among 6 little bowls and set aside.

2. Combine the marinade ingredients in a large bowl. Add the pork chops and toss to coat completely. Let rest covered at room temperature for 2 hours, turning a few times.

3. Combine the honey and sesame oil in a small bowl.

4. Place 2 nonstick skillets, large enough to hold 3 pork chops each, over medium heat. Brown the chops lightly, 5 minutes per side basting with the honey mixture. Reduce the heat to medium-low, cover, and cook, turning the chops after 8 minutes, until the chops are cooked through, about 15 minutes.

5. Serve each chop with a little bowl of dipping sauce.

Serves 6

Satay

Satays are spicy Indonesian bite-size meat or chicken barbecues. A selection of several satays is always an important component of a *rijsttaffel.* Peanut sauce, Indonesian soy sauce, and other sweet and savory sauces are served alongside for dipping. The choices of meat and distinctive marinades give each variety a unique character. Satays make great hors d'oeuvres because they're easily prepared ahead and then grilled or broiled just before serving. When placing the meat on a bamboo skewer, place it closer to the pointed end so that it can be taken off easily—in three bites. It's also very important to soak the little bamboo skewers in water for at least an hour before using them so that they don't burn under the broiler. Use your creativity, play with different combinations, and enjoy these delicious flavors.

PORK SATAY

Scallions, ginger, garlic, and cumin give a rich distinctive flavor to this pork satay. Let the pork marinate at least 2 hours before grilling or broiling. Serve with peanut sauce for dipping.

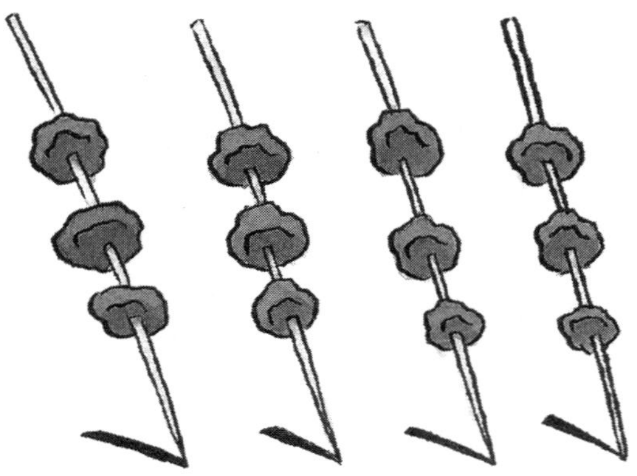

1 pound boneless pork loin
4 scallions (3 inches green left on), minced
1 tablespoon minced peeled fresh ginger
2 teaspoons minced garlic
½ cup Indonesian Soy Sauce (page 79)
Finely grated zest and juice of 1 lime
½ teaspoon ground cumin
Saus Kacang (page 71)

1. Cut the pork into ¾-inch cubes.

2. Combine the remaining ingredients except the *saus kacang* in a mixing bowl. Add the pork and toss well. Cover and let marinate at room temperature for 2 hours.

3. Soak 24 thin bamboo skewers, 3 to 4 inches long, in water for 1 hour while the pork is marinating.

4. Preheat the broiler.

5. Thread 3 pieces of marinated pork on each skewer, leaving a bit of space between the pieces. Place the skewers on a broiling pan.

Broil 4 inches from the heat source, basting and turning once, until just browned and cooked through, about 3 minutes per side. Serve hot or warm with *saus kacang* (peanut sauce) for dipping.

Makes 20 to 24 skewers; serves 5 to 6

LE COLIBRI PORC COLOMBO

Rich Curried Pork

When I headed for Martinique, I was on the lookout for the great Creole food that I knew could be found at remote porch restaurants scattered in the hills on the island. Typically these porch restaurants are simply an extension of the home kitchen. A few tables are set out on the porch attached to the house.

After driving several hours north from Fort-de-France through the sugar cane to Morne d'Esses, we reached Le Colibri (the hummingbird) for a 12:30 luncheon reservation. Three tables were covered with simple flowered cotton cloths. Brown-and-white checked napkins rested in wineglasses and flopped charmingly over the edges. No two tables had the same linen, and the effect was extremely homey. I knew I would find exactly what I was looking for, which was a great *colombo,* rich curried stew. Traditionally it is made with baby goat in the Caribbean, but I chose the pork.

The *colombo,* served family style, was rich in both color and flavors. And I learned a secret. After the meat is marinated in fresh lime juice and garlic to flavor and tenderize, it is sprinkled with sugar and spices before being browned in oil, which caramelizes it. What a taste! I've thickened this sauce by adding sweet potatoes. Try making your own *colombo* (curry powder) for great authentic flavor.

3 pounds boneless pork shoulder, cut into 2-inch pieces
4 cloves garlic, minced
½ cup fresh lime juice
¾ cup sugar
1½ teaspoons ground allspice
¾ teaspoon ground cinnamon
2 tablespoons olive oil, or more if needed
1 large onion, coarsely chopped
2 tablespoons Colombo Curry Powder (page 259) or best-quality curry powder
6 cups defatted Chicken Broth (page 127)
6 carrots, peeled and cut into ½-inch-thick rounds
3 sweet potatoes (about 12 ounces), peeled and cut into 1-inch chunks
1 green bell pepper, stemmed, seeded, and cut into 1-inch pieces
2 bay leaves
2 fresh thyme sprigs, or 1 teaspoon dried
5 to 6 cups cooked white rice

1. Combine the pork, garlic, and lime juice in a bowl. Cover and let marinate at room temperature for 1 hour.

2. Preheat the oven to 350°F.

3. Combine the sugar, allspice, and cinnamon in a large bowl. Remove the pork from the marinade and coat it with the sugar mixture, rubbing it into the meat well.

4. Heat the oil in a large heavy pot over medium-high heat. Brown the pork in small batches, adding more oil if necessary. Remove the browned pork pieces to a bowl.

5. Add the onion to the pot and cook, stirring, over medium-low heat until wilted, 10 minutes. Sprinkle the curry powder over the onion and cook, stirring, for 1 minute. Add 2 tablespoons chicken broth if the onions begin to stick.

6. Return the pork to the pot along with the carrots, sweet potatoes, and green pepper. Add the bay leaves, thyme, and chicken broth. Bring to a boil, reduce the heat, and simmer, partially covered, for 30 minutes. Uncover and simmer over medium heat until the pork is tender, about 45 minutes. Remove the thyme and bay leaves and serve with white rice.

Serves 6 to 8

RIO'S FEIJOADA

There is nothing like a cold snowy day for making Brazil's famous national dish, *feijoada*. Simply put, this is really a large hearty pot of pork and beans, but the Brazilians have elevated the combination to great heights. Make it and invite company over for a feast. This recipe lists the cuts of meat I used to make this dish, but you may vary your choices, according to your taste and what is available. The pork selection should include some smoked cuts, some fresh cuts, some spicy, and some mild.

There are traditional side dishes to serve with *feijoada*, such as collard greens (try Copacabana Collards, see Index), peeled and thinly sliced oranges, and a large bowl of white rice. In Brazil, I was served tiny hot red peppers soaked in oil to spice things up even more.

I added a halved orange to the beans and pork as the cooking began, so that a fresh citrus flavor would permeate the beans, the sauce, and all the meats. In my *feijoada*, it is the secret ingredient. Straying further from tradition, I also added sweet red bell peppers, onions, and garlic to enrich the sauce as it finishes cooking.

This recipe will feed about eight people, but if you want to feed more, simply increase the amount of sausages and other small meats. If the beans get dry and you need to add more liquid, be sure it is boiling before you add it. Chicken broth is a good choice instead of water for more flavor. I have not added any salt because some of the meat may be salty. But then I never add salt to beans while they're cooking, because I believe it keeps them from softening.

Serve *feijoada* with a robust, full-bodied Rioja red wine and have plates of watermelon and ripe cantaloupe on hand for a perfect finale.

1½ pounds dried black beans, rinsed, then soaked overnight in water to cover
1 pork knuckle (about 1 pound)
8 ounces slab bacon, rind discarded, cut into ½-inch pieces
8 ounces Polish kielbasa, cut into 2-inch lengths
8 ounces spicy frankfurters
8 ounces uncooked sausages, such as bratwurst
12 ounces lightly smoked Westphalian ham, cut into 2 thick slices
1 pound pork belly
1 to 1½ pounds smoked boneless pork chops, or more if you are serving more than 8, each chop halved
4 medium onions, chopped
1 orange, halved
3 bay leaves
Coarsely ground black pepper, to taste
4 tablespoons olive oil
8 cloves garlic, coarsely chopped
1 large red bell pepper, stemmed, seeded, and cut into small dice

1. Drain and rinse the beans and place them in a very large heavy casserole. Add all the meat, half the chopped onions, the orange, bay leaves, and black pepper.

2. Cover the ingredients with water by about 1 inch. Bring to a boil, skimming off any scum that rises to the top. Reduce the heat to medium-low and simmer uncovered until the beans are tender and meats are cooked, about 1½ hours.

3. While the meat and beans are cooking, heat the olive oil in a large nonstick skillet over low heat. Add the remaining onions, the garlic, and bell pepper and cook until wilted, about 10 minutes. Set aside.

4. When the meat is done, remove it to a large bowl. Cover to keep warm. Remove and discard the orange halves.

5. Purée 1 cup of the beans in a food processor with on and off pulses, and stir the purée back into the beans. Stir in the cooked onion mixture.

6. To serve, heat the beans through. Place the meat in a large, decorative, rustic serving bowl. Spoon the beans over the meat or serve them directly from the casserole.

Serves 8

THE WINES OF

Argentina and Brazil

Argentina is Latin America's largest wine producer, ranking fifth in the world in terms of quantity. Most of it is consumed by the Argentines themselves, and considerable amounts elsewhere on the continent. Until recently, Argentine wine producers have concentrated more on quantity than quality, producing a great deal of wine in bulk, including huge quantities of sparkling wine. Moët et Chandon has a large facility in Argentina (M. Chandon), as does Piper-Heidsieck.

The best Argentinian wines come from the province of Mendoza, situated at an elevation of 2,000 feet in the Andean foothills. Irrigated by run-off from the snow-capped mountains, vineyards planted to Cabernet Sauvignon, Merlot, Malbec, Chardonnay, and Sauvignon Blanc have shown the greatest potential for quality.

After a typical ranch barbecue (asado), entertainment is provided by the gauchos. Love the background fabric.

Argentines love red wine. Most of the better wines, particularly the sturdy Cabernets and Malbecs made to accompany Argentina's prized beef, come from smaller wineries, such as Bodegas Weinert, Canale, Luigi Bosca, and San Telmo, all noted for Cabernet and red blends. The giant firm of Peñaflor, however, has several premium labels, such as Trapiche or Fond de Cave reserved styles, which are among Argentina's best values. Italian red grapes are plentiful, including the workhorse red, Barbera, but Sangiovese and Nebbiolo also show potential in cooler microclimates.

White wines have become more stylish in recent years. Argentina grows a good deal of Riesling, Pinot Blanc, Gewürztraminer, and Chenin Blanc as well as prolific lesser varieties, such as Palomino and Torrontes. White wines made from Chardonnay and Sauvignon Blanc (often with Sémillon in the blend), however, have begun to approach international standards for these varieties. The result is attractive wines that are versatile with food and moderately priced.

Brazil aspires to winegrowing, but the warm, humid climate on either side of the equator makes it somewhat difficult. There are sizeable vineyards in the extreme south, but the most success in terms of quality has been at higher, cooler elevations that are well drained. Italian immigrants had some impact in southern Brazil, and in recent decades some progress has been made with Cabernet, Zinfandel, and Barbera. Little is exported, however, and in Brazil's cities, still wines from Argentina, Chile, California, and Europe are favored. Domestic sparkling wines are popular; Moët has one of its largest sparkling wine facilities in Brazil.

"The best Argentinian wines come from the province of Mendoza, situated at an elevation of 2,000 feet in the Andean foothills."

***Left to right:** One of the notable red blends from Bodegas Weinert. A great "steer" to the Cabana restaurant in Buenos Aires. At La Cinacina ranch, a gaucho sets up for games on horseback.*

JERK PORK RIBS

When you're shopping for ribs, look for a slab of pork barbecue ribs. Cut them into 2- to 3-rib portions before marinating. By prebaking the ribs in the oven for 45 minutes, they will cook to perfection on the grill without burning to a crisp. What you'll end up with are succulent ribs flavored throughout with Jamaican jerk sauce. Wonderful! If you've made extra jerk sauce, serve some alongside for dipping.

1 slab pork ribs for barbecuing (about 3 pounds), cut into 2- or 3-rib portions
2 cups Jamaican Jerk Sauce (recipe follows)

1. Coat the ribs with the jerk sauce and rub it in well, using rubber gloves if hot chilies are in the sauce. Cover and refrigerate overnight.

2. Preheat the oven to 350°F.

3. Remove the ribs and any excess marinade to a shallow roasting pan. Bake for 45 minutes, turning the ribs and basting them occasionally.

4. Prepare a grill with medium-hot coals.

5. Grill the ribs until browned and cooked through, 25 to 30 minutes. Turn them 4 or 5 times and baste often with jerk sauce. Serve hot.

Serves 6

SOUVENIR TO SAVOR

Island Secrets

In Montego Bay I spent lots of lunchtimes at the Pork Pit, sitting with the locals at green picnic tables under palm trees heavy with ripe coconuts eating jerk pork and chicken (my favorite). At this roadside joint (literally), with trucks and buses rattling by, the great Jamaican barbecue was served up in plastic baskets lined with paper. Along with the pork and chicken, I devoured yellow yams roasted in foil and deep-fried cornmeal crullers. All this we washed down with cold bottles of Red Stripe beer.

During one of the times I lined up to place my order, I tried to convince some of the staff to give me the recipe for their jerk sauce, which they were selling for $30 (Jamaican) a jar. No dice. They weren't giving away any secrets, just selling the sauce and T-shirts and yellow baseball caps with the Pork Pit logo emblazoned on the front.

Fortunately I met Norma Shirley, an extraordinary, talented woman, who recently had opened two splendid restaurants in Kingston and Montego Bay after moving back to her native Jamaica from New York. After spending many evenings together, I finally felt I knew her well enough to ask her for a jerk sauce recipe.

Norma was delightfully forthcoming with the ingredients, but I had to wait until I got home to figure out the proportions. If she hadn't told me, I never would have guessed soy sauce and orange juice in combination with allspice, thyme, and Scotch bonnet chilies. Spicy, sweet, and sour flavors comprise this great island barbecue sauce.

JAMAICAN JERK SAUCE

Here's an island-spiced, fiery jerk marinade thanks to Norma Shirley, who shared the ingredients to her great jerk sauce with me. She said for the best jerk, chicken, pork, and ribs are marinated and then slowly barbecued between pimento (allspice) leaves. Her recipe is really hot, so add the chilies to your own taste—but don't be too timid!

6 scallion greens, thinly sliced (reserve the white bulbs for another use)
2 large shallots, minced
2 large cloves garlic, minced
1 tablespoon minced peeled fresh ginger
½ Scotch bonnet or habanero chili, seeds and ribs removed, minced
1 tablespoon ground allspice
1 teaspoon freshly ground black pepper
¼ teaspoon cayenne pepper
1 teaspoon ground cinnamon
½ teaspoon ground nutmeg
1 tablespoon fresh thyme leaves, or 1 teaspoon dried
1 teaspoon coarse salt
1 tablespoon (packed) dark brown sugar
½ cup fresh orange juice
½ cup rice wine vinegar
¼ cup red wine vinegar
¼ cup soy sauce
¼ cup olive oil

1. In a bowl, combine the scallion greens, shallots, garlic, ginger, and chili. Set aside.

2. In another bowl, combine the spices, thyme, salt, and sugar. Into the spices, whisk the orange juice, both vinegars, and the soy sauce. Slowly drizzle in the oil, while whisking constantly. Add the scallion mixture and stir to combine. Let rest at least 1 hour before marinating meat and poultry.

Makes 2½ cups

SOUVENIR TO SAVOR

Jamaican Jerk

The hot stuff coming from the smoky, brightly painted barbecue stands that line Jamaica's beaches is their great jerk. Pork or chicken, soaked in a spicy hot marinade, then barbecued, is as Jamaican as reggae and rum.

They say the jerk tradition goes back to the 17th century when the Maroons, fugitive African slaves, combined their skills for slow pit-roasting with the native Arawak Indians' talent for spicing with local allspice and hot chilies. The Maroons combined the blazing marinade with salt and used it to preserve the wild boars they hunted in the remote mountains of Jamaica. Techniques and spicing secrets were handed down through generations.

Today competition and pride run high among the best jerk cooks. Some use dry marinades, while others swear by their devilishly wet mixtures. But all the cooks baste the meat religiously as it cooks.

In Jamaica, allspice wood is plentiful, and the island's best jerk is grilled over it for a unique flavor. Whatever the method, jerk dishes fire up the palate and leave you craving for more.

RACK OF LAMB WITH TARRAGON HERB RUB

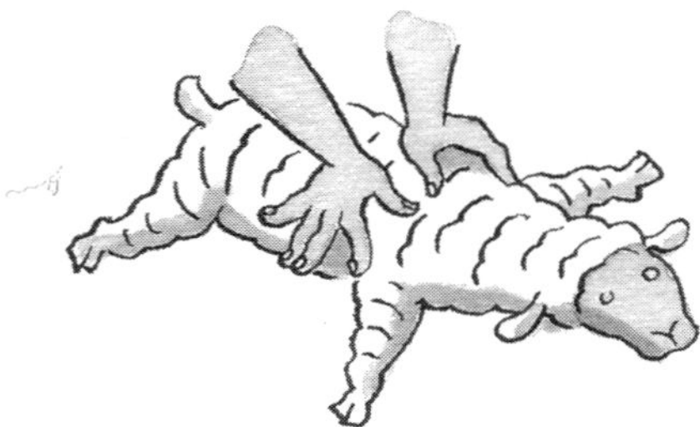

There was nothing I enjoyed more in Denmark than their tender rosy lamb embellished with delicious tarragon sauces or rubs. In honor of those much enjoyed meals, I've made a simple yet fragrant rub to enhance a delicate rack of lamb. It is elegant for a small dinner party or a romantic meal, served with Rhubarb Compote and Delicate Herbed Potato Pancakes (see Index). When shopping for a rack, look for a small one, about 1½ to 2 pounds. That's where you'll find the small loin chops, which are the most tender and delicious.

1 small rack of 8 loin lamb chops (about 1½ pounds), bones frenched
1 large clove garlic, slivered
½ orange
2 tablespoons olive oil
2 tablespoons dried tarragon
1 tablespoon dried thyme
1 tablespoon coarsely ground black pepper
1 teaspoon coarse salt

1. Preheat the oven to 500°F.

2. Cut deep slits all over the lamb with the tip of a small sharp knife and insert the garlic slivers. Squeeze the orange half all over the lamb, then brush lightly with the oil. Combine the dried herbs, pepper, and salt in a bowl and pat all over the lamb.

3. Place the lamb, fat side up, in a roasting pan. Place the pan on the center rack of the oven and roast for 10 minutes. Reduce the heat to 400°F and roast another 20 minutes for rare meat. Remove from the oven and let rest for 5 minutes before carving. Serve immediately.

Serves 4

HERB ROASTED LEG OF LAMB

There is nothing delicate or quiet about this succulent Greek roasted leg of lamb. Garlic, oregano, and black pepper have a natural affinity for one another, and the aroma permeating the air while the lamb cooks is extraordinary. Rare to medium-rare lamb has the greatest appeal for me. Once you take it out of the oven, it continues to cook for about 10 to 15 minutes. Save the leftovers for lamb salads and pita sandwiches filled with lots of fresh vegetables and Spiced Yogurt Slather (see Index).

1 leg of lamb (6½ to 7 pounds)
4 cloves garlic, slivered
2 tablespoons olive oil
1 tablespoon dried oregano
1 tablespoon coarsely ground black pepper
1 cup dry white wine

1. Preheat the oven to 400°F.

2. Place the leg of lamb in a large roasting pan. Cut deep slits all over the lamb with the tip of a small sharp knife and insert the garlic slivers. Brush the entire surface with the olive oil.

3. Mix the oregano and pepper together in a small bowl and rub this all over the lamb. Pour the wine into the bottom of the pan.

4. Place the lamb in the oven and reduce the heat to 350°F. Roast, basting occasionally, about 1½ hours. A meat thermometer inserted in the lamb should read about 140°F for rare meat. Let rest for 10 minutes before carving. The temperature will rise a bit.

5. Defat the pan juices in a gravy separator, heat through, and serve alongside the meat.

Serves 8

LAMB SATAY

Lamb loves marinades. In this one, the pungent tastes of Indonesian soy sauce, chili paste, ginger, and garlic are brightened with fresh lime juice and cilantro. The lamb should marinate at least 1 hour, but if you want to prepare it a few hours ahead, it will be fine. When serving satay for hors d'oeuvres, be sure that the pieces of meat are no larger or smaller than ¾-inch cubes. If they're too small, they'll dry out when they're cooked; if too large, they're hard to eat in one bite.

1 pound lean boneless lamb shoulder
1 small onion, minced
1 tablespoon minced peeled fresh ginger
2 teaspoons minced garlic
½ cup Indonesian Soy Sauce (page 79)
1 tablespoon fresh lime juice
1 teaspoon chili paste
2 tablespoons finely chopped cilantro leaves and stems
Saus Kacang (page 71), for dipping

1. Cut the lamb into ¾-inch cubes.

2. Combine the remaining ingredients except the *saus kacang* together in a mixing bowl. Add the lamb and coat well with the marinade. Cover and let stand at room temperature for 1 hour.

3. While the lamb is marinating, soak 24 thin bamboo skewers, 3 to 4 inches long, in water for 1 hour.

4. Preheat the broiler.

5. Thread 3 pieces of the marinated lamb on each skewer, leaving a bit of space between the pieces. Set the skewers on a broiling pan. Broil 4 inches from the heat source, basting and turning once, until browned and just cooked through, 2 to 3 minutes per side. Serve hot, warm, or at room temperature with *saus kacang* (peanut sauce) for dipping.

Makes 20 to 24 skewers, serves 5 to 6

EXOTIC LAMB CURRY

There is nothing I love more than combining unexpected ingredients to create magical flavors. Such is the case with this stew. Lamb always makes a wonderful stew base because of its rich and succulent flavor. Once the spices are added and mellowed, the sauce is further enriched with fresh ginger and thickened with tart apples and—here's the unexpected—sweet bananas. This curry uses a lot of curry powder. Not to worry—it's splendid.

¼ cup olive oil, or more if needed
3 pounds boneless lamb shoulder or leg, cut into 2 x 1½-inch cubes
2 onions, coarsely chopped (about 3 cups)
6 cloves garlic, minced
1 piece (1 inch) fresh ginger, peeled and minced
2 Granny Smith or other tart apples, cored and cut into ½-inch cubes (about 4 cups)
2 slightly underripe bananas, sliced ¼ inch thick (about 2 cups)
5 tablespoons all-purpose flour
½ cup best-quality curry powder
2 teaspoons ground nutmeg
1 teaspoon ground cardamom
1 teaspoon salt
2 cinnamon sticks (each 3 inches long)
5 cups defatted Chicken Broth (page 127)
½ cup coconut milk, (page 252 or available in specialty food stores)
½ cup chopped fresh cilantro leaves

1. Heat the oil in a large heavy pot over medium-high heat. Brown the lamb cubes in the hot oil in small batches. Remove to a bowl and set aside.

2. To the oil remaining from the lamb, add the onions, garlic, ginger, apples, and bananas. Add more oil, if necessary. Sauté, stirring often, over medium heat until tender and lightly colored, about 10 minutes.

3. Sprinkle the flour, curry powder, nutmeg, cardamom, and salt over the onion mixture, add the cinnamon sticks, and combine well. Cook, stirring constantly, for 5 minutes to mellow and bring out the flavors of the spices.

4. Return the browned lamb cubes to the pot and add the chicken broth. Mix well. Bring the mixture to a boil over medium-high heat. Reduce the heat, cover, and simmer for 1 hour, stirring occasionally. The sauce should have a creamy, thick consistency.

5. Remove the curry from the heat and gradually stir in the coconut milk and then the fresh cilantro. Serve warm over Spicy Marigold Rice and accompany with Raita Cool Down (see Index).

Serves 8

SPICED PELOPONNESIAN LAMB SHANKS

One doesn't expect to find North African influences in Greek cooking, but when I was served a casserole of lamb and prunes slowly cooked in a white wine sauce, I learned that this particular dish was rooted in regional Peloponnesian tradition. Lamb shanks have an affinity for long slow cooking with wine-based sauces and dried fruits. The foreshanks are from the front legs, and their long thin appearance makes for elegant single servings. The woodsy flavor of sage marries well with honey, cloves, and cinnamon. Fresh mint stirred in just before serving adds a bright note. Serve these lamb shanks with Lemon Orzo or Seven Vegetable Couscous (see Index).

4 lamb foreshanks (about 1 pound each)
1 teaspoon coarse salt
1 teaspoon coarsely ground black pepper
3 tablespoons olive oil
1 medium onion, cut in half lengthwise and slivered
1 cup defatted Rich Beef Broth (page 128)
1 cup dry red wine
2 tablespoons honey
4 large cloves garlic, lightly bruised (page 153)
2 cinnamon sticks (each 3 inches long)
4 fresh sage leaves
Pinch of ground cloves
1 cup seeded and coarsely chopped ripe plum tomatoes
1½ cups pitted prunes
¼ cup chopped fresh mint leaves

1. Preheat the oven to 350°F.

2. Sprinkle the lamb shanks all over with the salt and pepper. Heat 2 tablespoons of the oil in a large heavy casserole over medium heat. Add the lamb shanks, 2 at a time, and sauté until well browned, about 8 minutes per side. Remove the lamb and pour off the fat.

3. Add the remaining 1 tablespoon oil to the casserole and place over low heat. Add the onion and cook, stirring occasionally, until wilted, about 10 minutes.

4. Return the lamb shanks to the casserole. Add the beef broth, red wine, honey, garlic, cinnamon sticks, sage, and cloves. Bring to a boil. Cover the casserole and bake until the meat is soft, 1 hour.

5. Stir in the chopped tomatoes and prunes and cook uncovered until both are blended into the sauce, 45 minutes longer. Before serving, stir in the fresh mint.

Serves 4

YOGURT KEBABS

When I started my eating tour of Turkey, I began hearing about these great yogurt kebabs. They're a terrific idea and easily prepared with pitas, some tomato sauce, yogurt, and leftover lamb warmed up or your favorite kebab right off the grill. For summer entertaining, this becomes a most dramatic presentation. I've made this recipe with leftover lamb from a roast and tossed it with lemon juice and zest for extra freshness. If lamb is not your favorite, shredded chicken or grilled vegetables would make a lovely substitute. A crisp cucumber salad is all you need to complete the meal.

2 tablespoons extra virgin olive oil
1 tablespoon finely grated lemon zest
1 tablespoon fresh lemon juice
¼ teaspoon coarse salt
¼ teaspoon freshly ground black pepper
3 cups cubed (½ inch) roasted leg of lamb, warmed
4 pita breads (6 inches in diameter), cut into 1-inch squares
3 cups Grecian Tomato Sauce (page 309), hot
1½ cups nonfat plain yogurt
2 tablespoons coarsely chopped flat-leaf parsley
4 ripe plum tomatoes, seeded and cut into ½-inch dice
4 scallions (3 inches green left on), sliced ¼ inch thick on the diagonal

1. Place the olive oil, lemon zest, lemon juice, salt, and pepper in a bowl and whisk to blend. Add the lamb and toss to cover the cubes completely.

2. Spread the pita squares on the bottom of a large serving platter. Cover the pita evenly first with the tomato sauce and then with the yogurt.

3. Distribute the lamb pieces evenly over the yogurt layer. Sprinkle with 1 tablespoon of the parsley. Scatter the tomatoes evenly over the parsley and sprinkle the remaining tablespoon of parsley and the scallions over the top.

Serves 4

LAMB AND PRUNE TAGINE

There is something quite special about Moroccan *tagines,* and they deserve a much wider audience in America. In essence, these are slowly simmered pungent and sweet stews that truly require less fuss and bother than your basic beef stew. One saving grace is that it is not necessary to brown the meat. Another is that there's no call for any complicated butter and flour roux, because dried fruits, such as prunes, dates, and figs, both flavor and thicken the sauce. In this tagine, blanched almonds add another interesting texture to the lamb and fruit, and the addition of the whole lemon peel brings just the right balance to the sweet fruits. Once the ingredients are added to the pot, all you'll have to do is stir and taste occasionally. Tagines are wonderful served in shallow bowls over couscous or another favorite grain. Once you've made one, you'll be able to create your own versions with other seasonings and ingredients.

¼ cup olive oil
1 large onion, grated
2 tablespoons minced garlic
1 teaspoon ground cinnamon
1 teaspoon ground cumin
½ teaspoon ground coriander
½ teaspoon ground ginger
½ teaspoon salt
¼ teaspoon coarsely ground black pepper
3 pounds boneless lamb shoulder, cut into 3-inch chunks
2½ cups defatted Rich Beef Broth (page 128)
2 cinnamon sticks (each 3 inches long)
Peel of 1 lemon
1½ cups pitted prunes
1 cup whole blanched almonds

1. Place the olive oil, grated onion, garlic, cinnamon, cumin, coriander, ginger, salt, and pepper in a large heavy pot. Stir them together, then add the meat. Roll the meat into the spice mixture to coat well.

2. Add the broth, cinnamon sticks, and lemon peel. Bring to a boil over high heat, then reduce the heat and gently simmer, partially covered, over medium-low heat for 30 minutes. Stir in the prunes and almonds and continue to cook until the lamb is tender, about 30 minutes longer. Remove the cinnamon sticks and lemon peel before serving.

Serves 6

S O U V E N I R   T O   S A V O R

Restaurant "Yacout"

From time to time throughout my amazing journey, I fell in love with a particular market or restaurant. So it was with Yacout, a restaurant secreted within the sienna-hued medina of Marrakech, which captured my everlasting adoration.

From the time we made the reservation, which is essential, we felt completely cared for. On the evening of October 13, 1992, there was a perfect full moon. Richard and I left our hotel in a "petit taxi" for the restaurant. After slowly meandering through the medina, we came to a stop precisely in front of a gentleman dressed in a white *djellaba* (caftan) and wearing a dark red fez on his head. He opened the door of the cab and escorted us through a door we never would have noticed. Once inside, we were in another world. First we were led up a flight of winding stairs to a rooftop terrace covered from one end to the other in magnificent kilim rugs. Chairs were brought to us along with a small table inlaid with mother of pearl. We ordered aperitifs, which arrived in cranberry cut-crystal glasses. From our chairs we viewed the moonlit medina and heard the faint exotic sounds of a distant oud, a hauntingly beautiful musical instrument.

Our descent to the dining room led to only more splendor. Round tables draped in white linen were surrounded by lush, small blue velvet banquettes. The room was lit by ecru candles held in ornate, antique brass candlesticks. Each table was heavily scattered with pink and red rose petals, which subtly shared their perfume.

In preparation, our hands were washed with rose water from a long-necked silver pitcher. The feast began with a startling array of small salads in the style of Fez. There were sweetened tomato marmalade, mashed carrots sprinkled with fresh mint, puréed eggplant and green peppers, sautéed zucchini with mint, finely diced and sautéed chicken livers sprinkled with cinnamon, warm phyllo triangles filled with minced meat, and onions served on a bed of fresh mint sprigs. To accompany the salads, bread was graciously passed in a green and red velvet *port au pain*—a conical bread basket—embroidered in gold.

For my entrée, I chose succulent pigeons, stuffed with giblets, livers, and ground almonds and stewed in a delicate broth. Richard chose a tagine of lamb, smothered in green beans and preserved lemons; tomatoes and black peppers infused the sauce. Wine was poured throughout the meal from a blood-red etched, cut-glass decanter.

For dessert we shared an amazing dessert *bisteeya,* with the layers of crisply fried *warka*—a phyllo-like pastry—drizzled with thick, rich almond milk. We ended our dinner with glasses of mint tea poured in a steady confident stream from a silver pitcher, held high to aerate the tea.

Once again, our hands were washed with rose water and we were led to the door and into an awaiting taxi. The entire experience was so perfect, so dreamlike, it was almost as if the evening hadn't really existed—but no illusion could have left us with such vivid memories.

INDIVIDUAL MOUSSAKAS

I hadn't eaten moussaka since its trendy heyday in the 1960s. Then during a recent visit to Crete, Christopher Veneris, chef/owner of Kalypso, a beachside taverna, prepared, upon my request, a sensational moussaka for two. This moussaka was light, wonderfully seasoned, and seemed very new. The delicate individual servings in this recipe should put the dish back on the menu.

2 Idaho potatoes (about 8 ounces each), peeled and cut into 1/4-inch slices
4 tablespoons (1/2 stick) unsalted butter
6 tablespoons all-purpose flour
3 cups defatted Chicken Broth (page 127), hot
1/4 teaspoon ground nutmeg
Salt and freshly ground black pepper, to taste
4 tablespoons olive oil, plus more for oiling the ramekins
3 medium zucchini, ends trimmed, cut into 1/4-inch slices
2 small onions, coarsely chopped
1 tablespoon minced garlic
2 pounds ground lamb
1 cup Grecian Tomato Sauce (page 309) or other tomato sauce
1 tablespoon tomato paste
1 bay leaf
2 teaspoons ground cinnamon
2 teaspoons dried oregano
4 tablespoons chopped flat-leaf parsley, plus more for garnish
1/4 cup dry red wine
4 ripe medium tomatoes, sliced 1/4 inch thick
4 ounces Kasseri cheese or other semihard cheese, grated
1 cup Creamy Yogurt (page 248), for garnish

1. Place the potato slices in a medium-size saucepan and add cold water to cover. Bring to a boil, lower the heat slightly, and boil gently, partially covered, until tender, 8 to 10 minutes. Drain and set aside.

2. To make the sauce, melt the butter in a medium-size heavy saucepan over medium heat until it begins to bubble. Whisking constantly, add the flour and cook until the mixture is lightly colored but not browned, 1 to 2 minutes. Add the chicken broth slowly, whisking constantly to make a smooth paste. Bring the mixture to a gentle boil and cook, whisking constantly, until the mixture is thickened and smooth, 3 to 4 minutes. Remove from the heat and season with the nutmeg, salt, and pepper. Set aside.

3. Heat 2 tablespoons of the oil in a large skillet over medium heat. Add the zucchini in batches and sauté until golden brown, about 3 minutes per side. Drain on paper towels and sprinkle with salt and pepper. Set aside.

4. Add the remaining 2 tablespoons oil to the skillet. Add the onions and cook for 5 minutes over low heat. Add the garlic and cook 5 minutes longer.

5. Add the lamb to the onions and break up the meat well. Cook, stirring, over medium-high heat until well browned, about 10 minutes. Remove any liquid and fat in the pan, then stir in the tomato sauce, tomato paste, bay leaf, cinnamon, oregano, 2 tablespoons of the parsley,

and the wine. Season with salt and pepper. Simmer, stirring occasionally, until the liquid is absorbed, about 10 minutes. Remove and discard the bay leaf. Set aside.

6. Preheat the oven to 400°F. Lightly oil six 8-ounce ramekins, and set them on a baking sheet.

7. Spoon about ½ cup of the meat mixture into the bottom of each ramekin. Cover each one with a layer of potato slices, about 4 depending on their size; add several slices of zucchini and then 2 slices of tomato. Sprinkle all the ramekins with salt and pepper and the remaining 2 tablespoons parsley. Spoon ¼ cup sauce over each moussaka and sprinkle each with 1 tablespoon grated cheese.

8. Bake the moussakas until heated through and the cheese is melted, about 30 minutes. Sprinkle with chopped parsley and dollop with creamy yogurt. Serve hot.

Serves 6

MEXICAN POT ROAST

Pot roast is a time-honored and satisfying meal, but when braised deliciously with the wonderful ingredients that go into a classic Mexican *picadillo,* it becomes memorable. In this recipe tomatoes, cinnamon, raisins, capers, and olives blend with sweet carrots, onions, and garlic to blanket a lean first-cut brisket. I'll have to answer to my mother, Berta, for this one because I've strayed from her recipe, but I'm sure she'll understand. Serve this pot roast over wide noodles.

2 tablespoons olive oil
1 first-cut beef brisket (about 4½ pounds)
Coarsely ground black pepper, to taste
2 medium onions, halved and slivered
6 medium carrots, and cut into 1-inch lengths
4 cloves garlic, minced
1 teaspoon ground cinnamon
2 cans (28 ounces each) plum tomatoes
1 cup pitted green olives, chopped
½ cup golden raisins
2 tablespoons drained tiny capers
1 tablespoon (packed) dark brown sugar
1 dried small hot chili, or to taste
Coarse salt, to taste

1. Preheat the oven to 375°F.

2. Heat the oil in a large ovenproof casserole over medium-high heat. Add the meat and brown it well on both sides, sprinkling it generously with black pepper. Remove the meat to a large plate.

3. Pour off most of the fat in the casserole. Add the onions and carrots; cook, stirring and scraping up any browned bits on the bottom, over medium heat until the onions are golden, about 10 minutes. Add the garlic and cinnamon; cook 1 minute longer, stirring constantly.

4. Drain the tomatoes, reserving 1 cup of the juices. Crush the tomatoes with your fingers and add them to the casserole along with the reserved juices, the olives, raisins, capers, brown sugar, chili, salt, and a pinch of pepper. Bring to a boil and remove from the heat.

5. Return the meat to the casserole, placing it on the vegetables, and spoon some of the sauce over the top. Cover and bake for 2 hours.

6. Remove the pot roast to a board, scrape off the sauce, and cut it into thin slices on the diagonal and against the grain. Gather the roast back together and return it to the casserole. Cover the meat completely with the sauce and season with salt and pepper.

7. Bake uncovered, basting the meat occasionally with the sauce, until it is tender, about 1½ to 2 hours longer. Serve hot with lots of sauce on top or alongside.

Serves 8 to 10

MAGYAR GOULASH

Goulash, or shepherd's stew, the national dish of Hungary, calls for the best-quality paprika that you can find. *Edes nemes* (noble sweet) is the best choice for this recipe. Poppy red and delicate, it lends the most marvelous color, aroma, and flavor to the cooking broth. The addition of wide egg noodles towards the end of the cooking time makes this robust stew a perfect one-pot meal.

4 ounces slab bacon, rind discarded, cut into ¼-inch dice
1 tablespoon lard
1 large onion, coarsely chopped
1 tablespoon minced garlic
2 tablespoons sweet paprika
½ teaspoon caraway seeds
2 pounds beef rump, cut into 2-inch cubes
1 medium parsnip, peeled and cut into 1-inch pieces
4 cups defatted Rich Beef Broth (page 128), warmed
2 pale green Italian frying peppers, stemmed, seeded, and cut into 1-inch pieces
1 red bell pepper, stemmed, seeded, and cut into 1-inch pieces
2 medium Idaho potatoes, peeled and cut into ½-inch cubes
4 plum tomatoes, peeled, seeded, and cut into 1-inch pieces
Salt, to taste
4 ounces wide, short dried egg noodles
½ cup chopped flat-leaf parsley

1. Place the bacon and lard in a large heavy pot and cook over low heat until the bacon browns slightly, about 5 minutes.

2. Add the onion and cook, stirring, over low heat for 5 minutes. Add the garlic and continue to cook until the onion is wilted, about 5 minutes longer.

3. Off the heat, stir in the paprika and caraway seeds. Add the beef, parsnip, and broth. Bring to a boil, reduce the heat, cover, and gently simmer over low heat 1½ hours.

4. Add all the peppers, the potatoes, tomatoes, and salt. Increase the heat to medium and cook uncovered for 30 minutes.

5. Stir in the noodles and cook until the noodles are tender, about 10 minutes longer.

6. Stir in the parsley. Serve piping hot in shallow bowls with coarse black bread and creamy butter.

Serves 6

SOUVENIR TO SAVOR

Gundel of Budapest

In a glorious mansion on the fringes of the City Park near Heroes' Square in Budapest, sits what is a remarkable landmark restaurant that Karoly Gundel opened in 1910. Not far away is the zoo and an enormous lake which serves as an ice-skating rink in the winter, looking for all the world like a Norman Rockwell's best *Saturday Evening Post* cover. On its reopening on May 22, 1992, after a complete restoration, George Lang has clearly brought the magic of Gundel back.

The main dining room with George Lang, proprietor extraordinaire.

In the summer when the weather is fine, one can dine *al fresco* in the restaurant's fabulous garden, but dining anytime in the elegant main dining room brings one back to a time past. The room reminded me of what dinner on a grand ocean liner might have been like at the turn of the century. Silky blue banquettes lined the rosewood-paneled walls, which were adorned with a stunning collection of ornately framed paintings by Hungarian artists. Polished Biedermeier-style chairs surrounded crisp white linen-covered tables. A richly patterned carpet and huge Chinese vases filled with fresh flowers warmed the room. Near the kitchen doors on a slightly raised platform stood a small gypsy band whose violins sang throughout the meal. The handsome waiters dashed about in black jackets and long white aprons, hoisting large trays above their heads and creating plenty of excitement. The knowledgeable sommelier, with his large silver *tastevin* hanging from a silver chain around his neck, produced a never-ending succession of delicious and exciting Hungarian wines.

I looked forward to a splendid meal based on Gundel's marvelous original recipes. My dinner began with Hungarian housewife's-style foie gras served with small baked potatoes and was followed by a second appetizer of a poached mushroom cap filled with a delicious chopped mushroom mixture and set atop a rich sweet sauce. My main course was fried carp in a red sauce served with buttered noodles. For dessert, I couldn't resist the famous *palacsinta*—crêpes spread with a rum-laced walnut, raisin, orange zest, and cream filling, folded in quarters, and doused in chocolate sauce. Coffee served in small cups with a tiny pitcher of warm milk alongside provided the perfect ending. I loved the accompanying silver sectioned holder filled with granulated sugar, dark and light crystallized sugars, and shavings of dark chocolate. Finally, to avoid a sleepless night, I accepted the generous offering of *csepp,* or "60 drops"; this grape and juniper berry drink was served icy cold and purported to aid digestion. It worked—I returned to the hotel for a night of sweet dreams and exceptional memories.

PASTITSIO

Pastitsio (Corfu macaroni) combines the best of the two pasta dishes that have been comforting American palates for years—pasta with meat sauce and macaroni and cheese. Real Greek home cooking, which holds no aspirations to lofty elegance, shines through in this dish, but in deference to our eating habits today, I've omitted the thick cheese sauce from the classic preparation.

For this pastitsio, I begin with a small piece of beef brisket and cook it like a slowly braised pot roast in a tomato sauce infused with cinnamon and orange zest. Spooned over penne or ziti and sprinkled with coarsely grated Kasseri cheese (or another semihard cheese like provolone), this is a completely satisfying dish. Serve it with a crisp colorful Greek salad.

1 first-cut beef brisket (2½ pounds)
Salt and coarsely ground black pepper, to taste
2 tablespoons olive oil
2 medium onions, halved lengthwise and slivered
2 carrots, peeled and quartered
2 cloves garlic, lightly bruised (page 153) and peeled
1 can (28 ounces) plum tomatoes, crushed, with their juices
1 tablespoon tomato paste
½ cup dry red wine
¼ cup honey
2 cinnamon sticks (each 3 inches long)
1 teaspoon dried oregano
1 long strip of orange peel, pith removed
1 pound tube-shaped dried pasta, cooked
4 ounces Kasseri cheese or other semihard cheese such as provolone or Emmental, grated

1. Preheat the oven to 350°F.

2. Sprinkle the brisket generously with salt and pepper. Heat the oil in a heavy ovenproof casserole over medium-high heat, add the brisket, and brown it well on all sides. Remove the meat to a plate.

3. Reduce the heat to low. Add the onions and cook until softened, about 10 minutes, scraping up any browned bits on the bottom. Add the brisket, carrots, garlic, tomatoes and juices, tomato paste, wine, honey, cinnamon sticks, oregano, and orange peel. Stir to combine.

4. Bake covered for 1½ hours. Remove the meat to a plate and slice it thinly on the diagonal and against the grain. Return the sliced meat to the casserole and gently combine it with the sauce. Bake covered for another 30 minutes, then remove the cover and bake 1 hour longer. Before serving, remove the cinnamon sticks and orange peel.

5. Divide the cooked pasta between 8 shallow pasta bowls. Ladle the meat sauce over the pasta and sprinkle with the grated cheese.

Serves 8

ANDALUSIAN STEAK ROLLOS

In this recipe butterflied flank steak is marinated in Spain's intensely aromatic sherry vinegar from Andalusia, the country's southernmost region. Garlic and fruity olive oil flavor the mixture along with fresh cilantro. The steak is filled in the center with a pungent stuffing of roasted peppers, raisins, olives, and cured ham. When sliced, the pattern in the center of the meat resembles a rich mosaic. Serve with small bowls of Orange-Rosemary Mayonnaise and Fiesta Corn Salsa (see Index) for velvety and crisp contrasts.

MARINADE:
1/4 cup sherry vinegar
1/4 cup extra virgin Spanish olive oil
3 cloves garlic, minced
5 tablespoons chopped fresh cilantro leaves
Coarsely ground black pepper, to taste

1 flank steak (1 to 1 1/4 pounds), butterflied (see Note)
2 red, yellow, or orange bell peppers, halved lengthwise and roasted (page 202)
3 tablespoons chopped fresh cilantro leaves
8 thin slices prosciutto or other cured ham
1/4 cup coarsely chopped pitted Spanish Manzanilla olives
1/2 cup golden raisins
12 to 16 small fresh spinach leaves, stems removed
Freshly ground black pepper, to taste
Flat-leaf parsley or watercress, for garnish

1. For the marinade, combine the vinegar, olive oil, garlic, cilantro, and black pepper in a shallow baking dish. Add the flank steak and turn it to coat. Cover the dish and marinate at room temperature for about 2 hours, turning the steak twice.

2. After the steak has marinated, scrape it clean and lay it open on a piece of aluminum foil on a flat surface.

3. Preheat the oven to 350°F. Reserve the marinade.

4. Cover the steak with the roasted pepper halves. Sprinkle with 2 tablespoons of the cilantro. Cover with prosciutto. Sprinkle the entire surface evenly with the olives and raisins. Top with the spinach leaves, remaining 1 tablespoon cilantro, and black pepper to taste.

5. With the long side of the steak facing you, carefully lift the end from the foil and roll it tightly away from you, in jelly-roll fashion. Tie the steak roll at 2- to 3-inch intervals, using kitchen string.

6. Place the meat in a shallow baking dish and pour the marinade over the top. Bake until browned and cooked through, about 30 minutes, basting once or twice. Remove from the oven and let rest for 10 minutes before slicing.

7. To serve, cut the steak into 1/2-inch slices and arrange on a decorative platter. Garnish with parsley or watercress.

Serves 6 to 8

Note: Have your butcher butterfly the flank steak or do it yourself: With one long side of the steak facing you, run a thin sharp knife horizontally through the middle thickness of the meat, stopping 1/2 inch before reaching the opposite long side to create a hinge. Open the meat to resemble a butterfly.

SRI LANKAN DEVILED BEEF RIBS

Sri Lanka, a jewel of a country formerly known as Ceylon, rests in the Indian Ocean off the southern tip of India. Famous for tea, Sri Lanka also has a distinctive spiced cuisine of its own. Cardamom, one of the great Asian aromatics, perfumes these devilishly spiced beef ribs. Each diner can increase the intensity of heat to their own taste by adding a splash of chili sauce. Serve the ribs and sauce along with Spicy Marigold Rice and Mango Chutney (see Index) for an exotic cold-weather meal.

6 pounds beef short ribs, cut into pieces (2 meaty ribs per serving)
2 large onions, halved and slivered
1 tablespoon seeded, ribbed, and finely diced jalapeño or other fresh hot chili, or according to the heat of the chili and personal taste
2 tablespoons minced garlic
2 tablespoons minced peeled fresh ginger
8 whole cloves
1 tablespoon chili powder
2 teaspoons ground cardamom
½ teaspoon ground turmeric
1½ teaspoons salt
⅓ cup red wine vinegar
Asian chili sauce (available in Asian markets), for serving (optional)

1. Combine the ribs with all the other ingredients except the chili sauce in a large heavy pot. Add enough water to cover by 1 inch.

2. Bring to a boil uncovered over medium-high heat. Reduce the heat to medium, skim any foam that rises to the surface, and simmer, partially covered, until the beef is tender, about 2 hours. Let the fat rise to the top and carefully skim it off with a metal spoon.

3. Serve immediately. Pass the chili sauce.

Serves 6

SWEDISH MEATBALLS

The hallmark of a true "gourmet" cook in the late sixties was the freshly polished copper chafing dish on any buffet table, filled with Swedish meatballs in a creamy dill sauce. I scoured Sweden for the real McCoy but, alas, all I found were meekly spiced meatballs with no sauce. Nostalgia won out, so I made a version that will send you searching for that chafing dish. These meatballs are also just right as an entrée, spooned over mashed potatoes.

1 pound ground beef
1 small onion, finely grated
1 tablespoon finely chopped garlic
1 teaspoon ground allspice
¼ teaspoon plus a pinch ground nutmeg
¼ cup plus 3 tablespoons chopped fresh dill
1 large egg, lightly beaten
¼ cup dried bread crumbs
Salt and coarsely ground black pepper, to taste
2 tablespoons vegetable oil
½ cup defatted Rich Beef Broth (page 128)
1 tablespoon Cognac
1 cup crème fraîche
Coarsely ground white pepper, to taste

1. Mix the beef, onion, garlic, allspice, ¼ teaspoon nutmeg, ¼ cup chopped dill, the egg, bread crumbs, salt, and pepper. Form into 30 walnut-size meatballs.

2. Heat the oil in a large nonstick skillet over medium heat. Sauté the meatballs in 2 batches, shaking the skillet occasionally, until browned on all sides and cooked through, 8 to 10 minutes. Remove to a paper towel to drain.

3. Pour off any oil in the skillet. Add the broth and Cognac to the skillet and cook over high heat, scraping up any browned bits on the bottom, until slightly reduced, about 1 minute. Whisk in the crème fraîche, 2 tablespoons of the remaining dill, the remaining pinch of nutmeg, and white pepper to taste. Cook, stirring, over medium heat for 4 minutes. Add the meatballs to the pan and cook for 10 minutes, spooning the sauce over the meatballs as it thickens. Before serving, sprinkle with the remaining 1 tablespoon dill.

Makes 30 cocktail meatballs, serves 6 as an entrée

MEAT LOAF A LA LINDSTROM

Strolling through the markets in Sweden, I kept seeing bright pink hamburger-like patties being sold in the butcher stands. According to the signs accompanying the patties, they were called "Lindstroms." A closer look revealed beets in the mixture. I couldn't get to the bottom of who Lindstrom is or was, but it seems that these hamburgers are a favorite in Sweden and are often served with a fried egg on top! I think the meat mixture makes a better meat loaf than a hamburger. Served with Garlicky Mashed Potatoes and Dilled Cucumber Salad (see Index), it's great Sunday night eating. Many thanks to the Lindstrom family.

1 pound ground beef
1 pound ground pork
1 small onion, grated
1 medium Roasted Beet (page 194), peeled and coarsely grated
1 Idaho potato, cooked, peeled, and cut into small dice
1 tablespoon minced garlic
1 large egg, lightly beaten
1/4 cup chopped fresh dill
1 teaspoon ground allspice

1. Preheat the oven to 350°F.

2. Place the meats in a bowl. Add the remaining ingredients and gently toss to combine. Do not overmix.

3. Form the mixture into a thick round loaf and place it in a shallow ovenproof dish. Bake until cooked through, about 1 hour. Let rest for 10 to 15 minutes before slicing.

Serves 8

SOUVENIR TO SAVOR

Café Lumskebugten

Before we talk hash, a bit must be said about Café Lumskebugten, a perfectly charming restaurant in Copenhagen that reminded me of a cross between Scandinavian Victorian and a parlor scene out of a Chekhov story. Established in 1854 by Karen Marguerita Krog and located at the end of the Esplanaden along the harbor, the restaurant was a haven for sailors and originally served just hash, homemade beer, and schnapps. As the restaurant's reputation grew, aristocrats, artists, and members of the Danish royal family joined the enthusiastic diners. There is still a beautiful private room set aside for Queen Margrethe and her guests.

The food—all four dishes I sampled—was excellent. I particularly loved their renowned hash and offer their recipe, below.

LUSCIOUS BEEF HASH

Totally unlike any I've tasted, the hash at the Café Lumskebugten was lavish with large shreds of boiled beef mixed into coarsely mashed potatoes. Four small bowls of garnishes arrived: one with snipped fresh chives, another with diced cooked beets, one with butter balls, and the fourth with crème fraîche.

For myself, I'd omit the butter garnish. Don't even think of serving this "hash" for breakfast. It's fancy enough to go to the best dinner party.

1 tablespoon olive oil, or more if needed
4 pounds beef short ribs, cut into about 3-inch pieces
Coarsely ground black pepper, to taste
1 medium onion, peeled and halved
4 whole cloves
1 medium carrot, scrubbed and cut into chunks
4 cloves garlic, lightly bruised (page 153) and peeled
1 bay leaf
10 cups water
4 Idaho potatoes, peeled and cut into 1-inch cubes
Coarse salt, to taste
2 tablespoons unsalted butter
3 tablespoons snipped fresh chives
1½ cups diced (¼ inch) Roasted Beets (about 2 medium, page 194), for serving
1 cup sweet gherkins or cornichons, for serving
½ cup drained prepared white horseradish, for serving
¼ cup Dijon mustard, for serving

1. Heat the oil in a large heavy pot over medium-high heat. Add the short ribs in batches and brown well on all sides, about 3 to 4 minutes. Sprinkle the ribs with pepper as they cook. Remove with a slotted spoon to a bowl. If the pan becomes too dry, add more oil.

2. Return the meat to the pot. Stud the onion with the cloves and add it along with the carrot, garlic, bay leaf, and water to the meat. Bring to a boil, reduce the heat, and simmer gently, partially covered, for 2 hours. Skim off any foam that rises to the top during cooking.

3. Remove the meat to a bowl and set aside. Strain the broth, measure and reserve 2½ cups broth, and return the remaining broth to the pot. Add the potatoes to the remaining broth in the pot with enough water to cover. Bring to a boil, lower the heat slightly, and boil gently, partially covered, until the potatoes are tender enough for mashing, 25 to 35 minutes.

4. Shred the meat into large pieces (about 1 inch). Season with salt and pepper and toss with 1 cup of the reserved broth. Place in an ovenproof dish, cover, and keep warm in a low (250°F) oven.

5. Drain the potatoes and coarsely mash them so that some chunks remain. Add the butter, 1 cup of the reserved broth, and salt and pepper to taste; stir until well mixed.

6. To serve, remove the shredded meat from the oven. If it seems dry, toss it with the remaining ½ cup of reserved broth. Divide the mashed potatoes between 6 plates. Spoon the meat with the juices atop the potatoes and sprinkle with the chives. Place the roasted beets, pickles, horseradish, and mustard in small bowls and serve with the hash.

Serves 6

GRANNY REESMAN'S STUFFED CABBAGE

My Granny Reesman made the best sweet-and-sour cabbage ever. My sister Elaine was smart enough to spend a day taking notes as Granny cooked. So when I left an emergency message on Elaine's answering machine asking her if she had the recipe, she was able to produce a little index card with the recipe which said "Quoted by Rose Reesman to Elaine Block Yanell."

1 medium head green cabbage (about 3 pounds)
1 pound ground beef
1 large egg, lightly beaten
½ cup cooked barley
¼ cup chopped fresh dill
½ teaspoon salt
¼ teaspoon freshly ground black pepper
2 tablespoons unsalted butter
3 medium onions, halved and slivered
½ cup golden raisins
Juice of 2 lemons
2 tablespoons (packed) brown sugar
1 can (28 ounces) plum tomatoes, crushed, with their juices

1. Remove the tough outer leaves and core from the cabbage and discard.

2. Bring a large pot of lightly salted water to a boil. Add the cabbage and cook until the leaves pull apart easily, about 5 minutes. Remove the cabbage and drain upside down.

3. Carefully separate the large leaves, saving the smaller leaves, and pat dry with paper towels. Sliver the small firm center of the cabbage and set aside.

4. Combine the beef, egg, barley, dill, salt, and pepper in a small bowl. Set aside.

5. With a small sharp knife, cut out the tough center rib of each of the large leaves in a V shape.

6. Place a large cabbage leaf on a work surface with the core end facing you. Lay a smaller leaf on top to cover the cut-out V area. Place 2 tablespoons of the meat mixture in the center, about 1 inch from the edge closest to you. Fold the right and left sides over the filling, then roll the leaf up from the bottom to make a cabbage roll, similar to an egg roll. Secure with a toothpick.

7. Melt the butter in a large heavy pot over low heat. Add the onions and slivered cabbage; cook, stirring, for 5 minutes. Add the raisins, lemon juice, and sugar; continue to cook, stirring, 10 minutes more. Add the tomatoes and juices and bring to a boil. Remove from the heat.

8. Ladle 1 cup of the tomato mixture into the bottom of a large heavy pot. Arrange about 8 cabbage rolls, seam side down, loosely in the bottom of the pot. Layer the remaining rolls on top and cover with the remaining tomato sauce. Bring to a boil, then reduce the heat to low. Cover and cook for 2 hours, checking the pot occasionally. If the sauce boils too hard, reduce the heat further. If the liquid seems to be drying up, add a bit of water.

9. To serve, place the cabbage rolls in a large shallow bowl, remove the toothpicks, and spoon the sauce atop.

Serves 6 to 8

DUBLIN CORNED BEEF AND CABBAGE

To me, this pungent, satisfying dish has always been the ideal centerpiece for a splendid Sunday luncheon in March. When I visited Ireland, I expected to find it everywhere but to no avail. It is reserved primarily for those nostalgic Easter Sunday dinners. In addition to cabbage, I love the flourish of leeks, carrots, potatoes, and parsley served alongside the meat. For a more delicate flavor, I've perfumed the cooking liquid with whole cloves and orange zest. Ladle some of the liquid over the beef and vegetables before serving, then accompany the dish with Orange Horseradish Cream and garnet-hued Cumberland Sauce alongside.

1 lean corned beef brisket (4 to 5 pounds)
3 medium onions, peeled
9 whole cloves
14 carrots, peeled, 6 halved and 8 cut into 2-inch lengths
4 cloves garlic, peeled
3 ribs celery with leaves, halved
6 flat-leaf parsley sprigs
Strips of whole peel from 1 orange, pith removed
16 small new red potatoes
8 medium leeks (2 inches green left on), roots trimmed, rinsed well
1 medium-size green cabbage (3 to $3\frac{1}{2}$ pounds), cored and cut into 8 wedges
Salt and coarsely ground black pepper, to taste
4 tablespoons coarsely chopped flat-leaf parsley
Orange Horseradish Cream (recipe follows)
Cumberland Sauce (recipe follows)

1. Rinse the corned beef and pat dry. Place it in a large ovenproof casserole. Stud each onion with 3 cloves and add to the casserole along with the 6 halved carrots, the garlic, celery, parsley sprigs, and orange peel.

2. Cover the meat and vegetables with cold water and bring to a boil. Reduce the heat to medium and simmer, partially covered, until the meat is very tender, about 3 hours. Skim off any foam and turn the meat every 30 minutes. When the meat can easily be pierced with a fork, it is done. Remove to a plate, cover with aluminum foil, and keep warm.

3. Strain the broth and return it to the casserole. Discard the cooked vegetables. Add the potatoes, leeks, cabbage, 8 cut-up carrots, salt, and pepper. Bring the broth to a boil, then simmer uncovered over medium heat until the vegetables are tender, about 30 minutes. Stir in 2 tablespoons of the parsley.

4. Before serving, slice the corned beef and place on a large decorative serving platter. Arrange the vegetables around the corned beef. Ladle some hot broth over all to moisten. Sprinkle with the remaining parsley. Serve with the cumberland sauce and orange horseradish cream alongside.

Serves 6 to 8

ORANGE HORSERADISH CREAM

I serve this tangy horseradish cream with Cumberland Sauce alongside Dublin Corned Beef and Cabbage. Its lightly spiced flavor and texture are just right with the pungent taste of corned beef. Traditionally, horseradish cream sauces are served in Ireland and England alongside roast beef too. The addition of fresh orange zest enlivens all the flavors.

½ cup crème fraîche
½ cup mayonnaise
½ cup drained prepared white horseradish
2 tablespoons finely grated orange zest
2 tablespoons Dijon mustard
½ cup heavy (or whipping) cream
Pinch of sugar
Salt and freshly ground black pepper, to taste

1. Combine the crème fraîche, mayonnaise, horseradish, orange zest, and mustard in a bowl.

2. In another bowl, whip the heavy cream until it forms soft peaks.

3. Using a rubber spatula, fold the whipped cream into the crème fraîche mixture. Add the sugar, salt, and pepper; stir well. Transfer to a serving bowl. Serve immediately or store covered in the refrigerator for up to 4 hours.

Makes about 2½ cups

CUMBERLAND SAUCE

This sweet and savory sauce, made from ruby port and red currant jelly, was first introduced to me by Barry Wine, chef-owner of the former Quilted Giraffe restaurant. Fresh shallots and thinly slivered orange and lemon zests contribute texture and sparkle to the ruby-hued condiment. Throughout the British Isles you'll find Cumberland sauce served with game pâtés and cold meats. It's a nice alternative to the sweet mint jelly that often accompanies lamb.

2 cups red currant jelly
½ cup ruby port wine
1 tablespoon finely slivered orange zest
1½ tablespoons finely slivered lemon zest
¼ cup fresh orange juice
¼ cup fresh lemon juice
½ cup finely chopped shallots
1 tablespoon dry mustard
1½ teaspoons ground ginger
1½ teaspoons coarsely ground black pepper
½ teaspoon salt

1. Combine all the ingredients in a small saucepan over medium-low heat. Stir frequently until the jelly has melted, 5 to 10 minutes. Remove to a bowl and cool to room temperature.

2. Refrigerate until the sauce sets to the consistency of jelly, about 2 hours. Cumberland sauce will keep covered in the refrigerator for up to 2 days.

Makes about 3½ cups

THE BEERS OF

The British Isles

Beer is the national beverage of the British Isles, the drink of commoners and royals alike. When the British say beer, they mean ale, the traditional brew throughout England, Scotland, Ireland, and Wales. It may be "pale ale" (actually a coppery-reddish color), dark brown, as in porter or brown ale, or almost black, as in stout. The darker the roast of the barley, the deeper the color, and usually, the richer and stronger the taste. Lager is also made in Britain, but to a much lesser extent than in America or Germany (where lager originated). The technical distinction between ale and lager is the type of yeast used in fermentation. With ale the yeast used rises to the top of the vat, with lager the yeast used settles to the bottom.

"A good ale must not be served too cold. Most pubs in England serve ale at cellar temperature, around 55°F . . . a bit warmer than Americans are used to, but to the British, any chillier would mask the flavors."

The more important differences, however, have to do with flavor, weight, and mouth-feel. Generally, lagers are crisp and zesty, better perhaps for quenching thirst. Pale ales will do the same, but ales in general have more complexity and nuance of character—exceptional ones, in fact, are savored like fine wines. A good ale must not be served too cold. Most pubs in England serve ale at cellar temperature, around 55°F since most are in buildings old enough to have dark, cool cellars. That temperature is a bit warmer than Americans are used to, but to the British, any chillier would mask the flavors. Lagers are generally served colder, worth remembering perhaps when you're traveling in England.

There are some 70,000 pubs in Britain, nearly half of them serving the most tradi-

Wouldn't you look in at your local if he tended bar?

tional and individual of brews: cask-conditioned ale. Ale is put into barrel with a bit of residual sugar and live yeast, promoting a light secondary fermentation that creates a mild natural carbonation. Cask-conditioned ales are matured at the pub, with different barrels offering slightly different nuances of flavor and carbonation levels. At peak, which ideally is the only time the cask is broached, the brew is fresh and lively, fruity, slightly yeasty, faintly sweetish, but countered with the bitter accent of fine hops. It is served only on draft, hand-pulled, of course.

This is the "real" ale that was in danger of disappearing during the 60s as the large breweries (Britain's Big Six) swallowed up small breweries, standardized styles, and reduced the amount of malted barley by using cheaper adjuncts like corn. Beer lovers nationwide rose in protest, organizing the Campaign for Real Ale (CAMRA) to restore traditional standards—and launched the brewpub and microbrewery movement that has now spread worldwide. There is great regional loyalty to local pubs and breweries and the cask-conditioned ales they produce. Some pubs

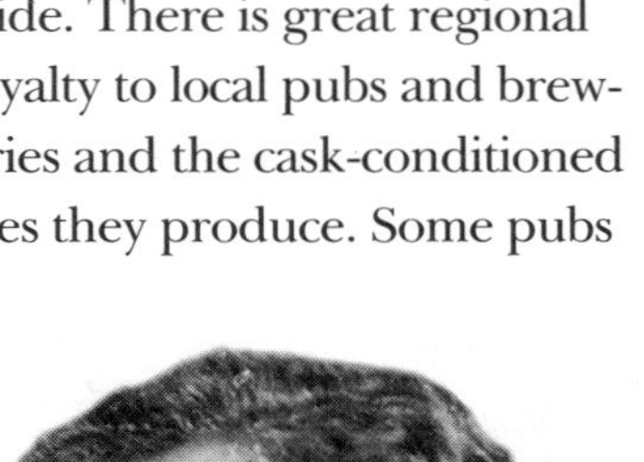

opt for "bright" ale, which is cask-conditioned at the brewery then decanted into new casks for the pub, but purists don't consider this "real" ale.

Cask-conditioned ale should not be confused with keg ale, a filtered, probably pasteurized draft that is mass-produced by large breweries. This is not to say that the "Big Six" (Bass, Allied Brewers, Whitbread, Watney, Courage, Scottish & Newcastle) don't produce good beer; most produce some well-regarded ales and dark beers. But with some sixty independent breweries in Great Britain, an equal number of microbreweries, as well as dozens of brewpubs cropping up (or disappearing), there is endless variety for the adventurous palate. Tops among the smaller operations are Samuel Smith (Yorkshire), Fuller, and Shepherd Neame (Kent), Young (London), Greene King (Suffolk), Timothy Taylor, Old Mill, Tetley, and Theakston (Yorkshire), to name just a few.

Ireland and Scotland

Dry stout is Ireland's claim to brewing fame, a uniquely satisfying brew, nearly black in color, rich in flavor, with creamy texture, and wonderful roasty, chocolatey

Top left to top right: The Jolly Judge in Edinburgh starts rocking at noon on Sunday. In Dublin the Lord Edward was filled at lunchtime, but only half the folks were eating. A coaster from one of my pub stops. Malt stacked up in a Scottish microbrewery. Ye Olde Masons Arms awaits the hungry in Devonshire. Samuel Smith is one of the better microbrewers in Great Britain. The Goblet, another one of my stops in Ireland.

"Scottish beers tend to be strong ales—rich and warming against the bone-chilling climate of Scotland."

flavors. Irish stout is drier than those made in England (such as Mackeson's). Guinness is the prototype for stout the world over, but Murphy's and Beamish are equally popular in the Emerald Isle. Guinness Extra Stout for export, interestingly, is stronger than the home product. Ireland makes good lager, such as Harp, but stout is the true Irish quaff.

Scottish beers tend to be strong ales from brewers, such as Belhaven, Broughton, McEwan, and Caledonian—rich and warming against the bone-chilling climate of Scotland. Some bear delightful names, such as Fowler's Wee Heavy from Bass, Broughton's Greenmantle Ale, or the Severe Strong of West Highland.

SOUVENIR TO SAVOR

Tales from the Pampas: Barbecue at a Gaucho Ranch

Buenos Aires, Argentina's capital, is as beautiful and majestic as any European city I've seen, with many historic and cultural sites, great restaurants, and widely varied and colorful neighborhoods. It's impossible to get your fill, but I was dying to visit *estancia,* or ranch, country, so we headed to San Antonio de Areco. There, in the capital of gaucho country, we lunched at La Cinacina, a typical gaucho ranch, known for its *asado* (barbecue). *Asado* is actually the Argentinean word for ribs.

We were greeted by five great-looking men, with jet black hair and very large black moustaches, dressed in white shirts tucked into blousy black pants, which were then tucked into great leather boots. They all had scarves jauntily tied around their necks and wore soft black gaucho hats, which are flatter on top and smaller than a typical cowboy hat. These guys were dashing.

There were large round stone grills everywhere and large iron wheels arranged over the burning embers to hold standing flanks of beef. They don't fool around here. Ribs, both pork and beef, and sausages threaded on very long skewers, and beef short ribs were grilling everywhere. A separate wood fire is kept going at all times for the embers that feed the grills. The beef cattle producing this cornucopia of beef are shorthorns. There are no marinades or special seasonings used on the meat, only salt.

As we and some other people were standing about hungrily, the cook began cutting up something on a massive wood board. This he offered to us as *matahambre,* or "kill hunger." They were small pieces of meat cut from between the skin and the ribs, along with some empanadas. Rather than assuage our hunger, the tasting seemed to whet our appetites for the feast ahead. In Argentina, red wine is always served with *asado*; so glasses were filled and we ventured into the dining hall—a rustic affair with long tables, checkered cloths, and cotton curtains decorated with cowboys on horses.

We finally sat down to lunch. Pitchers of red wine were brought to the tables. Beer and soda were also offered. After the arrival of two rather mundane salads came a perfectly grilled large chorizo, similar in taste to hot and sweet Italian sausages. Following this were large platters of *chinchulines,* beef tripe. Then the splendid medium rare steak arrived, thinly sliced.

Dessert seemed almost an afterthought—a piece of *queso blanco* (white cheese) topped with guava jelly—but it was quite good. The coffee rolled out as the entertainment began.

In traditional gaucho style, the host played music to welcome his guests after lunch. Out came the gauchos with accordions, guitars, and small congo drums. The samba rhythm is considered the most important in their songs. The men danced the *malembo,* the only dance in Argentina for men only. After the music came a brilliant display of horsemanship and then, sadly, it was time to say *adios.*

CARNAVAL CORNED BEEF

There's a marvelous small restaurant in Rio called Chalé that serves Brazilian regional dishes of every description. When you first walk in, the romantic sounds of bossa nova waft over you as a gentle guitar is deftly strummed. I ordered a dish of *carne seca* (also called *carne de sol*), which is beef, salted and left out in the sun to dry. This was accompanied by mashed calabaza, a vivid orange West Indian pumpkin somewhat like our Hubbard or butternut squash, along with some cooked greens, and a scoop of white rice. The combination was just splendid. The flavor of the meat reminded me of corned beef, and I thought I would put together a little American feast celebrating *Carnaval* in Rio de Janeiro.

To make things easier, the corned beef can be cooked ahead of time and then baked before serving. The squash and greens can be prepared ahead as well, and the bananas can bake as the corned beef is being finished.

1 lean corned beef brisket (about 4 pounds)
1 large onion, peeled
4 whole cloves
6 black peppercorns
6 cloves garlic
2 small dried chilies
Salt and freshly ground black pepper, to taste
1/2 cup bitter orange marmalade
Bahia Butternut Mash (page 217)
Copacabana Collards (page 198)
Lime Baked Bananas (page 509)

1. Place the corned beef in a large heavy pot and cover with water. Stud the onion with the cloves. Add the onion to the pot along with the peppercorns, garlic, and chilies. Bring to a boil over medium-high heat. Reduce the heat to low, partially cover the pot, and simmer until the meat is tender, about 2½ hours.

2. Preheat the oven to 350°F.

3. Remove the meat from the liquid and reserve ¾ cup. Place the corned beef in a small shallow baking dish. Sprinkle with salt and pepper. Spread the marmalade over the top of the corned beef. Pour the reserved cooking liquid into the pan. Bake for 25 minutes, basting occasionally. Remove the corned beef from the oven and let it rest for 15 minutes before slicing. Then thinly slice the beef and serve hot along with the squash, collards, and bananas.

Serves 6 to 8

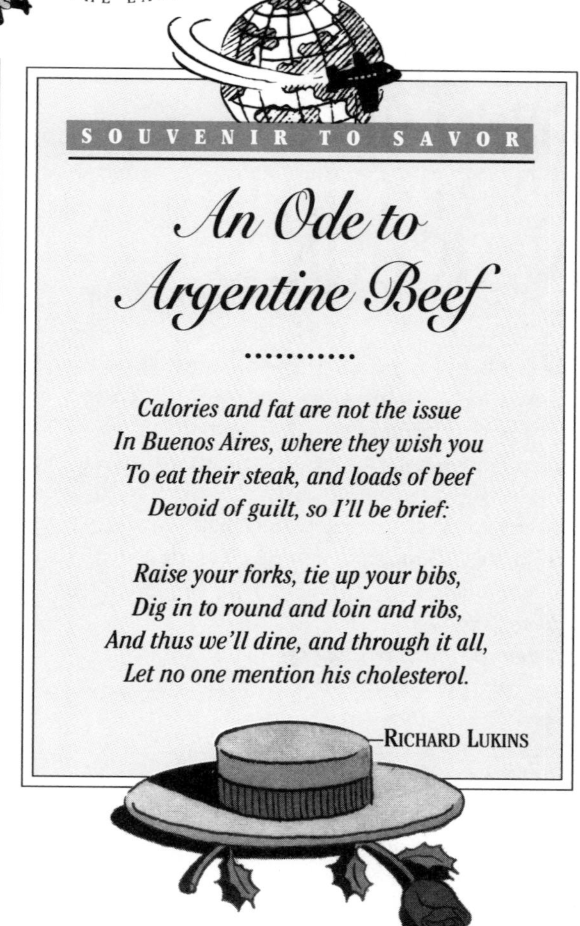

OSSO BUCO WITH BABY ARTICHOKES

Osso buco is about the only veal dish that I really love. It's moist and tender, and there is always the bonus of having the marrow to spread on toasted peasant bread when you've finished the meat. Gently stewed with artichokes in a sauce refreshed with orange zest, this dish is delicious served over delicate orzo.

1 lemon, halved
1¾ pounds baby artichokes
6 carrots, peeled, halved lengthwise, and cut into 1-inch lengths
1 cup all-purpose flour
Salt and freshly ground black pepper, to taste
8 pieces veal shank cut 1¼ to 1½ inches thick (about 5 pounds)
¼ cup olive oil, or more if needed
1 cup dry white wine
2 medium onions, halved and slivered
4 large cloves garlic, lightly bruised (page 153) and peeled
2 red bell peppers, stemmed, seeded, and cut into ¼-inch strips
2 cans (28 ounces each) plum tomatoes with their juices
2 tablespoons tomato paste
1½ teaspoons dried basil
1½ teaspoons dried oregano
½ cup chopped flat-leaf parsley
Strips of whole peel from ½ orange, pith removed

ORANGE GREMOLATA:
Finely grated zest of 1 orange
1 clove garlic, minced
2 tablespoons chopped flat-leaf parsley

1. Squeeze the lemon halves into a medium-size bowl and fill it with water. Remove the artichoke stems and cut about 1 inch off the tops. Remove any tough outer leaves at the base and trim the points from the remaining leaves with scissors. Cut the artichokes lengthwise in half and drop them into the acidulated water.

2. Bring a large pot of water to a boil. Add the artichokes and boil uncovered for 10 minutes. Add the carrots and continue boiling another 5 minutes. Drain the vegetables.

3. Combine the flour, salt, and pepper in a paper bag. Coat the veal with the seasoned flour and shake off any excess.

4. Heat the oil in a large heavy ovenproof casserole over medium-high heat. Add the veal in batches and brown well on both sides. Remove to a bowl. Continue until all the veal is browned, adding more oil if necessary.

5. Preheat the oven to 350°F.

6. Drain off any oil that remains in the casserole. Add the wine to the casserole and cook over medium-high heat, scraping up the browned bits from the bottom, for about 5 minutes. Return the veal to the casserole.

7. Add the artichokes, carrots, onions, garlic, and bell peppers. Next add the tomatoes and their juices, the tomato paste, basil, oregano, ¼ cup of the parsley, and the orange peel. Season to taste with salt and pepper.

8. Bring the mixture to a boil over medium-high heat. Cover and bake in the oven for 1 hour. Remove the cover, stir, and bake uncovered for 1 hour longer. Remove the orange peel, adjust the seasonings, and stir in the remaining ¼ cup parsley.

9. For the orange *gremolata,* chop the orange zest, garlic, and parsley together to combine well.

10. Serve the osso buco atop cooked orzo in shallow bowls with plenty of sauce and vegetables. Sprinkle with the *gremolata*.

Serves 8

VEAL SHANK "STIFADO"

While eating my way across Greece, I was amazed to see how often veal was on the menu. Most often it is cut into 1-inch cubes and cooked en papillote or in nondescript stews with peas, carrots, mushrooms, and dill. I decided upon another approach: I felt that the recipe should be boldly flavored with the tastes of Greece. What better choice than veal shanks cut for osso buco, which delivers the extra bonus of the marrow in the bones. Red and green peppers, tomatoes, onions, garlic, honey, and oregano, finished off with a dry red wine, are the basis for a rich sauce. *Gremolata,* the Italian garnish of fresh mint leaves, garlic, and fragrant lemon zest sprinkled on top just before serving, gives you the best of all worlds. This dish is lovely served with Oriental Pilaf (see Index) studded with pine nuts and currants.

1 cup all-purpose flour
1 teaspoon salt, plus more to taste
1 teaspoon coarsely ground black pepper, plus more to taste
6 pieces veal shank cut 1¼ to 1½ inches thick (about 4½ pounds)
¼ cup olive oil, or more if needed
1 large onion, cut into ¼-inch dice
2 red bell peppers, stemmed, seeded, and cut into ¼-inch strips
2 green bell peppers, stemmed, seeded, and cut into ¼-inch strips
6 carrots (about 8 ounces), peeled and cut into ½-inch lengths
4 cloves garlic, lightly bruised (page 153) and peeled
1 can (28 ounces) plum tomatoes, drained and crushed
2 tablespoons tomato paste
2 cups dry red wine
¼ cup honey
1½ teaspoons dried oregano
1½ teaspoons dried mint
Mint Gremolata (recipe follows), for serving

1. Preheat the oven to 350°F.

2. Combine the flour, 1 teaspoon salt, and 1 teaspoon pepper in a paper bag. Coat the veal with the flour mixture and shake off any excess.

3. Heat the oil in a large heavy casserole over medium-high heat. Add the veal in batches and brown well on both sides, about 5 minutes per side. Remove to a bowl. Continue until all the veal is browned, adding more oil if necessary.

4. Add the onion, peppers, and carrots to the casserole and cook, stirring and scraping up any browned bits on the bottom, over medium heat until the vegetables begin to soften, about 10 minutes. Stir in the garlic, then return the veal shanks to the pot. Season with salt and pepper to taste. Add the tomatoes, tomato paste, wine, honey, oregano, and mint.

5. Bring the mixture to a boil, then reduce

the heat and simmer for 15 minutes. Cover and bake in the oven for 1 hour. Remove the cover, stir, and bake uncovered for 1 hour longer. Serve the veal hot with the mint gremolata.

Serves 6

MINT GREMOLATA

A fresh mint gremolata is the perfect garnish for osso buco. Use sparingly—a teaspoon per serving is quite enough.

2 tablespoons finely chopped fresh mint leaves
1 teaspoon minced garlic
1 teaspoon finely grated lemon zest

Mix all the ingredients together in a small bowl. Serve immediately or store, covered, in the refrigerator for up to 4 hours.

Makes 2⅔ tablespoons

FRUITED RABBIT TAGINE

Once you perfect a marinade and make a few Moroccan-influenced *tagines,* you'll see how easy they are to create. Let your taste and imagination take over as you combine your favorite meat, poultry, or game with dried fruits and vegetables. Rabbit, a lean, delicate meat, stews up beautifully with dried apricots and dried cherries. Serve atop fluffy couscous on a chilly autumn evening and enliven it with a sprinkling of fresh mint just before serving.

1 rabbit (about 3 pounds), cut into 8 serving pieces, liver and kidneys reserved for another use
¼ cup olive oil
¼ cup fresh orange juice
1 medium onion, coarsely chopped
4 cloves garlic, minced
¾ cup chopped fresh mint leaves
1 teaspoon ground cinnamon
1 teaspoon ground cardamom
½ teaspoon ground cumin
1 cup dried apricots
¾ cup dried cherries
4 cups defatted Chicken Broth (page 127)
6 medium carrots, peeled, halved lengthwise, and cut into 2-inch lengths
4 to 5 cups cooked couscous

1. Rinse the rabbit pieces well and pat dry.

2. Place the olive oil, orange juice, onion, garlic, ½ cup of the chopped mint, the cinnamon, cardamom, cumin, apricots, and cherries in a large bowl. Add the rabbit and toss all the ingredients together, rubbing the rabbit pieces thoroughly with the marinade. Cover and let stand at room temperature for 2 hours or in the refrigerator overnight.

3. Place the rabbit with the marinade in a large heavy pot. Add the chicken broth and bring to a boil over medium-high heat. Reduce the heat and simmer, partially covered, for 20 minutes, stirring occasionally. Add the carrots and simmer covered until the rabbit is tender and cooked through, about 40 minutes longer.

4. Serve in shallow bowls over couscous or another grain. Garnish with the remaining ¼ cup chopped mint.

Serves 6

A TASTE OF THE WORLD

Moroccan Fruit Basket

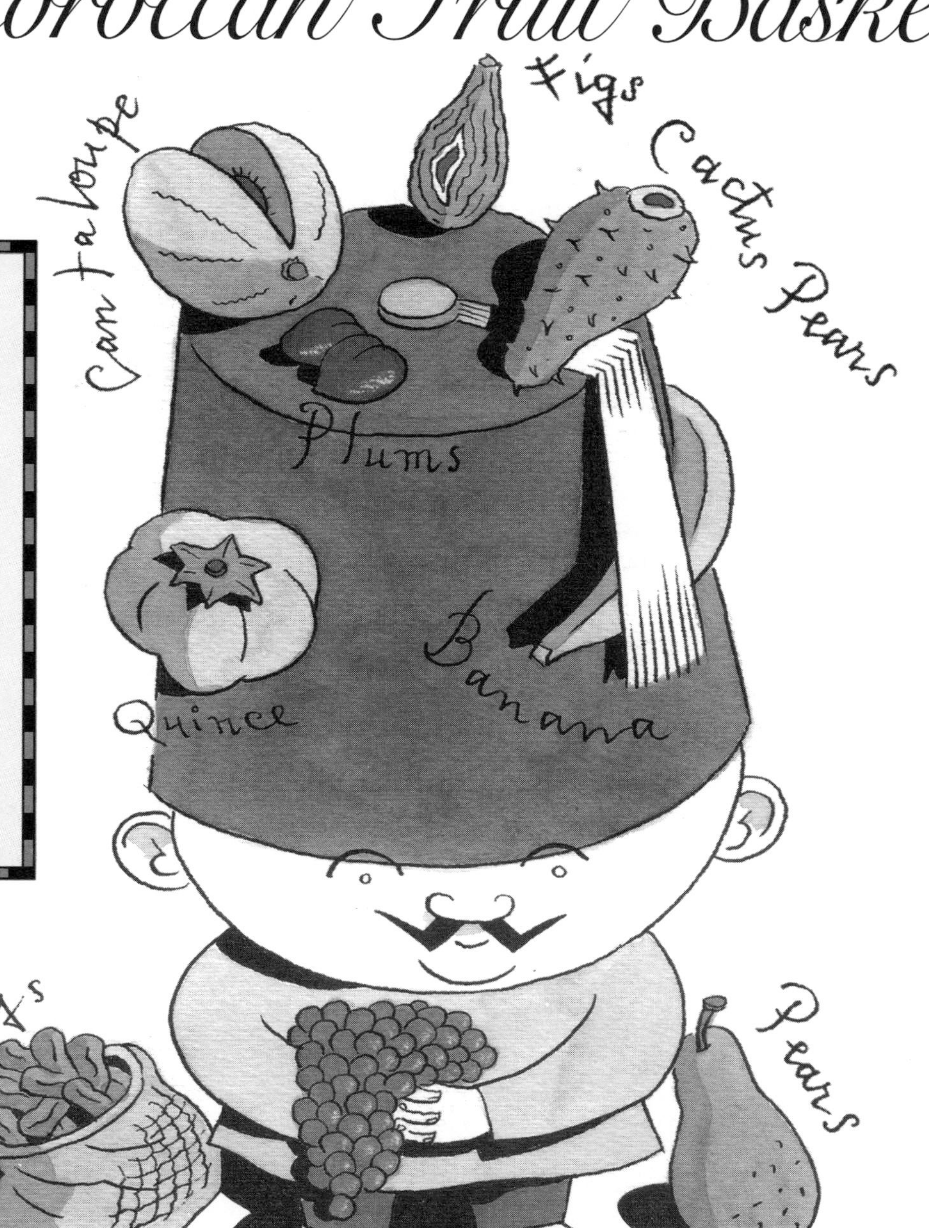

Apricots
Bananas
Cactus pears
Cantaloupes
Dates
Figs
Grapes
Honeydew melons
Lemons
Tangerines
Peaches
Pears
Plums
Pomegranates
Quinces
Strawberries
Watermelons

PROVENCAL RABBIT IN TAWNY PORT

Aromatic balsamic vinegar and tawny port blend with fruity olive oil and moist prunes to create a deep sensuous sauce for delicate young rabbit. With thyme and tarragon, this dish indulges my love for both Provençal and North African flavors. Serve in shallow bowls atop cooked wide noodles with roasted beets alongside. A Pinot Noir or Châteauneuf-du-Pape would be the perfect choice of wine.

1 rabbit (2½ to 3 pounds), cut into 8 to 10 serving pieces, liver and kidneys reserved
¼ cup plus 2 tablespoons extra virgin olive oil
4 cloves garlic, coarsely chopped
2 tablespoons balsamic vinegar
2 teaspoons dried thyme
2 teaspoons dried tarragon
½ teaspoon coarsely ground black pepper
2 cups (12 ounces) pitted prunes
1 large onion, halved and thinly sliced
2 tablespoons all-purpose flour
2 cups defatted Chicken Broth (page 127)
1 cup medium tawny port
1 tablespoon red currant jelly
Salt and freshly ground black pepper, to taste
1 tablespoon chopped flat-leaf parsley, for garnish

1. Rinse the rabbit pieces and pat dry. Trim the kidneys of fat and set aside.

2. In a large bowl, combine ¼ cup olive oil, the garlic, vinegar, thyme, tarragon, and pepper. Add the prunes and rabbit with kidneys and liver. Toss together well, cover, and let marinate at room temperature for 2 to 3 hours or in the refrigerator overnight.

3. Remove the rabbit pieces, kidneys, and liver from the marinade, scraping off any bits that stick. Reserve the marinade. Heat the remaining 2 tablespoons oil in a large heavy casserole over medium heat. Brown the rabbit and the liver and kidneys in small batches until golden, turning once or twice. Set the pieces aside.

4. Add the onion to the casserole, reduce the heat, and cook, stirring, until it begins to brown, about 2 minutes. Sprinkle with the flour and continue cooking, stirring constantly, for 2 minutes longer. Add the broth, port, and currant jelly; cook, stirring, another 2 minutes. Stir in the prunes and reserved marinade ingredients, then add the rabbit pieces and kidney. Set the browned liver aside.

5. Cook the rabbit, partially covered, over low heat for 20 minutes. Remove the cover and continue to cook until the rabbit is tender, 20 to 30 minutes more. Dice the liver and stir it into the casserole. Season with salt and pepper. Garnish with chopped parsley and serve.

Serves 4

The Air

As I traveled from country to country, arriving sometimes in languorous heat, and other times when it was briskly cool, I eagerly anticipated the next culinary find. How would local cooks transform the season's ingredients? How would they prepare their meats? And what about poultry and game? They were of particular interest to me for they provide such a perfect base for creative chefs. As they strutted their stuff, I continued to have a culinary field day.

In the Scottish highlands, I dined on lean pheasant that had been gently roasted in a honey and Drambuie sauce. In Sweden it was a meaty duck breast sauced with tangy black currants, berries common in Scandinavia during the summer months. In Hungary I ate creamy, rich *paprikás*; in Tokyo, a surprising fried chicken.

What gave all these birds their special flavor, and changed them so dramatically, were two things: the marinades and sauces that each of the cooks brought to them. India's lush chicken curry, Singapore's piquant satay, Jamaica's spicy jerk, Mexico's lively enchiladas—all wonderful variations of your basic baked and boiled poultry.

French Provençal Palette

...And

SAFFRON	PUMPKINS
NUTMEG	LEMONS
SHALLOTS	MELONS
OLIVES	APRICOTS
MUSHROOMS	PEACHES
EGGPLANTS	QUINCES
BELL PEPPERS	CHERRIES
ARTICHOKES	ALMONDS
POTATOES	PINE NUTS
BEANS	CHICKPEAS
LEEKS	SALT COD
FENNEL	HONEY
ZUCCHINI	WINE VINEGAR
SWISS CHARD	WINES

MEDITERRANEAN ROAST CHICKEN

I initially thought of this dish as Greek, but in fact it embodies the best flavors of Provence as well as Spain and North Africa. I prefer roasting two small chickens rather than one large bird because they are more tender and make for more delicate eating. The briny olives infuse the bird and potatoes as they roast, making for a one-dish meal. Seek out French Picholine, green Greek, or Spanish Manzanilla olives for their flavor and fleshy texture. Rosemary and garlic add their heady perfume to this lusty dish.

½ cup olive oil
Juice and grated zest of 2 lemons
4 cloves garlic, lightly bruised (page 153) and peeled
8 fresh rosemary sprigs
Salt and coarsely ground black pepper, to taste
2 chickens (about 2½ pounds each), rinsed well and patted dry
1½ pounds small new red potatoes, scrubbed and halved
1 cup imported green olives

1. Combine the olive oil, lemon juice and zest, garlic, rosemary, salt, and pepper in a large bowl. Coat the whole chickens well with the marinade and refrigerate covered overnight.

2. Preheat the oven to 400°F.

3. Place the chickens in a large roasting pan. Put the rosemary sprigs and garlic from the marinade in the cavities of the chickens. Surround the chickens with the potato halves and olives and drizzle the marinade over all.

4. Roast the chickens, basting occasionally, until the juices run clear when the thickest part of the thigh is pricked with a knife, about 1 hour. Let rest a few minutes before carving.

Serves 4 to 6

HERB-ROASTED CHICKEN, THE FRENCH WAY

Roasted chicken, with crisp skin and wonderfully moist meat, is a universal favorite. The French have the most divine way of cooking theirs, and here is a recipe for one of the very best. I have added my own flavorings, filling the cavity with fresh rosemary, garlic, and a wedge of lemon to perfume the bird as it cooks. This roasting method requires a good amount of attention because of the high oven temperature required, and the chicken should be basted every 10 minutes. In all good faith, I can definitely say it's well worth the effort.

1 roasting chicken (3½ to 4 pounds), with giblets
Salt and freshly ground black pepper, to taste
2 cloves garlic, peeled
1 large or 2 small fresh rosemary sprigs
1 lemon wedge
2 tablespoons unsalted butter, at room temperature
2 tablespoons olive oil
¼ cup defatted Chicken Broth (page 127)
Chopped flat-leaf parsley, for garnish

1. Preheat the oven to 425°F.

2. Rinse the chicken well, removing any excess fat, and pat dry.

3. Sprinkle the cavity with salt and pepper. Place the giblets (not liver), garlic, rosemary, and lemon in the cavity. Truss the chicken and place it in a small roasting pan. Rub it all over with the butter and drizzle with the oil. Season with salt and pepper.

4. Place the pan in the center of the preheated oven. Roast, basting with the accumulated juices every 10 to 15 minutes, for 1½ hours. The chicken is done when the juices run clear when the thickest part of the thigh is pricked with a knife. Remove from the oven and let rest 10 minutes before carving. Remove the trussing strings and stuffing ingredients. Save the giblets for another use.

5. Carve the chicken. Add the broth to the pan juices and heat. Pour through a gravy strainer, and pour over the carved chicken. Garnish with chopped parsley.

Serves 4 to 6

COQ AU VIN

A great coq au vin is as close as you can get to real French home cooking. Originating in Burgundy, a region known for its marvelous red wines, this hearty casserole was traditionally made with one of the best, Gevrey Chambertin. In classic versions salt pork or smoked bacon is used to render fat for sautéing the birds. I've substituted pancetta, a lightly spiced, salt-cured Italian bacon. Delicate-flavored pink shallots replace the expected tiny pearl onions, and *poussins* (French for baby chickens), instead of an older bird, make for succulent eating.

When choosing a wine for your coq au vin, don't feel the necessity to buy an extremely expensive Burgundy when other good-quality full-bodied, dry red wines will produce delicious results. It's quite acceptable to substitute a Pinot Noir, a Beaujolais, a red Zinfandel, a Rioja from Spain, or Chianti Classico from Italy. With wines of this caliber, buy more than one bottle and enjoy it along with the meal. Serve your coq au vin with parsleyed new potatoes, a buttery leaf lettuce salad, good cheeses, and a warm baguette. *Bon appétit!*

6 poussins (about 1 pound each) or 3 young chickens (about 2 pounds each), rinsed well and patted dry
2 cups defatted Chicken Broth (page 127)
3 tablespoons olive oil
8 ounces pancetta or slab bacon, rind discarded, cut into ¼-inch dice
1 pound medium carrots, peeled and cut into 1-inch lengths
12 ounces shallots, peeled
8 large cloves garlic, coarsely chopped
2 tablespoons unsalted butter
2 pounds white mushrooms, wiped clean, stems trimmed, caps quartered
2 tablespoons cornstarch
2 cups dry full-bodied red wine, such as Burgundy
¼ cup Cognac
2 tablespoons tomato paste
1 tablespoon red currant jelly
1 tablespoon (packed) light or dark brown sugar
1 tablespoon fresh thyme leaves or 1 teaspoon dried
1 bay leaf
1 teaspoon coarse salt
½ teaspoon freshly ground black pepper
6 tablespoons chopped flat-leaf parsley

1. Cut the *poussins* into quarters, removing the backbones and wing tips and setting these aside.

2. To enrich the broth, simmer it with the backs and wing tips in a large saucepan over low heat for 20 minutes. Strain the broth and reserve.

3. Heat the oil in a large heavy casserole over medium heat. Add the pancetta and cook, stirring occasionally, until the fat is rendered and the edges start to brown, about 10 minutes. Remove to a paper towel with a slotted spoon. Brown the *poussin* pieces in small batches, about 4 minutes on each side, and set aside.

4. Preheat the oven to 375°F.

5. Add the carrots and shallots to the casserole and cook, stirring occasionally, over medium-low heat until they just begin to brown, about 10 minutes. Stir in the garlic and cook 5 minutes longer.

6. Add the butter and mushrooms to the vegetables and cook over medium heat for 5 minutes.

7. Sprinkle the vegetables with the cornstarch and cook, stirring, for 1 minute longer.

8. Add the enriched chicken broth, the wine, and Cognac to the vegetables. Bring to a boil and cook, scraping the bottom occasionally to loosen browned bits, until the sauce thickens slightly, about 5 minutes.

9. Stir in the tomato paste, red currant jelly, brown sugar, thyme, bay leaf, salt, and pepper. Add the *poussins* and pancetta and gently fold these into the sauce.

10. Bake covered for 30 minutes. Remove the cover and bake, gently stirring occasionally, until the *poussins* are cooked through and the carrots are tender, about 30 minutes longer.

11. Adjust the seasonings to taste and fold in 4 tablespoons of the parsley. Serve hot, garnished with the remaining parsley.

Serves 8

THE WINES OF

France

It is no accident that when we think of wine, images of France are likely to surface—the vine-clad slopes along the Côte d'Or, the hills and valleys of the Loire, the stately châteaux of Bordeaux, the quaint villages of Alsace. France is home to the great prototypes of fine table wine: Bordeaux, Burgundy, Chablis, Champagne, Sauternes, Hermitage. These distinctive reds and whites are widely imitated around the world. Made from grapes such as Chardonnay, Cabernet Sauvignon, Merlot, Sauvignon Blanc, Sémillon, and Syrah—now favorites worldwide—French wines still provide the benchmarks for these varieties.

> *"The flavor and essence of French wine come out of earth that has known the vine for centuries."*

The nuts and bolts of French wine is its *appellation d'origine contrôlée* (AOC) system, which legally defines regions and vineyards, specifies grape varieties, limits production, and regulates certain aspects of winemaking and viticulture. But what we love about the wines goes way beyond that. The flavor and essence of French wine come out of earth that has known the vine for centuries.

While the traditional prototypes that make France the premiere wine-producing country are constantly challenged by ambitious winemakers everywhere, the French are not sitting passively on their laurels—a dangerous perch at any time. The new generation of growers and wine makers that has emerged in the last decade or so is much more in touch with the international wine community than previous ones. The wine industry in France today is one of the most dynamic anywhere, still evolving, experimenting (as much as AOC rules permit, at any rate), invigorating old styles, creating new ones.

Some of the most exciting developments have been in the general upgrading of wines from lesser regions, particularly those on the periphery of greater ones: Bordeaux's Entre-Deux-Mers or the Premières Côtes de Bordeaux, the Côte Chalonnaise in Burgundy, and in the southern reaches of the Rhône and Provence, both of which are coming up with some remarkable reds that rival the grander names. Even in the vast Midi, where

Left to right: A view of the walled city of Carcassone, in the Languedoc region. A good warm-weather red from the Loire. Harvesting grapes for Burgundy in the village of Monthélie.

regions such as Languedoc, Corbières, Côtes du Roussillon, and Minervois produced tons of mediocre wine, vineyards have been replanted to better varieties, technology has upgraded techniques in the vineyard and cellar, and quality, as a result, has taken a quantum leap. The flavorful, meaty Corbières of today is a far cry from the pale, lackluster reds of twenty years ago. The scintillating Syrahs of Provence and the Rhône, with their spicy herb and dark-berry flavors, work marvelously with Mediterranean styles of cooking.

Even the lowly *vins de pays* of several regions have benefitted from the new attention to quality—most notably those from the Midi. Stylish varietals—wines named for the dominant grape variety rather than the region—are offering some of the best values to be found in Cabernet Sauvignon, Merlot, Syrah, Sauvignon Blanc, and even Chardonnay. As for that perennial favorite—Chardonnay, the grape used for white Burgundy—we can look to very fine values from less exalted appellations. Rully, for example, from the Côte Chalonnaise, can be a most satisfying alternative to more expensive Meursault or Puligny-Montrachet.

In other areas there are new wines to try along-

"Some of the most exciting developments have been in the general upgrading of wines from lesser regions, particularly those on the periphery of greater ones…"

Facing page, left to right: This shop sign announces where to get your Alsatian wines. These gorgeous—but heavy—Gamay grapes will eventually become a Beaujolais. Vins de pays like this one are finally becoming worthy of attention. Above: It's mid-November, and the Beaujolais Nouveau has arrived. Right: There's nothing like a glass of wine or a demitasse at those great cafés in Paris.

side the old favorites. Sauvignon Blanc, for example, is subject to various interpretations—blended with Sémillon in regions of Bordeaux, racy and piquant along the Loire. And the lighter reds of the Loire, fruity, chillable, marvelous warm-weather reds, such as Chinon, Bourgueil, Ménétou-Salon, and Samur-Champigny, are finally getting their due as more wine drinkers switch to red wines.

When Hemingway wrote of Paris as "a moveable feast," all of France was really included in what he meant. Wine was ever-present in his recollections, the "crackling-cold" Sancerre, the rosy Beaujolais, the sturdy Bandol or St.-Emilion. As he well understood, what is a feast without wine?

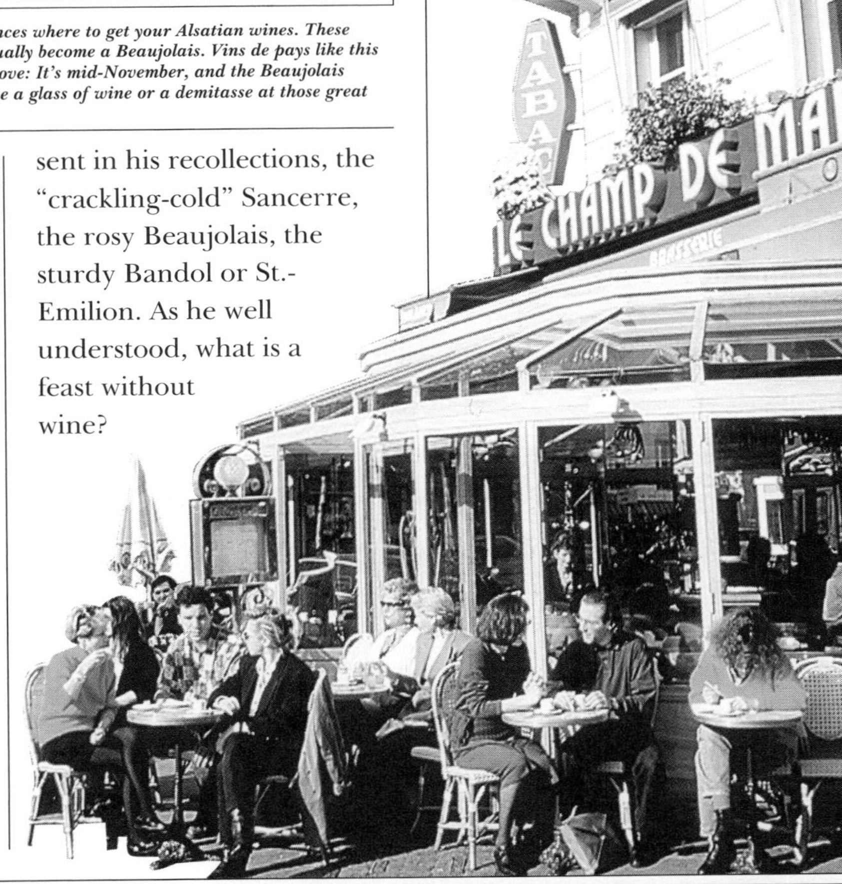

Know Your Soy Sauce

Soy sauce is the most important seasoning ingredient in both Chinese and Japanese cuisines. Although there are quite a few varieties of soy available in Asian markets and some supermarkets, for the most part I have used regular soy sauce in my recipes, and I find it to be absolutely fine.

Light soy sauce is delicately fragrant, pale amber in color, and often used to flavor soups, light sauces, and marinades. This variety may be saltier than regular or dark soy sauces.

Dark soy sauce is much darker in color than the lighter soy. It is best used for heavy dipping sauces and is often found in marinades for pickling vegetables.

HONEY AND GINGER-GLAZED CHICKEN

Golden honey and orange juice provide just the right amount of sweetness for this chicken when blended with the Asian flavors of soy sauce, ginger, garlic, and cilantro. Frequent basting glazes the meat in this simply prepared dish. Serve alongside warm brown rice, drizzled with some of the extra sauce.

MARINADE:
1 cup honey
½ cup fresh orange juice
¼ cup soy sauce
¼ cup fresh lemon juice
1 tablespoon minced garlic
1 tablespoon minced peeled fresh ginger
1 tablespoon chopped fresh cilantro stems

1 chicken (3 pounds), cut into 8 serving pieces, trimmed of wing tips
2 scallions (3 inches green left on), thinly sliced on the diagonal, for garnish

1. For the marinade, combine the ingredients in a bowl large enough to hold the chicken pieces.

2. Rinse the chicken well, removing any excess fat, and pat dry. Add to the marinade and toss well to coat. Cover and let rest at room temperature for 2 hours, turning the pieces once or twice.

3. Preheat the oven to 350°F.

4. Place the chicken pieces in a shallow baking dish large enough to hold it in a single layer and drizzle with 1 cup of the marinade. Bake, basting with the pan juices every 15 minutes, until the chicken is cooked through, about 45 minutes.

5. Remove the chicken to a serving platter and cover to keep warm. Reduce the cooking juices on the stove over medium heat until slightly thickened, about 15 minutes. Spoon a bit of sauce over the chicken and sprinkle with scallions. Serve the remaining sauce alongside.

Serves 4

CHICKEN ROGAN JOSH

The Moguls, known for the splendor and grandeur they brought to 16th-century India, originated this style of preparation as a lamb dish. I have substituted chicken for the lamb and marinated it in yogurt to tenderize the meat. India's great aromatics—coriander, cardamom, and cloves—impart their perfumes as the dish gently cooks. Serve this with Spicy Marigold Rice and Tomato Apricot Chutney (see Index).

2 chickens (2⅓ to 3 pounds each), cut into 8 serving pieces each, trimmed of wing tips
1¼ teaspoons salt
¾ teaspoon freshly ground black pepper
2 cups nonfat plain yogurt
1 large onion, minced
5 cloves garlic, minced
¼ cup minced peeled fresh ginger
1 teaspoon minced fresh red chili (seeds and ribs removed)
1 teaspoon ground coriander
1 teaspoon ground cardamom
½ teaspoon ground cloves
⅛ teaspoon ground turmeric
4 tablespoons (½ stick) unsalted butter
2 tablespoons vegetable oil
6 to 8 cups defatted Chicken Broth (page 127)
¼ cup coarsely chopped fresh cilantro leaves

1. Rinse the chicken well, removing any excess fat, and pat dry. Reserve the back and wing tips for another use.

2. Place the chicken in a bowl and toss with 1 teaspoon of the salt and ½ teaspoon of the pepper. Add the yogurt and coat the chicken pieces well. Let marinate at room temperature for 1 hour.

3. Combine the onion, garlic, ginger, chili, and spices, including the remaining salt and pepper, in a food processor. Pulse on and off 5 times to combine, then process until a smooth paste is formed, about 1 minute.

4. Heat the butter and oil in a large heavy pot over low heat. Add the onion and spice purée and cook, stirring, over medium heat for 5 minutes to color slightly and mellow the flavors.

5. Add the marinated chicken with the yogurt. Add enough chicken broth to cover and bring to a simmer. Reduce the heat to low, stir well, and cook covered until the chicken is cooked through, about 45 minutes. Stir in the cilantro and serve.

Serves 6

CHAKHOKBILI
Georgian Chicken Stew

Resplendent with herbs and perfumed with garlic and lemons, this Georgian stewed chicken is bold, yet remarkably fresh tasting. Only half the herbs, garlic, and lemon juice are added as the chicken cooks; the balance, just

before the dish is served—and the flavors dazzle. Serve with a big bowl of kasha and a bottle of chilled spicy white wine.

1 chicken (3 pounds), cut into 8 serving pieces, trimmed of wing tips
2 tablespoons olive oil
1 tablespoon unsalted butter
2 large onions, halved and slivered (about 4 cups)
2 tablespoons minced garlic
8 ripe plum tomatoes, each cut into 8 pieces
¼ cup defatted Chicken Broth (page 127)
5 tablespoons fresh lemon juice
½ cup finely chopped fresh cilantro leaves and stems
½ cup finely chopped fresh dill leaves and stems
¼ cup chopped fresh basil leaves
½ teaspoon sweet paprika
½ teaspoon coarsely ground black pepper
Coarse salt, to taste

1. Rinse the chicken well, removing any excess fat, and pat dry.

2. Heat the oil and butter in a heavy pot over medium-low heat. Add the chicken, a few pieces at a time, and sauté until pale golden. Remove to a plate. Pour off 2 tablespoons fat.

3. Add the onions and 1 tablespoon of the garlic to the pot. Cook, stirring, over medium heat for 2 minutes. Add the browned chicken to the onions and cook covered over medium-low heat for 15 minutes.

4. Add the tomatoes, chicken broth, 2 tablespoons of the lemon juice, half the fresh herbs, the paprika, pepper, and salt to the pot. Cook covered over low heat until the chicken is tender, about 30 minutes.

5. Add the remaining 1 tablespoon garlic, 3 tablespoons lemon juice, and fresh herbs. Adjust the seasonings to taste and heat through for 1 minute. Serve immediately.

Serves 4

HOME-STYLE JAMAICAN CHICKEN

Since it's so warm and balmy in Jamaica, one doesn't associate a cozy, long-stewed chicken dish with island cuisine. Jamaican home cooks have their versions, though, all spiced up and easily prepared once the chicken has marinated. As they say, "the flavors have gone right down to the bone." Serve with baked sweet potatoes and warm Miss Maud's Breakfast Banana Bread (see Index).

2 chickens (2½ to 3 pounds each), cut into 8 serving pieces each, trimmed of wing tips
2 large onions, coarsely chopped
6 scallions (3 inches green left on), sliced crosswise
3 ripe large tomatoes, cut into ½-inch pieces
¾ cup drained capers
1 tablespoon My Own Curry Powder (page 260)
½ teaspoon freshly ground black pepper
¾ teaspoon salt
½ teaspoon ground allspice
2 teaspoons sugar
⅛ teaspoon Tabasco or other hot pepper sauce
¼ cup olive oil
¼ cup red wine vinegar
2 bay leaves
1 fresh thyme sprig or 1 teaspoon dried
2 tablespoons snipped fresh chives, for garnish

Jamaican Allspice

Sweet and aromatic allspice is Jamaica's only indigenous spice. It was referred to as *pimento* by the Spanish and still often is in the Caribbean. The name "allspice" comes from the flavor, which tastes like a blend of cinnamon, cloves, and nutmeg. Allspice is an essential ingredient in Jamaica's famous jerk sauces, for its perfume seems to temper the blazing Scotch bonnet chilies. The berries, which are a bit larger than peppercorns, are harvested when green and then left to dry in the sun until they turn a rich purple brown. Underutilized in our country, this aromatic spice beautifully balances the acidity in tomato soups and sauces. I also love it in bean and rich dishes. Used in small amounts, it imparts a magical and somewhat mysterious flavor. All parts of the allspice tree are aromatic. When Jamaicans barbecue their jerk pork and chicken, they often throw allspice leaves on the fire for a richer essence. Throw a few berries into hot coals when preparing your barbecues.

1. Rinse the chicken well, removing any excess fat, and pat dry. Place the chicken in a large bowl and toss well with all the ingredients except the chives. Let marinate at room temperature 2 to 3 hours or refrigerate covered overnight.

2. Preheat the oven to 350°F.

3. Arrange the chicken pieces in a single layer in a roasting pan with 2-inch-high sides. With a slotted spoon, remove the vegetables from the marinade and scatter them over the chicken. Cover the roasting pan with aluminum foil, sealing the edges tightly, and bake for 1½ hours. Uncover the pan, move the chicken pieces around a bit, and turn the dark pieces of meat over. Re-cover with the foil and bake another 30 minutes.

4. Remove the chicken pieces to a deep serving platter or shallow bowl. With a slotted spoon, remove the vegetables from the sauce that forms and scatter them over the chicken. Pour the sauce into a gravy separator to remove any grease. Pour some of the sauce over the chicken to moisten it and serve the remaining alongside. Garnish with snipped chives.

Serves 6

JERK CHICKEN

As this chicken marinates overnight, it soaks up all the fire of the chilies and sweetness of the allspice. Because it's partially baked in the oven, only about 20 minutes is necessary on the grill and the taste of charcoal won't interfere with the deep flavors that the marinade imparts. Keep dabbing the chicken with marinade as it cooks, so that it glistens as it finishes cooking.

2 chickens (2½ to 3 pounds each), quartered, trimmed of wing tips
2 cups Jamaican Jerk Sauce (page 327)

1. Rinse the chicken well, removing any excess fat, and pat dry. Rub the jerk sauce into the pieces well, using rubber gloves to protect your skin from the hot chili. Cover and refrigerate overnight.

2. Preheat the oven to 350°F.

3. Arrange the marinated chicken in a single layer in a roasting pan. Bake for 45 minutes, turning the chicken pieces and basting occasionally.

4. Prepare a grill with medium-hot coals.

5. Grill the chicken, turning the pieces 4 or 5 times and dabbing with any remaining marinade, until golden brown and cooked through, 15 to 20 minutes. Serve hot.

Serves 6

OLIVE AND LEMON-STUDDED CHICKEN

The pleasant tang of two kinds of Mediterranean olives enhance a lemon sauce, and transform delicately simmered chicken into an unforgettable dish. This North African classic is refreshed with slivers of tender preserved lemons and lots of fresh parsley added just before serving. If you have a passion for fresh cilantro, substitute it for the parsley. Serve atop rice or couscous in shallow bowls.

2 tablespoons olive oil
2 medium onions, halved and slivered
1 tablespoon minced garlic
¼ teaspoon crumbled saffron threads
¼ teaspoon ground cumin
¼ teaspoon ground ginger
Pinch of cayenne pepper
2 chickens (3 to 3½ pounds each), cut into 10 serving pieces each, trimmed of wing tips
2 cups defatted Chicken Broth (page 127)
¼ cup fresh lemon juice
2 cinnamon sticks (each 3 inches long)
¾ cup each imported green and black olives, rinsed
1 Preserved Lemon (page 236), pulp discarded, rind cut into very thin slivers
Salt, to taste
½ cup chopped flat-leaf parsley

1. Heat the olive oil in a large heavy pot over medium-low heat. Add the onions and cook, stirring, until wilted, about 10 minutes. Add the garlic, saffron, cumin, ginger, and cayenne and cook, stirring, another 2 minutes.

2. Rinse the chickens well, removing any excess fat, and pat dry. Add the chicken, chicken broth, lemon juice, and cinnamon sticks to the pot. Bring to a boil, reduce the heat to medium-low, and cook, partially covered, for 30 minutes, stirring occasionally. If the liquid starts to boil, reduce the heat.

3. Add the olives and preserved lemon slivers. Continue to cook, partially covered, until the chicken is cooked through, about 20 minutes longer.

4. Just before serving, add salt and adjust the seasonings. Stir in the parsley. Serve hot.

Serves 6 to 8

POULET CHASSEUR

The French love their *poulet* with wild mushrooms during the fall hunting season. The Italians would call such a dish chicken cacciatore. We call it just delicious. This porcini-rich chicken stew is infused with a sprinkling of brandy, rich chicken broth, and the robust flavor of prosciutto di Parma. Serve it with Lemon Orzo (see Index).

1 ounce dried porcini mushrooms, rinsed of any dirt
1 cup defatted Chicken Broth (page 127), hot
6 tablespoons olive oil, or more if needed
4 ounces thinly sliced prosciutto, coarsely chopped
1 cup coarsely chopped onion
2 tablespoons finely chopped garlic
2 tablespoons finely chopped shallots
1 pound white mushrooms, stems trimmed, wiped clean, and sliced
½ cup all-purpose flour
1 teaspoon paprika
½ teaspoon salt
¼ teaspoon coarsely ground black pepper
2 chickens (2½ to 3 pounds each), cut into 8 serving pieces each, trimmed of wing tips, rinsed, excess fat removed, and patted dry
¼ cup brandy
1 can (28 ounces) plum tomatoes, lightly crushed, with their juices
1 cup chopped flat-leaf parsley

1. Soak the porcini mushrooms in the hot chicken broth for 1 hour. Drain, reserving the liquid, and chop the porcini.

2. Heat 3 tablespoons of the olive oil in a large nonstick skillet over medium heat. Add the prosciutto and porcini and sauté for 5 minutes. Add the onion, garlic, and shallots; sauté for an additional 5 minutes. Add the sliced mushrooms and cook until wilted, about 10 minutes. Set aside.

3. Combine the flour, paprika, salt, and pepper in a bowl. Heat the remaining 3 tablespoons olive oil in a large heavy pot over medium-high heat. Coat the chicken in the flour mixture, shaking off the excess. Sauté the chicken in batches until lightly browned, about 3 minutes per side, adding more oil if necessary. Remove the pot from the heat.

4. Heat the brandy in a small saucepan and pour it over the chicken. Carefully ignite the brandy with a long kitchen match and shake the pot until the flame subsides. Add the prosciutto and mushroom mixture and the tomatoes with their juices. Simmer, partially covered, over medium-low heat for 10 minutes.

5. Add the parsley, adjust the seasonings, and simmer an additional 30 minutes until the chicken is tender and cooked through. Serve hot.

Serves 8

TOKYO FRIED CHICKEN

Ellen White makes the best fried chicken in town, so when she came to visit, I lured her to my stove. There she put the finishing touches on the chicken I had marinated overnight in teriyaki sauce. The result was spectacular. When Ellen lived in Bangkok, she learned to dust the chicken with cornstarch before frying instead of flour, which makes for a slightly lighter crust.

2 chickens (2 to 2½ pounds each), cut into 8 serving pieces each, trimmed of wing tips, rinsed, excess fat removed, and patted dry
2 cups Basic Teriyaki Sauce (recipe follows)
½ cup cornstarch
Salt and coarsely ground black pepper, to taste
½ cup vegetable oil

1. Place the chicken pieces in a large bowl, pour the teriyaki sauce over the chicken, and toss to coat well. Marinate for 2 hours at room temperature or overnight in the refrigerator.

2. Remove the chicken from the marinade and drain on paper towels, blotting any excess moisture.

3. Dust the chicken pieces lightly with the cornstarch; do not coat them. Salt and pepper the chicken pieces.

4. Heat the oil in a large nonstick skillet over medium heat until hot, but not smoking. Reduce the heat slightly and add as many chicken pieces as will fit without crowding. Fry 6 to 7 minutes per side until golden brown and cooked through. Repeat with the remaining chicken. Serve hot.

Serves 6

BASIC TERIYAKI SAUCE

Teriyaki sauce is available in most markets, but it is easy to make your own and the result is much more delicious than the commercial version. This sauce, sweeter than regular soy, is logically named: In Japanese *teri* means shiny or glazed and *yaki* means baked or broiled. The sugar in the sauce creates the shine on poultry, meat, or fish as it caramelizes during cooking. This sauce is the basis for most Japanese barbecue done on the hibachi. Because of the fresh garlic and ginger, the sauce will last for only 3 to 4 days in the refrigerator, but it is easy enough to make so that you can stir up a fresh batch when you need it.

½ cup soy sauce
¼ cup dry sherry
¼ cup sugar
2 tablespoons vegetable oil
4 cloves garlic, coarsely chopped
1 tablespoon coarsely chopped peeled fresh ginger

Place all the ingredients in a food processor. Process until well combined. Transfer to a storage container, cover, and refrigerate until use.

Makes 1 cup

CHICKEN AND DATE TAGINE

When marinating chicken and lamb for tagines, I use a combination of ingredients that is considered classic in Morocco. The flavor the marinade imparts is quite delicious, and it serves as a basic palette for many stewed dishes. To this chicken tagine I've added a cinnamon stick, orange zest, dates, and tomatoes. A bit of broth and a slow simmer is all it really needs. Serve in bowls filled with couscous and you have an uncomplicated family dinner or a dish special enough for guests.

1 chicken (about 3½ pounds), cut into 10 serving pieces, trimmed of wing tips
1 cup chopped onion
6 cloves garlic, minced
1 cup chopped flat-leaf parsley
½ cup plus 3 tablespoons coarsely chopped fresh mint leaves
1 teaspoon ground cardamom
¼ teaspoon crumbled saffron threads
¼ cup extra virgin olive oil
¼ cup fresh lemon juice
1 cinnamon stick (3 inches long)
Strips of peel from 1 orange, pith removed
2½ cups defatted Chicken Broth (page 127)
Salt and freshly ground black pepper, to taste
1 can (15½ ounces) chickpeas (garbanzo beans), drained and rinsed
8 ounces pitted large dates, halved
6 ripe plum tomatoes, seeded and cut into ½-inch dice
4 to 5 cups cooked couscous

1. Rinse the chicken pieces well, removing any excess fat, and pat dry. Place the chicken in a large bowl. Add the onion, garlic, parsley, ½ cup mint, cardamom, and saffron, then the oil and lemon juice, and toss well to coat and combine. Cover and refrigerate 8 hours or overnight. Turn the pieces occasionally.

2. To cook the tagine, place the chicken with the marinade in a large heavy pot. Add the cinnamon stick, orange peel, broth, and salt and pepper. Slowly bring to a boil over medium-high heat, reduce the heat to medium low, and simmer, partially covered, for 30 minutes. Stir in the chickpeas, dates, and tomatoes; simmer, partially covered, for another 30 minutes.

3. To serve, remove the cinnamon stick and peel. Divide the couscous among 6 shallow bowls. Spoon the chicken and sauce atop and sprinkle with the 3 tablespoons chopped fresh mint.

Serves 6

THE WINES OF

Eastern Europe

As the countries of Eastern Europe emerge from the revolutionary changes of the late 80s, it will be interesting to see a resurgence of the wine industries of these regions. Several—notably Hungary, Bulgaria, and the former Yugoslavia—have a long history with the grape and, in some cases, illustrious wine traditions.

Hungary, for example, gave the world its unique dessert wine, Tokay Eszencia, an incredibly concentrated, honeyed ambrosia prized in the late 18th and 19th centuries by the crowned heads of Europe. Hungary was also Eastern Europe's leading producer of table wines—snappy, full-bodied white wines that seem to suit a cuisine based on the zesty paprika, plus muscular reds, like Egri Bikavér (*bikavér* means bull's blood).

"Hungary... gave the world its unique dessert wine, Tokay Eszencia, an incredibly concentrated, honeyed ambrosia..."

Future prospects for Hungary are exciting. Leading wine producers

Above: Badacsony near Lake Balaton is known for Hungary's fine white wine. Right: Harvesting for glorious Tokay—which certainly holds a candle to the best French Sauternes.

from Western Europe (France, Italy, Germany) have recently invested capital to expand Hungarian vineyards and provide the expertise needed to improve quality and style.

A sweet Tokay is an ideal aperitif when served lightly chilled.

The principal vineyards are situated on the hills around Lake Balaton, the great plain east of Budapest, and in the north, along the border of the former Czechoslovakia. Hungary's best whites are made from indigenous grapes, such as the Furmint (which produces dry as well as sweet Tokay), the Ezerjó, and Leányka. The brisk, almost peppery Kéknyelü is one of Hungary's most distinctive dry white wines, the best made from grapes grown on Mount Badacsony at Lake Balaton. Several more familiar varieties also produce lively, attractive white wines, including Pinot Gris (Szürkebarát in Hungary), Sauvignon Blanc, and Chardonnay.

The widely grown Kadarka grape is used now for Hungary's everyday reds, but it once yielded richly concentrated reds noted for ageability, particularly the Egri Bikavér (from the town of Eger in northern Hungary). The wine is still attractive, though milder in character than the old versions. Many wonder if some enterprising growers will attempt to produce it again in the old style. Merlot, know locally as Médoc Noir, is widely grown in Hungary, and more recently, Cabernet Sauvignon and Cabernet Franc have been planted there.

The Furmint grape, unique to Hungary, produces the famous Tokay. Tokay is made in a range of styles, from a young, fresh, quite dry white, known as Tokay Szamorodni, to varying degrees of sweetness that culminate in the Eszencia, or essence. Made from individually selected late-harvest grapes affected with Botrytis (noble rot, as in Sauternes), this intensely sweet nectar is produced in minute quantities and is expensive and rare. Less concentrated, sweet Tokay, known as Tokay Aszú when affected with noble rot, is more readily available. The degree of sweetness is noted on the label by the number of *puttonyos* or baskets enumerated—3 *puttonyos* is lightly sweet, 5 quite luscious, 6 exceptional.

Eastern Europe's largest wine producer is Bulgaria, which has the potential to produce the area's best quality wine as well. Bulgaria makes excellent Cabernet Sauvignon and Merlot, and agreeable Chardonnay, all highly regarded in Britain where they are considered exceptional values. With the demise of state control under the former U.S.S.R., many

> "Bulgaria makes excellent Cabernet Sauvignon and Merlot, and agreeable Chardonnay, all highly regarded in Britain where they are considered exceptional values."

Above: *Sopron, near the Austrian border, produces some of Hungary's finest red wine.* ***Right:*** *Aszú, one of the Tokays, ages in oak barrels.*

smaller Bulgarian vineyards have gone private with lofty aims toward upgrading quality, particularly for oak-aged, reserve-style red wines.

A real comer among the newly emergent regions is Moldova (formerly Moldavia), long a producer of big, sturdy red wines that were sometimes clumsy and heavy but often showed fine potential for character and complex flavor. Investors from Britain, Italy, and Germany are excited by the prospects of this region, with its gentle climate moderated by the nearby Caspian Sea. Recent infusions of capital and the introduction of modern techniques will help considerably. The best reds appear to be blends of Cabernet and Saperavi, but there are high hopes for Merlot, Pinot Noir, and Malbec. The dominant white variety is the Russian Rkatsiteli and also promising efforts with Pinot Gris, Riesling and Aligoté are most encouraging.

CSIRKE PAPRIKAS
Paprika Chicken

One of Hungary's most famous stews is *paprikás,* which is traditionally prepared with chicken or veal and has a rich sour cream sauce. Paprika, the indispensable Hungarian spice, adds its rosy color and flavor. The noble sweet variety, or *édes nemes,* is the paprika of choice for this chicken dish. Serve it with a bowl of thinly sliced sautéed green Italian frying peppers to sprinkle over the top and a steamy bowl of buttered egg noodles.

2 chickens (2½ pounds each), cut into 8 serving pieces each, trimmed of wing tips
2 tablespoons lard
2 medium onions, finely chopped
2 tablespoons sweet Hungarian paprika
4 ripe plum tomatoes, peeled and finely diced
1 red bell pepper, stemmed, seeded, and finely diced
½ cup defatted Chicken Broth (page 127)
Salt, to taste
½ cup sour cream
1 tablespoon all-purpose flour

1. Rinse the chickens well, removing any excess fat, and pat dry.

2. Heat the lard in a large heavy pot over low heat. Add the onions and cook, stirring, until wilted, 10 to 15 minutes. Do not brown. Sprinkle with the paprika and cook, stirring, for 1 minute.

3. Add the chicken, tomatoes, bell pepper, and broth. Season with salt and stir to combine. Bring to a boil, reduce the heat to medium-low, and simmer covered for 45 minutes, stirring occasionally. Do not let the sauce boil.

4. While the chicken is cooking, mix the sour cream and flour together in a small bowl. Set aside.

5. When the chicken has cooked for 45 minutes, remove the pieces to a bowl. Cook the sauce uncovered over medium heat for 10 minutes to reduce it slightly. Pour ¼ cup of the hot sauce into the sour cream and whisk until smooth. Gradually add the sour cream to the rest of the sauce, while whisking until smooth. Adjust the seasonings to taste.

6. Return the chicken pieces to the pot and cover them well with the sauce. Heat through gently over low heat. Do not let the sauce boil. Serve immediately.

Serves 6 to 8

STEWED CHICKEN UNDER A BLANKET

Before Richard and I left for Morocco, we had done such complete research, we not only knew which restaurants to eat in, we also knew what meals to order. We arrived in Marrakech, where we stayed for a few days before embarking on a long eight-hour drive to Fez. Richard had called The Palais Jamais restaurant ahead of time to order a *trid.* Knowing that we had a delicious dinner to look forward to certainly made the trip more bearable. Once in Fez, though, I was just too tired to show up in the

dining room. Naturally I was disappointed, but as it turned out, it didn't matter—Richard said the *trid* wasn't even very good.

Still intrigued with the idea, however, I began to experiment a bit with the dish when we got home. From his description it sounded like a free-form Moroccan *bisteeya* (an aromatic pigeon pie). The version I came up with is quite delicious and didn't involve an eight-hour drive! Whole boned pieces of herbed and spiced stewed chicken are nestled under leaves of phyllo pastry, making for a rather dramatic and delicious dish. I still prefer *bisteeya,* but this isn't quite as complicated a preparation. Be sure to plan ahead and marinate your chicken overnight for an intense flavor. I'm sure you'll find this well worth your effort.

MARINADE:
1 medium onion, coarsely chopped
¼ cup olive oil
¼ cup fresh lemon juice
½ cup chopped fresh cilantro leaves
½ cup chopped flat-leaf parsley
1 tablespoon ground cumin
1 tablespoon ground coriander
1 teaspoon coarsely ground black pepper
½ teaspoon crumbled saffron threads

1 chicken (3½ to 4 pounds), cut into 10 serving pieces, trimmed of wing tips
6 cups defatted Chicken Broth (page127)
2 tablespoons unsalted butter
2 tablespoons ground cinnamon
2 tablespoons confectioners' sugar
8 sheets phyllo pastry (see Note)

1. Combine all the marinade ingredients in a bowl.

2. Rinse the chicken pieces well, removing any excess fat, and pat dry. Add the chicken to the marinade and toss well, rubbing the chicken pieces so they absorb the flavors. Cover and marinate for 2 hours at room temperature or in the refrigerator overnight.

3. Place the chicken with the marinade ingredients in a large heavy pot. Add the broth and butter. Bring to a boil, reduce the heat, and gently simmer, partially covered, for 1 hour.

4. Remove the cooked chicken pieces to a bowl. Reduce the sauce over high heat to about 2 cups, about 30 minutes. Set aside.

5. When the chicken is cool enough to handle, remove the skin and bones, trying to avoid breaking up the meat too much.

6. Preheat the oven to 350°F. Lightly butter a 13 x 9 x 2-inch ovenproof dish.

7. Mix the cinnamon and sugar together in a bowl and set aside.

8. Ladle ½ cup of the sauce into the bottom of the dish. Cover with 1 sheet of phyllo, draping the excess over the sides of the dish. Brush well with some of the remaining sauce. Sprinkle with 1 teaspoon of the cinnamon sugar. Repeat with 3 more sheets of phyllo.

9. Lay the boned chicken in the dish, mounding it slightly in the center. Cover with the remaining 4 sheets of phyllo, brushing each one with sauce and sprinkling with 1 teaspoon cinnamon sugar. Gather up the pastry that is draped over the sides of the dish and mound it slightly on top. Spoon ½ cup sauce over the top and sprinkle to taste with the remaining cinnamon sugar.

10. Bake until the pastry is crispy and golden, 20 minutes.

Serves 6

Note: Phyllo dough is readily available frozen in 1-pound boxes. Follow the package directions for thawing the dough.

BABY BISTEEYAS

In Morocco, wonderful large, flaky, round *bisteeyas* are presented at the table and cut into wedges for a first course. They are so good, that during my visit, I found it difficult not to just keep eating this incredibly delicious pigeon pie, and forgo the rest of the meal. In this recipe I've satisfied my desire by creating smaller *bisteeyas* that make for generous entrée portions. Several lovely Moroccan vegetable salads would be the perfect start for an elegant dinner. What you do want is a moist, succulent meat for the filling. Instead of using pigeons, which are traditional, I have used chicken thighs. They make an ideal substitute.

12 chicken thighs, rinsed well and patted dry
1 medium onion, chopped
2 cloves garlic, minced
1 cup chopped flat-leaf parsley
1 tablespoon coarse salt
1 teaspoon ground coriander
½ teaspoon ground ginger
¼ teaspoon crumbled saffron threads
3 cups defatted Chicken Broth (page 127)
3 cinnamon sticks (each 3 inches long)
2 tablespoons unsalted butter
1 cup blanched almonds
¼ cup confectioners' sugar, plus more for garnish
1 teaspoon ground cinnamon, plus more for garnish
¼ cup fresh lemon juice
6 large eggs, well beaten
1 pound phyllo pastry (see Note)
¾ cup butter, melted

1. Place the chicken thighs, onion, garlic, parsley, salt, coriander, ginger, and saffron in a large bowl. Toss well, rubbing the chicken thoroughly with the spices. Cover and marinate for 2 hours at room temperature or in the refrigerator overnight.

2. Place the chicken with the marinade in a large heavy pot. Add the broth and cinnamon sticks. Bring to a boil, reduce the heat, cover, and gently simmer for 1 hour. Remove the chicken from the broth and set aside.

3. Strain the broth and return it to the pot. Boil the broth over high heat until reduced to 2 cups, about 10 minutes.

4. While the broth is reducing, melt the 2 tablespoons butter in a medium skillet over medium heat. Add the almonds and sauté, stirring, until golden brown, about 5 minutes. Drain on a paper towel. Finely chop the almonds and combine with the confectioners' sugar and cinnamon. Set aside.

5. After the broth has reduced, add the lemon juice and simmer gently another 10 minutes. Increase the heat to medium and, stirring constantly with a wooden spoon, slowly pour in the beaten eggs. Cook, stirring, until the eggs are set but not dry and most of the liquid has evaporated, 8 to 10 minutes. Season with salt if necessary. Cool to room temperature.

6. When the chicken is cool enough to handle, shred the meat from the bones and set aside.

7. Preheat the oven to 350°F.

8. Cut the phyllo pastry into 6-inch squares. You will need 60 squares. Keep the squares covered between damp dish towels while you are working. Place 1 square of phyllo in front of you and brush with melted butter. Repeat with 4 more squares of phyllo. Sprinkle with 1 tablespoon of the almond mixture, leaving a 1-inch border around the edges. Top with ⅓ cup of the egg mixture. Cover with 2 squares of phyllo, brushing each with melted butter. Add ⅓ cup of shredded chicken and sprinkle with 1 more tablespoon of the almond mixture. Fold up the edges about 1 inch to cover the topping. Lay 3 squares of phyllo over the top, brushing each square with melted butter, and then gently mold the top layers of phyllo under the mound to make a neat package. Place on a baking sheet. Repeat to make 6 packages.

9. Bake the *bisteeyas* until golden brown, about 20 minutes. Dust with confectioners' sugar and ground cinnamon and serve immediately.

Serves 6

Note: Phyllo dough is readily available frozen in 1-pound boxes. Follow the package directions for thawing the dough.

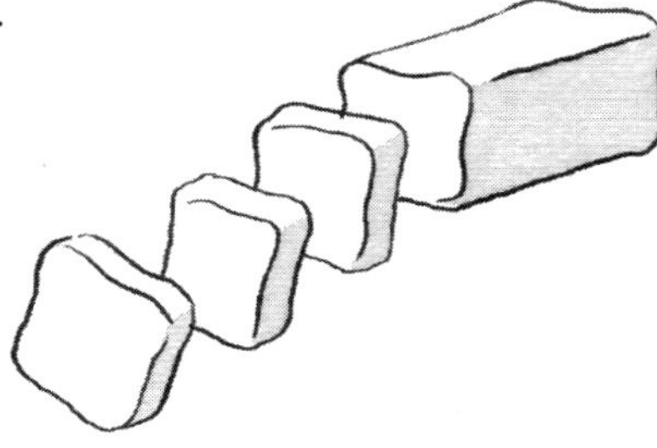

GOLDEN CHICKEN CURRY

Here is a delicious chicken curry that is both pungent and mellow. To achieve that smoothness, it is necessary to cook the curry powder briefly before adding it to the dish. Spicy heat is added with garlic and fresh ginger. Mango chutney and crème fraîche contribute velvety sweetness to the sauce, which is enlivened with carrots, tomatoes, and cilantro. A sprinkle of golden raisins before serving makes a lovely addition.

2 pounds boneless, skinless chicken breasts, cut crosswise on the diagonal into 1-inch strips
3 tablespoons all-purpose flour
3 tablespoons olive oil, or more if needed
1 cup chopped onion
1 tablespoon minced garlic
1 tablespoon minced peeled fresh ginger
¼ cup My Own Curry Powder (page 260)
2 cups defatted Chicken Broth (page 127)
2 tablespoons mango chutney
1 cup crème fraîche
4 cups cooked rice (1¼ cups raw), for serving
2 carrots, peeled, cut into ⅛-inch dice, and blanched, for garnish
3 ripe plum tomatoes, peeled, seeded, and cut into ⅛-inch dice, for garnish
¼ cup chopped fresh cilantro leaves, for garnish
About ½ cup golden raisins, for garnish (optional)

1. Coat the chicken strips with the flour, shaking off the excess. Heat 2 tablespoons of the olive oil in a large heavy pot over medium heat. Add half the chicken strips and sauté until just cooked through, about 5 minutes, shaking the pan often so that they cook evenly. Remove to a bowl with a slotted spoon. Repeat with the remaining chicken strips, adding more oil if necessary.

2. In the same pot, heat 1 tablespoon oil. Add the onion, garlic, and ginger. Cook, stirring often, until golden, 5 to 7 minutes. Sprinkle with the curry powder and cook, stirring constantly, 1 minute longer.

3. Add the chicken broth and simmer 8 to 10 minutes to reduce and thicken the sauce. Stir in the chutney and crème fraîche and simmer for 5 minutes to thicken the sauce. Do not boil. Add the chicken strips and heat through.

4. Serve immediately over hot cooked rice, garnished with the diced carrots and tomatoes and chopped cilantro. Sprinkle the raisins over all, if desired.

Serves 4 to 6

CHICKEN TIKKA

In India, *tikka* refers to fillets of chicken or other meats, but the key to this dish is the marinade. The chicken breasts are tenderized by being marinated in yogurt and lemon juice, which is intensely flavored with fresh ginger and garlic. Ideally the breasts are cooked in a tandoor oven, but by sautéing them quickly over high heat, a close result is reached. Usually, chicken *tikka* is served on a bed of raw onions. I prefer the onions softly grilled and golden from adding cumin and a pinch of turmeric. Serve with lots of lime halves for squeezing over all.

1 piece (2 inches) fresh ginger, peeled and coarsely chopped
6 cloves garlic, coarsely chopped
4 tablespoons fresh lemon juice
1 cup nonfat plain yogurt
6 tablespoons vegetable oil
2 teaspoons chili powder
2 teaspoons salt
4 whole boneless, skinless chicken breasts (about 12 ounces each; 3 pounds total), halved
3 medium onions, halved and slivered
1 teaspoon ground cumin
¼ teaspoon ground turmeric
2 tablespoons chopped flat-leaf parsley, for garnish
3 limes, halved crosswise, for serving

1. Place the ginger and garlic, 2 tablespoons lemon juice, and ¼ cup of the yogurt in a food processor and purée until smooth. Scrape the purée into a bowl with the remaining ¾ cup yogurt, 3 tablespoons of the oil, the chili powder, and 1 teaspoon of the salt. Stir well.

2. Cut each halved chicken breast crosswise into 3 pieces. Add the chicken to the yogurt mixture and toss to coat. Marinate at room temperature for 1 hour.

3. Meanwhile, place the onions in a large bowl and toss with the remaining 2 tablespoons lemon juice, the remaining 3 tablespoons vegetable oil, the remaining 1 teaspoon salt, and the cumin and turmeric. Set aside.

4. Fifteen minutes before the chicken is finished marinating, preheat the broiler.

5. Spread the onions in a single layer on a baking sheet and broil about 3 inches from the heat until they are golden, 10 minutes. Shake the pan and stir the onions after 5 minutes.

6. Remove the chicken pieces from the marinade with a fork (let some marinade remain on the pieces) and cook in small batches in a large cast iron skillet over medium-high heat until golden brown, about 5 minutes per side. Add a bit more marinade to the pan if necessary to prevent sticking.

7. Divide the onions evenly among 6 dinner plates. Top with chicken pieces and sprinkle each with 1 teaspoon of chopped parsley. Place a lime half on each plate and serve immediately.

Serves 6

MEE SOTO

Indonesian Chicken Noodle Curry

Any time you see *mee* in an Indonesian recipe, think noodles. This dish is a perfect example of the cross-cultural influences in Singapore's varied cuisine. Turmeric and curry powder contribute the hues and flavors of India. Lemongrass and coconut milk—Thai favorites—create a velvety sauce, which is sweetened with cinnamon and ripe tomatoes. Thin cooked noodles, scallions, and crispy mung bean sprouts provide a Chinese influence and a textural contrast to this complex and rich stew. Because the chicken is sliced into thin strips, it doesn't take long to cook it; so be sure not to overdo it.

½ cup coarsely chopped onion
2 tablespoons sliced peeled fresh ginger
2 cloves garlic, peeled
¼ cup roasted peanuts
¼ cup water
3 tablespoons peanut oil
2 cups coconut milk (page 252 or available in specialty food stores)
2 cups defatted Chicken Broth (page 127)
¼ cup thinly sliced fresh lemongrass
2 cinnamon sticks (each 3 inches long)
1 star anise, broken in half
⅛ teaspoon ground nutmeg
Finely grated zest of 1 lemon
3 tablespoons My Own Curry Powder (page 260)
1 tablespoon ground turmeric
3 cups diced (½ inch) seeded plum tomatoes
½ cup thinly sliced shallots, for garnish
2 pounds boneless, skinless chicken breasts
8 ounces linguine or spaghetti, cooked, warm
12 ounces mung bean sprouts
2 scallions (3 inches green left on), thinly sliced on the diagonal, for garnish
2 ribs celery, thinly sliced on the diagonal, for garnish

1. Place the onion, ginger, garlic, peanuts, and water in a food processor; pulse on and off to create a coarse paste.

2. In a large soup pot, heat 1 tablespoon of the peanut oil over medium-low heat. Add the paste and cook, stirring constantly, for 2 minutes. Add the coconut milk, chicken broth, lemongrass, cinnamon sticks, star anise, nutmeg, and lemon zest and bring to a boil. Turn the heat down slightly and simmer the sauce uncovered for 15 minutes.

3. In the meantime, heat 1 tablespoon peanut oil in a small nonstick skillet. Add the curry powder and turmeric and cook 1 minute, stirring constantly. Add this mixture to the sauce and stir well. Add the tomatoes and continue to simmer for 15 minutes longer.

4. While the sauce is cooking, fry the sliced shallots, in the remaining tablespoon peanut oil, in a small skillet over medium heat until they are nicely golden and crisp, about 10 minutes. Remove from the heat and drain on a paper towel. Reserve for garnish.

5. Halve the chicken breasts lengthwise, remove any cartilage, and cut the breasts on the diagonal into 1-inch strips. Add the chicken to the sauce and simmer until it is cooked through, about 5 minutes. Remove from the heat. Remove and discard the cinnamon sticks and star anise.

6. To serve, lay out 8 shallow soup or pasta bowls. Arrange the noodles on one side of each bowl and the bean sprouts on the other side. Ladle the curry over all, distributing the chicken pieces evenly. Garnish with the fried shallots, scallions, and celery. Serve immediately.

Serves 6 to 8

CHICKEN PICADILLO ENCHILADAS

When enchiladas are served in Mexico, they are often a bit heavy and meaty, but these chicken-filled tortillas are light and delicious and filled with the best flavors of the Mexican palette. Use chicken left over from a large roasted bird or poach some breasts for the filling. Olives and capers, with their briny bite, play against the flavorful sweetness of cinnamon and raisins. Enchiladas are easily prepared ahead of time and baked just before serving.

PICADILLO:
3 tablespoons olive oil
½ cup diced (¼ inch) red onion
½ cup diced (½ inch) red bell pepper
6 ripe plum tomatoes, seeded and diced
¼ cup coarsely chopped pitted green olives
½ cup golden raisins
¼ cup coarsely chopped almonds
2 tablespoons drained tiny capers
1 teaspoon dried thyme
½ teaspoon ground ginger
½ teaspoon ground cinnamon
3 cups cooked shredded chicken meat
Salt and freshly ground black pepper, to taste
¼ cup coarsely chopped flat-leaf parsley

6 cups Marinara Sauce (page 302) or other prepared tomato sauce
16 large flour tortillas (about 8 inches in diameter)
12 ounces Monterey Jack cheese, grated

1. For the picadillo, heat the oil in a large nonstick skillet over medium heat. Add the onion and bell pepper and cook, stirring, for 5 minutes. Add the tomatoes, olives, raisins, almonds, capers, thyme, ginger, and cinnamon; cook, stirring, over medium heat another 2 to 3 minutes. Remove from the heat and stir in the chicken. Season with salt and pepper and stir in the parsley.

2. Preheat the oven to 350°F.

3. Spread 2 cups of the marinara sauce over the bottom of a large shallow baking dish (or use 2 medium-size baking dishes each large enough to hold 8 enchiladas).

4. Spoon ¼ cup of the picadillo 1 inch from the edge of a flour tortilla. Roll up and place, seam side down, in the baking dish. Continue with the remaining tortillas and picadillo.

5. Pour the remaining 4 cups sauce evenly over the enchiladas, then sprinkle the grated cheese evenly over the top. Bake until the top is slightly browned and the cheese is melted, 20 to 25 minutes. Serve hot.

Makes 16 enchiladas or 8 entrée servings

MU SHU CHICKEN BURRITO

For good fun eating, try this new burrito inspired by the best Chinese mu shu pork and Mexican fajita. Shredded cooked chicken is enlivened in a quick stir fry, with fresh ginger and bell pepper, then rolled up in a flour tortilla spread with hoisin sauce. (I couldn't resist spooning a dollop of spicy Saus Kacang on top of the filling before closing up the tortilla.) Easy to prepare and a delight to eat, this is a terrific multicultural "fusion" sandwich where the "Far" and "South" Easts meet up with the "Southwest."

1 teaspoon plus 2 tablespoons peanut oil
2 large eggs, lightly beaten
½ cup water
¼ cup soy sauce
2 teaspoons (packed) light or dark brown sugar
1 medium red bell pepper, stemmed, seeds and ribs removed
1 medium leek, roots trimmed, rinsed well
1 piece (2 inches) fresh ginger, peeled
4 ounces white mushrooms, stems trimmed, caps wiped clean with a damp paper towel
¼ cup sliced bamboo shoots, rinsed
½ cup mung bean sprouts, rinsed
2 cups shredded cooked chicken
¼ cup chopped fresh cilantro leaves
⅓ cup hoisin sauce
8 large flour tortillas (8 inch diameter), at room temperature
8 teaspoons Saus Kacang (page 71)

1. Place 1 teaspoon peanut oil in a medium-size nonstick skillet over medium-high heat. To make a thin omelet, add the eggs to the skillet and cook until just set, using a spatula to lift the omelet around the edges and let the unset eggs run underneath. Once the eggs are completely set, slip the omelet onto a plate. Cut it in half and then into thin strips.

2. Combine the water, soy sauce, and brown sugar in a small bowl. Set aside.

3. Cut the pepper and leek into 3-inch-long matchsticks. Cut the ginger into matchsticks. Thinly slice the mushrooms. Cut the bamboo shoots into matchsticks. Arrange all the ingredients in separate piles.

4. Heat the remaining 2 tablespoons peanut oil in a wok over medium-high heat. Add the pepper, leek, and ginger and cook, stirring often, for 5 minutes. Add the mushrooms and cook 2 minutes longer. Add the bamboo shoots, bean sprouts, omelet strips, and chicken. Pour in the soy sauce mixture and cook over medium-high heat, tossing constantly, until the liquid nearly evaporates, 8 to 10 minutes. Remove from the heat and toss in the cilantro.

5. Spread 2 teaspoons hoisin sauce on each tortilla. Spoon ¼ cup of the filling about 1 inch from the edge of each tortilla. Dollop each with about 1 teaspoon *saus kacang* and roll up. Serve hot.

Serves 4

MADRAS CHICKEN SALAD

Some of the greatest blends of curry powder are from Madras in the south of India. Classically eight spices are blended to create a piquant yet warm flavor which radiates brilliant color. For a stew I find it best to cook the curry powder along with butter, onions, and garlic for a minute or so to soften and mellow the flavors. The base of my spice blend is cumin, fenugreek seeds, and ginger, to which I've added mace, turmeric, cardamom, hot mustard powder, and more. When buying commercial powders, it is important to search out the best quality and the freshest available. The fruity flavors and crisp textures of crisp tart apples, celery, and sweet red seedless grapes make an appealing contrast to the delicate poached chicken. Peanuts add the final crunch.

DRESSING:
1 cup mayonnaise
1 cup nonfat plain yogurt
2 tablespoons My Own Curry Powder (page 260)
⅛ teaspoon ground turmeric
½ cup toasted shredded coconut (page 514)
¼ cup mango chutney, finely chopped

POACHED CHICKEN:
1 carrot, halved
1 rib celery with leaves, halved
4 flat-leaf parsley sprigs
4 black peppercorns
1 bay leaf
8 cups water
4 whole boneless, skinless chicken breasts (about 12 ounces each; 3 pounds total)

SALAD:
1 cup halved red seedless grapes
2 ribs celery, cut into ¼-inch dice
1 Granny Smith apple, cored and cut into ¼-inch dice
½ cup roasted peanuts
2 tablespoons chopped fresh mint leaves, for garnish

1. For the dressing, stir all the ingredients together and set aside.

2. For the poached chicken, place the carrot, celery, parsley, peppercorns, bay leaf, and water in a large heavy pot and bring to a boil. Add the chicken breasts and simmer uncovered until cooked through, about 10 minutes. Remove from the cooking liquid, and let stand until cool enough to handle. Cut into 1-inch cubes, removing any cartilage.

3. For the salad, combine the chicken cubes, grapes, celery, apple, and peanuts in a large bowl. Add the curry dressing and combine well.

4. Refrigerate for at least 2 hours before serving to allow the flavors to meld. Sprinkle with chopped mint just before serving.

Serves 8

Suzy,
Explosive colors in the Agra market. Like vegetables are grouped together. And there is always a camel close by.
Sheila

A TASTE OF THE WORLD

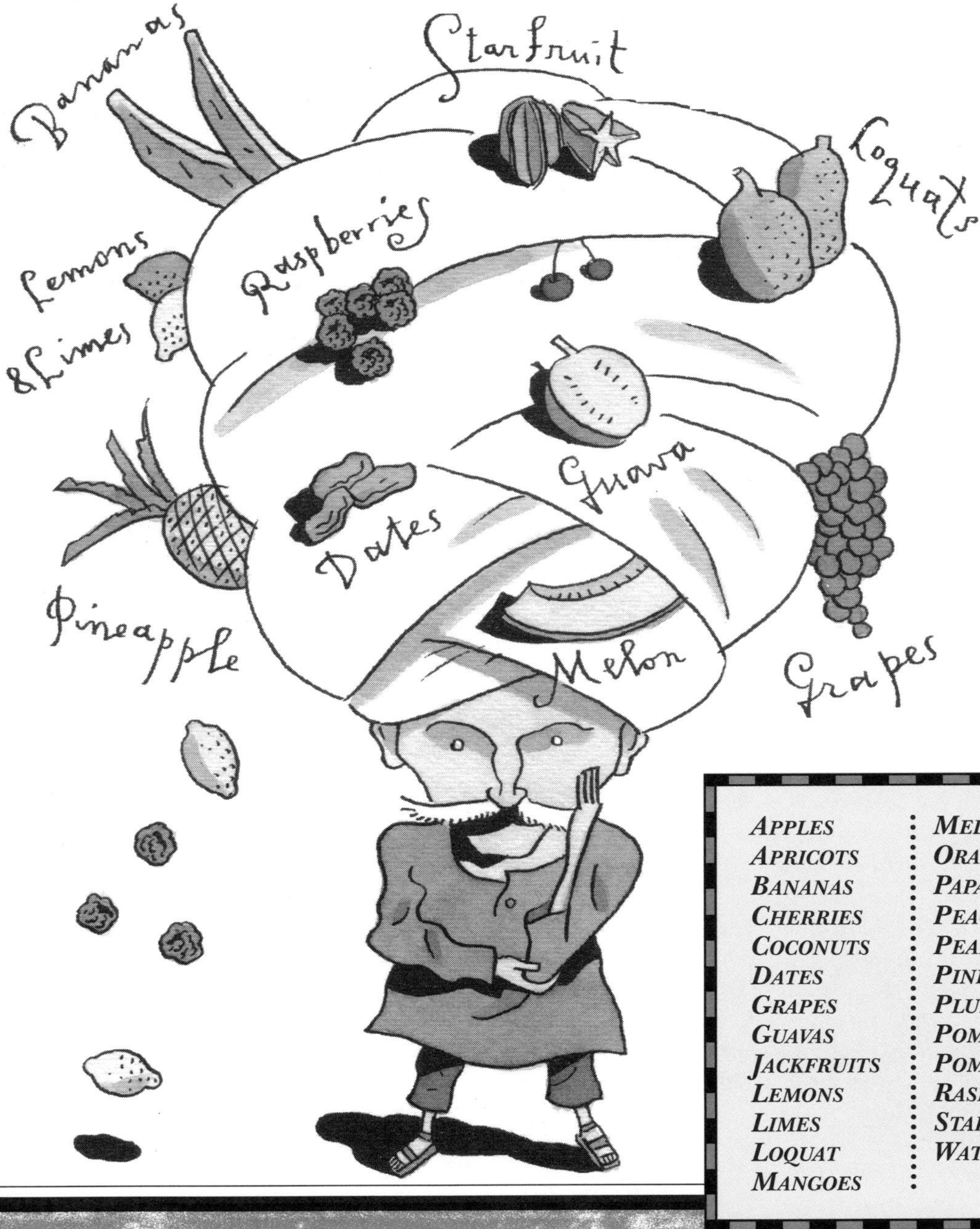

Bananas
Starfruit
Loquats
Lemons & Limes
Raspberries
Guava
Dates
Pineapple
Melon
Grapes

Apples	*Melons*
Apricots	*Oranges*
Bananas	*Papayas*
Cherries	*Peaches*
Coconuts	*Pears*
Dates	*Pineapples*
Grapes	*Plums*
Guavas	*Pomelos*
Jackfruits	*Pomegranates*
Lemons	*Raspberries*
Limes	*Starfruits*
Loquat	*Watermelon*
Mangoes	

HACKED CHICKEN SALAD

When Szechuan Chinese restaurants blossomed on every other street corner in cities across the U.S., they popularized a velvety, piquant peanut sauce for blanketing tender strips of chicken. This cold dish, known as "hacked chicken," very quickly began shutting out Chicken Cantonese style. Here it takes on a whole new freshness when quickly broiled chicken breasts are shredded, then tossed in a spicy sesame-peanut sauce and served over crisp watercress.

3 whole boneless, skinless chicken breasts (about 2 pounds total), halved
3 tablespoons Asian sesame oil
Salt and coarsely ground black pepper, to taste
¾ cup Spicy Peanut Sauce (page 294)
1 large bunch watercress, stems trimmed, rinsed well
2 ribs celery, cut into 2½-inch matchstick strips
½ hothouse (seedless) cucumber, peeled and cut into 2½-inch matchstick strips
4 scallions (3 inches green left on), cut into 2½-inch matchstick strips

1. Preheat the broiler. Line a baking sheet with aluminum foil.

2. Brush the chicken breasts with the sesame oil and sprinkle with salt and pepper. Fan out the little fillet on the underside of each breast half and place the chicken on the prepared baking sheet.

3. Broil the chicken breasts 3 to 4 inches from the heat until cooked through, about 4 minutes per side. Let cool to room temperature.

4. Shred the chicken into strips, about 2½ x ½ inch. Place in a bowl and toss with the peanut sauce.

5. To serve, spread the watercress on a large serving plate. Spoon the dressed chicken onto the center of the cress. Top with the celery, cucumber, and scallions.

Serves 6

CHINESE SQUABS

These gamy little birds are sweetened and delicately lacquered with a Chinese-inspired marinade of soy sauce, ginger, garlic, and honey. In the late 70s I would have cooked them at a very high heat for 15 to 20 minutes, but my tastes have changed and now I prefer them cooked through at a moderate heat for about 1 hour. The meat is tender and a bit stronger in flavor than Cornish game hens. They'd be lovely served with Sesame Butterfly Pasta (see Index) and a salad of frisée and Spanish blood oranges.

6 squabs (¾ to 1 pound each)
4 cloves garlic, peeled
1 piece (1 inch) fresh ginger, peeled and coarsely chopped
½ cup soy sauce
½ cup light honey
2 tablespoons peanut oil
2 tablespoons fresh orange juice
1 tablespoon finely minced orange zest

1. Rinse the squabs and pat dry. Place in a bowl. Trim off the wing tips, necks, and any excess fat from the neck cavity.

2. Place the garlic and ginger in a food processor and process until nearly smooth. Combine the soy sauce, honey, peanut oil, and orange juice and zest, then add the garlic and ginger mixture. Pour the marinade over the squabs and coat well.

3. Let marinate at room temperature for 4 hours or in the refrigerator overnight, turning the squabs in the marinade 3 or 4 times.

4. Preheat the oven to 350°F.

5. Place the squabs in a large roasting pan and pour the marinade over the top. Bake the squabs until cooked through and golden brown, 1 hour, basting every 15 minutes.

6. Remove the squabs to a serving platter. Pour the cooking juices into a small heavy saucepan and boil the sauce over high heat until it thickens slightly, about 5 minutes. Pour some of the sauce over the squabs and serve. Pass the remaining sauce alongside in a sauceboat.

Serves 6

BLACK CURRANT DUCK BREASTS

Fresh black currants, prolific in Sweden, have a great affinity for rich meats such as duck or lamb. As they are difficult to find fresh in the U.S., black currant preserves and syrups make good substitutes. After the duck breasts are trimmed of most of their fat and excess skin, I've quickly seared them in a nonstick skillet. The luscious mahogany sauce is easily prepared with chicken broth, black currant preserves, and a cassis syrup. For the most elegant presentation, slice each breast crosswise on the diagonal into thin slices. Arrange the slices decoratively on large dinner plates and spoon the currant sauce atop.

3 whole duck breasts, boned (about 1 pound each), rinsed, and patted dry
Coarse salt and coarsely ground black pepper, to taste
1 teaspoon olive oil
1 cup defatted Chicken Broth (page 127)
½ cup black currant preserves
2 tablespoons cassis syrup

1. Cut the whole duck breasts in half lengthwise. Trim the excess fat and skin from around the meat on each breast. Separate the long narrow fillets and reserve for another use. Score the skin of each breast 3 times on the diagonal with a sharp knife. Do not pierce the meat, only the skin. Salt and pepper both sides of the breasts.

2. Heat the oil in a large nonstick skillet over high heat. Place 3 breast pieces in the skillet, skin side down, and sauté, pressing down on the breasts with the back of a spatula, until well browned, 3 to 4 minutes. Turn and sauté the second side 3 to 4 minutes longer. Reduce the heat slightly if the pan seems too hot. Remove the cooked breasts to a plate and let rest, covered, until serving. Pour off any excess fat in the skillet and sauté the second batch.

3. Discard the fat in the skillet and lightly wipe it out with a paper towel. Heat the skillet over medium-high heat. Add the chicken broth and any accumulated juices that the duck gives off. Bring to a boil, scraping up any browned bits from the bottom of the pan, and boil for 1 minute. Reduce the heat to medium and stir in the black currant preserves and cassis. Cook, stirring, until slightly thickened, 5 to 6 minutes.

4. Slice the duck breasts on the diagonal and fan the slices on dinner plates. Spoon the sauce over the top and serve immediately.

Serves 6

Chinese Fruit Basket

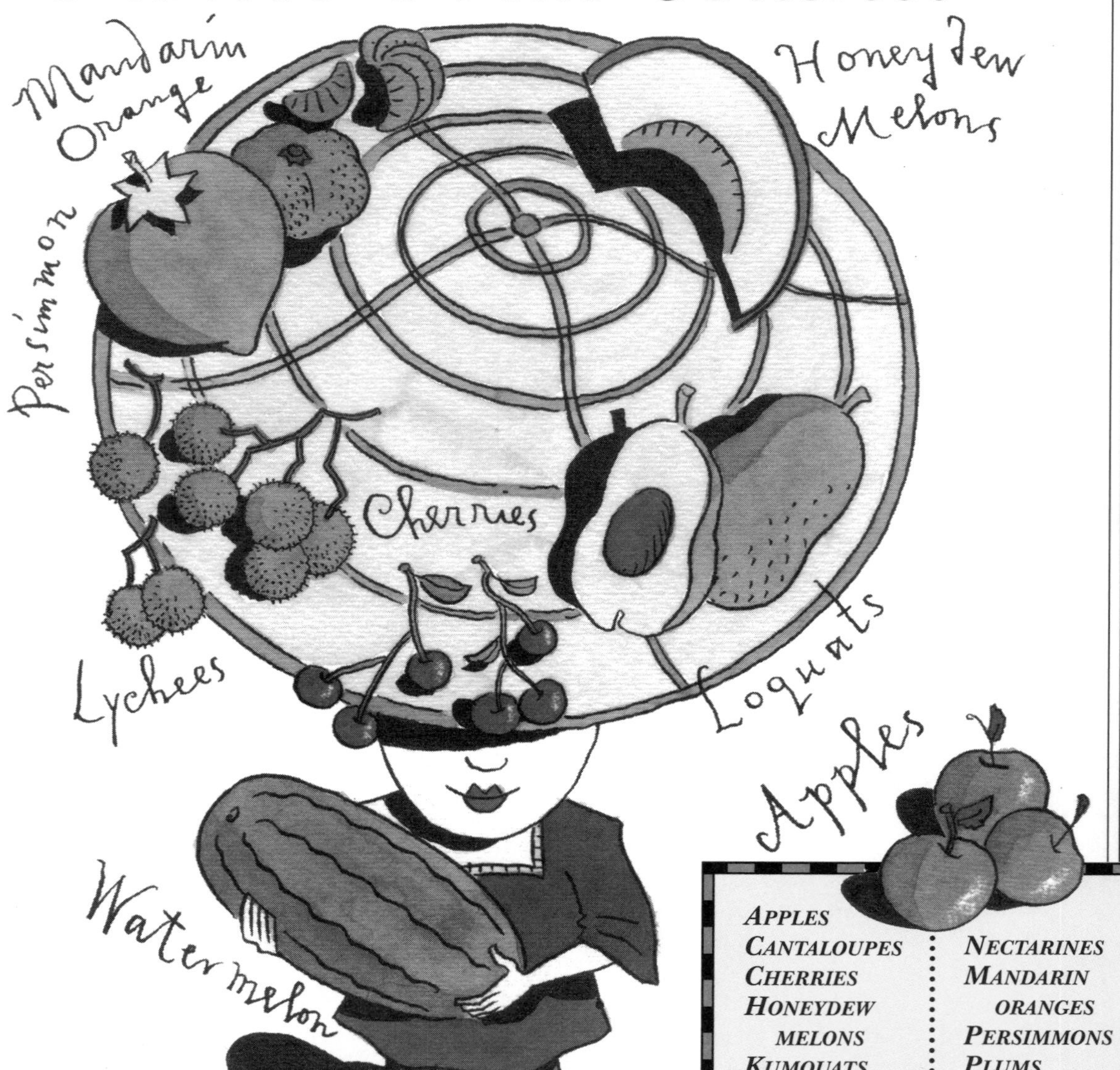

- *APPLES*
- *CANTALOUPES*
- *CHERRIES*
- *HONEYDEW MELONS*
- *KUMQUATS*
- *LOQUATS*
- *LYCHEES*
- *NECTARINES*
- *MANDARIN ORANGES*
- *PERSIMMONS*
- *PLUMS*
- *POMELOS*
- *WATERMELON*

MY KITCHEN DIARY

Roasting a Duck

Often cooks who never think twice about roasting chicken, shy away from roasting duck. Memories of being told duck needs extra care in order to avoid a fatty outcome still looms large, so many consider duck one of those dishes they only eat out.

Well, this shouldn't be the case. Roasting duck is not that difficult and the results can be spectacular. Even more so when you think of what you can do with the leftovers—Roast Duck, Melon, and Mango Salad, for example.

To successfully roast a duck, first remove the giblets and rinse the bird well under cold running water. Pat the bird dry and remove any excess fat from the cavity and around the neck area. Gently prick the skin all over, being careful not to cut into the flesh. Season the duck inside and out with salt and freshly ground black pepper; rub the inside with an orange or lemon half.

Place the duck, breast side up, on a rack in a roasting pan. Roast at 400°F for 30 minutes, then reduce the heat to 350°F and roast until the duck is done to your liking. Generally ducks cook a total of 15 to 18 minutes per pound. During the roasting, baste with the fat at regular intervals, so that the skin gets nicely browned and crisp. Then, pour off the extra fat that has accumulated in the roasting pan. Test for doneness, by pricking the thigh with a fork or skewer. If the juices run clear, the duck is done.

ROAST DUCK, MELON, AND MANGO SALAD

The trend toward leaner eating in China during the 1980s has given rise to dishes that are substantial yet light in flavor. This entrée salad of roast duck, tossed in a savory sauce and surrounded by fruit, is a typical example of new-wave Cantonese cooking. It's lovely to serve for a luncheon in late spring.

SAUCE:
6 tablespoons water
2 tablespoons peanut oil
4 teaspoons hoisin sauce
4 teaspoons soy sauce
4 teaspoons plum sauce
4 teaspoons sugar
2 teaspoons Asian sesame oil
2 teaspoons chili sauce
2 teaspoons oyster sauce

SALAD:
4 cups shredded cooked duck
1 bunch watercress, stems trimmed, rinsed well
1 Bosc pear, peeled, cored, and cut into 2½-inch matchstick strips
1 ripe mango, peeled, pitted, and cut into 2½-inch matchstick strips
½ small honeydew melon, peeled, seeded, and cut into 2½-inch matchstick strips
½ small cantaloupe, peeled, seeded, and cut into 2½-inch matchstick strips
1 hothouse (seedless) cucumber, peeled and cut into 2½-inch matchstick strips
¼ cup chopped roasted peanuts, for garnish
1 tablespoon chopped fresh cilantro leaves, for garnish

1. For the sauce, place the ingredients in a small saucepan over medium-low heat, and cook to blend the flavors and thicken slightly 2 minutes, swirling the pan occasionally.

2. Toss the sauce with the shredded duck meat and set aside.

3. Place the watercress in the center of a large serving platter. Arrange the matchstick strips of fruits and cucumber around the watercress in decorative small bunches. Place the shredded dressed duck in the center of the watercress and sprinkle with the chopped peanuts. Sprinkle the chopped cilantro over all and serve.

Serves 8

ST. MARTIN'S DAY ROASTED GOOSE

In Sweden, St. Martin's Day is celebrated on the 11th of November. Originally in memory of St. Martin of Tours, the festival has come to be associated with Martin Luther. Traditionally this day marks the end of autumn's work and the beginning of winter activities. Roast goose is *the* dish of the day, and there are celebratory goose banquets in both homes and restaurants all over the land.

Roast goose has always seemed special to me. I used to enjoy roasting geese and packing them up in antique baskets as Christmas presents for very special friends. They're very festive and well worth the time. Oven-Braised Red Cabbage and Delicate Herbed Potato Pancakes (see Index) marry beautifully with roasted goose.

STUFFING:
2 cups pitted prunes, halved
2 Granny Smith apples, cored and coarsely chopped
2 cups coarsely chopped red onions
Finely grated zest of 1 orange
2 tablespoons fresh orange juice

1 goose (10 to 12 pounds)
Juice of 1 orange
Coarse salt and coarsely ground black pepper, to taste
8 slices bacon
1 cup defatted Chicken Broth (page 127)
½ cup tawny port
1 tablespoon red currant jelly
1 tablespoon unsalted butter

1. For the stuffing, toss the prunes, apples, onions, and orange zest and juice together in a bowl. Set aside.

2. Preheat the oven to 325°F.

3. Rinse the goose well and pat dry. Prick the skin all over with the tines of a fork. Rub inside and out with orange juice, then sprinkle inside and out with salt and pepper.

4. Fill the cavities with the stuffing and close the cavities with poultry lacers.

5. Place the goose, breast side up, on a rack in a large roasting pan. Lay the bacon slices across the breast. Roast the goose for 1½ hours, removing any accumulated fat in the pan every 30 minutes.

6. Remove the bacon and roast the goose until an instant-read thermometer inserted deep into the thigh reads between 175° and 180°F, about 3 hours longer. Remove the excess fat occasionally. Transfer the goose to a platter, cover loosely with aluminum foil, and let rest for 20 minutes.

7. Pour off any remaining fat in the roasting pan. Add the chicken broth and port to the pan and bring to a boil, scraping up any browned bits on the bottom of the pan. Simmer over low

heat for 5 minutes. Add the red currant jelly and simmer for 2 minutes, stirring. Set aside.

8. Just before serving, warm the gravy over low heat. Add the butter and whisk until it is just mixed in. Serve the stuffing and gravy alongside the goose.

Serves 6

ROASTED PHEASANT WITH PRINCE CHARLES SAUCE

This splendid moist pheasant brings back memories of sitting by a roaring fire in Scotland, anticipating a romantic dinner for two. Don't let these little game birds intimidate, for they're certainly as easy to prepare as a small roast chicken. Because pheasant is a very lean bird, it is necessary to cover the breast with fat such as good smoky bacon, which also imparts beautiful flavor. I've added a bit of chicken broth and Drambuie to the pan for basting the bird as it cooks. For an extraordinary taste, serve the pheasant with warm and velvety Prince Charles Sauce alongside. Cumberland Sauce (see Index) served on the side is also a lovely accompaniment. This recipe is easily doubled to serve more. Be sure to choose an appropriate size roasting pan that will hold the pheasant comfortably.

1 pheasant (about 2¾ pounds)
1 orange, halved
2 tablespoons olive oil
Salt and coarsely ground black pepper, to taste
4 flat-leaf parsley sprigs
2 cloves garlic, peeled
1 bay leaf
6 slices bacon
¼ cup defatted Chicken Broth (page 127)
2 tablespoons Drambuie
Prince Charles Sauce (recipe follows)

1. Preheat the oven to 350°F.

2. Rinse the pheasant, cleaning the cavity well. Remove any excess fat. Pat dry.

3. Squeeze the orange all over the bird and inside the cavity. Brush the pheasant all over with the olive oil. Sprinkle inside and out with salt and pepper. Place the parsley, garlic, and bay leaf in the cavity.

4. Place the bird in a small roasting pan. Arrange the bacon slices across the pheasant, starting at the neck and working towards the back. Add the chicken broth and Drambuie to the pan.

5. Bake in the center of the oven for 1¼ hours, basting 2 or 3 times. Remove the bacon after 1 hour and continue to bake another 15 to 20 minutes until the breast is brown and the pheasant is cooked through (30 minutes per pound total time). When the thickest part of the thigh is tested with the tip of a knife, the juices should run clear. Let rest for 10 minutes, then carve and serve with a sauceboat of Prince Charles sauce.

Serves 2

PRINCE CHARLES SAUCE

This luxurious honey and Drambuie sauce was created for Scotland's Bonnie Prince Charlie in the mid 1700s. After brief low cooking, a pat of butter is swirled into the warm honey to smooth it to a velvety consistency. The combination of flavors, spooned warm over freshly roasted pheasant or rosy sliced leg of lamb, are lush.

½ cup pure clover honey
¼ cup Drambuie
2 tablespoons unsalted butter, at room temperature

Place the honey and Drambuie in a small heavy saucepan. Cook over low heat for 2 minutes until the honey thins out, stirring constantly. Swirl in the butter and cook, stirring, another 2 minutes until the butter melts and the sauce thickens. Warm through over low heat just before serving. This recipe is easily doubled.

Makes approximately ¾ cup

The Sea

It wasn't so long ago that the most glamorous fish dish served in fine restaurants was fillet of sole amandine, but the tide has changed and the variety available today is nothing short of a marvel. As I traveled, I began to feel liberated "fishwise" by the scope of preparations I encountered. An irresistible fresh cod, Russian style; a succulent sea bass baked in a salt crust as prepared in Seville; a perfect Jamaican red snapper grilled over thyme—all simply prepared and about as good as it gets.

With all the fish I've eaten around the world, I still find shrimp to be the universal favorite, and my travels inspired a sautéed shrimp salad Italian style, curried shrimp from Thailand, and avocado shrimp "boats" from Mexico—and that's just naming a few.

While I've generously peppered other chapters with dynamic fish recipes, the hot and cold seafood dishes here stand tall in my repertoire. Wait until you try the Turkish Halibut Lemon Kebabs, and all the other worldly recipes.

THAI SEAFOOD SALAD

Shellfish infused with lemongrass is the basis for this light and delicately spiced salad. Fresh lime juice, mint, and cilantro hold the many flavors together and contrast with the bite of ginger, shallots, and garlic. The beauty of this dish is in the presentation and the eating. You wrap the lettuce and herbs around the shellfish and that's it. No fork needed!

2 dozen littleneck clams
2 tablespoons cornmeal
4 cups water
2 tablespoons thinly sliced fresh lemongrass
1 to 3 tiny dried hot red chilies
1 pound bay scallops, rinsed and drained
1 pound large shrimp, peeled and deveined
2 tablespoons minced shallots
1 tablespoon minced garlic
1 tablespoon minced peeled fresh ginger
3 tablespoons fresh lime juice
2 tablespoons Thai Fish Sauce (page 254; see Note)
1 tablespoon finely grated lime zest
2 tablespoons coarsely chopped fresh mint leaves
2 tablespoons coarsely chopped fresh cilantro leaves
A Thai Centerpiece (see box)

1. Scrub the clams under cold water. Place them in a large bowl and cover with water. Add the cornmeal and let rest for 1 hour. Drain and rinse well.

2. Place the 4 cups of water, lemongrass, and chilies (to taste) in a large saucepan. Bring to a boil, reduce the heat, and simmer covered for 5 minutes. Add the clams and steam, partially covered, for 7 to 10 minutes, removing the clams as they open with a slotted spoon. When cool enough to handle, remove the clams from the shells. Place the meats in a large bowl and discard the shells and any clams that don't open.

3. Add the scallops to the broth and simmer until opaque, 2 to 3 minutes. Remove with a slotted spoon and add to the clams.

4. Add the shrimp to the broth and simmer until just cooked through, about 1½ minutes. Remove with a slotted spoon and add to the clams and scallops. Strain the broth and add the lemongrass to the shellfish.

A Thai Centerpiece

If you are preparing Thai or Vietnamese food, create an outrageously lavish edible centerpiece to accompany it. Begin with soft pale green lettuces. Remove the cores, rinse well, pat dry, and arrange back into the shape of the lettuce head in a basket lined with a linen napkin. Plant cleaned small bunches of fresh mint, fresh basil, and cilantro around the lettuce. Cut long, thin spears of crisp cucumbers and carrots and place decoratively around the greens. Invite your guests to dig into this miniature garden and use the lettuce leaves to enfold their main dish, along with the fresh herbs, cucumbers, and carrots.

5. In a separate bowl, combine the shallots, garlic, ginger, lime juice, fish sauce, and lime zest. Add to the shellfish and combine well. Let rest for 15 minutes.

6. Five minutes before serving, add the chopped mint and cilantro to the shellfish and toss to combine.

7. Serve the salad in a decorative bowl or individual bowls with the Thai centerpiece.

Serves 6 to 8

Note: If you'd rather buy fish sauce, it is available in Asian grocery stores or Asian sections of supermarkets.

SALAD PARADOR

In the early spring of 1991 I had the pleasure of visiting many of the magnificent olive plantations in Andalusia. After spending an enjoyable morning at one of them, my companions and I set off for the old village of Carmona and lunch at the Parador, a magnificent restored castle with great Moorish tile work set on top of a hill. The view of the valley was breathtaking—the patterns of all the olive trees resembling the design of a huge quilt. It seemed to me that something light was in order for lunch, and I chose this warm and luscious shrimp and vegetable salad—a perfect dish.

2 pounds Swiss chard, well rinsed
3 tablespoons plus 2 teaspoons extra virgin Spanish olive oil
1 tablespoon minced garlic (3 to 4 cloves)
8 ounces haricots verts (thin green beans), stem ends trimmed
Salt and freshly ground black pepper, to taste
8 ounces cherry tomatoes, halved
1 pound large shrimp, peeled and deveined
2 tablespoons chopped fresh thyme leaves
3 tablespoons balsamic vinegar
½ cup drained imported brine-marinated black olives
6 fresh thyme sprigs, for garnish
3 lemons, halved, for garnish

1. Cut the stems from the leaves of Swiss chard. Slice the stems on the diagonal ½ inch thick. Cut the leaves into ¼-inch-thick slivers.

2. Heat 1 tablespoon of the olive oil in a large nonstick skillet over medium heat. Add the garlic and cook about 1 minute. Add the Swiss chard stems and sauté to soften slightly, about 3 minutes. Transfer to a bowl and set aside.

3. Heat another 1 tablespoon olive oil in the skillet and add the haricots verts. Cook over medium heat until crisp-tender, shaking the pan occasionally for even cooking, 4 minutes. Add the beans to the Swiss chard stems and season with salt and pepper to taste.

4. Heat another 1 tablespoon olive oil in the skillet and add the cherry tomatoes, shrimp, chopped thyme, and salt and pepper to taste. Cook over medium heat, shaking the skillet and turning the shrimp once or twice, until the shrimp are cooked through, 4 to 5 minutes. Transfer to another bowl and set aside.

5. Heat 1 teaspoon olive oil in the skillet and add half the Swiss chard leaves. Sauté, stirring constantly, until nicely wilted but still slightly crunchy, 2 to 3 minutes. Transfer to a third bowl and repeat the process with the remaining oil and leaves. Toss the leaves with the balsamic

vinegar and season with salt and pepper.

6. To serve, divide the chard leaves among 6 plates. Top each with a portion of the stems and beans. Arrange the tomatoes and shrimp on top, sprinkle with a few olives, and garnish each plate with a sprig of thyme and half a lemon. Serve warm.

Serves 6

ITALIAN SHRIMP SALAD CROSTINI

This summery Italian salad of fresh tomatoes tossed with sautéed shrimp is enhanced by lemon juice and briny small capers. Spoon it atop garlicky crostini and crown it with crisp peppery greens. This quick preparation makes for a beautiful sun-bathed luncheon or dinner.

8 ripe plum tomatoes, cut into 8 pieces each
2 bunches arugula or watercress, rinsed and dried
1 pound large shrimp, peeled and deveined
5 tablespoons extra virgin olive oil
1 tablespoon drained tiny capers
1 tablespoon fresh lemon juice
Coarse salt and coarsely ground black pepper, to taste
4 slices (½ inch thick) crusty peasant bread, toasted
2 cloves garlic, halved

1. Place the tomatoes in a large bowl and set aside. Remove the tough stems from the greens. Pinch off and reserve the delicate stems and leaves. Cut the shrimp crosswise in half.

2. Heat 4 tablespoons of the oil in a large nonstick skillet over high heat. Add the shrimp and cook, shaking the skillet and tossing the shrimp, until cooked through, about 4 minutes. Add the shrimp to the tomatoes.

3. Toss the capers and lemon juice with the tomatoes and shrimp. Season with salt and pepper.

4. Brush 1 side of the toasted bread slices with the remaining tablespoon of oil. Rub the oiled sides of the bread with the cut side of the garlic cloves.

5. To serve, place each slice of toast, oiled side up, in the center of a large dinner plate. Spoon the shrimp and tomatoes over the toast, then top with the arugula or watercress. Serve immediately.

Serves 4

LISA'S ROSY SHRIMP SALAD

After a morning of wandering the food halls of Stockholm, I stopped for lunch at Lisa Elmquist's restaurant located at the heart of the bustling market. Among my selections was a very simple shrimp salad, all creamy and luxurious with a faint pink blush. For a dashing presentation, serve the salad nestled in red radicchio leaves, surrounded with deep-green, peppery arugula.

S O U V E N I R   T O   S A V O R

A Taste of the Baltic

One of the things I love most about traveling is visiting all the food markets. Stockholm's Saluhall is a gem of a place. Housed within a red brick building topped with oxidized bronze cupolas, this small market offers some usual market fare, but most impressive is the array of Baltic bounty that awaits. In season, trays filled with blazing red orange crayfish in their brine rest alongside delicate coral shrimp garnished with the greenest sprigs of dill. Sides of salmon on wooden fish-shaped boards glisten under the skylights. Slices of gravlax, delicately rimmed in finely chopped dill, are sold with a luscious dill mustard sauce. Customers wait in line to choose fresh crabs from huge wooden crates. Large tables covered with chopped ice display the vast variety of fish from northern waters—salmon, flounder, herring, cod, mackerel, haddock, halibut, coalfish, plaice. Small tins of caviar, tubes of fish paste, and other smoked fish delicacies are stacked abundantly in glass cases. A dozen or so other stalls offer fresh fruits and vegetables, different breads and cheeses, and fresh and smoked meats, including reindeer, moose, and elk.

After a wander through the market, Lisa Elmquist's restaurant provided a perfect spot for lunch. Sitting on bar stools perched over glass cases filled with the day's selection of seafood specialties, we ordered up a "tasting lunch" of Rosy Shrimp Salad, Salmon Caviar Egg Salad (see Index), a tureen of 12 crayfish and tall icy glasses of Sweden's Spendrups beer, to wash it all down. Waitresses, wearing crisp blue and white striped shirts emblazoned with a red crayfish logo, worked behind the counter artfully arranging the plates to be served to the eager Saturday morning crowd.

Saluhall In Stockholm.

POACHED SHRIMP:
6 cups water
½ cup dry white wine
4 black peppercorns
6 fresh dill sprigs
1 pound large shrimp, peeled and deveined

2 tablespoons finely chopped red onion
¼ cup finely chopped fresh dill, plus 2 tablespoons for garnish

DRESSING:
½ cup crème fraîche
½ cup mayonnaise
2 teaspoons ketchup
Salt, to taste
⅛ teaspoon ground white pepper

2 heads radicchio, leaves separated and rinsed
1 bunch arugula, rinsed, large stems trimmed

1. For the poached shrimp, in a large heavy pot, bring the water, wine, peppercorns, and dill sprigs to a boil. Add the shrimp, reduce the heat to medium-low and simmer until cooked through, about 1 minute. Drain. When cool enough to handle, cut the shrimp crosswise in half.

2. Place the shrimp, red onion, and ¼ cup dill in a mixing bowl and toss together gently.

3. For the dressing, combine the crème fraîche, mayonnaise, ketchup, salt, and pepper in a small bowl. Fold the dressing into the shrimp mixture. Cover the salad and refrigerate for at least 1 hour before serving.

4. To serve, divide the radicchio and arugula leaves among 4 large plates and spoon the shrimp salad into the radicchio cups. Sprinkle with the remaining 2 tablespoons chopped dill.

Serves 4

MINTY AVOCADO SHRIMP SALAD

Thai-inspired, this entrée salad of shrimp and avocado is pepped up with a lime vinaigrette and fresh mint leaves.

When working with avocados, especially in salads, toss them first with some lime or lemon juice to prevent discoloration.

2 ripe avocados, preferably Haas, pitted, peeled, and sliced in fairly large pieces
2 tablespoons fresh lime juice
1 pound large shrimp, peeled, deveined, and cooked
1 red bell pepper, stemmed, seeded, and cut into ⅛-inch dice
1 cup diced (⅛ inch) seeded ripe plum tomatoes
4 scallions (3 inches green left on), thinly sliced on the diagonal
½ cup Lily Lime Vinaigrette (recipe follows), or more for serving
3 tablespoons coarsely chopped fresh mint leaves

1. Place the avocados in a large bowl and toss with the lime juice.

2. Add the shrimp, bell pepper, tomatoes, and scallions; fold together. Toss gently with the vinaigrette. Just before serving, toss with the fresh mint leaves. Serve at once with extra vinaigrette if desired.

Serves 6

LILY LIME VINAIGRETTE

⅓ cup fresh lime juice
1 tablespoon Dijon mustard
Salt and freshly ground black pepper, to taste
½ cup olive oil
½ cup vegetable oil
1 tablespoon minced shallots
Finely grated zest of 1 lime
3 tablespoons snipped fresh chives

In a small bowl whisk together the lime juice, mustard, salt, and pepper. Slowly drizzle in the oils, whisking constantly, until thickened. Stir in the shallots and lime zest. Add the chives 15 minutes before use.

Makes 1⅓ cups

THE BEERS OF

Southeast Asia

The spicy cuisines of Southeast Asia call for cooling drinks, and beer is by far the beverage of choice with most dishes. It is the leading alcoholic drink in Asia since rice, barley, and buckwheat are plentiful in these climates, which are too humid for wine grapes. Though barley is the main component of regional beers, rice and other grains are used as adjuncts.

The Southeast Asian brewing industries, particularly those of Indonesia, Thailand, and Singapore, were influenced by German brewmasters after World War I. The best beers are ales and lagers, but dark-roasted barley stout is also popular. Among the favorites are Thailand's world-class Singha, a brisk, hop-flavored lager with its handsome stylized lion on the label; Singapore's two popular Tiger brands, a golden lager and a dark stout; and Malaya's ABC Extra Stout.

With tamer dishes, as well as French-influenced Vietnamese cuisine, dry but fruity white wines, such as dry Riesling, Pinot Gris, and Sauvignon/Sémillon blends, can be very appealing.

Merlot and Champagne *brut rosé* are popular with meat dishes.

Singha is the perfect cool down for those fiery Thai meals. If none is nearby—ask for spiritual advice!

SENORITA SHRIMP BOATS

Every restaurant in Mexico seemed to offer an avocado half stuffed with bay shrimp, but none I tasted was prepared with any originality. As soon as I came home, I decided to lighten and brighten this predictable salad. I scooped out the inside of the avocados with a small melon baller, and added the avocado balls to the shrimp along with diced tomatoes, and balls of cantaloupe and honeydew. All dressed in a lively orange and cilantro mayonnaise, it is lovely stuffed into the avocado shells.

1 bay leaf
2 ribs celery with leaves, halved
2 flat-leaf parsley sprigs
4 black peppercorns
1 pound large shrimp, peeled and deveined
3 plum tomatoes, seeded and cut into ¼-inch dice
Juice of 1 lime
3 ripe avocados, preferably Haas, halved and pitted
1 cup small ripe cantaloupe balls
1 cup small ripe honeydew balls
1 cup Cilantro Mayonnaise (recipe follows)
6 small fresh cilantro leaves, for garnish

1. Bring a large pot of water with the bay leaf, celery, parsley, and peppercorns to a boil. Add the shrimp, reduce the heat to medium-low, and simmer until the shrimp are just cooked through, about 1 minute. Drain.

2. When cool enough to handle, cut each shrimp crosswise into 3 or 4 pieces. Toss gently with the tomatoes in a large bowl.

3. Place the lime juice in another bowl. Using a small melon baller, remove 6 balls from each avocado half. Toss in the lime juice. Rub the remaining exposed avocado halves with lime juice to prevent discoloration. Set the shells aside.

4. Add the avocado and melon balls to the shrimp mixture. Add the cilantro mayonnaise and toss gently to combine.

5. Fill each avocado half with ½ cup shrimp salad and garnish with the cilantro leaves.

Serves 6

CILANTRO MAYONNAISE

A fresh herb mayonnaise adds zing to seafood, chicken, or fruit salad, instead of just acting as a moist binder. This recipe boasts the addition of orange zest as well. Feel free to substitute tarragon for the cilantro and lemon zest for the orange for a completely different flavor.

½ cup mayonnaise
½ cup sour cream
Finely grated zest of 1 orange
2 tablespoons chopped fresh cilantro leaves
2 tablespoons chopped flat-leaf parsley
Salt and coarsely ground black pepper, to taste

Mix all the ingredients together in a bowl.

Refrigerate covered until ready to use, but do not make more than 1 day in advance.

Makes approximately 1 cup

VELVETY CURRIED SHRIMP

Delicate and easy to prepare, shrimp curry is perfect for entertaining. Vegetable broth and coconut milk are flavored with onions, garlic, ginger, and my own blend of curry powder. Ripe tomatoes and fresh parsley add fresh dazzle to the sauce. The sauce can be made ahead of time and gently reheated. Just before serving, stir in the shrimp and cook for 5 minutes. This is the dish to serve in shallow bowls over Vegetable Sparkled Rice, with Apple-Pineapple Raita (see Index) and a sweet mango chutney.

2 tablespoons vegetable oil
2 medium onions, cut into ¼-inch dice
1 tablespoon minced peeled fresh ginger
1 tablespoon minced garlic
2½ tablespoons My Own Curry Powder (page 260) or best-quality curry powder
1 small fresh red chili, halved, seeds and ribs removed
3 ripe medium tomatoes, cored, seeded, and finely chopped
2 cups Fresh Vegetable Broth or defatted Chicken Broth (page 129 or 127)
2 cups coconut milk (page 252 or available in specialty food stores)
Salt, to taste
2 pounds medium shrimp, peeled and deveined
2 tablespoons chopped fresh cilantro leaves or flat-leaf parsley

1. Heat the oil in a heavy casserole over medium-low heat. Add the onions, ginger, and garlic; cook, stirring, until wilted, about 10 minutes.

2. Add the curry powder and continue to cook, stirring, over low heat for 2 minutes longer. Stir in the chili and tomatoes and cook, stirring, another 2 minutes.

3. Add the broth and bring to a boil. Reduce the heat to medium-low and gently simmer uncovered for 10 minutes. Whisk in the coconut milk and cook until the sauce thickens slightly, about 10 minutes more. Season the sauce with salt.

4. Before serving, heat the sauce over medium-low heat until it simmers. Discard the chili and add the shrimp. Simmer until just cooked through, 5 minutes. Do not overcook. Stir in the cilantro or parsley. Serve immediately.

Serves 6

HOT SHRIMP IN A POT

These little bubbling-hot dishes kept showing up as *mezes* throughout Greece and Turkey. Although there is a long list of ingredients, the recipe is easily prepared ahead of time up to the final baking. It makes a perfect centerpiece for a luncheon or dinner party.

2 tablespoons unsalted butter
2 tablespoons olive oil
1 pound medium-size white mushrooms, wiped clean, stems trimmed, quartered
¼ teaspoon ground nutmeg
Salt and coarsely ground black pepper, to taste
1 cup coarsely chopped onion
1 cup diced (¼ inch) red bell pepper
2 tablespoons minced garlic
1½ cups seeded and coarsely chopped ripe tomatoes
1 cup dry white wine
1 tablespoon honey
2 teaspoons dried oregano
1 bay leaf
1 pound medium shrimp, peeled and deveined
1 tablespoon finely grated orange zest
½ cup chopped flat-leaf parsley, plus 2 tablespoons for garnish
4 ounces Kasseri cheese or other semihard cheese, such as provolone, Gruyère, or Emmental, grated

1. Heat half the butter and half the olive oil in a large nonstick skillet over medium-high heat. Add the mushrooms and cook until softened, 4 to 5 minutes. Season with the nutmeg, salt, and pepper. Remove to a bowl and set aside.

2. Heat the remaining butter and olive oil in the skillet over low heat. Add the onion, bell pepper, and garlic; cook, stirring occasionally, until softened, about 10 minutes.

3. Add the tomatoes, white wine, honey, oregano, and bay leaf. Increase the heat to medium and cook uncovered for 30 minutes, stirring occasionally.

4. Add the shrimp and orange zest and cook until the shrimp is cooked through, 2 to 3 minutes. Drain the reserved mushrooms and add them to the shrimp along with ½ cup parsley. Remove the bay leaf and season with salt and pepper to taste.

5. Preheat the oven to 400°F.

6. Place six 8-ounce ramekins on a baking sheet and divide the shrimp mixture among them. Top with the grated cheese. Bake until the cheese is golden and bubbly, about 20 minutes. Sprinkle with the remaining chopped parsley and serve immediately.

Serves 6

JUMBO SHRIMP RAGOUT

Shrimp are the perfect ingredient for both delicate and robust preparations. Once the chopping is done, this Mediterranean-accented dish is quickly cooked to keep its fresh flavors. Swiss chard, which appears in many Niçoise and Spanish dishes, is a great substitute for escarole. Be sure to use only the tenderest part of the stems and the dark green leaves. Serve with hot crusty bread for dipping. A lightly chilled Provençal rosé is an ideal wine for this dish.

3 tablespoons extra virgin Spanish olive oil
3 cloves garlic, finely chopped
24 escarole leaves, rinsed well, cut crosswise into 1-inch strips
1 cup stuffed Spanish Manzanilla olives, rinsed
¾ cup defatted Chicken Broth (page 127)
1 cup coarsely chopped fresh basil leaves
Salt and freshly ground black pepper, to taste
18 jumbo shrimp, peeled and deveined
8 ripe plum tomatoes, seeded and cut into 1-inch pieces
¼ cup thinly sliced scallions, for garnish

1. Heat the oil in a large heavy pot over low heat. Add the garlic and cook to soften, 1 minute. Add the escarole and olives; cook, stirring constantly, until the escarole begins to wilt, about 1 minute.

2. Add the broth and basil and cook over low heat another 2 minutes. Season with salt and pepper.

3. Toss in the shrimp and tomatoes, cover the pot, and cook, stirring once, until the shrimp are cooked through, 3 to 4 minutes. Do not overcook.

4. Divide the shrimp among 6 shallow soup or pasta bowls. Spoon the sauce and vegetables over the top. Garnish with scallions and serve immediately.

Serves 6

GAENG KUA GOONG

Curried Pineapple and Prawns

Curry in Thailand is unlike the curry we are accustomed to in America. For the most part, Americans have eaten Indian curries, accompanied by yogurt and mango chutney. But now we are growing interested in Pacific Rim countries and their cuisines. Indonesia, Thailand, and Malaysia produce an extraordinary array of curry pastes, curry powders, and curry

MY KITCHEN DIARY

Shrimp Paste

Shrimp paste is one of those ingredients that is difficult to make at home or find a substitute for, so it is good to see it showing up in Asian and specialty food stores as the interest in Southeast Asian food increases. Basically, the paste is an intense mixture of fermented ground-up shrimp. The color, which ranges from purple to maroon, indicates how long a paste has cured and fermented in the sun. Because of its pungent flavor, most recipes just use a small amount. The heady taste enriches Thai and other Southeast Asian sauces, but you will be able to proceed with a recipe even if you can't find shrimp paste. If you find yourself making dishes that call for it, I would recommend that you write or call the following mail order suppliers to obtain a small jar. Once a jar is opened, it will last for 1 year in the refrigerator.

Adriana's Bazaar: 2152 Broadway, New York, NY 10023; (212) 877-5757.

K. Kalustyan: 123 Lexington Avenue, New York, NY 10016; (212) 685-3451; fax (212)683-8458.

sauces that are not based on the more familiar turmeric-laden blends. The curry paste in this recipe is pungent and aromatic. It flavors the coconut milk in a subtle yet exciting manner.

4 ounces flounder or sole fillet
6 fresh cilantro sprigs
3 large shallots, coarsely chopped (½ cup)
5 cloves garlic, coarsely chopped
1 piece (1 inch) fresh ginger, peeled and coarsely chopped
1 tablespoon minced fresh green chili, seeds and ribs removed
1 tablespoon thinly sliced fresh lemongrass
1 teaspoon shrimp paste (see box page 405)
½ teaspoon salt
3 cups coconut milk (page 252 or available in specialty food stores)
3 tablespoons fresh lemon juice
3 tablespoons Thai Fish Sauce (page 254; see Note)
3 cups diced (½ inch) fresh ripe pineapple
1½ pounds large shrimp, shelled, deveined, and halved lengthwise
4 tablespoons chopped fresh cilantro
4 cups hot cooked rice (1½ cups raw)

1. Rinse the fish and pat dry. Fill a skillet with water to the depth of 1 inch. Add the cilantro sprigs and bring to a boil. Reduce the heat, add the fish, and gently simmer until it is opaque, 2 minutes. Remove the fish to a bowl and break it into flakes. Discard the cooking liquid.

2. In a food processor, combine the shallots, garlic, ginger, chili, lemongrass, shrimp paste, and salt. Process until the mixture is almost a paste, about 30 seconds, stopping to scrape down the sides if necessary. With the machine running, add the fish through the feed tube and process another 30 seconds until combined. Remove to a bowl and set aside.

3. Place the coconut milk in a large heavy saucepan and slowly bring to a boil. Add the fish paste mixture and simmer, stirring constantly, over low heat until slightly thickened, about 2 minutes.

4. Add the lemon juice, fish sauce, and pineapple; cook, stirring, 1 minute. Add the shrimp and cook, stirring, until the shrimp are cooked through, 1½ to 2 minutes. Stir in 2 tablespoons of the cilantro.

5. Divide the rice between 6 shallow bowls. Ladle the hot curry atop the rice and garnish with the remaining chopped cilantro. Serve immediately.

Serves 6

How to Eat a Crayfish

Crayfish eating is a bit of an effort—but well worth it. Most of the meat is in the tail. To extract it, simply twist off the tail section from the rest of the body. Split the tail shell with your fingers; the meat lifts out easily. You can stop there or work on the two small claws. Twist them off and suck out the bit of meat inside. If you're *still* not ready to move on to the next crayfish, twist off the tiny legs and suck on them, too. Sip ice cold Aquavit or beer between crayfish and have plenty of napkins and a finger bowl on hand.

SWEDISH CRAYFISH

If you are lucky enough to come across fresh Swedish crayfish in the market around the middle of August, this is the classic Swedish method for preparing them. If the real thing isn't available, those delicious crayfish from Louisiana will do beautifully.

2 pounds fresh crayfish (about 30)
2½ quarts water
⅓ cup plus 1 tablespoon coarse salt
1 teaspoon sugar
2 large bunches fresh dill flowers, reserve some for garnish

1. Inspect the crayfish, making sure they're all alive and well. Rinse under cold water.

2. Combine 2½ quarts water, the salt, sugar, and dill flowers in a large pot and bring to a boil. Drop the crayfish in the boiling water and cover the pot immediately. Bring back to a boil and continue to boil for 7 minutes. Remove the cover and let the crayfish cool in the brine. Refrigerate overnight in the cooking brine.

3. Before serving, pour off the liquid and remove the dill. To serve, arrange the crayfish in an attractive bowl or on a platter and garnish with dill flowers. Then, dig in. (See How to Eat a Crayfish for tips on extracting every succulent bite.)

Serves 3 or 4

SOUVENIR TO SAVOR

The Swedish Crayfish Festival

I fell in love with crayfish not, as you might think, in New Orleans, but in Stockholm some twenty years ago. It was mid-August and Richard and I were there celebrating our wedding anniversary. We had such a wonderful vacation that I planned my recent visit to Sweden to coincide with the crayfish celebration and my own twenty-seventh anniversary celebration.

The crayfish festival starts with the beginning of the crayfish fishing season, the second Wednesday in August, and lasts until the end of the month. On the evening of the season's opening day, there are parties throughout the country. Paper lanterns decorate terraces and balconies, gently swaying above tables holding platters heaped high with Sweden's beloved delicacy. The Swedes take great delight in these delicious, vibrant, red orange crustaceans and favor a very simple preparation, boiling them in salted water seasoned with dill flowers. Black, whole-grain crisp breads and mild cheeses like Kryddost, spiced with caraway and cloves, accompany the feast along with iced aquavit and chilled beer. The only other element necessary is the best of Sweden's festive folk music.

A TASTE OF THE WORLD

Portuguese Palette

Photo: The fairyland castles of Sintra, outside of Lisbon.

...And

Chilies
Black pepper
Cilantro
Parsley
Garlic
Onions
Potatoes
Lemons
Oranges
Olives
Olive oil
Eggs
Cheese
Dried salt cod
Clams
Cured ham
Shrimp
Rice
Chorizo

STEAMED CLAMS ALENTEJO

The first time I ordered tiny steamed clams in Portugal, they came served with large pieces of pork. The dish was delicious and seemed to me to be unusual, but I quickly learned that this is a classic Portuguese preparation. To preserve the style of the Alentejo province, I've bathed the clams in olive oil, garlic, and cilantro, but I added shredded prosciutto—definitely not Portuguese. Yet it keeps the spirit of the original dish. Being a great fan of *linguine con vongole,* I serve the clams and broth in pasta bowls over linguine.

3 dozen littleneck clams, as small as possible
2 tablespoons cornmeal
¼ cup fruity extra virgin olive oil
4 ounces prosciutto di Parma, thinly shredded
8 cloves garlic, chopped
1 cup Fish Stock (page 130) or bottled clam juice
1 cup dry white wine
½ cup coarsely chopped fresh cilantro leaves
Crusty bread or 8 ounces linguine, cooked (optional)

1. Scrub the clams under cold water. Place them in a large bowl and cover with water. Add the cornmeal and let rest for 1 hour. Drain and rinse well.

2. Place the oil in a large heavy pot. Add the prosciutto and cook, stirring, over low heat for 2 minutes. Add the garlic, stock, wine, and cilantro. Cook over medium heat for another 2 minutes.

3. Add the clams, cover the pot, and increase the heat to medium. Cook, shaking the pan occasionally, until the clams open, about 10 minutes. Discard any unopened clams. Scoop the hot clams into shallow bowls, spoon the cooking broth over the top, and serve with crusty bread; or divide the linguine among 4 pasta bowls and spoon the clams and cooking broth on top.

Serves 4

STIR-FRIED SCALLOPS AND ASPARAGUS TERIYAKI

The light fresh tastes of springtime come together with sweet sea scallops and tender asparagus quickly sautéed in a pungent teriyaki sauce. If you're able to find some lavender chive blossoms, drape them over the scallops for an Asian flourish. Serve this dish with chive-flecked Lemon Orzo (see Index).

1½ pounds sea scallops
1 cup Basic Teriyaki Sauce (page 372)
1 tablespoon peanut oil
12 ounces asparagus, tough ends trimmed, sliced on the diagonal into 2-inch pieces
1 tablespoon snipped fresh chives, for garnish

1. Place the scallops in a small bowl, add the teriyaki sauce, and toss well. Marinate for 1 hour at room temperature.

2. Heat the peanut oil in a nonstick skillet over medium-high heat. Drain the scallops, reserving ½ cup of the marinade. Add the scallops to the skillet in small batches and cook about 1½ minutes per side until cooked through. Remove to a plate and keep warm.

3. Add the asparagus to the pan and cook for 3 minutes over medium-high heat, shaking the pan constantly. Remove the asparagus to the plate with the scallops.

4. Pour the reserved marinade into the skillet and cook over high heat until reduced by half, about 3 minutes. Return the scallops and asparagus to the skillet and coat well with the sauce. Garnish with the chives. Serve immediately.

Serves 6

MOULES MARINIERE

Moules marinière is a marvelous, simple French mussel preparation. The liquid the mussels are cooked in is delicately flavored with white wine, shallots, parsley, and fresh thyme. And as they cook, the mussels release their own liquid into the broth. I've added chopped tomatoes for both sweetness and color. Serve the mussels in shallow bowls with the broth and vegetables ladled atop, with a sprinkling of fresh parsley. This makes a lovely light meal, accompanied with crusty peasant bread for dipping in the broth, a green salad, and chilled white Burgundy.

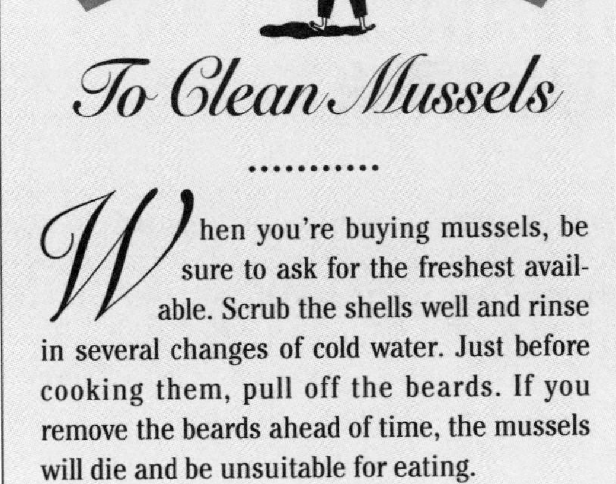

To Clean Mussels

When you're buying mussels, be sure to ask for the freshest available. Scrub the shells well and rinse in several changes of cold water. Just before cooking them, pull off the beards. If you remove the beards ahead of time, the mussels will die and be unsuitable for eating.

8 pounds fresh mussels (1⅓ pounds per person for a main course, about 16 per person)
4 tablespoons (½ stick) unsalted butter
1 large onion, cut into ¼-inch dice
4 shallots, finely chopped
¾ cup plus 3 tablespoons chopped flat-leaf parsley
3 large fresh thyme sprigs
Salt and coarsely ground black pepper, to taste
3 cups dry white wine
1 cup water
6 ripe plum tomatoes, seeded and cut into ¼-inch dice

1. Scrub the mussels well and rinse in several changes of cold water. Remove the beards just before cooking.

2. Melt the butter in a large heavy pot over medium heat. Add the onion and shallots; cook, stirring, until wilted and translucent, 6 to 8 minutes. Add ¾ cup parsley, the thyme, salt, pepper, wine, and water. Bring the mixture to a boil; lower the heat and simmer for 2 minutes.

3. Add the mussels and sprinkle with the tomatoes. Cover and cook over medium-high heat for about 15 minutes until the mussels open; shake the pan often for even cooking. Discard any unopened mussels.

4. Spoon the mussels into shallow bowls and ladle generously with the broth and chopped vegetables. Sprinkle with the remaining 3 tablespoons chopped parsley for garnish. Serve immediately.

Serves 6 to 8

SAVORY SALMON CROQUETTES

Flavors of the Turkish palette are so pervasive in all their dishes that they even make their way into fish *köfte,* small fried fish balls. For these croquettes I've combined salmon with toasted pine nuts, cinnamon, allspice, currants, and dill. The result is savory with just a hint of sweetness. These croquettes are well suited for a brunch entrée, served along with persimmon-hued Quince Spoon Sweet (see Index).

2 cups finely flaked poached fresh salmon, or canned salmon, drained, skin and bones removed
1 large egg, lightly beaten
½ cup plus 2 tablespoons dried bread crumbs
¼ cup mayonnaise
2 tablespoons grated onion
2 tablespoons pine nuts, toasted (see Note)
2 tablespoons currants
2 tablespoons chopped fresh dill
1 teaspoon finely grated lemon zest
⅛ teaspoon ground cinnamon
Pinch of ground allspice
¼ cup vegetable oil

1. Combine the salmon, egg, 2 tablespoons bread crumbs, the mayonnaise, onion, pine nuts, currants, dill, lemon zest, cinnamon, and allspice in a mixing bowl.

2. Form the salmon mixture into 8 patties about 2½ inches in diameter. Lightly coat the croquettes in the remaining ½ cup bread crumbs, shaking off any excess.

3. Heat the oil in a large nonstick skillet over medium heat. Fry the croquettes, turning once, until golden, about 6 minutes. Drain on paper towels and serve hot.

Makes 8 croquettes

Note: To toast pine nuts, preheat the oven to 350°F. Spread the nuts on a baking sheet and roast until golden and fragrant, 3 to 5 minutes. Check after 3 minutes as pine nuts burn very easily.

GRAVLAX

Gravlax is one of Scandinavia's great contributions to the culinary spectrum. The salmon, being both a salt and freshwater fish (it heads for "sweet" waters to spawn) is a perfect choice for this classic Nordic curing process which uses both salt and sugar. While sampling gravlax in Sweden, I often tasted fish cured in sugar alone. It's flavor was spectacular. In this recipe, I've leaned more heavily on the sugar than the salt. I think the result is delicious.

S O U V E N I R T O S A V O R

Dinner at Operakällaren with the Leimdorfers

During my stay in Sweden, Martin and Christine Leimdorfer invited me and my traveling companions to dinner at Stockholm's most beautiful dining room, Operakällaren. As we sat at our elegantly set table overlooking the Royal Palace on the banks of the Baltic, Martin filled us in on the restaurant's history. First opened in 1787 in the old Opera House built by King Gustav III, Operakällaren was a typical cellar restaurant in those days, and became an immediate success with the literary and art circles. It has since survived two centuries and several restorations and evolved into one of the most favored restaurants of Stockholm society, serving fabulous *smörgåsbords* at lunchtime and refined dinners in the evening.

The oak-paneled dining room is ornately decorated with gilt-framed cherubic paintings by the artist Oscar Bjorck. Our dinner began with warm fluffy blinis slathered with crème fraîche and topped generously with bleak roe caviar, the tiniest coral-colored beads from freshwater fish. Chopped red onion and lemon wedges were passed as we sipped our Champagne. Next came Swedish wild duck roasted in black currant sauce and served with rutabaga ("swedes" as the Swedes call them) and celery root purées. For dessert, we devoured cloudberry ice cream sandwiched between two hazelnut meringues, topped with fresh cloudberries and a cloudberry sauce. Cloudberries are orange-yellow raspberries that just about transported me to the clouds. You see, the meal was heavenly!

Stockholm's Royal Palace sits right on the Baltic.

Gravlax should be very thinly sliced on the diagonal with a long, thin, very sharp knife and daintily served with a sweet dilled mustard sauce spooned alongside. It is substantial enough to be the star of a late night supper, accompanied by a light cucumber salad, boiled new potatoes, and thin slices of pumpernickel bread in a small basket, lined with a lacy white napkin. Chilled Champagne and moonlight would certainly add the perfect final touch.

2 center-cut, best-quality fresh salmon fillets (1 pound each), of equal size and shape, skin left on
1 tablespoon Pernod
¾ cup sugar
¼ cup coarse salt
1 tablespoon white peppercorns, coarsely crushed
1 large bunch dill (about 2 ounces), coarsely chopped, reserve some sprigs for garnish
Sweet Dilled Mustard Sauce (recipe follows)

1. Wipe the fillets with a damp paper towel and remove any small bones with tweezers.

2. Sprinkle the flesh side of the fillets with the Pernod and rub it in well.

3. Combine the sugar, salt, and pepper together in a small bowl. Sprinkle one-third of the sugar mixture on the bottom of a nonreactive baking dish just large enough to hold the salmon in 2 layers. Cover with one-third of the dill. Lay one of the salmon fillets, skin side down, on top of the dill. Sprinkle with half the remaining sugar mixture, and rub it into the salmon well. Sprinkle with half the remaining dill and cover with the remaining salmon fillet, skin side up. Sprinkle with the remaining sugar mixture, then the remaining dill.

4. Cover tightly with plastic wrap, then a sheet of aluminum foil. Place a cutting board and several heavy cans or a brick on top of the salmon to weight it down. Marinate in the refrigerator for 36 to 48 hours, turning the salmon every 12 hours.

5. To serve, scrape the marinade off the salmon fillets. With the skin side down, very thinly slice the fillets with the grain. Allow about 4 slices for each serving. Garnish each serving with a dill sprig and spoon some mustard sauce alongside.

Serves 10

SWEET DILLED MUSTARD SAUCE

No matter where you travel in Scandinavia, a dilled mustard sauce always accompanies gravlax or other cured fish. Its smooth, velvety consistency comes from adding the oil drop by drop while whisking constantly. The choice of vinegar can vary from an assertive red or white wine vinegar to a sweeter and smoother apple cider variety. To accent the sauce's sweetness, I've used cider vinegar. In addition to gravlax, this sauce is delicious served with thinly sliced roasted lamb and cold smoked meats .

2 tablespoons Dijon mustard
2 tablespoons cider vinegar
2 tablespoons sugar
Salt and coarsely ground white pepper, to taste
½ cup vegetable oil
2 tablespoons chopped fresh dill

In a small bowl, combine the mustard, vinegar, sugar, salt, and pepper. While whisking constantly, slowly drizzle in the oil and continue to whisk until the mixture is thick and creamy. Stir in the chopped dill. The sauce keeps for up to 1 week stored in the refrigerator in an airtight container. Bring to room temperature and whisk again before serving.

Makes ¾ cup

SEARED GRAVLAX

This recipe should be entitled What to Do with Leftover Gravlax. As delicious as gravlax is, Americans find a little goes a long way. When I was testing the recipe, I had a 1-pound piece of cured salmon left. I was going to broil it but then decided that pan searing might be more convenient. The results were spectacular. The fish is seared, skin side down, in a skillet over high heat, then cooked covered a few minutes to just the right degree of doneness. As the salmon sears, the sugar from the marinade caramelizes, infusing the fish with a delicious sweetness. Because the fish has already been cured, it is perfect served rare, with no worries about eating undercooked fish. Serve with Roasted Tomatoes and Roasted Beets and your favorite potato salad (see Index).

1 tablespoon vegetable oil
1 piece (1 pound salmon) Gravlax (page 411)
Sweet Dilled Mustard Sauce (page 413)

1. Heat the oil in a large nonstick skillet for 30 seconds over medium heat. Add the gravlax, skin side down, and increase the heat to medium-high. Cook, shaking the pan and lifting the salmon with a spatula to loosen it from the pan, until the skin is brown, 2 to 3 minutes.

2. Reduce the heat to medium, cover the skillet, and cook, shaking the pan occasionally, until just cooked through, about 4 minutes. It should be crisp on the bottom.

Serves 4

PHUKET GRILLED SMOKED SALMON

While I dined at the Amanpuri on the island of Phuket in Thailand, I overlooked the golden spires of the buildings, the pale azure sea, royal palms, and dazzling orchids—it was pure heaven. The food was light and clear and the climate steamy. The restaurant served typically Thai dishes, which have many Chinese influences and a touch of the West about them. The menu offered an explanation of how the restaurant prepares its grilled smoked salmon, and although I didn't order it, I took notes, because it sounded delicious. When I returned home, I experimented. The result is succulent, piquant, and wonderful. The delicate smoked flavor comes through gently. Serve the salmon on very special occasions with pineapple and cucumber Cool Down Salsa (see Index).

2 pounds center-cut smoked salmon fillet in one piece, skin left on
2 tablespoons extra virgin olive oil
5 teaspoons fresh thyme leaves
2 teaspoons coarsely crushed white peppercorns
2 tablespoons fresh lime juice
4 limes, halved crosswise, for garnish

1. Place the salmon, skin side down, in a large shallow glass dish. Brush it with the olive oil and sprinkle the top evenly with 3 teaspoons of the thyme leaves and the crushed white peppercorns. Let rest, loosely covered, for 1 hour.

2. Preheat the broiler. Line a large broiling pan with aluminum foil.

3. Place the marinated salmon, skin side down, on the prepared broiling pan. Drizzle the top with the lime juice and any extra juices from marinating.

4. Broil 3 to 4 inches from the heat source until lightly browned and just crisp on top, 7 to 8 minutes. Watch it carefully so that it doesn't burn. Remove the salmon to a plate and let rest 10 to 15 minutes.

5. To serve, cut the salmon in half down the center (lengthwise) with a long, thin sharp knife. Then cut each half against the grain into 4 pieces crosswise. Garnish each serving with a lime half.

Serves 8

MY KITCHEN DIARY

Know Your Smoked Salmon

The variety of smoked fish available today has grown far beyond the familiar smoked salmon. Now succulent smoked mussels, scallops, spicy catfish, shrimp, and smoky tuna are an easy and elegant addition to any meal.

Fish and shellfish are smoked by one of two methods—hot or cold. Hot smoking is akin to slow gentle barbecuing and results in a moist, firm texture. The fish are cured with salt and then put into smokers where the temperature can range from 120° to 180°F. Depending on the size and desired cure, the fish is smoked from 20 minutes to 8 hours.

For cold smoking, the fish are cured with salt, or as in the Nova Scotia style, with a blend of salt and sugar. Many smokers also add a blend of spices to develop a complex flavor in the fish. After curing, the fish are exposed to smoke that never gets hotter than 90°F. Fish can be smoked for very short periods of time or for up to 3 weeks depending on the degree of preservation wanted. The luxurious texture of smoked salmon comes from being cold smoked.

The fish itself can be a deciding factor in the final taste and texture, particularly with smoked salmon. Different species of salmon are used in various parts of the world and contribute to the particular flavors associated with, say, a Scottish or Norwegian salmon. If you want true Scottish smoked salmon, make sure that it is imported and not just smoked and cured in the Scottish style.

Following are some labels you will find attached to smoked salmon and what they mean.

NOVA SCOTIA: This mild style of curing with salt and sugar originated in Nova Scotia. It is now the predominant method for curing both Pacific and Atlantic salmon. It delivers a very mild smoked flavor.

GASPÉ, ATLANTIC, CANADIAN, NOVA SCOTIA, FAEROE ISLAND: These terms usually reflect the place of origin for the fish. Styles of curing vary from smokehouse to smokehouse, but they generally are geared to the American taste for a balance of mild smoke and salt.

SCOTTISH: Produced in Scotland or cured in the Scottish style, this salmon is dry cured with salt, brown sugar, mixed spices, and rum. It has a firm texture and a smoky and slightly salty flavor.

NORWEGIAN: Farm-raised fish from Norway are cured in brine and assertively smoky. They have a very luscious texture and are rich tasting.

It must be the touch of brown sugar added during curing that makes Scottish salmon so smooth.

THE WINES OF

Germany

It's curious that Americans tend to ignore German wines, Germany being one of the oldest and noblest wine cultures in Europe. Many of us stay away from German wines because some are sweet—or perceived as sweet. But it's a shame to forgo some of the world's finest wines because of a mistaken perception. Actually, the latest trend in Germany are wines that are quite dry and highly suitable for the table. Even the sweet ones have their place, however.

Germany's most important wine regions are along the Rhine and Mosel rivers, where dramatically steep banks are home to some of the most impressive and picturesque wine estates in the world. Many people who have discovered the pleasures of German wine have done so at the source, say, on a boat trip along the Rhine or a drive along the curving Mosel, stopping at little *Weinstuben* (tasting cellars where growers offer wines by the glass). This is a delightful way to taste distinctions among the famous wine villages of the Mosel—

***This page, top:** This charming street in Rüdesheim is only open to pedestrians, who are attracted to its many bars, cafés, and restaurants. **Bottom:** Lush vineyards abound in the Rhine Valley. **Facing page, left:** Gorgeous grapes from the Lake Constance harvest. The Rhine from Cologne to Mainz.*

Bernkastel, Zell (as in Zeller Schwartze Katz), Ockfen, Wiltingen, Trier. The wines are light—only 7 or 8 percent alcohol—crisp, and snappy, perfect with a bit of Münster cheese or a good wurst.

The Rhine Valley has four leading districts: the Rheingau, with historic estates, such as Schloss Vollrads, Steinberg, Schloss Johannisberg, Rauenthal, and others; the Rheinhessen on the south bank, origin of a great deal of everyday table wine *(Tafelwein)* including Liebfraumilch; the Rheinpfalz, where slopes of the Harz Mountain range also have some of Germany's finest vineyards around the towns of Deidesheim, Ruppertsberg, and Bad Dürkheim; and the Nahe, a region bordering the Mosel-Saar-Ruwer, with exceptionally good wines across the board.

> *"To experience the best from German wines, look for Riesling on the label. . . . it is Riesling that offers the most distinctive aromas and flavors in German wines."*

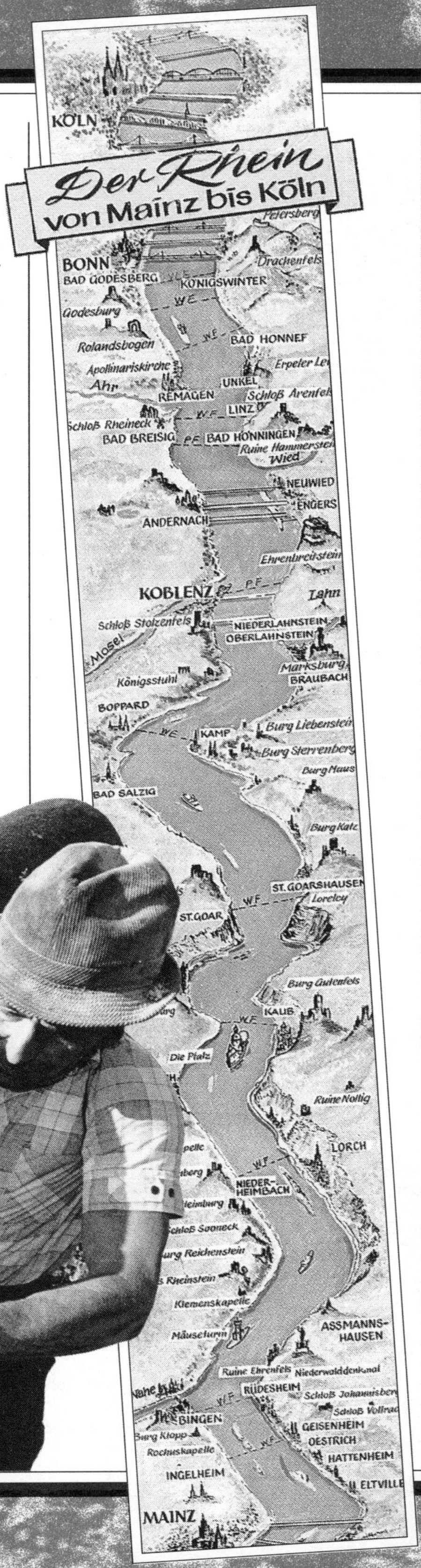

Der Rhein von Mainz bis Köln

Somewhat lesser in stature are the regions of Franconia and Baden, both of which offer traditionally drier wines and often very good value, if somewhat less noble and complex than Rhine and Mosel Rieslings. Baden in particular is producing attractive wines from grapes like Weissburgunder (Pinot Blanc), Rülander (Pinot Gris) and Gutedel (Chasselas).

To experience the best from German wines, look for Riesling on the label. If it is not specifically named, the wine may well be made from lesser varieties like Müller-Thurgau or Sylvaner. Though wines made from these grapes can offer pleasant drinking and good value (most Liebfraumilch and Moselblümchen are generic blends of these and other grapes, with some Riesling included in the better ones), it is Riesling that offers the most distinctive aromas and flavors in German wines.

The two significant quality levels for German wines are:

"Germany's most important wine regions are along the Rhine and Mosel rivers, where dramatically steep banks are home to some of the most impressive and picturesque wine estates in the world."

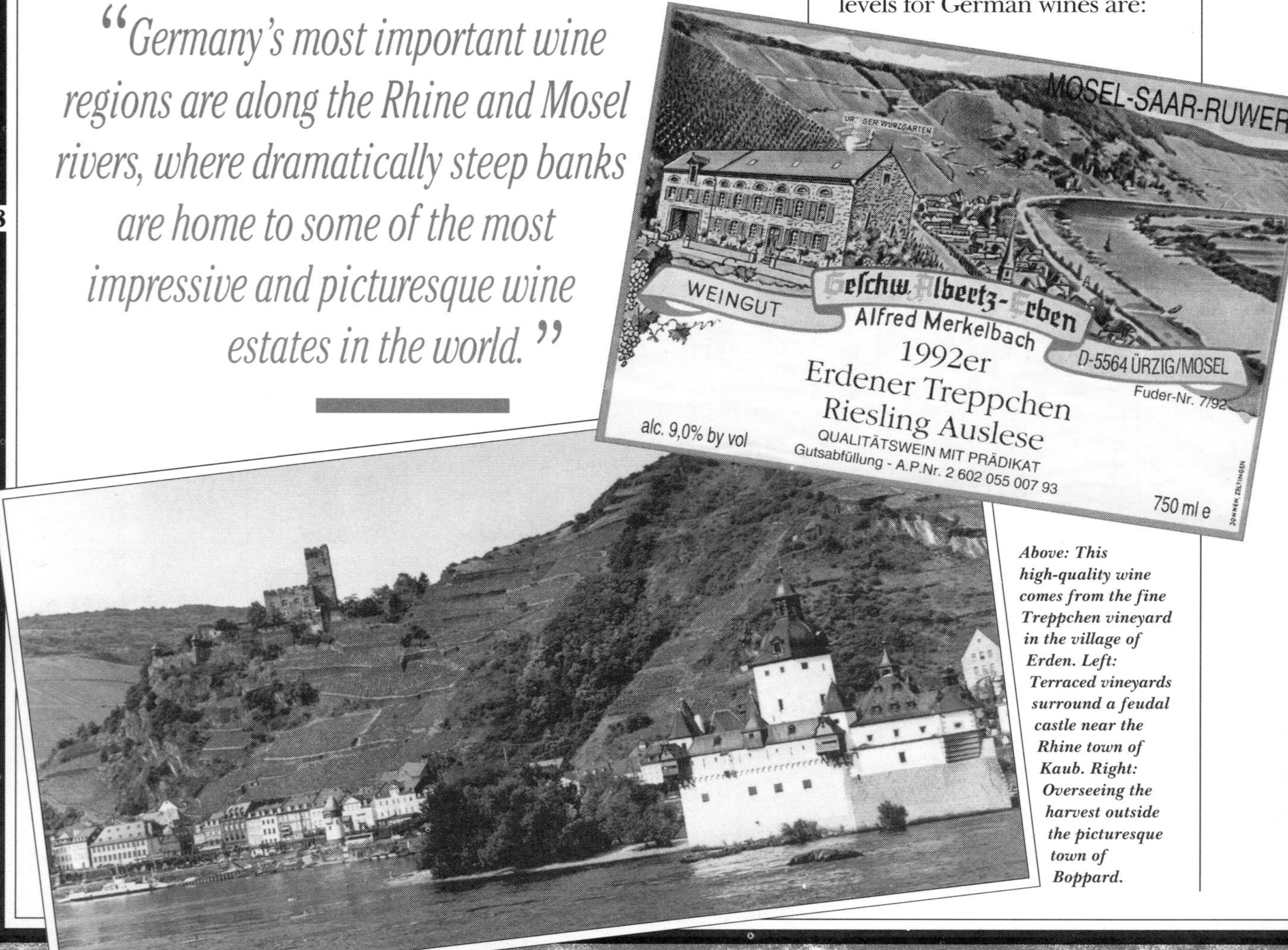

Above: This high-quality wine comes from the fine Treppchen vineyard in the village of Erden. Left: Terraced vineyards surround a feudal castle near the Rhine town of Kaub. Right: Overseeing the harvest outside the picturesque town of Boppard.

Qualitätswein (abbreviated QbA), wines of specific appellation (district, village, and/or vineyard), and *Qualitätswein mit Prädikat* (QmP), quality wine with special attributes, meaning extra degrees of ripeness that result in more intense character, richness, and sweetness. QbA offers the best value, a definite step up from *Tafelwein,* ordinary table wine that can be decent enough as a quaff or quite mediocre.

Germany's highest quality wines are at the QmP, or *Prädikat*, level, and there are four classifications ranging from driest to sweetest: Kabinett, Spätlese, Auslese, Beerenauslese, Trockenbeerenauslese, and Eiswein.

Kabinett is the driest, particularly when the term *halbtrocken* is attached.

The new drier Rieslings are excellent with a variety of foods, from fish to chicken to ham or pork—and to vegetable dishes. Riesling Kabinett, dry or off-dry, is superb with Oriental foods.

The sweeter Rieslings, which at this level are naturally sweet, are not the wines to choose for dishes better suited to Chardonnay or Sauvignon Blanc. Those labeled Spätlese may be lightly sweet, but they have a spicy character that goes very well with roast goose, breast of pheasant, or wild duck. They offer a change of pace from the red wines usually recommended with wild game. Kabinett or Spätlese Rieslings make delightful aperitifs, and are suited to grilled trout, catfish, ocean perch, or other mild fish as well.

The next level of quality, Auslese, is sweeter still. These, to my mind, are the most intriguing German wines. Very light in body (7 to 9 percent alcohol), they are harvested late, when the grapes are sweeter. The sweetness, combined with natural high acidity, intensifies the unique spicy-floral character of fine Riesling. These are lovely wines to sip just on their own, accompanied perhaps by fresh fruit or light crackers and creamy blue cheese. Sweet Riesling and blue cheese are, in fact, a delectable combination.

The pinnacles of German wines are the late-harvest, intensely sweet wines known as Beerenauslese (BA) and Trockenbeerenauslese (TBA). These honeyed, concentrated nectars are in very limited supply and consequently very expensive. Also in this category is the rarefied Eiswein. Sweet, utterly elegant, and refined, it is made in deep winter from grapes that have frozen on the vine. Most of these wines are bottled in smaller sizes (375 milliliters) but cost anywhere from $20 to over $100 or more. A glass after dinner is a dessert in itself.

BLACK SEA BASS BAKED IN A SALT CRUST

The first evening I spent in Seville, all I really wanted to do was cruise the beautiful old city and its great *tapas* bars. It didn't happen that night, but I was not disappointed. Instead I was feted at a marvelous seafood restaurant and had my very first taste of succulent dorade baked in a crust of coarse salt. It was moist and delicious, served with a drizzle of Spain's best extra virgin olive oil, a splash of fresh lemon juice, and a good grind of coarse black pepper. I managed to spend half the evening trying to extract the oven temperature and cooking time from the chef and finally left with instructions to bake the fish at 775°F for about 30 minutes. A year later I worked it out myself. Unable to find dorade, I settled on a small sea bass, although red snapper would have done nicely. The greatest effort required was carrying two large boxes of coarse salt home from the market. My result was superb. The fish was as moist and delicious as I had remembered. I baked it at 400°F for 25 minutes. As there is no way of testing the fish before it's finished, I would suggest adding another 5 minutes if you prefer your fish very well done. This size fish serves two perfectly. To serve more you could try baking two fish in a larger baking pan, although it would also be necessary to at least double the amount of salt.

1 black sea bass (1¾ pounds), cleaned
Coarsely ground black pepper, to taste
5 pounds coarse (kosher) salt
2 tablespoons extra virgin olive oil
2 lemons, halved crosswise, for garnish

1. Preheat the oven to 400°F.

2. Rinse and dry the fish. Season the cavity with pepper.

3. Spread 2 pounds of the salt in the bottom of a 13 x 9 x 2-inch baking dish. Press the fish lightly into the salt.

4. Pour the remaining salt on top of the fish to cover it completely. Spray the top of the salt with a plant mister filled with water or sprinkle the salt with water to help form a crust. Use the palm of your hand to pat down the surface, following the shape of the fish.

5. Bake in the center of the oven for 25 minutes. Remove the fish and let sit for 3 minutes.

6. Beginning at the side, carefully break the salt crust and discard the salt. Gently lift the fish to a cutting board with a long spatula.

7. Fillet the fish and transfer to a platter. Drizzle with olive oil and sprinkle with coarsely ground black pepper. Serve immediately, garnished with lemon halves.

Serves 2

HALIBUT LEMON KEBABS

I ate the most delicious sea bass kebab at Restaurant Han, along the Bosporus in the village of Rumelihisari, just outside downtown Istanbul. Lemon permeated the fish and vegetables. Pale green, mild chilies were delicious alongside the sweet ripe tomatoes. I've substituted Italian frying peppers for the chilies, but you can certainly add the heat if you prefer. This is an instance where I would beg, borrow, or steal fresh bay leaves because the presentation was spectacular. If none are available, use fresh sprigs of rosemary and entwine them between the fish and vegetables.

½ cup olive oil
¼ cup fresh lemon juice
2 cloves garlic, peeled and pressed through a garlic press
1 teaspoon dried oregano
½ teaspoon coarsely ground black pepper
4 thick (1 inch) halibut steaks, skin removed, each cut into 6 chunks
24 medium shrimp, peeled and deveined, tails left on
8 green Italian frying peppers, stemmed, seeded, and quartered
12 plum tomatoes, halved lengthwise
2 lemons, sliced ¼ inch thick, slices halved (you need 30 half slices)
24 bay leaves, preferably fresh
2 tablespoons chopped flat-leaf parsley
3 lemons, halved crosswise, for garnish

1. Combine the olive oil, lemon juice, garlic, oregano, and pepper in a large bowl. Add the halibut chunks and shrimp; toss gently in the marinade to coat the seafood well. Cover and refrigerate for 1 hour.

2. Prepare a grill with medium-hot coals or preheat the broiler.

3. Using 6 metal skewers, 18 inches long, thread the fish and vegetables in the following order: pepper quarter, tomato half, lemon slice, bay leaf, halibut chunk, and shrimp. Repeat 3 more times on each skewer, then add an additional lemon slice and green pepper quarter to the end of each. Make sure that the ingredients are evenly spaced on the skewers so that they cook properly.

4. Grill or broil the skewers 3 inches from the heat, brushing lightly with the marinade, until the fish and shrimp are cooked through, 6 to 8 minutes per side (2 sides).

5. Sprinkle with the chopped parsley and serve with the lemon halves.

Makes 6 kebabs

Dear Annabel,
Istanbul is fabulous!
Turquoise tiled walls
and colorful Kilims
decorate this splendid
restaurant in the
spice market.
Love,
mommy

TÜRKIYE CUMHURIYETI

ISLAND GRILLED RED SNAPPER

Bushes of thyme grow all over Jamaica just as they do in the south of France. The intense perfume marries beautifully with the island's fresh fish and when placed in the cavities of the snapper, it infuses the fish as it grills. When serving this fish, bring out the Sauce Chien to spoon atop for a typical island presentation.

4 small whole red snappers (1½ to 2 pounds each), cleaned
Olive oil
Salt and freshly ground black pepper, to taste
12 fresh thyme sprigs, plus 8 sprigs for garnish
4 limes, halved crosswise, for garnish
Sauce Chien (page 254; optional)

1. Prepare a grill with hot coals.

2. Rinse the snappers and pat dry with paper towels. Brush the fish, inside and out, with oil and sprinkle well, inside and out, with salt and pepper. Place 3 sprigs of thyme inside each fish. Close the openings with small metal skewers.

3. Lightly oil a grill rack and place the fish on the rack 4 inches from the coals. Grill, turning once, until cooked through, 4 to 6 minutes per side. Serve immediately, garnished with the fresh thyme sprigs and accompanied by the halved limes and *sauce chien*, if using.

Serves 4

PLA PREEO WAN
Sweet and Sour Flounder

Traveling throughout Southeast Asia means long plane rides between destinations and lots of airline magazines with an assortment of mystifying recipes and food descriptions. It was in one of these magazines that I came across a reference to a Thai dish, *pla preeo wan.* It sounded intriguing: broiled flounder or sole topped with a sweet and sour sauce of pineapple, cucumber, tomato, and onion. This description demanded a recipe. For kick I've added lots of fresh ginger and garlic. Serve the fish in shallow soup or pasta bowls with the sauce ladled atop.

2 pounds flounder fillets, cut into 4 pieces total
3 cups diced (¼ inch) ripe fresh pineapple
2 cups diced (¼ inch) seeded peeled cucumber
4 ripe large plum tomatoes, cored, seeded, and cut into ¼-inch dice (2 cups)
1 cup diced (¼ inch) onion
¼ cup pineapple juice
4 cloves garlic, minced
2 tablespoons minced peeled fresh ginger
Salt, to taste
1 teaspoon cornstarch
2 tablespoons olive oil
2 tablespoons fresh lime juice
½ cup coarsely chopped fresh cilantro leaves

1. Carefully remove any tiny bones from the flounder with a tweezers. Set the fish on a broiling pan lined with aluminum foil.

2. Preheat the broiler.

3. Combine the pineapple, cucumber, tomatoes, onion, and pineapple juice in a heavy saucepan. Simmer, stirring occasionally, over medium-low heat for 5 minutes. Reduce the heat, add the garlic and ginger, season with salt and continue simmering for another 5 minutes.

4. Pour ¼ cup of liquid from the saucepan into a small bowl, add the cornstarch, and mix until smooth. Stir the cornstarch back into the simmering fruit mixture and cook, stirring, until slightly thickened, about 2 minutes. Set aside.

5. Brush the fish fillets with the olive oil and drizzle with the lime juice. Sprinkle with salt. Broil 4 inches from the heat source until the fish is opaque and flakes easily, 4 to 5 minutes. Cut each piece of fish in half crosswise and place a piece in the bottom of each of 8 shallow bowls.

6. Heat the fruit sauce for 1 minute over medium heat, stir in the cilantro, and ladle it evenly over the fish. Serve immediately.

Serves 8

SOUVENIR TO SAVOR

Tokyo's Tsukiji Fish Market

You've got to get up real early to catch Tokyo's mammoth wholesale fish market in full swing but, believe me, it's worth it. More contained and colorful than New York's Fulton Fish Market and offering a wider selection of sea creatures than London's Billingsgate, Tsukiji feeds over 10 million fish-hungry Japanese daily. But turn up after 10, and you'll find the place deserted.

I arrived about 5 A.M. when I could rub shoulders with the best professional chefs in town. It was fun to see them in action and check up on what they were buying. Bring your camera and they'll happily pose for you along with their briny choices; tourists are barely in evidence at this hour.

As I wandered down the aisles of this vast shed, I passed bright pink octopi, squid of every size and shape, whale-sized tuna being divided into manageable chunks with the aid of a chain saw, dozens of varieties of sardine, mackerel, brilliantly hued carp, salmon, all manner of shellfish—freshwater and ocean going—slippery eels, yellowtail tuna, even a wide selection of red and black caviar. The majority of fish were fresh, but these days much is frozen as well. However, all were tightly packed and artfully arranged in rows in their custom-made wooden crates and boxes, often hammered together right on the spot. It was a mad scene, very wet and noisy, with the constant din of bargaining and bidding, slicing, chopping, cutting, weighing, and wrapping going on all around me.

Because there's water, water everywhere, high, shiny black rubber boots, shorts, and jeans are the fashion of the day. Put a bandana around your neck and tie on a headband, and you'll blend right in. Local shoppers carry their woven baskets for carting home their purchases, and many don sensible wooden clogs to keep the wet at bay.

If all the bustling activity gives you an appetite, you're in the right place. Tsukiji boasts some of the best seafood and sushi restaurants in the whole of Tokyo. And one thing is certain—everything is fresh.

A TASTE OF THE WORLD

Japanese Palette

Photo: These beautiful vats of sake are bought for special occasion parties.

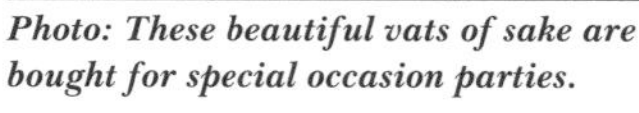

...And

GARLIC	SOY SAUCE
GINGER	SUGAR
SCALLION	TOFU (BEAN CURD)
CUCUMBER	FLUKE
DAIKON	SALMON
RICE WINE VINEGAR	SCALLOPS

RUSSIAN COD RAGOUT

This intriguing fish stew combines succulent codfish with kitchen staple vegetables. The magic comes from the Russian flavor palette—sweet and sour, fresh lemon juice and sugar, perfumed with cinnamon and cloves. Serve with good black bread, a bowl of roasted beets (see Index), and a chilled Chardonnay.

1 Idaho potato (about 8 ounces), peeled and cut into ½-inch dice
4 medium carrots, sliced ½ inch thick
1½ pounds cod fillets, 1 inch thick
4 tablespoons olive oil
1 medium onion, cut into ¼-inch dice
1 small parsnip (about 4 ounces), cut into ¼-inch dice
4 cloves garlic, chopped
1 cinnamon stick (3 inches long)
6 whole cloves
1½ pounds ripe tomatoes, seeded and cut into ½-inch dice
Salt and freshly ground black pepper, to taste
½ cup Fish Stock (page 130)
3 tablespoons fresh lemon juice
3 tablespoons sugar
½ cup, plus 2 tablespoons coarsely chopped flat-leaf parsley
1 bay leaf
¾ cup julienned seeded, peeled cucumber, for garnish

1. Bring a medium-size pot of water to a boil. Add the potato and boil gently for 3 minutes. Remove with a slotted spoon and set aside. Add the carrots, boil gently for 3 minutes, drain, and set aside.

2. Remove the bones and skin from the fish. With a tweezers, carefully pull out any small bones. Cut the fish into 2 x 1-inch pieces.

3. Heat 2 tablespoons of the oil in a large nonstick skillet over medium-high heat. Add the cod and sear for 1 minute on each side. Remove and set aside.

4. Spread the potato over the bottom of a medium-size heavy pot or Dutch oven. Cover with the carrots, then the fish in a single layer. Cover with the onion, parsnip, and garlic, then add the cinnamon stick and cloves. Top with the diced tomatoes. Drizzle with the remaining 2 tablespoons olive oil. Season with salt and pepper.

5. Mix the fish stock with the lemon juice and sugar and pour over the vegetables and fish. Simmer covered over low heat until the fish is opaque and cooked through, and the vegetables are tender, 20 minutes. Shake the casserole a few times during cooking to distribute the juices.

6. Gently fold ½ cup parsley and the bay leaf into the ragout and cook uncovered another 5 minutes. Serve directly from the pot into large, shallow soup or pasta bowls. Garnish with the remaining parsley and the julienned cucumber.

Serves 6

BAKED SWORDFISH PROVENCAL

Fragrant herbes de Provence perfume the vegetables in this robust fish preparation. If swordfish is unavailable, halibut steaks make an ideal substitute. Don't neglect the sprinkling of parsley and squeeze of fresh lime juice before serving. They add the final flourish.

6 tablespoons extra virgin olive oil
2 medium onions, slivered
2 red bell peppers, stemmed, seeded, and cut into ½-inch strips
2 yellow bell peppers, stemmed, seeded, and cut into ½-inch strips
1 fennel bulb, tough core removed, slivered
2 tablespoons balsamic vinegar
1 teaspoon herbes de Provence (French dried herb blend)
Salt and freshly ground black pepper, to taste
4 tablespoons chopped flat-leaf parsley
6 swordfish or halibut steaks (about 8 ounces each), cut 1 inch thick
3 limes, halved crosswise, for garnish

1. Preheat the oven to 400°F.

2. Heat 4 tablespoons of the olive oil in a large heavy pot over medium heat. Add the onions, peppers, and fennel and cook uncovered, stirring occasionally, until the vegetables are softened, 30 minutes. Stir in the vinegar and herbes de Provence. Cook until the vegetables are very tender, about 15 minutes more. Season with salt and pepper. Stir in 2 tablespoons of the parsley.

3. Spoon the vegetables into a 13 x 9 x 2-inch baking dish. Lay the swordfish over the vegetables and brush them with the remaining 2 tablespoons olive oil. Sprinkle with salt and pepper.

4. Bake the swordfish until cooked through, about 15 minutes. Sprinkle with the remaining 2 tablespoons parsley and serve immediately with the lime halves.

Serves 6

ZARZUELA

This dazzling red fish "soup" is the Catalonian version of the Provençal bouillabaisse so popular along the Mediterranean. Although traditionally made from the odds and ends of the day's catch, it can be prepared with any type of fish or shellfish in any proportion. The only rule of thumb is the greater the variety, the better. A very large heavy pot is essential. I prepared this in a huge copper pot, 12½ inches in diameter and 4½ inches deep. The rustic quality of this dish makes it ideal to go from the stove straight to the table. Be sure to have a few bowls on the table to hold the empty lobster shells and shrimp tails. Serve with warm chunks of crusty bread and a chilled white Zinfandel wine.

2 tablespoons olive oil
1 cup chopped onion
2 tablespoons minced garlic
2 medium red bell peppers, stemmed, seeded, and cut into ½-inch dice
3 ripe large tomatoes
¼ teaspoon saffron threads
1½ cups Fish Stock (page 130)
1½ cups dry white wine
2 tablespoons chopped blanched almonds
2 tablespoons plus ½ cup chopped flat-leaf parsley
Pinch of cayenne pepper
1½ pounds monkfish fillets, cut into large chunks
1 pound sea scallops
3 small lobsters (1¼ pounds each), claws removed and cracked, tails cut into 3 pieces
1 pound large shrimp, peeled and deveined, tails left on

1. Heat the oil in a very large heavy pot over medium heat. Add the onion, garlic, and peppers; cook, stirring, until the vegetables are wilted, about 10 minutes.

2. Meanwhile peel, seed, and coarsely chop the tomatoes, collecting about a tablespoon of juice as you go. Add the saffron to the tomato juice.

3. Add the tomatoes, saffron and juice, fish stock, wine, almonds, 2 tablespoons of the parsley, and the cayenne to the vegetables. Bring the mixture to a boil, reduce the heat slightly, and simmer uncovered for 10 minutes.

4. Add the monkfish and scallops, cover the pot, and cook over medium heat until the fish is opaque and cooked through, about 5 minutes. Remove the seafood to an ovenproof dish with a slotted spoon, cover with aluminum foil, and keep warm in a low (200°F) oven. (If working ahead, warm the seafood just before serving.)

5. Add the lobsters and shrimp to the pot. Cover, increase the heat slightly, and cook until the lobster shells turn bright red, 10 to 15 minutes. During cooking, shake the pan occasionally to distribute the seafood evenly and stir once or twice from the bottom. Sprinkle with the remaining ½ cup of parsley.

6. To serve, divide the fish and shellfish between 6 large shallow bowls and ladle the sauce over the top.

Serves 6 to 8

Molly,
A paella cookout with Adrian and Nani—heaps of langouste, Spanish sausage and fragrant saffron rice. The best!
XXX Mommy

MY KITCHEN DIARY

A Bit on Caribbean Beer

Several islands of the Caribbean have thriving breweries, most producing brisk, Pilsen-style lagers suited to the warmth of the tropics. Barbados has its Banks Lager, St. Thomas its agreeable Spinnaker, Jamaica its widely known Red Stripe (as well as the very strong, though not especially flavorful, Crucial Brew, also from the Red Stripe brewery).

Stout is produced in a few spots, notably Jamaica, where the dark, rich, somewhat sweetish Dragon Stout is popular. Haiti's drier Prestige Stout, fruitier in character, is excellent with roast chicken.

CARIBBEAN FISH POT

Caribbean seafood stews are the best, just bursting with native ingredients—fresh fish, okra, thyme, and hot, hot chilies. Orange zest sweetens the sauce and tames the heat. If fresh okra is unavailable, seek out the frozen variety. Serve in shallow bowls with a slice of Jamaican Gingerbread (see Index) alongside.

1 pound sliced bacon, cut crosswise into ½-inch pieces
1½ pounds okra, tops trimmed, sliced on the diagonal into ½-inch slices
2 tablespoons olive oil
2 red bell peppers, stemmed, seeded, and cut into ½-inch dice
1 large onion, cut into ½-inch dice
6 large cloves garlic, minced
2 cups canned plum tomatoes, with their juices, crushed
1 to 2 teaspoons minced Scotch bonnet or other hot chili (seeds and ribs removed), or to taste
¼ cup fresh thyme leaves or 1 tablespoon dried
3 bay leaves
½ teaspoon cayenne pepper, or to taste
3 cups Fish Stock (page 130) or bottled clam juice
2 cups defatted Chicken Broth (page 127)
2 pounds grouper or red snapper fillets, skinned and cut crosswise into 2-inch slices
1 pound sea scallops
1 pound large shrimp, peeled and deveined
8 ounces lump crabmeat, picked over for shell and cartilage
Grated zest of 2 oranges
¼ cup coarsely chopped fresh cilantro leaves, for garnish

1. In a large heavy pot, cook the bacon over medium heat until translucent. Add the okra and continue cooking until the bacon is slightly brown, about 5 minutes.

2. Add the oil, bell peppers, onion, and garlic; continue cooking until the vegetables are softened, 7 to 10 minutes.

3. Add the tomatoes, chili, thyme, bay leaves, and cayenne pepper; cook over medium-low heat for 15 minutes.

4. Add the fish stock and chicken broth, and cook, partially covered, for 30 minutes more.

5. Add the fish fillets and scallops; cook uncovered over medium-high heat for 2 minutes. Add the shrimp and cook 2 minutes longer. Add the crabmeat and cook 1 minute more. Stir gently after each addition.

6. Fold in the orange zest and sprinkle with the cilantro. Serve immediately.

Serves 8 to 10

GREAT TURKISH HAMBURGERS · YUMMY GRILLED CHEESE

SIDI BOU SAID MINTED TEA · CUMIN CURRY ROLLS

HERBED CHERRY CHICKEN SALAD TEA SANDWICHES

WHEAT BERRY BREAD · DORSET SCONES

VERA CRUZ VEGGIE SANDWICH

SPANISH CHEESES · PAO-DOCE · FINNISH CARDAMON TEA LOAF · LAVASH · CARIBBEAN CROQUE MONSIEUR

SCOTTISH OATCAKES

Side Trips
COPENHAGEN COD CAKES · ROSEMARY OLIVE BREAD
GALINA'S BERRY TEA · MOROCCAN PUMPKIN TEA LOAF
CHOCOLATE WITH COFFEE · CUCUMBER AND TINY SPROUT TEA SANDWICHES
HUNGARIAN CHERRY TEA CAKE
SPICE CAKE WITH COFFEE FROSTING · PROVENCAL PAN BAGNA · FOCACCIA
TWO PORTUGUESE CHEESES · SWEET BLINCHIKI · LIMPA BREAD
CAVIAR
MALOSSOL
BELUGA

SIDE TRIPS

Hands Across the Sea

As I traveled from country to country, I found myself eating everything from *bisteeyas* (in Morocco) to curry (in India) the traditional way—with my hands. I've recreated all these wonderful recipes in this book, but you should enjoy the results any way you wish. This chapter is the *real* hand-holding one!

Without question, the sandwich is America's favorite hand-held food, and it turns out the rest of the world has some pretty spectacular offerings for our repertoire. From Thailand comes crab layered between papaya slices; from Turkey, a pastrami "Reuben"; from Denmark, prettily presented *smørrebrød;* from France, a delicious, *pan bagna;* from Spain, the famous *pan con tomate*.

I've prepared fillings to be rolled in tortillas, stuffed into pitas, layered in phyllo, or simply sandwiched between two delicious bread slices. They are some of the tastes the world is holding in their hands. To me, they are bites of brilliance.

THAI CRAB "CLUB" WITH AVOCADO "MAYONNAISE"

Beach resorts, for me, are synonymous with daydreaming—in my case, not of sandcastles, but the luscious ripe and sparkling flavors local ingredients provide. I was lucky enough to visit Amanpuri (place of peace) on the island of Phuket off the west coast of Thailand. Exotic fruits—everything from pumelos, sapotes, and rambutans to pineapples, mangos, and bananas—were in abundance. Lingering over the fresh crabmeat I was having for lunch, I began thinking about how to combine the exotic fruits with crab, and how to bring back home the feeling and flavors of Southeast Asia together with a touch of the Caribbean. This fresh crab "club" is the result of my seaside reverie.

Slices of ripe papaya and tomato substitute well for extra slices of bread in this sandwich, and the "mayonnaise" is a creamy slather of avocado mixed with cilantro. Serve it with lots of plantain crisps alongside.

8 tablespoons Avocado "Mayonnaise" (recipe follows)
6 slices whole-grain or 7-grain bread, lightly toasted
1 ripe papaya (about 1 pound), peeled and seeded
2 cups jumbo lump crabmeat, picked over for shell and cartilage
6 teaspoons chopped fresh cilantro leaves
2 ripe large tomatoes
Coarsely ground black pepper, to taste

1. Spread 1 tablespoon of the avocado "mayonnaise" on one side of each slice of toast.

2. Cut the papaya into ¼-inch-thick slices and divide evenly among the bread. Top each with ⅓ cup crabmeat, then sprinkle each with 1 teaspoon cilantro.

3. Cut the tomatoes into ¼-inch-thick slices. Place the 6 largest center slices atop the crab. Reserve the rest for another use.

4. Sprinkle pepper to taste over the tomatoes and dollop a teaspoonful of the remaining avocado "mayonnaise" on the center of each sandwich.

Serves 6

AVOCADO "MAYONNAISE"

When looking for more of a dip or a dollop rather than an egg-based "tossing" mayonnaise, ripe avocados provide the perfect consistency. This is delicious served atop grilled seafood, eggs, steamed new potatoes, or with crisp, fresh seasonal vegetables.

1 ripe avocado (about 8 ounces), preferably Haas
2 tablespoons fresh lime juice
2 tablespoons extra virgin olive oil
3 tablespoons chopped fresh cilantro leaves
Salt and freshly ground black pepper, to taste

A TASTE OF THE WORLD

Scandinavian Palette

Photo: Some of the best street food can be found along the canal in Copenhagen.

434

...And

- CARAWAY SEEDS
- TARRAGON
- GARLIC
- CAPERS
- BEETS
- RED CABBAGE
- CLOUDBERRIES
- LINGONBERRIES
- RHUBARB
- RED CURRANTS
- SALMON
- SHRIMP
- SWEET MUSTARDS
- VENISON

Halve the avocado, remove the pit, and scoop the flesh into a bowl. Add the lime juice and mash it together with a fork. Scrape the mixture into a food processor and process until just smooth. With the machine running, slowly drizzle in the oil through the feed tube and continue to process until smooth. Remove the mixture to a bowl. Fold in the cilantro and season to taste with salt and pepper. Refrigerate for up to 1 hour before serving.

Makes about 1 cup

COPENHAGEN COD CAKES

Street food in Copenhagen does not appear on every corner, but when the occasional vendor does show up, he is likely to be grilling 12-inch-long hot dogs and buns. Nothing is particularly unusual about this—except the way they're eaten. Hungry customers take the hot dog in their left hand and the bun in their right and eat them separately—a bite of one and then a bite of the other!

I struck street-food gold along a beautiful canal street called Nyhavn (New Harbor), which was flanked on both sides by magnificent old yellow, rose, and chocolate-colored buildings trimmed in white. Restaurants and bars, with tables spilling out onto the sidewalks, were hugged by bright green hedges planted in wooden boxes. The cafés sported crisp white canvas umbrellas to dine under. Tall sailboats vied for docking space along the canal.

My find was a beautiful blond woman sautéing fish cakes, streetside, in a cast-iron skillet on an old iron stove. The cakes were made of a mixture of salmon and cod with a hint of fresh ginger. She served them up with a ginger-spiked carrot salad and a creamy dilled potato salad. All this rested atop hard, flat, whole-grain bread shells. A hollowed-out hard roll, toasted until crisp, would be a perfect substitute.

8 cups water
2 fresh dill sprigs
4 black peppercorns
1 pound cod fillets
8 ounces salmon fillet
½ cup cooked diced (¼ inch) Idaho potatoes
½ cup grated peeled carrots
1¼ cups dried bread crumbs
3 tablespoons chopped fresh dill
2 tablespoons minced peeled fresh ginger
2 tablespoons drained tiny capers
2 tablespoons grated onion
½ cup mayonnaise, plus additional for serving
1 large egg
1 tablespoon Dijon mustard
8 hard rolls
1 tablespoon vegetable oil, or more if needed
1 tablespoon unsalted butter, or more if needed
Copenhagen Carrots (page 197; optional)

1. Place the water, dill sprigs, and peppercorns in a large heavy pot and bring to a boil. Reduce the heat to medium and add the cod fillets. Simmer until the fish is opaque and flakes slightly, about 5 minutes. Remove with a slotted spoon. Return the water to a boil, reduce the heat, and add the salmon. Cook until the fish is opaque and flakes slightly, about 5 minutes. Remove with a slotted spoon. Let the fish cool to room temperature, then remove the skin and bones from the fish and coarsely flake the fish into a large bowl.

2. Add the potatoes, carrots, ¼ cup of the bread crumbs, the dill, ginger, capers, and onion to the fish and toss gently to combine.

3. In a small bowl, combine the mayonnaise, egg, and mustard; gently fold it into the fish mixture.

4. Form the fish mixture into 8 patties. Place the remaining 1 cup bread crumbs on a plate and coat the fish cakes well with the crumbs, patting them so that the patties are compact. Cover and refrigerate for at least 1 hour.

5. Just before frying the fish cakes, split the rolls in half and remove some of the excess bread from the centers. Toast the rolls and keep warm while you prepare the fish cakes.

6. Heat 1 tablespoon each oil and butter in a large nonstick skillet over medium heat. Add as many fish cakes as will fit in a single layer and cook until golden brown, 3 to 4 minutes on each side. Drain on paper towels. Keep warm. Fry the remaining cakes, adding more oil and butter to the skillet if necessary. Serve warm on toasted rolls with Copenhagen carrots and your favorite potato salad, or on their own. Pass mayonnaise to spread on the cod cakes.

Serves 8

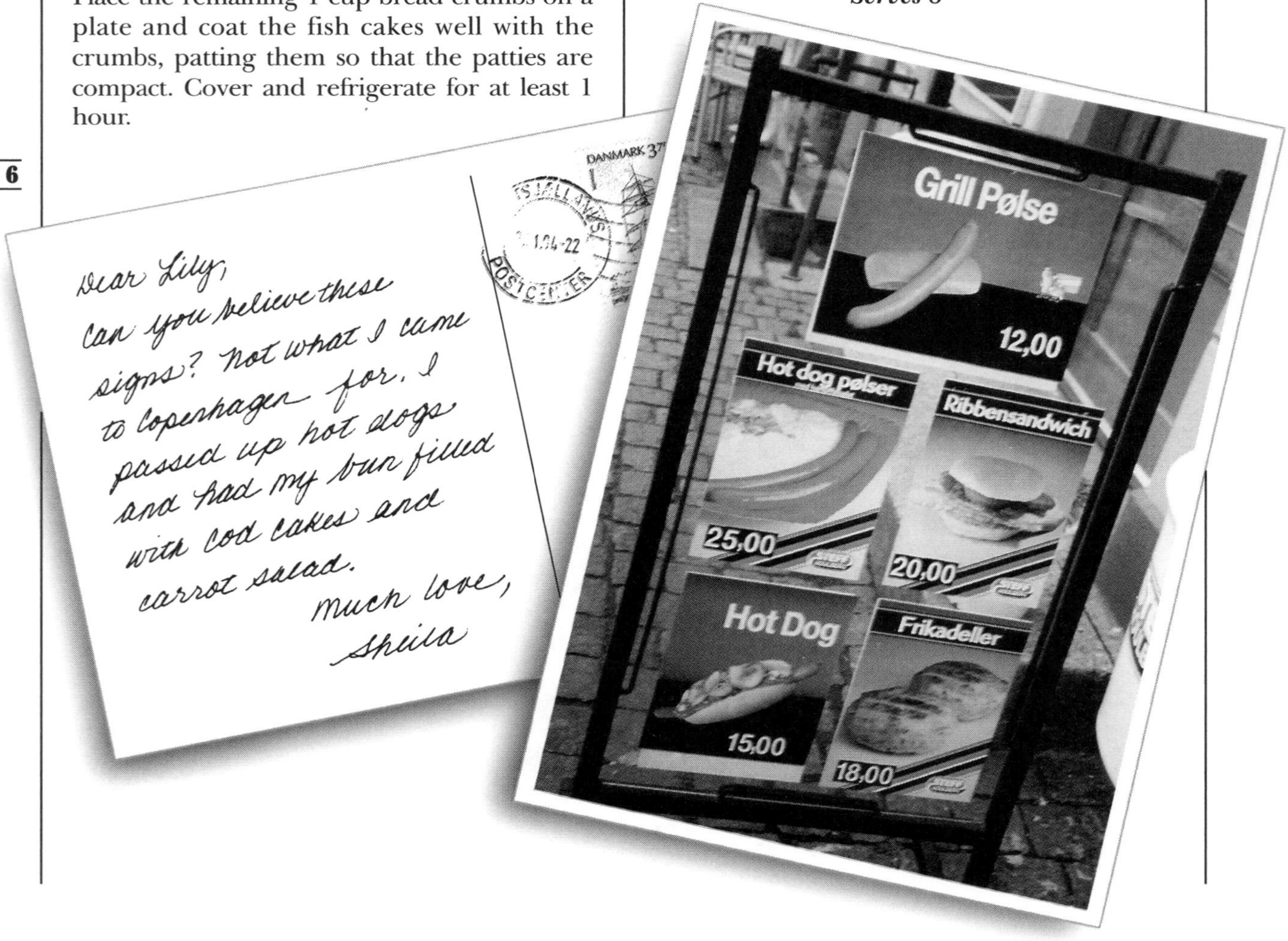

MY KITCHEN DIARY

Ida Davidsens' Smørrebrød

Fodor's guide to Scandinavia calls it "the most famous restaurant in Scandinavia . . . if you miss it you will never be able to look your traveled friends in the eye again."

When Ida Davidsen's grandfather originally set up shop in 1888, it was a bar he opened, but when customers were hungry, he or his wife would go in the back and fix up some sandwiches. Today the menu boasts 178 variations on a Danish theme—*smørrebrød*—a slice of bread served open-faced, and topped with the best ingredients. Over 56 inches long, the menu is the longest in the world and appears in the *Guinness Book of World Records.*

During my meal at her restaurant, Ida explained *smørrebrød* etiquette to me and my traveling companions. First of all, you never eat just one sandwich. You begin with the open-faced fish sandwiches, traditionally herring, shrimp, lobster, and so on. Then you continue with egg, vegetable, or meat sandwiches. None of these sandwiches are eaten casually; they are served at a well-set table and eaten with knives and forks. Traditionally cold schnapps and a beer chaser accompany the meal.

Good bread is essential to Ida's sandwiches, and she uses homemade sourdough, rye, white, and crisp breads. The bread is lightly spread on one side with sweet butter, and careful thought is given to arrangement of the ingredients on the bread. For instance, hard-cooked eggs are thinly sliced and fanned on either side of a slice of sourdough bread with a stripe of black caviar down the center. Fresh lobster meat is generously placed atop bread, sprinkled with chopped tarragon, and served with mayonnaise on the side.

Here are some other *smørrebrød* creations, inspired by Ida, to try at home:

■ Spread black bread with dill butter. Lay a thin slice of smoked salmon or other smoked fish on top. Scramble one egg and spoon it down the center. Sprinkle with snipped chives.

■ Hans Christian Andersen's favorite: Spread whole-grain bread with a smooth liver pâté flecked with truffles. Lay a crisp slice of bacon lengthwise on either side of the bread and line 6 slices of thinly sliced plum tomato down the center.

■ Butter a slice of rye bread and cover it with a thin slice of cooked roast beef. Place a slice of crisp bacon lengthwise and sprinkle finely chopped red onion down the center.

■ Butter a slice of sourdough bread. Cover with thinly sliced pork roast. Lay a row of thinly sliced plum tomato on either side. Sprinkle chopped dill down the center.

■ Butter a thin slice of black pumpernickel. Lay thinly sliced plum tomato lengthwise down either side and sliced hard-cooked egg down the center. Lay an anchovy fillet over each row of tomatoes.

■ Lay thin slices of meat loaf over buttered rye bread. Top with thin slices of boiled new potatoes lengthwise on either side. Spoon lingonberries down the center and sprinkle snipped chives over the top.

THE BEERS OF

Scandinavia

In countries too frigid for growing wine grapes, beers and spirits (like Aquavit) are the native alcoholic beverages. In Scandinavia, the brewing of beer, or beer-like drinks, dates to the days of the legendary Norsemen. Even mead, drink of the ancient Nordic gods, may have been a honey-flavored drink brewed mainly from grain. Scandinavia's modern brews took their cue from Germany, producing brisk golden lagers with clean, zesty flavors. Dark beers are also popular in Nordic lands but are not often seen in the United States.

Denmark boasts Scandinavia's oldest brewing tradition, with world-famous Carlsberg, the pioneer. Carlsberg is Denmark's internationally known brewer, producing half a dozen or more beers considered among the world's finest, as well as some of the most full-bodied. Carlsberg Elephant beer, for example, is a crisp brew with rich, creamy flavors, and at

Left to right: Although it's not Paris, there's a healthy café scene in Copenhagen. The Danish countryside is dappled with these wonderful inns. Sweden's Carnegie Porter and Denmark's Carlsberg are two impressively popular Scandinavian beers.

about 7 percent alcohol, is more powerful than Carlsberg Lager. Stronger yet is Carlsberg Special Strong Lager, 8.5 percent alcohol and very zesty indeed. The Carlsberg brewery in Copenhagen is one of the world's most impressive, well worth a visit when you are there.

Tuborg, another Danish beer that is known worldwide, is somewhat lighter than the Carlsberg brews but quite crisp, with stronger hop flavor. Other Danish beers to look for, mostly within Denmark, include Ceres Red Eric (a good dry lager), Faxe Fad, Giraf, and several dark, rich porters, bocks, and stouts, such as Albani Porter, Carlsberg Imperial Stout, and Tuborg Dark.

In Norway, a firm, dry lager and a popular Pilsner-style beer (clear lager with a strong accent of hops) are made by Ringnes, and are now widely distributed in the United States. Less well-known but also quite good are the beers from the Aass brewery near Oslo, whose best-loved brews are the seasonal Christmas beer, Aass Jule Øl, and a creamy bock, known as Aass Bokk. Some of Norway's most individual beers are brewed locally in small towns and available only there, so it is a good idea to ask about the local brewery when you are traveling in Norway.

"The Carlsberg brewery in Copenhagen is one of the world's most impressive, well worth a visit when you are there."

In Sweden, the largest brewer is Pripps, renowned for its very dark, almost toffee-flavored Carnegie Porter—highly rated by beer connoisseurs—and its Finnish Sinebrychoff Imperial Stout, a rich, dark-roast malt worth trying with venison. Sweden also produces a number of beers flavored with various herbs, such as the piney, juniper-flavored Spetsat—an acquired taste to say the least but a must for the adventurous palate.

PROVENCAL PAN BAGNA

The streets of Provence are lined with vendors selling the great local sandwich *pan bagna,* which means bathed bread. There are many variations, some more delicious than others, but the basics are canned tuna drenched in olive oil, with capers, anchovies, onions, tomatoes, olives, and greens.

I don't know whether it's the sun or the setting that makes this sandwich so special in the south of France, but I have never achieved quite the flavor sensation with the same ingredients in New York. I finally branched off and created my own version—which is truly excellent—by layering roasted garlic, tomatoes, and peppers with fresh seared tuna and the crisp crunch of haricots verts. My version is a bit more time consuming than the original, but all the ingredients can be prepared ahead of time and the sandwich assembled a few hours before eating. Be sure to leave enough time for the finished pan bagna to rest, as it should be moist when it's served.

1 head garlic
3 tablespoons olive oil
1 tablespoon dry white wine
Salt and freshly ground black pepper, to taste
8 ounces fresh tuna steak, 1½ inches thick
4 French bread rolls, about 5 inches long, or 1 long baguette (see Note)
¼ cup extra virgin olive oil
4 thin slices red onion
2 ounces haricots verts, trimmed and blanched
4 large slices Roasted Tomatoes (page 220)
1 red bell pepper, halved lengthwise and roasted (page 202)
1 tablespoon chopped flat-leaf parsley

1. Preheat the oven to 350°F.

2. Remove the papery outside layer of the head of garlic, cut off about ¼ inch from the top, exposing the cloves a bit, and place it in a small ramekin. Drizzle with 1 tablespoon of the olive oil and the white wine. Sprinkle with salt and pepper, cover with aluminum foil, and bake until softened, 1 hour. Remove and cool to room temperature.

3. Sprinkle both sides of the tuna with black pepper. Heat the remaining 2 tablespoons olive oil in a nonstick skillet. Over medium-high heat sear the tuna about 3 minutes per side for medium-rare. Remove from the pan, cool, and cut crosswise into 8 thin slices. Set aside.

4. Cut the top third off the rolls or baguette lengthwise and hollow out the centers. Brush the insides liberally with the extra virgin olive oil. Squeeze the roasted garlic from the skins and spread it over the bottom of the rolls.

5. To assemble the sandwiches, lay 2 slices of tuna on the bottom of each roll. Cover with the onion and then lay the haricots verts lengthwise. Top each with a slice of roasted tomato. Halve the roasted pepper halves and place a piece over each tomato slice; press down on the ingredients. Sprinkle evenly with black pepper and the parsley. Cover with the tops of the rolls and press down again. Wrap each sandwich tightly in plastic wrap and refrigerate for 2 to 3 hours before serving. Remove from the refrigerator 30 minutes before serving.

Serves 4

Note: If using a long baguette, cut the sandwich crosswise into 4 portions after it is assembled.

SOUVENIR TO SAVOR

A Pastrami Tale

A friend of mine, Sezer Tansug, tells me that we have Genghis Khan to thank for the delectable treat beloved in Turkey, *pastirma* (pastrami as we know it). Lore has it that during the early 13th century, Genghis Khan and his men tied seasoned sides of veal to the saddles of their horses as they rode across the central plains of Asia. The meat became tenderized as it constantly slapped against the sides of the horses and slowly dried out as it was exposed to the air.

Well, whether you believe this old tale is up to you, but the most renowned *pastirma* in Turkey comes from the Anatolian city of Kayseri. The nomadic ancestors of the Ottomans first brought *pastirma* to Kayseri, and it is now a favorite throughout Turkey.

"REUBEN" PITA

In Greece and Turkey, overflowing pita sandwiches are filled with moist lamb or pork shoulder kebabs right off the skewer. I'm so fond of my taste memories of these that I've been hesitant about trying even the most tempting-looking ones from the street vendors in New York City. Instead, in my own kitchen I cooked up a pastrami Reuben-style pita, which bursts with flavors from the Turkish palette.

4 pita breads, about 6 inches in diameter
2 tablespoons olive oil
4 tablespoons Zesty Yogurt Slather (page 56)
4 ounces thinly sliced pastrami
4 to 6 thin slices ripe tomato
½ small red onion, thinly slivered
2 teaspoons dried oregano
2 tablespoons chopped fresh mint leaves or flat-leaf parsley
Coarsely ground black pepper, to taste
2 red bell peppers, halved lengthwise and roasted (page 202)

1. Cut 4 pieces of waxed paper 12 inches long. Fold each one in half lengthwise to measure 12 x 6 inches.

2. Brush both sides of the pitas with olive oil. Place a nonstick skillet over medium heat. Cook the oiled pitas, flattening them with a metal spatula, until just golden but still soft, about 1 minute per side. Lay each pita on a folded piece of waxed paper.

3. Spread one side of each pita with 1 tablespoon of the yogurt slather. Divide the meat, tomato, onion, oregano, and mint evenly among the pitas. Season with pepper and top each with a roasted pepper half.

4. Carefully roll up the pitas with their fillings in the waxed paper, leaving the top third of the sandwich exposed. Serve rolled up in the paper.

Serves 4

CARIBBEAN CROQUE MONSIEUR

Sitting under a thatched roof in a restaurant on the beach in Martinique, I was amused to find amid all the exotic seafood and sauces listed on the menu a bit of French influence shining through—a Caribbean *croque monsieur*. My daughters ordered it, and it arrived bursting with ripe avocado and, unfortunately, lots of Cheddar cheese. I knew I could do better. And I did. Be sure to serve it with a large glass of pineapple juice to keep the mood.

4 thin slices French peasant bread, about 4 inches square
3 tablespoons unsalted butter, at room temperature
2 tablespoons honey mustard
4 slices Gruyère cheese
4 thin slices baked Virginia or Black Forest ham
2 tablespoons light honey
4 thin slices ripe tomato
½ ripe avocado, preferably Haas, peeled and thinly sliced

1. If desired, trim the crusts from the bread, then butter one side of each slice. Lay 2 slices of bread, buttered side down, on a work surface covered with waxed paper. Cover the 2 slices evenly with mustard. Top each with a slice of cheese, then 2 slices of ham. Drizzle the honey over the ham. Place the tomato slices on the ham and cover with the avocado slices. Finally top with the remaining 2 slices of bread, unbuttered side down.

2. Preheat the broiler.

3. Fry the sandwiches, one at a time, in a heavy skillet over medium heat until the bottom is golden. Carefully turn the sandwich over with a spatula and fry the other side. Place the sandwiches on a baking sheet and top each one with a remaining slice of cheese. Broil until the top slice of cheese just melts, 2 to 3 minutes. Cut the sandwiches in half or quarters and serve immediately.

Serves 2

CUBANA SANDWICH

In the late 70s there was nothing I liked better for lunch than a bowl of black bean soup and a Cubana sandwich from Victor's Cuban Café in New York. Cuban sandwiches are prepared on soft, chewy, bullet-shaped rolls. Once filled, the sandwiches are flattened and toasted in a *plancha,* a waffle-iron kind of cooking device. Over the years, I sought out variations in "Little Cuba" sections of Tampa and Key West in Florida, but they always seemed to have too much on them, including shredded lettuce. When I arrived in Havana, my search began anew. But even there, "No cigar!" And so I've resorted to making my own based on my memories of lunch at Victor's. I prefer my Cubana with sweet pickles, but you may substitute dill pickles. Although our bread isn't as soft as Cuban bread, a nice sourdough baguette makes an excellent substitute. This recipe is for one sandwich, but you can increase the ingredients depending on how many you want. The next time you roast pork, be sure to save the leftovers for this Latin treat.

1 teaspoon fresh orange juice
1 teaspoon red wine vinegar
2 teaspoons olive oil
1 sourdough baguette, cut into an 8-inch length, then lengthwise in half, inside scooped out a bit
1 teaspoon Dijon mustard
3 thin slices Monterey Jack cheese
Thin slices of sweet gherkins to cover length of sandwich
2 thin slices baked Virginia ham
2 to 3 very thin slices roasted pork

1. To make the vinaigrette, combine the orange juice, vinegar, and 1 teaspoon of the oil. Lightly brush the inside of the bread halves with the vinaigrette.

2. Spread the mustard over the bottom half of the bread. Cover with the cheese, pickles, ham, and pork; then cover with the top bread half.

3. Heat the remaining teaspoon oil in a nonstick skillet. Place the sandwich in the skillet, bottom side down. Weight the sandwich with a heavy pot lid and brown over medium heat until the cheese starts to melt, 1 to 2 minutes on each side. To serve, cut it in half diagonally, from corner to corner.

Makes 1 sandwich

SOUVENIR TO SAVOR

Street Food in the Tropics

Out looking for culinary thrills along bustling streets in Jamaica, I was taken by the brightly painted ramshackle carts selling snacks. Red, yellow, and turquoise carts and panel trucks painted with primitive birds and playing an energetic jumble of calypso and reggae music turned strolling into dancing.

Some carts were piled high with sugar cane, the tough outsides hacked off by a man sitting on a small stool, machete at his side. The soft pulp was ready for hours of sweet sucking and chewing. Bright yellow coconuts were set nearby, adorned with colorful straws, offering their sweet fresh liquid as a thirst-quencher in these hot climes. From other stands wafted the pungent island aromas of jerk chicken and pork, and spicy shrimp waiting to be nibbled. Irresistible food, irresistible music in a climate made for living outdoors—why go inside, ever?

SOUVENIR TO SAVOR

Ortaköy

Ortaköy is to Istanbul what Soho is to New York City. This district teems with the very trendiest Istanbul can serve up. The bustling area is packed with sprawling outdoor cafés, the tables spilling out onto a central square alive with the sounds of children playing ball and riding bicycles. Huge old trees are encircled by stone benches, where locals sit reading newspapers and books.

Unlike Soho, its setting is breathtaking. An 18th-century mosque provides the focal point, and an ornate bridge spanning the Bosporus delivers background. Smart bars, such as Memos with its melon and aqua wicker chairs, overlook the scene and serve up chilled glasses of Turkish white wine or raki accompanied by plates of greengage plums, ripe red cherries, salted pistachios, and hazelnuts.

The narrow streets are lined with art galleries and shops selling the latest hit songs, but I was taken by the fabulous array of street food to be found. Tastefully painted wooden carts sold modest baked potatoes, ready to be embellished by the toppings of your choice; grilled fish kebabs; Turkish heros filled with grilled lamb *köfte,* tomatoes, peppers, and shallots (see recipe); and *simit,* huge bread pretzels sprinkled with sesame seeds. A splendid feast for all the senses!

Wine, cherries, and plums at Café Memos in Ortaköy.

GREAT TURKISH HAMBURGERS

While on a leisurely walk through the small streets of Ortaköy I came upon beautifully painted wooden carts filled with incredibly good Turkish street food. One of my favorites was tended by a man with black curly hair and sporting a large dashing moustache. On one side of his cart was a grill, sizzling with lamb *köfte* (meat patties) alongside pencil-thin, sweet green peppers. His work space on the other side held sliced tomatoes and thinly sliced shallots tossed with parsley. To serve it all up, the man split baguettes in half lengthwise and scooped out the insides. First came the *köfte*, next the peppers, then tomatoes and generous sprinkles of salt and pepper. He topped it with the shallots and parsley and closed it with the top half of the bread. I planned on only having a small bite but quickly ate the whole thing (before dinner!). For a great Turkish burger, serve it the same way. The next time you grill, leave the ketchup in the fridge and serve this lusty Turkish treat.

1 pound ground lamb
1 pound ground beef
¼ cup coarsely grated onion
1 teaspoon minced garlic
1 tablespoon extra virgin olive oil
2 tablespoons chopped flat-leaf parsley
1 teaspoon dried oregano
1 teaspoon ground cinnamon
½ teaspoon ground cumin
1 teaspoon coarse salt
½ teaspoon coarsely ground black pepper
8 French bread rolls

TOPPINGS:
Sautéed thinly sliced strips Italian frying peppers
Thinly sliced tomatoes
Thinly sliced shallots tossed with minced parsley

1. Preheat a grill with medium-hot coals or the broiler.

2. Place all the burger ingredients through the pepper in a large bowl and work with your hands to just combine. Do not overmix.

3. Form the meat mixture into 8 oval patties, about 3 inches long, 2 inches across, and about 1 inch thick.

4. Grill or broil the patties, 8 minutes on the first side and 5 minutes on the second for rare.

5. Meanwhile split the rolls in half and remove some of the excess bread from the centers.

6. Place the patties in the rolls and serve immediately, with a platter of toppings.

Serves 8

SOUVENIR TO SAVOR

Broodjes

Broodjes, sandwiches, are great favorites throughout Holland, but in Amsterdam's renowned Van Dobben restaurant they reign supreme.

Opened in 1945, the Van Dobben's business *is* sandwiches. Every single *broodje* is a small masterpiece. The rolls are soft with a glazed top, similar to our hamburger buns, but so fresh they almost fly away. The list of sandwich fillings is extensive but you've got to be prepared to order fast.

As you walk through the door of this bustling little eatery with its oval counter, you hear other customers' choices being called out: "A *broodje* hot meat for me please." "Make mine a *broodje* healthy, a *broodje* chocolate confetti, and a glass of milk." "I'd like a *broodje* Russian salad and a *broodje* meatball." "I'll take a *broodje* steak tartare."

Everything goes between and around the bread. Other choices include:

Croquet: Ragout of beef coated with bread crumbs.

Spiegelei: An egg sunny side up.

Halfom: A mixture of liver and salt beef.

Versierde bal: Meatballs with the works—pickled onions and sliced pickles.

Gezond: Gouda cheese, ham, eggs, lettuce, and cucumbers.

Huzarensalade: Mashed potatoes, bacon, and mayonnaise.

Ossetong: Ox tongue.

THE BEERS OF

Belgium, The Netherlands, and Luxembourg

Belgium amazes beer lovers with its wide diversity of beers. There are six to eight hundred labels available at any one time. This array—surprising for such a small country—includes some of the most distinctive beers in the world, especially the "abbey" beers made at the country's five monastery breweries. Whether secular or Trappist, however, Belgian brewers produce all types of beer, from Pilsen-style golden lagers, to coppery ales like the classic malt, De Koninck of Flanders, to rich dark ales, such as Gouden Carolus and Oerbier.

Ancient traditions of brewing have evolved unique styles of beer—several have the fruity complexity of wine as well as the capacity to improve with age. The Trappist Saint Sixtus, for instance, produces the licorice-flavored Special and the rich, creamy, full-bodied Abbot. Another original style is lambic beer, which hails from the valley of the Senne River in central Belgium. Made mostly from wheat blended with lightly malted

Above: One of the beautiful canals in Bruges, Belgium. Right: Amsterdam's Heineken Brewery is as much a work of art as the beer is.

barley, lambic ferments spontaneously from wild yeasts born on the autumn wind. Some lambics remain in the barrel at least half a year (more likely one to three), undergoing a secondary fermentation that makes them slightly *pétillant,* or lightly sparkling.

Other distinctive Belgian beers to look for are the Trappist brews, such as Westmalle Triple, a strong, somewhat citrussy Pilsener; Orval; Chimay Red; Rochefort; Cuvée de l'Ermitage; cherry-flavored Kriek or Framboise (raspberry); the fruity, amber-hued Saison Dupont; and the dark reddish brown, slightly sour but highly prized Rodenbach Grand Cru, which devotees compare to fine Burgundy.

The Netherlands' Heineken was the first truly international beer, becoming so popular that breweries were established in numerous countries to handle demand. In recent years another Dutch beer has gained global popularity—Grolsch, a dry full-bodied Pilsener that comes in appealing bottles. The Netherlands has dozens of brewpubs and microbreweries producing flavorful beers and ales that never leave the country. The large brewers also make well-regarded specialty products, such as Heineken's Bock and Van Vollenhoven Stout.

Tiny Luxembourg, tucked between Belgium and France, has five breweries producing crisp, zesty Pilsen-style lagers. Included among them is one actually labeled Pils, as well as very fine Gambrinus, Royal-Altmünster, various Simon brews, and Diekirch Premium.

Above: The Amstel River in Amsterdam gave it's name to a crowd-pleasing brew. Right: Heineken's is so popular in the U.S., it is the number one imported beer.

PEPITO

Mexican Steak Sandwich

When I travel, every menu I see gets carefully scrutinized. As we moved across Mexico, I kept coming across a particular sandwich called *pepito*. I knew that *pepitas* were dried pumpkin seeds often served as a little snack with a tiny bowl of chili powder for dipping. So what was a *pepito*? I thought the university student who was our guide in Mexico City would know, so I asked him what a *pepito* was. He turned chili red and softly giggled, as did my daughters. Still blushing, he haltingly indicated that it referred to part of the male anatomy in a popular risqué joke. I dropped the discussion. When I saw it again on a menu in Ixtapa, I simply ordered it. A menu *pepito* turned out to be a great open-faced steak sandwich layered with refried red beans, guacamole, lettuce, and tomato. Nothing risqué about it at all!

MARINADE:
¼ cup extra virgin olive oil
¼ cup fresh orange juice
Juice of 1 lime
1 tablespoon chopped garlic
2 teaspoons ground cumin
1 teaspoon chili powder
Dash of Tabasco sauce
¼ cup chopped fresh cilantro leaves
Salt and coarsely ground black pepper, to taste

SANDWICHES:
1 skirt steak (about 1 pound)
8 slices peasant bread, about 4 inches square and ½ inch thick
¾ cup refried beans
8 romaine lettuce leaves, thinly shredded crosswise
4 ripe plum tomatoes, thinly sliced
¾ cup coarsely mashed avocado or Laurie's Basic Guacamole (page 61)
Salt and freshly ground black pepper, to taste

1. For the marinade, combine the olive oil, fruit juices, garlic, cumin, chili powder, Tabasco, cilantro, salt, and pepper in a large bowl.

2. For the sandwiches, cut the steak on the diagonal into 2 or 3 pieces depending on its length. Add the steak to the marinade and coat well. Cover and let marinate at room temperature for 2 hours or in the refrigerator overnight. Bring to room temperature before grilling.

3. Preheat a grill with hot coals.

4. Shortly before serving, grill the steak for about 5 minutes per side for medium rare. Let the meat rest about 10 minutes before slicing. Thinly slice on the diagonal and cover loosely with aluminum foil. Set aside.

5. Just before serving, assemble the sandwiches: Lightly toast the bread and spread one side of each slice with a heaping tablespoon of refried beans. Top each with shredded lettuce, and then tomato slices. With the back of a spoon, cover each sandwich with a heaping tablespoon of mashed avocado. Divide the steak slices evenly among the sandwiches, sprinkle with salt and pepper and serve immediately.

Serves 8

Adrian's Catalonian Snack

Adrian Forastier, my friend from Barcelona, says that his pleasant disposition can be traced back to the happiness he derived from his favorite after-school snack while growing up in Spain:

Take a piece of thin baguette, about 3 inches long. Cut it in half lengthwise and hollow out most of the inside. Brush lightly with olive oil and sprinkle both halves with granulated sugar. Lay a piece of chocolate in the bottom half and cover with the top.

Serves 1 happy *niño.*

YUMMY GRILLED CHEESE SANDWICH

If grilled cheese brings to mind white bread and processed cheese, this version will certainly dispel all such notions. The flavors and colors of the Mediterranean mingle with the Southwest and make this sandwich a totally satisfying light luncheon or late supper choice. When accompanied by a bowl of tomato soup, a roaring fire, and a good television movie, you've got the best of everything—warm weather tastes and cold weather comforts.

4 slices whole-grain bread, ½ inch thick
8 tablespoons Spanish Olive Tapenade (page 60)
2 yellow or red bell peppers, halved lengthwise, and roasted (page 202)
8 thin slices Monterey Jack cheese
2 teaspoons chopped fresh cilantro leaves, for garnish

1. Preheat the broiler.

2. Lightly toast the bread. Spread each slice with 2 tablespoons tapenade. Cover each with a roasted pepper half and top each with 2 slices cheese. Place the sandwiches on a baking sheet.

3. Broil the sandwiches until the cheese melts. Sprinkle with cilantro and serve immediately.

Serves 4

VERACRUZ VEGGIE SANDWICH

South-of-the border crunchy, colorful vegetables make the best fillings for warm-weather sandwiches served up on lightly toasted whole-grain bread. Here gossamer alfalfa sprouts top off a filling of creamy avocado, Monterey Jack, crispy cucumber, ripe tomato, and roasted peppers.

2 tablespoons mayonnaise
4 slices Wheat Berry Bread (page 485) or other multigrain bread, lightly toasted
½ ripe avocado, preferably Haas, pitted and peeled
½ teaspoon fresh lemon juice
2 teaspoons chopped flat-leaf parsley
2 slices Monterey Jack cheese
1 red bell pepper, halved lengthwise and roasted (page 202)
4 thin lengthwise slices peeled hothouse (seedless) cucumber
2 to 3 large slices ripe tomato
Salt and freshly ground black pepper, to taste
¼ cup alfalfa sprouts

1. Spread the mayonnaise on one side of each bread slice. Set 2 slices aside.

2. Mash the avocado with the lemon juice and spread some on the 2 remaining slices of bread. Sprinkle with the parsley.

3. Next top each with a cheese slice. Lay ½ roasted pepper over the cheese on each sandwich.

4. Cover the roasted pepper with the cucumber and tomato slices. Season with salt and pepper. Top each with sprouts and cover with reserved slices of bread. Cut each sandwich in half and serve.

Serves 2

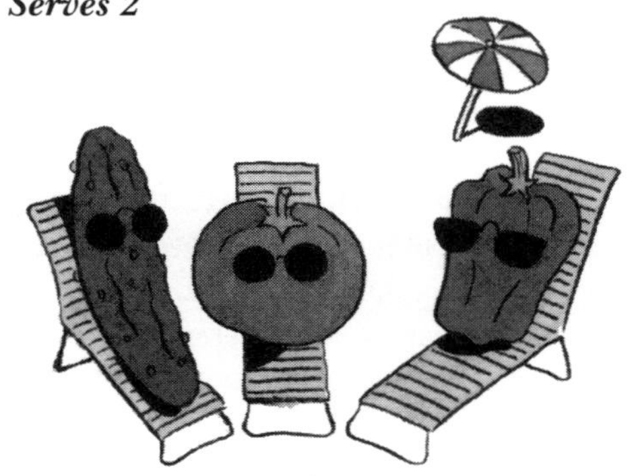

SOUVENIR TO SAVOR

Street Food Heaven

Street food was invented in Asia, I'm certain of it. It's virtually impossible to walk two blocks without coming across a small portable stall with a vendor tending a bubbling pan of hot oil, ladling out deep-fried squid, mysterious tantalizing meats, dumplings, or some other fragrant morsels. Office workers in Bangkok, Hong Kong, Taipei, and Singapore often take their lunch on the run at one of these ubiquitous dispensers of hot and cold concoctions. Hot chestnuts, rice cakes, pancakes, skewered baby cuttlefish, smelly deep-fried bean curd, corn on the cob, sticky rice, fish balls, and dozens of other delectable edibles sizzle and simmer on street corners ready to feed the bustling populace. Now that McDonald's has invaded Asian shores, let's hope that locals will continue to line up for grilled chicken legs at the corner stall. The food is simply too good to fade into the past.

THAI EGGPLANT SANDWICH

The sweetness in Thai cooking usually comes from brown sugar, but I couldn't resist using golden raisins instead in the roasted eggplant and basil base of this sandwich. Creamy chèvre adds tang and broiled ripe tomatoes, a lightly caramelized flavor. Serve with chilled Thai or Chinese beer or, for a true cross-cultural treat, a chilled Provençal rosé.

EGGPLANT SPREAD:
1 large eggplant (about 1¼ pounds)
1 tablespoon chopped fresh basil leaves
2 teaspoons finely grated lemon zest
1 teaspoon extra virgin olive oil
¼ cup coarsely chopped golden raisins
Salt and freshly ground black pepper, to taste

9 tablespoons (about 9 ounces) mild chèvre, such as Montrachet
3 tablespoons extra virgin olive oil
Salt and freshly ground black pepper, to taste
6 thick slices (¾ inch) peasant bread, lightly toasted
18 fresh large basil leaves, plus 2 tablespoons slivered, for garnish
6 large slices ripe tomato, ¼ inch thick

1. Preheat the oven to 400°F.

2. For the eggplant spread, pierce the eggplant in several places with the tines of a fork. Wrap in aluminum foil and bake for 1 hour. Unwrap the eggplant, let cool slightly, and cut it in half. Scoop the cooked pulp onto a cutting board, discarding as many seeds as possible. Coarsely chop the eggplant and place it in a mixing bowl. Add the basil leaves, lemon zest, oil, and raisins; combine well. Season with salt and pepper. Set aside.

3. In another bowl, mix the chèvre with 2 tablespoons of the oil and season to taste with salt and pepper.

4. Preheat the broiler.

5. Assemble the sandwiches: Divide the eggplant spread evenly atop the slices of toasted peasant bread. Cover evenly with the whole basil leaves. Spread the chèvre mixture over the basil and top each sandwich with a tomato slice. Brush the tomatoes with the remaining 1 tablespoon olive oil and sprinkle with salt and pepper.

6. Place the sandwiches on a baking sheet and broil 3 to 4 inches from the heat source until the tomato just starts to brown, 2 to 3 minutes. Sprinkle the tops with the slivered basil and serve immediately.

Serves 6

Whistle Stops: Time for Tea

In June 1968, nestled in a cozy tea parlor in the Dorset countryside, I was treated to my first proper English afternoon tea. The moment could not have been more idyllic. Tiny baskets of ripe strawberries and pitchers of clotted cream were brought to a pretty table set with delicate plates and cups decorated with pale pink roses.

The soothing warmth of those first few sips of steaming hot tea was all I needed—I was bewitched. Warm currant-studded scones arrived along with little dishes filled with strawberry preserves. I sipped, nibbled, and relaxed. That seemed to me to be the very essence of what the bewitching teatime hour was all about.

Over the twenty-six years since then, I've had many teas, including one in a tulip garden outside of Istanbul and one in the St. Petersburg home of a Russian friend. I've enjoyed tea in Paris, throughout Scotland, and in Ireland. The effect has always been comforting and there was no tradition I came to love, anticipate, and revere more in my travels. But, no matter how grand the setting, I think that I will always love best that cozy tea parlor in Dorset.

ANNE'S HAM AND CHEESE SALAD TEA SANDWICHES

When I was working on my tea sandwich recipes, I happened to ask New York food stylist Anne Disrude if she had any ideas for one using ham. She suggested this delightful ham and cheese combination. Crème fraîche combined with grainy mustard makes a luxurious dressing for this all-American favorite.

1 cup julienned baked Virginia ham
1 cup julienned Gruyère cheese
½ cup plus 2 tablespoons crème fraîche
2 teaspoons grainy mustard
Coarsely ground black pepper, to taste
16 very thin slices best-quality white bread
3 tablespoons unsalted butter, at room temperature

1. Place the ham and cheese in a small bowl.

2. In another bowl, mix together the crème fraîche and mustard. Add to the ham and cheese, season with pepper, and mix to combine.

3. Spread one side of each slice of bread with ½ teaspoon butter. Spread the buttered side of 8 slices of bread with a heaping tablespoon of the ham and cheese salad. Top with the remaining slices of bread, buttered side down.

4. Carefully cut the crusts from each sandwich with a long, sharp knife. Cut the sandwiches in half diagonally.

Makes 8 whole sandwiches or 16 halves

A Pretty Platter

When serving tea sandwiches, make sure they look their best. Line a small serving tray with a lacy doily and place the sandwiches in an attractive arrangement on the tray. Decorate with a tiny pink rosebud or small bunch of violets for a floral garnish.

CUCUMBER AND TINY SPROUT TEA SANDWICHES

Cucumber has always been, and remains today, the "Champagne" of tea sandwiches throughout the British Isles. These dainty bites are most often served in England peppered with tiny clover-shaped cress. To achieve that wonderful flavor of English cress, I've chopped up watercress and mixed it with butter to spread on the bread. I've also topped the cucumbers with alfalfa sprouts for just the right texture.

6 tablespoons (¾ stick) unsalted butter, at room temperature
½ cup coarsely chopped watercress leaves
16 very thin slices best-quality white bread
½ hothouse (seedless) cucumber, peeled and very thinly sliced (about 32 slices)
½ cup alfalfa sprouts

1. Mix the butter and watercress together in a small bowl.

2. Spread 1 teaspoon of the butter on one side of each slice of bread.

3. Lay about 4 cucumber slices on the buttered side of 8 slices of bread. Cover each with about 1 tablespoon alfalfa sprouts and top with the remaining 8 slices of bread, buttered side down.

4. Carefully cut the crusts from each sandwich with a long, sharp knife. Cut the sandwiches in half diagonally.

Makes 8 whole sandwiches or 16 halves

Tea Sandwich Musts

1. Allow 4 to 6 cut sandwich servings for each person.

2. Choose the thinnest, best-quality white or whole-wheat bread possible. Never serve end slices.

3. Bread slices should be lightly buttered no matter what the filling. Unsalted butter should always be used. Butter should be at room temperature before spreading.

4. Tea sandwiches are meant to be dainty, so don't overfill the bread.

5. I prefer cutting the crusts off the bread with a long, sharp knife after the sandwiches are filled. This keeps everything neater. The only exception to this rule is a smoked salmon sandwich. Remove the crusts first and trim any excess salmon carefully once the sandwich is made.

6. Since tea sandwiches should be delicate, cut each sandwich in half on the diagonal or into thirds before serving. Decorative shapes can be made with cookie cutters for special occasions.

7. If making tea sandwiches in advance, keep them fresh by first covering them loosely with a sheet of waxed paper and then laying a damp kitchen towel over the waxed paper. Never place a damp towel directly on top of the bread because the sandwiches will become soggy.

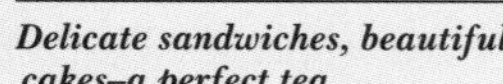

Delicate sandwiches, beautiful cakes–a perfect tea.

A TASTE OF THE WORLD

British Palette

Photo: Telephone kiosks in Edinburgh.

...And

GINGER	SALMON
MINT	TROUT
LEEKS	LAMB
CRESS	MALT VINEGAR
POTATOES	STILTON
PARSNIPS	CLOTTED CREAM
CABBAGE	RED CURRANT JELLY
MUSHROOMS	SHERRY
RHUBARB	MADEIRA
BARLEY	
OYSTERS	

RITZY EGG SALAD TEA SANDWICHES

Being a great lover of egg salad, I've tried many at home and around the world and always come back to my favorite—which is a rather pure version. I've added just a little fresh dill for a gentle lift. A dainty portion of this salad was my favorite teatime bite at the Ritz in London.

8 large eggs
½ cup mayonnaise
Salt and freshly ground black pepper, to taste
1 tablespoon finely chopped fresh dill
20 very thin slices best-quality white bread
3½ tablespoons unsalted butter, at room temperature

1. Place the eggs in a saucepan, cover with cold water, and bring to a boil. Once the eggs come to a boil, reduce the heat and simmer for 13 minutes.

2. Run the eggs under cold water until they are cool enough to handle. Peel them and place in a bowl.

3. Slice the eggs then coarsely mash them with the back of a fork. Stir in the mayonnaise, season with salt and pepper, and fold in the dill. (Refrigerate covered up to 2 days.)

4. Spread one side of each slice of bread with ½ teaspoon butter. Spread the buttered side of 10 slices of bread with 2 tablespoons egg salad. Top with the remaining slices of bread, buttered side down.

5. Carefully cut the crusts from sandwich with a long, sharp knife. Cut in half diagonally.

Makes 10 whole sandwiches or 20 halves

DATE AND NUT CREAM CHEESE TEA SANDWICHES

No tea is complete without a sandwich spread made with cream cheese and nuts. The addition of carrots is unexpected and colorful on this dainty whole-wheat sandwich. Dates add a welcome sweetness.

6 ounces cream cheese, at room temperature
¼ cup finely diced pitted dates (about 4 dates)
2 tablespoons finely chopped walnuts
1 tablespoon finely grated carrot
16 very thin slices best-quality whole-wheat bread
3 tablespoons unsalted butter, at room temperature

1. In a small bowl, mix together the cream cheese, dates, walnuts, and carrot.

2. Spread one side of each slice of bread with ½ teaspoon butter. Gently spread 1 tablespoon of the cream cheese mixture over the buttered side of 8 slices of bread. Top with the remaining 8 slices, buttered side down.

3. Carefully cut the crusts from each sandwich with a long, sharp knife. Cut the sandwiches in half diagonally.

Makes 8 whole sandwiches or 16 halves

HERBED CHERRY CHICKEN SALAD TEA SANDWICHES

Dried cherries complement the flavors of chicken and tarragon and add a pleasant texture. Toss all in a light dressing of mayonnaise and sour cream. Whole-wheat bread adds substance to these delicate tea sandwiches.

1½ cups shredded cooked white chicken meat
¼ cup dried cherries, coarsely chopped
1½ tablespoons chopped fresh tarragon leaves
Salt and coarsely ground black pepper, to taste
6 tablespoons mayonnaise
¼ cup sour cream
20 very thin slices best-quality whole-wheat bread
3½ tablespoons unsalted butter, at room temperature

1. Finely dice the shredded chicken and place it in a bowl. Add the cherries and tarragon. Season with salt and pepper.

2. In a small bowl, mix the mayonnaise and sour cream. Toss with the chicken.

3. Spread one side of each slice of bread with ½ teaspoon butter. Spread the buttered side of 10 slices with a heaping tablespoon of the chicken salad. Top with the remaining slices of bread, buttered side down.

4. Carefully cut the crusts from each sandwich with a long, sharp knife. Cut in half diagonally.

Makes 10 whole sandwiches or 20 halves, chicken salad yields about 1½ cups

Red Currants

These tart, red, jewel-like berries grow on a shrub in small, delicate clusters. Although red currants are native to northeastern Europe, they can be found in the United States during the summer months. They make delicious jams, jellies, and syrups. Added to a fruit salad, they provide a lovely burst of flavor and texture. A much cherished specialty from France is Bar-le-Duc jelly. The tiny seeds of red and white currants are removed by hand with a quill, and the sweet jelly produced is packaged in a magnificent little jar. The flavor is perfect atop biscuits for teatime.

A TASTE OF THE WORLD

Russian Fruit Basket

458

APPLES
BILBERRIES
CHERRIES
CRANBERRIES
CURRANTS
DATES
FIGS
GRAPES
HONEYDEW MELONS
PEACHES
PEARS
PLUMS
RASPBERRIES
SOUR CHERRIES

GASPE SMOKED SALMON TEA SANDWICHES

Smoked salmon sandwiches are a 4 o'clock favorite in the great tea parlors of England. Here I've blended cream cheese with fresh chives and lemon zest for my own New York touch. I think they'd still be welcome in the British Isles.

8 ounces cream cheese, at room temperature
2 tablespoons snipped fresh chives
1 teaspoon finely grated lemon zest
Coarsely ground black pepper, to taste
16 very thin slices best-quality whole-wheat bread
3 tablespoons unsalted butter, at room temperature
8 thin slices Gaspé or other favorite smoked salmon

1. In a small bowl, mix together the cream cheese, chives, lemon zest, and pepper.

2. Carefully remove the crusts from the bread with a long, sharp knife.

3. Spread one side of each slice of bread with ½ teaspoon butter. Spread the buttered side of 8 slices of bread with 1 tablespoon of the cream cheese mixture. Cover each with a slice of salmon and top with the remaining slices of bread, buttered side down.

4. Carefully cut each sandwich in half diagonally.

Makes 8 whole sandwiches or 16 halves

SWEET BLINCHIKI

Once you've mastered a basic crêpe recipe, there are endless dishes to be created from this thin pancake. Since I love the tart, sour flavor of buttermilk, I've used it in combination with whole milk to achieve a more interesting taste. With a well-seasoned crêpe pan and good wrist action, you'll be an expert in no time.

1 cup all-purpose flour
1 tablespoon sugar
Pinch of salt
3 large eggs
1⅓ cups milk
⅔ cup buttermilk
2 tablespoons melted clarified butter (page 53)

1. Sift the flour, sugar, and salt together into a mixing bowl. Make a well in the center of the dry ingredients. Break the eggs into the well and mix the eggs with a fork until well combined. Add the whole milk and buttermilk in a steady stream, while whisking constantly and drawing in the flour. The batter should have the consistency of cream. Let the batter rest for 30 minutes.

2. Heat a 7-inch nonstick skillet or crêpe pan over medium heat. Brush the pan lightly with a small amount of the clarified butter to prevent the crêpes from sticking.

3. Ladle ¼ cup batter into the pan and, working quickly, rotate the pan with a turn of the wrist so that the batter evenly coats the bottom. Cook the crêpe until it is set and the bottom is nicely golden brown, 30 to 45 seconds. Then loosen the crêpe with a spatula and turn it over. Cook the second side until just set, about 10 seconds. The underside should be paler than the first side. Continue with the remaining batter, adding more butter to the pan if the crêpes begin to stick.

4. Stack the finished crêpes on a plate, cover with a kitchen towel, and store at room temperature until ready to use.

Makes about twenty 6-inch blinchiki (crêpes)

MY KITCHEN DIARY

Bilberries

Small, tart, and magenta-colored, these are the little berries that we know as huckleberries in the United States. They are delicious just picked off the shrub and used in jams, jellies, syrups, and liqueurs. At a tea party in St. Petersburg, I rolled some, sprinkled with sugar, into buttery *blinchiki* and spooned bilberry purée atop. Both tangy and sweet, they often accompany game and meat dishes throughout Scandinavia and northern Germany.

DORSET SCONES

The first time I tasted scones was in a quaint tea parlor while visiting friends in Dorset, in southwest England. They were nothing like the heavy thick kind you might find in bakeries around America. My first deliciously warm scones were light and fragrant, and were served huddled together in a linen cloth in a sweet antique basket. Pots of freshly made strawberry jam rested alongside pitchers of thick clotted cream. And, since it was June, fresh strawberries were ripe for the picking and served in pretty flowered bowls along with the scones.

It was here, too, that I had my first "scone-eating lesson." Don't cut these delicate biscuits, but instead gently twist the top off and you'll create the ideal surface on which to spread your jam and cream. Brew a lovely pot of tea. Heaven!

This basic recipe includes currants but can be easily changed by adding another dried fruit or nuts. The cut dough can be refrigerated overnight or frozen well wrapped for up to 2 weeks. The thicker the dough is rolled, the higher the scone will be.

2 cups all-purpose flour
1 tablespoon baking powder
3 tablespoons sugar
½ teaspoon salt
½ teaspoon ground nutmeg
8 tablespoons (1 stick) unsalted butter, chilled and cut into cubes
1 large egg
Approximately ½ cup milk
¾ cup dried currants

1. Place the flour, baking powder, sugar, salt, and nutmeg in a food processor and pulse on and off to combine the ingredients. Add the cold butter and pulse 15 to 20 times until the mixture resembles coarse meal.

2. Break the egg into a small bowl and whisk lightly. Pour half the egg into a ½-cup measuring cup and fill to the top with milk. Pour the liquid over the flour mixture and process for about 10 seconds until the dough forms large curds. Scrape the dough onto a lightly floured work surface.

3. Quickly and gently knead in the currants. Pat or roll the dough ½ inch thick. Cut into 2¼-inch rounds with a biscuit cutter. Gently reroll the scraps and continue to cut all the dough. Place the scones on ungreased baking sheets and chill for 15 minutes. They can be covered and refrigerated at this point for as long as overnight.

4. Preheat the oven to 450°F.

5. Add 1 tablespoon milk to the remaining half egg and, using a pastry brush, moisten the top of each scone with the egg wash. Bake until the tops are lightly colored, about 15 minutes. Cool on wire racks for at least 10 minutes before serving.

Makes 12 scones

FINNISH CARDAMOM TEA LOAF

Cardamom is a spice that is highly favored in Scandinavian baking. It produces a marvelously exotic aroma that is reminiscent of its eastern origins. Cardamom is native to the tropical forests of India, where it grows on pod-bearing plants. These pods contain the black-brown seeds that are ground to a powder to release the full flavor. Because ground cardamom loses its flavor quickly, it is best to grind the seeds yourself with a mortar and pestle or a small coffee grinder (reserved for spices) just before using. The simplicity and sweet spiciness of this loaf make it the perfect companion to a steaming cup of smoky tea.

2 cups all-purpose flour
2 teaspoons ground cardamom
1½ teaspoons baking powder
1 teaspoon baking soda
½ teaspoon salt
3 large eggs
¾ cup sugar
1 cup sour cream
8 tablespoons (1 stick) unsalted butter, melted

1. Preheat the oven to 350°F. Lightly butter a 9 x 5 x 3-inch loaf pan and dust it with flour, shaking out the excess.

2. Combine the flour, cardamom, baking powder, baking soda, and salt in a bowl. Set aside.

3. In a mixing bowl, beat the eggs and sugar together with a hand-held mixer until creamy. Add the dry ingredients and mix until combined. Mix in the sour cream and melted butter.

4. Pour the batter into the prepared pan. Bake until a skewer inserted in the center comes out clean, about 1 hour.

5. Cool the cake in the pan for 15 minutes on a wire rack. Then run a knife around the edges of the pan to loosen the cake and turn it out onto the rack to cool completely.

Makes one 9-inch loaf, serves 8

HUNGARIAN CHERRY TEA CAKE

Hungarians, like most Central Europeans, take teatime seriously. Simple to prepare, this is the perfect cake to serve when fresh cherries are bountiful. It is a delicious treat served with a glass of hot tea with cherry preserves stirred in or a tall, cool glass of iced tea, garnished with mint sprigs.

8 tablespoons (1 stick) unsalted butter, at room temperature
½ cup plus 1 tablespoon sugar
3 large eggs, separated
Finely grated zest of 1 lemon
2 tablespoons fresh lemon juice
1 teaspoon pure vanilla extract
½ cup all-purpose flour
Pinch of salt
1½ cups pitted sweet dark cherries, fresh or well-drained jarred

SOUVENIR TO SAVOR

Gerbaud, A Model Coffeehouse

You can't go to Budapest without stopping for a leisurely afternoon respite at the legendary Gerbaud. This elegant coffeehouse has a series of ornately wood-paneled salons lit by crystal chandeliers that seem to go on for miles. Sun shines through the grand windows overlooking the square, while cigarette smoke rises eerily to the ceiling. An institution since 1858, Gerbaud has long been a gathering place for musicians, actors, artists, intellectuals, politicians, smart socialites, and the like. You can linger here for hours if you wish, watching the world go by. Located on the Vorosmarty Square, at the end of a long shopping street filled with book shops and great places to pick up a few souvenirs, this is an ideal atmospheric watering hole.

Central Europe has many gems like this, but Gerbaud is one of the stars. Sober-looking waitresses in white blouses and white aprons whisk about a sea of tiny green marble tables surrounded by stately chairs, taking orders and returning with the most luscious teatime savories, cakes, tea, coffee, hot chocolate, and more. I suggest the famous *dobostorta*—thin layers of genoise cake and luscious chocolate buttercream capped with a shiny caramel topping. Created at the turn of the century by pastry chef Jozef C. Dobos, it can be found throughout Central Europe in different forms, but surely it can be no better than at Gerbaud.

1. Preheat the oven to 350°F. Lightly butter an 8½-inch springform cake pan. Line the bottom with a round of waxed paper and butter the paper.

2. Cream the butter and ½ cup sugar in a mixing bowl with an electric mixer. Add the egg yolks, lemon zest, lemon juice, and vanilla. Mix well. Add the flour and mix well.

3. In a separate bowl, beat the egg whites with a pinch of salt until firm but not stiff. Stir one-third of the egg whites into the batter until well combined. Fold the remaining egg whites into the batter with a rubber spatula until just combined.

4. Scrape the batter into the prepared pan. Top evenly with the cherries, leaving about ½-inch border around the sides of the pan. Sprinkle the top evenly with the remaining 1 tablespoon sugar. Bake the cake until golden brown and the top springs back when lightly touched, about 35 minutes.

5. Cool the cake on a wire rack 10 minutes. Run a small knife around the cake to loosen it from the side of the pan. Remove the ring and let the cake cool completely. When it is completely cool, invert the cake onto a large plate. Remove the springform bottom and the waxed paper, then invert the cake onto a serving plate.

Makes one 8½-inch cake, serves 8

The Proper Way to Make Tea

A delicious cup of tea doesn't require much effort but there are several steps that must be followed religiously to obtain a delicious "cuppa" every time.

First, always start with cold fresh tap water. Bring a pot of water to a boil. Just as it begins to boil, remove it from the heat—overboiling the water causes it to lose oxygen and affects the flavor of the tea. Meanwhile, preheat a teapot with very hot tap water to warm it. Ceramic, china, silver, or nonreactive metal pots are the best. Let the water sit a minute or two in the pot, swirl it around a bit, then discard it. Add 1 teaspoon of tea leaves per cup plus 1 teaspoon "for the pot." Pour the boiling water into the pot over the tea, cover, and allow the tea to steep for 5 minutes. Steeping the tea is very important since the best flavors of the tea are extracted from the leaves during this time. To serve, give the tea a stir and strain it into teacups. Serve a second pot of hot water alongside to dilute the tea if it becomes too strong.

Tea Etiquette

Not until you've sipped around as much as I have can you truly understand the etiquette of British tea. To begin, a proper tutorial is necessary in the several categories of "tea" which are served at different times in the afternoon.

"Afternoon tea," which was reserved in the past for high society, is served from 3:00 to 5:00 P.M. A pot of tea is served along with delicate finger sandwiches on thin white or whole-wheat bread. The bread is always lightly buttered and crusts are trimmed. The sandwiches are filled with anything from egg salad, cucumbers and cress, cheese and tomatoes, thinly sliced tongue, cream cheese and nuts, to delicate slices of baked ham or turkey.

Next comes a basket of warm fresh scones served with strawberry jam and clotted or whipped heavy cream. Once the scones are cleared, a lovely choice of cakes and petits fours are brought to the table.

"Cream tea," the simplest of all, is served at 4:30 P.M. A pot of tea is served with scones, clotted or whipped cream and a pot of strawberry jam—never raspberry.

"High tea" is served between 5:00 and 7:00 P.M. This custom originated in the Victorian era and was originally eaten by the working class as the last meal of the day so that they could retire early and be up at dawn for the long day of labor ahead. The typical main course is either a mixed grill of sausages, lamb chops, boiled gammon (bacon), and tomatoes, or fried haddock, chicken salad, and chips. Lightly buttered bread and a selection of condiments are always served along with the main course. Cheeses, a large pot of tea, and a variety of home-baked cakes finish off this little feast.

Now that we've dotted our *I*s and crossed our *teas,* all that's necessary is a small primer on the best selections of teas to choose from. Remember tea can be served with a slice of lemon or a pitcher of milk but never cream. A pot of boiling water is always nearby to refresh the pot or to dilute tea that has steeped too long.

Breakfast Tea: This full-bodied blend of Indian and Ceylon teas is lovely any time of the day.

Darjeeling: My favorite, it is rightly known as the Champagne of teas. It has a delicate, wine-like Muscatel flavor.

Assam: A full-bodied Indian tea with a malty flavor.

Ceylon: This golden tea, grown at high altitudes, is both bright and reliable. Its rich quality makes it perfect for blending with other teas.

Lapsang Souchong: Smoky Chinese tea.

Rose Pouchon: A deep golden-hued, rose-scented tea, delectable served with pastries.

Jasmine: An extremely special tea, filled with the intoxicating perfume of the tiny white flower.

China Oolong: Burnished bronze in color with a slight almond taste.

Keemum: A delicate China tea with a slight floral hint to its flavor.

Earl Grey: This smoky-flavored, well-known tea is a perfect blend of China black tea and Darjeeling.

LITTLE SWEDISH LINGONBERRY TEA CAKE

Swedish lingonberries, small ruby-colored berries with a slightly sweet and slightly tart flavor, are a delicate addition to this flavorful spice cake. Lingonberries flourish in Scandinavian forests in the summer during the midnight sun. Similar to cranberries but smaller in size, lingonberries are also delicious stirred into yogurt, rolled into crêpes, spread on toast, or served as the condiment of choice with game birds and venison. Fresh lingonberries are hard to find in this country, but lingonberry preserves—Felix brand—are available in most specialty food shops. They are usually sold in 14½-ounce jars.

1½ cups all-purpose flour
2 teaspoons ground cinnamon
2 teaspoons ground ginger
1 teaspoon ground nutmeg
1 teaspoon ground cloves
1 teaspoon baking soda
8 tablespoons (1 stick) unsalted butter, at room temperature
¾ cup sugar
2 large eggs
½ cup sour cream
½ cup lingonberry preserves

1. Preheat the oven to 350°F. Lightly butter a 6-cup bundt pan and dust it with flour, shaking out the excess.

2. Combine the flour, cinnamon, ginger, nutmeg, cloves, and baking soda in a bowl. Set aside.

3. In a mixing bowl, beat the butter and sugar with an electric mixer until well combined. Add the eggs one at a time, mixing well after each addition. Beat in the sour cream. Add the dry ingredients and mix until just combined. Stir in the lingonberry preserves.

4. Pour the batter into the prepared pan. Bake until a skewer inserted into the center of the cake comes out clean, 45 to 55 minutes.

5. Cool the cake in the pan on a wire rack for 15 minutes. Then run a knife around the edges of the pan to loosen the cake and turn it out onto the rack to cool completely.

Makes 1 cake, serves 8

KUGELHOPF

This eggy, raisin-studded Alsatian yeast bread, traditionally baked in a crown-shaped ceramic mold, is great toasted for breakfast with dark cherry preserves and orange marmalade. The always clever French love it served in thick slices with rich hot chocolate for a Sunday afternoon *goûter* (snack). I think it is equally delicious with a cup of Darjeeling tea. I've plumped both golden and dark raisins in dark rum before adding them to the vanilla bean-scented dough. Sliced almonds are sprinkled into the baking pan so that they bake along with the bread, and decorate the top once it's turned out of its mold. Because of the length of time involved in preparation, it is perfectly fine to make the kugelhopf a day ahead of serving. It will be just as delicious the second day.

½ cup dark raisins
½ cup golden raisins
¼ cup dark rum
½ cup plus 2 tablespoons milk
1 teaspoon plus ⅔ cup granulated sugar
1 package active dry yeast
4 large eggs
1 vanilla bean, split
1 teaspoon salt
4½ cups all-purpose flour
8 tablespoons (1 stick) unsalted butter, very soft
½ cup sliced almonds
1 tablespoon confectioners' sugar

1. Place the raisins in a small bowl. Heat the rum in a small saucepan until hot but not boiling. Pour it over the raisins, stir, and set aside.

2. Heat ½ cup milk in a small saucepan until it is warm to the touch, about 110°F. Combine the milk, 1 teaspoon granulated sugar and the yeast in a small bowl and set aside in a draft-free place to proof about 10 minutes.

3. In a large bowl, whisk together the eggs, remaining ⅔ cup granulated sugar, the seeds from the vanilla bean, and the salt. Using a wooden spoon or rubber spatula, beat in 1 cup of the flour. Stir in the remaining 2 tablespoons of milk and the yeast mixture, then beat in a second cup of flour. (Beat vigorously after each addition of flour.) Drain the rum from the raisins, reserve the raisins, and pour the rum into the batter. Beat in a third cup of flour. Beat in the butter in 4 additions. When the butter is completely incorporated, add the fourth cup of flour and stir. When the dough becomes too stiff to mix, knead it with your hands. Turn the dough out onto a lightly floured surface and knead for 5 minutes, adding additional flour if necessary to prevent it from sticking too much. The dough should be soft and slightly sticky.

4. Form the dough into a ball and place it in a buttered bowl. Cover loosely with plastic wrap and let rise in a draft-free place until doubled in volume, 1½ to 2 hours. A finger pressed lightly into the dough should leave an indentation rather than springing back.

5. Turn the dough out onto a lightly floured surface, flatten it, and fold in the raisins. Knead a few minutes until the raisins are evenly distributed. Generously butter a 10-inch kugelhopf mold or bundt pan. Sprinkle the almonds into the bottom of the pan and rotate the pan so they adhere to the sides as well. Form the dough into a ball, poke a hole in the center with your finger, and slip the dough over the stem and into the pan. Press the dough evenly into the bottom of the pan. Cover loosely with plastic wrap and let rise in a draft-free place until doubled in volume, about 2 hours.

6. Preheat the oven to 375°F.

7. Place the pan in the center of the oven and bake 15 minutes. Cover the top with aluminum foil and bake until a wooden skewer inserted in the center comes out clean, about 15 minutes more. Remove the bread from the oven, cool on a wire rack for 5 minutes, then turn it out of the pan onto the rack to cool completely. Sift confectioners' sugar over the top before serving.

Makes one 10-inch bread, serves 8 to 10

SPICE CAKE WITH COFFEE FROSTING

I first tasted a version of this spice cake while sipping tea in front of a roaring fire on a rainy afternoon in southern Scotland. Not only suited to teas, the assertive flavor of this cake, laced with molasses and topped with a buttery coffee icing, can easily stand up to the strongest cup of coffee.

SPICE CAKE:
2 cups all-purpose flour
1¾ teaspoons baking soda
¾ teaspoon salt
1 tablespoon ground ginger
2 teaspoons ground cinnamon
½ teaspoon ground nutmeg
¼ teaspoon ground cloves
1½ cups milk
1½ cups granulated sugar
8 tablespoons (1 stick) unsalted butter, cut into pieces
⅓ cup molasses
2 large eggs, lightly beaten

COFFEE FROSTING:
2 tablespoons instant coffee crystals
1 teaspoon hot tap water
12 tablespoons (1½ sticks) unsalted butter, at room temperature
¼ teaspoon ground ginger
¼ teaspoon ground cinnamon
¼ teaspoon ground nutmeg
12 ounces cream cheese, at room temperature
1¼ cups confectioners' sugar

1. Preheat the oven to 325°F. Lightly butter a 9-inch round cake pan. Line the bottom of the pan with a round of waxed paper cut to fit and butter the paper.

2. Sift the flour, baking soda, salt, ginger, cinnamon, nutmeg, and cloves together into a large bowl. Whisk to combine and set aside.

3. Combine the milk and sugar in a saucepan and bring just to a boil. Remove from the heat and stir in the butter and molasses.

4. When the butter is melted, quickly whisk the liquids into the dry ingredients. Whisk in the eggs.

5. Pour the batter into the prepared pan. Bake until a toothpick inserted into the center of the cake comes out clean, about 50 minutes. Cool in the pan on a wire rack for 5 minutes, then invert the cake onto the rack to cool completely.

6. Meanwhile, make the frosting: Place the instant coffee in a small bowl and add the water. Stir to dissolve (it is fine if the coffee does not completely dissolve). In a mixing bowl, cream the butter with the spices, using a hand-held mixer. Gradually beat in the cream cheese and coffee. Combine thoroughly, scraping down the sides of the bowl occasionally with a rubber spatula. Gradually beat in the sugar and mix well. Set aside.

7. Using a long, sharp, serrated knife, even off the domed top of the cake. Place the cake, bottom side up, on a serving plate. Cut the cake horizontally in half, creating 2 layers. Lift off the top layer and set aside. Evenly spread about 1¼ cups of the icing over the bottom layer. Replace the top layer and frost the sides and top of the cake.

Makes one 9-inch cake, serves 8

Chocolate with Coffee

In Denmark, when you find a small piece of dark bitter chocolate resting on the saucer alongside a cup of coffee, do as the Danes do. Bite off a small piece, rest it behind your teeth, and sip the coffee through it. The chocolate melts in your mouth and flavors the coffee as you sip.

Skillet Cinnamon Toast

....

Spanish mothers have their own great equivalent of the American after-school classic, cookies and milk. My friend Laura MacArthur lived in Madrid during her childhood and enjoyed this treat upon returning from school at about 6 P.M. The snack satisfies a young child's sweet tooth, yet it is sophisticated with the savory addition of fruity and mild Spanish extra virgin olive oil.

Cut three to four ½-inch-thick slices from a round peasant bread. Then cut the slices crosswise in half. Fry until lightly brown in 2 tablespoons Spanish olive oil, adding more oil if necessary. Combine 1 tablespoon confectioners' sugar with ½ teaspoon ground cinnamon in a small bowl. Remove the bread when it is ready from the skillet, and using a strainer, sprinkle all over with the cinnamon sugar. Serve with a cozy cup of hot chocolate.

MOROCCAN PUMPKIN TEA LOAF

Although the North Africans usually reserve pumpkin for vegetable dishes, my thought was to incorporate it instead with the luscious dried fruits and nuts which overflow in their markets. The result is this cake-like sweet bread, which is wonderful served at teatime slathered with apricot preserves, or as a sweet and spicy accompaniment to Moroccan *tagines*, vegetable couscous, and other full-flavored stews and soups.

2 cups all-purpose flour
2 teaspoons baking powder
1 teaspoon baking soda
1 teaspoon ground cinnamon
½ teaspoon ground cloves
½ teaspoon ground nutmeg
½ teaspoon ground ginger
¼ teaspoon salt
8 tablespoons (1 stick) unsalted butter, at room temperature
¾ cup sugar
¼ cup honey
2 large eggs
1 cup canned pumpkin purée
½ cup nonfat plain yogurt
½ cup coarsely chopped pitted dates
½ cup coarsely chopped dried apricots
½ cup coarsely chopped walnuts

1. Preheat the oven to 350°F. Lightly butter a 9 x 5 x 3-inch loaf pan and dust it with flour, shaking out the excess.

2. Combine the flour, baking powder, baking soda, cinnamon, cloves, nutmeg, ginger, and salt in a bowl. Set aside.

3. In a mixing bowl, beat the butter, sugar, and honey together with an electric mixer until well combined. Add the eggs one at a time, mixing well after each addition.

4. Add the dry ingredients to the butter mixture and mix to combine. Add the pumpkin and yogurt and mix until just blended. Stir in the dates, apricots, and walnuts.

5. Pour the batter into the prepared pan. Bake until a skewer inserted into the center comes out clean, about 1¼ hours.

6. Cool the cake in the pan on a wire rack for 15 minutes. Then run a knife around the edges of the pan to loosen the cake and turn it out onto the rack to cool completely.

Makes one 9-inch loaf, serves 8

GALINA'S BERRY TEA

On a beautiful autumn Sunday morning while I was in St. Petersburg, my friends Galina and Irina brought me to see the newly restored Peter and Paul Fortress. As we walked through the garden, I noticed rose hips covering the bushes. They told me about the different teas they made from rose hips, berries, and apples. Galina described this tea and the sweet flavor that the apple skins imparted. When I came home I made a pot and found it quite delicious, with a subtle, gentle flavor.

½ cup coarsely chopped fresh raspberries
Peel of 1 Granny Smith apple
¼ cup dried cherries
2 whole cloves
4 peppermint tea bags
4 cups boiling water

1. Place the raspberries, apple peel, dried cherries, cloves, and tea bags in a large teapot or saucepan. Cover with the boiling water and allow to steep, covered, 5 to 10 minutes.

2. Strain and serve in teacups, adding more hot water if desired.

Serves 4

SOUVENIR TO SAVOR

Fruit Teas

During late September in St. Petersburg the rose hips are red and ripe on their bushes. With a slight chill in the air on a late afternoon, thoughts turn to the soothing teas they would make. I asked my friends Irina, Galina, and Rita how they made tea from rose hips. Here is what I learned. To make a fragrant drink, rinse the rose hips, cut them in half, and remove the seeds. Chop the fruit into very small pieces. You need about ⅓ cup in all. Place in a saucepan and cover with 5 cups water. Let sit for 10 minutes. Slowly bring to a boil and continue to cook at a slow boil for 5 minutes. Add 2 tablespoons golden raisins for aroma and up to 1 teaspoon each fresh lemon juice and sugar to taste. Strain and pour into teacups. Lovely!

A Georgian Wine and Cognac Tasting

On September 26, 1991, I was scheduled to depart from St. Petersburg to Tbilisi in Soviet Georgia. I received a phone call from the American Embassy in Moscow on the 25th urging me to change my plans. It was a time of great unrest and Americans had been advised to leave the area immediately. Crestfallen, I remained in St. Petersburg. To cheer me up, my hostess, Svetlana Antonova, arranged a wine tasting evening at Nektar, a wine bar specializing in Georgian wines. There were six of us attending. We were led downstairs to the cave and seated at a long table. At each place was a small round tray filled with small glasses. Instead of bread, two chocolate bars were placed beside each tray as palate cleansers. Little by little, wines from Georgia and other formerly restricted wine producers will be available in the United States. Following is a brief guide of what to ask for. *Na zdorovia!*

Vazisubani: Made from Georgian grapes, this wine is favored by Georgian women. We tasted a two-year-old dry white with a strong floral bouquet. A slightly acidic taste is characteristic of Vazisubani. Serve chilled in the summer with cold *zakuski.*

Gurdjiani: This wine was first developed in 1882 in the district of Gurdjiani and is considered one of the best from Georgia. This dry white is a strong "man's" wine and has a fruity bouquet with an undertaste of beets and aftertaste of almonds. It is excellent with spicy dishes.

Anakopia: Young and slightly sweet, this white wine is made from generic Georgian grapes that have an undertaste of honey. The sweetness comes from a concentration of the grapes. Its lightness makes this a lovely and simple table wine suitable for luncheons, sandwiches, and snacks.

Blue Lake: Considered the favorite of Hungarian women, this semisweet, white Hungarian wine has a bouquet of flowers and honey. It's light enough to serve with simple veal or pork dishes and light seafood stews.

Mukuzani: Made from European (Cabernet) and Georgian (Superavi) grapes, this is an excellent, full-bodied red wine of deep garnet hue. The special bouquet is reminiscent of black currants laden with crème fraîche. Excellent served with lamb dishes, especially shashlik.

Achmiadzinski: A very interesting port from Armenia, this fortified wine has a full, strong flavor and a deep bouquet of dried fruits and mushrooms. Achmiadzinksi should be served at room temperature as an aperitif, with no more than a small dish of almonds.

Russian "Nalivki": Homemade fruit liqueurs were the favorite drinks of Czarist Russians and Ukranians. Strawberries, Morello cherries, or raspberries were typically used as a base, mixed with sugar and allowed to ferment from two to four weeks, depending on the fruit. I tasted a strawberry Nalivki, resplendent with a sweet berry taste and extremely potent. Serve after dinner with little cakes, cookies, and a glass of tea.

Veber: This beet liqueur was first produced in Hungary in 1892. Veber is infused with fresh mint and other herbs. Its fascinating essence suggests small glasses and small sips with coffee.

SIDI BOU SAID MINTED TEA

My first sip of sweet mint and pignoli tea was at the Café des Nattes, in the magical azure hillside village of Sidi Bou Saïd in Tunisia. A long staircase, which led to the second-story terrace, was covered with richly patterned runners. The tables were filled with people lazily playing cards and drinking tea out of tiny tulip-shaped glasses. Occasionally someone with a very mellow expression on his face would take a puff from a beautifully painted hookah, (water pipe). I sipped on the extraordinary sweet, perfumed mint tea. I didn't get a strong flavor from the pignoli, but it was lovely having a small something to chew on as I drank my tea. Although you could easily enjoy this tea for hours served in a large mug, it's even more special when served in a small glass or tiny cup.

1 full bunch fresh mint (2 to 3 ounces), rinsed, stems slightly trimmed
2 tablespoons sugar
4 cups boiling water
4 teaspoons pignoli (pine nuts)

1. Place the mint and sugar in a teapot or a large saucepan. Pour in the boiling water. Stir, cover, and steep for 5 minutes.

2. Place 1 teaspoon nuts in each of 4 teacups or heatproof glasses. Strain the tea into the cups. Serve immediately.

Serves 4

Dear Annabel and Molly,

When leaving Tunis, saw this camel operating an olive press on the second floor of a tiny building in Sousse. Great way to make a living!

Love,
Mommy

A TASTE OF THE WORLD

Tunisian Fruit Basket

APPLES	*LEMONS*
APRICOTS	*ORANGES*
CRAB APPLES	*PEACHES*
DATES	*PLUMS*
FIGS	*QUINCES*
GRAPES	*WATERMELONS*

ORANGE SPICED TEA

At a Sunday afternoon tea party I attended in New York, my favorite cup was a brew called Russian tea. Although I was unable to obtain the recipe, this comes as close to the taste as I can remember. A drop of Grand Marnier liqueur would be lovely added to each cup.

Peel of 1 orange
Peel of 1 lemon
1 cinnamon stick (3 inches long)
4 spiced orange tea bags
4 cups boiling water

1. Remove as much white pith as possible from the orange and lemon peels to avoid a bitter taste. Place the peels, cinnamon stick, and tea bags in a large teapot. Cover with the boiling water and allow to steep, covered, 5 to 10 minutes.

2. Strain and serve in teacups, adding more hot water if desired.

Serves 4

SCOTTISH COFFEE

While the Irish fortify their smooth, classic after-dinner favorite, Irish coffee, with the best of Irish whiskey, the Scottish take a somewhat different tack. Velvety Drambuie graces this warming libation. While I was sipping mine after dinner on a rainy night in Edinburgh, I was given a couple of essential tips. My companion, Jake Campbell, told me that sugar cubes are a must in the preparation of this drink. He said that without them the cream will not float on top of the coffee. That layer of cream is the most fun and sets the tone for the dramatic coffee to follow. When you're choosing your glasses, be sure they're heatproof, as the coffee should be hot as you add it.

2 sugar cubes (2 teaspoons sugar)
1 cup hot strong coffee
3 tablespoons Drambuie liqueur
3 tablespoons lightly whipped heavy (or whipping) cream

1. Place the sugar cubes in a 12-ounce heatproof glass. Add the hot coffee and Drambuie and stir to dissolve the sugar.

2. Gently spoon the whipped cream over the top. Do not stir. Serve immediately.

Serves 1

SOUVENIR TO SAVOR

A Sweet Memory

Whenever my Granny Reesman sipped a cup of tea, she held half a sugar cube between her teeth to sweeten the potent brew. My grandfather preferred his tea in a glass with cherry preserves stirred in. Sweet holdovers of how they drank it when they lived in Russia.

MY FAVORITE

Afternoon Teas

Whenever I travel, I always try to make time for an afternoon tea stop. Sometimes it's nothing more than a quick cup, but I have also had my share of some pretty fabulous teas. I'd enjoy sharing a few favorites with you.

Tea at the Ritz

The stately mirrored and draped Palm Court Tearoom sits up a few steps off a main thoroughfare of grand hallways at the Ritz Hotel in the bustling Piccadilly section of London. A dazzling glass ceiling and crystal chandeliers make the room sparkle. Faux marble pillars, potted palms, and oriental rugs add an elegant ambiance while harp music fills the air. Damask-covered tables are set with white china rimmed with pale blue garlands and the tiny tea napkins are embroidered with "The Ritz" in royal blue. So elegant.

Seated on a dusty rose velvet settee at a small table, I reviewed the tea selection, then placed my order.

Tea sandwiches arrived first, thin and beautifully

> “Damask-covered tables are set with white china rimmed with pale blue garlands and the tiny tea napkins are embroidered with THE RITZ in royal blue.”

trimmed into elongated ovals and dainty triangles: the finest sliced salmon on wheat bread, smoked turkey on white, walnut-and-date-studded cream cheese on wheat, egg salad and watercress on white, and the classic—cucumber on wheat. The entire plate was showered with tiny cress leaves.

Once the waiter had rewarmed my pot of Darjeeling with hot water, the scones arrived accompanied by a little dishes of clotted cream and fresh strawberry preserves. A platter of fancy pastries brought this charming afternoon to a delicious end.

The Cringletie in Scotland

I spent a blustery April day touring the Border Country—some of the finest scenery in Scotland—not far from Edinburgh. The rolling hills were lush green and generously dappled with sheep and pheasant. The River Tweed, rippling with trout and salmon, cut a winding path through the countryside. But, for me, the pleasures of the day peaked upon my arrival at The Cringletie House Hotel just in time for afternoon tea.

Built in 1861, this large stone house sits on a hill, surrounded by white and yellow daffodils and hugged by an impressive two-acre walled kitchen garden. Inside, glowing fires keep the sitting room warm and cozy. It's an ideal setting for tea.

I sank into a deep, well-worn armchair near the fireplace anxiously awaiting the offerings. A large tray arrived stacked with floral tea cups,

Top left: Inside the magnificent Ritz Hotel. Bottom left: You'll be glad you're hungry when the Ritz tea arrives. Right: A properly outfitted Scottish piper.

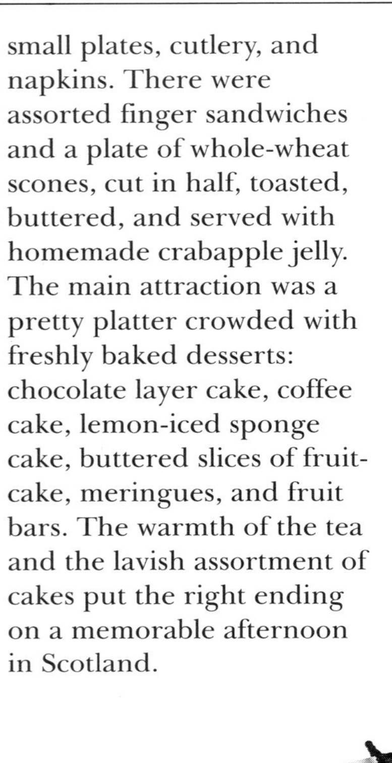

small plates, cutlery, and napkins. There were assorted finger sandwiches and a plate of whole-wheat scones, cut in half, toasted, buttered, and served with homemade crabapple jelly. The main attraction was a pretty platter crowded with freshly baked desserts: chocolate layer cake, coffee cake, lemon-iced sponge cake, buttered slices of fruitcake, meringues, and fruit bars. The warmth of the tea and the lavish assortment of cakes put the right ending on a memorable afternoon in Scotland.

The Caledonian

At the end of Prince's Street in Edinburgh stands the stately red sandstone Caledonian Hotel (known as The Caley to locals), built in 1903. The hotel is rich in history and Edwardian elegance, and I nestled in while visiting Scotland. I couldn't wait to have my first traditional afternoon tea in the sitting room.

Assorted finger sandwiches, crusts removed and cut into dainty triangles, appeared first on a pretty plate garnished with potato chips. There was a choice of egg salad, cheese and tomato, tongue, and ham. I ate them all. Next

Left and right: If you're not in the mood for a full Caledonian tea, enjoy the wee plate of shortbread and decanter of sherry waiting for you in your pretty room.

came a plate laden with warm scones, both currant and plain. I split them open, slathered them with raspberry preserves (the English would only have strawberry preserves), and topped them with a dollop of thick double cream. An array of cakes and pastries ended this traditional repast, and steaming hot Darjeeling tea was poured throughout.

The nicest treat of all was waiting on my table when I went to my room for a quick nap. A silver tray held a small decanter of sherry and a wee glass along with a wedge of Scottish shortbread garnished with a sprig of heather.

After a morning at the Louvre and a stroll through the beautiful Tuileries, stop for a luxurious cup of hot chocolate and a pastry at Angelina.

"... women outfitted in black skirts and frilly white blouses and aprons carry enormous silver trays of gem-like pastries through a maze of pretty but tiny, marble-topped tables ..."

Tea at Angelina

Parisians take the business of tea and cakes rather seriously, but nowhere is the institution more relished than at Angelina on the rue de Rivoli facing the beautiful Tuileries Gardens. Here, at 4 P.M. on any day, a team of energetic women outfitted in black skirts with frilly white blouses and aprons (all part of the effect) carry enormous silver trays of gem-like pastries through a maze of tiny, marble-topped tables surrounded by Louis XVI-style chairs. As the tray is presented, you choose the pastry most appealing, a rather difficult choice. If it's not on the tray, habitués know to ask for the *mont blanc,* a mound of chestnut purée, whipped cream, and meringue. It's Angelina's signature pastry. Then decide whether to accompany your dessert with a cup of smoky Lapsong Souchong tea, coffee, or even more sybaritically, a cup of hot chocolate. Angelina's hot chocolate is like none I've ever tasted—unbelievably thick and rich. It comes to the table in a little china pitcher on its own tray with a dainty china cup and saucer, a tiny silver spoon, a folded linen napkin, a pot of whipped cream to dollop atop, and a tall glass of water. After a visit to the Louvre or a walk in the Tuileries, install yourself in an elegant chair at Angelina and sip in pure luxury.

Teatime in Ipanema

South America's traditional teatime between 4 P.M. and 8 P.M. is not only refined and pleasurable but eminently practical. Most Brazilians eat their dinner at about 10 P.M. and therefore something substantial is necessary to sustain the wait.

Tea parlors abound in the city. The tables are daintily set, primarily with sweets, but scattered about are satisfying savories, such as delicious meat and cheese empanadas, tiny meatballs coated with fine bread crumbs and lightly fried, and small tea sandwiches ranging from ham and cheese to greens and tomatoes. Besides enjoying the wide selection of teas that are usually offered, this is the time to take an afternoon cocktail. As you're enjoying your tea, you'll most likely be serenaded by the swaying rhythms of the bossa nova, giving new dimensions to that old tune "The Girl from Ipanema."

An Afternoon at Irina Esimova's Home

Gracious and endearing are the best ways to describe my first tea party in St. Petersburg. Irina Esimova, a friend and professional pastry baker, escorted me into the living room of her small but lovely flat where a large dining table, covered with a pretty embroidered cloth, was set for five guests. Small plates and teacups were decorated with green flowers, and white paper napkins were arranged in fan shapes through the handles of the cups. One end of the table held a brass and enamel samovar painted with wild red berries, gold and green leaves, and swirls of black. It was filled with boiling water. Atop the samovar was a small teapot brewing an orange tea, covered with a "naive" tea cosy in the shape of a chicken. Another pot of very strong peppermint tea was offered first. Poured one-third full in the cups, it was then diluted with hot water from the

"We ate, talked politics, gossiped a bit, and tried every berry combination with lots of honey on our blinchiki."

samovar. In the center of the table was a plate of warm, sweet *blinchiki,* folded in quarters and overlapping slightly. In the center, one *blinchik* was arranged to resemble a flower.

All around the plate were small gold, red, green, and black lacquered wood bowls decorated in flower and fruit motifs. Each bowl was filled with different berries or preserves—strawberries, red and black currants, tiny cranberries, bilberries, and a puréed bilberry sauce. The seventh bowl was filled with a delicious honey. We ate, talked politics, gossiped a bit, and tried every berry combination with lots of honey on our *blinchiki*. Then came the apple cake with a bit of sour cream—a perfect party. Entertaining friends at home is a way of life and a great source of pride and pleasure for Russians. There is always enough food for these occasions. One day *blinchiki,* another day little cookies and cakes—sensitive, delicate, and sweet with the greatest attention paid to each detail.

Left to right: Beautiful Irina Estimova, my St. Petersburg friend. St. Basil's in Moscow's Red Square. The samovar on this Russian menu invites customers to tea.

SOUVENIR TO SAVOR

Tea in the Tulip Garden

After an intoxicating day of sightseeing in Istanbul, I relaxed with a cup of tea in a lovely tulip garden in Emirgan Park, along the shores of the Bosporus. The two-story white teahouse, all trimmed in golden yellow paint and standing like a Victorian maiden, was perched atop a hill with a perfect view of the park. My assistant Laurie and I sat under a parasol at a table surrounded by garden chairs and savored our cups of tea.

The teatime menu was great, unlike others I had seen which tended to echo the cakes and pastries most often associated with this 4 o'clock tradition. A nice tea selection would include meat and feta *böreks,* sliced cucumbers and tomatoes, and a slice of watermelon.

Mönu
(Menu)

SOGUK SANDVIÇLER *(Cold Sandwiches):*
Beyaz peynirli: *Feta cheese*
Kaşer peynirli: *Cheddar cheese*
Tavuk etli: *Chicken*
Soğuk etli: *Meat*
Karişik: *Mixed filling (Cheddar and chicken)*

....

SICAK SANDVIÇLER *(Toasted Sandwiches):*
Kaşer peynirli: *Chedder cheese toast*
Salami: *Salami toast*
Karişik: *Mixed toasted sandwich (Cheddar and salami)*

....

KOMPLE KAHVALTI
(*Continental Breakfast*):
Çay veya süt, kaşer peynir, beyaz peynir, zeytin, tereyağ, reçel: *Tea with milk, Cheddar and feta cheese, olives, butter, and jam*

BOREKLER *(Savory Pastries):*
Peynirli börek: *Feta cheese börek*
Kiymali börek: *Meat börek*

....

Yoğurt: *Yogurt*

....

Söğüş salata: *Sliced cucumbers and tomato*

....

Mevsim meyvalari: *Seasonal fruits*

....

ÇAY SAATI *(High Tea):*
Meyvali pastalar: *Fruit cake*
Çikolatali pasta: *Chocolate cake*
Tuzlu büsküi: *Savory biscuits*
Tatli büsküi: *Cookies*
Dondurma: *Ice cream*

Tea accompanied by a colorful array of tulips in full bloom—a perfect combination.

SIDE TRIPS

Oven-Fresh Bread

During my travels, I ate my fill of, and found pleasure in, the world's spectacular breads. I marveled over densely textured wheat berry loaves in Denmark and the well-spiced Limpa of Sweden. On chilly mornings in Ireland, I could be found appreciatively devouring thick slices of warm Irish soda bread and cups of coffee, while in Lisbon, Pão-Doce, the Portuguese sweet bread, and hot chocolate kept me at table. Maybe you can resist Italy's fragrant rosemary-olive bread, but not me. Nor could I stop myself from nibbling on freshly baked Lavash while in Moscow or tasty little oatcakes while in Scotland.

No selection I put together could possibly reflect the diversity of the breads I tasted around the world. This is just a small sampling, but it includes some of my favorites. If you feel that breads are just too difficult for most mortals to attempt, cast that concern aside. I've tried to lead you gently through each recipe. The time that it takes to bake fresh bread is truly worth it.

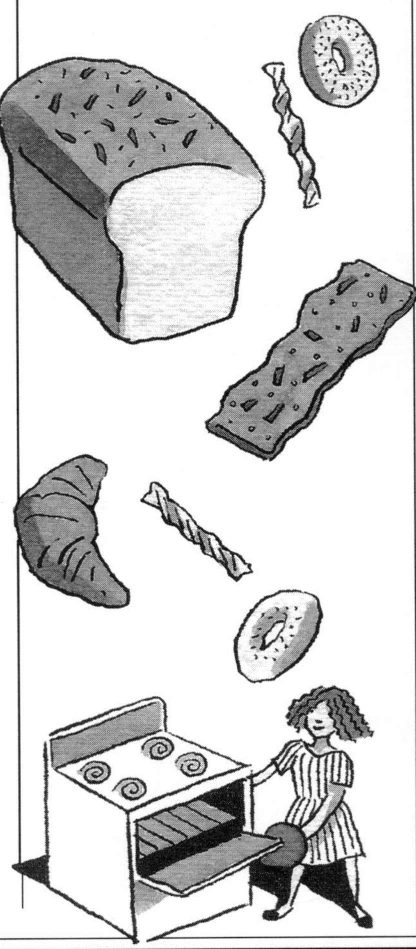

A TASTE OF THE WORLD

Portuguese Fruit Basket

APRICOTS
BANANAS
CHERRIES
FIGS
GRAPES
LEMONS
ORANGES
PEACHES
PEARS
PINEAPPLES
PLUMS
QUINCES
STRAWBERRIES

PAO-DOCE
Portuguese Sweet Bread

There are not too many breads that I think wonderful served at all meals—and I do mean breakfast, lunch, tea, and dinner—but this traditional festival bread of Portugal certainly fits the bill. Although the bread is often braided for Easter and studded with candied fruits for Christmas, I prefer it baked as a perfect round loaf with a deep brown lacquer surface encrusted with coarse sugar. I enjoy this sweet bread most served for breakfast with a cup of thick hot chocolate.

½ cup milk
1 teaspoon plus ⅓ cup granulated sugar
1 package active dry yeast
2 large eggs
1 teaspoon salt
2¼ to 2½ cups all-purpose flour
4 tablespoons (½ stick) unsalted butter, very soft
1 tablespoon coarse (or raw) sugar

1. Heat the milk in a small saucepan until warm to the touch, about 110°F. Remove to a small bowl and stir in 1 teaspoon sugar. Sprinkle the yeast over the milk and let sit to proof, about 10 minutes.

2. In a large bowl, whisk together the remaining ⅓ cup sugar, 1 egg, and the salt. Stir in 1½ cups of the flour and the yeast mixture with a wooden spoon. Beat vigorously for 25 strokes. Beat in the soft butter in 3 additions until completely incorporated. Stir in another ½ cup of the flour, kneading with your hands when the dough becomes too stiff to handle with a spoon. Turn the dough out onto a lightly floured surface and knead for 5 minutes, adding the remaining flour only as needed to prevent the dough from sticking. It should be smooth and elastic.

3. Form the dough into a ball, place it in a buttered bowl, and turn to coat completely. Cover loosely with plastic wrap. Let rise in a draft-free place until doubled in volume and a finger, lightly pressed into the dough, leaves an indentation, about 1 hour.

4. Butter a 9-inch pie plate. Knead the dough briefly to deflate it and form into a tight ball. Center the dough in the pie plate, cover loosely with plastic wrap, and let rise again until doubled in volume and the dough does not spring back when lightly pressed, about 1½ hours.

5. Preheat the oven to 350°F.

6. Lightly beat the remaining egg. Use a pastry brush to evenly cover the surface of the bread with the egg wash. Sprinkle the top with coarse sugar.

7. Bake the loaf until nicely browned and a toothpick inserted in the center comes out clean, about 35 minutes. Cool on a wire rack for 5 minutes, then remove from the pan and cool completely on the rack.

Makes 1 round loaf

ROSEMARY-OLIVE BREAD

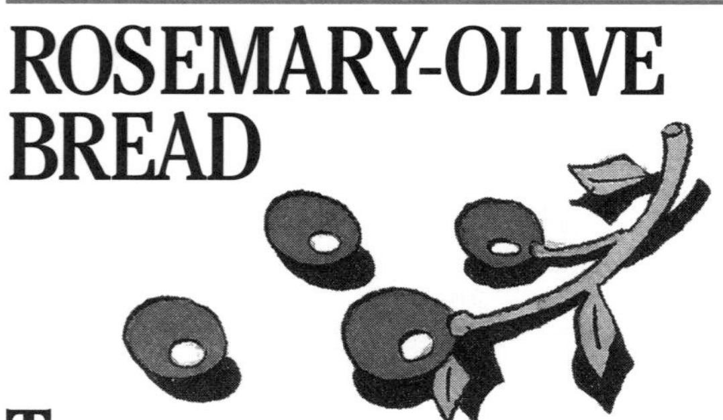

There is nothing more gratifying on a cold winter weekend than baking bread and savoring the warm results. This Italian beauty is close to a meal in itself served with prosciutto di Parma, a runny Taleggio, and ripe pears or persimmons. A rustic red Chianti Classico is a lovely accompaniment to this comforting meal. Gaeta olives are plump, moist, and perfect for the bread.

1½ teaspoons plus ⅛ teaspoon active dry yeast (see Note)
2¼ cups warm water
5 cups unbleached all-purpose flour
2 teaspoons salt
1 tablespoon fresh rosemary, coarsely chopped
⅔ cup pitted imported black and green olives, cut into large pieces
Olive oil

1. Make a sponge: In a small bowl stir ⅛ teaspoon yeast into ¾ cup warm water. Stir in 1½ cups flour and mix for a few minutes. It will be very sticky. Cover with plastic wrap and set in a draft-free place for about 6 hours. The mixture will actually resemble a porous-looking sponge. It will be sticky and stringy when you pull on it.

2. In a large bowl stir the remaining 1½ teaspoons yeast into 1½ cups warm water and let sit to proof for 10 minutes. Add the sponge and squeeze with your fingers to break it up. Using a large rubber spatula or wooden spoon, stir in 1 cup flour. Add another 1 cup flour and the salt and beat vigorously. Add another 1 cup flour and stir and fold for 3 minutes. The batter will be very gloppy. Fold in the rosemary and olives. Turn the dough out onto a heavily floured work surface and, scraping up the dough with a dough scraper, knead in the remaining ½ cup flour, a little at a time. The dough will remain quite sticky.

3. Shape the dough into a ball, brush the top lightly with olive oil, and place in an oiled bowl. Cover with plastic wrap and refrigerate overnight.

4. The following morning, remove the dough from the bowl, punch it down, and reshape it into a ball. Place it on a generously floured baking sheet. Cover loosely with plastic wrap and let rise until the dough doesn't spring back when pressed, about 2 hours.

5. Turn the dough out onto the work surface, flatten it, and fold in both the sides. Roll it up, starting from the top, using your thumbs to press against the roll to create a little tension on the dough surface. Turn the dough 90 degrees and repeat. Round it into a ball by cupping the dough in your hands as you roll it against the table. Pinch the bottom closed. Line a wide bowl with a dish towel dusted heavily with flour. Place the dough in the bowl so that the pinched bottom is facing up, sprinkle the exposed side lightly with flour, and fold the ends of the towel over the dough to cover it. Let rise in a draft-free place until doubled in volume, about 45 minutes.

6. Place a heavy baking sheet or baking stone in the oven and preheat the oven to 450°F.

7. When the bread is ready, gently turn it out onto the hot sheet or stone and remove the cloth. Using a sharp serrated knife or razor blade, cut a slit (½ inch deep) across the top (the smooth side). Spritz the oven a few times with water from a plant mister and close the door. Spritz again a few minutes later, and turn the oven down to 425°F. Bake for 30 minutes, reduce the heat to 350°F and bake until the loaf sounds hollow when tapped on the bottom, about 30 minutes more. Transfer to a wire rack to cool.

Makes 1 loaf

Note: This bread begins with a sponge, which is simply a thick batter made from a mixture of yeast, water, and just the right amount of flour to get a proper consistency for a starter batter. A sponge allows for longer dough fermentation, which results in a more flavorful bread with a nice coarse texture.

WHEAT BERRY BREAD

One of Scandinavia's great gifts to the culinary scene is its marvelous whole-grain breads filled with seeds and berries of every description. This loaf filled with golden crisp wheat berries, flax, and sunflower seeds approximates one of the best that I ate in Denmark. The rich flavor of molasses combined with whole-wheat and white flours gives the loaf interesting depth. Sliced thin and toasted, it's a perfect choice to serve with satiny smooth slices of gravlax, herring, and other cured and smoked fish. Mild cheeses are lovely atop it too, especially for breakfast.

⅓ cup wheat berries
1 package active dry yeast
1½ cups warm water
½ cup plus 1⅓ cups all-purpose flour
2 tablespoons oil
3 tablespoons molasses
¼ cup honey
1 tablespoon salt
2¼ cups whole-wheat flour
¼ cup flax seeds
2 tablespoons sunflower seeds

1. Place the wheat berries in a strainer, rinse well under running water, and drain. Bring 1½ cups tap water to a boil in a small saucepan and add the berries. Cover the pan, reduce the heat to low, and simmer until the berries are soft and the water is absorbed, about 1 hour.

2. Meanwhile, after the berries have cooked for 20 minutes, stir together the yeast, ½ cup of the warm water, and ½ cup all-purpose flour in a large bowl. Let rise for about 40 minutes.

3. Stir the remaining 1 cup warm water, the oil, molasses, honey, salt, and whole-wheat flour into the yeast mixture. Add the flax seeds, sunflower seeds, and 1 cup all-purpose flour. When the mixture becomes too stiff to stir, turn it out onto a floured work surface and knead. Flatten the dough and press in the cooked wheat berries. Knead in the remaining ⅓ cup all-purpose flour until the dough is elastic and springs back when lightly pressed, about 6 minutes.

4. Form the dough into a ball, place it in an oiled bowl, and turn the dough in the bowl to coat it well with oil. Cover with plastic wrap and let rise until the dough does not spring back when lightly pressed, about 2 hours.

5. Turn the dough out onto a lightly floured work surface, press it flat, fold both the sides in and roll the dough into a log. Pinch the seam closed and set it into an oiled 10 x 4 x 3-inch loaf pan. Push the dough down flat. Place the pan in a plastic bag and tuck the bag opening under the pan to close. Let rise until the dough domes up and does not spring back when lightly pressed, about 1½ hours.

6. Preheat the oven to 425°F.

7. Remove the pan from the plastic bag. Using a sharp serrated knife, cut 3 diagonal slashes across the top of the loaf. Place the bread in the oven, spritz the inside of the oven a few times with water from a plant mister, and quickly close the door. Bake 15 minutes. Reduce the oven temperature to 350°F and bake for another 15 minutes. To test for doneness, remove the bread from the pan and rap the bottom. It should sound hollow. If it is not quite done, continue baking out of the pan up to 10 minutes more. Cool on a wire rack.

Makes 1 large loaf

LIMPA BREAD

If you were spending Christmas in Scandinavia, you would no doubt have the pleasure of trying a variety of *limpa* breads. That's when bakers prepare their most coveted versions of this classic rye bread. Widely loved in Sweden, *limpa* is a flattened doughnut-shaped bread that varies in both sweetness and spiciness from family to family. At holiday time, some bakers even combine four types of rye flour, ranging from dark to light to get just the right *limpa* for the family festivities. The subtle sweetness of the bread comes from the addition of molasses, orange zest, and golden raisins. Spices range from caraway and anise seeds to more pungent fennel seeds. *Limpa* is lovely served at any meal, along with cured salmon and delicate game birds. I've shaped my *limpa* into a loaf, so that it can be sliced for toasting and served for sandwiches.

2 tablespoons plus ½ cup warm water
1 teaspoon plus 2 tablespoons honey
1¼ teaspoons (½ package) active dry yeast
Finely grated zest of 1 orange
½ cup fresh orange juice
1 tablespoon molasses
1 teaspoon salt
1 tablespoon ground anise seeds
1 tablespoon caraway seeds
1 tablespoon unsalted butter, at room temperature
1 cup rye flour
2 cups all-purpose flour
½ cup golden raisins
1 tablespoon cornmeal, for dusting

1. In a small bowl, combine 2 tablespoons warm water, 1 teaspoon honey, and the yeast. Let sit to proof for about 10 minutes.

2. In a large bowl stir together the ½ cup water, the 2 tablespoons honey, the orange zest, orange juice, molasses, salt, anise, caraway seeds, butter, rye flour, and the yeast mixture. Stir in ½ cup of the all-purpose flour. Cover with plastic wrap and let rise in a draft-free place until doubled in volume, about 1½ hours.

3. Stir in 1 cup all-purpose flour. When the dough becomes too stiff, knead it with your hands. Turn the dough out onto a floured surface and knead, adding the remaining ½ cup flour as needed to keep the dough from sticking. Knead until the dough springs back when pressed with a finger, about 5 minutes. It will be slightly sticky. Place in a buttered bowl, turn to coat the dough well with butter, cover with plastic wrap, and let rise in a draft-free place until it no longer springs back when lightly touched and has doubled in volume, about 2 hours.

4. Flatten the dough on a lightly floured surface and knead in the raisins. Flatten the dough again into a rectangular form and fold both sides into the center, then roll the dough into a log shape. Press down on the ends and roll to taper, so that the shape is like an elongated football. Pinch the seam closed. It should be about 9 inches long. Generously flour a dish towel and wrap the dough loosely in the towel, covering it completely. Secure the loaf between two objects of the same length (2 large books, for example) so that the bread rises up, rather than spreads out. Let rise until doubled in volume, about 45 minutes. The dough surface should be taut and not spring back when lightly pressed.

5. Place a heavy baking sheet in the oven and preheat to 375°F.

6. When the dough is fully risen, remove the hot baking sheet from the oven, dust it with cornmeal, and gently place the loaf on the sheet. Using a serrated knife, cut 3 diagonal slashes across the top. Return the sheet to the oven and spritz the inside of the oven with water from a plant mister. Bake until the bread sounds hollow when tapped on the bottom, about 45 minutes. Transfer the bread to a wire rack and cool.

Makes 1 loaf

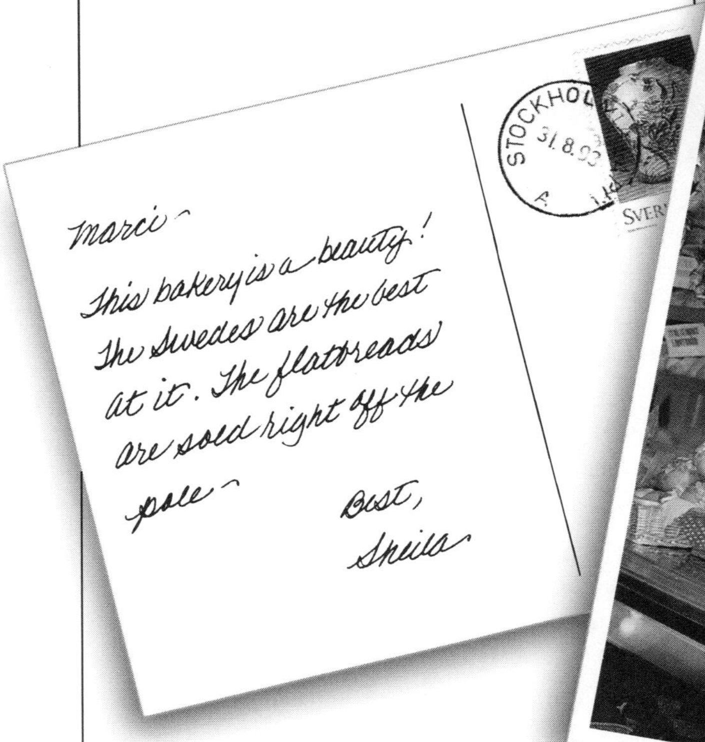

Marci –
This bakery is a beauty! The Swedes are the best at it. The flatbreads are sold right off the pole.
Best,
Sheila

THE WINES OF

North Africa

The French influence still lingers when it comes to the wine industry in Tunisia, Algeria, and Morocco. Although the Gallic demand has waned, red wines are produced in good quantity, ranging in style from claret-like Cabernets to dark, intense Rhône-style reds. Several Rhône grape varieties—Grenache, Mourvèdre, Cinsaut and Syrah—are grown in all three countries. Vineyards around ancient Carthage in Tunisia and the coastal hills are planted to such varieties, producing sturdy red wines, such as Koudiat, Magon, and Château Feriani, as well as Gris de Tunisie and Sidi Rais, appealingly fresh, dry rosés.

Casablanca in the sun. Where's the mystique? Where's Rick's?

Tunisia also produces North Africa's best dessert Muscats.

Algeria still has the largest vineyards and production in North Africa, most of it concentrated on slopes about 50 miles inland of the provinces of Alger and Oran. Cuvée le Président is a stylish, firmly structured red that has drawn kudos for its Bordeaux pretentions. And the robust, deep-purple reds of Dahra also have a following. Most versatile, however, are the country's fragrant, dry rosés.

Morocco, of course, gets the lion's share of Western tourists, seduced by the post-war film classic *Casablanca*. While Champagne appears to be the most popular wine in the movie, Moroccan *vin gris*, palest of all rosés, is the favored wine today. Morocco has vineyards in the foothills of the Atlas Mountains, which produce medium-bodied reds, and south of Casablanca, origin of a quite decent red known as Ourika and the popular Gris de Boulaouanem, a pale dry rosé that is consumed in great quantity with meals and on its own.

FOCACCIA

More rustic and thicker than a pizza dough, this robust Italian bread has been coming into its own all over the United States. There are so many ways to serve *focaccia*: In its basic form, baked with fresh coarse herbs such as rosemary, thyme, and sage; as a perfect palette for toppings such as roasted peppers, tomatoes, a pungent *olivida*, or pesto; as an open-faced sandwich bread; as a substitute for pizza crust, arranged with your favorite ingredients atop. Be creative with your fillings and toppings. In the autumn, the Florentines top theirs with sweet Concord grapes, creating their famous *schiacciata con l'uva*. The sky's really the limit with America's favorite new bread.

1 package active dry yeast
1½ cups warm water
¾ cup plus 2⅔ cups unbleached all-purpose flour
2 tablespoons olive oil, plus more for the loaves
2 teaspoons salt
1 tablespoon fresh sage leaves
1 tablespoon fresh rosemary leaves
1 tablespoon fresh thyme leaves
Cornmeal, for dusting

PESTO TOPPING (for 1 focaccia):
2 tablespoons pesto (see Pesto box, page 490)
⅓ cup pitted imported black and green olives, coarsely chopped

OLIVE OIL TOPPING (for 1 focaccia):
1 tablespoon extra virgin olive oil
1 small onion, halved, slivered, and sautéed with 1 clove minced garlic in the oil
⅛ teaspoon coarse salt

1. Make a sponge: In a large bowl stir together the yeast, ½ cup warm water, and ¾ cup flour. Scatter the remaining 2⅔ cups flour over the sponge. Do not stir. Set the bowl aside in a draft-free place until the sponge rises up through the flour, about 30 minutes.

2. Add the remaining 1 cup warm water, the olive oil, and salt to the bowl. Stir to combine. Stir in the fresh herbs. Turn the dough out onto a lightly floured work surface and knead until smooth and elastic, 4 to 5 minutes. The dough will be very soft and slightly sticky.

3. Shape the dough into a loose ball, place it in an oiled bowl, and turn the dough in the bowl to coat it well with oil. Cover with plastic wrap and let rise in a draft-free place until the dough does not spring back when lightly pressed, about 1 hour. Punch the dough down, reshape it into a ball, and refrigerate covered 8 hours or overnight.

4. Turn the dough out onto a lightly floured work surface, gently press out the air, and cut the dough into 2 equal pieces. Shape each half into a ball and place at least 6 inches apart on a heavily floured tray or table. Lightly brush the tops with oil, cover loosely with plastic wrap, and let rise until doubled in volume, 1¼ to 1½ hours.

5. Put a baking stone or heavy baking sheet (rimless) in the oven and preheat to 450°F.

6. Once the dough has risen, use floured hands to stretch and flatten each ball into a

Pesto

Heady, vibrant pesto as we know it today varies little in flavor from the original Genovese basil sauce. Traditionally, a mortar and pestle was used to pound summer's lushest crop of basil leaves, the finest garlic, pine nuts, extra virgin olive oil, and Parmigiano-Reggiano cheese into a pasta sauce. Today, thanks to the food processor, the task has become much quicker. Now, too, pesto is used for more than saucing pasta. I find a spoonful splendid in salad dressings, on coarse breads, and *focaccia.* The other change these days is that chefs are substituting fresh mint, cilantro, and parsley for the basil. As far as I'm concerned, when summer comes along, I still want basil in my pesto.

To make 1 cup of pesto, place about 2 cups of basil leaves, 2 garlic cloves, and 1 cup of pine nuts in a food processor. Process until just smooth, leaving a bit of texture. With the motor running, slowly drizzle in ½ cup of olive oil through the feed tube. Add ½ cup of freshly grated Parmesan cheese and a grind of black pepper. Process to combine and serve. Pesto will keep covered in the refrigerator for up to 2 days. Bring to room temperature before serving.

10-inch disk. Dust 2 rimless baking sheets or the backs of 2 regular baking sheets with cornmeal and transfer each disk to a baking sheet. Prick the dough all over with a fork. Brush each disk with the pesto or olive oil topping (or another topping of your choice), and press the topping into the surface.

7. Cover one *focaccia* and place it in the refrigerator while the other one bakes. Shake the dough around on the sheet to be sure the dough slides easily. With a quick jerking motion, slip the dough onto the hot sheet in the oven. Spritz the oven a few times with water from a plant mister and quickly close the door. Bake until the *focaccia* is nicely colored, about 25 minutes. Remove the finished focaccia from the sheet to a wire rack for cooling. Leave the sheet in the oven. Repeat with the remaining focaccia.

Makes two 10-inch rounds, serving 6 each

CUMIN CURRY ROLLS

I was so seduced by India's golden spices that when I returned from my visit to that country, I began adding them to everything I cooked. That's when I came up with these rolls. Onions add interesting texture and moistness to the

rolls as they cook. They are just right served warm with Mulligatawny Soup (see Index) accompanied by thick slices of sharp Cheddar cheese and a dish of mango chutney.

3 tablespoons vegetable oil
1½ cups thinly sliced onions
¼ cup millet
1 package active dry yeast
1¾ cups warm water
3 teaspoons sugar
3½ cups all-purpose flour, approximately
2½ teaspoons salt
2 tablespoons bran
1½ teaspoons best-quality curry powder
1 teaspoon ground cumin
Cornmeal, for dusting

1. Heat the oil in a large skillet over medium heat. Add the onions and cook until they begin to brown, about 10 minutes. Add the millet and cook, stirring, until the onions are nicely browned, about 10 minutes more.

2. Meanwhile, in a large bowl, stir together the yeast, ½ cup of the water, and 1 teaspoon of the sugar. Let proof while the onions cook.

3. When the onions finish cooking, stir the remaining 2 teaspoons sugar, remaining 1¼ cups water, and 2¼ cups of the flour into the yeast mixture. Add the salt, bran, curry powder, cumin, and onion mixture and stir until combined. Stir in 1 cup of the remaining flour and turn the dough out onto a lightly floured surface. Knead until the dough is smooth and elastic, about 5 minutes, adding the remaining ¼ cup flour as needed. The dough will be quite soft and a little sticky.

4. Place the dough in an oiled bowl and turn the dough to coat. Cover the bowl and set in a draft-free place to rise until doubled in volume, about 1¼ hours. The dough should not spring back when lightly pressed with a finger.

5. Punch the dough down, and on a heavily floured surface, roll it into a coil. Cut the coil into 16 pieces, each weighing a little over 2 ounces. Flatten a piece of dough slightly and fold and pinch the edges in towards the center to create a ball. Turn the ball over and roll it on the table, cupping the palm of your hand around the ball as you roll it. Repeat with the remaining pieces. Lightly sprinkle 2 baking sheets with cornmeal. Place the rolls at least 2½ inches apart on the sheets. Lightly sift flour over the top of the rolls, cover the trays loosely with plastic wrap, and let rise in a draft-free place until doubled in volume, about 1 hour.

6. Preheat the oven to 450°F.

7. When the rolls have risen properly, they will be taut on the surface and will not spring back when lightly pressed. Use a sharp serrated knife to cut a slash across the top of each roll. Place the rolls in the oven and spritz the oven a few times with water from a plant mister. Close the oven door. Spritz again after 1 minute. Bake until the bottom of the rolls are golden brown and sound hollow when tapped, about 20 minutes. Cool on a wire rack or serve immediately.

Makes 16 rolls

LAVASH

I was served freshly baked *lavash* in a Georgian restaurant in Moscow, along with a bowlful of *satsivi*. There is absolutely no comparison between the widely sold little packets of this Middle Eastern cracker bread and the home-baked version. Light and crispy, I love *lavash* sprinkled with both sesame and poppy seeds. They are also terrific served with Tarama Slather and Riad's Baba Ghanouj (see Index). Store *lavash* carefully in airtight tins.

1 package active dry yeast
1 cup warm water
1 teaspoon granulated sugar
2½ tablespoons olive oil
3¼ cups unbleached all-purpose flour
1¾ teaspoons salt
3 tablespoons toasted sesame seeds (see Sesame Butterfly Noodles, step 1, page 294)
3 tablespoons poppy seeds

1. In a small bowl stir together the yeast, water, and sugar. Let sit to proof about 10 minutes. Add the oil.

2. Combine the flour and salt in a food processor. With the machine running, add the yeast mixture through the feed tube and process for 20 seconds. Stop to scrape down the sides of the bowl with a rubber spatula, then continue to process to form a stiff ball. Turn the dough out onto a work surface and knead for a few minutes until the dough is smooth.

3. Transfer to an oiled bowl, turn to coat, cover tightly with plastic wrap, and let rise in a draft-free place until doubled in volume and a finger pressed gently into the dough leaves an indention, 1 to 1¼ hours.

4. Preheat the oven to 350°F.

5. Combine the sesame and poppy seeds in a small bowl. Turn the dough out onto a table, flatten it into a rectangle, and divide into 16 pieces. Keep the pieces that you are not working with covered with plastic wrap.

6. On an unfloured surface, roll a section to as thin a sheet as possible. Lift it up, flip it over, and roll paper thin. It should be about 8 x 3 inches. Peel the dough off the table and place on an ungreased baking sheet. (It is stiff and should lift easily without tearing.) Prick holes in the dough with the tines of a fork. Brush it lightly with water and sprinkle with about a teaspoon of the mixed seeds. Repeat with the remaining pieces, fitting as many sections as possible without touching on the sheet—3 to 4 sections should fit on one sheet. They may be cut in half to fit the sheet better.

7. Bake until golden brown, about 20 minutes. Repeat until all the dough is used. Cool completely, on wire racks.

Makes 16 large squares

IRISH SODA BREAD

Ken and Cathleen Buggy run a marvelous inn in Kinsale, Cork, Ireland, called The Old Presbytery. Every morning guests enjoy a special treat of Ken's celebrated homemade Irish soda bread. Ken invited me into his charming red-and-white gingham kitchen for a demonstration. He said that the secret to soda bread is that there is no secret! It's so quick and easy that it can practically be made on a moment's notice since it only takes about 5 minutes to put together. Soda bread is just great warm from the oven or toasted and spread with sweet butter and preserves or topped with silky Irish smoked salmon. Since the bread doesn't keep long, it is best to serve it immediately or let it cool, wrap well, and store in the freezer. Here is my version of Irish soda bread with the not-so-traditional addition of raisins and caraway seeds for a special treat.

2 cups all-purpose flour
¼ cup sugar
1½ teaspoons baking soda
½ teaspoon salt
½ cup golden raisins
2 tablespoons caraway seeds
1¼ cups nonfat plain yogurt
1 large egg, beaten
1 tablespoon unsalted butter, melted

1. Preheat the oven to 350°F.

2. Sift the flour, sugar, baking soda, and salt into a bowl. Add the raisins and caraway seeds and mix well.

3. In another bowl combine the yogurt, egg, and butter. Add to the dry ingredients and, using a wooden spoon, combine until just mixed.

4. Form the dough into a disk about 6 inches across (about 2½ inches thick in the center), dusting with more flour if it is too sticky. Place on an ungreased baking sheet. Using a sharp knife, cut an X on the surface.

5. Bake until golden brown and the bread sounds hollow when the bottom is tapped, about 50 minutes.

Makes 1 loaf

SCOTTISH OATCAKES

It took me many tries to get this recipe just right, but I think you'll love these homey, simple oatcakes. They are great with Highland Pâté (see Index) for an hors d'oeuvre or with cheese and a dollop of chutney at teatime. To finish an elegant dinner, serve them with Stilton cheese, freshly shelled walnuts, celery stalks, and a glass of port. Their wonderful, earthy flavor balances well with rich toppings and they're much more special than an ordinary cracker.

2¼ cups rolled oats
½ teaspoon baking powder
1 teaspoon salt
2 tablespoons unsalted butter, melted
⅓ cup water

1. Preheat the oven to 350°F.

2. Place 2 cups of the oats in a food processor and process until they resemble coarse flour. Transfer to a bowl.

3. Add the baking powder and salt to the ground oats and mix well. Add the melted butter and combine with a wooden spoon, using the back of the spoon to break up the clumps of dough. Add the water, a little bit at a time, mixing well, until the dough is combined.

4. Scatter the remaining ¼ cup oats on a work surface. Gather the dough in a ball and roll it in the oats, using your hands to press the oats into the dough.

5. Roll the dough out to a sheet ⅛ inch thick. Using a cookie cutter, cut the dough into 2½-inch rounds. Using a spatula, transfer the rounds to baking sheets, placing them 1 inch apart. Gather up and reroll the dough to cut out more oatcakes. Bake the oatcakes for 15 minutes. Their edges may become lightly golden, but they hardly color at all. Cool on a wire rack at least 15 minutes before serving. Store in an airtight container. The oatcakes keep for up to 1 week.

Makes 20 oatcakes

SIDE TRIPS

The New Cheese Plate

Until recently, France and Italy's spectacular cheeses were my favorites. I had savored them both here and on native soil, and of all the cheeses I had tasted during my travels over the years, they were the only ones you could get in this country in any meaningful way.

But finally many of the other cheeses I fell in love with are becoming readily available throughout the U.S. From Spain there's delicious Manchego to drizzle with honey and serve with almonds and green olives; from Crete, velvety white Manouri cheese to accompany fresh figs; from Lisbon, Serpa to serve with soft, warm bread; and from Scandinavia, buttery, mild cheeses some with wonderful names that are impossible to pronounce. Keep your eye out for these cheeses at your local market. And enjoy this "new" cheese sampler.

Spanish Cheeses

Today Spain produces over 300 varieties of earthy, full-flavored cheese, of which seven have been designated a *Denominación de Origen* by the government. The *Denominación de Origen* is awarded to only the finest cheeses that have unique characteristics and meet the highest standards in their given category. At this point the number of cheeses that qualify is small, but as other Spanish cheeses gain greater recognition, they will be added to the list.

As with Spain's great wines and olive oils, this country's varied terrain, climate, and soil conditions set the stage for a wide array of delicious regional cheeses. The difference in production methods—many are still produced by hand—distinguish the cheeses further.

....

MANCHEGO: The best known and most widely available Spanish cheese is Manchego from La Mancha, the land of Don Quixote and windmills. This robust sheep's milk cheese is made of raw milk from Manchega ewes, the local sheep capable of tolerating the extreme weather conditions and rugged terrain of central Spain. The cheese has a firm texture and a hard, straw-colored rind that carries a distinctive herringbone design produced by the mold it is matured in. At present the production of Manchego closely resembles the traditional cheese-making methods which date back centuries. Manchego can range from tender and mild to hard and sharp depending on how long it's been aged. Traditionally in Spain, a slice of Manchego is served with a bit of quince jelly for a delicious play of flavors.

> *"As with Spain's great wines and olive oils, this country's varied terrain, climate, and soil conditions set the stage for a wide array of delicious cheeses."*

Left and above: Manchego is as important in Spain as Parmesan is in Italy. Right: Gaudí's magnificent La Sagrada Família is not to be missed when visiting Barcelona.

Apple butter, Quince Spoon Sweet (see Index), grapes, and honey are divine served with Spain's prize-winning Roncal.

In La Mancha, it is often dipped in a batter of eggs, garlic, and fresh herbs and then fried. Served with ripe pears, peaches, figs or apples, roasted red bell peppers, and Serrano or another cured ham, this dish is divine.

....

RONCAL: Roncal was the first cheese to receive the Spanish *Denominación de Origen* in 1981. It is one of the most prized and expensive cheeses in Spain. The firm, aromatic, and slightly piquant cheese has a cylindrical shape and a straw-colored rind. It has been made for centuries in the rugged hills of the Roncal Valley in Navarra, nestled high in the Pyrenees. Roncal is made from the milk of the Rasa sheep, which are rather small and adjust well to the extreme weather conditions. They produce small amounts of very rich milk that has a wonderful aroma because they graze on wild grasses. The cheese is usually made from December to July. Since it is difficult to find shepherds who continue to produce Roncal, a factory was set up in 1974 to ensure continued production (under strict regulations) of this wonderful cheese. It is delicious served with a coarse bread, honey, apple butter, and green grapes.

....

MAHÓN: The Balearic island of Menorca (not far from better-known Majorca) has been home to this cheese for hundreds of years. Traditionally Mahón cheese was made seasonally from sheep's milk, sometimes with the addition of a small amount of cow's milk. Now the cheese is made primarily from cow's milk, sometimes with some sheep's milk added. It is made twice a day, just after milking. After maturing for one month, the rind is slathered in a mixture of butter, olive oil, and paprika and left to age one month longer. This cheese is firm, scattered with small eyes, and has a square shape with rounded edges. Most often Mahón is served sliced, drizzled with olive oil, and sprinkled with freshly ground pepper and chopped

"... it is the cow's milk that gives Cabrales its tartness, goat's milk its piquantness, and sheep's milk its richness and aroma."

fresh tarragon, or grated and mixed with eggs for a luscious soufflé. Serve it with plump, crisp red radishes, a crock of sweet butter, a baguette, and some coarse salt alongside in which to dip the radishes.

....

Cabrales: Spain's regal blue cheese is made primarily with cow's milk (the best milk in Spain comes from Asturias in the North) and a small addition of goat's and sheep's milk. It is then matured in the caves of the Asturias region in the Picos de Europa. Local inhabitants of this region say that the best cheese is made in the late spring using the milk from the cows, goats, and sheep that have grazed in the highland pastures. And, further, that it is the cow's milk that gives Cabrales its tartness, goat's milk its piquantness, and sheep's milk its richness and aroma. Because the milk available from the different animals varies from season to season, it is certainly possible to find a Cabrales made only of cows's milk. Cabrales is delicious served with fresh fruit and nuts, or mixed with a little softened butter and cream and served atop a grilled fish or toasted peasant bread, or blended into a stuffing for baked potatoes, or added to a dressing to top an endive salad.

....

Cantabria: For hundreds of years, a creamy cow's milk cheese with a soft yellow rind has been produced in Cantabria, the region of northern Spain tucked in between the sea and the mountains and one of Spain's major milk producing areas. Only whole unpasteurized cow's milk goes into this cheese. Cantabria usually comes in a 1- to 6-pound cylinder. The cheese has a soft, dense interior with a very fresh, clean taste. Its mild and buttery flavor makes it appealing to any palate. It is especially lovely served with candied fruits and a dessert sherry.

....

Liébana: Liébana is the generic name given to several different cheeses, each made with one or a combination of sheep's, goat's and cow's milk. It is handmade on farms in the eastern slopes of the Picos de Europa, and the production is fairly small and varied. Picón is a creamy blue cheese wrapped in a chestnut leaf. It can be made with any combination of goat's, sheep's, or

Serve Cabrales with almonds, apples, and sweet grapes.

cow's milk or with just one. There is also a smoked cheese usually made with cow's milk, although sheep's and goat's milk are used if necessary. The smoking of these cheeses is usually done over juniper wood. Also within the Liébana denomination are tiny cheeses that can be fresh as well as aged. If fresh, they are made with pasteurized milk. Any combination of cow's, goat's, or sheep's milk is used for these cheeses and aging usually lasts at least two months.

....

Idiazábal: This hard cheese, made with full-fat sheep's milk, comes from the hilly Basque region. Both handmade and industrially produced, the cylindrical, firm, light yellow cheese is surrounded by a hard yellow rind and is cured for about two months. The cheese has an intense, sharp, and buttery flavor. The best ones are made from early summer milk, when the highlands make for luscious grazing after a harsh winter. Some of the cheeses are smoked after curing. Idiazábal is delicious served with roasted peppers, Serrano ham, *pipérade* tarts, sliced oranges, green Manzanilla olives, and crusty bread drizzled with fruity extra virgin olive oil.

Two Portuguese Cheeses

....

Every once in a while, as I continued on my extraordinary world journey, I discovered a wonderful food that to date is rarely found in America. Serra and Serpa—two cheeses I adored in Portugal—are particular favorites that should be snapped up if you come upon them.

Most often, cheese is best served at room temperature laid out on a board or marble slab. The Portuguese cover their exposed cheeses with delicate white tulle. With all the inexpensive lace available, why not cover your cheeses with a slightly stiff piece for a magnificent presentation.

....

Serra: From the mountains in the northeast of the country, it is the best known of Portugal's sheep's milk cheeses. This luscious, nutty-flavored cheese is soft and runny, much like perfectly ripe French Brie or Camembert.

....

Serpa: Another noteworthy sheep's milk cheese from central Portugal. Serpa is pie-sized with a delicate orange rind that develops from being rubbed with olive oil and paprika. When young, Serpa's buttery flavor and consistency is very much like France's Vacherin Mont d'Or. Aged, it is tangy and similar to a good Parmesan.

"Serra and Serpa—two cheeses I adored in Portugal—are particular favorites that should be snapped up if you come upon them."

Danish Cheeses

....

A mild climate in both spring and summer, lots of rain, and fertile soil set the scene for Denmark's famous dairy products. In that country, there seems to be a cheese for every taste, every occasion, and every hour of the day. The Danes begin with delicate

slices of buttery cheese at the breakfast table. Thin slices are draped atop open-faced sandwiches, called *smørrebrød,* at lunchtime. Cheese turns up again at teatime, after dinner, and for late-night snacks.

....

SAMSOE: Named for an island off the east Jutland coast, it is Denmark's national cheese. A semifirm, golden, mild cheese with scattered holes, Samsoe most resembles Cheddar with its rich, sweet, nutty flavor. Aged, the cheese becomes stronger and slightly piquant. Samsoe is lovely on whole-grain bread and ideal for cooking because it melts nicely.

....

DANBO: Much like Samsoe but paler and softer with scattered large holes. Its flavor is mild and aromatic, and it comes in a variety of shapes and sizes. Sometimes it is flavored with caraway seeds, which is lovely at breakfast.

HAVARTI, a.k.a. **TILSIT:** One of the best known and loved Danish cheeses. Mild, yellow, and soft with scattered holes, it has a buttery flavor that pleases everyone. A creamier, spreadable variety of Havarti can be found plain or flavored with caraway seeds, mustard seeds, dill, peppercorns, jalapeños, and so on.

***Top:** I can just visualize sitting down to fresh baked grainy bread and mild creamy cheese in this typical house in the Danish countryside. **Above:** Built in the 1500s, Egeskov is one of the most beautiful manor houses in Denmark. It seems to be floating right on the water.*

A TASTE OF THE WORLD

Scandinavian Fruit Basket

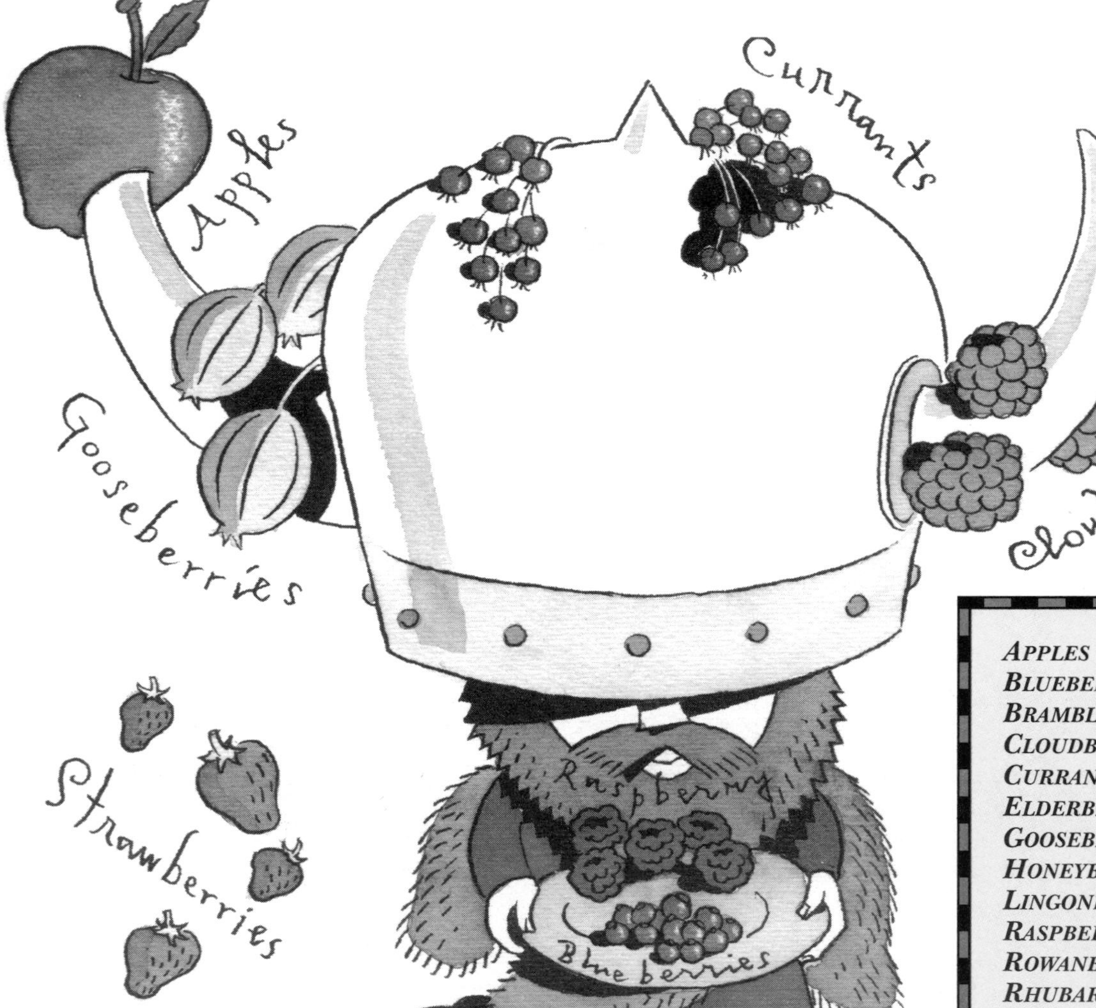

500

APPLES
BLUEBERRIES
BRAMBLEBERRIES
CLOUDBERRIES
CURRANTS
ELDERBERRIES
GOOSEBERRIES
HONEYBERRIES
LINGONBERRIES
RASPBERRIES
ROWANBERRIES
RHUBARB
STRAWBERRIES

ESROM: A pale yellow, semisoft cheese scattered with small holes, it is also known as Danish Port Salut. Mild and aromatic with a rich flavor, Esrom is perfect for slicing. It is sometimes spiced with caraway seeds.

> *"Denmark—there seems to be a cheese for every taste, every occasion, and every hour of the day."*

DANABLU: Even though quite different from French Roquefort, Danablu was developed as a substitute for it at the turn of the century. This Danish blue is sharper, more crumbly, and slightly more piquant that its French counterpart.

....

CASTELLO: A lusciously rich triple-cream blue cheese. Creamy and spreadable and made only at Tolstrop Dairy, it makes a superb hors d'oeuvre with sliced pears, walnuts, and dried Muscat grapes.

The Danes are also famous for their flavored fresh cream cheeses. Soft, luscious, and easy to spread, they come in many different flavors: plain, smoked, or with herbs, liqueurs, fruits, shrimp, ham, or mushrooms. They are excellent for topping crisp flatbreads as a savory addition to teatime fare.

Swedish Cheeses

....

Cheese is an important part of any Swedish *smörgåsbord* as well as a staple item in a Swedish breakfast. Wonderful grainy wholesome breads and crunchy crisp breads make perfect partners to this sampler of Swedish cheeses.

....

GREVÉ: Much like Swiss cheese with a sweet nutty flavor.

....

HERRGÅRDHOST: Similar to Jarlsberg, this cheese was originally made on small farms on the island of Gotland. Now it is a very popular cheese that is produced all over Sweden. Aged for about six months, the flavor is fresh and mellow.

The flower stalls in Copenhagen are a rainbow of lush colors.

Hushållsost: Literally "household cheese," a popular typical Swedish country cheese. It has a mild, slightly sour taste.

....

Kryddost: Spiced with caraway and cloves and ripened for several months. Traditionally served with crayfish during the season.

....

Mesost: A favorite among Swedish children. A firm cheese made from the leftover whey obtained in cheese making. Light brown in color and subtle sweet in flavor.

....

Prästost: Literally "priest's cheese," this classic has been around for over two centuries. It is well aged and has a strong, assertive flavor.

....

Sveciaost: "Swedish cheese," the best-selling cheese in Sweden. When fresh, it has a mild flavor; aged, the taste is sharper and stronger. Sometimes it is found flavored with caraway and cloves. This cheese is the everyday cheese of Sweden.

....

Västerbottenost: Often served as part of a *smörgåsbord*. Aged for a year, its flavor is strong and sharp. Occasionally it is found spiced.

Cheese bearers at the Alkmaar market. The men always wear white, but their hats are beautiful colors.

"Stacks of Edam cheese are carried on barrows to the weigh house by cheese bearers clad in white outfits that are topped off with wonderful, colorful hats."

Dutch Cheeses

....

The Netherlands, with its lush green meadows and grazing cattle, has been the world's largest cheese exporter for centuries. A rich architectural heritage is evident in many beautiful Dutch towns where splendid 16th- and 17th-century cheese "weigh houses" used for inspecting the cheeses prior to sale still stand. The town of Haarlem was the first to receive "weighing rights," which were granted to it by Floris V in 1266. Shortly thereafter Leiden, Oudewater, and Alkmaar followed suit. Today, Alkmaar is the site of one of the most famous cheese markets; it can be visited every Friday, from April to

September. Stacks of Edam cheese are carried on barrows to the weigh house by cheese bearers clad in white outfits that are topped off with wonderful, colorful hats.

There are many varieties of Dutch cheeses, the best known being Gouda and Edam.

....

Gouda: Derives its name from the town where farmers have brought their cheeses to market for centuries. The wheel-shaped cheese, coated in yellow wax, has a mild flavor and creamy texture when young. As it ages it becomes firmer, richer, darker, and tangier. The cheese, often flavored with herbs or cumin, is lovely served with grain breads, sweet butter, scallions, watercress, and tomato slices.

....

Edam: Characterized by its festive red wax coating and distinctive round shape, Edam hails from the town of the same name in northern Holland. The creamy yellow cheese has a firm, smooth texture and mild, fresh flavor when young. Aged Edam, coated in black wax, becomes robust, drier, and saltier. Like Gouda, Edam is often flavored with cumin seeds, herbs, or peppercorns. Sliced, it is delicious layered on lightly buttered crisp flatbreads spread with mustard and served with crisp celery and radishes.

Greek Cheeses

....

When we think about Greek cheese, feta is probably the first, and perhaps only, one that comes to mind. But this should change over the next few years because more cheeses are becoming available in the United States as interest in global foods increases. So, it really is up to the consumer to create the demand.

My most marvelous experience with Greek cheese was on the island of Crete when I first tasted a smooth, delicious, velvety piece of Manouri. This cheese is so very special that it didn't seem possible that the taste could be enhanced. I

Dick –

Crete is glorious – but that great Manouri cheese with ripe figs runs a close second!

Much love,

Sheila

was wrong. The next time I tasted it was when I was back home. I bought a large slice and served it at room temperature with wild thyme honey and large ripe purple figs. Pure heaven!

....

FETA: The best known of all Greek cheeses. Most often made from sheep's milk, it has a soft, crumbly texture with a pungent and slightly salty flavor. This white cheese is stored in a brine to keep it moist. *Feta* means "slice," which is how this cheese is usually sold—sliced into slabs or blocks. Feta is delicious served as a *meze*—drizzled with a fruity olive oil, then sprinkled with fresh herbs. It is wonderful, as well, cut up in chunks and tossed into a delicious Greek salad.

GRAVIERA: Resembles Gruyère with its mild flavor, semihard texture, and straw color. It is usually made from cow's milk, although sometimes sheep's milk is added. Its nutty sweet flavor and aroma make it a lovely table cheese for any occasion.

"My most wonderful experience with Greek cheese was on the island of Crete, when I first tasted a smooth, delicious, velvety, piece of Manouri."

KASSERI: A mild, yellowish, white, semihard cheese with a slightly sharp taste. Usually made from sheep's milk, it is a very versatile cheese that can be used for grating, baked atop casseroles, or grilled. If you have difficulty finding Kasseri, Italian provolone makes a suitable substitute.

....

MANOURI: One of my favorites, it is a soft, full-fat,

white cheese made from sheep's milk and has a smooth velvety texture.

....

MIZITHRA: A cheese from Crete, similar to Manouri, it is made with the whey from feta and sheep's or goat's milk. Sold fresh, it resembles pot cheese and makes a delightful addition to the breakfast table. Aged, it is semihard with a mild flavor, making it a perfect grating cheese.

....

KOPANISTI: A soft blue cheese made from full-fat sheep's milk. Salt and very finely ground pepper are mixed into the curds before aging. Kopanisti has a strong flavor, which makes it an excellent addition to a *meze* selection.

....

KEFALOTIRI: A hard sheep's and/or goat's milk cheese; it is pale yellow in color with irregular holes. Kefalotiri is shaped in the form of a head, from where it derives its name—*kefali* is the Greek word for head.

***Left:** This man stands before a gorgeous display of Greek cheeses. **Below:** Sheep graze peacefully under the hot sun and olive trees of Greece. **Right:** Milk from this charming goatherder's flock may eventually produce Mizithra.*

VELVETY TARTE AU CITRON · PINEAPPLE RUM UPSIDE-DOWN CAKE
INDONESIAN RIBBON CAKE
CRANACHAN
COPENHAGEN BUTTER COOKIES · BANANA BLISS
DENSE CHOCOLATE CAKE · GINGERSNAPS
BANANA RUM ICE CREAM · CHERRY COMPOTE
BERTA'S CARROT CAKE CARIBE · GALATOBOUREKO
COCONUT CREAM ICE CREAM
Grand Marnier

PAVLOVA
SUGAR
ANGEL BERRY TRIFLE
MELON COUPE SASHA
DUTCH GOLD
PURE HONEY
The Light
PROFITEROLES
COCOA
LINZER TART
CHOCOLATE CHOCOLATE CHUNK ICE CREAM · SCARLET SUMMER PUDDING
Fantastic
ORANGE POUND CAKE · TURKISH FIG PASTRIES
IRISH OATMEAL COOKIES · MEXICAN COCONUT RICE PUDDING
IRISH OATMEAL

A World of Desserts

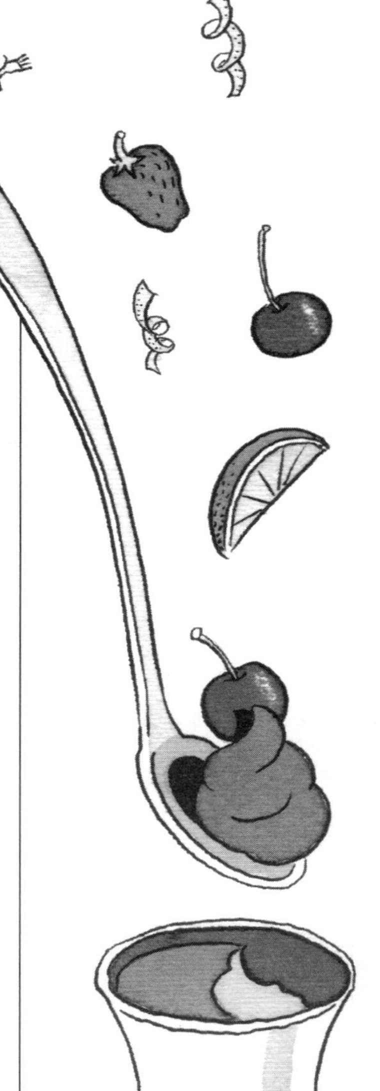

When I began traveling and dining for this book, I always ordered dessert just to have that little something at the end. But as I became more knowledgeable about how chefs around the world created their menus, the more particular I became about dessert. It was a wonderful sort of revelation and I came to appreciate sweet endings in a whole new way. In Spain, I couldn't get enough velvety smooth Orange Flan. In Mexico, a creamy Coconut Rice Pudding pressed all the right buttons. Tarte au Citron and Tarte Tatin were brilliant in Paris, and Banana Bliss from Istanbul was a fabulous suprise. Havana offered up thick slices of jelly-roll cake, and Bali, fresh papaya and incredible fruit sorbets.

Here they are—lush, intoxicating, gooey, totally satisfying—all the things great desserts should be. And they are even more enjoyable at home because there is the added bonus of seconds (maybe even thirds) available for everyone, including the cook.

BANANA BLISS

Kumkapi, the taverna area in Istanbul, teems with cafés that are embraced by the haunting serpentine sounds of Turkish music. Waiters bring forth huge trays of *meze* to begin the evening feast. Raki and chilled white wines are liberally poured.

At the end of a Turkish meal everyone is eager to think about dessert—but not me! I'm usually too stuffed. Then, one evening a Turkish friend with whom I was dining disappeared into the restaurant's kitchen. Out came a splendid banana dessert, golden and sparkling in a pool of scented honey. Slices of *kaymak,* a hard Turkish cream, covered the bananas, and ripe apricot halves garnished the plate. It was just about the best dessert I have ever tasted. Here's my version. I exercised restraint with the honey, but if you're feeling extravagant, use more. *Kaymak* is unavailable in America, so I've substituted a tangy fresh chèvre, which adds a lovely contrast to the sweetness. If you have the patience to shell them, chopped pistachio nuts would be delicious sprinkled atop.

6 medium bananas
1 cup plus 2 tablespoons honey, preferably wild thyme, plus extra for serving
¾ cup finely chopped walnuts
12 fresh ripe apricots, halved and pitted
8 ounces fresh chèvre, cut into 12 thin slices
Chopped pistachio nuts, for garnish (optional)

1. Peel the bananas and thinly slice each one on the diagonal, allowing 1 per serving.

2. Divide the slices among 6 dessert plates, arranging them decoratively. Drizzle each portion with about 3 tablespoons honey.

3. Sprinkle each serving with 2 tablespoons walnuts. Place 4 apricot halves around the sides of each plate. Top each portion with 2 slices of chèvre. Sprinkle each portion with the chopped pistachio nuts if desired and serve with extra honey on the side.

Serves 6

LIME BAKED BANANAS

Sometimes I think bananas are a greatly underused fruit. They make beautiful salads and desserts all year round. And they are easily accessible and always in season. This succulent sweet and tangy preparation would be delicious at the end of a meal served with Coconut Cream Ice Cream or as a side dish with savory meat dishes such as Carnaval Corned Beef and Copacabana Collards (see Index).

2 tablespoons unsalted butter
6 slightly underripe bananas
Juice of 2 limes
2 tablespoons (packed) light brown sugar

1. Preheat the oven to 375°F.

2. Using some of the butter, butter a shallow baking dish large enough to hold the bananas.

3. Peel the bananas and lay them in the prepared dish. Drizzle with the lime juice and sugar, and dot with the remaining butter.

4. Bake for 30 minutes, basting once or twice with the butter sauce. Serve hot, carefully removing the bananas to a platter with a long spatula. Spoon the sauce over the top.

Serves 6

CHERRY COMPOTE

Visiting Greece or Turkey not only offers the opportunity to feast your eyes on the Aegean, but if you visit in June, also on a far-reaching sea of ripe red cherries. Every market and decorative painted wooden street cart displays the harvest with exuberant respect. Small green leaves dapple the crop, imbuing it with a just-picked freshness. After falling in love with a bowl of cherry compote topped by scoops of thick creamy yogurt, I longed to make my own. You, too, should seize the season! Buy a cherry pitter and prepare this delectable "spoon sweet." As the cherries cook, they plump and look like small plums. I've cooked them with a vanilla bean and lemon juice to accent their natural flavor. While they're lovely eaten with yogurt, they'll reach celestial heights when spooned over vanilla ice cream or simply served on their own in small cut-crystal bowls.

1½ pounds Bing cherries, stems and pits removed
3 cups sugar
1 vanilla bean, split lengthwise in half
¾ cup water
1 tablespoon fresh lemon juice
16 ounces nonfat plain yogurt or Vanilla Bean Ice Cream (page 556), for serving

1. In a medium-size heavy, nonreactive saucepan, make a layer of half the cherries and top them with a layer of half the sugar. Place the vanilla bean on top of the sugar and cover with the remaining cherries and remaining sugar. Set the saucepan aside and allow the cherries to macerate for at least 1 hour.

2. Add the water to the pan and bring the cherries to a boil over high heat, stirring occasionally. Reduce the heat slightly and simmer, skimming off any scum that rises to the surface, until the mixture starts to thicken, about 15 minutes. Stir in the lemon juice and remove from the heat. Remove the vanilla bean and cool the compote to room temperature, then refrigerate until ready to serve. I enjoy the compote dolloped with plain yogurt or Vanilla Bean Ice Cream.

Makes 4 cups

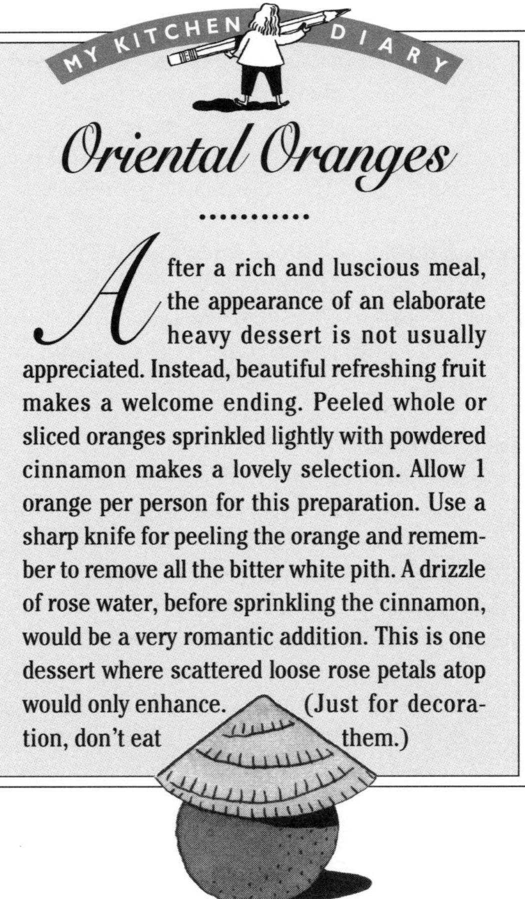

Oriental Oranges

After a rich and luscious meal, the appearance of an elaborate heavy dessert is not usually appreciated. Instead, beautiful refreshing fruit makes a welcome ending. Peeled whole or sliced oranges sprinkled lightly with powdered cinnamon makes a lovely selection. Allow 1 orange per person for this preparation. Use a sharp knife for peeling the orange and remember to remove all the bitter white pith. A drizzle of rose water, before sprinkling the cinnamon, would be a very romantic addition. This is one dessert where scattered loose rose petals atop would only enhance. (Just for decoration, don't eat them.)

A TASTE OF THE WORLD

Greek Fruit Basket

APPLES	*NECTARINES*
APRICOTS	*ORANGES*
CACTUS PEARS	*PEACHES*
CHERRIES	*PEARS*
DATES	*PLUMS*
FIGS	*POMEGRANATES*
GRAPES	*QUINCES*
LEMONS	*STRAWBERRIES*
MELONS	*WATERMELONS*

QUINCE SPOON SWEET

In Greece, fruits are plucked at the peak of ripeness for maximum flavor. When these fruits are poached in a thick syrup, they are known as "spoon sweets" throughout the country. One that I enjoyed particularly was a quince conserve spooned atop a bed of creamy, thick yogurt. Back home, I had to bide my time until quinces were in season—September and October are the best months to look for these golden fruits. Although quinces are difficult to cut because they're quite firm, making this sweet is well worth the effort. Cooked in a sugar syrup spiced with cinnamon and cloves, the fruit is gently simmered to a persimmon-hued tenderness. Chilled before serving, this spoon sweet is delectable as a dessert or served in place of applesauce alongside roast meats and Delicate Herbed Potato Pancakes or Banana Cinnamon Pancakes (see Index).

6 quinces (about 3 pounds), quartered, peeled, and cored
Juice and finely grated zest of 2 lemons
3 cups water
2 cups sugar
1 piece (1 inch) fresh ginger, peeled
2 cinnamon sticks (each 3 inches long)
4 whole cloves

1. Place the quinces in a large heavy, nonreactive pot with the lemon juice, grated zest, and water. Add the sugar, ginger, cinnamon sticks, and cloves. Bring the mixture to a boil, reduce the heat, and simmer until the fruit is tender and the color has changed to pale orange, about 1¼ hours.

2. Cool to room temperature. Remove the ginger, cinnamon sticks, and cloves. Store covered in the refrigerator up to 2 weeks.

Serves 8 to 10

PECHES AU BANDOL

There is no better way to end an outdoor summertime meal than with peaches blushed with Bandol, the fruity wine of Provence. Peaches and Bandol are just two of the many ingredients cherished in Provence during the summer months. Combined, they achieve the sublime. Accompany with a basket of biscotti.

1 bottle (750 ml) red Bandol wine
3 cups water
1½ cups sugar
Juice of 1 lemon
1 cinnamon stick (3 inches long)
8 peaches (just underripe and unblemished), rinsed

1. Combine the wine, water, sugar, lemon juice, and cinnamon stick in a large heavy, nonreactive pot. Bring to a boil, stirring once or twice until the sugar dissolves. Reduce the heat to a gentle simmer.

2. Add the peaches to the wine and cover the surface with a piece of parchment paper. Simmer until the tip of a small paring knife pierces the flesh with little resistance, 10 to 15 minutes, depending on their size and ripeness. Remove the peaches from the liquid with a slotted spoon and let rest until cool enough to handle.

3. Strain the wine syrup into a large serving bowl. Gently remove the skin from the peaches and return the peaches to the syrup in the bowl.

4. To serve, place the peaches in individual compote dishes. Ladle ¼ to ½ cup of the wine syrup over each peach.

Serves 8

MELON COUPE SASHA

At the conclusion of my friend Sasha's six-course dinner in his private restaurant in St. Petersburg, he suggested a dessert on the light side. Already feeling pleasantly stuffed, I agreed. So out came long-stemmed glasses filled with chilled honeydew balls laced with Cognac and rum. I've diluted the sauce slightly with sugar syrup and brightened the flavors with mint.

½ cup water
¼ cup sugar
2 tablespoons dark rum
1 tablespoon Cognac
4 cups melon balls, such as Crenshaw, cantaloupe, honeydew, or a mixture of two or three
2 tablespoons chopped fresh mint leaves
8 small fresh mint sprigs, for garnish

1. Combine the water and sugar in a small saucepan. Bring to a boil and cook until the sugar dissolves, about 1 minute. Remove from the heat, cool slightly, and stir in the rum and Cognac.

MY KITCHEN DIARY

Quince: An Autumn Specialty

In the autumn, you may come across a quince tree, its golden yellow fruit just ripe for picking. Rare as they are, I was lucky enough to have one in my backyard in northwest Connecticut. Unfortunately, I lost it in a storm, but till then it afforded me many years of quinces, perfect for compote-making.

I have never come across a fresh uncooked quince that was edible. For the most part, this fruit, which proliferates in Greece, is best cooked up into soft compotes and preserves. Preparing quinces can be a chore and should be done very carefully because they are so hard. They must be peeled and cored before they're ready for use. And it takes quite a while for the hard fruit to cook to the right consistency, resembling a chunky applesauce. Besides being ideal for compotes, quinces are also quite delicious when baked, drizzled with maple syrup, honey, or cooked up for pies and tarts.

2. In a bowl, mix the melon balls and chopped mint together. Pour the syrup atop and combine gently. Refrigerate covered up to 3 hours, stirring once or twice.

3. To serve, divide the melon balls between 8 coupes (stemmed goblets) with a slotted spoon. Spoon some syrup atop each and garnish with a mint sprig.

Serves 6 to 8

Toasting Coconut

Toasting coconut brings out all its natural sweetness, enhancing it for use in many desserts. The method is really quite simple. Spread no more than 1 cup shredded coconut on a baking sheet. Bake in a preheated 350°F oven until golden, about 5 minutes, shaking the pan once or twice. Watch the coconut carefully so that it does not burn. Bring it to room temperature and store in an airtight container in a cool dark place. Repeat the process if your recipe calls for more than 1 cup toasted coconut. Do not try to brown coconut under a broiler; the high sugar content will cause it to burn very quickly.

SALADE TROPICALE DE FRUITS

It's great to finish off a piquant meal with a scooped-out coconut filled with sweet, ripe tropical fruits echoing the tastes and colors of the island's bounty. It's best to make this summer salad when seasonal fruit is at its peak. As citrus juice enlivens flavors, it may discolor the fresh mint, so toss the mint into the fruit just before serving. Besides fresh mint sprigs for garnish, scatter some fresh nasturtium blossoms about.

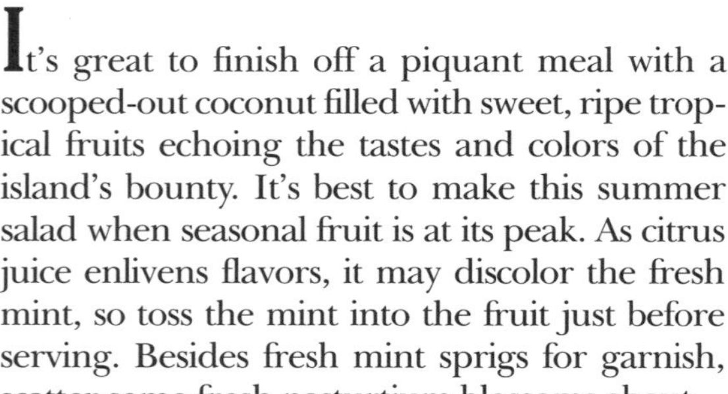

2 cups cubed (½ inch) ripe pineapple
2 cups ripe cantaloupe balls
2 cups seeded watermelon balls
2 cups sliced (¼ inch thick) bananas
¼ cup fresh lime juice
¼ cup fresh orange juice
1 tablespoon sugar
¼ cup chopped fresh mint leaves
¼ cup shredded coconut, toasted (see box)
6 fresh mint sprigs, for garnish

1. Place the pineapple, cantaloupe, watermelon, and bananas in a large bowl.

2. In a small bowl, combine the lime and orange juices and sugar. Pour over the fruit and fold all ingredients together gently.

3. Right before serving, fold in the chopped mint, sprinkle the toasted coconut atop, and garnish the salad with fresh mint sprigs.

Serves 6

SOUVENIR TO SAVOR

Carmen Miranda

When I was growing up, I loved going to the movies on Saturday afternoons, and for me there was nothing more spectacular than seeing Carmen Miranda in a film. Follow that with a Sunday night appearance by her on the Ed Sullivan Show singing "Cuanto le Gusta," and I was in heaven. As I got older I could emulate her by wearing platform shoes and styling my hair with a sleek roll in the front, but I could never imitate those headdresses, which resembled the best fruit baskets ever.

Once I set foot in Rio de Janeiro, I couldn't wait to visit the Carmen Miranda Museum. It did not disappoint. There were mannequins dressed up in all her glittery bejeweled costumes, each one topped off with an unbelievable headdress. My husband, Richard, was able to persuade the museum's curator to open one of the glass showcases so that I could have my picture taken with a Carmen mannequin without any reflection. I struck a Carmen pose, smiled, and found a dream come true!

1909: Maria do Carmo Miranda da Cunha is born in Portugal on February 9.

1910: Carmen and her family emigrate to Brazil.

1920: In Brazil, Carmen records two of her first records "Triste Jandaia" and "Iaia e Ioio."

1930: Already famous, Carmen records the big hit "Tai," by Joubert de Carvalho.

1933: Carmen makes her first screen appearance in A Voz do Carnaval!

1936: Carmen makes her debut at Cassino da Urca in Rio de Janeiro.

1935 to 38: Carmen appears in Alo, Alo Brazil, Estudantes, and Alo, Alo Carnaval.

1939: The costume known as "Baiana" is introduced in the film Banana de Terra, and "Baiana Style" (tropical fruit motif) become Carmen's trademark for the rest of her life. Traveling to the United States, she enjoys great success with the show Streets of Paris.

1940: Carmen is considered to be among the three most popular personalities in the United States. She sings and dances for President Roosevelt with her group Banda da Lua.

1941: Impressions of Carmen's hands and feet are made in the sidewalk in front of the famous Chinese Theater in Los Angeles.

1941 to 53: Carmen appears in fourteen Hollywood movies, plus radio and television shows and in nightclub, casino, and theatrical shows in the United States, Cuba, and Europe.

1946: Carmen pays the highest income tax bill of any actress in the United States.

1955: August 5, after an appearance on the "Jimmy Durante Show," Carmen dies of a heart attack in her Beverly Hills, California, home. She is 46 years old. She is buried at Cemitério São João Batista in Rio de Janeiro.

1976: Opening of the Carmen Miranda Museum, Avenida Rui Barbosa, Parque do Flamengo, Rio de Janeiro.

THE WINES OF

Australia and New Zealand

Australians dearly love good wine and take enormous pride in their own. In the last two decades Australia has won worldwide acclaim for its robust reds, like Cabernet and Shiraz, and full-blown Chardonnays. Explosive flavor is part of the attraction, flavors as ebullient and outgoing as the Australians themselves. Chardonnays, for instance, often have masses of fruit complemented by considerable oak, making them a great favorite with grilled shrimp. The sturdy Shiraz can be peppery and earthy, like Côte Rôtie, or taste of raspberries, reminiscent of Zinfandel. The best Cabernets are dark and concentrated, with excellent aging potential. Structure and balance are there as well, not only in the expensive wines but also in the moderate-priced Aussie Chardonnay and Shiraz wines that have made such a hit in the U.S.

"Current excitement centers on newer regions like Coonawarra and Padthaway, both cool districts of South Australia . . ."

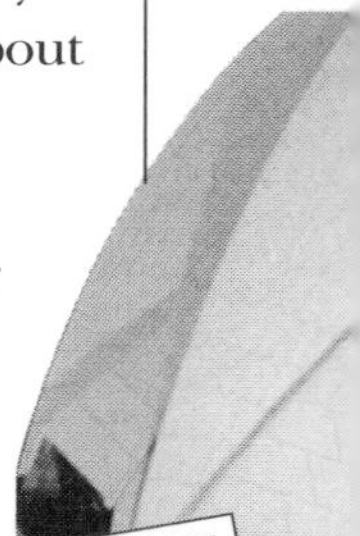

Australia's wine industry began in the mid-1800s, about the same time as that of its chief New World rival, the United States. By the latter part of the 19th century both industries were thriving. It is only in the last twenty or so years, however, that Australian wines became a significant export item. Australia's wine regions are scattered across the entire southern half of the continent, from the historic Hunter Valley north of Sydney to the west coast around Perth. In between are regions old and new. Barossa Valley, near the western city of Adelaide, for example, was one of the earliest areas to be developed a century ago. Barossa still produces the greatest total quantity of wine.

Current excitement centers on newer regions like Coonawarra and Padthaway, both cool districts of South Australia, as well as areas of the Southern Vales south of the city of Adelaide. Coonawarra, for example, produces what many consider the best Cabernet Sauvignon in Australia: bold but well-balanced reds with excellent aging potential. Fine Cabernets, Merlots, and intensely flavored Shiraz come from several regions, such as Goulburn Valley, Yarra Valley, McLaren Vale, and the upper Hunter Valley. Margaret River wineries produce stunning Chardonnays, as do Keppock and Padthaway just north of Coonawarra and, again, the upper Hunter.

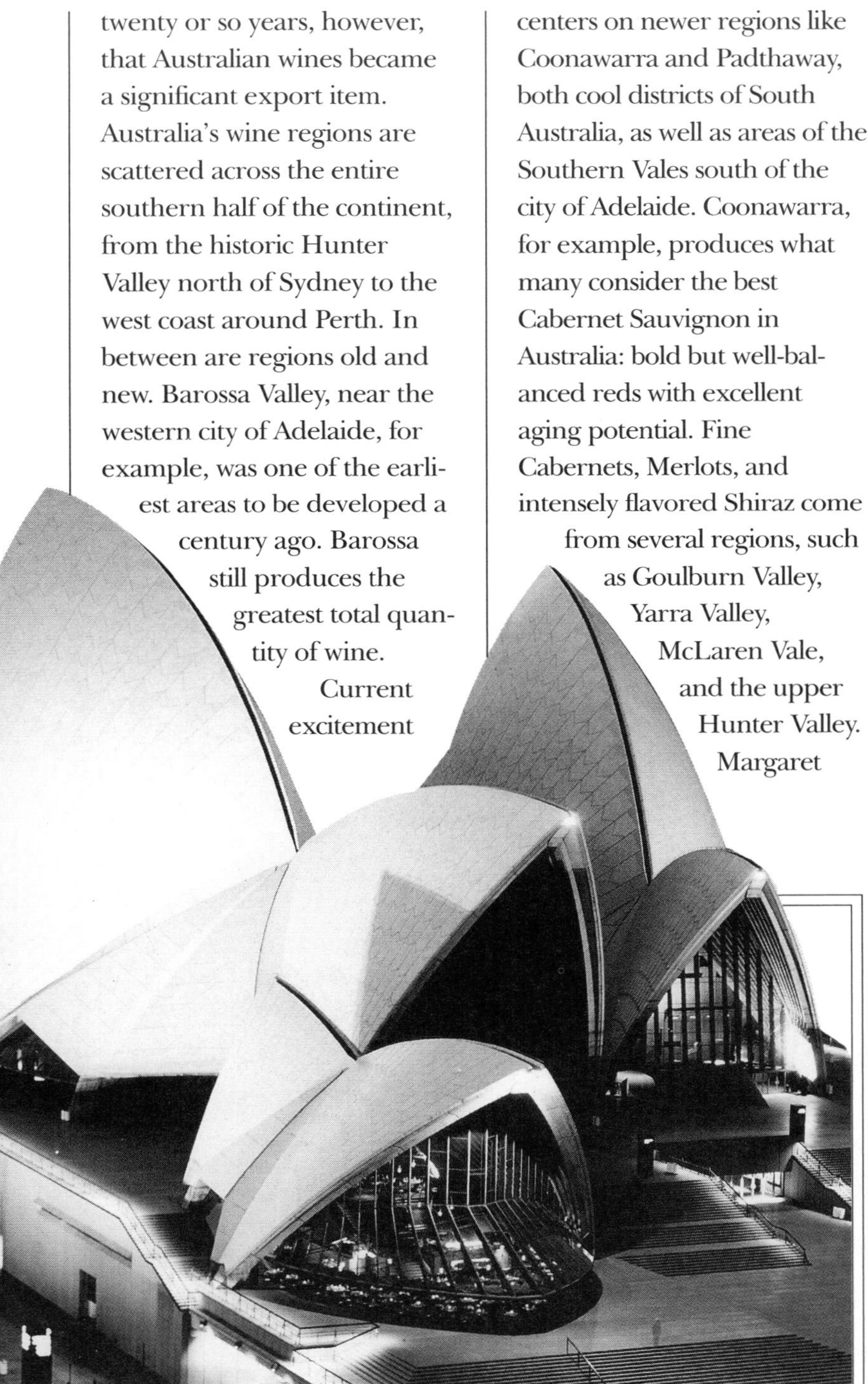

The venerable names in Australian wine still produce some of the country's best wines. Penfolds, for instance, continues to make its near-legend Grange Hermitage, a dark, dense concentrated Shiraz that ages decades, but its "Bin" wines, like the Bin 707 Cabernet, are also excellent values. Lindeman (bought by Penfolds in 1990 but independently run) produces appealing Chardonnay. Tyrrell of Hunter Valley, Wyndham Estate, Seppelt, Hardy's, Saltram, and a good dozen others produce sound varieties and Cabernet-Shiraz blends.

The new-era producers, largely responsible for thrusting Australia into the international arena include Rothbury Estate (Chardonnay), Rosemount (Chardonnay), Petaluma (Chardonnay, Cabernet, Pinot Noir,

Left: After years of neglect, the Yarra Valley, near Melbourne, is once again being developed as home to award-winning wineries. Right: There is no opera house more spectacular than the beauty in Sydney.

sparkling wine), Tim Knappstein (Cabernet-Shiraz, Fumé Blanc), Wolf Blass (Cabernet), Bannockburn (Chardonnay and Pinot Noir), Brokenwood (Cabernet-Shiraz, Chardonnay), Mountadam (Pinot Noir, Chardonnay), and Taltarni (Shiraz, Cabernet). Several younger innovators have lately come aboard with labels well worth seeking out if you are traveling Down Under, including Coldstream Hills, Cape Mentelle, Elgee Park, Grossett, Katnook Estate, Ashbourne, and Paul Conti.

> *"New Zealand is making impressive strides gaining international cachet for its intensely fruity, very stylish Sauvignon Blancs."*

New Zealand is making impressive wine strides gaining international cachet for its intensely fruity, very stylish Sauvignon Blancs. Chardonnay and Riesling also shine in the cool climate, and reds are beginning to show excellent character. Principal regions are Hawk's Bay on the North Island and the Marlborough region at the north end of the South Island, but other regions are emerging. Wineries such as Cloudy Bay, Kumeu River, Merlen, Jackson Estate, and other rising stars bode well for New Zealand wines and are increasingly stealing the thunder from neighboring giant Australia.

Above: The Rosemount Winery produces a Chardonnay that is popular worldwide. Right: Penfolds began producing its great red, Grange Hermitage, with the 1952 vintage.

Penfolds
Grange Hermitage
SOUTH AUSTRALIA
BIN 95
VINTAGE 1988 BOTTLED 1989

Grange Hermitage is generally recognised as Australia's finest red wine
and has received international acclaim. This great wine developed
by Max Schubert, commencing with the 1952 vintage, is made from
premium Hermitage grapes grown at selected vineyards in South
Australia and matured in small oak casks prior to bottling.
During an extensive tour of the Bordeaux region of France in 1950,
Max Schubert studied numerous wine-making practices that have now
become an integral part of Penfolds wine-making technique. He also
observed the practice of maturing wine in new oak casks, a method
previously untried in Australia. The development of Grange Hermitage
represented the beginning of a new era in Australia's red wine
making tradition.
This knowledge combined with Max Schubert's foresight, skill and
dedication has resulted in Grange Hermitage, the definitive
Australian dry red table wine, acknowledged to be amongst the
world's classic wine styles.
It is recommended that Grange Hermitage should always be decanted
before serving.

RED WINE PRODUCT OF AUSTRALIA 750mL VIN ROUGE PRODUIT D'AUSTRALIE
PRODUCED BY PENFOLDS WINES PTY. LTD., TANUNDA ROAD, NURIOOTPA, AUSTRALIA 5355 13.5% alc./vol.

PAVLOVA

Australia's most famous dessert was created in honor of the great Russian ballerina Anna Pavlova. This light and luxurious meringue and fruit confection is an ideal dessert to make in the spring. Strawberries and other gorgeous berries are just coming into season and the temperature is just right —try not to pick a humid day to work with meringues. If possible, make the meringues in small tart pans with removable bottoms for a lovely shape. While many people prefer to use all whipped cream for the filling, I've mixed it with an equal amount of crème fraîche, which adds a bit of tang to counterbalance the sweetness of the meringues.

MERINGUES:
4 large egg whites, at room temperature
¼ teaspoon cream of tartar
1 cup superfine sugar
½ teaspoon fresh lemon juice
2 tablespoons confectioners' sugar

FILLING:
1 cup heavy (or whipping) cream
1 cup crème fraîche
2 tablespoons confectioners' sugar
1 teaspoon pure vanilla extract
3 to 4 cups sliced ripe strawberries, kiwis, or other berries

MY KITCHEN DIARY

Fruit and Cheese

When the thought of a long dessert preparation gets me down, I remember the delicious simplicity of ripe fruit and cheese as served in both Italy and France—no *torta* or *gâteau* necessary.

For me this choice is best of all. I purchase a large piece of straw-hued Parmigiano-Reggiano, then flake it into little bits to savor. I choose seasonal fruits to serve alongside—usually ripe juicy pears, peaches, and figs afloat in a bowl of water. When ripe persimmons are in season, there is no better pleasure.

The sweet and nutty flavor of the cheese harmonizes with the naturally sweet nectars of the fruit. For an added dimension, I take the pale green innermost celery stalks, abundant with leaves, and place them in a jug of cold water for a crisp, savory nibble along with the cheese and fruit. Serve a bottle of Vin Santo alongside with small glasses for sipping.

1. Preheat the oven to 225°F. Line a baking sheet with waxed or parchment paper, or butter and lightly flour 6 small tart pans.

2. Make the meringues: In a very clean bowl, beat the egg whites until foamy. Add the cream of tartar and continue beating on medium speed until soft peaks form. Increase the speed to high and add the superfine sugar 1 tablespoon at a time, beating for at least 10 seconds after each addition. Beat in the lemon juice. Sift the confectioners' sugar over the whites and gently fold in with a rubber spatula.

3. Spoon the meringue in 6 equal mounds on the prepared baking sheet or in the prepared tart pans. Use the tip of a rubber spatula in a swirling motion to make a depression in the center of each. If using pans, place the filled pans on a baking sheet.

4. Bake for 1 hour. Reduce the heat to 200°F and bake for another 45 minutes. Turn off the oven. When the oven is completely cool, remove the meringues and allow them to cool completely at room temperature.

5. Carefully peel the meringues off the paper. If using tart pans, remove the outer ring, and slide a small knife between tart bottom and the meringue to separate them.

6. Make the filling: Beat the heavy cream, crème fraîche, sugar, and vanilla until soft peaks form.

7. Place the meringues on dessert plates. Spoon a little cream over the top of each. Cover each with ½ cup fruit and dollop with the remaining cream. Top evenly with the remaining fruit. Serve immediately.

Serves 6

COPENHAGEN BUTTER COOKIES

In the nibble department, there is nothing quite as delicious as a good Danish butter cookie. While they are lovely with cold milk, they're very luxurious served during afternoon tea following a selection of savory sandwiches and currant-studded scones. A proper butter cookie should melt in your mouth from the very first bite.

1 cup (2 sticks) unsalted butter, at room temperature
⅔ cup superfine sugar, plus more for sprinkling
1 teaspoon pure vanilla extract
¼ teaspoon salt
2 cups all-purpose flour

SOUVENIR TO SAVOR

The Konditoris of Denmark

Seek out the large, attention-getting golden pretzels hanging above the entrance of a Danish *konditori* and step inside. Take deep breaths to get the full buttery fragrance—this is a country of real bread- and pastry-lovers! The beckoning yeasty aroma reminds one of childhood visits to the bakery. Flaky, golden rounds of Danish pastry with cheese or jam fillings are strewn with white sugar icing and sliced almonds. There are rolls in every shape and size, each with a different topping. Golden loaves of bread and cakes, and cookies of every description line up proudly behind the sparkling glass cases. Choose from the huge selection (it's a tough decision), order a cup of coffee, and find yourself a sunny sidewalk table. Now this is what coffee and a Danish is all about.

1. Cream the butter, sugar, vanilla, and salt with an electric mixer until completely mixed. Do not overmix. (The butter should not be fluffy.) Stir in the flour in 2 additions, using a wooden spoon or a rubber spatula. Mix just until the flour is incorporated.

2. Form the dough into a log, cover well with plastic wrap, and refrigerate at least 2 hours or overnight.

3. Preheat the oven to 350°F. Line 2 baking sheets with waxed or parchment paper.

4. Remove the dough from the refrigerator and let it soften slightly before rolling.

5. Divide the dough into 4 quarters. On a well-floured work surface, roll out a quarter of the dough at a time ¼ inch thick. Run a long metal spatula under the dough to loosen it from the surface. Cut out shapes as close together as possible with a 3-inch cookie cutter. Transfer the cut dough to the prepared baking sheets with a spatula, leaving 1 inch between the cookies. Repeat with the remaining dough. Gather up all the scraps and roll them out to make more cookies.

6. Sprinkle the tops with sugar. Bake until the edges are golden brown, 15 to 20 minutes. Remove from the oven and cool for 10 minutes on the baking sheet. Transfer to a wire rack to cool completely. Store in an airtight container.

Makes about 2 dozen cookies

LEMON WAFERS

Lemon wafers—I've had them lacy, thin, crispy, and pale, pale white. The addition of egg whites in this recipe results in slightly puffy wafers resembling tissue-thin meringue cookies with a great burst of lemon pizzazz. They're lovely served at tea parties on frilly doilies.

8 tablespoons (1 stick) unsalted butter, at room temperature
1 cup sugar, plus more for sprinkling
¼ teaspoon salt
Finely grated zest of 1 lemon
4 teaspoons fresh lemon juice
½ teaspoon lemon extract
2 large egg whites, at room temperature, lightly beaten
1 cup all-purpose flour
¼ cup cornstarch

1. Preheat the oven to 375°F. Line 2 baking sheets with waxed or parchment paper.

2. Cream the butter, sugar, and salt with an electric mixer until fluffy. Beat in the lemon zest, juice, and extract. Gradually beat in the egg whites until completely incorporated. Scrape down the sides of the bowl with a rubber spatula and beat for a few more seconds.

3. Sift the flour and cornstarch into the bowl and stir it in by hand, using a wooden spoon or rubber spatula.

4. Transfer the dough to a pastry tube fitted with a ½-inch round tip. Pipe dollops of the dough about 1¼ inches in diameter, 2 inches apart, on the prepared baking sheets. Lightly sprinkle the tops with sugar.

5. Bake until the cookies have about a ¼-inch golden brown ring around the edges, about 15 minutes. Cool the cookies completely on the baking sheets and store in an airtight container.

Makes about 4 dozen cookies

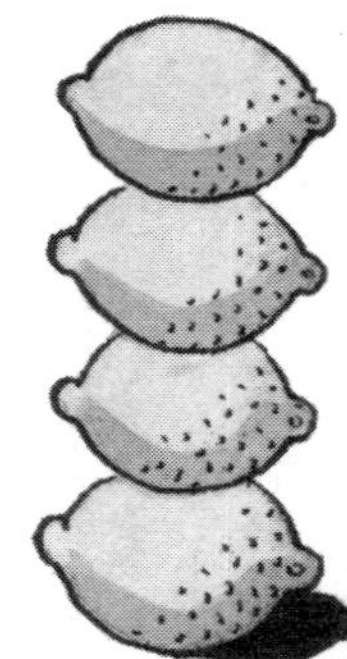

GINGERSNAPS

There is just the right bite of ginger in these spicy cookies. The intense flavors marry well with cooling Confetti Lemon Sorbet (see Index) or a soothing cup of Darjeeling tea.

12 tablespoons (1½ sticks) unsalted butter
¼ cup molasses
1 teaspoon pure vanilla extract
2 cups all-purpose flour
1 cup sugar, plus more for rolling
2 teaspoons baking soda
2 teaspoons ground ginger
2 teaspoons ground cinnamon
¼ teaspoon ground nutmeg
¼ teaspoon ground cloves
¼ teaspoon salt
1 large egg, lightly beaten

1. Preheat the oven to 375°F.

2. Melt the butter in a saucepan. Remove from the heat and stir in the molasses and vanilla. Set aside to cool.

3. Sift together all the dry ingredients (including 1 cup of the sugar) into a bowl. Add the egg to the cooled butter mixture and stir it into the dry ingredients. Combine well. Cover with plastic wrap and refrigerate the mixture until fairly firm, about 30 minutes.

4. Fill a small bowl with sugar. Using your hands, roll the dough into 1-inch balls. Roll each ball in the sugar and place 2 inches apart on ungreased baking sheets.

5. Bake until the bottoms begin to brown, about 10 minutes. Cool on the baking sheets for 5 minutes. Transfer to a wire rack to cool completely. Store in an airtight container.

Makes about 5 dozen cookies

HAZELNUT-ALMOND BISCOTTI

I've always found nut-filled biscotti a bit addictive. They are a wonderful side note with coffee or tea, though they taste best of all when dipped into a small glass of sweet Italian Vin Santo. Biscotti last for weeks stored in an airtight cookie tin—if they're not eaten up before then.

1¾ cups all-purpose flour
½ teaspoon baking powder
¼ teaspoon salt
¾ cup sugar, plus more for sprinkling
4 tablespoons (½ stick) unsalted butter, chilled and cut into small pieces
¾ cup blanched almonds
¾ cup toasted hazelnuts (see Note)
2 large eggs
1 teaspoon pure vanilla extract

1. Preheat the oven to 350°F. Lightly butter a baking sheet.

2. Combine the flour, baking powder, salt, and ¾ cup sugar in a food processor. Add the butter and pulse the machine on and off until the mixture resembles coarse meal. Add all the nuts and pulse about 10 times to coarsely chop.

3. Lightly beat together the eggs and the vanilla in a small bowl. Pour the egg mixture evenly over the dough in the food processor and pulse the machine on and off about 20 times to moisten the dough.

4. Scrape the mixture onto a very lightly floured work surface. Using the heel of your hand, mash the dough with a few quick strokes to moisten any dry spots in the dough. Gather up the dough, form into a ball, then flatten into a disk. Divide the disk into 4 quarters. Form each quarter into an 8-inch-long log.

5. Place the logs on the prepared baking sheet about 2 inches apart. Using the heel of your hand, flatten each log 2 inches wide. Sprinkle the tops with sugar.

6. Bake until golden brown, about 20 minutes. Remove from the oven (leave the oven on), and using a sharp knife, cut each log on the diagonal, into about ¾-inch-thick slices. Turn the biscotti cut side down on the baking sheet. Bake until they begin to color, 5 to 7 minutes. Transfer to a wire rack to cool completely. Store in an airtight container.

Makes about 32 biscotti

Note: To toast hazelnuts, spread them on a baking sheet and bake in a 350°F oven until the outer skins begin to crack off, about 15 minutes. The inside should be golden brown. Remove from the oven and rub the nuts in a kitchen towel to remove the outer skins.

STEFFI BERNE'S CHOCOLATE SKINNIES

While visiting the Caribbean, I was fascinated with the tropical sundae combinations. There were so many served with thin chocolate cookies, but none were as good as my friend Steffi Berne's Chocolate Skinnies, happily immortalized in her splendid book *The Cookie Jar Cookbook*—and now here, too.

1 cup sifted all-purpose flour
½ teaspoon baking soda
Pinch of salt
8 tablespoons (1 stick) unsalted butter, cut into small pieces
6 ounces bittersweet chocolate, broken into small pieces, or 1 cup (6 ounces) semisweet chocolate morsels
⅓ cup sugar
¼ cup light corn syrup
1 teaspoon instant good-quality expresso dissolved in 1 teaspoon hot water
1 extra-large egg, lightly beaten

1. Position two oven racks to divide the oven into thirds and preheat the oven to 350°F. Line baking sheets with parchment paper or aluminum foil.

2. Combine the flour, baking soda, and salt and set aside.

3. Combine the butter, chocolate, sugar, and corn syrup in a heavy medium-size saucepan and stir over low heat until almost all the chocolate is melted. Remove the pan from the heat and stir vigorously until smooth. Let cool for 5 minutes. Stir in the dissolved coffee and the egg. Add the dry ingredients and mix until thoroughly combined.

4. Using a measuring spoon and a tiny rubber spatula, drop level teaspoonfuls about 2½ inches apart onto the prepared baking sheets.

5. Bake 2 baking sheets at a time for 12 minutes, rotating the sheets from top to bottom and from front to back after the cookies puff up and then settle down (about halfway through the baking time). These cookies should be crisp, but they tend to burn if baked too long. Slide the paper with the cookies onto a flat surface and let the cookies cool for a few minutes before transferring them to a wire rack to cool completely. If the cookies are not crisp when cool, they can be returned to the oven for a minute or so. Store in a cookie jar with a loose-fitting lid.

Makes about 5 dozen very thin cookies

TURKISH FIG PASTRIES

Remember those great fig cookies you ate in rapid succession as a child? I've made a more refined version that is flavored with the best Turkey has to offer.

1½ cups coarsely chopped walnuts
1 cup best-quality dried figs, cut into ¼-inch dice
½ cup honey
1 tablespoon finely grated lemon zest
¼ teaspoon ground cinnamon
14 sheets phyllo pastry (see Note)
1 cup (2 sticks) unsalted butter, melted

1. Preheat the oven to 350°F.

2. Combine the walnuts, figs, honey, lemon zest, and cinnamon in a bowl. Set aside.

3. Remove the phyllo pastry from the box and lay the sheets on a clean dish towel. Cover the pastry with a sheet of waxed paper and then a slightly dampened dish towel. Keep the phyllo covered as you work.

4. Place 1 sheet of phyllo pastry, with the long side in front of you, on a clean work surface. Brush all over with melted butter. Cover with a second sheet of phyllo and brush it with butter. Cut the phyllo into six 3-inch-wide strips the short way. Place 1 teaspoon of the filling in the center of each strip 1 inch from the bottom. Fold a corner across the filling, then continue to fold as if you were folding a flag, until the strip is all folded. Tuck under the edges. Continue filling and folding the remaining strips, then repeat the process with the remaining phyllo and filling. Place the triangles on a baking sheet about ½ inch apart, and brush with the melted butter.

5. Bake until golden brown, 12 to 15 minutes. Cool the fig pastries on the baking sheet before serving. Store in an airtight container.

Makes 42 small pastries

Note: Phyllo dough is readily available frozen in 1-pound boxes. Follow the package directions for thawing the dough.

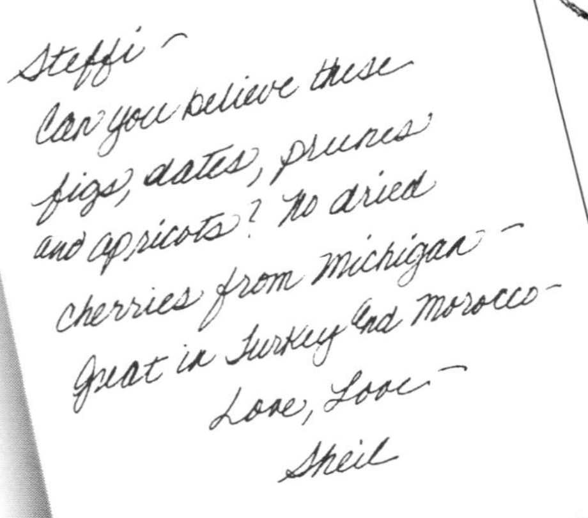
Steffi –
Can you believe these
figs, dates, prunes
and apricots? No dried
cherries from Michigan –
Great in Turkey and Morocco –
Love, Love –
Sheil

Turkish Fruit Basket

APPLES	*ORANGES*
APRICOTS	*PEACHES*
CHERRIES	*PLUMS*
FIGS	*POMEGRANATES*
GRAPES	*QUINCES*
LEMONS	*STRAWBERRIES*
MELONS	*WATERMELONS*

SCOTTISH SHORTBREAD

Every time I had tea in Scotland, a little plate of these delicious buttery biscuits was placed on the table. Although shortbread was traditionally associated with Christmas and Hogmanay (New Year's Eve), today it is eaten all year round. Lucky for me, since my visit to Scotland didn't coincide with the holiday season. If you don't have a shortbread mold, crimp the edges and make a nice pattern on the top with the tines of a fork. Before baking, it is essential to score the dough into serving wedges so that you can cut it easily as soon as it comes out of the oven.

1 cup (2 sticks) unsalted butter, at room temperature
1 cup confectioners' sugar, sifted
2½ cups all-purpose flour, sifted
1 teaspoon salt

1. Preheat the oven to 350°F. Lightly butter two 8-inch pie plates.

2. Cream the butter in a bowl with an electric mixer. Gradually beat in the confectioners' sugar and continue beating until light and fluffy.

3. Add the flour and salt. Using a wooden spoon, stir the mixture just to combine, then continue mixing with your hands to combine it thoroughly.

4. Divide the mixture in half. Press half the dough in the bottom of each pie plate, forming the dough into a smooth, flat disk.

5. Prick the surface of the shortbread all over in rows with the tines of a fork. Make a pretty border by using your index finger and thumb to crimp the edges. Using a sharp knife, score each disk halfway through to the bottom to make 8 wedges.

6. Bake until golden brown and firm, about 35 minutes.

7. While the shortbread is still hot, cut through along the scored lines with a knife. Allow the shortbread to cool completely in the pans. Remove to a plate and serve.

Makes 16 wedges

IRISH OATMEAL COOKIES

Chewy oatmeal-raisin cookies, are all-American favorites. This variation bakes up with a bit of a crunch as well as a nice chew. Have plenty of cold milk or a steaming pot of tea on hand when you serve them.

1¼ cups (2½ sticks) unsalted butter, at room temperature
¾ cup (packed) light brown sugar
¼ cup granulated sugar
1 large egg, lightly beaten
1 teaspoon pure vanilla extract
1½ cups all-purpose flour
1 teaspoon baking soda
1 teaspoon salt
1 teaspoon ground cinnamon
3 cups rolled oats
1 cup raisins

1. Preheat the oven to 375°F.

2. In a mixing bowl, cream the butter and both sugars with an electric mixer. Stir in the egg and vanilla.

3. Combine the flour, baking soda, salt, and cinnamon in a small bowl and stir it into the butter mixture. Add the oats and raisins and mix well.

4. Drop the cookie dough by rounded teaspoons 2 inches apart onto an ungreased baking sheet. Bake until golden brown, 10 to 12 minutes. Allow to cool slightly on the baking sheet, then remove to a wire rack to cool completely.

Makes about 42 cookies

ORANGE FLAN

Smooth. Creamy. Velvety. All good enough reasons to make this delicious Spanish classic. The addition of honey to the basic egg custard makes the texture extra creamy. This flan is particularly lovely accompanied by fresh fruit, such as ripe strawberries, raspberries, kiwis, and blueberries. To catch the custard as well as the caramel syrup, serve with a spoon rather than a fork. Chocolate-covered espresso beans are great served with the flan.

1 cup plus 2 tablespoons sugar
3 navel oranges
1 cup light cream or ½ cup milk and ½ cup heavy (or whipping) cream
2 cups milk
6 large egg yolks
4 large eggs
3 tablespoons honey, preferably orange-blossom

1. Preheat the oven to 325°F.

2. Place 1 cup of the sugar in a heavy 2-quart saucepan over medium-high heat and stir with a wooden spoon until it starts to melt. When it begins to melt, stir constantly until it turns a dark amber color and begins to smoke. Immediately pour the caramel into a shallow ovenproof dish, such as a Pyrex pie plate. Working quickly, tilt the dish to evenly coat the sides and bottom with the caramel. Set aside.

3. Using a vegetable peeler, remove all the peel from the oranges in long strips, being careful to avoid the bitter white pith. Place the orange peel, cream, and the milk into the same pot in which the caramel was made and scald it. Set aside to steep, stirring occasionally.

4. Squeeze the juice from the oranges and measure ⅔ cup. Place the juice in a small pot and bring to a boil. Reduce the heat and simmer, skimming any foam that rises to the top, until the juice is reduced to 2 tablespoons, 15 to 20 minutes. Transfer to a small bowl and set aside to cool.

5. Return the milk mixture to scalding hot. Meanwhile whisk together the egg yolks, eggs, honey, and remaining 2 tablespoons sugar in a bowl just to combine. Whisk in the reduced orange juice.

6. Whisking constantly, pour the hot milk mixture with the orange peel into the egg mixture in a slow stream. Strain the mixture into the prepared dish.

7. Place the dish in a slightly larger pan, so that it doesn't touch the sides, for a water bath. Pour hot water into the larger pan to about two-thirds of the way up the custard dish. Cover loosely with a piece of aluminum foil.

8. Bake until a knife inserted near the edge comes out clean, about 1½ hours. The custard should look set but jiggle slightly in the center when shaken. Remove the dish from the water bath and cool to room temperature on a rack. Refrigerate covered overnight.

9. To unmold the flan, place a large serving plate over the custard and quickly invert it onto the plate. Remove the dish and chill the flan until ready to serve.

Serves 12

A TASTE OF THE WORLD

Spanish Fruit Basket

APPLES
BANANAS
BLOOD ORANGES
DATES
FIGS
GRAPES
LEMONS
LIMES
MELONS
PEACHES
PEARS
STRAWBERRIES

SCARLET SUMMER PUDDING

Those English are just full of surprises! They may still tend to cook lamb and Brussels sprouts too much to suit our taste, but they are absolute wizards with desserts and quite the "berries" with berries! Few desserts that I've eaten of late compare to an English summer pudding, bursting with raspberries and strawberries.

As I was testing this recipe, I kept thinking this will never work. Twenty-four hours later, to my delight, I unmolded a perfect *bombe*-shaped pudding that miraculously held together. When lining your pudding bowl or mold, it helps to be a bit of a puzzlemaster, as it is necessary to trim each slice of bread to fit perfectly into a shell to hold the berries. Once it's unmolded, the bread really doesn't show because it's been saturated with the scarlet fruit. It is a must to weight down the pudding overnight so that it sets properly. I simply used a 28-ounce can of peeled tomatoes set on a plate for the task. It was just right. After you have cooked up the berries, you'll have lots of "sauce" left over to spoon atop the pudding and serve alongside. Dollops of sweetened whipped cream are a "must serve" garnish for the pudding, and sprigs of fresh mint make it so pretty.

4 tablespoons (½ stick) unsalted butter, or more if needed, at room temperature
20 slices day-old white bread, crusts removed
4 pints ripe strawberries, rinsed and hulled
2 pints raspberries, picked over
½ cup sugar
1 cup heavy (or whipping) cream, whipped with 1 tablespoon sugar, for garnish
8 fresh mint sprigs, for garnish

1. Lightly butter 1 side of each slice of bread. Set aside.

2. Place the strawberries in a large bowl and coarsely crush with the back of a fork. Remove to a large nonreactive pot. Simmer over medium-low heat until the berries soften and release some of their juices, 15 minutes, stirring occasionally. Skim off any foam that rises to the surface. Reduce the heat to low if the berries boil too rapidly. Remove from the heat. Stir the raspberries and sugar into the strawberries.

3. Using a 2-quart bowl or mold with rounded sides (see Note), trim the bread slices to fit the bottom and sides of the mold and place in the bowl with the unbuttered sides against the sides of the bowl.

4. Place 1 cup of the berry mixture in the bottom of the mold over the bread. Cover with a layer of bread, trimmed to fit. Add a second cup of berries and cover with another layer of bread. Cover with a third cup of berries and layer with bread. Cover with a fourth cup of berries and end with a final layer of bread to fit. (Save any leftover berries to serve with the pudding.)

5. Fit a plate that fits exactly inside the bowl over the pudding. It must fit just inside the bowl. Place the bowl on a large plate to catch any juices that run over. Weight the pudding with a 2-pound (approximately) can on top of the plate and set the bowl in the refrigerator. Refrigerate overnight so that the bread absorbs the berry mixture and the pudding sets.

6. Before serving, carefully invert the pudding onto a large serving platter. If there are any spots on the surface where the bread didn't absorb the berry juices, dab with some of the reserved sauce.

7. Serve the pudding with additional berry sauce spooned atop. Slice it as you would a round cake, from the center out. Dollop the slices with the sweetened whipped cream and garnish each with a fresh mint sprig.

Serves 8

Note: Your bowl or mold should hold 2 to 2½ quarts and be 6 inches deep and 6 inches across at the top.

MEXICAN CHRISTMAS BREAD PUDDING

Christmas in Mexico is one long festival, and this festive fruit-studded bread pudding fits in perfectly, combining bright colors and sweet flavor. Easily made ahead of time, this is an ideal finale to any Christmas dinner. If panettone is not available, seek out another fruit-studded, sweet, eggy bread. Just before serving, spoon the Grand Marnier sauce over the pudding and brown until golden and bubbly.

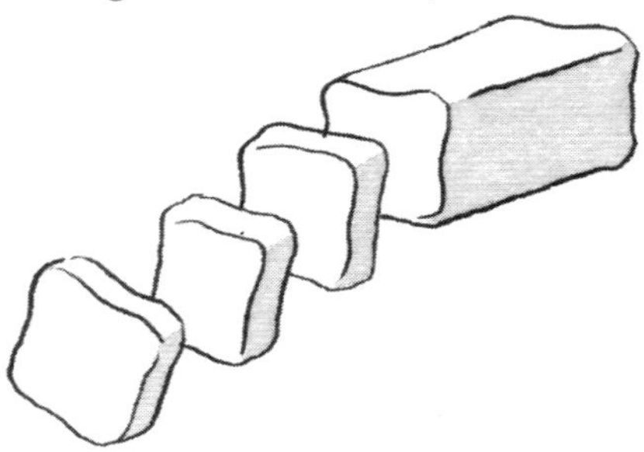

1 panettone or other fruit-studded sweet bread (about 1 pound), cut into 1-inch-thick slices
4 cups half-and-half
2 ounces candied orange peel, cut into ¼-inch dice
2 ounces dried cherries
2 ounces golden raisins
2 ounces dried apricots, cut into ¼-inch pieces
3 tablespoons Grand Marnier or other orange-flavored liqueur
1 tablespoon unsalted butter
3 large eggs
1 cup granulated sugar
1 tablespoon pure vanilla extract

GRAND MARNIER SAUCE:
8 tablespoons (1 stick) unsalted butter
1 cup confectioners' sugar
3 tablespoons Grand Marnier or other orange-flavored liqueur
2 large egg yolks

2 ounces semisweet chocolate, coarsely grated or shaved, for garnish

1. Preheat the broiler.

2. Arrange the bread slices on 2 baking sheets and toast 2 inches from the heat for about 1 minute per side, until lightly browned. Watch carefully as this bread burns very easily.

3. Tear the toasted panettone into 1½-inch pieces and place in a large bowl. Pour the half-and-half over the bread and toss gently to make sure all the pieces are moistened. Set aside for 1 hour, tossing occasionally.

4. Place the candied peel and dried fruits in a bowl and toss with 2 tablespoons of the Grand Marnier. Set aside.

5. Preheat the oven to 325°F. Butter the bottom and sides of a 13 x 9 x 2-inch baking dish with 1 tablespoon butter and set aside.

6. In a medium-size bowl, whisk the eggs

with the sugar, vanilla, and the remaining 1 tablespoon Grand Marnier. Mix well with the soaked bread, then fold in the reserved dried fruits.

7. Transfer the mixture to the prepared baking dish and bake in the middle of the oven until the pudding is set and the top is golden brown, about 1 hour. Let cool to room temperature. (The pudding can be prepared 1 day ahead. Cover and set aside at room temperature.)

8. While the pudding is baking, prepare the Grand Marnier sauce: In a medium-size bowl set over a saucepan of simmering water or in the top of a double boiler, melt the butter. Slowly whisk in the sugar until the mixture is creamy, about 30 seconds. Add the Grand Marnier and then the egg yolks one at a time, whisking constantly. Cook, whisking constantly, until the sauce is the consistency of honey, about 4 minutes. Let cool to room temperature.

9. Preheat the broiler.

10. Just before serving, spoon the Grand Marnier sauce over the pudding and broil 3 to 4 inches from the heat until bubbly and lightly browned, about 2 minutes. Sprinkle the grated chocolate evenly over the top. Cut the pudding into 12 rectangular pieces and serve immediately.

Serves 12

MEXICAN COCONUT RICE PUDDING

Rice pudding is to Mexicans what mashed potatoes are to Americans—the ultimate comfort food. There are few restaurants in Mexico where you won't find this creamy luscious dessert on the menu. The addition of velvety coconut milk smoothes the pudding and candied orange peel adds a pleasant zest. I serve this pudding with toasted coconut sprinkled on top. If you prefer, for a real splurge serve it with a pitcher of heavy cream alongside to be stirred in before eating.

3 cups water
Whole peel of 1 orange, pith removed
2 cinnamon sticks (each 3 inches long)
Pinch of salt
1½ cups long-grain rice
¼ cup golden raisins
¼ cup candied orange peel, cut into ¼-inch dice
¾ cup shredded coconut
¼ cup dark rum
5 cups milk
1 cup coconut milk (page 252 or available in specialty food stores)
1¼ cups sugar
1 teaspoon pure vanilla extract
½ cup half-and-half

1. In a large heavy pot, combine the water, orange peel, cinnamon sticks, and salt. Bring to a boil, add the rice, and stir. Reduce the heat to low, cover the pot, and simmer until all the liquid is absorbed, about 20 minutes.

2. While the rice is cooking, toss the raisins, candied orange peel, and ¼ cup of the shredded coconut with the rum. Set aside.

3. When the rice is ready, add the milk,

coconut milk, sugar, and dried fruits with rum to it. Increase the heat to medium-low and cook, stirring frequently, until the mixture has thickened, about 50 minutes. If the liquid boils rapidly, reduce the heat to low.

4. When the pudding is done, carefully skim off the thin layer of skin that may have formed on the top. Remove from the heat and discard the orange peel and cinnamon sticks. Stir in the vanilla. Cool the pudding slightly.

5. While the pudding cools, preheat the oven to 350°F.

6. Toast the remaining ½ cup shredded coconut in a small pan in the oven until golden, about 5 minutes (watch it carefully).

7. When the pudding has cooled slightly, stir in the half-and-half. Serve lightly chilled or at room temperature, sprinkled with the toasted coconut.

Serves 10 to 12

ANGEL BERRY TRIFLE

The English reached perfection with this dish. Berry trifle is definitely worthy of several deep bows. This is best made in the summer when all the ripe berries are in season for the best flavor. It's a lovely dessert for a party since the cake can be prepared ahead and left to rest overnight before adding the final touches. I've made a light delicate angel food cake as the base for this trifle, but Orange Pound Cake (see Index) or a good store-bought pound cake would serve equally well.

ANGEL FOOD CAKE:
½ cup cake flour
¾ cup superfine sugar
6 large egg whites, at room temperature
½ teaspoon cream of tartar
⅛ teaspoon salt
1 teaspoon pure vanilla extract
¼ cup cream or other sweet sherry

TRIFLE CREAM:
2½ cups Basic Pastry Cream (page 550), chilled
1 cup crème fraîche

MIXED BERRY MASH:
6 cups fresh strawberries
3 cups fresh mixed berries, such as blueberries, raspberries, and/or blackberries
¾ cup granulated sugar

½ cup heavy (or whipping) cream
2 teaspoons confectioners' sugar
½ cup fresh mixed berries, for garnish

1. Preheat the oven to 300°F. Oil or butter the sides of a 10½ x 5½-inch sheet pan, then line the pan with waxed or parchment paper, letting the edges overhang slightly. Press the paper down into the corners.

2. Make the angel food cake: Sift the flour twice and set aside. Sift the sugar. Return half the sugar (6 tablespoons) to the measuring cup. Place the egg whites in a very clean bowl and beat at low speed with an electric mixer until foamy. Add the cream of tartar and salt and beat at medium speed until soft peaks form. Gradually increasing the speed of the mixer, slowly sprinkle in half the sugar 1 tablespoon at a time and beat after each addition, until the sugar is incorporated. Using a rubber spatula, fold in the remaining sugar 1 tablespoon at a time until incorporated. Add the flour, sifting a few tablespoons of it over the mixture at a time and gently folding it in. Fold in the vanilla.

3. Pour the batter into the prepared sheet pan and tilt so that the batter flows evenly into all corners. Bake until the center springs back when lightly touched, about 30 minutes. Cool on a wire rack. Leave uncovered overnight to dry out.

4. Invert the cake onto a clean surface and carefully peel off the waxed paper. Using a serrated knife, cut the cake into 1-inch cubes. Place the cubes in a large bowl, sprinkle with the sherry, and toss well.

5. Make the trifle cream: Whisk the basic pastry cream in a bowl until it is just smooth. Place the crème fraîche in another bowl and whisk until it holds soft peaks. Fold the crème fraîche into the pastry cream. Refrigerate covered until assembly time.

6. Make the mixed berry mash: Rinse, hull, and halve the strawberries. If they are very large, quarter them; if small, leave them whole. In a large saucepan, stir together the strawberries, blueberries if using, and sugar. Cook, stirring occasionally, over medium-high heat until the sugar dissolves, 2 to 3 minutes. Add delicate berries, such as raspberries or blackberries, stir gently, and cook another minute just until they soften but do not fall apart. Remove from the heat and drain the berries, reserving the syrup.

7. Assemble the trifle: Place half the cake cubes in the bottom of a 10-cup glass bowl (see Note). Spoon half the drained mixed berries over the top and drizzle with ½ cup of the berry syrup. Cover with half the trifle cream. Repeat this procedure once again. Refrigerate overnight or up to 24 hours.

8. Before serving, whip the heavy cream with the confectioners' sugar until it holds its shape. Spread a layer of the whipped cream over the top of the trifle or use a pastry bag to pipe a decorative border or rosettes. Garnish with fresh berries. Serve the remaining berry syrup in a small sauceboat alongside.

Serves 12

Note: If your glass bowl has slanted rather than straight sides, use less than half the ingredients for the first layer, and more than half for the second.

CRANACHAN

This dessert ended a wonderful pub lunch at The Horse Shoe Inn in Peebleshire, Scotland, along the river Tweed. Although different berries and other liqueurs could certainly stand in for the raspberries and Drambuie in this recipe, I chose to keep this distinctly Scottish creation intact. The toasted oats give the cream body, adding a crunchy texture. Frozen berries may be substituted if fresh are not available. Serve cranachan in small portions.

½ cup rolled oats
2 cups heavy (or whipping) cream
⅓ cup sugar
1 tablespoon Drambuie liqueur
½ pint fresh raspberries, set aside several berries, for garnish
Fresh mint sprigs, for garnish

1. Preheat the oven to 350°F.

2. Place the oats in a small baking pan and bake in the oven until lightly browned, about 15 minutes. Shake the pan once or twice during cooking. Set aside.

3. Place the cream in a medium-size bowl and beat with an electric mixer, gradually adding the sugar and Drambuie, until stiff. With a rubber spatula, fold in the toasted oats and the raspberries until well combined.

4. Scrape the mixture into a serving bowl, garnish the top with the reserved raspberries and the mint sprigs. Refrigerate 4 to 6 hours before serving.

Serves 6

CARIBBEAN COCONUT TART

When I was in Martinique, I enjoyed this perfect dessert at the end of a spicy tropical island dinner. With a scoop of Coconut Cream Ice Cream (see Index), what could be better?

8 tablespoons (1 stick) unsalted butter, cut in pieces
¼ cup granulated sugar
1½ teaspoons pure vanilla extract
1 cup all-purpose flour
⅛ teaspoon salt
2 large egg whites, at room temperature
1 cup confectioners' sugar, sifted
Finely grated zest of 1 lime
¼ teaspoon ground cinnamon
1 cup shredded coconut

1. Place the butter in a food processor and process a few seconds until creamy. Add the granulated sugar and process until the mixture is light and fluffy, about 20 seconds. Stop to scrape the sides of the bowl once or twice with a rubber spatula. Add ½ teaspoon of the vanilla. Combine the flour and salt and add it to the food processor. Process until the dough comes together around the sides of the bowl, scrape down once, and process for a few more seconds.

2. With lightly floured hands, press the dough evenly over the bottom and up the sides of a 9-inch tart pan with a removable bottom. Press a finger around the bottom edge of the tart to make sure that the dough is not too thick.

3. Trim any excess dough draping over the top of the tart pan with a knife. Lightly press the dough around the inside of the rim with your thumb so that it extends about ⅛ inch above the rim of the pan. Prick the bottom of the dough all over with a fork. Cover with plastic wrap and chill the dough in the freezer for 30 minutes or overnight.

4. Preheat the oven to 375°F.

5. Bake the partially or fully frozen tart shell until fully baked and golden brown, about 25 minutes. Cool the tart shell on a wire rack. Reduce the oven temperature to 350°F.

6. In a bowl, beat the egg whites with an electric mixer until they begin to hold soft peaks. Gradually add the confectioners' sugar and continue beating until the whites are stiff. Mix in the remaining 1 teaspoon vanilla extract, the lime zest, and cinnamon, then fold in half the coconut.

7. Fill the tart shell with the egg white mixture. Sprinkle the remaining ½ cup coconut evenly over the top. Bake for 25 minutes. Cool on a wire rack. The tart is delicious served slightly warm.

Makes one 9-inch tart, serves 8 to 10

SUMMER PLUM TART

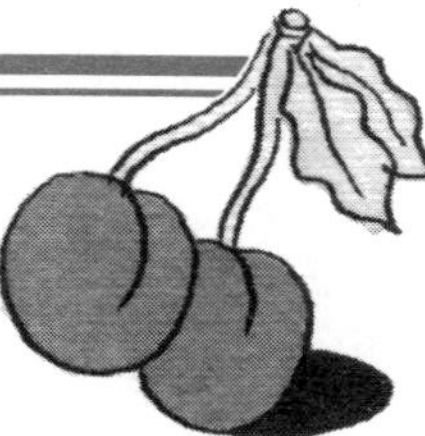

When ripe red plums are in season, it's time to make some fruit tarts. This is a divine summer dessert. Serve with Banana Rum Ice Cream (see Index) on top to enhance with the flavors of the Caribbean.

8 tablespoons (1 stick) unsalted butter, cut into pieces
¼ cup plus 3 tablespoons sugar
½ teaspoon pure vanilla extract
1 cup all-purpose flour
⅛ teaspoon salt
1½ pounds red plums, pitted and quartered
½ teaspoon ground cinnamon
¼ cup red currant jelly, melted

1. Place the butter in a food processor and process a few seconds until creamy. Add ¼ cup sugar and process until the mixture is light and fluffy, about 20 seconds, stopping to scrape the sides of the bowl once or twice. Add the vanilla. Combine the flour and salt and add it to the food processor. Process until the dough comes together around the sides of the bowl, scrape the sides of the bowl, and process for a few more seconds.

2. With lightly floured hands, press the dough evenly over the bottom and up the sides of a 9-inch tart pan with a removable bottom. (Press around the bottom edge of the tart with your finger, making sure that the dough is not too thick.)

3. Trim any excess dough at the top of the tart pan with a knife. Lightly press the dough around the inside of the rim with your thumb so that it extends about ⅛ inch above the pan. Prick the bottom of the dough all over with a fork. Chill the dough in the freezer at least 30 minutes or overnight.

4. Place the quartered plums in a bowl with the remaining 3 tablespoons sugar and the cinnamon. Mix well and set aside.

5. Preheat the oven to 375°F.

6. Bake the partially or fully frozen tart shell until fully baked and golden brown, 25 minutes. Cool the tart shell on a wire rack. Reduce the oven temperature to 350°F.

7. Brush the inside of the baked tart shell all over with half the red currant jelly. Arrange the plums in the tart shell, skin side up, starting at the outside rim and working toward the center. The plums should overlap slightly. Brush the plums all over with the remaining jelly.

8. Place the tart on a baking sheet. Cover the rim of the tart shell with aluminum foil to prevent the crust from overbrowning. Bake the tart until the plums are tender, about 30 minutes longer. Cool slightly on a wire rack and serve slightly warm.

Serves 8

LINZER TART

This luscious tart, a traditional favorite throughout the coffeehouses all over Central Europe, hails from the Austrian town of Linz.

Although the tart is traditionally made with almonds, I've substituted hazelnuts, which marry beautifully with the raspberry jam filling. A touch of cocoa powder adds rich color and flavor to the wonderful shortbread crust. Once it's baked, the raspberry jam glistens like antique garnets.

2 cups all-purpose flour
1 teaspoon baking powder
1 teaspoon ground cinnamon
½ teaspoon salt
1 tablespoon unsweetened cocoa powder
1 cup (2 sticks) unsalted butter, at room temperature
¾ cup sugar
1¼ cup ground toasted hazelnuts (see Note)
1 large egg
1 teaspoon pure vanilla extract
1 cup raspberry jam

1. In a medium-size bowl, whisk together the flour, baking powder, cinnamon, salt, and cocoa powder. Set aside.

2. In a large mixing bowl, cream the butter and sugar until light and fluffy with an electric mixer. Add the hazelnuts and mix to combine. Beat in the egg and vanilla. Scrape down the sides of the bowl with a rubber spatula and mix again briefly.

3. With the mixer on low speed, add the dry ingredients in 3 parts, scraping down the sides of the bowl after each addition. When the flour mixture is completely incorporated, form the dough into a ball and cover in plastic wrap. Refrigerate at least 4 hours or overnight.

4. Let the chilled dough sit at room temperature until soft and pliable. Form the dough into a log and cut into thirds. Pat one-third of the dough into the bottom of an ungreased 10-inch springform or tart pan with a removable bottom. Pat the dough out ¼ inch thick to within ½ inch of the side of the pan.

5. Using another third of the dough, roll about twenty-eight 1-inch balls between the floured palms of your hands. Place these balls around the edge of the tart pan. It will take about 28 to go around.

6. For the lattice top, form the remainder of the dough into a rectangle and roll it between 2 sheets of waxed paper to form a rectangle that is approximately 8 inches long, 4 inches wide, and ¼ inch thick. Chill the tart mold and the rolled dough (still in its waxed paper) in the refrigerator until firm, about 1 hour.

7. Preheat the oven to 350°F.

8. Spread the jam evenly into the center of the tart. Remove 1 sheet of the waxed paper from the chilled dough. Use a pizza or pastry cutter to cut six ½-inch-wide strips of dough. Peel off the waxed paper and place 3 of the strips over the jam in a lengthwise direction, spacing them out evenly and allowing any extra dough to drape over the sides. Place the other 3 strips on top in a crosswise direction to create a lattice pattern. Don't attempt to weave the strips. Trim the strips just at the edges so that they neatly meet the balls around the edge.

9. Bake the tart until the jam bubbles and the dough begins to color, 60 to 70 minutes. Cool for 15 minutes on a wire rack. Remove the sides of the tart pan and cool completely.

Makes one 10-inch tart, serves 8 to 10

Note: To toast hazelnuts, preheat the oven to 350°F. Place the nuts in a single layer on a baking sheet and bake until lightly colored and the skins begin to blister, about 15 minutes. Wrap the nuts in a kitchen towel and rub between the palms of your hands to remove the outer skins. Grind the nuts in a food processor by pulsing the machine on and off to obtain a medium grind. Do not overprocess. One cup whole nuts will yield about 1¼ cups ground nuts.

TARTE TATIN

The most delicious of all apple pies, this rustic French work of art is cooked upside down in a skillet, with the apples under a lid of pastry. Then it is inverted and served with the pastry underneath gorgeous caramelized, buttery apples. If you're visiting Paris, you certainly can have this marvel in any number of restaurants, but it is the specialty of the house at the beautiful art nouveau Maxim's. To cut the sweetness, this is delicious served with dollops of whipped cream or crème fraîche.

PASTRY:
1¼ cups all-purpose flour
2 teaspoons sugar
¼ teaspoon salt
6 tablespoons (¾ stick) unsalted butter, chilled and cut into small pieces
¼ cup ice water

APPLES:
1½ to 2 pounds Granny Smith apples (about 4)
Juice of 1 lemon
4 tablespoons (½ stick) unsalted butter
⅔ cup sugar

1. For the pastry, place the flour, sugar, and salt in a food processor and pulse on and off to mix. Add the butter and pulse the machine on and off 15 to 20 times until the butter is the size of peas. Remove the lid and pour the ice water over the mixture. Pulse the machine until the dough resembles curds and holds together when gathered. Remove the dough from the machine and form it into a disk. Place the disk between 2 sheets of waxed paper and roll it into a 10-inch circle, flipping the dough over once or twice to obtain an even thickness. Refrigerate for at least 1 hour.

2. Preheat the oven to 400°F.

3. For the apples, core, peel, and halve the apples. Place them in a bowl and toss with the lemon juice. Set aside.

4. Melt the butter in a 9-inch ovenproof skillet. Add the sugar and cook over medium heat, stirring constantly, until the mixture just reaches a golden caramel color. Remove the skillet from the heat.

5. Cut each apple half into 4 wedges. Arrange the slices, rounded side down, in concentric circles, starting from the outside of the skillet. Be careful not to touch the hot sugar mixture, with your fingers. Stack more apple slices to fill in all the gaps. You may have to trim the ends off some slices to fit in the center. Dice the remaining apples and fill in the center.

6. Remove the dough from the refrigerator, peel away the waxed paper, and set the dough over the apples in the skillet. Using scissors, trim any overhanging dough. When the pastry softens a bit, lightly tuck the edges down between the apples and the skillet.

7. Bake until the crust is golden brown, about 50 minutes. Remove from the oven and cool on a rack for 5 minutes.

8. Place a serving dish over the skillet and quickly invert the tart onto the dish. Serve immediately.

Serves 8

VELVETY TARTE AU CITRON

I don't remember how I first came to eat lunch at Cartet, a tiny Paris bistro in the 11th arrondissement, but I do know that once I ate there, I never forgot it. Madame Cartet appeared from the kitchen in her apron carrying a large pot brimming with duck and fresh figs that had stewed all morning. This exquisite dish—which she proudly served up right at the table—followed a grand feast of charcuterie, salads, and fresh foie gras. I'm not quite sure which magnificence was her signature dish but the golden *tarte au citron* was high on my list. When I began working on a lemon tart for this book, I wanted all the crisp tartness for a filling that she delivered, and I felt that a soft-textured buttery sugar crust would be the perfect complement. When making the dough, it is essential to press it to an even thickness throughout the tart pan so that it bakes evenly. The tangy, buttery lemon curd is not like Madame Cartet's original but is totally delicious. I think you'll find this dessert a perfect ending to a lusty, full-flavored meal.

8 tablespoons (1 stick) unsalted butter, cut into pieces
¾ cup sugar
½ teaspoon pure vanilla extract
1 cup all-purpose flour
⅛ teaspoon salt
⅔ cup fresh lemon juice, strained
2 tablespoons heavy (or whipping) cream
3 large eggs
2 large egg yolks

1. Place the butter in a food processor and process a few seconds until creamy. Add ¼ cup of the sugar and process until the mixture is light and fluffy, about 20 seconds, stopping to scrape the sides of the bowl once or twice. Add the vanilla. Combine the flour and salt and add it to the food processor. Process until the dough comes together around the sides of the bowl, scrape the sides of the bowl, and process for a few seconds.

2. With lightly floured hands, press the dough evenly over the bottom and up the sides of a 9-inch tart pan with a removable bottom. (Press around the bottom edge of the tart with your finger, making sure that the dough is not too thick.)

3. Trim any excess dough at the top of the tart pan with a knife. Lightly press the dough around the inside of the rim with your thumb so that it extends about ⅛ inch above the pan. Prick the bottom of the dough all over with a fork. Chill the dough in the freezer at least 30 minutes or overnight.

4. Preheat the oven to 375°F.

5. Bake the partially or fully frozen tart shell until fully baked and golden brown, about 25 minutes. Cool the tart shell on a wire rack. Leave the oven on.

6. Whisk the remaining ½ cup sugar and the lemon juice together in a bowl. Gradually whisk in the heavy cream, then the eggs and the egg yolks. Combine thoroughly. Pour the mixture into a saucepan and cook over medium heat, whisking constantly until the filling thickens and the whisk leaves a trail, about 4 minutes.

7. Strain the filling into a bowl, then pour it into the baked tart shell. Bake for 4 minutes.

8. Cool thoroughly on a rack and serve at room temperature. Before serving, carefully remove the sides and bottom of the pan and carefully slide the tart onto a decorative plate.

Makes one 9-inch tart, serves 8 to 10

CHOCOLATE PECAN CAKE

A thin slice of this delicious cake is all that is needed to satisfy any chocolate lover's craving. Made with the slightest amount of flour, the addition of ground pecans gives the cake the right texture while subtly enhancing the flavor. Once the cake goes in the oven, it is important not to overbake it so that it retains a fudgy texture. Remove the cake from the oven as soon as it is nearly firm. Finishing the cake off with an easy-to-make glaze adds just the right elegance. Pecan halves, candied violets, or rose petals placed decoratively around the top edge of the cake lends a perfect touch. This cake gets even better and slightly denser one day after it's baked.

CAKE:
1½ cups pecan halves
1 cup (2 sticks) unsalted butter
12 ounces best-quality bittersweet chocolate, broken into small bits
¼ cup milk
6 large eggs, separated
1 cup confectioners' sugar
½ cup all-purpose flour, sifted
Pinch of salt

CHOCOLATE GLAZE:
6 ounces best-quality bittersweet chocolate, broken into small bits
¼ cup heavy (or whipping) cream
2 tablespoons unsalted butter

1. Preheat the oven to 350°F. Butter a 9½-inch springform pan. Line the bottom of the pan with a round of waxed or parchment paper. Butter the paper and dust the pan lightly with flour, tapping out any excess.

2. Place the pecans in a food processor. Pulse the machine on and off until the pecans resemble coarse meal. Measure the ground pecans; the yield should be 1¼ cups. Set aside.

3. Place the butter, chocolate, and milk in a heavy small saucepan over very low heat to melt the chocolate. Stir occasionally until the mixture is completely smooth. Set aside.

4. In a large bowl, beat the egg yolks and confectioners' sugar together with an electric mixer until thick and pale yellow. Slowly add the melted chocolate mixture to the eggs and beat until well combined. Add the flour and the reserved pecans and mix to combine.

5. In another large bowl, beat the egg whites with a pinch of salt until they hold soft peaks. Stir one-third of the egg whites into the chocolate mixture until completely combined. Gently fold in the remaining egg whites with a rubber spatula until just combined.

6. Scrape the batter into the prepared pan and bake in the center of the oven until the cake is just set and a toothpick inserted in the center comes out nearly clean but with some crumbs attached, 35 to 40 minutes. The center of the cake should not be completely dry. Place the cake on a wire rack to cool completely. When cool, remove the cake from the pan, peel off the paper, and carefully place it on a serving plate.

7. To make the chocolate glaze, place the chocolate, cream, and butter in a heavy small saucepan over very low heat to melt the chocolate. Stir occasionally until the mixture is completely smooth. Cool just slightly.

8. Pour the glaze over the cake and use an icing spatula to smooth it gently across the top and down the sides. Let rest for at least 2 hours before serving. If serving the next day, cover loosely and refrigerate overnight. Bring to room temperature before serving.

Serves 10 to 12

BERTA'S CARROT CAKE CARIBE

After years of making and loving Berta's Carrot Cake, and including it in all my books, I figured there was no way I could leave it out of this one without slighting my darling mother. Here it appears as a luscious two-layer cake slathered with a creamy pineapple icing and decorated with toasted coconut, evoking the best of the Caribbean.

CAKE:
2 cups all-purpose flour
2 cups granulated sugar
2 teaspoons baking soda
2 teaspoons ground cinnamon
1 cup corn oil
3 large eggs, lightly beaten
2 teaspoons pure vanilla extract
1⅓ cups puréed cooked carrots
1 cup chopped walnuts
1 cup shredded coconut
¾ cup drained canned crushed pineapple

CARIBBEAN CREAM CHEESE ICING:
8 ounces cream cheese, at room temperature
4 tablespoons (½ stick) unsalted butter, at room temperature
3 cups confectioners' sugar
1 teaspoon pure vanilla extract
1 tablespoon fresh lemon juice
¼ cup drained canned crushed pineapple, finely chopped

½ cup shredded coconut, toasted (page 514), for garnish

1. Preheat the oven to 350°F. Lightly butter two 9-inch round cake pans. Line the bottoms of the pans with rounds of waxed paper and butter the paper.

2. To make the cake, sift the flour, sugar, baking soda, and cinnamon together in a large mixing bowl. Add the oil, eggs, and vanilla; beat well. Fold in the carrots, walnuts, coconut, and pineapple.

3. Divide the batter evenly between the prepared pans. Place on the middle rack of the oven and bake until the edges have pulled away from the sides of the pan and a toothpick inserted in the center comes out clean, about 1 hour.

4. Cool the layers in the pans for 10 minutes. Invert the pans onto a wire rack, carefully remove the waxed paper, and cool completely.

5. Meanwhile make the icing: cream the cream cheese and butter together in a mixing bowl with an electric mixer.

6. Slowly sift in the confectioners' sugar and continue beating until fully incorporated (there should be no lumps). Stir in the vanilla, lemon juice, and pineapple.

7. Place a cake layer on a pretty serving plate and ice the surface. Top with the remaining cake layer and ice the top and sides. Pat the toasted coconut gently around the sides of the cake.

Serves 12

CHEVRE CHEESECAKE

When I think of cheesecake, I think heavy and sweet, but a tart chèvre from France provides just the right bite to contrast with any sweetness in this recipe. Instead of being heavy, you'll find this cake light as a feather. Because of its tartness, it is lovely served with Quince Spoon Sweet or Cherry Compote (see Index) or lightly sweetened raspberries.

1 teaspoon unsalted buttter, for greasing pan
1 teaspoon all-purpose flour, for dusting pan
22 ounces soft chèvre without ash, such as Montrachet, at room temperature
1¼ cups granulated sugar
5 eggs, at room temperature, lightly beaten
1 cup sour cream
2 tablespoons confectioners' sugar

1. Preheat the oven to 325°F. Lightly butter a 7-inch springform pan and dust with the flour, shaking out the excess.

2. Place the chèvre and granulated sugar in a food processor and process until completely smooth, stopping occasionally to scrape down the sides of the bowl.

3. With the machine running, add the eggs through the feed tube; process until completely smooth, stopping occasionally to scrape the sides of the bowl.

4. Pour the mixture into the prepared pan and set the pan into a larger pan, such as a small roasting pan or a 10-inch cake pan. Fill the larger pan with warm water to reach halfway up the cheesecake pan. Place in the oven and bake until the cake is set and slightly domed in the center, about 1½ hours. Remove from the oven; leave the oven on. Remove the cake from the water bath and cool on a rack for 10 minutes.

5. Meanwhile combine the sour cream and confectioners' sugar in a bowl. Spread this mixture over the top of the baked cheesecake and return to the oven for 5 minutes. Cool the cake for 30 minutes on a rack, then refrigerate overnight in the pan.

6. The following day, slide a small knife around the edge of the cake to loosen it and remove the sides of the springform pan.

Makes one 7-inch cake, serves 10 to 12

ORANGE POUND CAKE

Moist and delectable, this cake is lovely served in small pieces with an ice cream sundae or used as a base for Angel Berry Trifle (see Index) laden with summer berries and sweet cream.

12 tablespoons (1½ sticks) unsalted butter, at room temperature
1¼ cups sugar
3 large eggs
¼ cup sour cream
1 teaspoon pure vanilla extract
1 tablespoon finely grated orange zest
6 tablespoons fresh orange juice
1½ cups all-purpose flour
1 teaspoon baking powder
Pinch of salt

1. Preheat the oven to 350°F. Butter a 9 x 4 x 2½-inch loaf pan. Line the bottom with a piece of parchment or waxed paper and butter the paper. Lightly dust the pan with flour, shaking out the excess.

2. In a mixing bowl, cream the butter and ¾ cup of the sugar with an electric mixer. Add the eggs one at a time, mixing well after each addition. Add the sour cream, vanilla, orange zest, and 2 tablespoons of the orange juice; mix well.

3. Sift the flour, baking powder, and salt over the batter and fold it in with a rubber spatula until just incorporated.

4. Spread the batter in the prepared pan. Bake until a toothpick inserted into the center of the cake comes out clean, about 40 minutes.

5. While the cake is baking, prepare the orange glaze: Place the remaining ½ cup sugar and remaining 4 tablespoons orange juice in a small saucepan. Cook the syrup over medium heat until the sugar is dissolved, then cook 1 minute longer. Remove the pan from the heat and set aside.

6. When the cake is finished, let it cool in the pan on a wire rack for 5 minutes. Then remove it from the pan, peel off the paper, and return it to the rack to cool completely. Brush the glaze onto the surface of the cake while it is warm.

Serves 8 to 10

JAMAICAN GINGERBREAD

Not too sweet, this gingerbread is excellent served for dessert with ice creams and fruit salads. All the flavors are reminiscent of those calypso Caribbean nights. On cooler nights, this gingerbread is best served warm with a scoop of Vanilla Bean Ice Cream or Banana Rum Ice Cream (see Index) right on top. Served warm, it makes an excellent accompaniment to savory dishes as well. Try gingerbread alongside Caribbean Fish Pot and Le Colibri Porc Colombo (see Index).

8 tablespoons (1 stick) unsalted butter, at room temperature
½ cup molasses
¼ cup honey
½ cup (packed) dark or light brown sugar
3 large eggs
½ cup sour cream
1 tablespoon finely grated lemon zest
1 teaspoon pure vanilla extract
2 cups all-purpose flour
1 teaspoon baking soda
½ teaspoon salt
1½ teaspoons ground ginger
1 teaspoon ground cinnamon
½ teaspoon ground allspice
¼ teaspoon ground cloves
¼ teaspoon ground nutmeg

1. Preheat the oven to 350°F. Lightly butter a 9 x 4 x 2½-inch loaf pan. Line the bottom with a piece of parchment or waxed paper and butter the paper. Lightly dust the pan with flour, shaking out the excess.

2. In a mixing bowl, cream the butter, molasses, honey, and brown sugar with an electric mixer until smooth. Add the eggs one at a time, mixing well after each addition. Add the sour cream, lemon zest, and vanilla extract and beat to combine.

3. Sift the flour, baking soda, salt, and spices together and fold into the batter with a rubber spatula.

4. Spread the batter in the prepared pan. Bake until a toothpick inserted into the center comes out clean, 50 to 55 minutes. Cool the gingerbread in the pan on a wire rack for 15 minutes. Remove from the pan and peel off the paper. Cool completely if not serving immediately.

Serves 8 to 10

HAVANA JELLY-ROLL CAKE

When I started planning the desserts for this book, I never imagined I'd be making a jelly roll, but after having strawberry ice cream served with a generous slice of jelly roll alongside at La Heladeria Coppelia in Havana, I decided that a delicious homemade version was a must. This cake stays fresh for a few days when well covered, and it is worth any effort it entails. It truly is a special treat. I used raspberry preserves in this recipe, but strawberry preserves would be equally delicious. Work carefully when removing the cake from the pan. A thin slice is perfect served at teatime with a cup of your favorite brew, steaming hot or iced.

1½ tablespoons unsalted butter, cut into small pieces
¼ cup milk
½ teaspoon pure vanilla extract
⅔ cup cake flour, sifted
¾ teaspoon baking powder
⅛ teaspoon salt
3 large eggs
2 large egg yolks
⅔ cup sugar
⅔ cup raspberry preserves

1. Preheat the oven to 350°F. Grease the sides of a 15½ x 10½-inch jelly-roll pan with butter, then grease an X from corner to corner in the pan. Line the pan with a sheet of parchment or waxed paper so that it overhangs the pan slightly.

2. In a small saucepan, combine the butter, milk, and vanilla. Scald the mixture over medium-low heat but do not allow it to boil. Set aside.

3. Sift together the flour, baking powder, and salt.

4. In a medium-size heatproof bowl, whisk together the eggs, egg yolks, and sugar. Hold the bowl over a very low flame and whisk the eggs constantly until they are lukewarm. Remove from the heat and, using an electric mixer, beat until the mixture is light in color and as thick as whipped cream, 5 to 6 minutes. Reheat the milk mixture over low heat.

5. Sift one-third of the flour mixture over the whipped eggs and gently fold together, using a large rubber spatula. Fold in the remaining flour mixture in two additions. Add the hot milk in a slow stream as you continue folding. Fold to incorporate all the liquid. Pour the batter into the prepared pan and tilt the pan to evenly distribute it.

6. Bake the cake until the center springs back when lightly touched, about 20 minutes. Cool completely on a wire rack. Carefully remove the cake from the pan, flip it over, and peel off the paper. Reverse it onto a piece of aluminum foil so that the browned top of the cake faces up. Spread the preserves evenly over the surface. Roll the cake up as tightly as possible and then enclose it in the foil. Refrigerate, seam side down, for at least 3 hours. To serve, using a sharp serrated knife, trim off the ends, then cut into 1-inch-thick slices.

Serves 12

PINEAPPLE-RUM UPSIDE-DOWN CAKE

The Caribbean islands overflow with a cornucopia of extraordinary tropical fruits. There, pineapples ripen on their spiky leaves surrounded by fields thick with sugarcane. That feeling of abundance is what I was looking for when I created this moist upside-down cake. When left to sit, the pineapple's natural juices flavor the cake, and it becomes even more delicious. Serve warm with homemade tropical ice cream.

6 tablespoons (¾ stick) unsalted butter, plus 1 cup (2 sticks), at room temperature
½ cup (packed) light brown sugar
½ cup dark rum
6 slices (¼ inch thick) fresh pineapple, halved crosswise
1 cup granulated sugar
2 large eggs
2 teaspoons pure vanilla extract
2 cups all-purpose flour
1½ teaspoons baking powder
1 teaspoon salt
Vanilla Bean or Banana Rum Ice Cream (page 556 or 553)

1. Preheat the oven to 350°F.

2. Melt 6 tablespoons butter with the brown sugar and ¼ cup of the rum in a 13 x 9 x 2-inch flameproof baking dish on top of the stove over low heat. Arrange the pineapple slices decoratively over the melted butter mixture and set aside.

3. In a mixing bowl, cream the remaining 1 cup butter with the granulated sugar with an electric mixer. Add the eggs one at a time, mixing well after each addition. Then, stir in the vanilla.

4. Combine the flour, baking powder, and salt in a small bowl. Add to the batter, a bit at a time, mixing well after each addition. Add the remaining ¼ cup of rum and stir well.

5. Spread the batter evenly over the pineapple slices and smooth it with a spatula. Bake until a toothpick inserted in the center of the cake comes out clean, about 35 minutes.

6. Let the cake cool for 5 minutes, then invert it onto a pretty serving plate. Serve warm or at room temperature with a scoop or two of ice cream.

Serves 10 to 12

INDONESIAN RIBBON CAKE

I first discovered this cake in an Indonesian restaurant in Amsterdam many years ago. A tiny wedge was served with coffee after a *rijsttafel*. One of the things I always look forward to when returning to Amsterdam is a taste of this cake. Although I've never been able to discern its exact origins, several of the spices used are native to Indonesia's Moluccan Islands—the famous Spice Islands—which were an important source for nutmeg and cloves for centuries. A lavish array of spices are an indispensable part of Indonesian cooking and this cake, laced with cinnamon, nutmeg, cardamom, ginger, and cloves, pays tribute to that spice tradition. Although time-consuming to prepare, the different layers create a beautiful effect.

1 cup (2 sticks) unsalted butter, at room temperature
1 cup (packed) light brown sugar
10 large eggs, at room temperature, separated
Pinch of salt
1 cup all-purpose flour, sifted
1 tablespoon ground cinnamon
1 teaspoon ground nutmeg
1 teaspoon ground cardamom
1 teaspoon ground ginger
½ teaspoon ground cloves
½ cup (1 stick) unsalted butter, melted
2 tablespoons confectioners' sugar

1. Preheat the oven to 300°F. Butter a 9-inch round cake pan. Line the bottom with a round of waxed paper and butter the paper.

2. In a mixing bowl, cream the softened butter and sugar with an electric mixer. Add the egg yolks and mix well. Set aside.

3. In another bowl, beat the egg whites and salt until they are firm but not stiff.

4. Stir one-third of the egg whites into the yolk mixture until combined. Fold in the remaining whites using a rubber spatula. Fold in the flour.

5. Scrape half the batter into another bowl. Add the ground spices to one of the bowls of batter and stir well.

6. Spread ½ cup of the spiced batter over the bottom of the prepared cake pan, using a rubber spatula to smooth it neatly.

7. Bake until the surface is set enough to be brushed lightly with a pastry brush, about 10 minutes. Remove from the oven and lightly brush the entire surface with melted butter. Spread ½ cup of the plain batter over the top and bake until set, about 10 minutes. Remove from the oven, brush with butter, and top with ½ cup of the spiced batter. Bake 10 minutes. Repeat this process until all the batter is used. You'll have about 12 layers in all.

8. Cool the cake in the pan on a wire rack for about 15 minutes, then invert the cake onto the rack to cool completely. Remove the waxed paper.

9. Sift confectioners' sugar over the top of the cake and serve in very thin slices.

Serves 12

A TASTE OF THE WORLD

Southeast Asian Fruit Basket

BANANAS
CANTALOUPES
COCONUTS
DURIANS
JACKFRUITS
KIWIS
LEMONS
LIMES
LYCHEES
MANGOES
ORANGES
PALMYRA FRUITS
PAPAYAS
PINEAPPLES
POMELOS
RAMBUTANS
ROSE APPLES
SOURSOPS
STARFRUITS
WATERMELONS

SACHERTORTE

A visit to Vienna would not be complete without a visit to the Sacher Hotel to sample the famous Sachertorte, perhaps one of the best known cakes in the world, created in 1832 by Franz Sacher. I sat at a tiny marble table in the red velvet-draped tearoom facing Vienna's grand Opera House. The luscious slice of torte, glistening with apricot preserves under a shiny chocolate glaze, arrived on a silver tray with a Sacher-Hotel-emblazoned paper napkin folded into a triangle tucked underneath the plate. The smallest dessert fork rested on the side of the plate and was accompanied by a bowl of whipped cream, a cup of coffee, and a tiny glass of water with a small spoon balanced atop, obviously a long-standing ritual. The fork, however, was barely large enough to hold the delicious mouthfuls.

SOUVENIR TO SAVOR

Condiments with Coffee

After dinner at the Taj View Hotel in Agra, India, coffee was served with great flair. The most wonderful four-tiered brass tray holding every little thing you might want to accompany your cup was brought to the table along with the coffee. The top tier held almonds and golden raisins. The second tier, divided into four sections, held cashews, large rough pieces of crystallized sugar, whole cloves, and cardamom seeds to flavor your coffee. The third tier, covered with paper lace, held an assortment of chocolate and butter cookies dusted with confectioners' sugar. The fourth and largest tier on the bottom held clementines, sweet green grapes, and small ripe bananas. With a presentation such as this, a formal dessert is hardly necessary.

CAKE:

6 ounces best-quality bittersweet chocolate, coarsely chopped
12 tablespoons (1½ sticks) unsalted butter, at room temperature
⅔ cup superfine sugar
5 large egg yolks, at room temperature
1 teaspoon pure vanilla extract
¾ cup all-purpose flour, sifted
6 large egg whites
⅛ teaspoon salt
½ cup apricot preserves

CHOCOLATE GLAZE:

6 ounces best-quality bittersweet chocolate, finely chopped
1 tablespoon unsalted butter, cut into small pieces
2 tablespoons granulated sugar
¼ cup water

1. Preheat the oven to 350°F. Butter and flour an 8-inch springform pan.

2. Prepare the cake: Warm the chocolate in the top of a double boiler over simmering water until almost melted. Remove from the heat and stir to melt completely. Be sure that no water gets into the chocolate. Set aside.

3. In a large mixing bowl, cream the butter

and half the sugar until light and fluffy with an electric mixer. Add the egg yolks one at a time, beating well after each addition and scraping the sides of the bowl with a rubber spatula. Add the melted chocolate and vanilla and mix on low speed. Sprinkle in the flour and mix on low speed until just incorporated. Set aside in a warm, draft-free place.

4. In a very clean bowl, beat the egg whites on medium speed until foamy. Add the salt and continue to beat until they hold soft peaks. Increase the speed to high and add the remaining sugar 1 tablespoon at a time, beating for 10 seconds after each addition. When all the sugar has been incorporated, beat an additional 30 seconds on high speed until the whites are stiff and glossy.

5. With a rubber spatula, stir one-quarter of the egg whites into the chocolate mixture until combined. Fold in the remaining whites in 3 additions.

6. Pour the batter into the prepared pan. Bake until a toothpick inserted into the center comes out clean, about 50 minutes. Cool the cake on a wire rack for 20 minutes, then remove the sides of the pan. Invert the cake onto the rack and remove the pan bottom. Cool completely.

7. Using a serrated knife, slice the cake horizontally in half and remove the top half. Spread the bottom half with ⅓ cup of the apricot preserves. Replace the top of the cake. Heat the remaining apricot preserves in a small pan and then press through a small strainer. Use a pastry brush to brush the top and sides of the cake with the warm jam.

8. Make the chocolate glaze: Place the chocolate and butter in a small bowl. Combine the sugar and water in a small pot and bring to a boil. Add the hot sugar syrup to the chocolate and whisk until all the chocolate has melted. Use a metal icing spatula to smooth the glaze over the top and sides of the cake.

Makes one 8-inch cake, serves 8 to 10

GALATOBOUREKO

When my friend Wende Sasse married Aristedes Kambanis, Greek dishes became a delicious part of their dinner parties. Wende pulled out all the stops on New Year's Eve 1991. As the grand finale to dinner, she served this custard-laden phyllo confection. If you lightly score the top layer of phyllo before baking, serving the lush portions is much easier.

CUSTARD AND PASTRY:
2 quarts whole milk
1½ cups granulated sugar
1 cup (2 sticks) unsalted butter
1 cup Cream of Wheat cereal
10 large eggs
1 tablespoon pure vanilla extract
16 sheets phyllo pastry (see Note)

SYRUP:
1½ cups water
2 cups granulated sugar
¼ cup Grand Marnier liqueur
1 cinnamon stick (3 inches long)

1 tablespoon confectioners' sugar, for garnish
½ teaspoon ground cinnamon, for garnish

1. Preheat the oven to 350°F.

2. For the custard, scald the milk in a large heavy pot over low heat. Add the sugar and stir until dissolved. Add ½ cup of the butter and the Cream of Wheat. Increase the heat to medium and cook, whisking constantly, until thick, 10 to 12 minutes. Remove the mixture from the heat and cool slightly.

3. In a bowl, beat the eggs until fluffy. Add the vanilla. Whisking constantly, gradually mix some of the hot cereal mixture into the eggs. Then, whisking constantly, gradually add the egg mixture to the remaining cereal mixture. Set aside.

4. Melt the remaining ½ cup butter in a small saucepan over low heat. Use a pastry brush to lightly coat an 18 x 12-inch baking dish or pan with melted butter.

5. Remove the phyllo pastry from the box and lay the sheets on a dish towel. Cover the pastry with a sheet of waxed paper and a slightly dampened dish towel.

6. Place 8 sheets of phyllo pastry in the bottom of the baking dish, brushing each sheet first with melted butter. Pour the custard evenly over the phyllo. Top with 8 more sheets of phyllo, brushing each sheet with melted butter.

7. Score the top layers of phyllo into 24 squares. Bake for 1 hour.

8. For the syrup, combine the water, sugar, Grand Marnier, and cinnamon stick in a saucepan. Bring to a boil, then reduce the heat and simmer for 5 minutes. Cool slightly, remove the cinnamon stick, and pour the syrup evenly over the hot pastry. Place the confectioners' sugar and cinnamon in a fine strainer and dust the top of the pastry, tapping lightly on the side of the strainer. Let rest for at least 1 hour. Cut into squares to serve.

Serves 24

Note: Phyllo dough is readily available frozen in 1-pound boxes. Follow the package directions for thawing the dough.

PROFITEROLES

For years I have thought of profiteroles as the most luxuriant, outrageous, and festive dessert, and with good reason. Just look at what they're made from: a light textured choux pastry, a well set but not stiff pastry cream, great chocolate sauce, and perfectly whipped sweet cream. There are a few variations and the puffs are lovely filled, just before serving, with vanilla or strawberry ice cream, if you would rather not make a pastry cream. They can be served one, two, or three on a plate or all piled dramatically in a tall decorative mound (which is how I like mine) with chocolate sauce drizzled over the top and dolloped with whipped cream.

CHOUX PUFFS:
1 cup water
6 tablespoons (¾ stick) unsalted butter
¼ teaspoon salt
1 teaspoon sugar
1 cup all-purpose flour, sifted
4 to 4½ large eggs

2½ cups Basic Pastry Cream (recipe follows)
1 cup Chocolate Sauce (recipe follows), warmed
Whipped cream, for garnish (optional)

1. Preheat the oven to 400°F. Butter a baking sheet or line it with waxed or parchment paper.

2. For the choux puffs, place the water, butter, salt, and sugar in a heavy medium-size saucepan. Bring to a boil and, stirring with a wooden spoon, add the sifted flour all at once. Stir the paste until it pulls away from the sides of the pan in a mass. Reduce the heat and continue to cook 1 minute longer, stirring and mashing the mixture with the back of the spoon. Remove the pan from heat and transfer the mixture to a bowl. Let sit for about 2 minutes, stirring occasionally, to cool slightly.

3. In a small bowl, beat each of the 4 eggs briefly before adding it to the warm paste. Add the eggs one at a time to the warm paste, beating well with a wooden spoon after each addition. The paste should be soft but still able to hold a peak. If the mixture can take a little more egg, break the fifth one into a small bowl and add only as much as needed.

4. Using two soup spoons, heap 18 mounds, about 1¾ inches wide, 1 inch high, and about 1½ inches apart onto the prepared baking sheet. Use a slightly wet finger to smooth down the peaks.

5. Bake until puffed, set, and lightly colored, about 25 minutes. Remove from the oven and prick each puff with a sharp knife along the crack. Return the puffs to the oven until golden brown, about 10 minutes more. At the end of the baking time, if there are little beads of water on the outside of the puffs, turn the oven off and let them stay in for another few minutes until they are dry. (They are best used within a few hours but may be made ahead and frozen; see Note.)

6. If filling with pastry cream, assemble the puffs within a few hours of serving so that they remain crisp. Using a sharp serrated knife, slice the top third off of each puff, leaving it hinged on if possible. Remove any moist strands of dough from the interior.

7. Place the pastry cream in a bowl and stir vigorously with a rubber spatula until smooth. With a small spoon, fill the puffs, and replace the tops.

8. To serve, arrange 2 or 3 filled puffs per plate and drizzle the warm chocolate sauce over them. For a more dramatic presentation, pile all the filled puffs onto a large serving plate, drizzling a little chocolate sauce over each layer as you construct the stack. Dollop with whipped cream.

Makes 18 pastries, serves 6 to 12

Note: Freeze the puffs on the baking sheet. Once frozen, transfer them to a plastic bag. They will keep for up to 1 month in the freezer. To defrost, place frozen puffs on a baking sheet in a preheated 375°F oven for about 8 minutes.

BASIC PASTRY CREAM

This rich, velvety custard is delicate to make, but any good cook will work hard to perfect it. Basically it is not served on its own but rather used as a filling for a tart or a choux puff. Most people will recognize it as an eclair filling. The essential ingredient for a luscious pastry cream is a fresh vanilla bean.

2 cups milk
12 tablespoons sugar
1 vanilla bean, split
6 large egg yolks
⅓ cup all-purpose flour

1. Scald the milk with 6 tablespoons of the sugar and all the seeds scraped from the vanilla bean in a heavy medium-size saucepan.

2. Using an electric mixer, beat the yolks and the remaining 6 tablespoons sugar in a mixing bowl until pale lemon in color and thick. A ribbon should form when the beater is lifted from the batter. Beat in the flour.

3. Strain the seeds from the milk. Then while whisking constantly, slowly add ½ cup of the hot milk to the egg mixture in a slow stream. Whisking constantly, pour the egg mixture back into the hot milk in a slow stream.

4. Place the saucepan over medium heat and cook the mixture, whisking constantly, until it becomes thick and starts to boil. Continue to cook for 1 minute, whisking constantly. Remove from the heat and strain the pastry cream into a bowl. Place a piece of plastic wrap directly onto the surface to prevent a skin from forming. Refrigerate until completely chilled. The pastry cream may be made up to 2 days in advance.

Makes 2½ cups

CHOCOLATE SAUCE

Every kitchen must have a chocolate sauce to drizzle over profiteroles, ice cream, or anything else your heart desires. The butter makes this sauce a velvety smooth and delicious basic. I've added rum, but you may change the flavor of the sauce by adding another compatible liqueur, such as Amaretto, Grand Marnier, Frangelico, or Chambord. Most important is to use the best-quality chocolate for the best results. If you'd like to double the quantity of sauce, I would recommend making two batches separately.

4 ounces best-quality semisweet chocolate
½ cup heavy (or whipping) cream
1 tablespoon sugar
1 tablespoon unsalted butter
1 tablespoon rum (optional)

1. Chop the chocolate into small pieces.

2. In a small saucepan over medium heat, scald the cream with the sugar. When it is just about to boil, remove from the heat and stir in the chocolate, butter, and rum. Stir until smooth and all the chocolate is melted. Let cool slightly, then whisk briefly. The sauce is best served warm but may be made ahead and reheated in a double boiler before serving.

Makes 1 cup

CONFETTI LEMON SORBET

Refreshing, smooth, and sparkled with a confetti of citrus zest, this simply prepared sorbet will quickly become a staple in your culinary repertoire all year round. It's particularly delicious served in a small bowl alongside a wedge of Summer Plum Tart (see Index).

1½ cups fresh lemon juice (about 6 lemons)
1 tablespoon finely grated lemon zest
1 teaspoon finely grated lime zest
1 teaspoon finely grated orange zest
3 cups Simple Sugar Syrup for Sorbets (recipe follows)

Combine all the ingredients in a medium-size bowl, then transfer to an ice cream maker and freeze according to the manufacturer's instructions.

Makes 5 cups

SIMPLE SUGAR SYRUP FOR SORBETS

This syrup is very easy to make and is convenient to have on hand when making sorbets. It lasts indefinitely in the refrigerator.

4 cups sugar
4 cups water

Place the sugar and water in a saucepan; bring to a boil. Reduce the heat and gently simmer until the sugar has dissolved, about 5 minutes. Cool to room temperature. Use immediately or store refrigerated in a covered container until use.

Makes 5 cups

RASPBERRY RUBY SORBET

When fresh raspberries are in season, this sorbet is a must to make. But take a tip from me: After I puréed the berries, I tried to strain them to remove the seeds. This turned out to be a rather thankless task, so I proceeded with the unstrained purée. The seeds were hardly noticeable once the sorbet was finished. I think you'll come to the same conclusion.

2 pints fresh raspberries, or 24 ounces frozen unsweetened raspberries, thawed
1¼ cups Simple Sugar Syrup for Sorbets (this page)
2 tablespoons fresh orange juice

1. Purée the raspberries with ¼ cup of the simple sugar syrup in a food processor until smooth.

2. Stir in the remaining sugar syrup and the orange juice, then transfer to an ice cream maker and freeze according to the manufacturer's instructions.

Makes 4 cups

RUM RAISIN ICE CREAM

Aged dark Jamaican rum—an essential flavor to great tropical sundaes—electrifies this luscious ice cream studded with macerated golden raisins. When preparing your custard base, have patience and stir constantly for a velvety smooth consistency.

½ cup golden raisins
½ cup dark rum
3 cups heavy (or whipping) cream
1 cup milk
½ cup sugar
1 tablespoon pure vanilla extract
4 large egg yolks

1. Soak the raisins in the rum for 30 minutes.

2. Combine the cream, milk, sugar, and vanilla in a heavy saucepan over medium heat. Cook until the milk is hot but not boiling and the sugar is dissolved, about 10 minutes. Remove from the heat.

3. Place the egg yolks in a bowl and whisk to mix. Whisking constantly, slowly pour in 1 cup of the hot milk mixture and whisk until smooth.

4. Slowly pour the egg mixture into the saucepan, whisking constantly until well combined. Place the saucepan over medium heat and stir the mixture constantly until it is thick enough to coat the back of a spoon, 6 to 8 minutes. The mixture should never boil.

5. Strain the mixture into a bowl and cool to room temperature. Strain the raisins and rum and stir the rum into the custard.

6. Freeze in an ice cream maker according to the manufacturer's instructions. Five minutes before the ice cream is finished freezing, add the raisins and complete the freezing process.

Makes 1 quart

BANANA RUM ICE CREAM

As one of the Caribbean's prime agricultural crops, bananas are used throughout the islands with great creativity. I've always thought they were underutilized and underappreciated in the United States. This sensational ice cream should help to remedy that. I keep the bananas from turning color by puréeing them with fresh lime juice. It also helps to enhance the flavor.

6 to 8 very ripe bananas (2 cups banana purée)
2 tablespoons fresh lime juice
3 cups heavy (or whipping) cream
1 cup milk
½ cup sugar
1 tablespoon pure vanilla extract
4 large egg yolks
¼ cup dark rum

1. Place the bananas and lime juice in a food processor and purée until smooth. Set aside.

2. Combine the cream, milk, sugar, and vanilla in a heavy medium-size saucepan over medium heat. Cook until the milk is hot but not boiling and the sugar is dissolved, about 10 minutes. Remove the pan from the heat.

3. Place the egg yolks in a bowl and whisk to mix. Whisking constantly, slowly pour in 1 cup of the hot milk mixture and whisk until smooth.

4. Slowly pour the egg mixture into the saucepan, whisking constantly until well combined. Place the saucepan over medium heat and stir the mixture constantly until it is thick enough to coat the back of a spoon, 6 to 8 minutes. The mixture should never boil.

5. Strain the mixture into a bowl and stir in the rum and mashed bananas. Cool to room temperature.

6. Freeze in an ice cream maker according to the manufacturer's instructions.

Makes about 1½ quarts

SOUVENIR TO SAVOR

La Heladeria Coppelia

When I was planning my trip to Cuba, I knew I had to include a stop at the Coppelia, a must-visit ice cream parlor in Havana.

In the center of town, directly across from the Havana Libra Hotel and in the heart of a lush palm tree park, sits a large cement structure that evokes memories of a World's Fair pavilion. When I arrived, there was a serpentine line of hundreds of people waiting outside. I looked at my guide and at the line. He said, "You're in if you show hard currency." I thought, "How often will I visit Cuba?" Out came the dollars and in I went.

Once inside, we walked up a massive winding staircase surrounded by a dark gray lattice wall inset with Mondrian-style primary-colored glass panels. It was an amazing contrast to see a dish of brightly colored peach or apricot ice cream being carried up the stairs by a waiter. Looking around at what people were eating, it seemed that the choice would be wonderfully extensive. But by the time I ordered, hardly any flavors were still available I ultimately had scoops of chocolate, vanilla, and strawberry ice cream—rich, creamy, and very delicious—with a slice of white jelly-roll cake alongside.

Still, the lists of sodas and sundaes on Coppelia's menu delight the imagination. I've created some combinations based on the choices I saw there, so that next time an ice cream party or a great summer dessert are in order, you can look to Coppelia for tropical guidance. Recipes for many of the ice creams, toppings, and cakes appear in this book. Check the Index for page numbers.

SUNDAE SUPREMA

1 scoop of Banana Rum Ice Cream and 1 scoop of Rum Raisin Ice Cream drizzled with rum raisin sauce, and accompanied by a slice of Havana Jelly-Roll Cake.

SUNDAE PRIMAVERA

2 scoops of Vanilla Bean Ice Cream topped with Salade Tropicale de Fruits drizzled with tutti frutti sauce. Serve with two Lemon Wafers.

BANANA SPLIT

1 banana, split lengthwise, topped with 2 scoops of Banana Rum Ice Cream, drizzles of caramel sauce, and dollops of whipped cream. Serve two Copenhagen Butter Cookies alongside.

PINEAPPLE SPLIT

1 wedge of fresh ripe pineapple topped with 2 scoops of Coconut Cream Ice Cream, drizzled with Chocolate Sauce, and sprinkled with toasted coconut. Serve two Gingersnaps alongside.

INDIAN'S CANOE

1 slice of chocolate pound cake topped with sliced strawberries, 2 scoops of Tia Maria Ice Cream, and a drizzle of Chocolate Sauce.

COPA LOLITA

2 slices of Havana Jelly-Roll Cake, one topped with a scoop of Vanilla Bean Ice Cream and drizzled with red berry sauce and the other topped with Chocolate Chocolate Chunk Ice Cream and drizzled with Chocolate Sauce. Dollop with whipped cream and top with fresh sweet cherries.

SUNDAE UNICORNO

1 slice of chocolate pound cake, cut in half, topped with 2 scoops of Vanilla Bean Ice Cream and drizzled with Chocolate Sauce and rum raisin sauce.

TIA MARIA ICE CREAM

When coffee ice cream is your choice, it is most delicious flavored with Jamaica's world-famous Tia Maria liqueur, made from their very best coffee beans. Try this with lots of coarsely grated unsweetened chocolate on top.

3 cups heavy (or whipping) cream
1 cup milk
½ cup sugar
1 tablespoon pure vanilla extract
3 tablespoons good-quality instant espresso
½ teaspoon ground cinnamon
4 large egg yolks
½ cup Tia Maria coffee liqueur

1. Combine the cream, milk, sugar, vanilla, instant espresso, and cinnamon in a heavy saucepan over medium heat. Cook until the milk is hot but not boiling and the sugar is dissolved, about 10 minutes. Remove the pan from the heat.

2. Place the egg yolks in a bowl and whisk to mix. Whisking constantly, slowly pour in 1 cup of the hot milk mixture and whisk until smooth.

3. Slowly pour the egg mixture into the saucepan, whisking constantly until well combined. Place the saucepan over medium heat and stir the mixture constantly until it is thick enough to coat the back of a spoon, 6 to 8 minutes. The mixture should never boil.

4. Strain the mixture into a bowl and stir in the Tia Maria. Cool to room temperature.

5. Freeze in an ice cream maker according to the manufacturer's instructions.

Makes 1 quart

COCONUT CREAM ICE CREAM

While visiting the Caribbean I just couldn't get enough coconut ice cream. Its velvety white consistency, punctuated by a hint of rum, made it irresistible. Sprinkle large scoops with toasted coconut and let this luscious treat become your new vanilla.

14 ounces coconut milk (page 252 or available in specialty food stores)
1 cup heavy (or whipping) cream
1 cup milk
½ cup sugar
1 tablespoon pure vanilla extract
4 large egg yolks
¼ cup dark rum
½ cup shredded coconut

1. Combine the coconut milk, cream, milk, sugar, and vanilla in a heavy saucepan over medium heat. Cook until the milk is hot but not boiling and the sugar is dissolved, about 10 minutes. Remove from the heat.

2. Place the egg yolks in a bowl and whisk to mix. Whisking constantly, slowly pour in 1 cup of the hot milk mixture and whisk until smooth.

3. Slowly pour the egg mixture into the saucepan, whisking constantly until well combined. Place the saucepan over medium heat and stir the mixture constantly until it is thick enough to coat the back of a spoon, 6 to 8 minutes. The mixture should never boil.

4. Strain the mixture into a bowl and stir in the rum and coconut. Cool to room temperature.

5. Freeze in an ice cream maker according to the manufacturer's instructions.

Makes 1 quart

VANILLA BEAN ICE CREAM

In order to make a spectacular vanilla ice cream, the quality of ingredients is paramount. Although recipes do not vary dramatically, fresh, moist vanilla beans and pure vanilla extract make all the difference in the world. There is simply nothing like homemade. Try a scoop of this on a slice of Caribbean Coconut Tart (see index) for heaven on earth.

3 cups heavy (or whipping) cream
1 cup milk
½ cup sugar
2 vanilla beans, split lengthwise in half
1 tablespoon pure vanilla extract
4 large egg yolks

1. Combine the cream, milk, sugar, vanilla beans, and vanilla extract in a heavy saucepan over medium heat. Cook until the milk is hot but not boiling and the sugar is dissolved. Remove from the heat.

MY KITCHEN DIARY

Two More Tropical Sundaes

COUPE TRINIDAD

Place 1 or 2 scoops of Rum Raisin Ice Cream and 1 or 2 scoops of Tia Maria Ice Cream in a dish. Drizzle with rum raisin sauce and top with dollops of whipped cream. Place 1 Gingersnap on each side. Serves 1, of course.

ANTILLES BANANA SPLIT

Top 1 banana, split lengthwise, with 1 scoop each of Coconut Cream Ice Cream, Banana Rum Ice Cream, and Chocolate Chocolate Chumk Ice Cream. Place 1 Copenhagem Butter Cookie on each end. Drizzle with Chocolate Sauce. Slice half of a banana on top and dollop with whipped cream. This only serves 1 also.

2. Place the egg yolks in a bowl and whisk to mix. Whisking constantly, slowly pour in 1 cup of the hot milk mixture and whisk until smooth.

3. Slowly pour the egg mixture into the saucepan, whisking constantly until well combined. Place the saucepan over medium heat and stir the mixture constantly until it is thick enough to coat the back of a spoon, 6 to 8 minutes. The mixture should never boil.

4. Strain the mixture into a bowl and cool to room temperature.

5. Freeze in an ice cream maker according to the manufacturer's instructions.

Makes 1 quart

CHOCOLATE CHOCOLATE CHUNK ICE CREAM

Chocolate ice cream is wonderful no matter where you eat it, and each country seems to have its own favorite variety. For years I was told the best to be had came from Tre Scalini on the Piazza Navona in Rome, but that information could have only come from someone who had not tried the chocolate ice cream at Berthillon on the Ile Saint-Louis in Paris. Never mind. Here is my chunky version, which I've gotten more than a few compliments on, too. When making this rich-flavored ice cream, I use only the best-quality bittersweet chocolate—a chocolate with a high cocoa content—for the most intense flavor. I buy it in one-pound chunks at specialty food stores and store it well wrapped in a cool dark place. If you can't find chocolate sold this way, imported bar chocolate, such as Lindt, is an adequate substitute. For this recipe, the chocolate chunks should be added just as the ice cream has finished freezing.

3 cups heavy (or whipping) cream
1 cup milk
½ cup sugar
4 large egg yolks
11 ounces best-quality bittersweet chocolate, broken into small chunks

1. Combine the cream, milk, and sugar in a heavy saucepan over medium heat. Cook until the milk is hot but not boiling and the sugar is dissolved, about 10 minutes. Remove from the heat.

2. Place the egg yolks in a small bowl and whisk to mix. Whisking constantly, slowly pour 1 cup of the hot milk mixture into the eggs and continue to whisk until smooth. Slowly pour the egg mixture into the saucepan, whisking constantly until well combined. Place the saucepan over medium heat and stir the mixture constantly until it is thick enough to coat the back of a spoon, 6 to 8 minutes. The mixture should never boil.

3. Place 8 ounces of the chocolate chunks (about 1 cup) into a heavy large saucepan over very low heat until just melted, stirring until smooth.

4. Strain the ice cream mixture into the melted chocolate, whisking until completely combined. Cool to room temperature.

5. Freeze in an ice cream maker according to the manufacturer's instructions. Just before the mixture has completed freezing, with the motor off, add the remaining dark chocolate chunks and stir to combine. Once frozen, be prepared to eat and swoon.

Makes 1½ quarts

Conversion Table

U.S. WEIGHTS AND MEASURES

1 pinch = less than ⅛ teaspoon (dry)
1 dash = 3 drops to ¼ teaspoon (liquid)
3 teaspoons = 1 tablespoon = ½ ounce (liquid and dry)
2 tablespoons = 1 ounce (liquid and dry)
4 tablespoons = 2 ounces (liquid and dry) = ¼ cup
5⅓ tablespoons = ⅓ cup
16 tablespoons = 8 ounces = 1 cup = ½ pound
16 tablespoons = 48 teaspoons
32 tablespoons = 16 ounces = 2 cups = 1 pound
64 tablespoons = 32 ounces = 1 quart = 2 pounds
1 cup = 8 ounces (liquid) = ½ pint
2 cups = 16 ounces (liquid) = 1 pint
4 cups = 32 ounces (liquid) = 2 pints = 1 quart
16 cups = 128 ounces (liquid) = 4 quarts = 1 gallon
1 quart = 2 pints (dry)
8 quarts = 1 peck (dry)
4 pecks = 1 bushel (dry)

APPROXIMATE EQUIVALENTS

1 quart (liquid) = about 1 litre
8 tablespoons = 4 ounces = ½ cup = 1 stick butter
1 cup all-purpose presifted flour = 5 ounces
1 cup stoneground yellow cornmeal = 4½ ounces
1 cup granulated sugar = 8 ounces
1 cup brown sugar = 6 ounces
1 cup confectioners' sugar = 4½ ounces
1 large egg = 2 ounces = ¼ cup = 4 tablespoons
1 egg yolk = 1 tablespoon + 1 teaspoon
1 egg white = 2 tablespoons + 2 teaspoons

TEMPERATURES: °FARENHEIT (F) TO °CELSIUS (C)

–10°F = –23.3°C (freezer storage)
0°F = –17.7°C
32°F = 0°C (water freezes)
50°F = 10°C
68°F = 20°C (room temperature)
100°F = 37.7°C
150°F = 65.5°C
205°F = 96.1°C (water simmers)
212°F = 100°C (water boils)
300°F = 148.8°C
325°F = 162.8°C
350°F = 177°C (baking)
375°F = 190.5°C
400°F = 204.4°C (hot oven)
425°F = 218.3°C
450°F = 232°C (very hot oven)
475°F = 246.1°C
500°F = 260°C (broiling)

CONVERSION FACTORS

If you need to convert measurements into their equivalents in another system, here's how to do it.

ounces to grams: multiply ounce figure by 28.3 to get number of grams

grams to ounces: multiply gram figure by .0353 to get number of ounces

pounds to grams: multiply pound figure by 453.59 to get number of grams

pounds to kilograms: multiply pound figure by 0.45 to get number of kilograms

ounces to milliliters: multiply ounce figure by 30 to get number of milliliters

cups to liters: multiply cup figure by 0.24 to get number of liters

Fahrenheit to Celsius: subtract 32 from the Fahrenheit figure, multiply by 5, then divide by 9 to get Celsius figure

Celsius to Fahrenheit: multiply Celsius figure by 9, divide by 5, then add 32 to get Fahrenheit figure

inches to centimeters: multiply inch figure by 2.54 to get number of centimeters

centimeters to inches: multiply centimeter figure by .39 to get number of inches

ALL AROUND THE WORLD

Cookbook Index

A

Aamar, Riad, 66
Aass, 439
ABC Extra Stout, 401
Achmiadzinski, 470
Aegina, 45
Afternoon tea, 464
  favorite stops for, 474-80
  see also Tea; Tea fare; Teas
Agra (India):
  coffee at Taj View Hotel in, 547
  market in, 228
A-jaad (Thai cucumber cool down), 248
Albani, 439
Albariño, 317
Ale, 340, 341-42
Algeria, wines of, 488
Ali, Aziza, 132, 257
All Around the World Cocktails (menu), 178
Allied Brewers, 348
Allspice, 369
Almacenista, 317
Almond(s):
  Catalan romesco "sauce" rotelli, 303
  hazelnut biscotti, 522-23
  kugelhopf, 465-66
  skordalia sauce, 65
Altbiers, 204
Amandari Hotel (Bali), 263
Amandari smoked salmon angel pasta, 289
Amanpuri (Thailand), 414
Amarone, 298
Amontillado, 316
Amsterdam:
  broodjes at Van Dobben in, 445
  Dutch breakfast in, 26
  Japanese-style breakfast in, 25
Anakopia, 470
Andalusian and Andalusian-inspired dishes:
  The Andalusian (dinner menu), 181
  salad Parador, 397-98
  steak rollos, 338-39
Angel berry trifle, 532-33
Angelina (Paris), 477
Angel pasta, Amandari smoked salmon, 289
Anne's ham and cheese salad tea sandwiches, 453
Antilles banana split, 556
Antinori, 297
Antipasto, menu for, 176
Aperitifs, 30-41
  banana daiquiri, 33-34
  basic daiquiri, 33
  Chilean white peach melba sangria, 40
  Cuba Libre, 35
  Le Dauphin, 38-39
  Emotion, 38
  fresh grapefruit spritz, 31-32
  Margaritas, 31
  Mojito, 34
  Napoleon Bonaparte, 39-40
  ouzo, 31
  Piña Martinique, 35
  Planteur, 37
  punch Martinique, 35
  raki, 31
  Rhumlet, 39
  Rouge Tropical, 39
  strawberry or mango daiquiri, 33
  vermouth cassis, 37
  La Vie en Rose, 37-38
Appellation d'origine contrôlée (AOC) system, 363
Appetizers and hors d'oeuvres, 42-90
  All Around the World Cocktails (menu), 178
  badam sandheko (spiced roasted peanuts), 46
  bhel poori, 48-49
  blini, 53
  braised globe artichokes, 193
  brandade, 62-63
  Brazilian onion bites, 43
  bruschetta with Sevilla *tapas* salad, 102
  buckwheat blini, 54
  caviar eggs à la Russe, 51-52
  chèvres bathed in herbs and extra virgin olive oil, 47-48
  chicken satay Singapore style, 71
  Chilean empanadas, 82-83
  Creole crab slather, 58-59
  feroce, 62
  goong waan (spicy sweetened shrimp), 68-69
  Gordon's quesadillas, 86

herbed orange chèvre slather, 56
Highland pâté, 46-47
hot shrimp in a pot, 403-4
island pan-barbecued shrimp, 68
Kalamata olive purée, 60-61
Laurie's basic guacamole, 61
Mediterranean spiced olives, 44-45
meze, 67, 113
Oaxaca tostada bites, 43-44
pastrami böreks, 87
pissaladière, 80-81
pita chips, 66
plaka tsatsiki (cucumber and yogurt dip), 65-66
polenta with Cremini mushroom sauce, 272-73
prathaad lom (prawn rolls), 79-80
Provençal chickpea slather, 58
Riad's baba ghanouj, 66-67
rigani, white bean, and garlic slather, 57-58
salmon caviar egg salad, 51
salmon ribbon bites, 44
satsivi (chicken bathed in walnut sauce), 72-74
savory mint and coriander chutney, 49-50
skordalia sauce, 65
spanakopita, 90
Spanish olive tapenade, 60
tapas, 67, 316
tarama slather, 59-60
Thai crab spring rolls, 77-78
thod mun pla (tiny Thai croquettes), 74-75
tiny potato croquettes, 76
tuna Niçoise briks, 81-82
wild mushroom blinchiki, 55
yakitori, 74
zakuski, 67, 110
zesty yogurt slather, 56-57
see also Salads, first-course or accompaniment
Apple:
berry tea, Galina's, 469
cider vinaigrette, 109
crab cocktail, Sasha's, 115-16
herring, Palterovich creamy, 118
pineapple raita, 250
samba Waldorf salad, 100
tarte tatin, 537
Après Ski (dinner menu), 180
Apricot(s):
banana bliss, 509
tomato chutney, 242
Aquavit, 89
Argentina:
barbecue at gaucho ranch in, 350
chicken soup in style of, 143
palette of, 199
wines of, 324-25
Arienzo, Marqués de, 317
Artichokes:
baby, osso buco with, 352-53
globe, braised, 193
Arugula:
garlic mashed potatoes with, 209
insalata d'estate, 92-93
Leslie Russo's summer puttanesca, 303-4
sunshine salad, 98
Asado, at gaucho ranch, 350
Asahi, 134
Ashbourne, 518
Asia:
street food in, 450
see also specific countries
Asparagus:
Bali sunrise brunch, 6-7
sauté, 193
softly scrambled eggs with cured ham and, 10
stir-fried scallops and, teriyaki, 409-10
Assam tea, 464
Assyrtiko grape, 107
Auslese, 418, 419
Australia, wines of, 516-18
Austrian dishes:
Linzer tart, 535-37
Sachertorte, 547-48
Avgolemono soup, Wende's, 157-58
Avocado(s):
butter, 255
Caribbean croque monsieur, 442
Chilean quinoa tabouleh, 281
cream, 86
feroce, 62
Laurie's basic guacamole, 61
mambo fruit salad, 97-98
"mayonnaise," 433-35
Oaxaca tostada bites, 43-44
preventing discoloration of, 400
salad, Chilean, 102-3
señorita shrimp boats, 402
shrimp salad, minty, 400
sunshine salad, 98
Thai fruit salsa, 246
Vera Cruz veggie sandwich, 449-50
Azerbaijan, wines of, 117
Aziza's Restaurant (Singapore), 132, 257

Baba ghanouj, Riad's, 66-67
Baby bisteeyas, 380-81
Bacon, in English mixed grill, 13-14
Badam sandheko (spiced roasted peanuts), 46
Baden, 417-18
Bahia butternut mash, 217-18
Bali, Amandari Hotel in, 263
Balikcilar Carsisi fish market (Istanbul), 231
Balinese and Balinese-inspired dishes:
Amandari smoked salmon angel pasta, 289
citrus cream, shrimp, and papaya salad, 122
primavera potato salad, 113-14
sunrise brunch, 6-7
Ballymaloe (County Cork, Ireland), 27
Baltic sturgeon salad, 123
La Bamba rice, 264
Banana(s):
bliss, 509
bread, Miss Maud's breakfast, 16-17
brunch soup, 4
cinnamon pancakes, 15-16
coconut raita, minted, 249-50
daiquiri, 33-34
Emotion (aperitif), 38
lime baked, 509

Mexican lentils with pineapple and, 285-86
rum ice cream, 553
salade tropicale de fruits, 514
samba Waldorf salad, 100
split, 554
split, Antilles, 556
Banana Leaf Apolo (Singapore), 224, 225
Banana Leaf vegetable curry, 224-25
Banks Lager, 428
Bannockburn, 518
Barbados, beer of, 428
Barbara Ensrud's red wine sangria, 40-41
Barbaresco, 298
Barbecue, at gaucho ranch, 350
Barbera, 298
Barco Reale, 298
Bar-le-Duc jelly, 457
Barley:
black-eyed peas and, 284-85
chicken, and leek soup, Scottish (cock-a-leekie), 138-39
Barolo, 298
Basil:
pasta arrabiata, 300
pesto, 490
Bass, 348
Bayo, Chef, 241
Beamish, 349
Bean(s):
black-eyed peas and barley, 284-85
blazing squash chili, 218-19
fava, in Chilean pistou with cilantro pesto, 151-52
fava, skinning, 151
lima, in hearty Irish beef soup, 131
Montego red pea soup, 165-66
Provençal chickpea slather, 58
and rice, calypso, 283-84
two-, and duck pasta, Mediterranean, 299
white, rigani, and garlic slather, 57-58
white, soup, Mediterranean, 164-65
see also Black bean(s); Green beans; Lentil(s)
Beck's, 204
Beef, 335-51
Andalusian steak rollos, 338-39
broth, rich, 128-29
corned, and cabbage, Dublin, 343-44
corned, Carnaval, 351
corned, in Chilean empanadas, 82-83
Granny Reesman's stuffed cabbage, 342-43
great Turkish hamburgers, 444-45
hash, luscious, 341-42
hot Russian borscht, 132-33
meat loaf à la Lindstrom, 341
Mexican pot roast, 335-36
pastitsio, 338
pepito (Mexican steak sandwich), 448
ribs, Sri Lankan deviled, 339-40
roast, *smørrebrød*, 437
soup, hearty Irish, 131
Swedish meatballs, 340
Beerenauslese, 419
Beers:
of Belgium, Netherlands, and Luxembourg, 446-47
of British Isles, 346-49
of Caribbean, 428
of China and Japan, 134-35
of Czechoslovakia, 196
of Germany, 204-5
of India and Pakistan, 256
of Latin America, 84-85
of Scandinavia, 438-39
of Southeast Asia, 401
Beet(s):
Blushing Beet Bash (dinner menu), 185
bread pudding, 195
La Coupole salad, 95
hot Russian borscht, 132-33
Nordic Cobb salad, 114-15
rhubarb compote, 240
roasted, 194-95
Russian salad, 108-9
salad, Ida's, 194
Belgian endive:
Caribe crudités, 92
La Coupole salad, 95
Belgium, beers of, 446-47
Bellhaven, 349
Beluga, 52
Berliner Weisse, 204
Berne, Steffi, 523
Berra's Turkish leeks, 200-201
Berry(ies):
angel trifle, 532-33
Pavlova, 519-20
tea, Galina's, 469
see also Strawberry(ies)
Berta's carrot cake Caribe, 540
Berta's really rich noodle pudding, 307
Berthillon (Paris), 557
Beverages:
aquavit, 89
chocolate with coffee, 467
hot chocolate (chocolate a la taza), 5
Jamaican Blue Mountain coffee, 15
Scottish coffee, 473
see also Aperitifs; Beers; Teas; Wine(s)
Bhel poori, 48-49
Bilberries, 460
Biscotti, hazelnut-almond, 522-23
Bisteeyas, baby, 380-81
Bites Before the Bolshoi (dinner menu), 184
Black bean(s):
frijoles negros, 284
Oaxaca tostada bites, 43-44
and rice (Moros y Cristianos), 282-83
Rio's feijoada, 322-23
soup, Carlos', 166-67
Black cherry soup, Hungarian, 169-70
Black currant duck breasts, 389
Black-eyed peas and barley, 284-85
Black Label, 256
Black sea bass baked in salt crust, 420
Blazing squash chili, 218-19
Bleecker Luncheonette (New York), 150
Blinchiki:
sweet, 459-60
wild mushroom, 55

Blini, 53
buckwheat, 54
Blue cheese:
Cabrales, 497
Castello, 501
Danablu, 501
salad dressing, 115
Blue Lake, 470
Blue Mountain coffee, Jamaican, 15
Blushing Beet Bash (dinner menu), 185
Bock beer (bockbier):
of Denmark, 439
of Germany, 204, 205
of Netherlands, 447
Bodegas de Santo Tomás, 255
Bodegas Fernandez, 317
Bodegas Palacio Glorioso, 317
Bodegas Weinert, 324
La Bodeguita del Medio (Havana, Cuba), 282, 313, 315
Bohemia (beer), 85
Boiled potatoes and sliced tomatoes, 210-11
Böreks, pastrami, 87
Borges & Irmão, 154
Borscht, hot Russian, 132-33
Botvinya (sorrel potato soup), 163-64
Boutari, 107
Braised:
globe artichokes, 193
red cabbage, 195-96
Brandade, 62-63
Brazil:
beers of, 84, 85
breakfast on beach in Rio in, 22
palette of, 199
tea in, 478
wines of, 325
Brazilian and Brazilian-inspired dishes:
Bahia butternut mash, 217-18
Carnaval corned beef, 351
chicken soup, 142
Copacabana collards, 198
onion bites, 43
Rio's feijoada, 322-23
Rio Revelry (dinner menu), 188
Bread(s), 481-93
banana, Miss Maud's breakfast, 16-17
cumin curry rolls, 490-91
Finnish cardamom tea loaf, 461
focaccia, 489-90
garlic croutons, 96-97
Irish soda, 492-93
kugelhopf, 465-66
lavash, 491-92
limpa, 486-87
Moroccan pumpkin tea loaf, 468-69
pan con tomate, 219-20
Portuguese sweet (pao-doce), 483
pudding, beet, 195
pudding, Mexican Christmas, 530-31
pudding, scarlet summer, 529-30
rosemary-olive, 484-85
Scottish oatcakes, 493
soup, garlic and cilantro (sopa alentejana), 152-53
soup, Italian tomato (pappa al pomodoro), 155-57
soups, 156
torrijas (Spanish "French" toast), 17
wheat berry, 485-86
Breakfast and brunch fare, 2-17
Bali sunrise brunch, 6-7
Baltic sturgeon salad, 123
banana bread, Miss Maud's, 16-17
banana brunch soup, 4
banana cinnamon pancakes, 15-16
Café Tacuba Breakfast (menu), 172
Caribe Breakfast on the Balcony (menu), 172
Caribe Western omelet, 7
English mixed grill, 13-14
hot chocolate (chocolate a la taza), 5
Irish Country Breakfast (menu), 172
Irish porridge, 3
Jamaican Blue Mountain coffee, 15
kugelhopf, 465-66
morning muesli, 3
Nani's tortilla de patatas, 9-10
odja (Tunisian Western omelet), 12-13
Palterovich creamy apple herring, 118
Scottish fried rice, 271-72
scrambled egg and salt cod hash, 10-11
softly scrambled eggs with asparagus and cured ham, 10
Summer Mediterranean Brunch (menu), 172
Swedish pancakes, 14
torrijas (Spanish "French" toast), 17
Tunisian Brunch (menu), 173
Turkish Western omelet, 12
Breakfasts, memorable, 18-27
at Ballymaloe (County Cork, Ireland), 27
on beach in Rio de Janeiro, 22
at Café Tacuba (Mexico City), 21-22
Dutch, in Amsterdam, 26
at Hotel d'Angleterre (Copenhagen), 26
at Hotel Doma (Chania, Crete), 23-24
at Hotel Gellert (Budapest), 19-20
at Inglaterra (Havana), 20-21
at Istanbul Hilton, 24-25
Japanese-style, in Amsterdam, 25
at Mamounia Hotel (Marrakech), 18-19
Nordic-style, in Helsinki, 23
at Okura Hotel (Tokyo), 25
Russian menu for, 11
Breakfast tea, 464
Brigl, 297
British Isles:
beers of, 346-49
palette of, 455
tea in, 452, 464, 474-77
see also English and English-inspired dishes; Scottish and Scottish-inspired dishes
Brokenwood, 518
Broodjes, 445
Broths:
chicken, 127
defatting, 128

fresh vegetable, 129-30
rich beef, 128-29
see also Stocks
Broughton, 349
Brunch fare, *see* Breakfast and brunch fare
Brunello, 298
Bruschetta:
Greek, 220
with Sevilla *tapas* salad, 102
Buckwheat blini, 54
Budapest:
afternoon respite at Gerbaud in, 462
breakfast at Hotel Gellert in, 19-20
dinner at Gundel in, 337
Budvar, 196
Buggy, Ken and Cathleen, 492
Bulgaria, wines of, 376-77
Burrito, mu shu chicken, 384-85
Butter(s):
avocado, 255
clarified, 53-54
cookies, Copenhagen, 520-21
curry, 257
dill caper, 44
rum sauce, 16
Butterfly noodles, sesame, 293-94
Butternut squash:
chili, blazing, 218-19
mash, Bahia, 217-18
Byzantine pilaf, 269-70

Cabbage:
Dublin corned beef and, 343-44
hearty Irish beef soup, 131
hot Russian borscht, 132-33
red, braised, 195-96
red, in Caribe crudités, 92
stuffed, Granny Reesman's, 342-43
sweet pickled, 237-38
Cabernet Sauvignon, 256
of Australia, 516, 517-18
of Chile, 278-79
Cabrales, 497
Ca' del Bosco, 297
Caesar salad, 96
Café des Nattes (Sidi Bou Saïd, Tunisia), 471
Café Lumskebugten (Copenhagen), 341
Café Tacuba (Mexico City), 21-22
Café Tacuba Breakfast (menu), 172
Cakes (savory), Copenhagen cod, 435-36
Cakes (sweet):
angel food, 532, 533
carrot, Berta's Caribe, 540
chèvre cheesecake, 540-41
chocolate pecan, 539
Havana jelly-roll, 543-44
Hungarian cherry tea, 462-63
Indonesian ribbon, 545
Jamaican gingerbread, 542-43
orange pound, 541-42
pineapple-rum upside-down, 544
Sachertorte, 547-48
spice, with coffee frosting, 466-67
tea, little Swedish lingonberry, 465
Caledonian (beer), 349
Caledonian Hotel (Edinburgh), 476-77
Caliterra, 280
Calypso beans and rice, 283-84
Campo Fiorin, 298
Canale, 324
Canepa, 280
Cantabria, 497
Cantaloupe:
Chilean avocado salad, 102-3
mambo fruit salad, 97-98
salade tropicale de fruits, 514
salsa Carnaval, 245
Cape Mentelle, 518
Caper dill butter, 44
Cardamom tea loaf, Finnish, 461
Caribbean:
beers of, 428
fruit basket of, 99
palette of, 36
Caribbean and Caribbean-inspired dishes:
Berta's carrot cake Caribe, 540
calypso beans and rice, 283-84
Caribbean Carnivale (dinner menu), 189
Caribe Breakfast on the Balcony (menu), 172
Caribe crudités, 92
Caribe Western omelet, 7
chicken soup, 143
citrus cream, shrimp, and papaya salad, 122
coconut cream ice cream, 555-56
coconut tart, 534-35
colombo curry powder, 259-60
croque monsieur, 442
daiquiris, 33-34
Emotion (aperitif), 38
fish pot, 428-29
island pan-barbecued shrimp, 68
mambo fruit salad, 97-98
mambo mango pork, 318
Paradise Island Dinner (menu), 188
pineapple-rum upside-down cake, 544
Rhumlet, 39
sunny sweet potato salad, 212
sunshine salad, 98
La Vie en Rose, 37-38
see also Jamaican and Jamaican-inspired dishes; Martinique and Martinique-inspired dishes
Carlos' black bean soup, 166-67
Carlsberg, 438-39
Carnaval corned beef, 351
Carras, Château, 107
Carresquera, Carlos, 166-67
Carrot(s):
Banana Leaf vegetable curry, 224-25
Byzantine pilaf, 269-70
cake Caribe, Berta's, 540
Copenhagen, 197-98
dilled, 196-97
gingered crème de Crécy, 161
minted sweet, 198
Russian salad, 108-9
seven vegetable couscous, 276-77
soup, Casbah, 160-61
sugared mashed, 197
Thai pickled, 236-37

Carta Blanca, 84, 85
Cartet (Paris), 538
Carvalho, 154
Casbah carrot soup, 160-61
Castello, 501
Casual Mexican Summer Supper (menu), 187
Catalan and Catalan-inspired dishes:
  chocolate sandwich, 449
  romesco "sauce" rotelli, 303
  spinach, 217
  zarzuela, 426-27
Catfish, in thod mun pla (tiny Thai croquettes), 74-75
Cauliflower, in Banana Leaf vegetable curry, 224-25
Cavas de San Juan, 255
Cavas São João, 154
Caviar, 52
  buckwheat blini and, 54
  eggs à la Russe, 51-52
  salmon, egg salad, 51
  tarama salmon blush, 118
  tarama slather, 59-60
Celebrations, menus for, 176-78
  All Around the World Cocktails, 178
  Ice Cream Dream Party for the Kids, 178
  Italian Antipasto Festival, 176
  Meze Celebration, 178
  Rijsttafel, 177
  Russian *Zakuski* Party, 177
Central Market (Budapest), 232
Cereals:
  Irish porridge, 3
  morning muesli, 3
Ceres Red Eric, 439
Cetto, Luis, 255
Ceylon tea, 464
Cha-cha corn gazpacho, 169
Chakhokbili (Georgian chicken stew), 367-68
Chandon, M., 324
Chardonnay:
  of Australia, 516, 517-18
  of Chile, 280
  of France, 364
  of Italy, 297
Cheese(s), 494-505
  blue, salad dressing, 115
  cream, date and nut, tea sandwiches, 456-57
  cream, icing, 540
  Danish, 499-501
  Dutch, 502-3
  feta, in Greek salad, 112
  feta, in spanakopita, 90
  feta, in Turkish Western omelet, 12
  fruit and, as dessert, 519
  Gordon's quesadillas, 86
  Greek, 503-5
  Gruyère, in Caribbean croque monsieur, 442
  and ham salad tea sandwiches, Anne's, 453
  Monterey Jack, in Vera Cruz veggie sandwich, 449-50
  Monterey Jack, in Oaxaca tostada bites, 43-44
  pastitsio, 338
  Portuguese, 498
  sandwich, yummy grilled, 449
  Spanish, 494-98
  Swedish, 501-2
  tarte Provençale, 221-22
  see also Chèvre(s)
Cheesecake, chèvre, 540-41
Cherry(ies):
  black, soup, Hungarian, 169-70
  chicken salad tea sandwiches, herbed, 457
  compote, 510
  sour, pickled (griottes), 238-39
  tea cake, Hungarian, 462-63
Chèvre(s):
  banana bliss, 509
  bathed in herbs and extra virgin olive oil, 47-48
  cheesecake, 540-41
  orange slather, herbed, 56
  Thai eggplant sandwich, 451
Chez Henri (Paris), 101
Chianti, 298
Chicken, 357-88
  baby bisteeyas, 380-81
  bathed in walnut sauce (satsivi), 72-74
  broth, 127
  broth, defatting, 128
  cherry salad tea sandwiches, herbed, 457
  coq au vin, 360-61
  and corn chowder, Chilean, 144-45
  curry, golden, 381
  and date tagine, 372-73
  Gordon's quesadillas, 86
  hacked, salad, 388
  harira soup, 136-38
  herb roasted, the French way, 359-60
  home-style Jamaican, 368-69
  honey and ginger-glazed, 366
  jerk, 369-70
  leek, and barley soup, Scottish (cock-a-leekie), 138-39
  Mediterranean roast, 359
  mulligatawny soup, 139-40
  mu shu, burrito, 384-85
  noodle curry, Indonesian (mee soto), 382-83
  noodle soup, Indonesian (soto banjar), 145-46
  olive and lemon-studded, 370
  paprika (csirke paprikás), 378
  picadillo enchiladas, 384
  poulet chasseur, 371
  rogan josh, 367
  salad, Madras, 385-86
  satay Singapore style, 71
  stew, Georgian (chakhokbili), 367-68
  stewed, under a blanket, 378-79
  tikka, 382
  Tokyo fried, 371-72
  wings, in Oriental pilaf, 269
  yakitori, 74
Chickpea slather, Provençal, 58
Chile:
  palette of, 199
  wines of, 278-80
Chilean and Chilean-inspired dishes:
  avocado salad, 102-3
  chicken soup, 142
  Chilean Tastings (dinner menu), 188
  corn and chicken chowder, 144-45
  empanadas, 82-83
  pistou with cilantro pesto, 151-52

quinoa tabouleh, 281
white peach melba sangria, 40
Chili, blazing squash, 218-19
Chili(es) (peppers):
harissa, 239
Jamaican pepper sauce, 253-54
sauce chien, 254
Scotch bonnet, 253
Chimay Red, 447
China:
beers of, 134
fruit basket of, 390
palette of, 295
soy sauce in, 366
wines of, 135
China Oolong tea, 464
Chinese and Chinese-inspired dishes:
chicken soup, 142
Chinese Cook-in Dinner (menu), 186
Ellen's hot and sour soup, 136
hacked chicken salad, 388
mu shu chicken burrito, 384-85
roast duck, melon, and mango salad, 391-92
serving wine or beer with, 135
spicy peanut sauce, 294
squabs, 388-89
vinaigrette, 95
Chips, pita, 66
Chocolate:
chocolate chunk ice cream, 557
coffee with, 467
glaze, 539, 547, 548
hot (chocolate a la taza), 5
pecan cake, 539
sandwich, 449
sauce, 551
skinnies, Steffi Berne's, 523
Chorizo sausages, in La Bamba rice, 264
Choux puffs, 549
Chowder, Chilean corn and chicken,144-45
Christmas, Mexican "Night of the Radishes" festival and, 168
Christmas beers, 85, 439
Christmas fare:
Mexican bread pudding, 530-31
red pepper soup, 159
Chutneys, 241
green tomato, Chef Bayo's Tanzanian, 240-41
savory mint and coriander, 49-50
tomato apricot, 242
Cicek Pasaji (Istanbul), 231
Cider vinaigrette, 109
Cilantro:
and garlic bread soup (sopa alentejana), 152-53
mayonnaise, 402-3
pesto, Chilean pistou with, 151-52
La Cinacina (San Antonio de Areco, Argentina), 350
Cinnamon:
banana pancakes, 15-16
skillet toast, 468
Citrus cream, shrimp, and papaya salad, 122
Clams:
steamed, Alentejo, 409
Thai seafood salad, 396
Clarified butter, 53-54
Clement, Domaine, 32
Cloudy Bay, 518
"Club sandwich," Thai crab, with avocado mayonnaise, 433
Cobb salad, Nordic, 114-15
Cock-a-leekie soup (Scottish chicken, leek, and barley soup), 138-39
Cocktail coulibiac, 87-88
Coconut:
banana raita, minted, 249-50
cream ice cream, 555-56
Le Dauphin, 38-39
milk, rich, 252
Piña Martinique, 35
ratatouille, Thai, 212-13
rice pudding, Mexican, 531-32
salade tropicale de fruits, 514
serunding, 257
tart, Caribbean, 534-35
toasting, 514
Cod:
cakes, Copenhagen, 435-36
feroce, 62
ragout, Russian, 425
see also Salt cod
Coffee:
chocolate with, 467
condiments with, in India, 547
frosting, 467
Jamaican Blue Mountain, 15
Scottish, 473
Coffeehouses, Hungarian, 462
Cognacs, of Georgia, 470
Coldstream Hills, 518
Le Colibri porc colombo, 321-22
Collards, Copacabana, 198
Colombo curry powder, 259-60
Commemorativa, 85
Compotes:
cherry, 510
rhubarb-beet, 240
Concha y Toro, 280
Condiments, 235-61
a-jaad (Thai cucumber cool down), 248
apple-pineapple raita, 250
avocado butter, 255
Chef Bayo's Tanzanian green tomato chutney, 240-41
clarified butter, 53-54
with coffee, in India, 547
colombo curry powder, 259-60
cool down salsa, 247
creamy yogurt, 248
curry butter, 257
dill caper butter, 44
fiesta corn salsa, 246
griottes (pickled sour cherries), 238-39
harissa, 239
kiwi salsa, 245-46
mango-tomato raita, 250
masala for mildly spiced sauces, 257-58
minted banana-coconut raita, 249-50
mint gremolata, 354
my own curry powder, 260
orange gremolata, 352
preserved lemons, 236
quince spoon sweet, 512
raita cool down, 248-49
ranchero salsa rosa, 242-43
rhubarb-beet compote, 240
rich coconut milk, 252
salsa Carnaval, 245
Saun's fresh salsa verde, 246-47
savory masala for meat, 258-59

savory mint and coriander chutney, 49-50
savory plum conserve, 239-40
serunding, 257
shrimp paste, 405
sweet garam masala, 259
sweet pickled cabbage, 237-38
Thai fruit salsa, 246
Thai pickled carrots, 236-37
Thai pickled cucumbers, 237
tomato apricot chutney, 242
see also Salad dressings; Sauces; Vinaigrettes
Confetti lemon sorbet, 551-52
Conserve, savory plum, 239-40
Conti, Paul, 518
Cookies:
Copenhagen butter, 520-21
gingersnaps, 522
hazelnut-almond biscotti, 522-23
Irish oatmeal, 526-27
lemon wafers, 521
Steffi Berne's chocolate skinnies, 523
Cool downs:
apple-pineapple raita, 250
mango-tomato raita, 250
minted banana-coconut raita, 249-50
raita, 248-49
salsa, 247
Thai cucumber (a-jaad), 248
Copa Lolita, 554
Copenhagen:
breakfast at Hotel d'Angleterre in, 26
butter cookies, 520-21
Café Lumskebugten in, 341
carrots, 197-98
cod cakes, 435-36
Coq au vin, 360-61
Coriander and mint chutney, savory, 49-50
Corn:
cha-cha gazpacho, 169
and chicken chowder, Chilean, 144-45
Chilean quinoa tabouleh, 281
salsa, fiesta, 246
Corned beef:
and cabbage, Dublin, 343-44
Carnaval, 351
Chilean empanadas, 82-83
Cornmeal, *see* Polenta
Corona, 84
La Costa Del Sol (dinner menu), 181
Costadolio, 298
Côtes de Meliton, 107
Coulibiac, cocktail, 87-88
Coupe Trinidad, 556
La Coupole salad, 95
Courage (beer), 348
Couscous:
Moroccan Couscous Dinner (menu), 181
seven vegetable, 276-77
Cousino Macul, 280
Cozy Fireside Supper (menu), 187
Crab(meat):
apple cocktail, Sasha's, 115-16
Caribbean fish pot, 428-29
"club" with avocado mayonnaise, Thai, 433
pad Thai, 293
salad composée, Jamaican, 121-22
slather, Creole, 58-59
spring rolls, Thai, 77-78
Cranachan, 533-34
Crayfish:
eating, 406
Swedish (recipe), 407
Swedish festival of, 407
Cream:
avocado, 86
basic pastry, 550-51
orange horseradish, 345
Cream cheese:
date and nut, tea sandwiches, 456-57
icing, 540
Creamed spinach, Indian, 215-16
"Cream tea," 464
Creamy:
paprika potatoes, 206
wild mushroom soup, 163
yogurt, 248
Créme de menthe, in Le Dauphin, 38-39
Creole crab slather, 58-59
Crêpe pans, seasoning, 54
Crêpes:
Swedish pancakes, 14
sweet blinchiki, 459-60
wild mushroom blinchiki, 55
Crete, breakfast at Hotel Doma on, 23-24
Cringletie House Hotel (Scotland), 475-76
Croque monsieur, Caribbean, 442
Croquettes:
savory salmon, 411
tiny potato, 76
tiny Thai (thod mun pla), 74-75
Crostini, Italian shrimp salad, 398
Croutons, garlic, 96-97
Crucial Brew, 428
Crudités, Caribe, 92
Csirke paprikás (paprika chicken), 378
Cuba:
La Bodeguita del Medio in, 315
breakfast at Inglaterra in (Havana), 20-21
origin of daiquiri in, 34
Cuba Libre, 35
Cuban and Cuban-inspired dishes:
Cubana sandwich, 442-43
Habana Libra pork roast, 313-14
Mojito, 34
Moros y Cristianos (black beans and rice), 282-83
Soup and Sandwich Cuban Style (luncheon menu), 174
Viva Havana (dinner menu), 189
Cucumber(s):
cha-cha corn gazpacho, 169
Chilean quinoa tabouleh, 281
cool down, Thai (a-jaad), 248
cool down salsa, 247
Mexican gazpacho, 167
raita cool down, 248-49
Russian garden salad, 109-10
Russian salad, 108-9
salad, dilled, 103-4
salsa Carnaval, 245
Thai pickled, 237
and tiny sprout tea sandwiches, 453-54
and yogurt dip (plaka tsatsiki), 65-66
Cumberland sauce, 345
Cumin curry rolls, 490-91
Currant(s), 37
black, duck breasts, 389
red, 457

Curries and curried dishes:
- Banana Leaf vegetable, 224-25
- butter, 257
- Casbah carrot soup, 160-61
- Le Colibri porc colombo, 321-22
- cumin rolls, 490-91
- exotic lamb, 329-30
- garam masalas for, 257-59
- golden chicken, 381
- golden squash soup, 158
- Indonesian chicken noodle (mee soto), 382-83
- Madras chicken salad, 385-86
- Malay noodles, 290-91
- mulligatawny soup, 139-40
- pineapple and prawns (gaeng kua goong), 405-6
- savory plum conserve, 239-40
- in Singapore's Little India, 225
- velvety shrimp, 403

Curry powders, 258
- colombo, 259-60
- my own, 260
- *see also* Garam masalas

Custards:
- basic pastry cream, 550-51
- orange flan, 527

Cuvée de l'Ermitage, 447
Cuvée le Président, 488
Czechoslovakia, beers of, 196

Dahra, 488
Daiquiris, 33-34
- banana, 33-34
- basic, 33
- origins of, 34
- strawberry or mango, 33

Dal, spiced vegetable, 286-87
Danablu, 501
Danbo, 499, 501
Dandelion greens, in spanakopita, 90
Danish and Danish-inspired dishes:
- Copenhagen butter cookies, 520-21
- Copenhagen carrots, 197-98
- creamy wild mushroom soup, 163
- dilled carrots, 196-97
- Ida's beet salad, 194
- Nordic Cobb salad, 114-15
- rack of lamb with tarragon herb rub, 328

Darjeeling tea, 464
Date:
- and chicken tagine, 372-73
- and nut cream cheese tea sandwiches, 456-57

Le Dauphin, 38-39
Ida Davidsen's Restaurant (Copenhagen), 194, 437
Defatting chicken broth, 128
Déjeuner sur l'Herbe (menu), 175
De Koninck of Flanders, 446
Delicate herbed potato pancakes, 202-3
Denmark:
- beers of, 438-39
- breakfast at Hotel d'Angleterre in (Copenhagen), 26
- Café Lumskebugten in (Copenhagen), 341
- cheeses of, 499-501
- chocolate with coffee in, 467
- *konditori* in, 520

Desserts, 508-57
- angel berry trifle, 532-33
- banana bliss, 509
- cherry compote, 510
- confetti lemon sorbet, 551-52
- cranachan, 533-34
- fruit and cheese, 519
- galatoboureko, 548-49
- lime baked bananas, 509
- melon coupe Sasha, 513-14
- Mexican Christmas bread pudding, 530-31
- Mexican coconut rice pudding, 531-32
- orange flan, 527
- Pavlova, 519-20
- peches au Bandol, 512-13
- peeled whole or sliced oranges, 510
- profiteroles, 549-50
- quince spoon sweet, 512
- raspberry ruby sorbet, 552
- scarlet summer pudding, 529-30
- Scottish shortbread, 526
- Turkish fig pastries, 524
- *see also* Cakes (sweet); Cookies; Ice cream; Ice cream sundaes; Tarts (sweet)

Dessert wines:
- of Crimea, 117
- of Hungary, 374

Deviled beef ribs, Sri Lankan, 339-40
Diekirch Premium, 447
Dill(ed):
- caper butter, 44
- carrots, 196-97
- cucumber salad, 103-4
- sweet mustard sauce, 413

Dîner en Ville (menu), 180
Dinner menus, 178-89
- Andalusian, 181
- Après Ski, 180
- Bites Before the Bolshoi, 184
- Blushing Beet Bash, 185
- Caribbean Carnivale, 189
- Casual Mexican Summer Supper, 187
- Chilean Tastings, 188
- Chinese Cook-in Dinner, 186
- La Costa Del Sol, 181
- Cozy Fireside Supper, 187
- Dîner en Ville, 180
- Dinner for the Gods, 182
- Dinner with Japanese Influences, 185
- Dubliner, 183
- Flavors of Summer, 180
- Heavenly Harvest Dinner, 180
- Homey Mediterranean Dinner, 179
- Magyar Magic, 185
- Malay Festival Nights, 186
- Mardi Gras Magic, 188
- Mediterranean Tastes, 178
- Mediterranean Pasta Dinner, 179
- Mexican Fiesta, 187
- Midnight Sun Celebration, 183
- Moroccan Couscous Dinner, 181
- Nordic Nosh, 184
- 1,001 Nights, 181
- Paradise Island Dinner, 188
- Plaka Supper, 182
- Portuguese Tango Dinner, 182

Provençal Supper, 179
Reggae Evening, 189
Rio Revelry, 188
Russian Nights, 184
St. Martin's Day Feast, 184
Santa Lucia Dinner, 179
Santorini Splendor, 182
Singapore Supper, 186
Sultan's Feast, 183
Taj Table, 187
Thai Table, 186
Tokyo Tailgate, 185
Tropicana al Fresco, 189
Turkish Delight, 183
Viva Havana, 189
Dipping sauce, 318, 319
Dips:
cucumber and yogurt (plaka tsatsiki), 65-66
Kalamata olive purée, 60-61
Laurie's basic guacamole, 61
pita chips for, 66
skordalia sauce, 65
Disrude, Anne, 453
Djemaa el Fna (Marrakech), 137
Dobos, Jozef C., 462
Doc's Restaurant (New Preston, Ct.), 66, 272
Dolcetto d'Alba, 298
Domecq, 255
Dorset scones, 460-61
Dos Equis, 84, 85
Dragon Stout, 428
Drohojowski, Saun and Pancho, 246-47
Dry Sack, 317
Dublin corned beef and cabbage, 343-44
Dubliner (dinner menu), 183
Duck:
breasts, black currant, 389
Gordon's quesadillas, 86
roast, melon, and mango salad, 391-92
roasting, 391
tomato, and pineapple soup, Peranakan (itek tim), 146-47
and two-bean pasta, Mediterranean, 299
Durian, 319

E

Earl Grey tea, 464
Eastern Europe, wines of, 374-77
Edam, 503
Edinburgh, tea at Caledonian Hotel in, 476-77
Egg(s):
Bali sunrise brunch, 6-7
Caribe Western omelet, 7
caviar, à la Russe, 51-52
English mixed grill, 13-14
hard-cooked, *smørrebrød*, 437
Jamaican crab salad composée, 121-22
Khaled Kouhen's salad michwiya (grilled vegetable salad), 119
Nani's tortilla de patatas, 9-10
Nordic Cobb salad, 114-15
odja (Tunisian Western omelet), 12-13
poached, 6
salad tea sandwiches, Ritzy, 456
and salmon caviar salad, 51
scrambled, and salt cod hash, 10-11
softly scrambled, with asparagus and cured ham, 10
Thai fried rice and, 271
torrijas (Spanish "French" toast), 17
tuna Niçoise briks, 81-82
Turkish Western omelet, 12
Wende's avgolemono soup, 157-58
whites, in meringues, 519-20
Eggplant, 212
ratatouille, 213-14
Riad's baba ghanouj, 66-67
salad, Turkish, 112-13
sandwich, Thai, 451
Thai coconut ratatouille, 212-13
Egri Bikavér, 374, 376
Egyptian Spice Market (Istanbul), 46
Eiswein, 418, 419
Elgee Park, 518
Ellen's hot and sour soup, 136
Elmquist, Lisa, 398, 399
Emigren Park (Istanbul), 480
Emotion (aperitif), 38
Empanadas, Chilean, 82-83
Enchiladas, chicken picadillo, 384
Endive, *see* Belgian endive
England:
beers of, 346-48
palette of, 455
tea in, 452, 464, 474-75
English and English-inspired dishes:
angel berry trifle, 532-33
chicken soup, 143
cucumber and tiny sprout tea sandwiches, 453-54
Cumberland sauce, 345
Gaspé smoked salmon tea sandwiches, 459
mixed grill, 13-14
orange horseradish cream, 345
Ritzy egg salad tea sandwiches, 456
scarlet summer pudding, 529-30
Ensrud, Barbara, 171
Errazuriz, 280
Esimova, Irina, 478-79
Esrom, 501
Exotic lamb curry, 329-30
Ezerjó grape, 375

F

Farina, in galatoboureko, 548-49
Fava beans:
Chilean pistou with cilantro pesto, 151-52
skinning, 151
Faxe Fad, 439
Fennel:
pasta arrabiata, 300
Provençal chickpea slather, 58
spanakopita, 90
Feriani, Château, 488
Fernandes, 154
Feroce, 62
Ferreira, 154
Feta cheese, 503, 504

Greek salad, 112
spanakopita, 90
Turkish Western omelet, 12
Fez-style tomato soup, 159-60
Fiesta corn salsa, 246
Fig pastries, Turkish, 524
Finland:
beers of, 439
Nordic-style breakfast in (Helsinki), 23
Fino, 316
Finnish cardamom tea loaf, 461
First courses, *see* Appetizers and hors d'oeuvres; Salads, first-course or accompaniment; Soups
Fish, 395, 411-29
baked swordfish Provençal, 425-26
Baltic sturgeon salad, 123
black sea bass baked in salt crust, 420
Copenhagen cod cakes, 435-36
halibut lemon kebabs, 420-21
island grilled red snapper, 422
pla preeo wan (sweet and sour flounder), 422-23
pot, Caribbean, 428-29
Provençal pan bagna, 440
Russian cod ragout, 425
salmon ribbon bites, 44
sauce, Thai, 254-55
smoked, in Scottish fried rice, 271-72
smoking, 415
stock, 130
thod mun pla (tiny Thai croquettes), 74-75
zarzuela, 426-27
see also Crab(meat); Salmon; Salt cod; Shellfish; Shrimp
Flaccianello, 298
Flageolet salad, 104
Flan, orange, 527
Flavors of Summer (dinner menu), 180
Floridita Bar (Havana), 32, 34
Flounder, sweet and sour (pla preeo wan), 422-23
Flying Horse, 256
Focaccia, 489-90
Fond de Cave, 324
Fonseca, J. M. da, 154
Fontodi, 297
Food markets, 226-34
in Agra (India), 228
Balikcilar Carsisi fish market (Istanbul), 231
Budapest's Central Market, 232
in Hong Kong, 233-34, 319
konditori of Denmark, 520
Marrakech's spice market, 276
Martinique's spice market, 260
Mercado Central de Abastos (Oaxaca, Mexico), 226-29
Mercado da Riberia (Lisbon), 229-30
Misir Carsisi spice bazaar (Istanbul), 231-33
Saluhall (Stockholm), 399
Tsukiji market (Tokyo), 26, 423
Forastier, Adrian, 9, 449
Forastier, Nani, 9
France:
palette of, 94
tea at Angelina in (Paris), 477
wines of, 362-65
Franconia, 417-18
Frascati, 296
French and French-inspired dishes:
chèvre cheesecake, 540-41
chicken soup, 143
coq au vin, 360-61
La Coupole salad, 95
Dîner en Ville (menu), 180
French Goûter d'Hiver (lunch menu), 176
gratin dauphinois, 206
griottes (pickled sour cherries), 238-39
Heavenly Harvest Dinner (menu), 180
herb roasted chicken, 359-60
kugelhopf, 465-66
moules marinière, 410
poulet chasseur, 371
profiteroles, 549-50
Resto des Amis' onion soup gratinée, 155
roasted peppers and haricots verts, 101
Sunday farmhouse roast pork, 313
tarte tatin, 537
torrijas (Spanish "French" toast), 17
vermouth cassis, 37
see also Niçoise and Niçoise-inspired dishes; Provençal and Provençal-inspired dishes
Frescobaldi, 297
Fried:
chicken, Tokyo, 371-72
rice, Scottish, 271-72
rice and egg, Thai, 271
Frijoles negros, 284
Frosting, coffee, 467
Fruit(s):
of Caribbean, 99
and cheese, as dessert, 519
of China, 390
dried, display of nuts and, 46
of Greece, 511
of India, 387
of Italy, 306
of Morocco, 355
of Portugal, 482
rabbit tagine with, 354
of Russia, 458
salad, mambo, 97-98
salade tropicale de, 514
salsa, Thai, 246
of Scandinavia, 500
of Southeast Asia, 546
of Spain, 528
of Tunisia, 472
of Turkey, 525
see also specific fruits
Fuller, 348
Furmint grape, 375, 376

Gaeng kua goong (curried pineapple and prawns), 405-6
Gaja, 297
Galatoboureko, 548-49
Galina's berry tea, 469
Gambrinus, 447

Game:
- Chinese squabs, 388-89
- fruited rabbit tagine, 354
- Provençal rabbit in tawny port, 356
- roasted pheasant with Prince Charles sauce, 393-94

Garam masala,sweet, 259
Garbure, 156
Garlic:
- bruising, 153
- and cilantro bread soup (sopa alentejana), 152-53
- croutons, 96-97
- glazed roasted shallots and, 214-15
- lemon vinaigrette, 102
- lime vinaigrette, 98
- linguine with oil and, Liguria, 304
- mashed potatoes with arugula, 209
- rigani, and white bean slather, 57-58
- sauce, sweet, 79
- skordalia sauce, 65

Gaspé smoked salmon tea sandwiches, 459
Gattinara, 298
Gavi, 296
Gazpacho:
- cha-cha corn, 169
- Mexican, 167

Genghis Khan, 441
Georgia, wines and Cognacs of, 470
Georgian and Georgian-inspired dishes:
- chakhokbili (chicken stew), 367-68
- satsivi (chicken bathed in walnut sauce), 72-74

Gerbaud (Budapest), 462
German potato salad, 203
Germany:
- beers of, 204-5
- wines of, 416-19

Gibbs Farm (Tanzania), 240-41
Ginger(ed):
- crème de crécy, 161
- and honey-glazed chicken, 366

Gingerbread, Jamaican, 542-43
Gingersnaps, 522
Giraf, 439
La Gitana, 316
Glaze, chocolate, 539, 547, 548
Glazed roasted shallots and garlic, 214-15
Golden chicken curry, 381
Golden Eagle, 256
Goong waan (spicy sweetened shrimp), 68-69
Goose, St. Martin's Day roasted, 392-93
Gordon's (Aspen, Co.), 86
Gordon's quesadillas, 86
Gouda, 503
Gouden Carolus, 446
Goulash, Magyar, 336
Goumenissa, 106
Grains, 262-87
- black-eyed peas and barley, 284-85
- Chilean quinoa tabouleh, 281
- classic polenta, 273
- Granny's mushroom kasha, 281-82
- polenta with crimini mushroom sauce, 272-73
- quick-cooking polenta, 273-74
- seven vegetable couscous, 276-77
- *see also* Pasta; Rice

Grand Marnier sauce, 530, 531
Gran Fuedo, 317
Granny Reesman's stuffed cabbage, 342-43
Granny's mushroom kasha, 281-82
Grapefruit:
- fresh, spritz, 31-32
- Napoleon Bonaparte (aperitif), 39-40

Grapes, in samba Waldorf salad, 100
Gratin dauphinois, 206
Graviera, 504-5
Gravlax, 411-13
- seared, 413-14

Greece:
- breakfast at Hotel Doma in (Chania, Crete), 23-24
- cheeses of, 503-5
- fruit basket of, 511
- *meze* in, 67
- ouzo in, 31
- palette of, 64
- visit to Aegina in, 45
- wines of, 105-7

Greek and Greek-inspired dishes:
- bruschetta, 220
- chicken soup, 143
- Dinner for the Gods (menu), 182
- galatoboureko, 548-49
- herb roasted leg of lamb, 328-29
- hot shrimp in a pot, 403-4
- individual moussakas, 334
- *Meze* Celebration (menu), 178
- pastitsio, 338
- Plaka Supper (menu), 182
- plaka tsatsiki (cucumber and yogurt dip), 65-66
- quince spoon sweet, 512
- rigani, white bean, and garlic slather, 57-58
- salad, 112
- Santorini Splendor (dinner menu), 182
- skordalia sauce, 65
- spanakopita, 90
- spiced Peloponnesian lamb shanks, 330-31
- tomato sauce, 309
- veal shank "stifado," 353-54
- Wende's avgolemono soup, 157-58

Green beans:
- flageolet salad, 104
- hearty Irish beef soup, 131
- Martinique, 200
- roasted peppers and haricots verts, 101
- salad Parador, 397-98
- thod mun pla (tiny Thai croquettes), 74-75

Greene King, 348
Greens, in spanakopita, 90
Gremolata:
- mint, 354
- orange, 352

Greve, 502
Grilled:
- cheese sandwich, yummy, 449
- halibut lemon kebabs, 420-21
- jerk chicken, 369-70

pork satay, 320-21
red snapper, island, 422
smoked salmon, Phuket, 414
vegetable salad (Khaled Kouhen's salad michwiya), 119
yakitori, 74
yogurt kebabs, 331-32
Griñon, Marqués de, 317
Griottes (pickled sour cherries), 238-39
Gris de Boulaouanem, 488
Gris de Tunisie, 488
Grolsch, 447
Grossett, 518
Grouper, in Caribbean fish pot, 428-29
Gruyère cheese, in Caribbean croque monsieur, 442
Guacamole, Laurie's basic, 61
Guillen, Nicolas, 315
Guinness, 349
Gundel (Budapest), 337
Gundel, Karoly, 337
Gurdjiani, 470
Gymkhana, 256

H

Habana Libra pork roast, 313-14
Hacked chicken salad, 388
Haiti, beer of, 428
Halibut:
baked, Provençal, 425-26
lemon kebabs, 420-21
Ham:
Caribbean croque monsieur, 442
and cheese salad tea sandwiches, Anne's, 453
Cubana sandwich, 442-43
cured, softly scrambled eggs with asparagus and, 10
Hamburgers, great Turkish, 444-45
Hardy's, 517
Haricots verts:
Mediterranean duck and two-bean pasta, 299
penne pasta salade niçoise, 289-90
roasted peppers and, 101
salad Parador, 397-98
Harira soup, 136-38
Harissa, 239
Harp, 349
Hash:
beef, luscious, 341-42
salt cod, scrambled egg and, 10-11
Havana:
La Bodeguita del Medio in, 315
breakfast at Inglaterra in, 20-21
origin of daiquiri in, 34
Havana jelly-roll cake, 543-44
Havarti, 501
Hazelnut(s):
almond biscotti, 522-23
Linzer tart, 535-37
toasting, 523, 536-37
Hearty Irish beef soup, 131
Heavenly Harvest Dinner (menu), 180
Heineken, 447
La Heladeria Coppelia (Havana), 543, 554
Helsinki, Nordic-style breakfast in, 23
Herb(ed)(s):
cherry chicken salad tea sandwiches, 457
chèvres bathed in extra virgin olive oil and, 47-48
orange chèvre slather, 56
potato pancakes, delicate, 202-3
roasted chicken, the French way, 359-60
roasted leg of lamb, 328-29
wild mushrooms, 201-2
Herdade de Esporão, 154
Herrgårdhost, 502
Herring, Palterovich creamy apple, 118
Highland pâté, 46-47
Highland Winter Luncheon (menu), 173
"High tea," 464
Holland, *see* Netherlands
Home Mediterranean Dinner (menu), 179
Honey and ginger-glazed chicken, 366
Hong Kong:
markets in, 233-34, 319
pork chops, 318-20
Hors d'oeuvres, *see* Appetizers and hors d'oeuvres
Horseradish orange cream, 345
Horse Shoe Inn (Peebleshire, Scotland), 533
Hot:
chocolate (chocolate a la taza), 5
Russian borscht, 132-33
shrimp in a pot, 403-4
and sour soup, Ellen's, 136
Hotel d'Angleterre (Copenhagen), 26
Hotel Doma (Chania, Crete), 23-24
Hotel Gellert (Budapest), 19-20
Huckleberries, 460
Hungarian and Hungarian-inspired dishes:
black cherry soup, 169-70
cherry tea cake, 462-63
chicken soup, 142
creamy paprika potatoes, 206
csirke paprikás (paprika chicken), 378
Magyar goulash, 336
Magyar Magic (dinner menu), 185
Hungary:
afternoon respite at Gerbaud in (Budapest), 462
breakfast at Hotel Gellert in (Budapest), 19-20
Central Market in (Budapest), 232
dinner at Gundel in (Budapest), 337
palette of, 208
paprika in, 207
wines of, 374-76
Hushållsost, 502

I

Ice cream:
banana rum, 553
chocolate chocolate chunk, 557
coconut cream, 555-56
rum raisin, 552-53
Tia Maria, 555
vanilla bean, 556-57
see also Sorbets
Ice Cream Dream Party for the Kids (menu), 178
Ice cream sundaes:
Antilles banana split, 556
banana split, 554
Copa Lolita, 554
Coupe Trinidad, 556
at La Heladeria Coppelia (Havana), 554
Indian's Canoe, 554
pineapple split, 554
primavera, 554
suprema, 554
Unicorno, 554
Icing, cream cheese, 540
Ida's beet salad, 194
Idiazabal, 498
La Ina, 316
Indage India Ltd., 256
India:
Agra market in, 228
chutneys in, 241
coffee at Taj View Hotel in (Agra), 547
condiments with coffee in, 547
fruit basket of, 387
palette of, 251
wines and beers of, 256
Indian and Indian-inspired dishes:
apple-pineapple raita, 250
badam sandheko (spiced roasted peanuts), 46
bhel poori, 48-49
blazing squash chili, 218-19
chicken rogan josh, 367
chicken soup, 142
chicken tikka, 382
creamed spinach, 215-16
cumin curry rolls, 490-91
curried golden squash soup, 158
curry butter, 257
Madras chicken salad, 385-86
mango-tomato raita, 250
masala for mildly spiced sauces, 257-58
minted banana-coconut raita, 249-50
mulligatawny soup, 139-40
not-really tamarind sauce, 50
raita cool down, 248-49
savory masala for meat, 258-59
savory mint and coriander chutney, 49-50
serving wines with, 256
spiced vegetable dal, 286-87
sweet garam masala, 259
Taj Table (dinner menu), 187
Indian's Canoe (sundae), 554
Indian Summer Mid Day (menu), 173
Indio Oscura, 84
Individual moussakas, 334
Indonesia:
Amandari Hotel in (Bali), 263
fruit basket of, 546
palette of, 148
Indonesian and Indonesian-inspired dishes:
Amandari smoked salmon angel pasta, 289
Bali's sunrise brunch, 6-7
chicken soup, 142
citrus cream, shrimp, and papaya salad, 122
cool down salsa, 247
itek tim (Peranakan duck, tomato, and pineapple soup), 146-47
lamb satay, 329
mee soto (chicken noodle curry), 382-83
pork satay, 320-21
prathaad lom (prawn rolls), 79-80
primavera potato salad, 113-14
ribbon cake, 545
rijsttafel, 270
satays, 320
saus kacang (peanut sauce), 71-72
soto banjar (chicken noodle soup), 145-46
soy sauce, 79
spiced prawn and pineapple soup, 149
sweet garlic sauce, 79
Inglaterra (Havana), 20-21
Insalata d'estate, 92-93
Ireland:
beers of, 349
breakfast at Ballymaloe in (County Cork, Ireland), 27
Irish and Irish-inspired dishes:
Dublin corned beef and cabbage, 343-44
Dubliner (dinner menu), 183
hearty beef soup, 131
Irish Country Breakfast (menu), 172
Irish Lace Tea (menu), 176
oatmeal cookies, 526-27
orange horseradish cream, 345
porridge, 3
soda bread, 492-93
Island grilled red snapper, 422
Island pan-barbecued shrimp, 68
Istanbul:
Balikcilar Carsisis fish market in, 231
breakfast at Hilton in, 24-25
Cicek Pasaji in, 231
Egyptian Spice market in, 46
lunch at Pandeli in, 231
Misir Carsisi spice bazaar in, 231-33
Ortaköy district of, 444
tea at Emigren Park in, 480
Italian and Italian-inspired dishes:
chicken soup, 143
focaccia, 489-90
hazelnut-almond biscotti, 522-23
insalata d'estate, 92-93
Italian Antipasto Festival (menu), 176
Leslie Russo's summer puttanesca, 303-4
linguine with garlic and oil Liguria, 304
marinara sauce, 302

Mediterranean Tastes, (dinner menu), 178
Mediterranean duck and two-bean pasta, 299
minestrone, 149-50
osso buco with baby artichokes, 352-53
pappa al pomodoro (tomato bread soup), 155-57
pasta arrabiata, 300
pesto, 490
rosemary-olive bread, 484-85
rustic tomato-pancetta pasta, 299-300
Santa Lucia Dinner (menu), 179
shrimp salad crostini, 398
spinach risotto, 265
summer tomato risotto, 266
Vineyard Luncheon (menu), 174
Italy:
fruit basket of, 306
palette of, 301
wines of, 296-98
Itek tim (Peranakan duck, tomato, and pineapple soup), 146-47

J, K

Jackfruit, 78
Jackson Estate, 518
Jade soup, 161-62
Jamaica:
allspice in, 369
beers of, 428
jerk in, 326, 327
Pork Pit in (Montego Bay), 326
street food in, 443
Jamaican and Jamaican-inspired dishes:
banana brunch soup, 4
Caribe Western omelet, 7
crab salad composée, 121-22
fresh grapefruit spritz, 31-32
gingerbread, 542-43
home-style chicken, 368-69
island grilled red snapper, 422
jerk chicken, 369-70
jerk pork ribs, 326
jerk sauce, 327
Lunch on the Lanai (menu), 174
Montego red pea soup, 165-66
pepper sauce, 253-54
Reggae Evening (dinner menu), 189
Jamaican Blue Mountain coffee, 15
Japan:
beers of, 134-35
breakfast at Okura Hotel in (Tokyo), 25
noodles at Narita Airport in, 291
palette of, 424
soy sauce in, 366
Tsukiji market in (Tokyo), 26, 423
wines of, 135
Japanese and Japanese-inspired dishes:
basic teriyaki sauce, 372
at breakfast in Amsterdam, 25
chicken soup, 142
Dinner with Japanese Influences (menu), 185
serving wine or beer with, 135
stir-fried scallops and asparagus teriyaki, 409-10
Tokyo fried chicken, 371-72
Tokyo Tailgate (dinner menu), 185
yakitori, 74
Jasmine tea, 464
Jelly-roll cake, Havana, 543-44
Jerk, 327
chicken, 369-70
at Pork Pit (Montego Bay, Jamaica), 326
pork ribs, 326
sauce, Jamaican, 327
Jubilee, 256
Jumbo shrimp ragout, 404-5

Kabinett, 418-19
Kadarka grape, 376
Kalamata olive purée, 60-61
Kambanis, Aristedes, 548
Kasha, Granny's mushroom, 281-82
Kasseri, 505
Katnook Estate, 518
Kebabs:
halibut lemon, 420-21
yogurt, 331-32
Keemum tea, 464
Kefalotiri, 505
Kéknyelü, 375-76
Khaled Kouhen's salad michwiya (grilled vegetable salad), 119
Kidney beans:
blazing squash chili, 218-19
calypso beans and rice, 283-84
Montego red pea soup, 165-66
Kingfisher, 256
Kirin, 134
Kiwi(s):
Pavlova, 519-20
salsa, 245-46
Knappstein, Tim, 518
Koc, Berra, 200
Kölsch, 204
Konditori, 520
Kopanisti, 505
Koudiat, 488
Kouhen, Khaled, 119
Kourtakis Kritikos, 107
Kriek, 447
Kryddost, 502
Kugelhopf, 465-66
Kumeu River, 518

Lacryma Rosa, 298
Lageder, 297
Lager, 205, 340-41
Lagrein Rosato, 298
Lalli's Turkish pilaf tomatoes, 267
Lamb, 328-35
chops, in English mixed grill, 13-14

curry, exotic, 329-30
great Turkish hamburgers, 444-45
harira soup, 136-38
individual moussakas, 334
leg of, herb roasted, 328-29
Prince Charles sauce for, 394
and prune tagine, 332
rack of, with tarragon herb rub, 328
satay, 329
shanks, spiced Peloponnesian, 330-31
stock, 130-31
yogurt kebabs, 331-32
Lambic beer, 446-47
Lancer's, 154
Lapsang Souchong tea, 464
Lar de Barros, 317
Latin America:
beers of, 84-85
palette of, 199
see also specific countries
Laurie's basic guacamole, 61
Lavash, 491-92
Leányka grape, 375
Leek(s):
Berra's Turkish, 200-201
chicken, and barley soup, Scottish (cock-a-leekie), 138-39
seven vegetable couscous, 276-77
Leimdorfer, Martin and Christine, 412
Lemon(s):
garlic vinaigrette, 102
mint yogurt dressing, 103
and olive-studded chicken, 370
orzo, 307
preserved, 236
sorbet, confetti, 551-52
velvety tarte au citron, 538
wafers, 521
Wende's avgolemono soup, 157-58
Lentil(s):
with pineapple and bananas, Mexican, 285-86
salad, savory, 287
vegetable soup, Mediterranean, 150-51
Leslie Russo's summer puttanesca, 303-4
Liebana, 497-98
Liebfraumilch, 417, 418
Lily lime vinaigrette, 400
Lima beans, in hearty Irish beef soup, 131
Lime:
baked bananas, 509
basic daiquiri, 33
Cuba Libre, 35
garlic vinaigrette, 98
lily vinaigrette, 400
Margaritas, 31
punch Martinique, 35
Rhumlet, 39
Limpa bread, 486-87
Lindeman, 517
Lingonberry tea cake, little Swedish, 465
Linguine:
with garlic and oil Liguria, 304
with steamed clams Alentejo, 409
Linzer tart, 535-37
Lion (beer), 256
Lisa's rosy shrimp salad, 398-400
Lisbon, Mercado da Riberia in, 229-30
Little India (Singapore), 225
Little Swedish Lingonberry tea cake, 465
Liver pâté:
Highland, 46-47
smørrebrød, 437
Lobsters, in zarzuela, 426-27
London (beer), 256
London, tea at Ritz in, 474-75
Lunch menus, 173-75
Déjeuner sur l'Herbe, 175
Highland Winter Luncheon, 173
Indian Summer Mid Day, 173
Lunch at the Beach, 174
Lunch from a Swedish Market, 173
Lunch on the Lanai, 174
Riviera Luncheon, 175
Soup and Sandwich Cuban Style, 174
Summer Sunday Luncheon, 175
Vineyard Luncheon, 174
Luscious beef hash, 341-42
Lustau, 317
Luxembourg, beers of, 447

M

MacArthur, Laura, 468
McEwan, 349
Mâche, in La Coupole salad, 95
McKenna, Sally and John, 27
Mackeson's, 348
Maculan, 297
Madras chicken salad, 385-86
Magon, 488
Magyar goulash, 336
Magyar Magic (dinner menu), 185
Mahon, 496-97
Malaya, beers of, 401
Malay and Malay-inspired dishes:
curried noodles, 290-91
Malay Festival Nights (dinner menu), 186
oxtail soup, 132
Malvasia, 297
Mambo fruit salad, 97-98
Mambo mango pork, 318
Mamounia Hotel (Marrakech), 18-19
Manchego, 495-96
Mango:
daiquiri, 33
Jamaican pepper sauce, 253-54
mambo pork, 318
roast duck, and melon salad, 391-92
Thai fruit salsa, 246
tomato raita, 250
Manouri, 504, 505
Manzanilla, 316
Manzanilla olives, 60
Mardi Gras Magic (dinner menu), 188
Margaritas, 31
Marinades:
for beef, 339, 448
for chicken, 71, 366, 379
for pork, 319
Marinara sauce, 302

Markets, *see* Food markets
Marmalade, Yacout tomato, 219
Marrakech:
breakfast at Mamounia Hotel in, 18-19
dinner at Yacout in, 333
Djemaa el Fna in, 137
spice market in, 276
Martinique:
rum of, 32
spice market in, 260
Martinique and Martinique-inspired dishes:
boiled potatoes and sliced tomatoes, 210-11
Caribbean coconut tart, 534-35
Le Colibri porc colombo, 321-22
Creole crab slather, 58-59
Le Dauphin, 38-39
feroce, 62
green beans, 200
Napoleon Bonaparte (aperitif), 39-40
Piña Martinique, 35
Planteur, 37
punch Martinique, 35
sauce chien, 254
Masalas, 257-259
for mildly spiced sauces, 257-58
savory, for meat, 258-59
sweet garam, 259
Massandra, 117
Mateus, 154
Mavrodaphne, 107
Maxim's (Paris), 537
Mayonnaise:
avocado, 433-35
cilantro, 402-3
orange-rosemary, 76-77
sunrise orange, 101
Meat:
loaf à la Lindstrom, 341
loaf *smørrebrød*, 437
savory masala for, 258-59
see also Beef; Ham; Lamb; Pork; Sausages; Veal
Meatballs, Swedish, 340
Mediterranean and Mediterranean-inspired dishes:
duck and two-bean pasta, 299
Flavors of Summer (menu), 180
Homey Mediterranean Dinner (menu), 179
jumbo shrimp ragout, 404-5
lentil vegetable soup, 150-51
Mediterranean Pasta Dinner (menu), 179
Mediterranean Tastes, (dinner menu), 178
roast chicken, 359
spiced olives, 44-45
Summer Mediterranean Brunch (menu), 172
white bean soup, 164-65
yummy grilled cheese sandwich, 449
see also specific countries
Mee soto (Indonesian chicken noodle curry), 382-83
Melon:
coupe Sasha, 513-14
roast duck, and mango salad, 391-92
see also Cantaloupe; Watermelon
Menus, 171-89
for breakfasts and brunches, 172-73
for celebrations, 176-78
for dinners, 178-89
for lunches, 173-75
for teas, 175-76
Mercado Central de Abastos (Oaxaca, Mexico), 226-29
Mercado da Riberia (Lisbon), 229-30
Meringues, 519-20
Merlen, 518
Merlot, 135, 256, 401
of Chile, 278-79
Mesost, 502
Meursault, 364
Mexican and Mexican-inspired dishes:
La Bamba rice, 264
blazing squash chili, 218-19
Café Tacuba Breakfast (menu), 172
Casual Mexican Summer Supper (menu), 187
cha-cha corn gazpacho, 169
chicken picadillo enchiladas, 384
chicken soup, 142
Christmas bread pudding, 530-31
Christmas red pepper soup, 159
coconut rice pudding, 531-32
gazpacho, 167
Gordon's quesadillas, 86
Laurie's basic guacamole, 61
lentils with pineapple and bananas, 285-86
Margaritas, 31
Mexican Fiesta (dinner menu), 187
mu shu chicken burrito, 384-85
Oaxaca tostada bites, 43-44
pepito (steak sandwich), 448
pot roast, 335-36
ranchero salsa rosa, 242-43
salsa Carnaval, 245
Saun's fresh salsa verde, 246-47
señorita shrimp boats, 402
Vera Cruz veggie sandwich, 449-50
Mexico:
beers of, 84-85
breakfast at Café Tacuba in (Mexico City), 21-22
festival of radishes in, 168
Mercado Central de Abastos in (Oaxaca), 226-29
palette of, 244
wines of, 255
Mexico City, breakfast at Café Tacuba in, 21-22
Meze, 67, 113
Berra's Turkish leeks, 200-201
hot shrimp in a pot, 403-4
Meze Celebration (menu), 178
skordalia sauce, 65
tarama slather, 59-60
Turkish mussel salad, 121
zesty yogurt slather, 56-57
Middle Eastern and Middle Eastern-inspired dishes:
Chilean quinoa tabouleh, 281
lavash, 491-92
Mediterranean lentil vegetable soup, 150-51
Oriental pilaf, 269
Riad's baba ghanouj, 66-67
Midnight Sun Celebration (dinner menu), 183
Milmanda, 317

Minestrone, 149-50
Mint(ed)(y):
  avocado shrimp salad, 400
  banana-coconut raita, 249-50
  and coriander chutney, savory, 49-50
  gremolata, 354
  jade soup, 161-62
  lemon yogurt dressing, 103
  Mojito, 34
  sweet carrots, 198
  sweetened emerald zucchini, 223-24
  tea, Sidi Bou Saïd, 471
  zesty yogurt slather, 56-57
Miranda, Carmen, 515
Misir Carsisi spice bazaar (Istanbul), 231-33
Miss Maud's breakfast banana bread, 16-17
Mixed grill, English, 13-14
Mizithra, 505
Moët et Chandon, 324, 325
Mohan Meakin, 256
Mojito, 34
Moldova, wines of, 377
Monkfish, in zarzuela, 426-27
Monte Antico, 298
Montego red pea soup, 165-66
Montepulciano d'Abruzzo, 298
Monterey Jack:
  Oaxaca tostada bites, 43-44
  sandwich, yummy grilled, 449
  Vera Cruz veggie sandwich, 449-50
Morning muesli, 3
Moroccan and Moroccan-inspired dishes:
  baby bisteeyas, 380-81
  Casbah carrot soup, 160-61
  chicken and date tagine, 372-73
  chicken soup, 143
  Fez-style tomato soup, 159-60
  fruited rabbit tagine, 354
  harira soup, 136-38
  lamb and prune tagine, 332
  minted sweet carrots, 198
  Moroccan Couscous Dinner (dinner menu), 181
  preserved lemons, 236
  pumpkin tea loaf, 468-69
  stewed chicken under a blanket, 378-79
  sugared mashed carrots, 197
  sweetened emerald zucchini, 223-24
  Yacout tomato marmalade, 219
Morocco:
  breakfast at Mamounia Hotel in (Marrakesh), 18-19
  dinner at Yacout in (Marrakech), 333
  Djemaa el Fna in (Marrakech), 137
  fruit basket of, 355
  Marrakech's spice market in, 276
  palette of, 275
  wines of, 488
Moros y cristianos (black beans and rice), 282-83
Moselblümchen, 418
Moules marinière, 410
Mountadam, 518
Moussakas, individual, 334
Muesli, morning, 3
Mukuzani, 470
Mulligatawny soup, 139-40
Murphy's, 349
Murree Brewery, 256
Murrieta, Marqués de, 317
Mushroom(s):
  crimini, sauce, polenta with, 272-73
  kasha, Granny's, 281-82
  Oriental spinach salad, 93
  spinach risotto, 265
Mushroom(s), wild:
  blinchiki, 55
  herbed, 201-2
  hunting for, 201
  soup, creamy, 163
Mu shu chicken burrito, 384-85
Mussel(s):
  cleaning, 410
  moules marinière, 410
  salad, Turkish, 121
Mustard sauce, sweet dilled, 413
My own curry powder, 260

Naccarato, Gordon, 86
Nahe, 417
Nani's tortilla de patatas, 9-10
Naoussa, 106, 107
Napoleon Bonaparte (aperitif), 39-40
Narita Airport (Tokyo), 291
Negra Modelo, 85
Nemea, 107
Netherlands:
  beers of, 447
  broodjes in, 445
  cheeses of, 502-3
  Dutch breakfast in, 26
  Japanese-style breakfast in, 25
New Zealand, wines of, 518
Niçoise and Niçoise-inspired dishes:
  penne pasta salade niçoise, 289-90
  pissaladière, 80-81
  Riviera Luncheon (menu), 175
  tuna briks, 81-82
Noche Buena, 85
La Noche de los Rábanos, 168
Nonya cuisine, 145
  itek tim (Peranakan duck, tomato and pineapple soup), 146-47
Noodle(s):
  butterfly, sesame, 293-94
  and chicken curry, Indonesian (mee soto), 382-83
  fresh crab pad Thai, 293
  Indonesian chicken soup with (soto banjar), 145-46
  Malay curried, 290-91
  pudding, Berta's really rich, 307
Nordic and Nordic-inspired dishes:
  Cobb salad, 114-15
  Nordic Nosh (dinner menu), 184

see also Scandinavian and Scandinavian-inspired dishes; Swedish and Swedish-inspired dishes
North Africa, wines of, 488
North African and North African-inspired dishes:
harissa, 239
Mediterranean lentil vegetable soup, 150-51
olive and lemon-studded chicken, 370
Provençal rabbit in tawny port, 356
savory masala for meat, 258-59
sweet garam masala, 259
see also Moroccan and Moroccan-inspired dishes; Tunisian and Tunisian-inspired dishes
Norway, beers of, 439
Not-really tamarind sauce, 50
Nut(s):
and date cream cheese tea sandwiches, 456-57
display of dried fruit and, 46
see also specific nuts

Oat(meal)(s):
cookies, Irish, 526-27
cranachan, 533-34
Irish porridge, 3
morning muesli, 3
Scottish oatcakes, 493
Oaxaca (Mexico), Mercado Central de Abastos in, 226-29
Oaxaca tostada bites, 43-44
Odja (Tunisian Western omelet), 12-13
Oerbier, 446
Okra, in Caribbean fish pot, 428-29
Okura Hotel (Tokyo), 25
Old Mill, 348
Old Presbytery (Kinsdale, Cork, Ireland), 492
Olive(s):
bell pepper, and tomato pasta, Spanish, 308
Kalamata, purée, 60-61
and lemon-studded chicken, 370
Mediterranean spiced, 44-45
penne pasta salade niçoise, 289-90
rosemary bread, 484-85
Spanish, 60
Spanish, tapenade, 60
Olive oil:
extra virgin, chèvres bathed in herbs and, 47-48
topping for focaccia, 489-90
Oloroso, 316
Omar Khayyám (wine), 256
Omelets:
Caribe Western, 7
Tunisian Western (odja), 12-13
Turkish Western, 12
1,001 Nights (dinner menu), 181
Onion(s):
bites, Brazilian, 43
Nani's tortilla de patatas, 9-10
pissaladière, 80-81
seven vegetable couscous, 276-77
soup gratinée, Resto des Amis' French, 155
Operakällaren (Stockholm), 412
Orange(s):
chèvre slather, herbed, 56
Emotion (aperitif), 38
flan, 527
gremolata, 352
horseradish cream, 345
insalata d'estate, 92-93
mayonnaise, sunrise, 101
peeled whole or sliced, 510
Planteur, 37
pound cake, 541-42
rosemary mayonnaise, 76-77
spiced tea, 473
sunshine salad, 98
zesty yogurt slather, 56-57
Oriental dishes:
pilaf, 269
spinach salad, 93
see also Chinese and Chinese-inspired dishes; Japanese and Japanese-inspired dishes
Oriental Hotel (Bangkok), 68
Ortaköy (Istanbul), 444
Orval, 447
Orvieto, 296
Orzo, lemon, 307
Ossetra, 52
Osso buco with baby artichokes, 352-53
Ourika, 488
Ouzo, 31
Oxtail soup, Malay, 132

Pad thai, fresh crab, 293
Pakistan, wines and beers of, 256
Palladin, Jean-Louis, 155
Palterovich creamy apple herring, 118
Paltrow, Bruce, 86, 118
Pan bagna, Provençal, 440
Pancakes, 53
banana cinnamon, 15-16
buckwheat blini, 54
delicate herbed potato, 202-3
Swedish, 14
see also Crêpes
Pancetta-tomato pasta, rustic, 299-300
Pan con tomate, 219-20
Pandeli (Istanbul), 231
Pans, seasoning, 54
Pao-doce (Portuguese sweet bread), 483
Papaya:
citrus cream, and shrimp salad, 122
fiesta corn salsa, 246
kiwi salsa, 245-46
Pappa al pomodoro (Italian tomato bread soup), 155-57
Paprika, 207
chicken (csirke paprikás), 378
potatoes, creamy, 206
Paradise Island Dinner (menu), 188
Parador (Carmona, Spain), 397
Paris, tea at Angelina in, 477
Parmigiano-Reggiano with fruit, 519
Pasta, 288-309
angel, Amandari smoked salmon, 289
arrabiata, 300
Catalan romesco "sauce" rotelli, 303

Grecian tomato sauce for, 308
lemon orzo, 307
Leslie Russo's summer puttanesca, 303-4
linguine with garlic and oil Liguria, 304
linguine with steamed clams Alentejo, 409
marinara sauce for, 302
Mediterranean duck and two-bean, 299
Mediterranean Pasta Dinner (menu), 179
pastitsio, 338
penne, salade niçoise, 289-90
rustic tomato-pancetta, 299-300
Spanish bell pepper, tomato, and olive, 308
spicy peanut sauce for, 294
see also Noodle(s)
Pastitsio, 338
Pastrami, 441
böreks, 87
"Reuben" pita, 441
Turkish Western omelet, 12
Pastries (savory):
baby bisteeyas, 380-81
Chilean empanadas, 82-83
cocktail coulibiac, 87-88
Gordon's quesadillas, 86
pastrami böreks, 87
pissaladière, 80-81
prathaad lom (prawn rolls), 79-80
spanakopita, 90
stewed chicken under a blanket, 378-79
sultan's pillows, 223
tarte Provençale, 221-22
Thai crab spring rolls, 77-78
tuna Niçoise briks, 81-82
Pastries (sweet):
galatoboureko, 548-49
profiteroles, 549-50
Turkish fig, 524
see also Tarts (sweet)
Pastry, phyllo, *see* Phyllo pastry
Pastry cream, basic, 550-51
Pastry dough, 537
Pâté:
Highland, 46-47
smørrebrød, 437
Patras, 107
Pavlova, 519-20
Pea(s):
La Bamba rice, 264
black-eyed, and barley, 284-85
jade soup, 161-62
red, soup, Montego, 165-66
soup, Scandinavian smoky, 162
Peach(es):
peches au Bandol, 512-13
melba sangria, Chilean white, 40
Peanut(s):
sauce, Indonesian (saus kacang), 71-72
sauce, spicy, 294
spiced roasted (badam sandheko), 46
Pecan chocolate cake, 539
Peches au Bandol, 512-13
Pelican, 256
Peloponnesian spiced lamb shanks, 330-31
Peñaflor, 324
Penfold's, 517
Penne pasta salade niçoise, 289-90
Pepito (Mexican steak sandwich), 448
Pepper(s) (bell):
Bali sunrise brunch, 6-7
calypso beans and rice, 283-84
Catalan romesco "sauce" rotelli, 303
Chilean avocado salad, 102-3
Khaled Kouhen's salad michwiya (grilled vegetable salad), 119
Leslie Russo's summer puttanesca, 303-4
Mexican gazpacho, 167
odja (Tunisian Western omelet), 12-13
ratatouille, 213-14
red, Christmas soup, 159
red, roasted, vinaigrette, 92
roasted, 202
roasted, and haricots verts, 101
sauce, Jamaican, 253-54
sultan's pillows, 223
tomato, and olive pasta, Spanish, 308
Pepper(s), chili, *see* Chili(es)
Peranakan and Peranakan-inspired dishes, 145
itek tim (duck, tomato, and pineapple soup), 146-47
spiced prawn and pineapple soup, 149
Periyali (New York City), 65
Pesto, 490
cilantro, Chilean pistou with, 151-52
topping for focaccia, 489-90
Petaluma, 517
Pheasant, roasted, with Prince Charles sauce, 393-94
Phuket grilled smoked salmon, 414
Phyllo pastry:
baby bisteeyas, 380-81
Chilean empanadas, 82-83
cocktail coulibiac, 87-88
galatoboureko, 548-49
pastrami böreks, 87
spanakopita, 90
stewed chicken under a blanket, 378-79
sultan's pillows, 223
Turkish fig pastries, 524
working with, 82
Picadillo enchiladas, chicken, 384
Pickled:
cabbage, sweet, 237-38
carrots, Thai, 236-37
cucumbers, Thai, 237
sour cherries (griottes), 238-39
Pickles, in Nordic Cobb salad, 114-15
Pilaf(s):
Byzantine, 269-70
Oriental, 269
tomatoes, Lalli's Turkish, 267
Pils, 447
Pilsener Urquell, 196
Piña Martinique, 35
Pineapple:
apple raita, 250
cool down salsa, 247
cream cheese icing, 540
curried prawns and (gaeng kua goong), 405-6
Le Dauphin, 38-39
duck, and tomato soup,

Peranakan
(itek tim), 146-47
mambo fruit salad, 97-98
mambo mango pork, 318
Mexican lentils with bananas and, 285-86
Piña Martinique, 35
Planteur, 37
and prawn soup, spiced, 149
rum upside-down cake, 544
salade tropicale de fruits, 514
samba Waldorf salad, 100
split, 554
La Vie en Rose, 37-38
Pine nuts, toasting, 411
Pinot Bianco, 296
Pinot Blanc, 256
Pinot Grigio, 135, 296
Pinot Gris, 135, 256, 401
Pinot Noir, 135
Piper-Heidsieck, 324
Pires, João, 154
Pissaladière, 80-81
Pistou with cilantro pesto, Chilean, 151-52
Pita:
chips, 66
"Reuben," 441
Plaka Supper (menu), 182
Plaka tsatsiki (cucumber and yogurt dip), 65-66
Planteur, 37
Pla preeo wan (sweet and sour flounder), 422-23
Plum:
conserve, savory, 239-40
tart, summer, 535
Poached egg, 6
Polenta, 274
classic, 273
with Cremini mushroom sauce, 272-73
quick-cooking, 273-74
Pomelos, 97
Poori, bhel, 48-49
Pork, 313-27
chops, Hong Kong, 318-20
Le Colibri porc colombo, 321-22
Cubana sandwich, 442-43
mambo mango, 318
meat loaf à la Lindstrom, 341
ribs, jerk, 326
Rio's feijoada, 322-23
roast, Habana Libra, 313-14
roast, *smørrebrød*, 437
roast, Sunday farmhouse, 313
satay, 320-21
see also Ham; Sausages
Pork Pit (Montego Bay, Jamaica), 326
Porridge, Irish, 3
Port, 154
tawny, Provençal rabbit in, 356
Portugal:
cheeses of, 498
fruit basket of, 482
Mercado da Riberia in (Lisbon), 229-30
palette of, 408
wines of, 154
Portuguese and Portuguese-inspired dishes:
chicken soup, 143
pao-doce (sweet bread), 483
Portuguese Tango Dinner (menu), 182
scrambled egg and salt cod hash, 10-11
sopa alentejana (garlic and cilantro bread soup), 152-53
steamed clams Alentejo, 409
Potato(es):
baked, with garnishes, 211
Baltic sturgeon salad, 123
Banana Leaf vegetable curry, 224-25
boiled, and sliced tomatoes, 210-11
creamy paprika, 206
croquettes, tiny, 76
garlic mashed, with arugula, 209
gratin dauphinois, 206
Nani's tortilla de patatas, 9-10
pancakes, delicate herbed, 202-3
penne pasta salade niçoise, 289-90
primavera salad, 113-14
Russian salad, 108-9
salad, German, 203
seven vegetable couscous, 276-77
sorrel soup (botvinya), 163-64
Stockholm street, 209-10
Pot roast, Mexican, 335-36
Poulet chasseur, 371
Poultry, 357-88
Chinese squabs, 388-89
roasted pheasant with Prince Charles sauce, 393-94
St. Martin's Day roasted goose, 392-93
see also Chicken; Duck
Pound cake, orange, 541-42
Poussins, in coq au vin, 360-61
Prathaad lom (prawn rolls), 79-80
Prästost, 502
Prawn(s):
curried pineapple and (gaeng kua goong), 405-6
and pineapple soup, spiced, 149
rolls (prathaad lom), 79-80
see also Shrimp
Preserved lemons, 236
Prestige Stout, 428
Primavera potato salad, 113-14
Prince Charles sauce, 394
Pripps, 439
Profiteroles, 549-50
Provençal(e) and Provençal(e)-inspired dishes:
baked swordfish, 425-26
brandade, 62-63
chèvres bathed in herbs and extra virgin olive oil, 47-48
chickpea slather, 58
Déjeuner sur l'Herbe (menu), 175
pan bagna, 440
peches au Bandol, 512-13
Provençal Supper (menu), 179
rabbit in tawny port, 356
ratatouille, 213-14
tarte, 221-22
tiny potato croquettes, 76
tomatoes, 221
Provençe, palette of, 358
Prune(s):
and lamb tagine, 332
spiced Peloponnesian lamb shanks, 330-31
sultan's pillows, 223
Puddings:
beet bread, 195
Mexican Christmas bread, 530-31
Mexican coconut rice, 531-32
noodle, Berta's really rich, 307
scarlet summer, 529-30

Puffs, choux, 549
Puligny-Montrachet, 364
Pumpkin tea loaf, Moroccan, 468-69
Punches:
 Barbara Ensrud's red wine sangria, 40-41
 Chilean white peach melba sangria, 40
 Martinique, 35
Purée, Kalamata olive, 60-61
Purslane, 215
Puttanesca, Leslie Russo's summer, 303-4

Quesadillas, Gordon's, 86
Quince, 513
 spoon sweet, 512
Quinoa tabouleh, Chilean, 281
Quinta de Bacalhõa, 154
Quinta do Cotto, 154

Rabbit(s), 354-56
 tagine, fruited, 354
 in tawny port, Provençàl, 356
Rack of lamb with tarragon herb rub, 328
Radishes:
 Mexican festival of, 168
 Russian garden salad, 109-10
Ragouts:
 jumbo shrimp, 404-5
 Russian cod, 425
Raimat, 317
Raisin(s):
 Jamaican pepper sauce, 253-54
 kugelhopf, 465-66
 rum, ice cream, 552-53
Raitas:
 apple-pineapple, 250
 cool down, 248-49
 mango-tomato, 250
 minted banana-coconut, 249-50
Raki, 31
Ranchera salsa rosa, 242-43
Ras el hanout, 276
Raspberry(ies):
 Chilean white peach melba sangria, 40
 cranachan, 533-34
 Galina's berry tea, 469
 Linzer tart, 535-37
 preserves, in Havana jelly-roll cake, 543-44
 ruby sorbet, 552
 scarlet summer pudding, 529-30
Ratatouille, 213-14
 Thai coconut, 212-13
Rauchbier, 204
Rauenthal, 417
Red cabbage:
 braised, 195-96
 Caribe crudités, 92
Red snapper:
 Caribbean fish pot, 428-29
 island grilled, 422
Red Stripe, 428
Reggae Evening (dinner menu), 189
Reguengos de Monsarraz, 154
Reiss, Adam, 66
Restaurant Bergere (Hammamet, Tunisia), 12
Restaurant Han (near Istanbul), 420
Resto des Amis (Atlanta, Ga.), 155
Resto des Amis' French onion soup gratinée, 155
Retsina, 105-6
"Reuben" pita, 441
Rheingau, 417
Rheinhessen, 417
Rheinpfalz, 417
Rhubarb-beet compote, 240
Rhumlet, 39
Riad, Chef, 272
Riad's baba ghanouj, 66-67
Ribalaiqua, Constante, 34
Ribeiro & Ferreira, 154
Ribollita, 156
Ribs:
 beef, Sri Lankan deviled, 339-40
 pork, jerk, 326
Rice:
 La Bamba, 264
 and black beans (moros y cristianos), 282-83
 Byzantine pilaf, 269-70
 calypso beans and, 283-84
 coconut pudding, Mexican, 531-32
 fried, and egg, Thai, 271
 fried, Scottish, 271-72
 Lalli's Turkish pilaf tomatoes, 267
 Oriental pilaf, 269
 spicy marigold, 263
 spinach risotto, 265
 vegetable sparkled, 264-65
Rich beef broth, 128-29
Rich coconut milk, 252
Riesling:
 of Chile, 280
 with Chinese food, 135
 of Germany, 416-19
 with Indian food, 256
 with Southeast Asian food, 401
Rigani, white bean, and garlic slather, 57-58
Rijsttafel, 270
 menu for, 177
Ringnes, 439
Rio de Janeiro, breakfast on beach in, 22
Rioja, 316, 317
Rio Revelry (dinner menu), 188
Rio's feijoada, 322-23
Riscal, Marqués de, 317
Risottos:
 spinach, 265
 summer tomato, 266
Ritz (London), 474-75
Ritzy egg salad tea sandwiches, 456
Riviera (beer), 256
Riviera Luncheon (menu), 175
Rkatsiteli grape, 117, 377
Roast(ed):
 beets, 194-95
 bell peppers, 202
 chicken, Mediterranean, 359
 chicken with herbs, the French way, 359-60
 duck (method), 391
 duck, melon, and mango salad, 391-92
 goose, St. Martin's Day, 392-93
 leg of lamb, herb, 328-29
 peppers and haricots verts, 101

pheasant with Prince Charles sauce, 393-94
pork, Habana Libra, 313-14
pork, mambo mango, 318
pork, Sunday farmhouse, 313
rack of lamb with tarragon herb rub, 328
red pepper vinaigrette, 92
tomatoes, 220
Robola, 107
Rochefort, 447
Rodenbach, 447
Roditys, 107
Roe, *see* Caviar
Rolls:
cumin curry, 490-91
prawn (prathaad lom), 79-80
Romesco "sauce" rotelli, Catalan, 303
Roncal, 496
Rosato dei Masi, 298
Rose hip tea, 469
Rosemary:
olive bread, 484-85
orange mayonnaise, 76-77
Rose Pouchon tea, 464
Rosés:
of Greece, 107
of Italy, 298
of North Africa, 488
of Portugal, 154
Rosso di Montalcino, 298
Rotelli with Catalan romesco "sauce," 303
Rothbury Estate, 517
Rouge Tropical, 39
Royal-Altmünster, 447
Rubesco, 298
Ruffino, 297
Rully, 364
Rum:
banana daiquiri, 33-34
banana ice cream, 553
basic daiquiri, 33
butter sauce, 16
Cuba Libre, 35
Le Dauphin, 38-39
Emotion, 38
of Martinique, 32
Mojito, 34
Piña Martinique, 35
pineapple upside-down cake, 544
Planteur, 37
punch Martinique, 35
raisin ice cream, 552-53
Rhumlet, 39
Rouge Tropical, 39
strawberry or mango daiquiri, 33
La Vie en Rose, 37-38
Russia:
breakfast menu from, 11
fruit basket of, 458
palette of, 111
tea at home in, 478-79
wines of, 117
zakuski in, 67, 110
Russian and Russian-inspired dishes:
Baltic sturgeon salad, 123
beet bread pudding, 195
Bites Before the Bolshoi (dinner menu), 184
blini, 53
botvinya (sorrel potato soup), 163-64
buckwheat blini, 54
caviar eggs à la Russe, 51-52
chicken soup, 142
cocktail coulibiac, 87-88
cod ragout, 425
Galina's berry tea, 469
garden salad, 109-10
Granny's mushroom kasha, 281-82
hot borscht, 132-33
melon coupe Sasha, 513-14
Moroccan pumpkin tea loaf, 468-69
Palterovich creamy apple herring, 118
rose hip tea, 469
Russian Nights (dinner menu), 184
Russian Samovar Tea (menu), 175-76
Russian *Zakuski* Party (menu), 177
salad, 108-9
salmon caviar egg salad, 51
Sasha's apple crab cocktail, 115-16
wild mushroom blinchiki, 55
Russian "Nalivki," 470
Rustic tomato-pancetta pasta, 299-300
Rye, in limpa bread, 486-87

Sacher Hotel (Vienna), 547-48
Sachertorte, 547-48
St. George grape, 107
St. Martin's Day Feast (dinner menu), 184
St. Martin's Day roasted goose, 392-93
St. Pauli Girl, 204
St. Petersburg (Russia), tea at home in, 478-79
Saint Sixtus, 446
St. Thomas, beer of, 428
Saison Dupont, 447
Salad(s):
egg, tea sandwiches, Ritzy, 456
ham and cheese, tea sandwiches, Anne's, 453
herbed cherry chicken, tea sandwiches, 457
Italian shrimp, crostini, 398
Salad dressings:
blue cheese, 115
cilantro mayonnaise, 402-3
curry, 386
lemon-mint yogurt, 103
see also Vinaigrettes
Salade tropicale de fruits, 514
Salads, entrée:
Chilean avocado, 102-3
Greek, 112
hacked chicken, 388
Jamaican crab, composée, 121-22
Lisa's rosy shrimp, 398-400
Madras chicken, 385-86
minty avocado shrimp, 400
Parador, 397-98
penne pasta salade niçoise, 289-90

roast duck, melon, and mango, 391-92
señorita shrimp boats, 402
tarama salmon blush, 118
Thai seafood, 396-97
Salads, first-course or accompaniment, 92-123
a-jaad (Thai cucumber cool down), 248
Baltic sturgeon, 123
braised globe artichokes, 193
Caesar, 96
Caribe crudités, 92
citrus cream, shrimp, and papaya, 122
La Coupole, 95
dilled cucumber, 103-4
flageolet, 104
German potato, 203
Greek, 112
Ida's beet, 194
insalata d'estate, 92-93
mambo fruit, 97-98
michwiya, Khaled Kouhen's (grilled vegetable salad), 119
Nordic Cobb, 114-15
Oriental spinach, 93
Palterovich creamy apple herring, 118
potato primavera, 113-14
Russian, 108-9
Russian garden, 109-10
samba Waldorf, 100
Sasha's apple crab cocktail, 115-16
savory lentil, 287
Sevilla *tapas*, 102
sunny sweet potato, 212
Sunshine, 98
sweetened emerald zucchini, 223-24
Turkish, 113
Turkish eggplant, 112-13
Turkish mussel, 121
Salice Salentino, 298
Salmon:
cocktail coulibiac, 87-88
croquettes, savory, 411
gravlax, 411-13
potato primavera salad, 113-14
ribbon bites, 44
seared gravlax, 413-14
tarama blush, 118
Salmon, smoked, 415
angel pasta, Amandari, 289
Gaspé, tea sandwiches, 459
Phuket grilled, 414
smørrebrød, 437
Salmon caviar:
egg salad, 51
eggs à la Russe, 51-52
tarama salmon blush, 118
Salsas:
Carnaval, 245
cool down, 247
fiesta corn, 246
kiwi, 245-46
ranchero, rosa, 242-43
Thai fruit, 246
verde, Saun's fresh, 246-47
Salt cod, 63
brandade, 62-63
hash and scrambled egg, 10-11
Salt crust, black sea bass baked in, 420
Saltram, 517
Saluhall (Stockholm), 399
Samba Waldorf salad, 100
Samos, 107
Samsoe, 499
Sancho, Martin, 317
Sandwiches, 432-51
Caribean croque monsieur, 442
chocolate, 449
Copenhagen cod cakes, 435-36
Cubana, 442-43
Dutch (*broodjes*), 445
great Turkish hamburgers, 444-45
Khaled Kouhen's salad michwiya (grilled vegetable salad), 119
Mexican steak (pepito), 448
Provençal pan bagna, 440
"Reuben" pita, 441
salmon ribbon bites, 44
smørrebrød, 437
Soup and Sandwich Cuban Style (menu), 174
Thai crab "club" with avocado mayonnaise, 433
Thai eggplant, 451
Vera Cruz veggie, 449-50
yummy grilled cheese, 449
see also Tea sandwiches
Sangria:
Barbara Ensrud's red wine, 40-41
Chilean white peach melba, 40
San Michaele, 297
Santa Carolina, 280
Santa Lucia Dinner (menu), 179
Santa Margherita, 297
Santa Rita, 280
San Telmo, 324
Santorini Splendor (dinner menu), 182
Saperavi grape, 117
Sapporo, 134
Saraswat, Arvind, 241
Sarria, Señorío de, 317
Sasha's apple crab cocktail, 115-16
Sasse, Wende, 548-49
Satay, 320
chicken, Singapore style, 71
lamb, 329
pork, 320-21
Satsivi (chicken bathed in walnut sauce), 72-74
Sauces:
avocado cream, 86
avocado "mayonnaise," 433-35
basic teriyaki, 372
butter rum, 16
chien, 254
chocolate, 551
cilantro pesto, 152
Cumberland, 345
Grand Marnier, 530, 531
Grecian tomato, 309
Indonesian peanut (saus kacang), 71-72
Indonesian soy, 79
Jamaican jerk, 327
Jamaican pepper, 253-54
mildly spiced, masala for, 257-28
not-really tamarind, 50
orange horseradish cream, 345
orange-rosemary mayonnaise, 76-77
pesto, 490
Prince Charles, 394
skordalia, 65
spicy peanut, 294

sunrise orange mayonnaise, 101
sweet dilled mustard, 413
sweet garlic, 79
Thai fish, 254-55
Thai sweet and sour, 75-76
walnut, 73
see also Salad dressings; Salsas; Vinaigrettes
Saun's fresh salsa verde, 246-47
Sausages:
chorizo, in La Bamba rice, 264
English mixed grill, 13-14
pasta arrabiata, 300
Rio's feijoada, 322-33
Saus kacang (Indonesian peanut sauce), 71-72
Sauvignon Blanc, 256, 297, 401
of Chile, 278-80
of France, 365
Savory:
lentil salad, 287
masala for meat, 258-59
mint and coriander chutney, 49-50
plum conserve, 239-40
salmon croquettes, 411
Scallops:
Caribbean fish pot, 428-29
stir-fried asparagus and, teriyaki, 409-10
Thai seafood salad, 396
zarzuela, 426-27
Scandinavia:
aquavit in, 89
beers of, 438-39
fruit basket of, 500
palette of, 434
see also specific countries
Scandinavian and Scandinavian-inspired dishes:
chicken soup, 142
dilled cucumber salad, 103-4
Finnish cardamom tea loaf, 461
gravlax, 411-13
limpa bread, 486-87
Midnight Sun Celebration (dinner menu), 183
Nordic Nosh (dinner menu), 184
primavera potato salad, 113-14
rhubarb-beet compote, 240
smoky pea soup, 162
smørrebrød, 437
sweet dilled mustard sauce, 413
wheat berry bread, 485-86
see also Swedish and Swedish-inspired dishes
Scarlet summer pudding, 529-30
Schloss Johannisberg, 417
Schloss Vollrads, 417
Scones, Dorset, 460-61
Scotch bonnet chilies, 253
Scotland:
beers of, 349
tea at Caledonian Hotel in (Edinburgh), 476-77
tea at Cringletie House Hotel in, 475-76
Scottish and Scottish-inspired dishes:
chicken, leek, and barley soup (cock-a-leekie), 138-39
coffee, 473
cranachan, 533-34
fried rice, 271-72
Highland pâté, 46-47
Highland Winter Luncheon (menu), 173
oatcakes, 493
roasted pheasant with Prince Charles sauce, 393-94
shortbread, 526
spice cake with coffee frosting, 466-67
Scottish & Newscastle, 348
Scrambled egg(s):
and salt cod hash, 10-11
softly, with asparagus and cured ham, 10
Sea bass, black, baked in salt crust, 420
Seafood, 395-429
tarama slather, 59-60
see also Crab(meat); Fish; Salmon; Salt cod; Shellfish; Shrimp
Seared gravlax, 413-14
Seasoning pans, 54
Seeger, Guenter, 155
Sémillon, 256, 401
Señorita shrimp boats, 402
Sephardic spinach stems, 217
Seppelt, 517
Serpa, 498
Serra, 498
Serunding, 257
Sesame butterfly noodles, 293-94
Seven vegetable couscous, 276-77
Sevilla *tapas* salad, 102
Sevruga, 52
Shallots, glazed roasted garlic and, 214-15
Shellfish, 395-411
Caribbean fish pot, 428-29
moules marinière, 410
smoking, 415
steamed clams Alentejo, 409
stir-fried scallops and asparagus teriyaki, 409-10
Swedish crayfish, 407
Thai seafood salad, 396-97
Turkish mussel salad, 121
zarzuela, 426-27
see also Crab(meat); Shrimp
Shepherd Neame, 348
Sherry, 316-17
Shiraz, 135, 516, 517, 518
Shirley, Norma, 326, 327
Shortbread, Scottish, 526
Shrimp:
avocado salad, minty, 400
boats, señorita, 402
Caribbean fish pot, 428-29
citrus cream, and papaya salad, 122
gaeng kua goong (curried pineapple and prawns), 405-6
island pan-barbecued, 68
jumbo, ragout, 404-5
Nordic Cobb salad, 114-15
paste, 405
in a pot, hot, 403-4
prathaad lom (prawn rolls), 79-80
salad, Lisa's rosy, 398-400
salad crostini, Italian, 398
salad Parador, 397-98
spicy sweetened (goong waan), 68-69
Thai fried rice and egg, 271
Thai seafood salad, 396
velvety curried, 403
zarzuela, 426-27
Sidi Bou Saïd minted tea, 471

Sidi Rais, 488
Simon, 447
Sinebrychoff, 439
Singapore:
  beers of, 401
  Little India in, 225
Singapore and Singapore-inspired dishes:
  Banana Leaf vegetable curry, 224-25
  chicken satay, 71
  Malay curried noodles, 290-91
  Singapore Supper (menu), 186
Singha, 401
Skillet cinnamon toast, 468
Skordalia sauce, 65
Slathers, 56
  see also Spreads
Samuel Smith, 348
Smoked fish and shellfish, 415
  see also Salmon, smoked
Smørrebrød, 437
Snacks:
  bhel poori, 48-49
  chocolate sandwiches, 449
  skillet cinnamon toast, 468
Soda bread, Irish, 492-93
Softly scrambled eggs with asparagus and cured ham, 10
Sole, sweet and sour (pla preeo wan), 422-23
Sopa alentejana (garlic and cilantro bread soup), 152-53
Sorbet(s):
  confetti lemon, 551-52
  raspberry ruby, 552
  simple sugar syrup for, 552
Sorrel potato soup (botvinya), 163-64
Soto banjar (Indonesian chicken noodle soup), 145-46
Soups, 126-53
  avgolemono, Wende's, 157-58
  banana brunch, 4
  beef, hearty Irish, 131
  black bean, Carlos', 166-67
  black cherry, Hungarian, 169-70
  bread, 156
  carrot, Casbah, 160-61
  cha-cha corn gazpacho, 169
  chicken broth, 127
  chicken noodle, Indonesian (sota banjar), 145-46
  Chilean corn and chicken chowder, 144-45
  Christmas red pepper, 159
  cock-a-leekie (Scottish chicken, leek, and barley), 138-39
  creamy wild mushroom, 163
  curried golden squash, 158
  duck, tomato, and pineapple, Peranakan (itek tim), 146-47
  fish stock, 130
  fresh vegetable broth, 129-30
  frijoles negros, 284
  garlic and cilantro bread (sopa alentejana), 152-53
  gingered crème de crécy, 161
  harira, 136-38
  hot and sour, Ellen's, 136
  hot Russian borscht, 132-33
  jade, 161-62
  lamb stock, 130-31
  lentil vegetable, Mediterranean, 150-51
  Mexican gazpacho, 167
  minestrone, 149-50
  mulligatawny, 139-40
  onion, gratinée, Resto des Amis' French, 155
  oxtail, Malay, 132
  pea, Scandinavian smoky, 162
  red pea, Montego, 165-66
  rich beef broth, 128-29
  sorrel potato (botvinya), 163-64
  Soup and Sandwich Cuban Style (luncheon menu), 174
  spiced prawn and pineapple, 1 49
  tomato, Fez-style, 159-60
  tomato bread, Italian (pappa al pomodoro), 155-57
  white bean, Mediterranean, 164-65
  world-class chicken, 141-43
  zarzuela, 426-27
South America:
  beers of, 84-85
  palette of, 199
  tea in, 478
  see also specific countries
Southeast Asia:
  beers of, 401
  palette of, 70
  shrimp paste in, 405
  see also specific countries
Southeast Asian and Southeast Asian-inspired dishes:
  chicken soup, 142
  Rijsttafel menu, 177
  serving wines or beers with, 401
  see also Indonesian and Indonesian-inspired dishes; Thai and Thai-inspired dishes
Soviero, Donaldo, 37, 304
Soy sauce, 366
  Indonesian, 79
Spain:
  cheeses of, 494-98
  fruit basket of, 528
  olives of, 60
  palette of, 8
  tapas in, 67, 316
  wines of, 316-17
Spanakopita, 90
Spanish and Spanish-inspired dishes:
  The Andalusian (dinner menu), 181
  Andalusian steak rollos, 338-39
  Barbara Ensrud's red wine sangria, 40-41
  bell pepper, tomato, and olive pasta, 308
  black sea bass baked in salt crust, 420
  Catalan romesco "sauce" rotelli, 303
  chicken soup, 143
  "French" toast (torrijas), 17
  hot chocolate (chocolate a la taza), 5
  Nani's tortilla de patatas, 9-10
  pan con tomate, 219-20
  salad Parador, 397-98
  Sevilla *tapas* salad, 102
  skillet cinnamon toast, 468
  softly scrambled eggs with asparagus and cured ham, 10
  Spanish olive tapenade, 60
  spinach Catalan, 217
  zarzuela, 426-27

Sparkling wines:
of Argentina and Brazil, 324, 325
of Russia, 117
with sushi, 135
Spätlese, 419
Spetsat, 439
Spice cakes:
with coffee frosting, 466-67
Indonesian ribbon, 545
little Swedish lingonberry tea, 465
Spiced:
olives, Mediterranean, 44-45
orange tea, 473
Peloponnesian lamb shanks, 330-31
prawn and pineapple soup, 149
roasted peanuts (badam sandheko), 46
vegetable dal, 286-87
Spices:
colombo curry powder, 259-60
Jamaican, 369
in Martinique market, 260
masala for mildly spiced sauces, 257-58
at Misir Carsisi bazaar (Istanbul), 231-33
Moroccan, 276
my own curry powder, 260
savory masala for meat, 258-59
sweet garam masala, 259
Spicy:
marigold rice, 263
peanut sauce, 294
sweetened shrimp (goong waan), 68-69
Spinach:
Catalan, 217
Indian creamed, 215-16
risotto, 265
salad, Oriental, 93
stems, Sephardic preparation of, 217
Spinnaker, 428
Spreads:
brandade, 62-63
Creole crab slather, 58-59
eggplant, 451
feroce, 62
herbed orange chèvre slather, 56
Provençal chickpea slather, 58
Riad's baba ghanouj, 66-67
rigani, white bean, and garlic slather, 57-58
Spanish olive tapenade, 60
tarama slather, 59-60
Turkish eggplant salad, 112-13
zesty yogurt slather, 56-57
Spring rolls, Thai crab, 77-78
Spritz, fresh grapefruit, 31-32
Sprout and cucumber tea sandwiches, 453-54
Squabs, Chinese, 388-89
Squash:
Bahia butternut mash, 217-18
chili, blazing, 218-19
Moroccan pumpkin tea loaf, 468- 69
soup, curried golden, 158
Sri Lankan and Sri Lankan-inspired dishes:
deviled beef ribs, 339-40
spicy marigold rice, 263
Steak:
rollos, Andalusian, 338-39
sandwich, Mexican (pepito), 448
Steamed clams Alentejo, 409
Steffi Berne's chocolate skinnies, 523
Steinberg, 417
Stewed chicken under a blanket, 378-79
Stews:
Caribbean fish pot, 428-29
chicken and date tagine, 372-73
Le Colibri porc colombo, 321-22
csirke paprikás (paprika chicken), 378
exotic lamb curry, 329-30
fruited rabbit tagine, 354
Georgian chicken (chakhokbili), 367-68
home-style Jamaican chicken, 368-69
jumbo shrimp ragout, 404-5
lamb and prune tagine, 332
Magyar goulash, 336
mee soto (Indonesian chicken noodle curry), 382-83
olive and lemon-studded chicken, 370
osso buco with baby artichokes, 352-53
poulet chasseur, 371
Provençal rabbit in tawny port, 356
Russian cod ragout, 425
veal shank "stifado," 353-54
Stir-fried scallops and asparagus teriyaki, 409-10
Stockholm:
dinner at Operakällaren in, 412
Lisa Elmquist's Restaurant in, 399
Saluhall market in, 399
street potatoes, 209-10
Stocks:
fish, 130
lamb, 130-31
see also Broths
Stout, 349
Strawberry(ies):
daiquiri, 33
Pavlova, 519-20
Piña Martinique, 35
scarlet summer pudding, 529-30
Street food:
in Asia, 450
at Djemaa el Fna in Marrakech, 137
in Istanbul, 444
in Jamaica, 443
Stockholm potatoes, 209-10
Stuffed cabbage, Granny Reesman's, 342-43
Stuffing, fruit, 392
Sturgeon salad, Baltic, 123
Sugared mashed carrots, 197
Sugar syrup, 34
for sorbets, 552
Sultan's Feast (dinner menu), 183
Sultan's pillows, 223
Summer Mediterranean Brunch (menu), 172
Summer plum tart, 535
Summer Sunday Luncheon (menu), 175
Summer tomato risotto, 266
Sundaes, *see* Ice cream sundaes
Sunday farmhouse roast pork, 313
Sunny sweet potato salad, 212
Sunrise orange mayonnaise, 101
Sunshine salad, 98
Suntory, 134

Sushi, serving sparkling wines with, 135
Sveciaost, 502
Sweden:
- beers of, 439
- cheeses of, 501-2
- crayfish "festival" in, 407
- dinner at Operakällaren in (Stockholm), 412
- Lisa Elmquist's Restaurant in, 399
- Saluhall market in (Stockholm), 399

Swedish and Swedish-inspired dishes:
- braised red cabbage, 195-96
- Copenhagen cod cakes, 435-36
- crayfish, 407
- delicate herbed potato pancakes, 202-3
- gravlax, 411-13
- limpa bread, 486-87
- Lisa's rosy shrimp salad, 398-400
- little lingonberry tea cake, 465
- Lunch from a Swedish Market (menu), 173
- meatballs, 340
- meat loaf à la Lindstrom, 341
- pancakes, 14
- St. Martin's Day roasted goose, 392-93
- Stockholm street potatoes, 209-10

Sweet:
- blinchiki, 459-60
- bread, Portuguese (pao-doce), 483
- dilled mustard sauce, 413
- emerald zucchini, 223-24
- garam masala, 259
- garlic sauce, 79
- pickled cabbage, 237-38

Sweet and sour:
- flounder (pla preeo wan), 422-23
- sauce, Thai, 75-76

Sweet potato salad, sunny, 212
Swiss chard:
- salad Parador, 397-98
- spanakopita, 90

Swiss morning muesli, 3
Swordfish Provençal, baked, 425-26
Syrah, 135
Syrups, 34
- for sorbets, 552

Szürkebarát, 376

Tabouleh, Chilean quinoa, 281
Tagines:
- chicken and date, 372-73
- fruited rabbit, 354
- lamb and prune, 332

Taj Table (dinner menu), 187
Taj View Hotel (Agra, India), 547
Taltarni, 518
Tamarind sauce, not-really, 50
Tansug, Sezer, 441
Tanzanian green tomato chutney, Chef Bayo's, 240-41
Tapas, 67, 316
- salad, Sevilla, 102

Tapenade, Spanish olive, 60
Tarama:
- salmon blush, 118
- slather, 59-60

Tarts (savory):
- pissaladière, 80-81
- tarte provençal, 221-22

Tarts (sweet):
- Caribbean coconut, 534-35
- Linzer, 535-37
- summer plum, 535
- tarte au citron, 538
- tarte tatin, 537

Taurasi, 298
Taurino Rosato, 298
Timothy Taylor, 348
Tea, 452
- at Angelina (Paris), 477
- at Caledonian Hotel (Edinburgh), 476-77
- at Cringletie House Hotel (Scotland), 475-76
- at Emigren Park (Istanbul), 480
- etiquette for, 464
- at Gerbaud (Budapest), 462
- in Ipanema, 478
- at Irina Esimova's Home (St. Petersburg), 478-79
- at Ritz (London), 456, 474-75

Tea, menus for, 175-76
- French Goûter d'Hiver, 176
- Irish Lace Tea, 176
- Russian Samovar Tea, 175-76
- Tea and Sympathy, 176

Tea fare, 452-80
- Dorset scones, 460-61
- Finnish cardamom tea loaf, 461
- Hungarian cherry tea cake, 462-63
- kugelhopf, 465-66
- little Swedish lingonberry tea cake, 465
- Moroccan pumpkin tea loaf, 468-69
- Scottish oatcakes, 493
- spice cake with coffee frosting, 466-67
- sweet blinchiki, 459-60

Teas:
- Galina's berry, 469
- making, 463
- orange spiced, 473
- rose hip, 469
- Sidi Bou Saïd minted, 471
- sweetening, 473
- types of, 464

Tea sandwiches:
- Anne's ham and cheese salad, 453
- cucumber and tiny sprout, 453-54
- date and nut cream cheese, 456-57
- Gaspé smoked salmon, 459
- herbed cherry chicken salad, 457
- musts for, 454
- Ritzy egg salad, 456
- serving, 453

Tecate, 85
Teifenbrunner, 297
Tequila, in Margaritas, 31
Teriyaki:
- sauce, basic, 372
- stir-fried scallops and asparagus, 409-10

Tetley, 348

Thai and Thai-inspired dishes:
- a-jaad (cucumber cool down), 248
- coconut ratatouille, 212-13
- crab "club" with avocado mayonnaise, 433
- crab spring rolls, 77-78
- edible centerpiece, 396
- eggplant sandwich, 451
- fresh crab pad Thai, 293
- fried rice and egg, 271
- fruit salsa, 246
- gaeng kua goong (curried pineapple and prawns), 405-6
- goong waan (spicy sweetened shrimp), 68-69
- honey and ginger-glazed chicken, 366
- Phuket grilled smoked salmon, 414
- pickled carrots, 236-37
- pickled cucumbers, 237
- pla preeo wan (sweet and sour flounder), 422-23
- seafood salad, 396-97
- spiced prawn and pineapple soup, 149
- sweet and sour sauce, 75-76
- Thai Table (dinner menu), 186
- Thod mun pla (tiny croquettes), 74-75

Thailand:
- beers of, 401
- fish sauce in, 254-55
- sauces and dips in, 292

Theakston, 348
Thod mun pla (tiny Thai croquettes), 74-75
Tia Maria ice cream, 555
Tiger, 401
Tignanello, 298
Tikka, chicken, 382
Tilsit, 501
Tiny potato croquettes, 76
Tiny Thai croquettes (thod mun pla), 74-75
Tio Pepe, 316
Toast:
- skillet cinnamon, 468
- Spanish "French" (torrijas), 17

Tokay, 374, 376
Tokyo:
- breakfast at Okura Hotel in, 25
- noodles at Narita Airport in, 291
- Tsukiji market in, 26, 423

Tokyo fried chicken, 371-72
Tokyo Tailgate (dinner menu), 185
Tomatillos, in Saun's fresh salsa verde, 246-47
Tomato(es):
- apricot chutney, 242
- La Bamba rice, 264
- bell pepper, and olive pasta, Spanish, 308
- bread soup, Italian (pappa al pomodoro), 155-57
- Chilean avocado salad, 102-3
- duck, and pineapple soup, Peranakan (itek tim), 146-47
- green, chutney, Chef Bayo's Tanzanian, 240-41
- insalata d'estate, 92-93
- Lalli's Turkish pilaf, 267
- mango raita, 250
- marmalade, Yacout, 219
- Mexican gazpacho, 167
- pancetta pasta, rustic, 299-300
- pan con tomate, 219-20
- peeling, 242
- Provençale, 221
- ranchero salsa rosa, 242-43
- risotto, summer, 266
- roasted, 220
- sauce, Grecian, 309
- seven vegetable couscous, 276-77
- Sevilla *tapas* salad, 102
- sliced, boiled potatoes and, 210-11
- soup, Fez-style, 159-60
- sultan's pillows, 223
- tarama salmon blush, 118
- tarte Provençale, 221-22
- Thai coconut ratatouille, 212-13

Torres (winery), 317
Torres, Miguel, 280
Torrijas (Spanish "French" toast), 17
Tortilla de patatas, Nani's, 9-10
Toscano Bianco, 296
Tostada bites, Oaxaca, 43-44
Trapiche, 324
Trappist beers, 446
Traverso, Sergio, 280
Trebbiano grape, 296
Tre Scalini (Rome), 557
Trifle, angel berry, 532-33
Trockenbeerenauslese, 419
Tropicana al Fresco (dinner menu), 189
Tsingtao, 134
Tsukiji market (Tokyo), 26, 423
Tuborg, 439
Tuna:
- Khaled Kouhen's salad michwiya (grilled vegetable salad), 119
- Niçoise briks, 81-82
- penne pasta salade niçoise, 289-90
- Provençal pan bagna, 440

Tunisia:
- fruit basket of, 472
- palette of, 120
- wines of, 488

Tunisian and Tunisian-inspired dishes:
- chicken soup, 143
- Khaled Kouhen's salad michwiya (grilled vegetable salad), 119
- odja (Western omelet), 12-13
- Sidi Bou Saïd minted tea, 471
- tuna Niçoise briks, 81-82
- Tunisian Brunch (menu), 173

Turkey:
- Balikcilar Carsisis fish market in (Istanbul), 231
- breakfast at Istanbul Hilton in, 24-25
- Cicek Pasaji in (Istanbul), 231
- fruit basket of, 525
- Istanbul's Egyptian Spice market in, 46
- Istanbul's Ortaköy district in, 444
- lunch at Pandelil in (Istanbul), 231
- *meze* in, 67
- Misir Carsisi spice bazaar in (Istanbul), 231-33
- palette of, 268
- pastirma (pastrami) in, 441
- raki in, 31
- salads in, 113
- tea at Emigren Park in (Istanbul), 480

Turkish and Turkish-inspired dishes:
- banana bliss, 509
- Berra's leeks, 200-201
- chicken soup, 143
- eggplant salad, 112-13
- fig pastries, 524
- great hamburgers, 444-45
- halibut lemon kebabs, 420-21
- hot shrimp in a pot, 403-4
- Lalli's pilaf tomatoes, 267
- *Meze* Celebration (menu), 178
- mussel salad, 121
- pastrami böreks, 87
- "Reuben" pita, 441
- savory salmon croquettes, 411
- Sultan's Feast (dinner menu), 183
- sultan's pillows, 223
- Turkish Delight (dinner menu), 183
- Western omelet, 12
- yogurt kebabs, 331-32

Turnips, in seven vegetable couscous, 276-77
Tyrrell, 517

U, V

Ukraine, wines of, 117
Undurraga, 280
Upside-down cake, pineapple-rum, 544
Uzbekistan (wine), 117

Van Dobben (Amsterdam), 445
Vanilla bean ice cream, 556-57
Los Vascos, 280
Västerbottenost, 502
Vazisubani, 470
Veal, 352-54
- osso buco with baby artichokes, 352-53
- shank "stifado," 353-54

Veber, 470
Vegetable(s):
- dal, spiced, 286-87
- fresh, broth, 129-30
- grilled, salad (Khaled Kouhen's salad michwiya), 119
- lentil soup, Mediterranean, 150-51
- minestrone, 149-50
- sandwich, Vera Cruz, 449-50
- seven, couscous, 276-77
- sparkled rice, 264-65

Vegetable dishes, 192-225
- asparagus sauté, 193
- Bahia butternut mash, 217-18
- baked potatoes with garnishes, 211
- Banana Leaf vegetable curry, 224-25
- beet bread pudding, 195
- Berra's Turkish leeks, 200-201
- blazing squash chili, 218-19
- boiled potatoes and sliced tomatoes, 210-11
- braised globe artichokes, 193
- braised red cabbage, 195-96
- Copacabana collards, 198
- Copenhagen carrots, 197-98
- creamy paprika potatoes, 206
- delicate herbed potato pancakes, 202-3
- dilled carrots, 196-97
- garlic mashed potatoes with arugula, 209
- German potato salad, 203
- glazed roasted shallots and garlic, 214-15
- gratin dauphinois, 206
- herbed wild mushrooms, 201-2
- Ida's beet salad, 194
- Indian creamed spinach, 215-16
- Martinique green beans, 200
- minted sweet carrots, 198
- pan con tomate, 219-20
- ratatouille, 213-14
- roasted beets, 194-95
- roasted bell peppers, 202
- roasted tomatoes, 220
- Sephardic spinach stems, 217
- spinach Catalan, 217
- Stockholm street potatoes, 209-10
- sugared mashed carrots, 197
- sultan's pillows, 223
- sunny sweet potato salad, 212
- sweetened emerald zucchini, 223-24
- tarte Provençale, 221-22
- Thai coconut ratatouille, 212-13
- tomatoes Provençale, 221
- Yacout tomato marmalade, 219

Velvety:
- curried shrimp, 403
- tarte au citron, 538

Vera Cruz veggie sandwich, 449-50
Verdejo grape, 317
Verdicchio, 296
Vermouth cassis, 37
Victor's Cuban Café (New York), 442-43
La Vie en Rose, 37-38
Vietnamese cuisine, serving wines with, 401
Vinaigrettes:
- apple cider, 109
- Chinese, 95
- lemon-garlic, 102
- lily lime, 400
- lime-garlic, 98
- roasted red pepper, 92
- walnut oil, 96

Viña Magaña, 317
Vineyard Luncheon (menu), 174
Vin gris, 488
Vinho verde ("green wine"), 154
Viva Havana (dinner menu), 189
Van Vollenhoven, 447

W

Wafers, lemon, 521
Waldorf salad, Samba, 100
Walnut(s):
- sauce, chicken bathed in (satsivi), 72-74
- Turkish fig pastries, 524

Walnut oil vinaigrette, 96

Watercress:
cucumber and tiny sprout tea sandwiches, 453-54
sunshine salad, 98
Watermelon:
salade tropicale de fruits, 514
salsa Carnaval, 245
Watney, 348
Weizenbier, 205
Wende's avgolemono soup, 157-58
Western omelets:
Caribe, 7
Tunisian (odja), 12-13
Turkish, 12
Westmalle Triple, 447
Wheat berry bread, 485-86
Whitbread, 348
White, Ellen, 136, 371
White bean(s):
Mediterranean duck and two-bean pasta, 299
rigani, and garlic slather, 57-58
soup, Mediterranean, 164-65
Wine(s):
of Argentina and Brazil, 324-25
of Australia and New Zealand, 516-18
of Chile, 278-80
Chilean white peach melba sangria, 40
of China and Japan, 135
with Chinese food, 135
of Eastern Europe, 374-77
of France, 362-65
of Georgia, 470
of Germany, 416-19
of Greece, 105-7
of India and Pakistan, 256
with Indian food, 256
of Italy, 296-98
with Japanese food, 135
of Mexico, 255
of North Africa, 488
peches au Bandol, 512-13
of Portugal, 154
red, sangria, Barbara Ensrud's, 40-41
of Russia, 117
with Southeast Asian food, 401
of Spain, 316-17
Wine, Barry, 345
Wolf Blass, 518
Wolfert, Paula, 276
World-class chicken soup, 141-43
Wyndham Estate, 517

X, Y, Z

Xingu, 85
Xinomavro grape, 107
Xinotroulia, Janette "Hilde," 45

Yacout (Marrakech), 197, 333
Yacout tomato marmalade, 219
Yakitori, 74
Yogurt:
apple-pineapple raita, 250
banana brunch soup, 4
cherry compote, 510
creamy, 248
and cucumber dip (plaka tsatsiki), 65-66
kebabs, 331-32
lemon-mint dressing, 103
mango-tomato raita, 250
minted banana-coconut raita, 249-50
raita cool down, 248-49
slather, zesty, 56-57
Young (beer), 348
Yummy grilled cheese sandwich, 449

Zakuski, 67, 110
Baltic sturgeon salad, 123
caviar eggs à la Russe, 51-52
Palterovich creamy apple herring, 118
Russian salad, 108-9
Russian *Zakuski* Party (menu), 177
salmon caviar egg salad, 51
Sasha's apple crab cocktail, 115-16
satsivi (chicken bathed in walnut sauce), 72-74
wild mushroom blinchiki, 55
Zarzuela, 426-27
Zenato, 297
Zeni, 297
Zesty yogurt slather, 56-57
Zucchini:
ratatouille, 213-14
seven vegetable couscous, 276-77
sweetened emerald, 223-24

Photo Credits

INTRODUCTION: AROUND THE WORLD IN 730 DAYS

Pages xi-xv: Sheila Lukins and Sheila Lukins Collection.

ROOM SERVICE

Pages xvi-1: Food photographs, Walt Chrynwski; travel photographs, Sheila Lukins and Sheila Lukins Collection.

A PERFECT START

Page 4: Sheila Lukins. Page 8: Sheila Lukins.

BREAKFAST IN BED

Page 18: Sheila Lukins. Page 19: (top left) Courtesy of The Mamounia Hotel; (bottom left) Sheila Lukins; (right) courtesy of the Casablanca Ritz Café Restaurant. Page 20: (top) Sheila Lukins Collection; (middle and bottom) Sheila Lukins. Page 22: Sheila Lukins. Page 23: The Bettmann Archive. Page 24: (top left) Sheila Lukins; (top right) Sheila Lukins Collection; (bottom) courtesy of the Turkish Culture and Information Office. Page 25: Both photos courtesy of the Hotel Okura. Page 26: Courtesy of The Danish Tourist Board. Page 27: (left) Photo by Catherine Karnow; both photos courtesy of Ballymaloe House.

WISH YOU WERE HERE

Pages 28-29: Food photographs, Walt Chrynwski; travel photographs, Sheila Lukins and Sheila Lukins Collection.

APERITIFS

Page 36: Sheila Lukins. Page 41: Sheila Lukins.

FIRST BITES & SMALL PLATES

Page 49: Sheila Lukins. Page 52: New York Public Library Picture Collection. Page 64: Jeffrey D. Sherwin. Page 69: Sheila Lukins. Page 83: Sheila Lukins. Page 84: Sheila Lukins. Page 85: (top and bottom left) Sheila Lukins. Page 89: Courtesy of Jim Beam Brands Co.

SALADS

Page 100: Sheila Lukins. Page 105: Courtesy of the Greek National Tourist Office. Page 106: (top) The Bettmann Archive. Pages 106-107: (bottom) Jeffrey D. Sherwin. Page 107: (top) Courtesy of the Greek National Tourist Office. Page 108: Sheila Lukins. Page 110: Sheila Lukins. Page 111: Sheila Lukins Collection. Page 117: Sheila Lukins Collection.

GREAT MELTING POT

Pages 124-125: Food photographs, Walt Chrynwski; travel photographs, Sheila Lukins and Sheila Lukins Collection.

SOUPS

Pages 134-135: Courtesy of Kirin U.S.A. Inc. Page 140: Sheila Lukins, Page 148: Sheila Lukins. Page 154: UPI / Bettmann. Page 168: Sheila Lukins.

MARKETPLACE

Pages 190-191: Food photographs, Walt Chrynwski; travel photographs, Sheila Lukins and Sheila Lukins Collection.

VEGETABLES

Pages 204-205: Courtesy of the German Information Center. Page 207: Sheila Lukins. Page 216: Sheila Lukins. Page 222: Sheila Lukins. Page 226: Sheila Lukins. Page 227: (left to right) Sheila Lukins; Sheila Lukins; David Hiser/Tony Stone Worldwide. Page 228: Sheila Lukins Collection. Page 229: H. Armstrong Roberts. Page 230: Sheila Lukins. Page 231: Courtesy of the Turkish Culture and Information Office. Page 233: H. Armstrong Roberts. Page 234: Sheila Lukins.

CONDIMENTS AND SPICES

Page 243: Sheila Lukins. Page 244: Sheila Lukins. Page 251: Sheila Lukins Collection. Page 252: Sheila Lukins. Page 253: Sheila Lukins. Page 255:© F. Gohier/Photo Researchers, Inc. Page 256: Sheila Lukins Collection. Page 258: Sheila Lukins.

GRAINS AND BEANS

Page 266: Sheila Lukins. Page 268: Sheila Lukins. Page 275: Sheila Lukins. Page 278: UPI / Bettmann. Page 279: (top left) Courtesy of ProChile, N.Y., Chilean Government Trade Bureau; (right) Walt Chrynwski. Page 280: (left) Walt Chrynwski; (right) The Bettmann Archive.

NOODLING AROUND

Page 292: Sheila Lukins. Page 295: Sheila Lukins. Page 296: New York Public Library Picture Collection. Page 297: Nancy Murray. Page 298: UPI/Bettmann. Page 301: Lori S. Malkin. Page 302: Jeffrey D. Sherwin. Page 305: Jeffrey D. Sherwin.

THE GRAND TOUR

Pages 310-311: Food photographs, Walt Chrynwski; fish photograph, Howard Earl Simmons; travel photographs, Sheila Lukins and Sheila Lukins Collection.

THE LAND

Page 314: Sheila Lukins. Page 316: (top) Carlos Navajas, (bottom) P. Sancho-Mata/both courtesy of ICEX Wines from Spain. Page 317: P. Sancho-Mata/courtesy of ICEX Wines from Spain. Page 323: Sheila Lukins. Page 324: Sheila Lukins. Page 325: Sheila Lukins Collection; Sheila Lukins. Page 337: Courtesy of George Lang office. Page 344: Sheila Lukins. Page 347: Courtesy of The British Tourist Authority. Page 348: Sheila Lukins. Page 349: (top) Sheila Lukins; (bottom left to right) Sheila Lukins; courtesy of The British Tourist Authority.

THE AIR

Page 361: Jeffrey D. Sherwin. Page 362: H. Armstrong Roberts. Page 363: Courtesy of the French Governnent Tourist Office. Page 364: Courtesy of the French Government Tourist Office. Page 365: Reuters/Bettmann; Bruno De Hogues/Tony Stone Worldwide. Page 373: Sheila Lukins. Page 374: Arpád Patyi/courtesy of the Embassy of the Hungarian Republic, Office of the Commercial Counselor. Page 375: (left) The Bettmann Archive; (right) courtesy of the Embassy of the Hungarian Republic, Office of the Commercial Counselor. Pages 376-377: Arpád Patyi/courtesy of the Embassy of the Hungarian Republic, Office of the Commercial Counselor. Page 386: Sheila Lukins.

THE SEA

Page 399: Sheila Lukins. Page 401: (top) Courtesy of Paleewong Trading and Siam Enterprise Office; (bottom) Sheila Lukins. Page 408: Sheila Lukins. Page 412: © Chad Ehlers/Tony Stone Worldwide. Pages 416-419: Courtesy of German Information Center. Page 421: Sheila Lukins. Page 424: Nancy Murray. Page 427: Sheila Lukins.

SIDE TRIPS

Pages 430-431: Food photographs, Walt Chrynwski; cheese photograph, courtesy of Embassy of Spain, Foods from Spain; travel photographs, Sheila Lukins and Sheila Lukins Collection.

HANDS ACROSS THE SEA

Page 434: Sheila Lukins. Page 436: Sheila Lukins. Page 438: Courtesy of the Danish Tourist Board. Page 439: Courtesy of Pripps. Page 444: Sheila Lukins. Page 446: H. Armstrong Roberts. Page 447: (left and right) Courtesy of Heineken International; (middle) courtesy of the Netherlands Board of Tourism.

WHISTLE STOPS

Page 454: Sheila Lukins. Page 455: Lori S. Malkin. Page 471: Sheila Lukins.

MY FAVORITE AFTERNOON TEAS

Page 475: (top left) Courtesy of The Ritz: (right) H. Armstrong Roberts. Page 476: Courtesy of The Caledonian Hotel. Page 477: Lori S. Malkin. Page 478: Courtesy of VARIG; Sheila Lukins. Page 479: Sheila Lukins; Sheila Lukins Collection. Page 480: Kent and Donna Dannen.

OVEN-FRESH BREAD

Page 487: Laurie Griffiths. Page 488: Courtesy of the Moroccan National Tourist Office.

THE NEW CHEESE PLATE

Page 495: (left) Courtesy of Embassy of Spain, Foods from Spain; (right) Sylvain Grandadam/Photo Researchers Inc. Pages 496-497: Courtesy of Embassy of Spain, Foods from Spain. Page 499: (top) Sheila Lukins; (bottom) courtesy of The Danish Tourist Board. Page 501: Sheila Lukins. Page 502: Courtesy of the Netherlands Board of Tourism. Page 503: Sheila Lukins. Pages 504-505: Courtesy of Greek National Tourist Office.

THE LIGHT FANTASTIC

Pages 506-507: Food photographs, Walt Chrynwski; travel photographs, Sheila Lukins and Sheila Lukins Collection.

A WORLD OF DESSERTS

Page 516: Courtesy of Marine Trading Consultants/Australian Wine Importers Association. Page 517: H. Armstrong Roberts. Page 518: (left) Courtesy of Australian Wine Importers Association. (right) Courtesy of Penfolds Wine Group. Page 524: Sheila Lukins.